Lecture Notes in Computer Science   9341

Commenced Publication in 1973
Founding and Former Series Editors:
Gerhard Goos, Juris Hartmanis, and Jan van Leeuwen

More information about this series at http://www.springer.com/series/7411

Fabien Gandon · Christophe Guéret
Serena Villata · John Breslin
Catherine Faron-Zucker
Antoine Zimmermann (Eds.)

The Semantic Web: ESWC 2015 Satellite Events

ESWC 2015 Satellite Events
Portorož, Slovenia, May 31 – June 4, 2015
Revised Selected Papers

 Springer

Editors
Fabien Gandon
Inria
Sophia Antipolis
France

Christophe Guéret
Data Archiving and Networked Services
Den Haag
The Netherlands

Serena Villata
Inria - Sophia Antipolis-Méditerran
Sophia Antipolis
France

John Breslin
Eng-3047, Engineering
National University of Ireland
Galway City
Ireland

Catherine Faron-Zucker
Laboratoire I3S
Polytech Nice Sophia
Sophia Antipolis
France

Antoine Zimmermann
École des Mines de Saint-Étienne
Saint-Étienne
France

ISSN 0302-9743   ISSN 1611-3349   (electronic)
Lecture Notes in Computer Science
ISBN 978-3-319-25638-2   ISBN 978-3-319-25639-9   (eBook)
DOI 10.1007/978-3-319-25639-9

Library of Congress Control Number: 2015952051

LNCS Sublibrary: SL5 – Computer Communication Networks and Telecommunications

Springer Cham Heidelberg New York Dordrecht London

Printed on acid-free paper

Springer International Publishing AG Switzerland is part of Springer Science+Business Media
(www.springer.com)

Preface

The 12th edition of ESWC took place in Portorož (Slovenia), from May 31 to June 4, 2015. Its program included three keynotes by: Lise Getoor (University of California), Viktor Mayer-Schönberger (Oxford University), and Massimo Poesio (University of Essex).

The main scientific program of the conference comprised 43 papers: 34 research and nine in-use, selected out of 166 submissions (146 research plus 20 in-use submissions), which corresponds to an acceptance rate of 23 % for research papers and of 45 % for in-use papers. It was completed by a demonstration and poster session, in which researchers had the chance to present their latest results and advances in the form of live demos. In addition, the conference program included 16 workshops, nine tutorials, a PhD Symposium, a Hackfest, four challenges, the Semantic Web Evaluation Track, an EU Project Networking Session, a "Minute of Madness," and Networking Networking Women Lunch Tables. The PhD Symposium program included 12 contributions, selected out of 16 submissions.

This volume includes the accepted contributions to the demonstration and poster track: 12 poster and 22 demonstration papers, selected out of 50 submissions (25 demo and 25 posters), which corresponds to an overall acceptance rate of 68 %. Each submission was reviewed by at least two, and on average 2.9, Program Committee members. During the poster session the students from the PhD Symposium were invited to display a poster about their work. This resulted in 12 additional posters being presented during the session.

Additionally, this book includes a selection of the best papers from the workshops co-located with the conference, which are distinguished meeting points for discussing ongoing work and the latest ideas in the context of the Semantic Web. From 24 workshop submissions originally, the ESWC 2015 Workshops Program Committee carefully selected 16 workshops focusing on specific research issues related to the Semantic Web, organized by internationally renowned experts in their respective fields:

- The Fourth International Workshop on Detection, Representation, and Exploitation of Events in the Semantic Web (DeRiVE 2015)
- The ESWC 2015 Developers Workshop (ESWCDev 2015)
- The First Workshop on Managing the Evolution and Preservation of the Data Web (Diachron 2015)
- The Third International Workshop on Human Semantic Web Interaction and the First International Workshop on Summarizing and Presenting Entities and Ontologies (HSWI+SumPre 2015)
- The Fourth Workshop on Knowledge Discovery and Data Mining Meets Linked Open Data (Know@LOD 2015)
- The Second Workshop on Linked Data Quality (LDQ 2015)
- The Workshop on Legal Domain And Semantic Web Applications (LeDA-SWAn 2015)

- The Fourth Workshop on the Multilingual Semantic Web (MSW 2015)
- The Workshop on Negative or Inconclusive rEsults in Semantic web (NoISE 2015)
- The Workshop on Politicizing the Future of the Semantic Web (PhiloWeb 2015)
- The Second International Workshop on Dataset PROFIling and fEderated Search for Linked Data (PROFILES 2015)
- The Workshop on RDF Stream Processing (RSP 2015)
- The Workshop on Services and Applications over Linked APIs and Data (SALAD 2015)
- The Workshop on Semantic Web for Scientific Heritage (SW4SH 2015)
- The Fifth International Workshop on Using the Web in the Age of Data (USEWOD 2015)
- The Third Workshop on Semantic Web Enterprise Adoption and Best Practice (WaSABi 2015)

From the overall set of papers that were accepted for these workshops (from 140 submissions), a selection of the best papers has been included in this volume. Each workshop Organizing Committee evaluated the papers accepted in their workshop to propose those to be included in this volume. The authors of the selected papers improved their original submissions, taking into account the comments and feedback obtained during the workshops and the conference. As a result, 22 papers were selected for this volume.

As General Chair, Poster and Demo Chairs, and Workshop Chairs, we would like to thank everybody who has been involved in the organization of ESWC 2015.

Special thanks go to the Poster and Demo Program Committee, to the challenge reviewers, and to all the workshop organizers and their respective Program Committees who contributed to making the ESWC 2015 Workshops a real success.

We would also like to thank the Organizing Committee and especially the local organizers and the Program Chairs for supporting the day-to-day operation and execution of the workshops.

A special thanks also to our Proceedings Chair, Antoine Zimmermann, who did a remarkable job in preparing this volume with the kind support of Springer.

Last but not least, thanks to all our sponsors listed in the next pages, for their trust in ESWC.

August 2015

Fabien Gandon
Christophe Guéret
Serena Villata
Catherine Faron-Zucker
John Breslin

Organization

Organizing Committee

General Chair
Fabien Gandon   Inria, France

Program Chairs
Marta Sabou   Vienna University of Technology, Austria
Harald Sack   Hasso Plattner Institute for IT Systems Engineering,
                            University of Potsdam, Germany

Local Chair
Marko Grobelnik   Jožef Stefan Institute Ljubljana, Slovenia

Workshops Chairs
John Breslin   National University of Ireland, Galway, Ireland
Catherine Faron   University of Nice Sophia Antipolis, France

Poster and Demo Chairs
Christophe Guéret   Data Archiving and Networked Services, The Netherlands
Serena Villata   Inria, Sophia Antipolis, France

Tutorials Chairs
Elena Simperl   University of Southampton, UK
Antoine Isaac   Vrije Universiteit Amsterdam, The Netherlands

PhD Symposium Chairs
Claudia d'Amato   Università degli Studi di Bari, Italy
Philippe Cudré-Mauroux   University of Fribourg, Switzerland

Challenge Chairs
Elena Cabrio   Inria, Sophia Antipolis, France
Milan Stankovic   Sépage and STIH, Université Paris-Sorbonne, France

Semantic Technologies Coordinators
Andrea Giovanni   University of Bologna/STLab ISTC-CNR, Italy
  Nuzzolese
Luca Costabello   Fujitsu, Galway, Ireland

Lionel Medini   University of Lyon, France
Fuqi Song   Inria, Sophia Antipolis, France
Anna Lisa Gentile   University of Sheffield, UK

EU Project Networking Session Chairs

Frédérique Segond   Viseo, Grenoble, France
Jun Zhao   Lancaster University, UK
Erik Mannens   Multimedia Lab - iMinds - Ghent University, Belgium
Sergio Consoli   STLab ISTC-CNR, Italy

Publicity Chair

Mauro Dragoni   Fondazione Bruno Kessler, Italy

Sponsor Chair

Blaž Fortuna   Ghent University, Belgium

Web Presence

Serge Tymaniuk   STI International, Austria

Proceedings Chair

Antoine Zimmermann   École nationale supérieure des mines de Saint-étienne,
                       France

Treasurer

Ioan Toma   STI International, Austria

Local Organization and Conference Administration

Špela Sitar   Jožef Stefan Institute Ljubljana, Slovenia
Monika Kropej   Jožef Stefan Institute Ljubljana, Slovenia

Program Committee

Program Chairs

Marta Sabou   Vienna University of Technology, Austria
Harald Sack   Hasso Plattner Institute for IT Systems Engineering,
                       University of Potsdam, Germany

Track Chairs

Silvio Peroni   University of Bologna, Italy and National Research
                       Council, Italy
Pavel Shvaiko   Informatica Trentina SpA, Italy
Pascal Hitzler   Wright State University, USA
Stefan Schlobach   Vrije Universiteit Amsterdam, The Netherlands

Sören Auer	University of Bonn, Germany
Stefan Dietze	L3S Research Center, Germany
Miriam Fernandez	Knowledge Media Institute, The Open University, UK
Markus Strohmaier	GESIS and University of Koblenz-Landau, Germany
Olivier Curé	Université Pierre et Marie Curie, France
Axel Polleres	Vienna University of Economics and Business, Austria
Kalina Bontcheva	University of Sheffield, UK
Simone Paolo Ponzetto	University of Mannheim, Germany
Bettina Berendt	Katholieke Universiteit Leuven, Belgium
Heiko Paulheim	University of Mannheim, Germany
Alasdair Gray	Heriot-Watt University, UK
Terry Payne	University of Liverpool, UK
Carlos Pedrinaci	Knowledge Media Institute, The Open University, UK
Aba-Sah Dadzie	The HCI Centre, The University of Birmingham, UK
Andreas Nürnberger	Otto von Guericke University Magdeburg, Germany
Lora Aroyo	Vrije Universiteit Amsterdam, The Netherlands
Gianluca Demartini	University of Sheffield, UK
Vanessa Lopez	IBM Research, Ireland
Giovanni Tumarello	SindiceTech/Fondazione Bruno Kessler, Italy

Steering Committee

Chair

| John Domingue | The Open University, UK and STI International, Austria |

Members

Claudia d'Amato	Università degli Studi di Bari, Italy
Grigoris Antoniou	FORTH, Greece
Philipp Cimiano	Bielefeld University, Germany
Oscar Corcho	Universidad Politécnica de Madrid, Spain
Marko Grobelnik	Jožef Stefan Institute Ljubljana, Slovenia
Axel Polleres	Vienna University of Economics and Business, Austria
Valentina Presutti	CNR, Italy
Elena Simperl	University of Southampton, UK

Workshops Organization

Workshops Chairs

| John Breslin | National University of Ireland, Galway, Ireland |
| Catherine Faron | University of Nice Sophia Antipolis, France |

DeRIVE Workshop Organizers

Marieke van Erp	Vrije Universiteit Amsterdam, The Netherlands
Raphaël Troncy	EURECOM, France
Marco Rospocher	Fondazione Bruno Kessler, Italy

Willem Robert van Hage   SynerScope B.V., The Netherlands
David A. Shamma   Yahoo!, USA

Developers Workshop Organizers

Ruben Verborgh   Ghent University - iMinds, Belgium
Miel Vander Sande   Ghent University - iMinds, Belgium

Diachron Workshop Organizers

Mathieu d'Aquin   Knowledge Media Institute, The Open University, UK
Jeremy Debattista   University of Bonn, Germany
Christoph Lange   University of Bonn, Germany

KnowLOD Workshop Organizers

Johanna Völker   University of Mannheim, Germany
Heiko Paulheim   University of Mannheim, Germany
Jens Lehmann   University of Leipzig, Germany
Vojtěch Svátek   University of Economics, Prague, Czech Republic

LDQ Workshop Organizers

Anisa Rula   University of Milano-Bicocca, Italy
Amrapali Zaveri   University of Leipzig, Germany
Magnus Knuth   Hasso Plattner Institute, University of Potsdam, Germany
Dimitris Kontokostas   University of Leipzig, Germany

LeDA-SWAn Workshop Organizers

Serena Villata   Inria, Sophia Antipolis, France
Silvio Peroni   University of Bologna and ISTC-CNR, Italy

Multilingual Workshop Organizers

Jorge Gracia   Universidad Politécnica de Madrid, Spain
John P. McCrae   Bielefeld University, Germany
Gabriela Vulcu   Insight Centre for Data Analytics,
                          National University of Ireland, Galway, Ireland

NoISE Workshop Organizers

Anastasia Dimou   Ghent University - iMinds, Belgium
Jacco van Ossenbruggen   Vrije Universiteit Amsterdam, The Netherlands
Maria-Esther Vidal   Universidad Simón Bolívar, Venezuela
Miel Vander Sande   Ghent University - iMinds, Belgium

PhiloWeb Workshop Organizers

Alexandre Monnin   Inria, Sophia Antipolis, France
Harry Halpin   W3C and MIT, USA

PROFILES Workshop Organizers

Elena Demidova	L3S Research Center, Germany
Stefan Dietze	L3S Research Center, Germany
Julian Szymanski	Gdansk University of Technology, Poland
John Breslin	National University of Ireland Galway, Ireland

RSP Workshop Organizers

Jean-Paul Calbimonte	EPFL, Switzerland
Alasdair Gray	Heriot-Watt University, UK
Alejandro Llaves	Universidad Politécnica de Madrid, Spain
Alessandra Mileo	Insight Centre for Data Analytics, National University of Ireland, Galway, Ireland

SALAD Workshop Organizers

Maria Maleshkova	Karlsruhe Institute of Technology, Germany
Ruben Verborgh	Ghent University - iMinds, Belgium
Steffen Stadtmüller	Karlsruhe Institute of Technology, Germany

HSWI+SumPre Workshops Organizers

Gong Cheng	Nanjing University, China
Kalpa Gunaratna	(Kno.e.sis) Wright State University, USA
Andreas Thalhammer	Karlsruhe Institute of Technology, Germany
Heiko Paulheim	University of Mannheim, Germany
Martin Voigt	Ontos GmbH, Germany
Roberto Garcia	Universitat de Lleida, Spain

SW4SH Workshop Organizers

Arnaud Zucker	University of Nice Sophia Antipolis, France
Isabelle Draelants	CNRS, France
Catherine Faron	University of Nice Sophia Antipolis, France
Alexandre Monnin	Inria, Sophia Antipolis, France

USEWOD Workshop Organizers

Bettina Berendt	Katholieke Universiteit Leuven, Belgium
Laura Drăgan	University of Southampton, UK
Laura Hollink	Vrije Universiteit Amsterdam, The Netherlands
Markus Luczak-Roesch	University of Southampton, UK

WaSABI Workshop Organizers

Marco Neumann	KONA LLC, USA
Sam Coppens	IBM Research, Ireland
Karl Hammar	Jönköping University, Linköping University, Sweden

Magnus Knuth   Hasso Plattner Institute, University of Potsdam, Germany
Dominique Ritze   University of Mannheim, Germany
Miel Vander Sande   Ghent University - iMinds, Belgium

Sponsoring Institutions

Contents

ESWC2015 Developers Workshop

Demo and Poster Papers

3XL News: A Cross-lingual News Aggregator and Reader

Evgenia Belyaeva[1,2], Jan Berčič[1], Katja Berčič[1], Flavio Fuart[1(✉)],
Aljaž Košmerlj[1], Andrej Muhič[1], Aljoša Rehar[3], Jan Rupnik[1],
and Mitja Trampuš[1]

[1] Jožef Stefan Institute, Jamova Cesta 39, 1000 Ljubljana, Slovenia
{evgenia.belyaeva,jan.bercic,katja.bercic,flavio.fuart,aljaz.kosmerlj,
andrej.muhic,jan.rupnik,mitja.trampus}@ijs.si
[2] JSI International Postgraduate School, Jamova Cesta 39, 1000 Ljubljana, Slovenia
[3] Slovenian Press Agency, Tivolska Cesta 50, 1000 Ljubljana, Slovenia
aljosa.rehar@ijs.si

Abstract. We present *3XL News*, a multi-lingual news aggregation
application for iPad that provides real-time, comprehensive, global and
multilingual news coverage. Using methods, developed within the XLike
project, for semantic data extraction from news articles and linking of
news stories we are able to construct a concise, yet in-depth view of current news stories and their semantic relation. This enables users real-time
monitoring of current global events and analysis of diverse reporting in
different languages and navigation across related news stories.

1 Introduction and Motivation

Real-time access to the latest news any time and from any location has become
possible with widespread adaptation of mobile networks and devices. Increasingly, users of such devices expect custom-made, native applications to access
their information. In this article we describe **3XL News**: a system stemming
from the **XLike** EU project, offering **X(cross)**Lingual analysis of eXtra Large
News. *3XL News* is an iOS application targeting news professionals and the
general public. It shows how semantic technologies can be used in a real-world
scenario to provide real-time global news monitoring and analysis across several
languages. The main novelty is the linking of stories across six languages using
semantic data derived from multi-lingual entity detection and cross-language
news linking.

Related Work: A multitude of news monitoring mobile applications is available
on the market, broadly divided into two groups: publishers' own applications (like
BBC, Al-Jazeera and RTV Slovenija) and news aggregators (like News Republic,
Yahoo News, EMM mobile app [7] and iDiversiNews [8]). Those services reduce
the overwhelming amount of information by summarizing news events and filtering them according to predefined user preferences or reading habits, however,
they do not link news stories across languages. There are systems that perform

© Springer International Publishing Switzerland 2015
F. Gandon et al. (Eds.): ESWC 2015, LNCS 9341, pp. 3–8, 2015.
DOI: 10.1007/978-3-319-25639-9_1

cross-language linking such as NewsReader [10] and SPIGA [4] but support only four and two languages respectively and lack the capability to explore news along other dimensions (sentiment, location etc.).

2   Technological Background

XLike Project. XLike stands for Cross-LIngual Knowledge Extraction. The main goal of the project[1] was to develop technology to monitor and aggregate knowledge spread across mainstream and social media, as well as across different languages. This is achieved by applying computational linguistics and semantic technologies to extract formal knowledge from multilingual texts.

Developed methods were integrated into an extensive linguistic and semantic text analysis pipeline [2], which provides input data for *3XL News*. News is gathered from the Internet [9], annotated with semantic data [2], similar articles are linked across languages [5], news articles are clustered into stories and finally, news stories are linked across languages using content (i.e. text) and semantic data. We have performed manual evaluation of the obtained clusters [1] but we omit it here due to lack of space.

Cross-Lingual Similarity Function. To compute similarities between documents written in different languages, we model them in a latent, language-independent vector space [6]; projections into the latent space are inferred using techniques from linear algebra and statistics. The method [5] is related to Canonical Correlation Analysis (CCA) [3], which we apply on a multilingual corpus of documents obtained from Wikipedia[2].

Semantic Data Extraction. Semantic annotation consists of *named entity recognition* [2] and *Wikipedia Miner Wikifier* [11]. The former detects named entities (persons, organisations, locations), while the later relates them to Wikipedia entries. For each entity a list of identifiers across all supported languages is provided. Thus, semantic annotation is used not only to better present data to users, but also to identify the same entity across different languages.

Linking News Stories Across Languages. Automatic linking of news stories (clusters of closely related news articles describing about the same event) across languages is an important addition to existing aggregation approaches. The main goal is to interconnect many influential and often related news that are reported constantly by numerous news outlets in different languages. We use CCA and semantic data (entities) to link stories as described in [1].

---

[1] http://www.xlike.org.
[2] http://www.wikipedia.org.

3   *3XL News* Application

The application consists of the following views:

Languages Overview (Fig. 1, left). The graph represents stories grouped by language (colour-coded) with images of the top-mentioned entities for each language. Node size corresponds to the number of articles in each language, while the width of each edge is computed from the overall similarity of stories in the two corresponding languages. News sources are shown on the world map, in which the display of any language can be switched *on* or *off*.

Entity Overview (Fig. 1, right). Top-mentioned entities are aggregated across all languages, with possible filtering for major categories. Furthermore, users can choose a single entity to read related stories. Selected entities are shown on the world map below where news sources can be compared.

News Stories List. Contains a list of news stories filtered by language or entity and ordered by relevance with basic information for each story: title, summary, photo, publication date, number of news articles and related stories per language. The user can select a story and explore it.

News Story Exploration (Fig. 2). Components representing different aspects of a story are shown. The graph represents related stories across languages, with

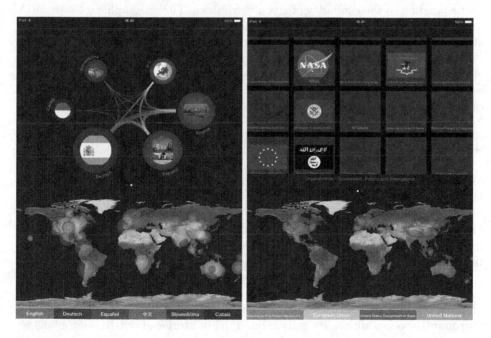

Fig. 1. Overview screens: by language and by entities (Color figure online)

Fig. 2. NASA story exploration (left) and Middle East story exploration (right)

node sizes corresponding to the number of articles in a story and edge widths corresponding to the similarity of given two stories. The geographic selector sorts articles according to sources, while the last section gives a quick overview of the story by giving its top-mentioned entities, summary and keywords.

Articles List. Contains a list of articles for a selected story, ordered by user selection, is shown on a separate screen. Each article can be selected and the original web page, from which the text was extracted from, is displayed.

4   Demonstration

We will demonstrate a typical user session by selecting and analysing few news stories as shown in the figures.

Katja checks the overview screen (Fig. 1, left) and top-mentioned entities (Fig. 1, right). She then compares several entities by reporting locations. Being interested in space-related news, she selects "NASA" to view a list of related news stories (screen-shot not provided).

Katja now explores the main story she selected, together with its semantically related stories. A thick connection shows strongly related stories, while thin connections represent weak relations. For example, stories related to NASA astronauts space-walk are strongly related, while stories about Russian plans to get to the moon are weakly connected (Fig. 2, left).

Switching to earthly events (Fig. 2, right), Katja finds an abundance of inter-connected stories from all languages. Compared to space-related news, current events are more widely covered by the world media. Finally, she can list all the articles making up the current story and read them in the integrated browser (screen-shot not provided).

5   Conclusion

In this article we presented *3XL News*, an iPad news aggregation app that deliv-ers a global view on the news media landscape by applying advanced compu-tational linguistics and semantic approaches. The main advantage compared to similar systems is semantic linking of stories across six languages.

3XL News currently supports six languages, but the system is being extended to twelve languages with more planned. Through xLiMe[3], a research project ded-icated to fusing the knowledge from different media content in different modali-ties, we plan to include annotated video and audio materials.

The demonstration video is available from the *3XL News* homepage[4]. The application will also be submitted to the *Apple App Store* and available free of charge.

Acknowledgements. This work was funded by the European Union through project XLike (FP7-ICT-2011-288342).

References

1. Belyaeva, E., Košmerlj, A., Muhič, A., Rupnik, J., Fuart, F.: Using semantic data to improve cross-lingual linking of article clusters. J. Web Seman. (submitted)
2. Carreras, X., Padró, L., Zhang, L., Rettinger, A., Li, Z., García-Cuesta, E., Agić, V., Bekavec, B., Fortuna, B., Štajner, T.: Xlike project language analysis services. In: Proceedings of EACL 2014, pp. 9–12. Gothenburg, Sweden, April 2014
3. Hardoon, D.R., Szedmak, S., Szedmak, O., Shawe-Taylor, J.: Canonical correlation analysis; an overview with application to learning methods. Technical report (2007)
4. Hennig, L., Ploch, D., Prawdzik, D., Armbruster, B., De Luca, E.W.: Spiga - a multilingual news aggregator. In: Proceedings of GSCL 2011 (2011)
5. Rupnik, J., Muhič, A., Škraba, P.: Cross-lingual document retrieval through hub languages. xLiTe: Cross-Lingual Technologies, NIPS 2012 Workshop (2012)
6. Salton, G., Buckley, C.: Term-weighting approaches in automatic text retrieval. In: Information Processing and Management, pp. 513–523 (1988)
7. Steinberger, R.: Multilingual and cross-lingual news analysis in the europe media monitor (EMM) (Extended Abstract). In: Lupu, M., Kanoulas, E., Loizides, F. (eds.) IRFC 2013. LNCS, vol. 8201, pp. 1–4. Springer, Heidelberg (2013)
8. Trampuš, M., Fuart, F., Pighin, D., Tadej, Š., Berčič, J., Novak, B., Rusu, D., Stopar, L., Grobelnik, M.: Diversinews: surfacing diversity in online news. AI Mag-azine (2015, accepted for publishing)

---

[3] http://xlime.eu/.
[4] http://ailab.ijs.si/tools/3xl-news/.

9. Trampuš, M., Novak, B.: The internals of an aggregated web news feed. In: Proceedings of IS-2012. Ljubljana, Slovenia (2012)
10. Vossen, P., Rigau, G., Serafini, L., Stouten, P., Irving, F., Hage, W.V.: Newsreader: recording history from daily news streams. In: Proceedings of LREC 2014 (2014)
11. Zhang, L., Rettinger, A.: Semantic annotation, analysis and comparison: a multilingual and cross-lingual text analytics toolkit. In: Proceedings of EACL 2014, pp. 13–16 (2014)

Towards Scalable Visual Exploration of Very Large RDF Graphs

Nikos Bikakis[1,2]([✉]), John Liagouris[3], Maria Kromida[1],
George Papastefanatos[2], and Timos Sellis[4]

[1] NTU Athens, Athens, Greece
bikakis@dblab.ntua.gr
[2] ATHENA Research Center, Athens, Greece
[3] ETH Zürich, Zürich, Switzerland
[4] RMIT University, Melbourne, Australia

Abstract. In this paper, we outline our work on developing a disk-based infrastructure for efficient visualization and graph exploration operations over very large graphs. The proposed platform, called graphVizdb, is based on a novel technique for indexing and storing the graph. Particularly, the graph layout is indexed with a spatial data structure, i.e., an R-tree, and stored in a database. In runtime, user operations are translated into efficient spatial operations (i.e., window queries) in the backend.

Keywords: graphVizdb · Graph data · Disk based visualization tool · RDF graph visualization · Spatial · Visualizing linked data · Partition based graph layout

1 Introduction

Data visualisation provides intuitive ways for information analysis, allowing users to infer correlations and causalities that are not always possible with traditional data mining techniques. The wide availability of vast amounts of graph-structured data, RDF in the case of the Data Web, demands for user-friendly methods and tools for data exploration and knowledge uptake. We consider some core challenges related on the management and visualization of very large RDF graphs; e.g., the Wikidata RDF graph has more than 300M nodes and edges.

First, their size exceeds the capabilities of memory-based layout techniques and libraries, enforcing disk-based implementations. Then, graph rendering is a time consuming process; even drawing a small part of the graph (containing a few hundreds of nodes) requires considerable time when we assume real-time systems. The same holds for graph interaction and navigation. Most operations, such as zoom in/out and move, are not easily implemented to large dense graphs, as their implementations require redrawing and re-layout large parts of them.

Related works in the field handle very large graphs through hierarchical visualization approaches. Although hierarchical approaches provide fancy visualizations with low memory requirements, their applicability is heavily based on the

© Springer International Publishing Switzerland 2015
F. Gandon et al. (Eds.): ESWC 2015, LNCS 9341, pp. 9–13, 2015.
DOI: 10.1007/978-3-319-25639-9_2

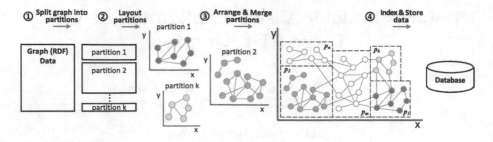

Fig. 1. Preprocessing overview

particular characteristics of the input dataset. In most cases, the hierarchy is constructed by exploiting clustering and partitioning methods [1,4,5,14,19]. In other works, the hierarchy is defined with hub-based [15] and destiny-based [22] techniques. [3] supports ad-hoc hierarchies which are manually defined by the users. Some of these systems offer a disk-based implementation [1,14,19] whereas others keep the whole graph in main memory [3–5,15,22].

In the context of the Web of Data [2,7–9,16,17,20], there is a large number of tools that visualize RDF graphs (adopting a node-link approach); the most notable ones are *ZoomRDF* [21], *Fenfire* [12], *LODWheel* [18], *RelFinder* [13] and *LODeX* [6]. All these tools require the whole graph to be loaded on the UI. Several tools that follow the same non-scalable approach have also been developed in the field of ontology visualization [10,11].

In contrast to all existing works, we introduce a generic platform, called graphVizdb, for scalable graph visualization that do not necessarily depend on the characteristics of the dataset. The efficiency of the proposed platform is based on a novel technique for indexing and storing the graph. The core idea is that in a preprocessing phase, the graph is drawn, using any of the existing graph layout algorithms. After drawing the graph, the coordinates assigned to its nodes (with respect to a Euclidean plane) are indexed with a spatial data structure, i.e., an R-tree, and stored in a database. In runtime, while the user is navigating over the graph, based on the coordinates, specific parts of the graph are retrieved and send to the user.

2   Platform Overview

The graphVizdb platform is built on top of two main concepts: (1) it is based on a "spatial-oriented" approach for graph visualization, similar to approaches followed in browsing maps; and (2) it adopts a disk-based implementation for supporting interaction with the graph, i.e., a database backend is used to index and store graph and visual information.

Partition-Based Graph Layout. Here we outline the partition-based approach adopted by the graphVizdb in order to handle very large graph. Recall that, for graph layout, the graph is drawn once in a preprocessing phase, using any of the existing graph layout algorithms. However several graph layout algorithms require large amount of memory in order to draw very large graphs. In order to overcome this problem, our partition-based approach (outlined in Fig. 1) is described next.

(1) Initially, the graph (RDF) data is divided into a set of smaller sub-graphs (i.e., partitions) using a graph partitioning algorithm. At the same time, the graph partitioning algorithm tries to minimize the number of edges connecting nodes in different partitions. (2) Then, using a graph layout algorithm, each of the sub-graph resulted from the graph partitioning, is visualized into a Euclidean plane, excluding (i.e., not visualizing) the edges connecting nodes through different partitions (i.e., crossing edges). (3) The visualized partitions are organized and combined into a "global" plane using a greedy algorithm whose goal is twofold. First, it ensures that the distinct sub-graphs do not overlap on the plane, and at the same time it tries to minimize the total length of the crossing edges. (4) Based on the "global" plane, the coordinates for each node and edge are indexed and stored in the database.

Spatial Operations for Graph Exploration. In graphVizdb, most of the user's requests are translated into simple spatial operations evaluated over the database. In this context, *window queries* (i.e., spatial range queries that retrieve the information contained with in a specific spatial region) are the core operation for most user's requests. The user navigates on the graph by moving the viewing window. When the window is moved, its new coordinates with respect to the whole canvas are tracked on the client side, and a window query is sent to the server. The query is evaluated on the server using the R-tree indexes. This way, for each user request, graphVizdb efficiently renders only visible parts of the graph, minimizing in this way both backend-frontend communication cost as well as rendering and layout time. Additionally, more sophisticated operations, e.g., abstraction/enrichment zoom operations are also implemented using spatial operations.

Implementation. We have implemented a graphVizdb prototype[1] which provides interactive visualization over large graphs. The prototype offers three main operations: (1) interactive navigation, (2) multi-level exploration, and (3) keyword search. We use MySQL for data storing and indexing, the Jena framework for RDF data handling, Metis[2] for graph partitioning, and Graphviz[3] for drawing the graph partitions. In the front-end, we use mxgraph[4], a client-side JavaScript visualization library. A video presenting the basic functionality of our prototype is available at: vimeo.com/117547871.

Acknowledgement. This research has been co-financed by the European Union (European Social Fund - ESF) and Greek national funds through the Operational Pro-

---

[1] graphvizdb.imis.athena-innovation.gr.
[2] glaros.dtc.umn.edu/gkhome/views/metis.
[3] www.graphviz.org.
[4] www.jgraph.com.

grams "Education and Lifelong Learning" - Funding Program: THALIS and "Competitiveness and Entrepreneurship" (OPCE II) - Funding Program: KRIPIS of the National Strategic Reference Framework (NSRF).

References

1. Abello, J., van Ham, F., Krishnan, N.: ASK-GraphView: a large scale graph visualization system. IEEE Trans. Vis. Comput. Graph. **12**(5), 669–676 (2006)
2. Alonen, M., Kauppinen, T., Suominen, O., Hyvönen, E.: Exploring the linked university data with visualization tools. In: Cimiano, P., Fernández, M., Lopez, V., Schlobach, S., Völker, J. (eds.) ESWC 2013. LNCS, vol. 7955, pp. 204–208. Springer, Heidelberg (2013)
3. Archambault, D., Munzner, T., Auber, D.: GrouseFlocks: steerable exploration of graph hierarchy space. IEEE Trans. Vis. Comput. Graph. **14**(4), 900–913 (2008)
4. Auber, D.: Tulip - a huge graph visualization framework. In: Jünger, M., Mutzel, P. (eds.) Graph Drawing Software, pp. 105–126. Springer, Heidelberg (2004)
5. Bastian, M., Heymann, S., Jacomy, M.: Gephi: an open source software for exploring and manipulating networks. In: ICWSM (2009)
6. Benedetti, F., Po, L., Bergamaschi, S.: A visual summary for linked open data sources. In: ISWC (2014)
7. Bikakis, N., Skourla, M., Papastefanatos, G.: rdf:SynopsViz – a framework for hierarchical linked data visual exploration and analysis. In: Presutti, V., Blomqvist, E., Troncy, R., Sack, H., Papadakis, I., Tordai, A. (eds.) ESWC Satellite Events 2014. LNCS, vol. 8798, pp. 292–297. Springer, Heidelberg (2014)
8. Brunetti, J.M., Auer, S., García, R., Klímek, J., Necaský, M.: Formal linked data visualization model. In: IIWAS (2013)
9. Dadzie, A., Rowe, M.: Approaches to visualising linked data: a survey. Semant. Web **2**(2), 89–124 (2011)
10. Dudáš, M., Zamazal, O., Svátek, V.: Roadmapping and navigating in the ontology visualization landscape. In: Janowicz, K., Schlobach, S., Lambrix, P., Hyvönen, E. (eds.) EKAW 2014. LNCS, vol. 8876, pp. 137–152. Springer, Heidelberg (2014)
11. Fu, B., Noy, N.F., Storey, M.-A.: Eye tracking the user experience - an evaluation of ontology visualization techniques. Semant. Web J. (2015)
12. Hastrup, T., Cyganiak, R., Bojars, U.: Browsing linked data with fenfire. In: WWW (2008)
13. Heim, P., Lohmann, S., Stegemann, T.: Interactive relationship discovery via the semantic web. In: Aroyo, L., Antoniou, G., Hyvönen, E., ten Teije, A., Stuckenschmidt, H., Cabral, L., Tudorache, T. (eds.) ESWC 2010, Part I. LNCS, vol. 6088, pp. 303–317. Springer, Heidelberg (2010)
14. Rodrigues Jr., J.F., Tong, H., Traina, A.J.M., Faloutsos, C., Leskovec, J.: GMine: a system for scalable, interactive graph visualization and mining. In: VLDB (2006)
15. Lin, Z., Cao, N., Tong, H., Wang, F., Kang, U., Chau, D.H.P.: Demonstrating interactive multi-resolution large graph exploration. In: ICDM (2013)
16. Mazumdar, S., Petrelli, D., Ciravegna, F.: Exploring user and system requirements of linked data visualization through a visual dashboard approach. Semant. Web **5**(3), 203–220 (2014)
17. Mazumdar, S., Petrelli, D., Elbedweihy, K., Lanfranchi, V., Ciravegna, F.: Affective graphs: the visual appeal of linked data. Semant. Web **6**(3), 277–312 (2015)
18. Stuhr, M., Roman, D., Norheim, D.: LODWheel - JavaScript-based visualization of RDF data. In: Workshop on Consuming Linked Data (2011)

19. Tominski, C., Abello, J., Schumann, H.: CGV - an interactive graph visualization system. Comput. Graph. **33**(6), 660–678 (2009)
20. Vocht, L.D., Dimou, A., Breuer, J., Compernolle, M.V., Verborgh, R., Mannens, E., Mechant, P., de Walle, R.V.: A visual exploration workflow as enabler for the exploitation of linked open data. In: IESD (2014)
21. Zhang, K., Wang, H., Tran, D.T., Yu, Y.: ZoomRDF: semantic fisheye zooming on RDF data. In: WWW (2010)
22. Zinsmaier, M., Brandes, U., Deussen, O., Strobelt, H.: Interactive level-of-detail rendering of large graphs. IEEE Trans. Vis. Comput. Graph. **18**(12), 2486–2495 (2012)

SmartKeepers: A Decentralized, Secure, and Flexible Social Platform for Coworkers

Romain Blin[1], Charline Berthot[1], Julien Subercaze[2], Christophe Gravier[2], Frederique Laforest[2(✉)], and Antoine Boutet[2]

[1] SmartKeepers, Saint-Etienne, France
{romain.blin,charline.berthot}@univ-st-etienne.fr
[2] CNRS, Laboratoire Hubert Curien, Saint-Etienne, France
{julien.subercaze,christophe.gravier,frederique.laforest,
antoine.boutet}@smartkeepers.com

Abstract. Coworking (style of work that involves a shared working environment and networking) has emerged as an attractive model for organizations. It relies on a highly dynamic collaboration among different partners. Traditional centralized social platforms lack fundamental requirements for such a collaboration that are the management of the dynamic topology of such professional networks, privacy, data exchanges and ownership. In this paper, we present SmartKeepers, a decentralized and secure environment for coworking activities. Each user physically owns his node that he plugs in and out as he moves from one collaborative space to another. The system supports a large variety of network topologies and is fully interoperable with W3C compliant solutions. We showcase the cogency of the Semantic Web for building decentralized and secure services while keeping every user at the core of the data ownership process.

1 Introduction

Coworking has emerged as an attractive model for organizations [4]. The rise of coworking spaces in the past decade has brought new challenges for adapted collaborative social platforms. Coworking spaces offer support for remote working, freelance and entrepreneurial activities. Coworkers share physical resources such as desks, Internet accesses, printers, conference rooms or kitchen, to name a few. The dynamic and collaborative nature of coworking pushes freelancers, entrepreneurs and independent contractors to collaborate and start new projects. As a consequence, individuals might belong to several projects or organizations such as bootstrapping a startup with a few partners and managing a freelance activity at the same time. The same individuals may integrate two other collaborative projects several weeks later. To follow this dynamics, digital assets management requires flexibility, fine-grained control and a high level of security.

Traditional enterprise social network services such as Yammer[1] are originally designed to manage large companies. They are therefore not adapted for the

---
[1] https://www.yammer.com.

© Springer International Publishing Switzerland 2015
F. Gandon et al. (Eds.): ESWC 2015, LNCS 9341, pp. 14–19, 2015.
DOI: 10.1007/978-3-319-25639-9_3

paradigm shift introduced by coworking [5]. Moreover, using well known social networks or a myriad of different public solutions for a business activity most likely represents a risky solution in case of a leak of privacy [1]. The usage of such solutions can also be prohibited in case of confidential documents which must not be disseminated outside the working group. In the last few years, decentralization has become an appealing solution to address the challenges of privacy and data ownership [2,3,6].

In this demonstration we present SmartKeepers, a cost-effective and scalable decentralized social network solution for coworkers looking for flexibility. Smart-Keepers addresses two main challenges raised by the organizational revolution introduced by coworking: decentralization and security. SmartKeepers offers all the required tools for daily IT activities of every business such as shared calendars, collaborative documents, real-time discussion, backup or communication services. SmartKeepers leverages the elastic nature of decentralized solutions to be cost-effective and flexible, adapting the infrastructure to the need of dynamic companies. The solution is based on W3C standards at every level of its architecture. It relies on Semantic Web standards for data representation and exchange. It implements state-of-the-art cryptographic protocols and standards to ensure security. Fine-grained access control is realized through Web Access Control and WebID. Based on a decentralized model, the SmartKeepers system allows users to regain complete ownership and control over their data.

The lightweight version of SmartKeepers is bundled on a low-consumption device (the Raspberry Pi in this demonstration) and is called a KeepBox. This allows any user to host his own data for low starting and running costs. Different coworkers' boxes can interact with each other to offer shared spaces and communication features while respecting privacy using fine grained security policies. In this demonstration we present the capabilities of SmartKeepers to operate with one KeepBox as well as with multiple KeepBoxes to scale the infrastructure of a growing business. It also illustrates how the shared collaborative tools work between different partners.

2   Decentralized Openness

SmartKeepers is designed to support the full range of real life situations that emerge from the paradigm shift introduced by coworking. For this purpose, the network architecture of SmartKeepers is highly flexible and supports various network topologies. Communication between users is supported by the communication between the KeepBoxes. Each user is identified by the URI of his FOAF profile. Each user is hosted on a single box. However a box can host several users. This model enables the decoupling from the user and the hosting of his data. SmartKeepers grants elasticity in two ways:

User relation: Relations between users evolve over time. This is a standard feature of social networks. In traditional centralized networks such a Facebook, this relation is represented by a value in a database. In SmartKeepers this relation is represented through cryptographic certificate authorization (See Sect. 3.1).

Data migration: SmartKeepers offers the users to migrate their data from one KeepBox to another. For instance, a user who is leaving a company to start as a freelancer can transfer his data from the company box to a privately hosted box. A user who is unsatisfied by the quality of a hosting service may decide to migrate his data to another one.

For interoperability purposes, SmartKeepers is fully committed to support W3C standards in every piece of its architecture: security, data, protocols. In SmartKeepers, the following standards are implemented in different parts of the architecture:

Protocols: To expose data on the Web, SmartKeepers is using the Read Write Web protocol (RWW) over HTTPS. RWW defines performatives to access and modify data over the Web. SmartKeepers utilizes notifications in order to keep users updated of the news from their network. Notifications are implemented upon the Pingback protocol and its related ontology.

Data: Every service of SmartKeepers, such as calendar, group management, message board, file exchange, has an underlying data format defined by a standard ontology. FOAF is used to describe a person. Message stream uses the SIOC ontology to describe users' posts and comments. Calendar is based upon NCAL[2], contact management is backed by NCO[3].

Security: Security is a key service of SmartKeepers. WebID and Web Access Control are the two standards implemented to harness security. We detail the usage of these standards to implement secure services in the next section.

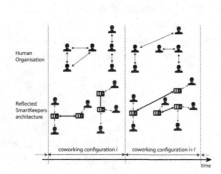 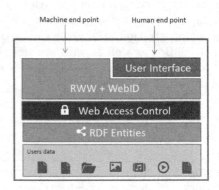

Fig. 1. Example of evolving human coworking organisation (left) and the SmartKeepers stack that supports such configurations (right)

---

[2] Nepomuk Calendar Ontology.
[3] Nepomuk Contact Ontology.

3 Secure Services

3.1 WebID

The authentication in SmartKeepers relies on WebID over TLS sessions. This is a paradigm under consideration as a W3C specification[4] that allows distributed authentication. In our system, a WebID is an URI which denotes a person. When Bob wants to access Alice's data on her box in order to post new triples, Bob needs to authenticate on Alice's box. A preliminary is for Bob to create a certificate store within its Web browser for authentication purposes. Both private and public keys are stored within Bob's in-browser keystore. This step is usually performed on Bob's KeepBox that Bob controls. Then, when Bob accesses Alice's services, his browser first initiates a TLS connection with Alice's Keep-Box. Then, the latter issues a `CertificateRequest` message, a performative already present in TLS protocol. Bob's browser provides the certificate without any user interaction, and the authentication scheme is run on Alice's KeepBox. For this purpose, the WebID provided at sign-in is dereferencable using the specified protocol in this URI. Then, Alice's KeepBox checks if the returned profile relates the WebID to the certificate public key. When this authentication process successfully terminates, Bob is connected to Alice's KeepBox, without having to create an account on it. Bob can synchronize his WebIDs on different browsers for every terminal he owns. This is of the utmost practical interest in the Smart-Keepers distributed system – authentication is performed without Bob having to either create an account, or use a login/password pair as the certificate is stored in Bob's browser and served automatically on `CertificateRequest` messages.

3.2 Web Access Control

Linking WebID with other ontologies natively supports privacy settings for the user controlling his identity on the Web. This is similar to common user and role based access control policies in most Web systems, except that each user is authenticated using an URI. On her KeepBox, Alice manages the access control list of users allowed to access her services (calendar, social stream, posts, notifications, . . .). This access control list is a sequence of triples that explicits the rights given to a user u identified by his URI to operate Alice's services. The supported operations are the performatives from RWW for trusted read and write operations. This includes Read, Write, and Append triples to existing RDF graph for each Alice's service. At this stage, it is important to note that the profile of a user $u \in U$ stays on the server of u. The information about u is not duplicated, which leaves out any profile synchronicity issue. Moreover, this enforces a government of u profile by u only.

---

[4] http://www.w3.org/2005/Incubator/webid/spec/tls/.

4   Demonstration of the System

Our demonstration is a Web-based server implemented in Java[5]. As the protocols implemented in the system are particularly lightweight, the system itself can run on a low cost and credit-card sized computer – the Raspberry Pi, which only needs 3.5 Watts per hour.

The unifying thread throughout our demonstration involves two KeepBoxes at the conference site and it evolves around the following scenario. The first KeepBox is configured and hosts the user profile and services of one of the authors – denoted Alice in what follows. The second KeepBox is reset to factory default for each presentation, so that we can showcase the zero-configuration deployment of a new node in the decentralized social network. Other already running KeepBoxes are also connected to the Internet – this represents as many additional nodes to connect to in this demonstration. This central thread holds together the showcase of three different aspects of the SmartKeepers system as follows.

Signing up and adding friends: At the first stage, we showcase the creation of a new user named Paul on a KeepBox. This includes the browser-side generation and storage of the user certificate. Paul is able to use enterprise-ready services (calendar, mail, ...) but also to search for new friends in the decentralized on-site architecture. He ultimately adds Alice (on-site box) and Carol (remote box) as friends.

Collaborative agenda and pingbacks: Users then enter a collaborative task with their friends. Paul suggest a meeting with both Alice and Carol, who are notified using the pingback ontology and its service. In their calendar module, Alice, Paul and Carol view the newly created event.

Meeting follow-up online discussion and file sharing: Right after the meeting, Paul wants to share his meeting minutes with Alice and Carol. He uploads his minutes through the file manager module, and he is able to share it with Alice and Carol only if he edits his web access control list in order to grant them the right to access the file on his box. This illustrates the RWW, WebID and Web Access Control stack, all implemented using TLS sessions.

5   Conclusion

We demonstrate the cogency of the Semantic Web for building an enterprise-ready decentralized and secure social platform. The SmartKeepers system makes it possible for any user to wield control of his identity in the social network, as well as manage the access control list for the different social services he exposes to his peers. The demonstration showcases services including WebID sign-in on the box of a peer using TLS sessions and certificates, without the need to memorize a login and a password per peer, collaborative distributed social services based

---

[5] A screencast is available at http://smartkeepers.com/files/screencast.ogv.

on the pingback ontology for notifications, and Web Access Control ontology for managing peers rights. The SmartKeepers system is also easy to deploy and run on commodity boxes, like the Raspberry Pi, roughly a hundred times less energy consuming than a refrigerator.

References

1. Giffin, D.B., Levy, A., Stefan, D., Terei, D., Mazières, D., Mitchell, J.C., Russo, A.: Hails: protecting data privacy in untrusted web applications. In: Operating Systems Design and Implementation (2012)
2. Koll, D., Li, J., Fu, X.: Soup: an online social network by the people, for the people. In: Middleware (2014)
3. Seong, S.-W., Seo, J., Nasielski, M., Sengupta, D., Hangal, S., Teh, S.K., Chu, R., Dodson, B., Lam, M.S.: PrPl: a decentralized social networking infrastructure. In: Mobile Cloud Computing (2010)
4. Spinuzzi, C.: Working alone together, coworking as emergent collaborative activity. J. Bus. Tech. Commun. **26**(4), 399–441 (2012)
5. Townsend, S.: What are you working on?: global knowledge sharing at deloitte. eLearn **2012**(1) (2012). doi:10.1145/2090108.2090109
6. Xu, T., Chen, Y., Zhao, J., Fu, X.: Cuckoo: towards decentralized, socio-aware online microblogging services and data measurements. In: Hot Topics in Planet-scale Measurement (2010)

How to Stay Ontop of Your Data: Databases, Ontologies and More

Diego Calvanese, Benjamin Cogrel, Sarah Komla-Ebri, Davide Lanti,
Martin Rezk, and Guohui Xiao(✉)

Faculty of Computer Science, Free University of Bozen-Bolzano, Bolzano, Italy
xiao@inf.unibz.it

Abstract. *Ontop* is an Ontology Based Data Access system allowing
users to access a relational database through a conceptual layer provided by an ontology. In this demo, we use the recently developed NPD
benchmark (+4 billion triples) to demonstrate the features of *Ontop*.
First we use *Ontop* as a SPARQL end-point to load the ontology and
mappings, and answer SPARQL queries. Then, we will show how to use
Ontop to check inconsistencies and exploit SWRL ontologies.

Keywords: *Ontop* framework · OBDA · SPARQL · R2RML · OWL ·
OWL 2 QL

1 Introduction

As databases grow in volume and complexity, finding and interpreting the information stored in them becomes a challenging task. As a result, there has been a
growing trend to use a conceptual layer containing a vocabulary that is familiar
to the users, to capture the domain knowledge and hide the complexity of data
storage. This gives rise to the setting of *Ontology-Based Data Access* (OBDA) [2],
illustrated in Fig. 1. In an nutshell, in an OBDA setting users access data through
a conceptual layer, which provides a convenient query vocabulary. Usually the
conceptual layer is expressed in the form of an RDF(S) [7], SWRL [11], or
OWL 2 [10] ontology, and the data is stored in relational databases. Terms in
the conceptual layer (classes and properties in the ontology) are populated with
elements from the data sources using mappings. Mappings define triples (subject, property, object) out of SQL queries. In the virtual approach these triples
do not need to be materialized and are accessible at query time using SPARQL.
Alternatively these triples can be materialized and loaded into a triplestore, but
we will not explore this approach here.

In this demo, we illustrate *Ontop* [5], which is a platform that implements
the OBDA paradigm, by allowing users to query relational databases as *Virtual
RDF Graphs* using SPARQL [4], through a domain ontology expressed in the
OWL 2 QL fragment [8] of the OWL 2 ontology language.

© Springer International Publishing Switzerland 2015
F. Gandon et al. (Eds.): ESWC 2015, LNCS 9341, pp. 20–25, 2015.
DOI: 10.1007/978-3-319-25639-9_4

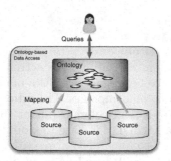

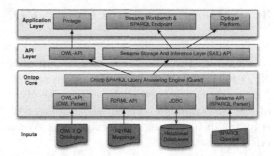

Fig. 1. OBDA paradigm   **Fig. 2.** Architecture of *Ontop* system

This demo, unlike its predecessors [1,9], will challenge *Ontop* with a real world scenario: the NPD Benchmark [6][1]. This benchmark contains thousands of axioms and mappings, and its dataset exposes several billion triples. In addition we will show the new extensions of the system: mapping language (new native syntax, and support for the W3C standard R2RML), query language (SPARQL 1.1), ontology language (SWRL), optimization techniques, accessibility (SPARQL end-point), consistency check, among others. Attendants will learn how to build an OBDA system from scratch using *Ontop*, and which are the benefits and the limitations of this approach. The files used for the demonstration are available online[2].

2   Ontop

Ontop is an open-source[3] project released under the Apache license, and developed at the Free University of Bozen-Bolzano[4]. The *Ontop* system answers SPARQL queries by rewriting them into SQL queries over the underlying database. Its architecture is depicted in Fig. 2. To the best of our knowledge, *Ontop* is currently the only OBDA system supporting all the relevant W3C standards (OWL 2 QL,SWRL, R2RML, SPARQL) and all major relational databases (PostgreSQL, MySQL, H2, DB2, ORACLE, HSQL, and MS SQL Server). *Ontop* can be used as: *(i)* a *plugin for Protégé* , which provides a graphical interface for mapping editing, SPARQL query execution, and inconsistency checking, *(ii)* a *SPARQL end-point* through Sesame Workbench, and *(iii)* a *Java library*, which implements both the OWL API and the Sesame API interfaces, available as Maven dependencies. In addition, *Ontop* acts as the core query transformation component of the Optique platform [3].

In [9] we showed how to use *Ontop* in Protégé over a small dataset. In this demo we will focus on how to use *Ontop* as a SPARQL end-point over a real world dataset.

---

[1] The benchmark is based on the commercially used dataset **N**orwegian **P**etroleum **D**irectorate FactPages, available at http://factpages.npd.no/factpages/.

[2] https://github.com/ontop/ontop-examples/tree/master/eswc-2015.

[3] http://github.com/ontop/ontop.

[4] http://ontop.inf.unibz.it/.

3 A Demo of Ontop Over NPD

NPD[5] is a governmental organization whose main objective is to contribute to maximize the value that society can obtain from the oil and gas activities. NPD FactPages contains information regarding the petroleum activities on the Norwegian continental shelf, and is actively used by oil companies. The **schema** of the NPD dataset consists of 70 tables with 276 distinct columns (about 1000 columns in total), and 94 foreign keys. We use a MySQL database to store the NPD dataset.

To ease the access of end-users to this dataset, we will show how to set up an OBDA framework using *Ontop* as a SPARQL endpoint. The user can access the dataset using the vocabulary specified in the NPD **ontology**. The NPD ontology contains OWL axioms specifying comprehensive information about the underlying concepts in the dataset; specifically hierarchies of classes (e.g., *Wellbore, ProductionWellbore*), and properties (e.g., *wellboreAgeHc, wellboreAgeHcLevel1*). In this demo, we use an OWL 2 QL fragment of the NPD ontology that contains 343 classes, 142 object properties, 238 data properties, and 1451 axioms. The NPD **mapping** set consists of 1190 assertions, mapping a total of 464 classes, objects properties, and data properties, exposing +4 billion triples[6].

To illustrate these concepts, we will take a simple query that retrieves all the wellbores[7]:

```
SELECT * WHERE {?w rdf:type epds:Wellbore}
```

and show how this simple query over the ontology gets translated into a complex SQL query over the database, with five unions and accessing three different tables. Intuitively, the generated SQL query has the following form:

```
SELECT uri(wellb-at1) FROM wellbore_exploration_all WHERE filter... UNION
SELECT uri(wellb-at1) FROM wellbore_development_all WHERE filter... UNION
SELECT uri(wellb-at2) FROM wellbore_exploration_all WHERE filter... UNION
SELECT uri(wellb-at2) FROM wellbore_development_all WHERE filter... UNION
SELECT uri(wellb) FROM wellbore_npdid_overview WHERE filter...
```

where *uri(attr)* builds the URIs specified by the mappings. The average execution time for the fastest executing queries in this benchmark (with +4B triples) is 6.7 s. There are queries, however, that take much longer to execute. For instance, query 11 in the benchmark already takes 10 s in a dataset with only 25 million triples [6]. One of the main tasks of an OBDA system is to optimize redundant joins and unions that often appear during the SPARQL to SQL translation. We will show how we have been tackling these issues in *Ontop* to allow for scalability of OBDA over real world data.

---

[5] http://www.npd.no/en/.

[6] In NPD$_{1500}$, see [6].

[7] A wellbore is a hole drilled for the purpose of exploration or extraction of natural resources.

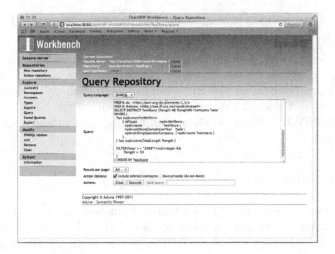

Fig. 3. Query a repository in Sesame Workbench

3.1   Ontop as a SPARQL Endpoint

Ontop extends the Sesame Workbench to create and manage *Ontop* repositories, which can then be used as standard SPARQL HTTP endpoints. A SPARQL endpoint is a (referenceable) entity over which SPARQL queries can be posed and that is compliant with the SPARQL Protocol for RDF specification. Sesame OpenRDF Workbench is a web application for administrating Sesame repositories.

In this demo we demonstrate how to use *Ontop* with the Sesame Workbench over NPD. We will use a pre-configured Jetty web server including the Sesame workbench with the *Ontop* extension. We will show how to create a Virtual RDF Store using the NPD ontology and mappings, how to explore it, and query it (depicted in Fig. 3). We will also show how the SPARQL queries are translated into SQL, what are the semantic and structural optimizations applied to the SQL query, and what are the main challenges in this approach.

3.2   New Features in Ontop

We will present two new features of the system:

Consistency Check. Ontology languages, such as OWL 2, allow for the specification of constraints on the data. If the data exposed by the database through the mappings does not satisfy such constraints, then we say that the ontology is *inconsistent w.r.t. the mappings and the data*. The OWL 2 QL profile of OWL 2, which is specifically designed to be used in the context of OBDA, allows for expressing *disjointness constraints* between classes and properties. Two disjoint classes cannot have individuals in common. For example, in NPD the class *OneDimensionalRegion* is declared to be disjoint from the class *TwoDimensionalRegion*. The notion of disjointness is extended in the obvious way to properties as well. The original NPD ontology contained inconsistencies, and it is possible to detect those using the *Ontop* Protégé plugin.

SWRL. The Semantic Web Rule Language (SWRL) is a widely used Semantic Web language combining a DL ontology component with rules (allowing only unary and binary predicates). SWRL is implemented in many systems, such as, Pellet, Stardog, and HermiT. We show how fragments of the NPD ontology can be expressed in SWRL, and how *Ontop* can handle it, including a weak form of linear recursion.

4   Conclusions

In this demonstration we present the *Ontop* framework over the NPD Benchmark, which offers a complex, authentic and challenging scenario for OBDA systems. We show how to set up an OBDA system from scratch using *Ontop*, and which are the benefits and the limitations of this approach. In addition, we explore several new interesting features of the system such as *Ontop* as a SPARQL end-point, support for additional relevant standards (SWRL, R2RML) and consistency checks.

Acknowledgement. This paper is supported by the EU under the large-scale integrating project (IP) Optique (Scalable End-user Access to Big Data), grant agreement n. FP7-318338.

References

1. Bagosi, T., et al.: The ontop framework for ontology based data access. In: Zhao, D., Du, J., Wang, H., Wang, P., Ji, D., Pan, J.Z. (eds.) CSWS 2014. CCIS, vol. 480, pp. 67–77. Springer, Heidelberg (2014)
2. Calvanese, D., De Giacomo, G., Lembo, D., Lenzerini, M., Poggi, A., Rodriguez-Muro, M., Rosati, R.: Ontologies and databases: the *DL-Lite* approach. In: Tessaris, S., Franconi, E., Eiter, T., Gutierrez, C., Handschuh, S., Rousset, M.-C., Schmidt, R.A. (eds.) Reasoning Web. LNCS, vol. 5689, pp. 255–356. Springer, Heidelberg (2009)
3. Giese, M., Soylu, A., Vega-Gorgojo, G., Waaler, A., Haase, P., Jiménez-Ruiz, E., Lanti, D., Rezk, M., Xiao, G., Özçep, Ö.L., Rosati, R.: Optique: zooming in on big data. IEEE Comput. **48**(3), 60–67 (2015)
4. Harris, S., Seaborne, A.: SPARQL 1.1 Query Language. W3C Recommendation, World Wide Web Consortium, March 2013. http://www.w3.org/TR/sparql11-query
5. Kontchakov, R., Rezk, M., Rodríguez-Muro, M., Xiao, G., Zakharyaschev, M.: Answering SPARQL queries over databases under OWL 2 QL entailment regime. In: Mika, P., et al. (eds.) ISWC 2014, Part I. LNCS, vol. 8796, pp. 552–567. Springer, Heidelberg (2014)
6. Lanti, D., Rezk, M., Xiao, G., Calvanese, D.: The NPD benchmark: reality check for OBDA systems. In: Proceedings of the 18th International Conference on Extending Database Technology (EDBT), pp. 617–628 (2015)

7. Manola, F., Mille, E.: RDF primer. W3C Recommendation, World Wide Web Consortium, February 2004. http://www.w3.org/TR/rdf-primer-20040210/
8. Motik, B., Grau, B.C., Horrocks, I., Wu, Z., Fokoue, A., Lutz, C.: OWL 2 web ontology language: Profiles. W3C Recommendation, World Wide Web Consortium (2012). http://www.w3.org/TR/owl2-profiles/
9. Rodriguez-Muro, M., Hardi, J., Calvanese, D.: Quest: efficient SPARQL-to-SQL for RDF and OWL. In: Proceedings of the ISWC 2012 Posters and Demonstrations Track (ISWC-PD 2012), CEUR Electronic Workshop Proceedings. http://ceur-ws.org/, vol. 914 (2012)
10. W3C OWL Working Group. OWL 2 Web Ontology Language document overview (second edition). W3C Recommendation, World Wide Web Consortium, December 2012. http://www.w3.org/TR/owl2-overview/
11. Xiao, G., Rezk, M., Rodríguez-Muro, M., Calvanese, D.: Rules and ontology based data access. In: Kontchakov, R., Mugnier, M.-L. (eds.) RR 2014. LNCS, vol. 8741, pp. 157–172. Springer, Heidelberg (2014)

This 'Paper' is a Demo

Sarven Capadisli[1,2]([✉]), Sören Auer[2], and Reinhard Riedl[1]

[1] E-Government-Institute, Bern University of Applied Sciences, Bern, Switzerland
info@csarven.ca, reinhard.riedl@bfh.ch
[2] Enterprise Information Systems Department, University of Bonn, Bonn, Germany
auer@cs.uni-bonn.de

Abstract. This 'paper', when viewed on the Web, is the demo itself, since the interactive and semantic features can be directly observed while reading and consuming. The demo showcases, how scholarly communication can adapt to the audience, whether the content is read on a screen or printed on paper, listen with a screen reader, watched as a movie, shown as a presentation, or even interacted with in the document. To experience the described features please open this document in your Web browser under its canonical URI: http://csarven.ca/this-paper-is-a-demo.

Keywords: Knowledge acquisition · Linked data · Semantic publishing · Technology demonstration

1 Introduction

One of the most widely debated questions in the scientific community is the impact of digitization on the scholarly communication and knowledge exchange. In this demo, we present a way how scholarly communication can truly digitize by means of living, interactive publications. Despite advances such as open and digital access to publications few has been changed yet with regard to the digitization of scientific publishing. Scientists still write static documents, which do not use the possibilities of digitization, such as interactivity, multimodality or semantic content annotation and representation.

In this demo, we present our linked scientific publication approach based on native Web technologies i.e., HTML, CSS, JavaScript, and RDFa for authoring and representing scholarly content. We demonstrate how multimodal content such as video and audio can be embedded. Especially for computer science, code examples are an important type of content, which can be integrated with these publications. We showcase, how different views of the content can be rendered for different devices (e.g. screen, print, mobile) or audiences (e.g. slideshows). A particular strength of our approach is the integration and linking of data, which can automatically update tables and diagrams when the underlying data changes. Also, all content can be annotated and represented using semantic knowledge representation formalisms to facilitate better search, exploration and retrieval of scholarly content. In the following subsections we explain and demonstrate each of these features.

© Springer International Publishing Switzerland 2015
F. Gandon et al. (Eds.): ESWC 2015, LNCS 9341, pp. 26–30, 2015.
DOI: 10.1007/978-3-319-25639-9_5

2   Technology and Design

Our work is called **Linked Research** as discussed in Enabling Accessible Knowledge [1]. There is a single template using the HTML 5 Polyglot markup. Different CSS are used to present the information for different media e.g., academic paper layouts following the ACM and LNCS authoring style guidelines, slideshow styles, or even as a W3C "Recommendation" (to only demonstrate the flexibility of semantic markup). JavaScript is applied to the document to *progressively enhance* the informations interactive components. In a nutshell, the minimum viable product encloses the following:

- Documents are human and machine-*friendly*.
- Using the *plain old semantic HTML* marking process, with further semantic annotations using microformats and RDF.
- No server required. Works on local machine.
- No installation. No account creation.
- No out-of-band tooling. A Web browser is the only requirement, whether it is a Line Mode Browser, or Firefox Nightly.
- Licenses and rights: Apache License and CC0.

The code for Linked Research is publicly available along with a demo site, with sample peer-reviewed and published 'paper'. Well-known LNCS and ACM authoring guidelines themselves are also available as examples. The ACM guidelines can be viewed or printed using LNCS, and vice-versa.

2.1   Structure and Semantics

Underneath the user interface, simple and flexible HTML patterns are used to encapsulate sectioning content. Listing 1 shows a common design pattern.

```
1  <section>
2      <h2>
3      <div>
```

Listing 1. h2 is an example heading used here for **section** titles, div as a typical wrapper for descriptions, as well as to contain further sub-sectioned content.

The available RDF and microformats of this 'paper' can be consumed using e.g., Linked Data URI Burner or RDFa 1.1 Distiller and Parser. Linked Research documents may typically include the following vocabularies: SKOS, FOAF, DC Terms, SIO, SPAR, PROV-O, OPMW, RO, Disco, QB, SIOC.

2.2   Presentation

The CSS are primarily tested using the Gecko browser engine e.g., Firefox, as it provides a more comprehensive and consistent CSS screen and print media support. The views are also tested for in other engines e.g., WebKit, and Trident. The single HTML is flexible such that it can presented in different ways (a CSS Zen Garden), using the browser or document options.

2.3　Interaction

Screen devices with interactive abilities can use the following:

- In browser editing without having to hand-code HTML or RDF syntaxes - partial support at the moment - and, sorting sections through table of contents.
- Embed data in HTML: Turtle and JSON-LD.
- Visible identifiers for sections and other important enough declared concepts. Fosters sharing and cross-linking of concepts, arguments, workflows etc.
- Document metadata for authors.
- Exporting to HTML. A (La)TeX export is planned.
- Local Storage (in the browser) for offline editing. Auto-save is available.
- View switching e.g., ACM, LNCS, W3C-REC, Slideshow, Native.

3　Multimedia Interactions

Different representations of this 'paper' and interactions are demonstrated:

3.1　Print

The view e.g., LNCS, in which the audience is experiencing this 'paper' is one of many. This document can be printed by inputting (typically keyboard or equivalent voice command): Ctrl + P or File -> Print.

3.2　Slideshow

This 'paper' can also be viewed as a slideshow.

3.3　Audio

An audio recording and its spectrogram of this 'paper' is available for supporting media. Otherwise, a complimentary spectrogram of the recording is visible in Fig. 1:

Fig. 1. Spectrogram of the audio recording of this paper.

3.4　Video

A video with captions of this 'paper' is available for supporting media. Otherwise, a screenshot or in audio only.

3.5 Statistical Displays

Inline-charts or sparkline are word-sized graphic with typographic resolution. For example, the GDP of Canada _____. This brief demonstration of Linked Stati stical Data Sparkline, (1) compliments the supporting text without breaking the readers flow, and (2) provides an opportunity for the reader to investigate further by clicking on the data-line to access the source. It is an SVG file which uses JavaScript to request data from a SPARQL Endpoint to build the datapoints and behaviour.

3.6 Linked Statistical Data Cube Designer

LSD (Linked Statistical Data) Cube Designer is a Web service with an user-interface for researchers to design their own statistical data cubes. It offers a way to search for dimensions (e.g., "reference"), measures (e.g., "value"), and attributes (e.g., "status") for their data structure and components, and then export the cubes structural information (in RDF Turtle). Figure 2 is this inter-active remote application.

Create and export a cube structure

Dimensions [+]   Measure [+]   Attribute [+]

Export Cube Structure

Make it so:

Esc key to cancel search
[+] to search and add property
[i] for more information
[✓] to select property
[x] to deselect property
[↓] to download cube structure

Fig. 2. Linked statistical data cube designer.

3.7   Executable Code

Web Science 'papers' can be far more engaging and useful to the community if we merely embrace what the Web offers. Figure 3 demonstrates the Yet Another SPARQL GUI application embedded to this document. For instance, the research paper itself creates an executable paper environment where some code can be rerun or observe the effects of changing parameters.

Fig. 3. Yet another SPARQL GUI

4   Conclusions

Our intentions with this 'paper' is primarily to emphasize the flexibility of native Web technologies for scientific publishing and communication. A comprehensive demonstration for what lies ahead naturally can not fit within an arbitrary (5) page limit. To get the most out of research communication in Web Science, it is only sensible to break-free from the archaic limitations of the print world. After all, as we have demonstrated, a PDF or print representation of this 'paper' can always be achieved. In the spirit of *open science* and to embrace the Webs values, all feedback are welcome at the canonical URL.

Reference

1. Capadisli, S., Riedl, R., Auer, S.: Enabling Accessible Knowledge, CeDEM (2015). http://csarven.ca/enabling-accessible-knowledge

Improving Semantic Relatedness in Paths for Storytelling with Linked Data on the Web

Laurens De Vocht[1]([✉]), Christian Beecks[2], Ruben Verborgh[1], Thomas Seidl[2], Erik Mannens[1], and Rik Van de Walle[1]

[1] Multimedia Lab, Ghent University - iMinds,
Gaston Crommenlaan 8 Bus 201, 9050 Ghent, Belgium
{laurens.devocht,ruben.verborgh,erik.mannens,rik.vandewalle}@ugent.be
[2] Department of Computer Science 9, Data Management and Data Exploration
Group, RWTH Aachen University, 52056 Aachen, Germany
{beecks,seidl}@cs.rwth-aachen.de

Abstract. Algorithmic storytelling over Linked Data on the Web is a challenging task in which many graph-based pathfinding approaches experience issues with *consistency* regarding the resulting path that leads to a story. In order to mitigate arbitrariness and increase consistency, we propose to improve the semantic relatedness of concepts mentioned in a story by increasing the relevance of links between nodes through additional domain delineation and refinement steps. On top of this, we propose the implementation of an optimized algorithm controlling the pathfinding process to obtain more homogeneous search domain and retrieve more links between adjacent hops in each path. Preliminary results indicate the potential of the proposal.

1 Introduction

Algorithmic storytelling can be seen as a particular kind of querying data. Given a set of keywords or entities, which are typically, but not necessarily dissimilar, it aims at generating a story by explicitly relating the query context with a path that includes semantically related resources. Storytelling is utilized for example in entertaining applications and visualizations [4] in order to enrich related Linked Data resources with data from multimedia archives and social media [1] as well as in scientific research fields such as bio-informatics where biologists try to relate sets of genes arising from different experiments by investigating the implicated pathways [3].

The most frequently encountered algorithm to determine a path between multiple resources is the A* algorithm [2]. This algorithm, which is based on a graph representation of the underlying data (i.e., resources and links between them define nodes and edges, respectively) determines an optimal solution in form of a lowest-cost traversable path between two resources. The optimality of a path, which is guaranteed by the A* algorithm, does not necessarily comply with the users' expectations. By considering for instance large real-world semantic graphs, such as Linked Data graphs, where links between nodes are semantically

© Springer International Publishing Switzerland 2015
F. Gandon et al. (Eds.): ESWC 2015, LNCS 9341, pp. 31–35, 2015.
DOI: 10.1007/978-3-319-25639-9_6

annotated, users are able to directly interpret the transitions between nodes and thus the meaning of a path. Caused by the inevitable increasing number of nodes and sometimes loosely related links among them in nowadays online datasets on the Web, optimal paths frequently show a high extent of *arbitrariness*: paths appear to be determined by chance and not by reason or principle and are often affected by resources that share many links.

In order to mitigate arbitrariness of a story, we propose a control algorithm that wraps an optimized version of our original core algorithm, which is embedded in the Everything is Connected Engine (EiCE) [1]. In fact, our contribution is twofold: (i) We outline the control algorithm which reduces arbitrariness by increasing the relevance of links between nodes through additional domain delineation and refinement steps; and (ii) we optimized the original core algorithm to support two-hop paths rather than directly linked nodes, this allows to define heuristics and weights on a broader context than a pair of directly linked nodes and predicates between them. We discuss how paths consisting of two-hop node steps are presented as building blocks for storytelling. We conclude our paper with preliminary results and an outlook on future work.

2   Pathfinding for Storytelling

Each path that contributes to a story is determined within a query context comprising both start and destination resources. Our algorithm reduces the arbitrariness of a path between these resources by increasing the *relevance* of the links between the nodes using a domain delineation step. The path is refined by controlling the iteratively application of the A* algorithm and with each iteration attempting to improve the overall semantic relatedness between the resources until a fixed number of iterations or a certain similarity threshold is reached.

2.1   Domain Delineation

Instead of directly initializing the graph as-is by including all links between the resources, we identify the relevance of predicates with respect to the query context. This is done by extracting and giving higher preference to the type of relations (predicates) that occur frequently in the query context. In this way, links leading to a story are of relevance since each predicate that describes the semantics of a link also occurs in the direct neighborhood of the query context. The goal is to determine a more homogeneous subgraph with more potentially relevant nodes to the user.

2.2   Core Algorithm

Determining a path between two nodes is carried out by means of the A* algorithm, because this algorithm provides an optimal solution, i.e., a (shortest) cost-minimal path between two nodes with respect to the weights of the links contained in the path. While the A* algorithm is able to compute an optimal solution within a computation time complexity of $\mathcal{O}(|E|)$, where E denotes the number of links to be examined, heuristics are able to reduce the runtime of this algorithm significantly and, thus, to achieve an improvement in efficiency when computing the lowest-cost path between two nodes. Our algorithm utilizes a bidirectional variant of the A* algorithm which turns out to have higher efficiency.

2.3   Refinement

After a path is determined by the A* algorithm, we measure the semantic relatedness between all resources occurring in the path with respect to the query context. This done by counting the number of overlapping predicates (i) among each other combined with those in the start and destination resources; and then (ii) averaging and normalizing this count over all resources. Depending on the threshold and the maximum number of iterations configured, typically between 3 and 10 times, the core algorithm is repeated excluding the middle hop in the path. Different outputs after each iteration are guaranteed by forcing the core algorithm to find a path without the excluded node. Finally, the path with the highest similarity score is selected for the story.

3   Presenting the Story

Obviously a set of paths is not a presentable story yet. We note that even if a path comprise just the start and destination (indicating they are linked via common hops or directly to each other), the story will contain interesting facts. This is because each step in the path is separated with at least one hop from the next node. For example, to present a story about *Carl Linnaeus* and *Charles Darwin*, the story could start from a path that goes via *J.W. von Goethe*. The resulting statements serve as basic facts, which are relation-object statements, that make up the story. It is up to the application or visualization engine to present it to end-users and enrich it with descriptions, media or further facts. Table 1 exemplarily explicates the idea of statements as story facts.

4   Preliminary Results

To determine whether the arbitrariness of a story is reduced, we validated that our optimization increased the semantic relatedness of the concepts mentioned

Table 1. The statements as story facts

About	Relation	Object
Carl Linnaeus and Charles Darwin	are	scientists
J.W. von Goethe	influenced	Carl Linnaeus and Charles Darwin
J.W. von Goethe and Charles Darwin	influenced	Karl Marx and Sigmund Freud

Table 2. The comparison between the original and optimzed algorithm shows that the semantic relatedness can be improved in all cases except for the last two when the entities were already closely related.

Query context	Original	NGD	Optimized	NGD
C._Linnaeus - C._Darwin	C._H._Merriam	0.50	J._W._Von_Goethe	**0.43**
C._Linnaeus - A._Einstein	Aristotle	0.70	J._W._Von_Goethe	**0.45**
C._Linnaeus - I._Newton	P._L._Maupertuis	0.48	D._Diderot	**0.40**
A._Einstein - I._Newton	Physics	0.62	D._Hume	**0.45**
C._Darwin - I._Newton	D._Hume	**0.38**	Royal_Liberty_School	0.40
C._Darwin - A._Einstein	D._Hume	**0.43**	B._Spinoza	0.44

in a story. To this end, we computed stories about the four highest ranked DBpedia scientists, according to their PageRank score[1], and have determined their pairwise semantic relatedness by applying the Normalized Google Distance (NGD). The results are shown in Table 2.

Table 2 shows that the entities *Aristotle* and *Physics* are included in the story when applying the original algorithm. These entities are perfect examples of *arbitrary* resources in a story which decrease the consistency. Except that they are related to science, it is unclear to the user why the algorithm 'reasoned' them to be in the story. When utilizing the optimized algorithm these entities are replaced by *J._W._Von_Goethe* and *D._Hume*.

In order to verify our results, we also include the total semantic similarity of a path by computing the semantic relatedness between all neighboring node pairs in that path. As can be seen in Table 2, the optimized algorithm is able to improve the semantic relatedness of the resulting paths.

5   Conclusions and Future Work

We proposed an optimized pathfinding algorithm for storytelling that reduces the number of arbitrary resources popping up in paths contained in the story. We added an additional resource pre-selection and a post-processing step that increases the semantic relatedness of resources. Preliminary evaluation results using the DBpedia dataset indicate that our proposal succeeds in telling a story featuring higher semantic relatedness, especially in cases where the previous algorithm did not make seemingly optimal choices in terms of semantic relatedness. Future work will mainly focus on developing the algorithm and making it available for use in applications. We will extend and verify our findings with additional semantic similarity measures besides the NGD and by investigating different weights and heuristics within the core algorithm. We will validate the correlation between the increased semantic relatedness and the impact on the

---

[1] http://people.aifb.kit.edu/ath#DBpedia_PageRank.

story consistency as perceived by users. Additionally, we will evaluate the scalability of our approach in a distributed client/server architecture.

Acknowledgment. This work is partially Funded by the Excellence Initiative of the German federal and state governments; Flanders (IWT, FWO); and the European Union.

References

1. De Vocht, L., Coppens, S., Verborgh, R., Vander Sande, M., Mannens, E., Van de Walle, R.: Discovering meaningful connections between resources in the web of data. In: Proceedings of the 6th Workshop on Linked Data on the Web (LDOW 2013) (2013)
2. Hart, P., Nilsson, N., Raphael, B.: A formal basis for the heuristic determination of minimum cost paths. IEEE Trans. Syst. Sci. Cybern. **4**, 100–107 (1968)
3. Kumar, D., Ramakrishnan, N., Helm, R.F., Potts, M.: Algorithms for storytelling. IEEE Trans. Knowl. Data Eng. **20**(6), 736–751 (2008)
4. Vander Sande, M., Verborgh, R., Coppens, S., De Nies, T., Debevere, P., De Vocht, L., De Potter, P., Van Deursen, D., Mannens, E., Van de Walle, R.: Everything is connected: using linked data for multimedia narration of connections between concepts. In: Proceedings of the 11th International Semantic Web Conference Posters and Demo Track, November 2012

Dataset Summary Visualization with LODSight

Marek Dudáš[(✉)], Vojtěch Svátek, and Jindřich Mynarz

University of Economics, Prague, Czech Republic
{marek.dudas,svatek}@vse.cz, mynarzjindrich@gmail.com

Abstract. We present a web-based tool that shows a summary of an RDF dataset as a visualization of a graph formed from classes, datatypes and predicates used in the dataset. The visualization should allow to quickly and easily find out what kind of data the dataset contains and its structure. It also shows how vocabularies are used in the dataset.

1 Introduction

In contrast to the RDBMS world, (RDF) datasets on the semantic web usually are not provided with a schema. There are of course RDFS/OWL vocabularies,[1] but those only define sets of concepts that *can* be used in a dataset rather than what combinations of concepts *should* be used to describe the data. The relationship between a vocabulary and a dataset is thus by far not as strict as the relationship between an SQL database and its schema. If users encounter an RDF *dataset* they are not familiar with, finding out what kind of data it contains is nontrivial since up-to-date and complete documentation of the dataset is usually not present. The other way around, when users encounter a *vocabulary* they are not familiar with, they can try to learn the proper usage of the vocabulary by reading the documentation and inspecting the axioms, labels and comments in the RDFS/OWL source code. However, even the vocabulary documentation may be insufficient or missing, and the axioms do not fully specify the usage, as said above. Then the only remaining option is to look at datasets where the vocabulary is used (provided they exist).

Users can obviously explore the dataset manually, e.g., using exploratory SPARQL queries. Several approaches to dataset summarization that makes such exploration easier have been implemented (discussed in Sect. 2). We present LODSight:[2] a dataset summary visualization tool based on those existing approaches. LODSight is aimed to be applicable to any RDF dataset available through a SPARQL endpoint and to show the whole dataset summary in one view. It searches the dataset for typical combinations of class instances and properties. The combinations are merged into one graph and displayed as an interactive node-link JavaScript-based visualization. The application is designed to allow a non-expert user to both (a) get an overview of the data and its structure in the dataset, and, (b) learn how the vocabularies are used in it.

---

[1] By vocabulary we mean ontology or vocabulary.

[2] Available at http://lod2-dev.vse.cz/lodsight.

© Springer International Publishing Switzerland 2015
F. Gandon et al. (Eds.): ESWC 2015, LNCS 9341, pp. 36–40, 2015.
DOI: 10.1007/978-3-319-25639-9_7

2 Related Research

The visualization in LODSight is based on the same principle as *maps of ontology usage* [3]. However, maps of ontology usage focus the visualization on entities from single namespace while we display all classes in one summarization regardless of namespace. Maps of ontology usage rely on YARS2 while we support remote summarization of theoretically any SPARQL endpoint. **ExpLOD** [4] offers a more complex approach based on bisimulation contraction. The result is a node-link visualization similar to ours but more accurate: showing a combination of links that reportedly exist in the dataset while we show combinations of links that *possibly* exist. Our visualization might be on the other hand more intuitive as it shows types of instances directly as node labels while ExpLOD shows types as separate nodes which might lead to clutter. In addition to both maps of ontology usage and ExpLOD we allow to show examples of existing combinations of instances represented by the generalized (sub)graph. An approach similar to ExpLOD is presented by Li [5]. None of the above mentioned tools seem to be publicly available. **SPARQture** [6] shows a summary of the dataset in the form of a mere list of classes but allows incremental exploration showing predicates and example instances related to a selected class. Incremental exploration is applicable on datasets of the size of DBpedia, which is simply too big for detailed view in LODSight. Somewhat similar results are offered by **Rhizomer** [1], which includes a method for displaying the hierarchy of classes used in the dataset in a treemap. We use the notion of *type-property paths* as mentioned by Presutti et al. [9] (and also as used in [10]), which aims at construction of prototypical SPARQL queries showing examples of typical data. Campinas et al. [2] discuss efficient graph summarization using MapReduce, but we aim at easier applicability accessing a SPARQL endpoint directly without the need to transform the data. Our approach is also inspired by the notion of characteristic sets [7] as used by Minh-Duc [8] to summarize a dataset into a relational schema.

3 Summarization Method

Summarization in LODSight is based on type-property and datatype-property paths. Type-property path of length 1 is a sequence `type1 - property - type2`. `Type1` and `type2` are the types of instances from the dataset that are connected by the property. We use the term path frequency to denote the number of triples `?s ?property ?o` in the dataset where `?s` is an instance of `type1` and `?o` of `type2`. We use the term *datatype-property path* for a sequence `type - data property - datatype`. Such path is present in the dataset if there is a triple `?s ?dataproperty ?l`, where `?s` is an instance of `type` and `?l` is a literal of type `datatype`. To create a dataset summary in LODSight we first find all type-property paths and merge them into one graph. Then we add datatype-property paths, whose subject type is present in the type-property paths.

The generalization is to some extent inaccurate. Each path has its instantiations existing in the dataset – there are instances typed and connected as the path shows. However, the graph created by merging the paths together may not necessarily have such instantiations in the dataset. This is explained on an example in Sect. 4. The benefit is that the final summarization is more compact, but the user has to interpret it correctly. The summarization algorithm is implemented as a Java application with Apache Jena library performing SPARQL queries on remote endpoints. The first step of the algorithm is done in a single query:

```
SELECT ?a ?p1 ?b (COUNT(*) AS ?count)
WHERE { [ a ?a ] ?p1 [ a ?b ] .} GROUP BY ?a ?p1 ?b
```

The datatype-property paths are then obtained through a series of additional queries. All paths are stored into a MySQL database and served through a script to a JavaScript application which uses D3.js library to show them in a node-link force-directed layout visualization. The summarization is not done on demand as it might be prohibitively time consuming. The JS app offers a list of prepared summarizations from which the user selects.

Evaluation. We tested LODSight on first 32 available datasets listed by default order at datahub.io.[3] In 17 cases the summarization worked, out of which in 10 cases only the type-property paths were retrieved, while queries for datatypes ended in errors.[4] Successful (including datatypes) summarizations of datasets with triple counts between 18,834 and 11,485,244 took between 4 and 44 s. Successful summarization of 117,000,000 triples took 5 min and 7 s.

4   Demonstration

An example of LODSight visualization is shown in Fig. 1. It displays a part of a public contracts dataset.[5] Each class is represented as one node, regardless of how many type-property paths it occurs in. However, the fact that a class node is in several paths does not automatically mean that there are actual instances linked as the visualization suggest. In Fig. 1 the nodes pc:Tender, gr:BusinessEntity and schema:ContactPoint are interlinked. That does not necessarily mean that each instance of gr:BusinessEntity with schema:ContactPoint specified is participating in some pc:Tender. It only means that there are some instances of pc:Tender linked to some instances of gr:BusinessEntity and some (possibly different) instances of gr:BusinessEntity that are linked to instances of schema:ContactPoint. Paths are represented by links labeled with predicates between the nodes. Technically, each link is split into two edges and the label is drawn as a diamond shaped node to avoid label and edge overlap. If there are multiple paths between two classes, they are drawn as one link with multiple labels to avoid clutter. The thickness of edges represents the frequency of

---

[3] The list was filtered to show only datasets provided with SPARQL endpoint.

[4] The problem seems to be in support of demanding queries and bind() and datatype() functions in specific endpoints.

[5] Available at http://lod2-dev.vse.cz/lodsight/?sumid=5024128&minfreq=1.

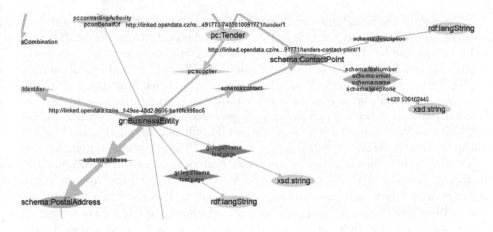

Fig. 1. An example of a "zoomed-in" summarization of public contracts dataset.

type-property paths (datatype-property frequency is not counted in the current implementation): in Fig. 1 there are more links from br:BusinessEntity to schema:PostalAddress than schema:ContactPoint. If more classes occur in a datatype-path with the same datatype the datatype node (and the link) is repeated for each such class to avoid edge crossings: see that xsd:string is displayed twice in Fig. 1. After the initial automatic layout is performed the visualization zooms out to show an overview of the whole summarization. The user can pan & zoom and drag & drop the nodes freely then.

Three main features contribute to the goals stated in the introduction: first, each node is colored according to its namespace. Therefore, the user can easily see which parts of the dataset structure are realized with which vocabularies. Second, the user can change the minimum frequency threshold of the type-property paths. A slider is provided that can change the threshold between 1 and a value near the maximum frequency in the dataset. The latter leads to displaying only the most frequent paths thus showing the "core" structure of the dataset. Third, the user can select any subset of the nodes (a subgraph) to retrieve example instantiations of it. The instantiations are retrieved on-line from the SPARQL endpoint and displayed above the corresponding nodes one combination at a time while the user can switch between them: see examples in Fig. 1 showing a combination of instances of pc:Tender, gr:BusinessEntity, schema:ContactPoint and the phone number literal that are actually present in the dataset and linked as the visualization suggests.

The demonstration will include showing visualizations of 17 datasets at various levels of detail and retrieving example instantiations for selected subgraphs.

5   Conclusions and Future Work

We presented LODSight: an RDF dataset summary visualization tool that displays typical combinations of types and predicates in a similar way as other existing approaches. There are four main advantages of our approach. First, it relies solely on SPARQL and thus allows to summarize (theoretically) any dataset accessible through a SPARQL endpoint. Second, it enables to dynamically change the level of detail and show summarizations of very large datasets. Third, it provides an option to load examples of instances and literals represented by a selected subgraph. Last, it makes the visualizations publicly available through a web browser. Real-time summarization might be considered for smaller datasets – preliminary results suggest that processing several hundred triples takes less than 20 s. For large datasets, implementing incremental exploration similar to SPARQture might be an option. We also plan to improve the reliability of the summarization: preliminary evaluation shows it worked on 53 % of tested datasets. A possible workaround for that is copying the dataset into a more reliable triple store and running the summarization there. Future evaluation will include tests with a group of users, students with basic knowledge of linked data, asked to describe displayed data or learn the usage of a vocabulary.

This research is supported by VŠE IGA No. F4/90/2015 and long-term institutional support of research activities by Faculty of Informatics and Statistics, University of Economics, Prague.

References

1. Brunetti, J.M., Garca, R., Auer, S.: From overview to facets and pivoting for interactive exploration of semantic web data. Int. J. Semantic Web Inf. Syst. **9**, 120 (2013). doi:10.4018/jswis.2013010101
2. Campinas, S., et al.: Efficiency and precision trade-offs in graph summary algorithms. In: Proceedings of the 17th International Database Engineering & Applications Symposium, pp. 38–47. ACM (2013)
3. Kinsella, S., et al.: An interactive map of semantic web ontology usage. In: 12th International Conference Information Visualisation, IV 2008, pp. 179–184. IEEE (2008)
4. Khatchadourian, S., Consens, M.P.: ExpLOD: summary-based exploration of interlinking and RDF usage in the linked open data cloud. In: Aroyo, L., Antoniou, G., Hyvönen, E., ten Teije, A., Stuckenschmidt, H., Cabral, L., Tudorache, T. (eds.) ESWC 2010, Part II. LNCS, vol. 6089, pp. 272–287. Springer, Heidelberg (2010)
5. Li, H.: Data profiling for semantic web data. In: Wang, F.L., Lei, J., Gong, Z., Luo, X. (eds.) WISM 2012. LNCS, vol. 7529, pp. 472–479. Springer, Heidelberg (2012)
6. Maali, F.: SPARQture: A More Welcoming Entry to SPARQL Endpoints. http://ceur-ws.org/Vol-1279/iesd14_9.pdf
7. Neumann, T., Moerkotte, G.: Characteristic sets: accurate cardinality estimation for RDF queries with multiple joins. In: 2011 IEEE 27th International Conference on Data Engineering (ICDE), pp. 984–994. IEEE (2011)
8. Pham, M.: Self-organizing structured RDF in MonetDB. In: 2013 IEEE 29th International Conference on Data Engineering Workshops (ICDEW), pp. 310–313. IEEE (2013)
9. Presutti, V., et al.: Extracting core knowledge from linked data. In: Proceedings of the Second Workshop on Consuming Linked Data, COLD 2011 (2011)
10. Svátek, V., et al.: B-Annot: supplying background model annotations for ontology coherence testing. In: 3rd Workshop on Debugging Ontologies and Ontology Mappings at ESWC 2014, Heraklion, Crete (2014)

The ProtégéLOV Plugin: Ontology Access and Reuse for Everyone

Nuria García-Santa[1], Ghislain Auguste Atemezing[2]([✉]),
and Boris Villazón-Terrazas[1]

[1] Expert System Iberia, Campo de las Naciones, Madrid, Spain
{ngarcia,bvillazon}@expertsystem.com
[2] MONDECA, 35 Boulevard de Strasbourg, Paris, France
ghislain.atemezing@mondeca.com

Abstract. Developing ontologies, by reusing already available and well-known ontologies, is commonly acknowledge to play a crucial role to facilitate inclusion and expansion of the Web of Data. Some recommendations exist to guide ontologists in ontology engineering, but they do not provide guidelines on how to reuse vocabularies at low fine grained, i.e., reusing specific classes and properties. Moreover, it is still hard to find a tool that provides users with an environment to reuse terms. This paper presents ProtégéLOV, a plugin for the ontology editor Protégé, that combines the access to the Linked Open Vocabularies (LOV) during ontology modeling. It allows users to search a term in LOV and provides three actions if the term exists: (i) replace the selected term in the current ontology; (ii) add the `rdfs:subClassOf` or `rdfs:subPropertyOf` axiom between the selected term and the local term; and (iii) add the `owl:equivalentClass` or `owl:equivalentProperty` between the selected term and local term. Results from a preliminary user study indicate that ProtégéLOV does provide an intuitive access and reuse of terms in external vocabularies.

Keywords: Ontology engineering · Ontology reuse · LOV · Protégé · Plugin

1 Introduction

So far, Linked Data principles and practices are being adopted by an increasing number of data providers, getting as result a global data space on the Web containing hundreds of LOD datasets [4]. There are already several guidelines for generating, publishing, interlinking, and consuming Linked Data [4]. An important task, within the generation process, is to build the vocabulary to be used for modelling the domain of the data sources, and the common recommendation is to reuse as much as possible available vocabularies [4,5]. This reuse approach speeds up the vocabulary development, and therefore, publishers will save time, efforts, and resources.

© Springer International Publishing Switzerland 2015
F. Gandon et al. (Eds.): ESWC 2015, LNCS 9341, pp. 41–45, 2015.
DOI: 10.1007/978-3-319-25639-9_8

There are research efforts, like the NeOn Methodology [7], the Best Practices for Publishing Linked Data - W3C Working Group Note [5], and the work proposed by Lonsdale et al. [6]. However, at the time of writing we have not found specific and detailed guidelines that describe how to reuse available vocabularies at fine granularity level, i.e., reusing specific classes and properties. Our claim is that this difficulty in how to reuse vocabularies at low fine grained level is one of major barriers to the vocabulary development and in consequence to deployment of Linked Data.

Moreover, the recent success of Linked Open Vocabularies (LOV[1]) as a central point for curated catalog of ontologies is helping to convey on best practices to publish vocabularies on the Web, as well as to help in the Data publication activity on the Web. LOV comes with many features, such as an API, a search function and a SPARQL endpoint.

In this paper we propose an initial set of guidelines for this task, and provide technological support by means of a plugin for Protégé, which is one of the popular frameworks for developing ontologies in a variety of formats including OWL, RDF(S), and XML Schema. It is backed by a strong community of developers and users in many domains. One success on Protégéalso depends on the availability to extend the core framework adding new functionalities by means of plug-ins. In addition, we propose to explore, design and implement a plug-in of LOV in Protégéfor easing the development of ontologies by reusing existing vocabularies at low fine grained level. The tool helps to improve the modeling and reuse of ontologies used in the LOD cloud.

2 Reusing Vocabulary Elements When Building Ontologies

In this section we describe the procedure of reusing available vocabulary terms when building ontologies. In a nutshell, the task of building vocabularies by reusing available vocabulary terms consists of

- Search for suitable vocabulary terms to reuse from the LOV repository. The search should be conducted by using the terms of the application domain.
- Assess the set of candidate terms from LOV repository. In this particular case the results coming from LOV repository include a score for each term retrieved.
- Select the most appropriate term taking into the account its score.
- Include the selected term in the ontology that has being developed. The selected term will be the external term. There are three alternatives in this case:
  - Include the external term and use it directly in the local ontology by defining local axioms to/from that term in the local ontology.
  - Include the external term, create a local term, and define the `rdfs:sub ClassOf` or `rdfs:subPropertyOf` axiom to relate both terms.
  - Include the external term, create a local term, and define the `owl:equival- entClass` or `owl:equivalentProperty` axiom to relate both terms.

---

[1] http://lov.okfn.org/dataset/lov/.

3   Related Work

The BioPortal Reference Plugin[2] allows the user to insert into the ontology references to external ontologies and terminologies stored in BioPortal[3]. The plugin allows to generate external reference of a selected term. Additionally, the BioPortal Import Plugin[4] allows users to import classes from external ontologies stored in the BioPortal ontology repository. The user can import entire trees of classes with a desired depth and choose which properties to import for each class. However, those plugins work only with Protégé3.x releases and are not ported yet to recent versions.

Most closely related to the ProtégéLOV plugin are approaches that use semantic search engine to support the process of editing an ontology and make large scale knowledge reuse automatically integrated in the tool. An example is the Watson Plugin [2] for the NeOn Toolkit [3], a plugin supporting the NeOn life-cycle management using the Watson [1] APIs[5]. However the similar plugin for Protege[6] is just a proof of concept rather than a real plugin.

4   Linked Open Vocabulaires (LOV)

The intended purpose of the LOV [8] is to help users to find and reuse terms of vocabularies in Linked Open Data. For achieving that purpose, the LOV gives access to vocabularies metadata and terms using programmatic access with APIs. LOV[7] catalogue is a hub of curated vocabularies used in the Linked Open Data Cloud, as well as other vocabularies suggested by users for their reuse. Some of the three main features of the LOV are for: (1) searching ontologies according to their scope, (2) assessing ontologies by providing a score for each term retrieved by a keyword search and (3) interconnecting ontologies using VOAF vocabulary[8]. The search function uses an algorithm based on the term popularity in LOD and in the LOV ecosystem. The matched resource set for each term should be the value of the (a) `rdfs:label` (b) `rdfs:comment`, or (c) `rdfs:description` property.

Futhermore, the LOV APIs give a remote access to the many functions of LOV through a set of RESTful services[9]. The APIs give access through three different type of services related to: (1) vocabulary terms (classes, properties, datatypes and instances), (2) vocabulary browsing and (3) ontology's creators.

5   ProtégéLOV

ProtégéLOV is an open source tool that provides support to the methodological guidelines described in Sect. 2. It is written in Java programming language as a

---

[2] http://protegewiki.stanford.edu/wiki/BioPortal_Reference_Plugin.
[3] http://bioportal.bioontology.org/.
[4] http://protegewiki.stanford.edu/wiki/BioPortal_Import_Plugin.
[5] http://watson.kmi.open.ac.uk/WS_and_API.html.
[6] http://protegewiki.stanford.edu/wiki/Watson_Search_Preview.
[7] http://lov.okfn.org/dataset/lov/.
[8] http://lov.okfn.org/vocab/voaf.
[9] http://lov.okfn.org/dataset/lov/apidoc/.

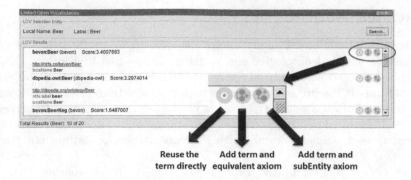

Fig. 1. Three actions currently available in the plugin after looking up a term in LOV catalogue: (a) reuse it directly, (b) add equivalent axiom and (c) add subEntity axiom

plugin for the Protégéontology editor. It can be easily installed by just copying the jar file provided at the ProtégéLOV website[10] into the plugins directory of an existing Protégéinstallation. Then upon a new start, the user should select *Linked Open Vocabularies* item, within the *Ontology views* menu item.

Currently, ProtégéLOV[11] provides the following five functionalities:

1. **Search for a particular term (class or property) in LOV repository.** The user selects a particular term from the *Class, Object property* or *Data property* navigator. Next, the user switches to the *Linked Open Vocabularies View* and performs a search on the LOV repository. The system takes as input the selected term, and calls the LOV REST API to get the LOV terms that match the criteria. The plugin provides the following information (if it is available) for each term (1) URI, (2) score, (3) label, (4) local name, and (5) usage note.

2. **Reuse directly a particular term from LOV repository.** The user selects the *reuse directly* option. Next, the system replaces the selected term from the *Class, Object property* or *Data property* navigator, and replaces by the selected term from LOV.

3. **Add the particular term and define the `owl:equivalentClass` or `owl:equivalentProperty` axiom.** The user selects the *add entity and equivalent axiom* option. Next, the system includes the new term on the local ontology, and defines `owl:equivalentClass` or `owl:equivalentProperty` axiom to relate both terms.

4. **Add the particular term and define the `rdfs:subClassOf` or `rdfs:subPropertyOf` axiom.** The user selects the *add entity and sub-entity axiom* option. Next, the system includes the new term on the local ontology, and defines `rdfs:subClassOf` or `rdfs:subPropertyOf` axiom to related both terms.

Figure 1 depicts the three main actions the user can perform.

---

[10] http://labs.mondeca.com/protolov/.
[11] A video is also available at https://www.youtube.com/watch?v=UgA17N5FNzA.

6   Evaluation

We have conducted an initial user driven evaluation of the tool. For this preliminary evaluation we keep the number of evaluators low; seven ontology engineers used our plugin and gave us an insight on their experience by filling in a questionnaire[12]. The results indicate that while the tool needs some minor improvements, the majority of the evaluators still consider the tool to be useful.

7   Conclusions and Future Work

In this paper we have presented (1) initial guidelines that describe how to reuse available vocabularies at low granularity level, i.e., by reusing specific classes and properties, and (2) a tool that provides technological support by means of a plugin for Protégéthat access LOV API. As future work we plan to fully evaluate the tool and guidelines.

During the demonstration we will show to potential users how to install the plugin and how to quickly build ontologies by reusing terms from LOV repository in Protégé.

Acknowledgments. Thanks to Pierre-Yves and the LOV team for maintaining the LOV catalog and the API access.

References

1. D'Aquin, M., Baldassarre, C., Gridinoc, L., Sabou, M., Angeletou, S., Motta, E.: Watson: Supporting next generation semantic web applications (2007)
2. D'Aquin, M., Suárez-Figueroa, M.C.: A Quick Guide to Knowledge Reuse with the Watson Plugin for the NeOn Toolkit (2008). http://watson.kmi.open.ac.uk/DownloadsAndPublications_files/WNTP-guide.pdf
3. Haase, P., Lewen, H., Studer, R., Tran, D., Erdmann, M., d'Aquin, M., Motta, E.: The neon ontology engineering toolkit. In: WWW (2008)
4. Heath, T., Bizer C.: Linked Data: Evolving the Web into a Global Data Space. Synthesis Lectures on the Semantic Web. Morgan & Claypool Publishers (2011)
5. Hyland, B., Atemezing, G., Villazon-Terrazas, B.: Best Practices for Publishing Linked Data. W3C Working Group Note (2014). http://www.w3.org/TR/ld-bp/
6. Lonsdale, D., Embley, D.W., Ding, Y., Xu, L., Hepp, M.: Reusing ontologies and language components for ontology generation. Data Knowl. Eng. **69**(4), 318–330 (2010). Including Special Section: 12th International Conference on Applications of Natural Language to Information Systems (NLDB2007) - Three selected and extended papers
7. Suárez-Figueroa, M.-C., Gómez-Pérez, A., Motta, E., Gangemi, A.: Ontology Engineering in a Networked World. Springer, Berlin (2012)
8. Vandenbussche, P.-Y., Atemezing, G.A., Poveda-Villalónc, M., Vatant, B.: LOV: a gateway to reusable semantic vocabularies on the Web. Semantic Web Journal (under review) (2015). http://www.semantic-web-journal.net/system/files/swj974.pdf

---

[12] http://goo.gl/H4YgBJ.

Controlling and Monitoring Crisis

Nuria García-Santa[1], Esteban García-Cuesta[2]([⊠]), and Boris Villazón-Terrazas[1]

[1] Expert System Iberia, Campo de las Naciones, Madrid, Spain
ngarcia@expertsystem.com, esteban.garcia@uem.es
[2] Universidad Europea de Madrid, Madrid, Spain
bvillazon@expertsystem.com

Abstract. Nowadays there is an increase interest on using social media contents for detecting and help during natural disasters. That interest is mainly based on the successful use of this type of data in the different phases of a disaster management process which ranges from early detection to efficient communication during the management of disasters. This paper focuses on the first phases of disasters' management and presents a system that allows to analyze, enrich, and detect on real time needs from a set of web sources. By using the concept of crowd as a sensors, this application can help, jointly with other traditional systems, to improve the current applied procedures during the initial phases of the disaster and detect demanded needs.

Keywords: Disaster management · Social media · Emergency assistance · Crowdsourcing

1 Introduction

The combination of recent advances of information technologies and communications, with the advent of social media applications has fueled a new landscape of emergency and disaster response systems, by allowing affected citizens to generate geo-referenced real time information on critical events. Moreover, information from social media is increasingly becoming an important source of knowledge not only for situation awareness but also for obtaining users experiences, feelings, and critical local knowledge through their post and comments about the event [4]. The identification and analysis of such events is not straightforward and the application of automatic tools is needed for both language processing and semantic interpretation.

In this scenario the concept of "crowd as a sensor" is very relevant due to it provides a larger coverage of the situation and its context. Furthermore the concept of 'crowd as journalist' which can also provide an initial interpretation of the event is an extra which is obtained by analyzing the comments that people provide. That terminology has its roots in the "crowdsourcing" term which can be defined as a process of obtaining needed services, ideas, or content by soliciting contributions from a large group of people, and especially from an online community, rather than from traditional employees or suppliers [4].

© Springer International Publishing Switzerland 2015
F. Gandon et al. (Eds.): ESWC 2015, LNCS 9341, pp. 46–50, 2015.
DOI: 10.1007/978-3-319-25639-9_9

At present, there are several crowdsourcing open platforms available on the web, which are being used by governments, crisis response teams, NGOs, bussiness organizations and other individuals to collect data and use it to develop new policies, innovative ideas for new products, help victims of natural calamities to find refuges, medicines, and other emergency needs [2]. Following that approach we present in this paper an ongoing system for helping during the initial phases of a crisis by relying on the contents and extraction of knowledge from social media channels such as Twitter[1] and Facebook[2], and using an open crowdsourcing platform so called Ushahidi[3]. Our motivation is to convert social media messages into actionable units of information (AUIs) which can be consumed directly by final users or by other machines in order to generate an automatic response to a particular crisis. The system is based on Linked Open Data [1] to alleviate the integration problems of crowdsourced data and to improve the exploitation of such new generated data by other crisis control systems.

2 Crowd Crisis Control

Crowd Crisis Control[4] is an under construction platform that aims at controlling and monitoring large areas humanitarian crisis within low-cost technologies. The platform makes use of XLike multi-linguistic pipelines, developed within the context of the XLike EU FP7 project[5], which, among other functionalities, provide basic linguistic state-of-the-art tokenization, lemmatization, part of speech tagging, and name entity recognition. Moreover, one of the main advantages of such infrastructure is that it provides a common framework for the four major languages worldwide: English, Spanish, Chinese, and German.

The system has been implemented and it is based on the platform Ushahidi[6], a framework that provides visualization, reporting, and data collection capabilities, and allows the interaction with external volunteers. During the training of the system we have collected a database of crisis alerts by monitoring in English and Spanish some agency channels from Twitter and Facebook, such as *112Madrid*[7,8], Emergency Center of Madrid, Spain and *nswpolice*[9,10], Police of Sydney, Australia.

Next, we present a high level overview of the complete workflow of the platform. The implemented system periodically monitors information from social networks channels such as Twitter and Facebook, extracts relevant data (considering relevant those posts or comments which contains any word considered

---

[1] https://twitter.com/.
[2] http://facebook.com/.
[3] http://www.ushahidi.com/.
[4] http://crowdcrisiscontrol.isoco.net/crowdmap/.
[5] http://www.xlike.org/.
[6] http://www.ushahidi.com/.
[7] https://twitter.com/112cmadrid.
[8] https://es-la.facebook.com/112ComunidadeMadrid.
[9] https://twitter.com/nswpolice.
[10] https://www.facebook.com/nswpoliceforce.

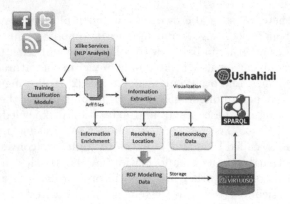

Fig. 1. Internal Workflow of CrowdCrisis Control

in the crisis vocabulary which has been previously defined automatically), analyzes the texts and automatically filter and enrich those that add value in the management of humanitarian crisis.

The Fig. 1 shows the system workflow which includes the following steps:

- **Identification and crawling of data sources:** it monitors social network channels through an API REST facilitated by these platforms. We have used the APIs provided by Twitter[11] and Facebook[12].
- **Analysis of text messages:** it processes texts obtained from the different sources by applying the natural language processing techniques which are provided by the multilingual XLike services [3].
- **Training at classification module:** it parses texts and uses machine learning techniques (e.g. naive bayes) to train and filter results for each one of the domains (fire, earthquake, flood, etc.).
- **Extraction of relevant information:** it includes the following tasks
  - modeling of the unstructured data to obtain information such as source, brief description, date, etc. and also include the predicted domain (type of emergency, fire, flood, etc.) of the texts which are obtained by the classifier module.
  - extraction of the location from mobile devices (whenever it is possible due to not all the users have this option activated); if that is not possible then the localization is extracted directly from the social networks platform whenever it is available.
  - extraction of cross-information by linking the analyzed data and the obtained entities with external sources of information. For example using named entities related to locations and link those to resources coming from Geonames[13] and OpenWeatherMap[14].

---

[11] https://api.twitter.com/1.1/.
[12] https://graph.facebook.com/.
[13] http://geonames.org.
[14] http://openweathermap.org/.

Fig. 2. Crowd Crisis Control Platform - map and report visualization of the incidents

- **Modeling and transformation of data:** it structures the analyzed data into RDF[15] format conforming to standard vocabularies and ontologies, such as MOAC[16] and WGS84[17].
- **Publication of analyzed and structured data:** it stores the RDF data in a publicly accessible Virtuoso[18] triplestore and also it is provided using Ushahidi platform[19] to manage easily the crisis information reports.
- **Visualization of the data:** it presents crisis reports on Ushahidi platform which provides an end-user appealing visualization at the Crowd Crisis Control website[20]. Ushahidi platform allows showing emergency reports, with textual and media resources, as temporal and spatial data. Besides it includes collaborative features, like the option of making comments or send reports by end users, it facilitates sending alerts about emergencies monitored to every registered user, and it supports PC and mobiles devices.

3 Evaluation

The presented system has been deployed within the context of C3 Spanish Project[21] and it is monitoring crisis located in the countries Spain and Australia. Figure 2 shows the geolocalization of the incidents and the obtained reports resulting from the classification of detected incidents. Despite the interface has been implemented in Spanish, due to the C3 Spanish project main coverage and clients are in Spain, we want to point out that the systems can also analyze other languages such as English or any other which is compliant with the APIs provided by the XLike multilingual pipeline [3].

---

[15] http://www.w3.org/RDF.
[16] http://www.observedchange.com/moac/ns/.
[17] http://www.w3.org/2003/01/geo/wgs84_pos.
[18] http://virtuoso.openlinksw.com/.
[19] http://www.ushahidi.com/products/ushahidi-platform.
[20] http://crowdcrisiscontrol.isoco.net/crowdmap.
[21] http://crowdcrisiscontrol.isoco.net/.

As can be seen, the system automatically extracts those comments or posts which are associated to any of the categories that has been trained for and in this case the ones shown belongs to a fire crisis and contain different information such as prevention information to avoid forest fires (second one from the top) or some consequences due to a fire which has already happened such as evacuation of people from their houses. It worth to highlight that this type of information belongs also to different phases of a crisis management process which currently we are not able to automatically categorize.

4   Conclusions

In this paper we have presented an ongoing system for managing crisis which is based on the assumption that the information provided by the crowd through the social media channels can complement the traditional sources of information. For this purpose we have analyzed to major social media platforms such as Twitter and Facebook and implemented a new crowdsourcing platform, which is based on the open source platform Ushahidi.

The presented system include all the needed functionalites in order to perform a complete knowledge extraction process in a crisis scenario covering the functionalities of extraction and access to the source data, filtering of useful post/comments, natural language processes, structuring of the data, classification and finally representation and interpretation. We are able to process this workflow for Spanish and English though it can be easily extended to any other language which is covered by services of the XLike EU project. Despite the current system has many of the needed funcionalities already implemented, the automatically categorization of the texts regarding its membership to one of the phases during the management of a crisis is proposed as the next most important challenge to be achieved.

Acknowledgments. This work was supported by X-Like project (ICT-288342-STREP) and Spanish CrowdCrisisControl project (IPT-2012-0968-390000).

References

1. Bizer, C., Heath, T., Berners-Lee, T.: Linked data - the story so far. Int. J. Semant. Web Inf. Syst. (IJSWIS) **5**, 1–22 (2009)
2. Halder, B.: Evolution of crowdsourcing: potential data protection, privacy and security concerns under the new media age. In: Democracia Digital e Governo Eletrônico, Florianópolis, vol. 10, pp. 1–17 (2014)
3. Padró, L., Agic, Z., Carreras, X., Fortuna, B., Garcia-Cuesta, E., Li, Z.: Language processing infrastructure in the xlike project. In: Proceedings of the Ninth International Conference on Language Resources and Evaluation (LREC 14) (2014)
4. Poblet, M., García-Cuesta, E., Casanovas, P.: Crowdsourcing tools for disaster management: a review of platforms and methods. In: Casanovas, P., Pagallo, U., Palmirani, M., Sartor, G. (eds.) AICOL 2013. LNCS, vol. 8929, pp. 261–274. Springer, Heidelberg (2014)

FAGI-gis: A Tool for Fusing Geospatial RDF Data

Giorgos Giannopoulos[✉], Nick Vitsas, Nikos Karagiannakis,
Dimitrios Skoutas, and Spiros Athanasiou

IMIS Institute, "Athena" Research Center, Athens, Greece
`giann@imis.athena-innovation.gr`

Abstract. In this demonstration, we present FAGI-gis, a tool for fusing geospatial RDF data. FAGI-gis is the core component of the FAGI framework, which handles all the steps of the fusion process of two interlinked RDF datasets in order to produce an integrated, aligned and richer dataset that combines data and metadata from both initial datasets. In the demonstation, we showcase how a user can use FAGI-gis's map based UI to perform several fusion actions on linked geospatial entities, considering both spatial and non-spatial properties of them.

1 Introduction

Languages and standards for organizing and querying semantic information, such as RDF(S) and SPARQL, are increasingly being adopted not only within academic communities but also by corporate vendors, which turn to semantic technologies to more effectively organize, expose and exchange their data as Linked Data. However, it is often the case that different data sources, although describing the same real world entities, provide different views of them, either by containing information on different subsets of attributes or even by providing different values on the same attributes. Typical reasons for this is that some sources may be outdated or may serve different purposes. For example, different maps of a city's roads and buildings, obtained from different sources (e.g., governmental, commercial, crowdsourced), may differ in the geometries and coordinates of the depicted geospatial features, as well as on the type, richness and correctness of the metadata associated with them (e.g. names and categories of buildings). As a result, information for the same real world entities is often spread across several heterogeneous datasets, each one providing partial and/or contradicting views of it. These need to be fused in order to acquire a unified, cleaner and richer dataset.

Fusion handles the merging of the linked entities, i.e., for each set of linked entities it produces a richer, more correct and more complete description w.r.t. to the properties describing it. It involves recognizing which properties of the entities correspond to each other and resolving potential conflicts or irregularities, such as different values for the same property, lack of values or properties, differences in metadata quality, etc.

© Springer International Publishing Switzerland 2015
F. Gandon et al. (Eds.): ESWC 2015, LNCS 9341, pp. 51–57, 2015.
DOI: 10.1007/978-3-319-25639-9_10

In this demonstration, we present a tool for fusing geospatial RDF data. Based on our findings on the shortcomings of previous works [1], we propose a fusion framework called FAGI (Fusion and Aggregation for Geospatial Information) that includes all the aspects of the process of fusing geospatial RDF data. Specifically, we present the implementation of the core component of the framework: *FAGI-gis*, a tool for performing geospatial processing transformations on RDF geometry features, so that they can be used on complex fusion actions, involving both spatial and non-spatial properties of the interlinked entities.

2   Related Work

Although several works exist on schema integration and interlinking of RDF data, fusion has received less attention and is still a field of ongoing research. Below, we provide a brief overview of the main existing tools. Also, none of the following tools deal with geospatial RDF data. FAGI-gis fills this gap as shown in this demonstration.

Sieve [2] focuses on quality assessment and fusion of Linked Data, being part of a larger framework for Linked Data integration [3] that provides state-of-the-art techniques for data fusion. Fusion takes into account factors such as timeliness of data, provenance, as well as user configurable preference lists on features of the dataset. ODCleanStore [4] is another framework that supports linking, cleaning, transformation and quality assessment operations on Linked Data. The fusion component supports several user configurable fusion strategies, that also consider provenance and quality metadata of the datasets. KnoFuss [5] is a framework for interlinking, conflict detection, and fusion, with main focus on interlinking. It implements several variations of the Jaro-Winkler string similarity metric and an adaptive learning clustering algorithm, which is applied in a configurable way.

3   Geospatial Fusion in FAGI-gis

The central part of the fusion process is the combination of different geometries into richer and more accurate ones. FAGI-gis is the component of our framework that provides the infrastructure for this task. The tool is implemented in Java and Javascript and can be operated either via a command line utility or via a web-based graphical user interface. Since complex geospatial operations are typically time consuming, a PostgreSQL/PostGIS database is used for efficient geospatial indexing and the support of a wide range of efficient calculation and transformation functions. FAGI-gis is publicly available on GitHub[1].

The input of FAGI-gis is two separate RDF datasets and a set of links that interlink entities from one dataset to the other. The output of the tool is a unified dataset, where the geometries of the linked entities, along with the rest, non-spatial properties, are fused according to selected fusion actions. Input and output data are read from SPARQL endpoints and written in Virtuoso RDF

---

[1] https://github.com/GeoKnow/FAGI-gis.

Store respectively. Also, the supported vocabularies for representing geospatial features include GeoSPARQL with WKT serialization of geospatial features and Basic Geo.

FAGI-gis supports a set of 15 fusion actions handling both spatial and non-spatial properties. Some of them are of general use and can be applied to both types of properties, while others apply on only one type. Indicatively, FAGI-gis allows the concatenation of strings and geometries, shifting and re-scaling of geometries and mutual handling of semantically related properties (e.g. separate properties that contain different elements of an address can be handled together). Table 1 presents each fusion action, along with the type of property it applies on and a short description of its functionality.

3.1 Tool Demonstration

Next, we demonstrate the usage of the software through its graphical user interface[2]. First, the user needs to input the connection information regarding the SPARQL endpoints containing the two datasets, the local Virtuoso and PostGIS databases and the file containing the pairs of interlinked entities.

Upon that, two processes are performed: (i) The RDF triples representing the links are loaded in an RDF graph in the local Virtuoso store and (ii) for each dataset, all possible classes that may characterize any of the linked entities are queried from the respective SPARQL endpoints and presented in two distinct lists (Fig. 1). The user is able to optionally choose specific classes from both datasets and filter the pairs of linked entities based on them.

After this task is performed, the linked entities are visualized on the map of the interface through points or polygons (see polygons in Fig. 2). Further, a straight line segment connects each pair of linked entities so that the user can explicitly see on the map the pairs of entities to be fused.

The next step regards property matching. FAGI-gis first selects some sample linked entities pairs and tries to automatically match the properties of the entities for each pair individually. To this end, it compares the namings of the properties based on their lexical/semantic, textual and literal type similarity. Eventually, the total of the properties for all selected link pairs are presented to the user divided into two lists, one for each of the two input datasets (see "Fusion" panel in Fig. 1). When the user selects a property from one list (dataset), the system marks with yellow colour the properties of the other list (dataset) that are found to match. The final selection of the matching is performed by the user who is also able to rename the final, fused property to be kept.

Eventually, the actual fusion task takes place. The user can select a pair of linked entities from the map by clicking on the line segments that represent links. Then, the fusion panel pops-up (Fig. 2), that allows to perform different fusion actions, for each pair of properties corresponding to the linked entities. Upon that, the system executes the required transformations and produces RDF triples, either to be output in a new graph, or to replace some of the initial triples of one of the input datasets.

---

[2] A screencast video is also available at http://vimeo.com/117606305.

Table 1. FAGI fusion actions

Action	Type	Functionality
Keep target	Both	Keeps the value of the first property
Keep source	Both	Keeps the value of the second property
Keep both	Both	Keeps both properties separately
Concatenate	Both	Keeps only one property that contains information from both initial properties
Keep complex geometry	Spatial	Keeps the geometry that consists of the most points
Keep most complete	Non-spatial	Keeps the literal of the property, if it contains a large part of the literal of the other property
Keep complex geometry and shift it	Spatial	Keeps the geometry that consists of the most points and shifts it so that it has as centroid the centroid of the other geometry
Keep the average of two points	Spatial	Keeps a new point geometry that is calculated by the average of the two initial points
Keep one geometry and scale it	Spatial	Keeps one of the geometries and rescales it according to some given factor
Multi-fusion	Non-spatial	Allows the handling of multiple properties describing sub-attributes of a more general attribute of an entity to be handled as a singular property
Chain-fusion	Non-spatial	Considers for fusion properties that describe an entity but are not directly connected with it

4   Evaluation

In the current version of the tool, automatic execution or recommendation of fusion actions is not yet implemented, thus an evaluation of the correctness and quality of the fusion results is not applicable. However, it is interesting to examine whether the tool runs in acceptable times, given large workloads.

The input used for the evaluation is two datasets extracted from Wikimapia[3], a crowdsourced, open-content collaborative mapping initiative. In particular, we considered a set of cities throughout the world (Athens, London, Leipzig, Berlin, New York) and downloaded the whole content provided by Wikimapia regarding the geospatial entities included in those geographical areas. The aforementioned dumps were transformed into RDF triples in a straightforward way. In order to create a synthetically linked dataset that can be fused, we split the Wikimapia RDF dataset, duplicating the geometries and dividing them into the two datasets in the following way: for each polygon geometry, we created another point geometry located in the centroid of the polygon and then shifted the point by a random (but bounded) factor. The polygon was left in the first dataset,

---

[3] http://wikimapia.org/.

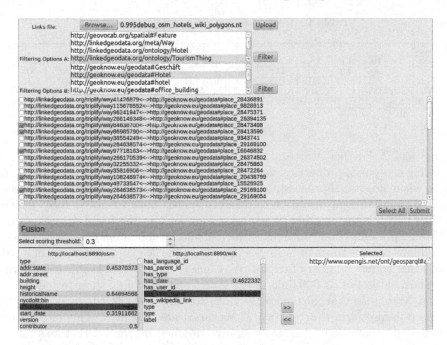

Fig. 1. Class filtering and property matching pane (Color figure online)

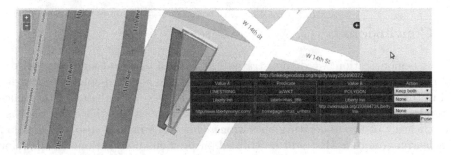

Fig. 2. Fusion pane

while the point was transferred to the second dataset. The rest of the properties where distributed between the two datasets. This way, every entity that exists in both datasets is considered interlinked among the datasets.

The software is tested in fusing 1000, 10,000 and 100,000 linked entity pairs. We note that these numbers actually correspond to a much higher number of total triples to be fused. The latter is represented by the size of each fused dataset in terms of number of triples that is recorded at each experiment. The second parameter is the size of property chains (sequences) that are considered as metadata of the linked entities. The available dataset had only property chains of depth 2, so our measurements were limited to chains of size 1 (no property

Table 2. Total runtimes and output triples.

chain=2						chain=1					
links	Total Time (QE)			Triples in fused graph			links	Total Time (QE)			Triples in fused graph		
	S	KL	KB	S	KL	KB		S	KL	KB	S	KL	KB
1000	20.06	16.13	15.13	21531	21513	23531	1000	14.86	14.34	13.92	16521	16521	18521
10000	96.02	42.46	87.01	222445	222445	242445	10000	30.27	26.42	27.94	132425	132425	152425
100000	276.29	295.47	252.22	4936015	4936015	5136015	100000	131.87	131.82	152.76	2381137	2381137	2581137

chains) and 2. Further, we tested the system on three different fusion actions regarding geospatial properties: keep left (denoted KL) which is a simple fusion action where no special processing is required; shift geometry (denoted S), which requires a spatial transformation to take place; keep both (denoted KB), which requires that a larger number of geometries are kept in the fused dataset.

Table 2 presents total runtimes of the tool and total number of output triples. All columns present times in seconds except from the last column (triples in fused graph) that counts number of triples. We can see that the tool is able to perform fusion on a dataset of 100000 links in less than 5 minutes for all three tested fusion actions. Note, also that, although the links are only 100000, the final triples of the fused datasets (in the "chain $= 2$" scenario) are 5 Million. This fact, along with the fact that the tool is unavoidably burdened by the RDF store's query execution overhead, which can be further optimized, shows the scalability of the tool and the potential for further improvement.

5 Conclusions

In this demonstration, we demonstrated FAGI-gis, a tool that supports geospatial processing and transformations for fusing spatial and non-spatial properties of interlinked RDF entities. Our future work focuses on enhancing the functionality of the tool, to support more fusion strategies, as well as to increase the efficiency of the underlying operations. Our plans include also the addition of a learning module that will be trained on previous user actions to allow for automatic fusion recommendations.

Acknowledgments. This work was supported by a grant from the EU's 7th Framework Programme (2007–2013) provided for the project GeoKnow (GA no. 318159).

References

1. Giannopoulos, G., Skoutas, D., Maroulis, T., Karagiannakis, N., Athanasiou, S.: FAGI: a framework for fusing geospatial RDF data. In: Proceedings of OTM, ODBASE (2014)
2. Mendes, P.N., Muhleisen, H., Bizer, C.S.: linked data quality assessment and fusion. In: Proceedings of the Joint EDBT/ICDT Workshops, pp. 116–123 (2012)
3. Schultz, A., Matteini, A., Isele, R., Mendes, P., Bizer, C., Becker, C.: LDIF-a framework for large-scale linked data integration. In: WWW, developer track (2012)

4. Michelfeit, J., Knap, T.: Linked data fusion in ODCleanStore. In: Proceedings of the International Semantic Web Conference (Posters & Demos) (2012)
5. Nikolov, A., Uren, V.S., Motta, E., De Roeck, A.: Integration of semantically annotated data by the KnoFuss architecture. In: Gangemi, A., Euzenat, J. (eds.) EKAW 2008. LNCS (LNAI), vol. 5268, pp. 265–274. Springer, Heidelberg (2008)

A Semantic, Task-Centered Collaborative Framework for Science

Yolanda Gil[1], Felix Michel[1(✉)], Varun Ratnakar[1],
and Matheus Hauder[2]

[1] Information Sciences Institute, University of Southern California,
Marina del Rey, CA 90292, USA
{gil,felixm,varunr}@isi.edu
[2] Software Engineering for Business Information Systems,
Technical University Munich, 85748 Munich, Germany
hauder@in.tum.de

Abstract. This paper gives an overview of the Organic Data Science framework, a new approach for scientific collaboration that opens the science process and exposes information about shared tasks, participants, and other relevant entities. The framework enables scientists to formulate new tasks and contribute to tasks posed by others. The framework is currently in use by a science community studying the age of water, and is beginning to be used by others.

Keywords: Organic data science · Semantic wiki · Collaborative web platforms

1 Introduction

The Web was originally developed to support collaboration in science. Although scientists benefit from many forms of collaboration on the Web (e.g., blogs, wikis, forums, code sharing, etc.), most collaborative projects are coordinated over email, phone calls, and in-person meetings.

We are interested in supporting scientific collaborations where joint work occurs on a concrete problem of interest, with many participants, and over a long period of time. Although the Web may be used to share information, there is no explicit support for the shared tasks involved. These tasks are discussed through email, phone calls, and occasional face-to-face meetings.

2 Organic Data Science

We are developing an Organic Data Science framework based on a task-centered organization of the collaboration, and that includes principles from social sciences for successful on-line communities. Figure 1 illustrates the representation of a task, which includes properties such as the owner, participants, start and end times, and expertise required. Users can create additional task properties, as is typical in semantic wikis. They can add subtasks, and sign up as participants in tasks created by others. These

© Springer International Publishing Switzerland 2015
F. Gandon et al. (Eds.): ESWC 2015, LNCS 9341, pp. 58–61, 2015.
DOI: 10.1007/978-3-319-25639-9_11

tasks capture the what, who, when, and how of the activities pursued by the collaboration, and capture a novel form of science processes that has not been explicitly captured before.

Our Organic Data Science framework is implemented as an extension of a semantic wiki, in particular the Semantic MediaWiki platform [1]. Users can add properties to tasks as needed, and can describe any entity of interest to the collaboration (datasets, software, papers, etc.) using semantic properties of the wiki. Every task has its own page, and therefore a unique URL, which gives users a way to refer to the task from any other pages in the site as well as outside of it. Semantic wikis provide an easy-to-use interface where users can define structured properties, which are then represented in RDF and exported as linked data. The framework is still under development, and it evolves to accommodate user feedback and to incorporate new collaboration features.

We view the scientific collaboration as an on-line community, and have designed the Organic Data Science framework following social design principles uncovered by research on successful on-line communities [2]. The community design aspects are described in [3]. The semantic aspects of the design are described in [4].

The Organic Data Science framework captures science processes that are not made explicit in publications, supports the formation of ad-hoc groups to work on tasks of interest, enables anyone to contribute to tasks that match their interests, and advertises ongoing work to potential newcomers.

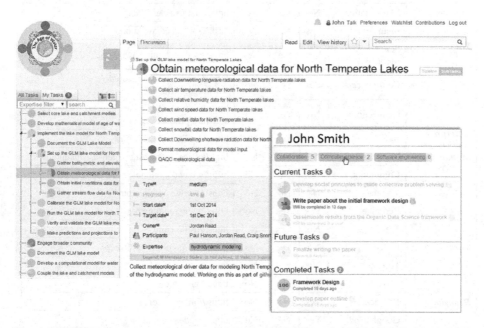

Fig. 1. Collaboration is organized around tasks in the Organic Data Science framework, represented through RDF properties in the underlying semantic wiki. These semantic properties are used by the system to generate content for other pages, such as the user page shown in the right side based on the tasks that this user is participating in. Status icons, shown as pie charts next to tasks, are also derived from the semantic properties that specify task type and deadlines.

Table 1 illustrates the features of the Organic Data Science framework (shown at the bottom), compared other collaborative tools on the Web that scientists use. Our framework is the only one that is designed to support on-line communities, is organized around tasks, and captures semantic structures for the entities involved in the collaboration.

Table 1. An overview of features supported by existing online collaboration tools.

Category	Tool	Community support	Task-oriented organization	Semantic structures	Link (last accessed on March 2015)
Forum	V-Bulletin Forum	Yes	No	No	http://www.vbulletin.com/forum
	WordPress bbPress	No	No	No	http://bbpress.org/
	WordPress p2 Theme	No	No	No	http://wordpress.org/themes/p2
	Stackoverflow	Yes	No	No	http://stackoverflow.com/
	Mathematics	No	Yes	No	http://math.stackexchange.com/
Wiki	MediaWiki	Yes	No	No	http://www.mediawiki.org/
	Semantic MediaWiki	Yes	No	Yes	https://semantic-mediawiki.org/
Enterprise Knowledge Management	Confluence	Yes	Yes	No	https://www.atlassian.com/de/software/confluence
	Connections	No	Yes	No	http://www-03.ibm.com/software/products/en/conn
	Jive	No	Yes	No	http://de.jivesoftware.com/
	MS SharePoint	No	Yes	No	http://office.microsoft.com/en-us/sharepoint/
	Communote	No	No	No	http://www.communote.com/ homepage/
	Yammer	No	No	No	https://www.yammer.com/
	Redmine	Yes	Yes	No	http://www.redmine.org/
ToDo Lists	Trello	No	Yes	No	https://trello.com/
	Keep	No	Yes	No	https://keep.google.com/keep/
	Todoist	No	Yes	No	http://todoist.com/
Repositories	GitHub	Yes	No	No	https://github.com/
	BitBucket	Yes	No	No	https://bitbucket.org/
	Google Code	Yes	No	No	https://code.google.com/
Organic Data Science	Organic Data Science Framework	Yes	Yes	Yes	http://organicdatascience.org/

3 Supporting Scientific Collaboration

The major user of the Organic Data Science framework is a community of hydrologists and limnologists that are studying the age of water in an ecosystem. Other communities are beginning to use the framework for neuroscience and geosciences research.

Table 2 shows the tasks defined so far in the age of water collaboration. In a 10-week time period started on 1st of October 2014, all task pages together were accessed more than 2,900 times. Person pages were accessed 328 times. We logged in total more than 19,000 events as users interacted with the system. Users have defined a total of 1047 RDF triples.

Table 2. Owner and participant's distribution of task types.

Type of task	Total tasks	Total owners	Total participants
High-level	7	7	8
Medium-level	110	109	82
Low-level	237	237	24
Unspecified	24	20	7

The Organic Data Science framework provides live collaboration data evaluation for every community with a dashboard. A community dashboard includes a collaboration graph and statistical task metadata. The oldest ODS community is the age of water community[1], followed by the Organic Data Science framework development community, geosciences community[2] and the private neuroscience community.

Acknowledgements. We gratefully acknowledge funding from the US National Science Foundation under grant IIS-1344272.

References

1. Krötzsch, M., Vrandecic, D., Völkel, M., Haller, H., Studer, R.: Semantic Wikipedia. Journal of Web Semantics 5(4), 251–261 (2007)
2. Kraut, R.E., Resnick, P.: Building Successful Online Communities. IT Press, Cambridge (2011)
3. Michel, F., Gil, Y., Ratnakar, V., Hauder, M.: A task-centered interface for on-line collaboration in science. In: Proceedings of the ACM International Conference on Intelligent User Interfaces, Atlanta, GA (2015)
4. Gil, Y., Michel, F., Ratnakar, V., Read, J., Hauder, M., Duffy, C., Hanson, P., Dugan, H.: Supporting open collaboration in science through explicit and linked semantic description of processes. In: Gandon, F., Sabou, M., Sack, H., d'Amato, C., Cudré-Mauroux, P., Zimmermann, A. (eds.) ESWC 2015. LNCS, vol. 9088, pp. 591–605. Springer, Heidelberg (2015)

---

[1] http://www.organicdatascience.org/ageofwater/index.php/Special:WTDashboard.

[2] http://www.organicdatascience.org/gpf/index.php/Special:WTDashboard.

QueryVOWL: Visual Composition of SPARQL Queries

Florian Haag[(✉)], Steffen Lohmann, Stephan Siek, and Thomas Ertl

Institute for Visualization and Interactive Systems, University of Stuttgart,
Universitätsstraße 38, 70569 Stuttgart, Germany
{florian.haag,steffen.lohmann,thomas.ertl}@vis.uni-stuttgart.de

Abstract. In order to make SPARQL queries more accessible to users, we have developed the visual query language QueryVOWL. It defines SPARQL mappings for graphical elements of the ontology visualization VOWL. In this demo, we present a web-based prototype that supports the creation, modification, and evaluation of QueryVOWL graphs. Based on the selected SPARQL endpoint, it provides suggestions for extending the query, and retrieves IRIs and literals according to the selections in the QueryVOWL graph. In contrast to related work, SPARQL queries can be created entirely with visual elements.

Keywords: Visual querying · QueryVOWL · VOWL · SPARQL · RDF · OWL · Visualization · Linked data · Semantic web

1 Introduction

As an increasing amount of Linked Data is becoming available, various visual concepts for specifying search queries on that data have been proposed. While some of them focus on visualizing the Boolean connections between filter criteria [4,7], others represent the structure of the object graph [3,6,11,12]. Examples from the latter group reflect the basic idea of queries specified in SPARQL, and the visualizations are often syntactically close to textual SPARQL queries. For instance, they explicitly show variable names or textual filter expressions.

We have developed QueryVOWL, a graph-based visual query language for SPARQL endpoints. QueryVOWL reuses graphical elements of VOWL, the Visual Notation for OWL Ontologies [9], and defines SPARQL mappings for them. We strive for expressing query restrictions in a way that does not require any knowledge of SPARQL and aim to reduce the learning effort by reusing elements that users of ontologies might already know from VOWL. Furthermore, we decided to reuse VOWL, as empirical results indicate that it is comparatively intuitive and understandable, also and especially to lay users [9].

In this demo, we present a web-based prototype of a visual query system that allows for the composition of queries in the QueryVOWL notation and retrieves results from a SPARQL endpoint. At ESWC 2015, we will demonstrate the idea and functionality of QueryVOWL by creating several SPARQL queries with the prototype. A more in-depth description of the QueryVOWL visual language and its SPARQL mappings has been presented at a workshop [5].

© Springer International Publishing Switzerland 2015
F. Gandon et al. (Eds.): ESWC 2015, LNCS 9341, pp. 62–66, 2015.
DOI: 10.1007/978-3-319-25639-9_12

2   QueryVOWL

VOWL, the Visual Notation for OWL Ontologies, provides a set of visual elements that represent concepts and components defined in OWL ontologies [9]. The meaning of the shapes, colors, labels, and combinations thereof is defined in a specification document [10], which maps graphical features to OWL constructs.

For QueryVOWL, we have redefined the graphical elements used in VOWL by mapping them to SPARQL fragments, while still conceptually adhering to the original definitions of the elements with respect to OWL. Moreover, we have slightly extended some of the visual elements to introduce interactive functionality that assists in the creation of SPARQL queries.

We developed a web-based prototype of QueryVOWL that implements the main elements of the visual query language. It is based on open web standards (HTML, JavaScript, CSS, SVG) and integrates some JavaScript libraries, most importantly D3 [2] for the visualization of the QueryVOWL graph. Figure 1 depicts a screenshot of the prototype, showing an exemplary QueryVOWL graph created on the DBpedia dataset [1].

The QueryVOWL concept focuses on a selected element—a class node, a literal node, or a property label—chosen by the user for retrieving results. In the exemplary query of Fig. 1, a user is looking for specific cars restricted by

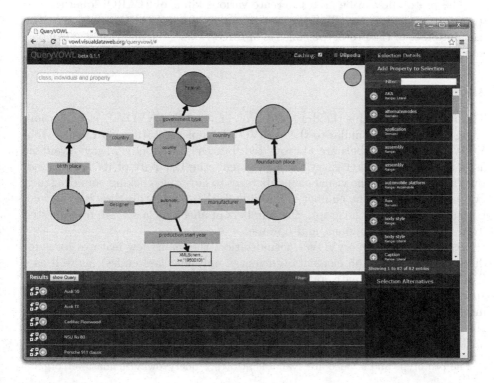

Fig. 1. Web-based implementation of QueryVOWL visualizing an exemplary query.

several attributes. The queries are automatically generated from the Query-VOWL graphs and sent to a SPARQL endpoint of choice in order to retrieve results. Listing 1 shows the SPARQL query generated by the prototype for the class *Automobile* selected in Fig. 1.

Listing 1. SPARQL query resulting from the QueryVOWL graph shown in Fig. 1.

```
1   SELECT ?Node1
2   WHERE {
3       ?Node1 a <http://dbpedia.org/ontology/Automobile>.
4       ?Node1 <http://dbpedia.org/property/manufacturer> ?Node2.
5       ?Node2 <http://dbpedia.org/ontology/foundationPlace> ?Node4.
6       ?Node4 <http://dbpedia.org/ontology/country> ?Node6.
7       ?Node3 <http://dbpedia.org/property/birthPlace> ?Node5.
8       ?Node5 <http://dbpedia.org/ontology/country> ?Node6.
9       ?Node6 a <http://dbpedia.org/ontology/Country>.
10      ?Node6 <http://dbpedia.org/ontology/governmentType>
11          <http://dbpedia.org/resource/Federalism>.
12      ?Node1 <http://dbpedia.org/property/designer> ?Node3.
13      ?Node1 <http://dbpedia.org/ontology/productionStartYear> ?Node7.
14      FILTER(?Node7 >="19500101"^^<http://www.w3.org/2001/XMLSchema#gYear>).
15      FILTER(datatype(?Node7) = <http://www.w3.org/2001/XMLSchema#gYear>).
16  }
```

The prototype can be used to create various kinds of SPARQL queries, and it can be applied to any RDF dataset that provides a SPARQL endpoint. The user interface of the prototype consists of three views—the main view, a sidebar, and a result list—which are described in the following.[1]

2.1   Main View

The main view contains the drag-and-drop enabled QueryVOWL visualization, using SVG graphics similar to the WebVOWL implementation [8]. Like in Web-VOWL, long class labels are abbreviated, but the full label is always available as a tooltip. If no label is set for an element, the last part of its IRI is used. Interactive spots on the visual elements react to hovering, clicking, and dragging. For each class node, the number of individuals that match this class is displayed. Upon any change to the graph, the numbers of affected classes are re-requested from the SPARQL endpoint and updated.

Apart from the QueryVOWL visualization, the main view features icons for directly inserting graph elements (currently, only for class nodes), as well as a search box equipped with auto-completion. The search box serves for finding specific entities in the dataset, such as classes or individuals, by their name, and inserting them into the QueryVOWL graph. It can also be used to directly input IRIs and add the corresponding element, should a user wish to copy and paste an IRI from another source.

---

[1] The prototype and a video are available at http://queryvowl.visualdataweb.org.

2.2   Sidebar

The sidebar is divided into three lists organized in an accordion widget. All the information shown in the lists is retrieved by means of SPARQL queries, which are processed in the background once the selection in the QueryVOWL graph changes.

The first list provides details about the selected element, which always includes a hyperlink to its IRI and some additional literal values if the selected element is an individual. The second list suggests properties that might be added to the selected class or individual in order to extend the query (cf. Fig. 1). The properties are all linked to the selected element in the accessed RDF data, so that the suggestions assist the users in defining restrictions that make it less likely that no results are returned. The third list suggests elements that might be used as a replacement for the currently selected element. For classes and individuals, other classes are listed that might be appropriate replacements; other properties are listed when a property is selected. These suggestions are again retrieved based on the modeled QueryVOWL graph and on how the elements are used in the RDF data. For the convenience of the user, the suggestions are also available in dropdown lists accessible directly on the QueryVOWL elements of the main view.

2.3   Result List

The result list shows the labels of all individuals that are valid replacements for the selected class node, along with hyperlinks to their IRIs. In other words, all individuals that match the focused property restrictions (i.e., the corresponding RDF subgraph) are displayed in the result list. Similar to the functionality of the sidebar, classes in the main view can be replaced by individuals from the result list to further restrict the QueryVOWL graph.

Moreover, the textual SPARQL query used to retrieve the individuals of the result list can be displayed and copied. This enables expert users to first create a SPARQL query visually with QueryVOWL and then edit it textually according to their needs.

2.4   Data Retrieval

The QueryVOWL prototype generates SPARQL queries like the one shown in Listing 1. We integrated an optional cache module, as the response time for complex queries may be noticeable on some endpoints. In addition, the cache module helps reduce the workload and resource use of those endpoints. Recently sent SPARQL queries and their results are stored in the cache, and the remote SPARQL endpoint is only accessed for non-cached queries.

In order to recognize equivalent but differently written SPARQL queries, the queries are normalized in the cache module. For this purpose, the graph patterns are brought into a specified order and names of variables are substituted based on a fixed scheme. This normalization is invisible to the caller of the module, as the original variable names are replaced in the returned result.

3   Conclusion

QueryVOWL supports the construction of SPARQL queries without the need to input any structured text. Once set up on a SPARQL endpoint, no particular RDF knowledge is required to use the approach. Since QueryVOWL reuses visual elements of the ontology notation VOWL, we expect it to be especially comprehensible to users who have previously come in touch with VOWL. However, it may also be easily understandable to people who never used VOWL before. This is at least indicated by the results of a preliminary user study we conducted to evaluate QueryVOWL [5].

The presented prototype demonstrates how the QueryVOWL concept can be used in practice for the visual composition of SPARQL queries. Currently, it does not support all envisioned graphical elements of QueryVOWL, but we plan to advance it in the future and to provide more options and features. Moreover, the QueryVOWL concept may be extended by adding enhanced capabilities for comparing literals, and for improved support of logical combinations of filter criteria to visually form conjunctions and disjunctions, among others.

References

1. Bizer, C., Lehmann, J., Kobilarov, G., Auer, S., Becker, C., Cyganiak, R., Hellmann, S.: DBpedia–a crystallization point for the web of data. Web Semant. **7**(3), 154–165 (2009)
2. Bostock, M., Ogievetsky, V., Heer, J.: D3 data-driven documents. IEEE Trans. Visual Comput. Graphics **17**(12), 2301–2309 (2011)
3. Groppe, J., Groppe, S., Schleifer, A.: Visual query system for analyzing social semantic web. In: WWW 2011, pp. 217–220. ACM (2011)
4. Haag, F., Lohmann, S., Ertl, T.: SparqlFilterFlow: SPARQL query composition for everyone. In: Presutti, V., Blomqvist, E., Troncy, R., Sack, H., Papadakis, I., Tordai, A. (eds.) ESWC Satellite Events 2014. LNCS, vol. 8798, pp. 362–367. Springer, Heidelberg (2014)
5. Haag, F., Lohmann, S., Siek, S., Ertl, T.: Visual querying of linked data with QueryVOWL. In: HSWI 2015. CEUR-WS (2015) (To appear)
6. Heim, P., Ziegler, J., Lohmann, S.: gFacet: a browser for the web of data. In: IMC-SSW 2008, vol. 417, pp. 49–58. CEUR-WS (2008)
7. Jarrar, M., Dikaiakos, M.D.: MashQL: a query-by-diagram topping SPARQL. In: ONISW 2008, pp. 89–96. ACM (2008)
8. Lohmann, S., Link, V., Marbach, E., Negru, S.: WebVOWL: web-based visualization of ontologies. In: Lambrix, P., Hyvönen, E., Blomqvist, E., Presutti, V., Qi, G., Sattler, U., Ding, Y., Ghidini, C. (eds.) EKWA 2014 Satellite Events. LNCS, vol. 8982, pp. 154–158. Springer, Heidelberg (2015)
9. Lohmann, S., Negru, S., Haag, F., Ertl, T.: VOWL 2: user-oriented visualization of ontologies. In: Janowicz, K., Schlobach, S., Lambrix, P., Hyvönen, E. (eds.) EKAW 2014. LNCS, vol. 8876, pp. 266–281. Springer, Heidelberg (2014)
10. Negru, S., Lohmann, S., Haag, F.: VOWL: visual notation for OWL ontologies (2014). http://purl.org/vowl/
11. OpenLink: iSPARQL. http://oat.openlinksw.com/isparql/
12. Russell, A., Smart, P., Braines, D., Shadbolt, N.: NITELIGHT: a graphical tool for semantic query construction. In: SWUI 2008, vol. 543. CEUR-WS (2008)

Merging and Enriching DCAT Feeds to Improve Discoverability of Datasets

Pieter Heyvaert$^{(\boxtimes)}$, Pieter Colpaert, Ruben Verborgh, Erik Mannens,
and Rik Van de Walle

Ghent University - iMinds - Multimedia Lab, Ghent, Belgium
{pheyvaer.heyvaert,pieter.colpaert,ruben.verborgh,
erik.mannens,rik.vandewalle}@ugent.be

Abstract. Data Catalog Vocabulary (DCAT) is a W3C specification to describe datasets published on the Web. However, these catalogs are not easily discoverable based on a user's needs. In this paper, we introduce the Node.js module 'dcat-merger' which allows a user agent to download and semantically merge different DCAT feeds from the Web into one DCAT feed, which can be republished. Merging the input feeds is followed by enriching them. Besides determining the subjects of the datasets, using DBpedia Spotlight, two extensions were built: one categorizes the datasets according to a taxonomy, and the other adds spatial properties to the datasets. These extensions require the use of information available in DBpedia's SPARQL endpoint. However, public SPARQL endpoints often suffer from low availability, its Triple Pattern Fragments alternative is used. However, the need for DCAT Merger sparks the discussion for more high level functionality to improve a catalog's discoverability.

Keywords: Data publishing · DCAT · Triple pattern fragments · Linked open data · Open data · Smart cities

1 Introduction

DCAT[1], short for Data Catalog Vocabulary, is a W3C specification for describing data catalogs, using Linked Data. It is a rather small vocabulary which has three main classes: *dcat:Catalog, dcat:Dataset* and *dcat:Distribution*. A *dcat:Catalog* is a class which can be used to describe the entire catalogue, e.g., who is the maintainer, when was it created, when was it last updated, what is the license of the metadata, and so on. The *dcat:Dataset* is a class to describe a dataset, a set of data facts which is published through one or more *dcat:Distributions*. A *dcat:Distribution* describes in its turn how data can be retrieved from the dataset it belongs to.

---

[1] http://www.w3.org/TR/vocab-dcat/.

F. Gandon et al. (Eds.): ESWC 2015, LNCS 9341, pp. 67–71, 2015.
DOI: 10.1007/978-3-319-25639-9_13

2 Problem Statement and Proposed Solution

The data catalogs are distributed over the Web. However, this distributed nature does not make it straightforward to reuse the catalogs directly, because discovering the catalogs (and its datasets), based on a certain need, is difficult for the following reasons:

1. it is not possible to query multiple feeds simultaneously,
2. different protocols are used for offering different feeds, and
3. additional information (e.g., themes and spatial coverage of datasets) provided by the different catalogs is not always interoperable, i.e. different ontologies are used.

In this paper, we introduce DCAT Merger[2], build using Node.js[3]. It aggregates DCAT feeds in one feed to solve the first two problems. It comes with three enrichment methods: determining the subjects and geographical areas of the datasets, and categorizing the datasets using a theme taxonomy. This is done using Named Entity Recognition (NER) on the descriptions and keywords of the datasets. These methods solve the third problem, and improve the general discoverability of the catalog.

3 Architecture

DCAT Merger module consists out the following six files: *dcat-merger.js*, *loader.js*, *cataloger.js*, *themeMatcher.js* and *spatialDetector.js* (Fig. 1). These files can be found in the folder */lib*. The entry point for the module is offered by *dcat-merger.js*, which uses *loader.js* and *cataloger.js*. The former is used to load the input feeds. Next, the latter merges them, which results in a single output feed. The *cataloger.js* makes use of *themeMatcher.js* and *spatialDetector.js* to enrich the output feed with theme and spatial information of the datasets.

4 Merging Feeds

First, we start by loading the different input feeds each in a separate triple store. Next, a triple store is created for the output feed, hence, containing the

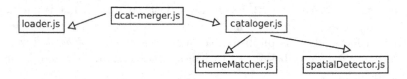

Fig. 1. The architecture of the DCAT Merger Node.js module.

---

[2] https://github.com/pheyvaer/dcat-merger.
[3] https://nodejs.org/.

information about the new catalog. After adding the basic information about the catalog, we add the information about the datasets from each input feed's triple store. However, during this process, for each dataset the necessary adjustments to the triples are made, so that they connect to the newly created catalog. The triple store-functionality was provided by the Node.js module n3[4].

5   Enriching Feeds

Besides only merging the different input feeds, we try to enrich them via three options: the *subjects* of the datasets, the *themes* of the datasets, and the *spatial coverage* of the datasets. We do this to improve the discoverability of (a group of) datasets in the catalog when keeping certain use cases and needs in mind.

5.1   Subjects

Based on the available keywords and descriptions, provided through *dcat:keyword* and *dcat:description*, we use NER to determine the (URI of the) subject(s) of each dataset. NER is facilitated by DBpedia Spotlight [3]. The request that is sent to the DBpedia spotlight server contains a string with a keyword or the description of a dataset. In return, a list of corresponding DBpedia resources is received, if any. This information is added to the resulting feed, hence, to its corresponding triple store.

5.2   Themes

The DCAT specification allows to denote the main themes (or categories) of a dataset using the property *dcat:theme*. Based on the subjects dissected in Sect. 5.1, we determine the themes of the datasets. To decide which themes are implicated by which subjects, we have created *themeMatcher.js*. It takes a subject as input and returns the corresponding theme, if any. All themes belong to the taxonomy defined at http://ns.thedatatank.com/dcat/themes. At the moment the mapping is manually defined. This information is added to the output feed's triple store. When using our module, the generation of themes is optional.

5.3   Spatial Coverage

If a subject, dissected in Sect. 5.1, refers to a geographical area, we also connect it to its dataset with the property *dcat:spatial*. To determine whether a subject represents a geographical area, we inspects its classes, i.e., check if the subject is an instance of the class http://dbpedia.org/ontology/Place. The relevant classes are configurable by the user. The functionality for detecting the spatial information is provided by *spatialDetector.js*. When using our module, the generation of the spatial coverage information is optional.

---

[4] https://www.npmjs.com/package/n3.

5.4 Triple Pattern Fragments

Both the *themeMatcher.js* and *spatialDetector.js* need additional information besides the (DBpedia) URI of a subject. That is, the classes that the subjects belong to. This information is available in DBpedia, which is accessible through a SPARQL endpoint[5]. However, the availability of such an endpoint is questionable [1]. That is why we opted to use its Triple Pattern Fragments (TPF) [4] alternative[6]. Using Node.js, there is a TPF client available through the module *ldf-client*[7].

6 Real-World Application: OTN

OpenTransportNet (OTN) is a project granted by the European Commission's CIP-ICT-PSP 2013-7 Call. By bringing together open geo-spatial data within City Data Hubs and enabling it to be viewed in new easy to understand ways, OTN enables new reuse of existing open datasets. In order to keep a relevant list of datasets, DCAT Merger was configured with various DCAT sources, and a new DCAT feed was generated for a certain city. The data was afterwards loaded in a virtuoso triple store, and published using The DataTank [2]. A demo of this can be viewed at http://ewi.mmlab.be/otn/.

7 Conclusion and Future Work

In practice, the use of DCAT Merger allows to create a single DCAT feed, which improves finding the catalogs that satisfy a user's needs. It is possible to enrich the feed with theme and spatial information, next to subject information. However, adding other custom extensions to DCAT Merger involves adding and changing the code in multiple places. To this extent, a plugin system should be developed to circumvent this. As a result, the functionality provided by *themeMatcher.js* and *spatialDetector.js* should be added as plugins. However, the need for DCAT Merger raises the questions if more (high level) functionality is required, e.g. on the server side, to solve the problems addressed by our module.

References

1. Buil-Aranda, C., Hogan, A., Umbrich, J., Vandenbussche, P.-Y.: SPARQL web-querying infrastructure: ready for action? In: Alani, H., Kagal, L., Fokoue, A., Groth, P., Biemann, C., Parreira, J.X., Aroyo, L., Noy, N., Welty, C., Janowicz, K. (eds.) ISWC 2013, Part II. LNCS, vol. 8219, pp. 277–293. Springer, Heidelberg (2013)

---

[5] http://dbpedia.org/sparql.
[6] Basic Triple Pattern Fragments server of DBPedia is available at http://fragments.dbpedia.org.
[7] https://www.npmjs.com/package/ldf-client.

2. Colpaert, P., Verborgh, R., Mannens, E., de Walle, R.V.: Painless URI dereferencing using the datatank. In: Presutti, V., Blomqvist, E., Troncy, R., Sack, H., Papadakis, I., Tordai, A. (eds.) ESWC Satellite Events 2014. LNCS, vol. 8798, pp. 304–309. Springer, Heidelberg (2014)
3. Mendes, P.N., Jakob, M., García-Silva, A., Bizer, C.: DBpedia spotlight: shedding light on the web of documents. In: Proceedings of the 7th International Conference on Semantic Systems, pp. 1–8. ACM (2011)
4. Verborgh, R., Hartig, O., De Meester, B., Haesendonck, G., De Vocht, L., Vander Sande, M., Cyganiak, R., Colpaert, P., Mannens, E., Van de Walle, R.: Querying datasets on the web with high availability. In: Mika, P., Tudorache, T., Bernstein, A., Welty, C., Knoblock, C., Vrandečić, D., Groth, P., Noy, N., Janowicz, K., Goble, C. (eds.) ISWC 2014, Part I. LNCS, vol. 8796, pp. 180–196. Springer, Heidelberg (2014)

Minimally Supervised Instance Matching: An Alternate Approach

Mayank Kejriwal$^{(\boxtimes)}$ and Daniel P. Miranker

University of Texas at Austin, Austin, USA
{kejriwal,miranker}@cs.utexas.edu

Abstract. Instance matching concerns identifying pairs of instances that refer to the same underlying entity. Current state-of-the-art instance matchers use machine learning methods. Supervised learning systems achieve good performance by training on significant amounts of manually labeled samples. To alleviate the labeling effort, this poster (The work presented herein is also being published as a full conference paper at ESWC 2015. This poster provides a more high-level overview and discusses supplemental experimental findings beyond the scope of the material in the full paper.) presents a *minimally supervised* instance matching approach that is able to deliver competitive performance using only 2 % training data. As a first step, a committee of base classifiers is trained in an ensemble setting using *boosting*. Iterative *semi-supervised learning* is used to improve the performance of the ensemble classifier even further, by *self-training* it on the most confident samples labeled in the current iteration. Empirical evaluations on real-world data show that, using a multilayer perceptron as base classifier, the system is able to achieve an average F-Measure that is within 2.5 % of that of state-of-the-art supervised systems.

Keywords: Instance Matching · Boosting · Semi-supervision · Self-training

Instance matching is the problem of matching pairs of instances that refer to the same *underlying* entity, with numerous documented applications in the Semantic Web community [4]. Current state-of-the-art instance matchers use a variety of machine learning techniques to achieve effective performance. Many of these systems are *supervised*, and require sets of manually annotated samples to train their classifiers. This manual effort is expensive in open communities.

In recent years, *minimally supervised* approaches have been devised to alleviate extensive labeling effort [2]. While such approaches perform reasonably in many cases, a comparative analysis shows that there is still a considerable gap between their performance and that of supervised systems. An additional problem is that such systems rely on the specification of a function called the *pseudo F-Measure* (PFM). Intuitively, the PFM serves as a proxy for the *true* F-Measure, with minimally supervised instance matchers heuristically attempting to optimize the PFM instead of the true (unknown) F-Measure [3]. A recent

© Springer International Publishing Switzerland 2015
F. Gandon et al. (Eds.): ESWC 2015, LNCS 9341, pp. 72–76, 2015.
DOI: 10.1007/978-3-319-25639-9_14

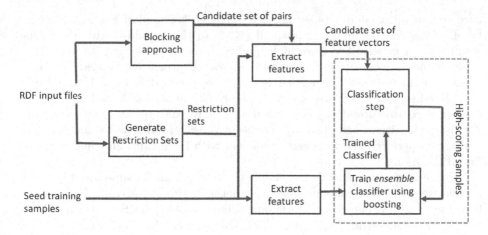

Fig. 1. The proposed instance matching system. The dotted component (the *classification step* of instance matching) is iteratively executed for a pre-defined number of rounds, and constitutes the key innovation of this work

study found the PFM to be uncorrelated (or *negatively* correlated) with the true F-Measure in several cases [2], raising concerns about whether currently defined PFMs are appropriate proxies.

This paper presents an alternate *minimally supervised* instance matching approach that offers a practical compromise between the two paradigms above. The architecture of the system is illustrated in Fig. 1. The proposed system expects a few input *seed* training samples to bootstrap itself. Some preprocessing that is often specific to instance matching systems (blocking and restriction set generation) is then performed. We implemented existing state-of-the-art modules for these steps to maximize system performance. Two sets of real-valued *feature vectors*[1] are output by the pipeline prior to the classification step (the dotted component in Fig. 1).

The first output is the set of seed training samples, with each (matching and non-matching) instance pair in the set converted to (positively and negatively labeled) feature vectors and are used to train an *ensemble* classifier. An ensemble classifier takes a *base* classifier as input and trains the classifier using a *meta-classification* strategy called *boosting* [1]. The goal is to obtain a committee (or *ensemble*) of base classifiers that use weighted majority voting to classify samples, which is shown to improve performance on many challenging tasks [1].

The second output is the *candidate set*, which represents the *unseen* (or test) data in the classification task. These are *unlabeled* feature vectors, with each vector representing an underlying instance pair. The trained ensemble classifier is used for *probabilistic* instance matching, where the classifier scores each fea-

---

[1] For a full description of features and preprocessing modules, we refer the reader to the full paper as well as the project website at https://sites.google.com/a/utexas.edu/mayank-kejriwal/projects/semi-supervised-im-using-boosting.

ture vector in the candidate set according to its likelihood of having a positive label. If the seed training set is small ($\leq 2\%$ of the ground-truth), the initial output is not expected to have high quality. Instead, the system assumes that a percentage of the top-scoring feature vectors are correctly labeled, and uses them to iteratively *self-train* itself in a *semi-supervised* fashion. In our work, we showed that an aggressive strategy (doubling the size of the self-training set in each successive iteration) performed well, with convergence achieved within 7 self-training iterations. The overall intent of self-training is to improve generalization performance with each iteration, with large gains anticipated in the initial iterations.

To the best of our knowledge, this is the first minimally supervised instance matching system that combines boosting methods with iterative semi-supervised learning to achieve effective performance. The ensemble classifier is trained using the *AdaBoost* algorithm, and with a choice of two base classifiers, *random forests* (RFs) and *multilayer perceptrons* (MLPs), both of which have been individually validated for good instance matching performance in related work.

Experiments: We compare the two settings of the proposed system (with RF and MLP as base classifier) on six real-world benchmarks covering domains of people (*Persons 1 & 2*), restaurants (*Restaurants*), bibliographies (*ACM-DBLP*) and e-commerce (*Amazon-GP, Abt-Buy*). In our original work (see footnote 1), the highest F-Measure (averaged over all the benchmarks) achieved by the MLP setting of the system (76.78%; see also Table 1) was within 2.5% of that of state-of-the-art supervised approaches (79.25%), and outcompeted various PFM optimization-based minimally supervised approaches (72.18%). This was not true of the RF-based setting. Table 1 directly compares the two settings. Essentially, we record the highest achieved F-Measure of each setting on each benchmark over 1–7 self-training iterations (equiv. *runs*) and report the run in which the highest F-Measure was recorded, along with the corresponding precision and recall. The table shows that, while the difference between the settings on *Amazon-GP, Abt-Buy* and on average is considerable, it is quite small on the other four test cases. RF even outperforms MLP by 5.32% on *Restaurants*.

An analysis of Table 1 shows that MLP is preferrable to RF. However, the recorded training times of both settings (Table 2) show that there is a cost to using MLP over RF. The training time of MLP depends at least linearly on the number of training samples, roughly doubling in a successive iteration (when the size of the self-training set also doubles), while RF training time grows slowly. To compare the difference, consider that, in Table 1, the best performance of MLP on *Abt-Buy* occurs in the fifth iteration, with training time being 887.28 s. RF achieves its best performance in the seventh iteration, at training time of 46.49 s. On large datasets, these differences (a factor of 19) will amplify even further, calling into question the practical feasibility of MLP.

Future Work: The excellent performance achieved by boosted MLP on the benchmarks showed that it is feasible to devise minimally supervised approaches that nearly equal the performance of supervised approaches requiring training on a non-trivially obtained manually labeled set ($\geq 10\%$ of ground-truth).

Table 1. A comparison of the highest achieved F-Measure (and corresponding precision and recall) over 7 self-training runs of the system when using MLP/RF as base classifier in the AdaBoost algorithm

Test case	Run	Recall	Precision	F-Measure
Persons-1	4/2	**100 %/100 %**	**100 %/100 %**	**100 %/100 %**
Persons-2	2/5	**95.25 %/88.25 %**	**99.22 %/96.19 %**	**97.19 %/92.05 %**
Restaurants	6/5	**100 %/100 %**	89.90 %/**100 %**	94.68 %/100 %
ACM-DBLP	1/1	95.50 %/**95.68 %**	**91.43 %/90.02 %**	**93.42 %/92.76 %**
Amazon-GP	2/6	**54.31 %/45.77 %**	**34.18 %/12.84 %**	**39.13 %/20.77 %**
Abt-Buy	5/7	29.08 %/**31.27 %**	**48.19 %/17.87 %**	**36.27 %/22.75 %**
Average	3.33/4.33	**79.02 %/76.83 %**	**77.15 %/69.49 %**	**76.78 %/71.39 %**

Table 2. A comparison of the training times (in seconds) over 7 self-training iterations of the system when using MLP/RF as base classifier in the AdaBoost algorithm. x indicates that reliable results could not be obtained for that run due to system-specific factors. Averages are computed over non-x values

Test case	Run 1	Run 2	Run 3	Run 4	Run 5	Run 6	Run 7
Persons-1	350.15/ 1.45	726.51/ 1.86	1428.42/ 2.06	3031.47/ 2.32	7219.10/ 3.60	x/5.13	x/6.35
Persons-2	562.21/ 3.82	498.75/ 4.48	1145.27/ 3.89	2291.79/ 4.08	5217.94/ 4.68	x/5.88	x/7.74
Restaurants	17.90/ 2.69	30.09/ 3.21	67.56/ 4.04	129.19/ 3.34	319.65/ 3.60	799.12/ 4.40	1062.20/ 5.01
ACM-DBLP	202.30/ 3.14	298.10/ 5.56	766.76/ 8.62	1325.83/ 12.76	2164.15/ 20.31	x/45.37	x/93.93
Amazon-GP	352.03/ 10.94	533.98/ 13.16	669.12/ 22.52	1111.33/ 28.18	2655.59/ 50.25	3579.75/ 115.98	6336.14/ 160.48
Abt-Buy	106.07/ 4.99	217.53/ 6.59	273.62/ 8.67	477.93/ 12.09	887.28/ 17.98	1761.89/ 32.17	x/46.49
Average	265.11/ 4.51	384.16/ 5.81	725.13/ 8.30	1394.59/ 10.46	3077.29/ 16.74	2046.92/ 34.82	3699.17/ 53.33

However, a close look at the training times of the MLP against a cheaper alternative, namely RFs, shows that the cost of training the MLP against the RF can be prohibitive. Future work will seek to make progress on this front by (i) predicting, through meta-strategies, when to use RF vs. MLP to secure the best cost-performance trade-off, and (ii) developing classifiers that can match the benefits of MLPs but without its prohibitive training times.

References

1. Freund, Y., Schapire, R.E.: A decision-theoretic generalization of on-line learning and an application to boosting. In: Vitányi, P.M.B. (ed.) EuroCOLT 1995. LNCS, vol. 904, pp. 23–37. Springer, Heidelberg (1995)
2. Ngomo, A.-C.N., Lyko, K.: Unsupervised learning of link specifications: deterministic vs. non-deterministic. In: OM, pp. 25–36 (2013)
3. Nikolov, A., d'Aquin, M., Motta, E.: Unsupervised learning of link discovery configuration. In: Simperl, E., Cimiano, P., Polleres, A., Corcho, O., Presutti, V. (eds.) ESWC 2012. LNCS, vol. 7295, pp. 119–133. Springer, Heidelberg (2012)
4. Scharffe, F., Ferrara, A., Nikolov, A., et al.: Data linking for the semantic web. Int. J. Seman. Web Inf. Syst. **7**(3), 46–76 (2011)

Discovering Types in RDF Datasets

Kenza Kellou-Menouer$^{(\boxtimes)}$ and Zoubida Kedad$^{(\boxtimes)}$

PRISM - University of Versailles Saint-Quentin-en-Yvelines, Versailles, France
{kenza.menouer,zoubida.kedad}@prism.uvsq.fr

Abstract. An increasing number of linked datasets is published on the Web, expressed in RDF(S)/OWL. Interlinking, matching or querying these datasets require some knowledge about the types and properties they contain. This work presents an approach, relying on a clustering algorithm, which provides the types describing a dataset when this information is incomplete or missing.

Keywords: Type extraction · Clustering · Semantic web · Linked data

1 Introduction

An increasing number of linked datasets is published on the Web. Understanding these datasets is crucial in order to exploit them. Having some knowledge about the content of a dataset, such as the types it contains, is crucial for users and applications as it will enable many tasks, such as creating links between datasets or querying them. Linked datasets are not always complete with respect to type information. Even when they are automatically extracted from a controlled source, type information can be missing: in DBpedia (extracted from Wikipedia), 63.7 % of type information is provided [8].

Our goal is to infer the types describing an RDF(S)/OWL dataset. Our main contribution is a deterministic and automatic approach relying on a clustering algorithm to extract types, where several types can be assigned to an entity. Our approach does not require any schema related information in the dataset. We have implemented our algorithms and we present some experimental evaluation results to demonstrate the effectiveness of the approach.

2 Type Discovery

In order to infer the types from a dataset, our approach relies on grouping entities according to their similarity. A group of similar entities corresponds to a type definition. The similarity between two given entities is evaluated considering their respective sets of both incoming and outgoing properties.

Our main requirements are the following: (i) the number of types is not known in advance, (ii) an entity can have several types, and (iii) the datasets may contain noise. The most suitable grouping approach is density-based clustering,

© Springer International Publishing Switzerland 2015
F. Gandon et al. (Eds.): ESWC 2015, LNCS 9341, pp. 77–81, 2015.
DOI: 10.1007/978-3-319-25639-9_15

introduced by [2], because it is robust to noise, deterministic and it finds classes of arbitrary shape. In addition, unlike the algorithms based on k-means and k-medoid, the number of classes is not required.

Our density-based algorithm has two parameters: the maximum radius of neighborhood ε and the minimum number of neighbors for an entity $MinPts$. ε represents the minimum similarity value for two entities to be considered as neighbors. We use Jaccard similarity to measure the closeness between two property sets describing two entities. $MinPts$ is the minimum number of similar entities required to form a core [2]: an entity is not assigned to a class if it is considered as noise, i.e. if it is neither a core itself nor the neighbor of a core.

In order to speed up the clustering process, we perform once and for all the calculation of the nearest neighbors of each entity [4]. We store a neighborhood matrix containing for each entity the ordered list of its neighbors. It is then straightforward to find the nearest neighbors for an entity at a distance lower than ε, with a linear complexity o(n) [5].

Each type is described by a profile, which is a property vector where each property is associated to a probability. The profile corresponding to a type T_i is denoted $TP_i = < (p_{i1}, \alpha_{i1}), ..., (p_{in}, \alpha_{in}) >$, where each p_{ij} represents a property and where each α_{ij} represents the probability for an entity of T_i to have the property p_{ij}. The type profile represents the canonical structure of type T_i.

An important aspect of RDF(S)/OWL datasets is that an entity may have several types [8]. We provide overlapping types by analyzing the type profiles: intuitively, if an entity e is described by properties characterizing several types, then these types could be assigned to e. However, the properties have different levels of confidence, which has to be considered. Indeed, if σ represents a threshold above which the probability associated to a property is considered as high, and if all the properties p of the type T_i having a probability $\alpha_i > \sigma$ are also properties of another type T_k, then T_i is also a type for the entities in T_k.

3   Related Works

Type inference from structureless and semi-structured data has been addressed by some works in the literature. In [10], an approximate DataGuide based on an incremental hierarchical clustering (COBWEB) is proposed in order to group similar nodes, i.e. the ones having the same incoming/outgoing edges. The approach considers both types of edges in the same way, which could be a problem if applied to RDF datasets as it will not differentiate between the domain and the range of properties. The resulting classes are disjoints, and the approach is not deterministic as it is based on COBWEB. The approach presented in [6] uses bottom-up grouping providing a set of disjoint classes. A similarity threshold has to be set, as well as the number of clusters, unlike in our approach. In [1] standard ascending hierarchical clustering is used to build structural summaries of linked data. Each instance is represented by its outgoing properties only and the property set of a class is the union of the properties of all its entities, unlike our approach where the probability of each property is computed for a type. The algorithm provides disjoint classes and it is costly, in addition, the method explores the hierarchical clustering tree to assess the best cutoff level. SDType [8] enriches an entity by several types using inference rules, and computes the confidence of a type for an entity. The focus of the approach is more on the evaluation of the relevance of the inferred types rather than finding these types. In addition, *rdfs:domain*, *rdfs:range* and *rdfs:subClassOf* properties are required. The approach does not introduce new types, but considers instead the ones already assigned to an entity in the dataset. Works in [3,7] infer types for the DBpedia dataset only: [7] uses K-NN and [3] finds the most appropriate type of an entity in DBpedia based on descriptions from Wikipedia and links with WordNet and Dolce ontologies. A Statistical Schema Induction approach [9] enriches a RDF dataset with the RDFS/OWL primitives, however the classes must be pre-defined and expressed as *rdf:type* declarations.

4   Evaluation

We have used the Conference[1] dataset, which exposes data for several semantic web related conferences and workshops. We have also used a dataset extracted from DBpedia considering the following types: Politician, SoccerPlayer, Museum, Movie, Book and Country.

We have extracted the existing type definitions from our dataset and considered them as a gold standard. We have then run our algorithm on the dataset without the type definitions and evaluated the precision and recall for the inferred types. We have annotated each inferred class C_i with the most frequent type label associated to its entities. For each type label L_j corresponding to type T_j in the dataset and each class C_i inferred by our algorithm, such that L_j is the label of C_i, we have evaluated the precision $P(T_j, C_i) = |T_j \cap C_i|/|C_i|$ and recall $R(T_j, C_i) = |T_j \cap C_i|/|T_j|$. We have set $\varepsilon = 0.5$ and $MinPts = 1$ so that an entity is considered as noise if it is completely isolated.

The resulting values of the metrics are shown in Fig. 1. For the Conference dataset, our approach gives good results and detects types which were not declared in the dataset, annotated as follows: classes 7, 8, 9 and 10 are labeled 'AuthorList', 'PublicationPage', 'HomePage' and 'City' respectively. In

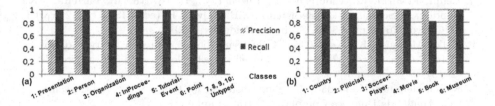

Fig. 1. Quality evaluation on the conference (a) and DBpedia (b) datasets.

---

[1] Conference: data.semanticweb.org/dumps/conferences/dc-2010-complete.rdf.

some cases, types have been inferred relying on incoming properties only. Indeed, for containers, such as 'AuthorList', it is necessary to consider these properties as they do not have any outgoing property. Classes 1 and 5 do not have a good precision because they contain entities with different types in the dataset: class 1, annotated 'Presentation', corresponds to three types with the same properties in the dataset: 'Presentation', 'Tutorial' and 'ProgrammeCommitteeMember'.

The results for the DBpedia dataset (see Fig. 1 (b)) show that the assignment of types to entities has achieved good precision and recall. The recall for types 'Book' and 'Politician' is not maximum because noisy instances were detected. Entities of the two types 'Politician' and 'SoccerPlayer' have not been grouped together despite having similar property sets, as it is shown by the corresponding type profiles generated by our algorithm, and presented below.

- Politician: $< (\overrightarrow{name}, 1), (\overrightarrow{party}, 0.73), (\overrightarrow{children}, 0.21), (\overrightarrow{birthDate}, 0.94), (\overrightarrow{nationality}, 0.15), (\overleftarrow{successor}, 0.78), (\overrightarrow{deathDate}, 0.68), ...>.$
- SoccerPlayer: $< (\overrightarrow{name}, 1), (\overrightarrow{height}, 0.46), (\overrightarrow{birthDate}, 1), (\overrightarrow{nationalteam}, 0.86), (\overleftarrow{currentMember}, 0.8), (\overrightarrow{surname}, 0.93), (\overrightarrow{deathDate}, 0.06), ...>.$

5 Future Works

In addition to type discovery, it is also useful to find the semantic links between them and the labels which best capture the semantics of this cluster. One of our perspectives is to tackle this issue, and provide a support for meaningful cluster annotation.

References

1. Christodoulou, K., Paton, N.W., Fernandes, A.A.: Structure inference for linked data sources using clustering. In: EDBT/ICDT (2013)
2. Ester, M., Kriegel, H.-P., Sander, J., Xu, X.: A density-based algorithm for discovering clusters in large spatial databases with noise. In: Kdd (1996)
3. Gangemi, A., Nuzzolese, A.G., Presutti, V., Draicchio, F., Musetti, A., Ciancarini, P.: Automatic typing of DBpedia entities. In: Cudré-Mauroux, P., Heflin, J., Sirin, E., Tudorache, T., Euzenat, J., Hauswirth, M., Parreira, J.X., Hendler, J., Schreiber, G., Bernstein, A., Blomqvist, E. (eds.) ISWC 2012, Part I. LNCS, vol. 7649, pp. 65–81. Springer, Heidelberg (2012)
4. Kellou-Menouer, K., Kedad, Z.: A clustering based approach for type discovery in RDF data sources. Revue des Nouvelles Technologies de l'Information, EGC (2015)
5. Kellou-Menouer, K., Kedad, Z.: Using clustering for type discovery in the semantic web. Fouille de Donnees Complexes (2015, to appear)
6. Nestorov, S., Abiteboul, S., Motwani, R.: Extracting schema from semistructured data. In: ACM SIGMOD Record (1998)
7. Nuzzolese, A.G., Gangemi, A., Presutti, V., Ciancarini, P.: Type inference through the analysis of Wikipedia links. In: LDOW (2012)

8. Paulheim, H., Bizer, C.: Type inference on noisy RDF data. In: Alani, H., Kagal, L., Fokoue, A., Groth, P., Biemann, C., Parreira, J.X., Aroyo, L., Noy, N., Welty, C., Janowicz, K. (eds.) ISWC 2013, Part I. LNCS, vol. 8218, pp. 510–525. Springer, Heidelberg (2013)
9. Völker, J., Niepert, M.: Statistical schema induction. In: Antoniou, G., Grobelnik, M., Simperl, E., Parsia, B., Plexousakis, D., De Leenheer, P., Pan, J. (eds.) ESWC 2011, Part I. LNCS, vol. 6643, pp. 124–138. Springer, Heidelberg (2011)
10. Wang, Q.Y., Yu, J.X., Wong, K.-F.: Approximate graph schema extraction for semi-structured data. In: Zaniolo, C., Grust, T., Scholl, M.H., Lockemann, P.C. (eds.) EDBT 2000. LNCS, vol. 1777, pp. 302–316. Springer, Heidelberg (2000)

Supporting Real-Time Monitoring in Criminal Investigations

Robin Keskisärkkä$^{(\boxtimes)}$ and Eva Blomqvist

Linköping University, Linköping, Sweden
{robin.keskisarkka,eva.blomqvist}@liu.se

Abstract. Being able to analyze information collected from streams of data, generated by different types of sensors, is becoming increasingly important in many domains. This paper presents an approach for creating a decoupled semantically enabled event processing system, which leverages existing Semantic Web technologies. By implementing the actor model, we show how we can create flexible and robust event processing systems, which can leverage different technologies in the same general workflow. We argue that in this context RSP systems can be viewed as generic systems for creating semantically enabled event processing agents. In the demonstration scenario we show how real-time monitoring can be used to support criminal intelligence analysis, and describe how the actor model can be leveraged further to support scalability.

Keywords: Semantic event processing · Event processing · RDF stream processing · Actor model · Criminal intelligence

1 Introduction

Semantic Web (SW) technologies provide flexible tools for working with heterogeneous data, and Linked Data principles enable information to be shared by explicitly articulating the underlying schemas and ontologies.

Traditional SW technologies have been developed to support slowly evolving (or static) data, and scale quite poorly when data is highly dynamic. In recent years, a number of RDF Stream Processing (RSP) systems have therefore been developed to support streaming Linked Data, focusing on timely execution of continuous queries over streams.

Unlike most types of event processing approaches, such as Drools fusion[1] and ESPER[2], RSP systems use the Linked Data principles to leverage the semantics in the streaming data. The available RSP systems, however, provide only a limited set of features out-of-the-box. For example, in the available versions of C-SPARQL [3], CQELS [5], INSTANS [8], and ETALIS/EP-SPARQL [1], streams, queries, and result listeners are closely coupled with their respective engine. This can make them difficult to use in settings where streams are not

---

[1] http://www.drools.org/.
[2] http://esper.codehaus.org/.

© Springer International Publishing Switzerland 2015
F. Gandon et al. (Eds.): ESWC 2015, LNCS 9341, pp. 82–86, 2015.
DOI: 10.1007/978-3-319-25693-9_16

under the direct control of the system itself, or when other technologies need to be included in the event processing pipeline.

In this paper we present an approach for creating decoupled semantically enabled event processing systems by leveraging existing technologies, and demonstrate its applicability in a criminal intelligence scenario.

2   Related Work

The Streaming Linked Data framework, based on C-SPARQL, allows publishers to stream data to a central server, where the data can be queried, stored, replayed, decorated, and republished as new streams [2]. This drastically improves the flexibility of the RSP system, making it possible to provide APIs and add functionality to the standard C-SPARQL system.

The Super Stream Collider is platform for combining semantically annotated Linked Stream and Linked Data sources [7]. It was constructed around the CQELS engine and supports registering of streams and queries in a web-based interface. This simplifies the querying of static and dynamic resources, and allows rapid development Linked Stream mashups that can be used by applications.

Both approaches significantly increase the flexibility of their respective RSP systems, but the frameworks are still closely coupled with the structure of the underlying engines. There are several issues related with closely coupled systems. For example, a close coupling with the data streams limits the ability to handle stream overload. Most engines naively attempt to handle the full set of streaming data, regardless of rate, volume, and number of registered queries, which can create bottlenecks that deteriorate performance across the entire system.

CQELS Cloud uses scalable parallel algorithms to support elastic parallelising of query execution [6]. This approach helps to scale processing, both in terms of parallel queries and stream rates, but the underlying assumption is still that it will be possible to scale up the processing to handle all the incoming data.

3   Architecture Overview

In a decoupled event processing system the states of event producers, events, and event consumers are independent of each other [4]. This demo implements the actor model to handle message based communication, which completely separates the states of the different parts of the event processing system.

We implemented the actor model using the Akka[3] toolkit and runtime environment, which supports efficient, lightweight, and scalable, asynchronous message communication between its actors. This approach supports a robust and possibly distributed system, which avoids slow-downs that may result from individual components.

Event producers generate internal event streams from event sources, which are typically outside the control of the system, and these event streams are then

---

[3] http://akka.io/.

fed to *event consumers*. Event Processing Agents (EPAs) are special in that they are both event consumers and event producers [4]. To handle the communication between producers and consumers we created an event distribution mechanism, which pushes data from event producers (identified by URIs) to the listening event consumers. Sequential processing of event streams is made possible by pipelining several EPAs, thus enabling event processing requiring multiple steps.

The novelty of this approach in the RSP context is that it allows us to abstract from the implementation specific aspects of individual RSP engines, facilitating the use of multiple different engines within the same system. We represent events as RDF graphs, which requires RSP engines that support only RDF triples streams to decompose the events into triples internally. To demonstrate our approach we integrated the CQELS engine by creating wrappers for its internal RDF stream and query listener.

We can view each registered RSP query together with its output stream as an EPA. This allows us to seamlessly integrate different RSP engines in the overall workflow, and we can use optimized EPA components for such things as text analysis, stream decoration, and statistical analysis.

4   Demonstration Scenario

Criminal investigations involve a wide range of data sources, ranging from criminal records, modus operandi descriptions, case files, criminal reports, videos, images and more. When large volumes of data need to be interpreted, analysts have to rely heavily on their own domain expertise and skill to detect potential patterns in the data. However, pure manual work scales poorly as the amount of accumulated and continuously delivered data increases. Although many of the tasks of the analysts are difficult to articulate some can be formalized as rules, for example, to filter, aggregate, or decorate events.

The task in the demonstration scenario is inspired by real-world investigative tasks of the police. Based on a stream of Automatic Number Plate Recognition (ANPR) observations, originating from CCTV footage, the task is to monitor vehicles to detect when two "persons of interest" are possibly meeting up.

The system generates an alert when two vehicles, belonging to persons of interest in an investigation, are observed in close proximity of each other within a small time window. All observations are visualized on a map, while detected events are persisted in a separate tab.

The available data is: (1) a stream of ANPR observations, (2) a dataset containing the locations of the ANPR cameras, and pre-calculated distances between them, (3) a dataset containing registered owners of vehicles, and (4) "persons of interest" within specific investigations. The static datasets (2–4) are represented as RDF, while the ANPR stream is converted into RDF (from csv) in real-time via a direct mapping by a designated event producer. A diagram of the demonstration setup can be seen in Fig. 1.

The data used in the demonstration was created artificially (by the authors), but care was taken to follow the format of the ANPR data available within

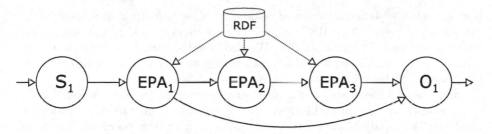

Fig. 1. An event producer, S_1, converts a stream of csv-strings into an RDF stream. The generated event stream is decorated with camera location information, EPA_1. Vehicle owner information is added to the stream, EPA_2, and finally, vehicles belonging to the same cases that are potentially meeting up are detected, EPA_3. The event streams generated by EPA_1 and EPA_3 are consumed by the output formatter, O_1, which converts them for use in the web-interface.

the VALCRI project[4], which in turn reflects the formatting of actual ANPR data used by the UK police. The locations of the ANPR cameras were set to street crossings in small section of London (UK), and possible paths were generated within and through this area. Observations of randomized registration plate numbers were assigned to paths, and the average delay between observations was approximated based on the distance between cameras. The number of observations were balanced against time of day to roughly correspond to the distribution of ANPR data in the VALCRI project. The queries and datasets used in the demo, and a recording of the running demo is available at http://valcri.ida.liu.se:8080/eswc2015/.

5 Scalability

The demonstration scenario was run on standard PC with a 1.7 GHz dual-core processor and 4 Gb RAM. In the scenario, the CQELS engine runs three parallel queries and processes up to 85 events per second, which is equivalent to approximately 285 triples per second. When benchmarking the system the same setup gives acceptable performance even when increasing the application time by up to 15 times, thereby processing more than 1200 events per second (corresponding to more than 4000 triples per second).

The Akka framework supports communication between different virtual machines running on the same machine, as well as communication in a peer-to-peer fashion. This means that the approach could be used to tackle several scalability issues, for example, to support more parallel queries by running and interlinking several instances of RSP engines on separate machines.

6 Conclusions

We have shown the potential of leveraging SW technologies and RSP engines in the context of semantic event processing. Our demo application demonstrates

---
[4] http://www.valcri.org/.

how an actor system can be used as a way of setting up a decoupled event processing system, where RSP engines can be viewed as a generic means for creating semantically enabled EPAs. We also describe how the same architecture can be used to distribute processing and leverage more than a single RSP system, for example, to take advantage of engine specific features.

In criminal investigations manually processing continuously delivered messages is often not possible. Limited resources means that data is often logged until need for analysis arises, thereby missing out on the potential benefit of detecting events in real-time. The demo scenario shows how event processing can be used to support some investigative tasks, and how RSP systems can be used to support semantically enabled event processing. The demo visualization shows how this has the potential to be used to develop tools for criminal investigations.

Acknowledgments. This work was supported by the EU FP7 project Visual Analytics for Sense-making in Criminal Intelligence Analysis (VALCRI) under grant number FP7-SEC-2013-608142.

References

1. Anicic, D., Fodor, P., Rudolph, S., Stojanovic, N.: EP-SPARQL: a unified language for event processing and stream reasoning. In: Proceedings of the 20th International Conference on World Wide Web (2011)
2. Balduini, M., Della Valle, E., Dell'Aglio, D., Tsytsarau, M., Palpanas, T., Confalonieri, C.: Social listening of city scale events using the streaming linked data framework. In: Alani, H., Kagal, L., Fokoue, A., Groth, P., Biemann, C., Parreira, J.X., Aroyo, L., Noy, N., et al. (eds.) ISWC 2013, Part II. LNCS, vol. 8219, pp. 1–16. Springer, Heidelberg (2013)
3. Barbieri, D.F., Braga, D., Ceri, S., Valle, E.D., Grossniklaus, M.: Querying RDF streams with C-SPARQL. SIGMOD Rec. **39**(1), 20–26 (2010)
4. Etzion, O., Niblett, P.: Event Processing in Action, 1st edn. Manning Publications Co., Greenwich (2010)
5. Le-Phuoc, D., Dao-Tran, M., Parreira, J.X., Hauswirth, M.: A native and adaptive approach for unified processing of linked streams and linked data. In: Aroyo, L., Welty, C., Alani, H., Taylor, J., Bernstein, A., Kagal, L., Noy, N., Blomqvist, E. (eds.) ISWC 2011, Part I. LNCS, vol. 7031, pp. 370–388. Springer, Heidelberg (2011)
6. Le-Phuoc, D., Quoc, H.N.M., Le Van, C., Hauswirth, M.: Elastic and scalable processing of linked stream data in the cloud. In: Alani, H., Kagal, L., Fokoue, A., Groth, P., Biemann, C., Parreira, J.X., Aroyo, L., Noy, N., et al. (eds.) ISWC 2013, Part I. LNCS, vol. 8218, pp. 280–297. Springer, Heidelberg (2013)
7. Quoc, H.N.M., Serrano, M., Le-Phuoc, D., Hauswirth, M.: Super stream collider-linked stream mashups for everyone. In: Proceedings of the Semantic Web Challenge Co-located with the 11th International Semantic Web Conference, Boston, MA, USA, November 2012
8. Rinne, M., Nuutila, E., Törmä, S.: INSTANS: high-performance event processing with standard RDF and SPARQL. In: Proceedings of the ISWC 2012 Posters and Demonstrations Track, Boston, US (2012)

FOODpedia: Russian Food Products as a Linked Data Dataset

Maxim Kolchin[(✉)], Alexander Chistyakov, Maxim Lapaev,
and Rezeda Khaydarova

Laboratory ISST, ITMO University, St Petersburg, Russia
kolchinmax@niuitmo.ru, {al.ol.chistyakov,mignolowa}@gmail.com,
m.lapaev@telemetria.ru

Abstract. Open and efficient sharing of information about food products and their ingredients is important for all parties of the chain ranging
from the manufactures to consumers. There exist a public catalogue of
some Russian food products (http://goodsmatrix.ru/) that is used by
some manufactures and consumers. Although the information is open,
there are many difficulties in using the site, e.g., interoperability, querying and linking that could be mitigated by Semantic Web technologies. This paper presents an approach and a project for extracting and
publishing information about food products and also linking it to existing
datasets in Linked Open Data Cloud.

Keywords: Knowledge graph · Linked open data · Semantic web

1 Introduction

The goal of this work is to create a 5-star[1] open data dataset about Russian food
products and their ingredients. Such work involves *(a)* food ontology development, *(b)* crawling of the existing sources, *(c)* publishing of the information as
Linked Data and *(d)* linking to existing LOD datasets, such as *AGROVOC* [1]
and *DBpedia* [2].

Based on the dataset that is created using Semantic Web technologies, new
applications and services can be built, e.g. manufacturers can uses it to stan-
dardise the names for the ingredients, retailers can reuse the information on their
e-shops, developers can built applications for customers that help them decide
which product to buy based on their health conditions or personal preferences.

2 Dataset Creation

The source of the information for FOODpedia is web site called GoodsMatrix[2] which is manually curated catalogue where information comes mainly from
manufacturers.

---

[1] http://5stardata.info/.
[2] http://goodsmatrix.ru.

© Springer International Publishing Switzerland 2015
F. Gandon et al. (Eds.): ESWC 2015, LNCS 9341, pp. 87–90, 2015.
DOI: 10.1007/978-3-319-25639-9_17

Extraction of food product information from GoodsMatrix goes through a pipeline that includes *(a)* crawling the web site using *Scrapy*[3] framework and set of XPath expressions, *(b)* parsing the resulting data to extract information about energy values, ingredients and E-additives, *(c)* translation of the name and description to English and *(d)* linking ingredients information to resource in *AGROVOC* and *DBpedia* datasets.

The source code of the crawler and other artifacts are available in Github repository[4].

Extraction of Ingredients. Ingredients are crawled as a list of ingredients separated by some character such as comma or semicolon. But there is an unsolved issue, it's rare when different manufacturers use the same names for the same ingredients, some ingredients can have more than dozen alternative names. Usually such names are different only because of word order, missing or extra words, therefore we apply the Ratcli-Obershelp algorithm [3] to measure string similarity and create single resource for similar names.

Extraction of E-additives. E-additives are food additives which have special identifiers called E numbers such as E-100, E-201, etc. and are used in Europe, Russia and other countries. Since the identifiers have well-defined structure, it's quite easy to find them in the ingredient list using regular expressions. The only issue is additives which have E-number, but written on the package without its number, e.g. Curcumin[5].

Multilingual Support. The name and description of food product crawled earlier are translated to English with help of *Yandex.Translate API*[6].

Linking. Extracted E-additives and ingredients are linked to similar resource in *AGROVOC* and *DBpedia* datasets.

AGROVOC is a multilingual agricultural thesaurus consisting of over 32 000 concepts available in 21 languages including Russian, therefore it's a good candidate for linking. Ingredients are mapped to AGROVOC concepts automatically, but it doesn't support E numbers because of that they are mapped manually.

DBpedia is a good source of human readable descriptions of concepts, therefore it's interesting to link E-additives and ingredients to its resources, but it's not so easy, because the ontology is generated semi-automatically. Therefore the mapping is performed manually.

---

[3] http://scrapy.org/.
[4] https://github.com/ailabitmo/foodpedia.
[5] http://dbpedia.org/resource/Curcumin.
[6] https://api.yandex.com/translate/.

3   Ontologies

To represent food products and their ingredients, Food Product Ontology[7] were developed which extends GoodRelations[8] and Food Ontology[9]. Below you find an example of food product in Turtle:

```
foodpedia:4601242311914 a food:Food;
    fpr:carbohydratesPer100gAsDouble "13.1"^^xsd:double;
    food:containsIngredient foodpedia:E952, foodpedia:E412,
                            foodpedia:E202;
    fpr:energyPer100gAsDouble "52.4"^^xsd:double;
    fpr:fatPer100gAsDouble "0.0"^^xsd:double;
    food:ingredientsListAsText "вода, томатная паста,
                                яблочное пюре, сахар, соль,
                                E412, уксусная кислота,
                                перец красный, E202, укроп,
                                E952"@ru;
    fpr:proteinsPer100gAsDouble "0.0"^^xsd:double;
    gr:description "Кетчуп второй категории с добавлением
                    фруктового пюре"@ru;
    gr:hasEAN_UCC-13 "4601242311914";
    gr:name "КЕТЧУП АРСЕНТЬЕВСКИЙ ОСТРЫЙ 900 Г"@ru,
            "KETCHUP ARSENIEVSKIY ACUTE 900 G"@en.
```

Also an example of ingredient with links to similar resource in *AGROVOC* and *DBpedia* datasets:

```
foodpedia: a food:Ingredient;
    rdfs:label "сахар"@ru, "сахар-песок"@ru, "sugar"@en;
    skos:exactMatch agrovoc:c_7498, dbpedia:Sugar .
```

4   Publishing

The dataset is published using *Pubby*[10]. The interface for human and machine consumption is available at http://foodpedia.tk. Using the SPARQL endpoint[11] provided by the underlying *Virtuoso Triple Store*[12], actors are able to satisfy complex information needs. In addition, actors are able to use another query interface through Linked Data Fragments [4] server[13] for high-availability querying. And last, human can use a simple search interface (see Fig. 1) to find food products by its barcode or name.

---

[7] @prefix fpr: <http://purl.org/foodontology#>.
[8] @prefix gr: <http://purl.org/goodrelations/v1#>.
[9] @prefix food: <http://data.lirmm.fr/ontologies/food#>.
[10] https://github.com/cygri/pubby.
[11] http://foodpedia.tk/sparql.
[12] http://virtuoso.openlinksw.com.
[13] http://data.foodpedia.tk.

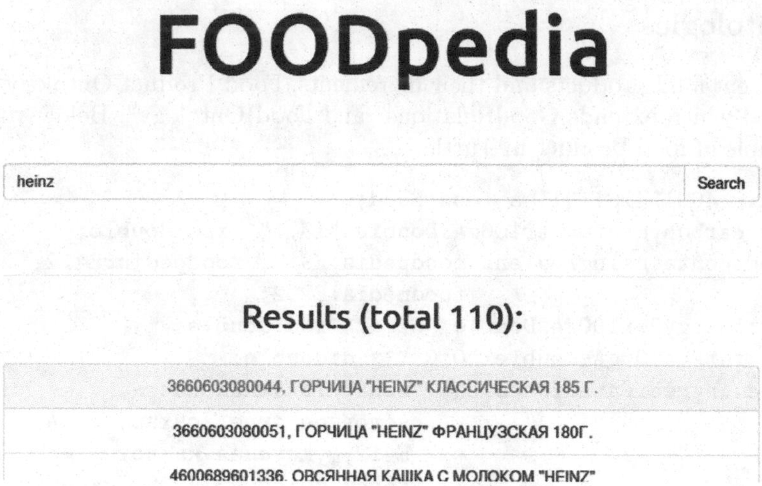

FOODpedia

heinz	Search

Results (total 110):

3660603080044, ГОРЧИЦА "HEINZ" КЛАССИЧЕСКАЯ 185 Г.

3660603080051, ГОРЧИЦА "HEINZ" ФРАНЦУЗСКАЯ 180Г.

4600689601336, ОВСЯННАЯ КАШКА С МОЛОКОМ "HEINZ"

Fig. 1. FOODpedia search interface

Licensing. All published data is openly licensed under Creative Commons Attribution License in accordance with the open definition[14].

Acknowledgements. This work has been partially financially supported by the Government of Russian Federation, Grant #074-U01.

References

1. Caracciolo, C., Stellato, A., Morshed, A., Johannsen, G., Rajbhandari, S., Jaques, Y., Keizer, J.: The agrovoc linked dataset. Semant. Web **4**(3), 341–348 (2013)
2. Lehmann, J., Isele, R., Jakob, M., Jentzsch, A., Kontokostas, D., Mendes, P.N., Hellmann, S., Morsey, M., van Kleef, P., Auer, S., Bizer, C.: Dbpedia - a large-scale, multilingual knowledge base extracted from wikipedia. Semant. Web **6**(2), 167–195 (2015)
3. Ratcliff, J.W., Metzener, D.E.: Pattern-matching-the gestalt approach. Dr. Dobbs J. **13**(7), 46 (1988)
4. Verborgh, R., et al.: Querying datasets on the web with high availability. In: Mika, P., et al. (eds.) ISWC 2014, Part I. LNCS, vol. 8796, pp. 180–196. Springer, Heidelberg (2014). http://dx.doi.org/10.1007/978-3-319-11964-9_12

---

[14] http://opendefinition.org.

SentiML++: An Extension of the SentiML Sentiment Annotation Scheme

Malik M. Saad Missen, Mohammed Attik, Mickaël Coustaty,
Antoine Doucet[✉], and Cyril Faucher

L3i Laboratory, Avenue Michel Crépeau, University of La Rochelle,
17042 La Rochelle, France
{malik.missen,mohammed.attik,mickael.coustaty,antoine.doucet,
cyril.faucher}@univ-lr.fr

Abstract. In this paper, we propose *SentiML++*, an extension of SentiML with a focus on annotating opinions answering aspects of the general question "who has what opinion about whom in which context?". A
detailed comparison with SentiML and other existing annotation schemes
is also presented. The data collection annotated with SentiML has also
been annotated with *SentiML++* and is available for download for
research purpose.

1 Introduction

The semantic annotation of opinions is one of the very important tasks of opinion mining. Semantic annotations are very important both for training machine
learning approaches and for evaluating opinion mining methods. Unfortunately,
there have been hardly any serious proposal attempts of appropriate annotation schemas until recently when SentiML [2], OpinionMiningML [9] and EmotionML [10] were proposed. In this paper, we discuss, compare and identify the
positives and negatives of these annotation schemes. Following this overview, we
propose SentiML++, an extension of SentiML that addresses several shortcomings of the state of the art.

SentiML. The SentiML annotation schema [2] follows a conventional sentiment
annotation style and is based on Appraisal Framework (AF) [5] which is a strong
linguistically-grounded theory. AF helps to define appraisal types (affect, judgments and appreciation) within the modifier tag which is another positive point
to be noted in SentiML. With a very simple annotation scheme, SentiML is
popular because adopting its annotation scheme does not require to acquire any
specific skills. However, concerns can be raised about SentiML.

OpinionMiningML. OpinionMiningML [9] is an XML-based formalism that
allows tagging of attitude expressions for features or objects as found in a textual
segment. It targets extraction of feature-based opinion expressions but its scope
is limited to proposing an annotation schema. Besides this, the structure of
OpinionMiningML is not straightforward and can be threatened by challenges

© Springer International Publishing Switzerland 2015
F. Gandon et al. (Eds.): ESWC 2015, LNCS 9341, pp. 91–96, 2015.
DOI: 10.1007/978-3-319-25639-9_18

for feature and relation extraction while developing an automatic tagger for this annotation scheme.

EmotionML. EmotionML [10] aims to make concepts from major emotion theories available in a broad range of technological contexts. Being informed by the effective sciences, EmotionML recognises the fact that there is no single agreed representation of effective states, nor of vocabularies to use. Therefore, an emotional state *<emotion>* can be characterised using four types of descriptions: *<category>*, *<dimension>*, *<appraisal>* and *<action − tendency>*. Furthermore, the vocabulary used can be identified.

SentiML Example. Throughout the article, we will use the following sentence as a running example: *"The U.S. State Department on Tuesday (KST) rated the human rights situation in North Korea "poor" in its annual human rights report, casting dark clouds on the already tense relationship between Pyongyang and Washington."* Relevant annotations in *SentiML* are given below:

```
<APPRAISALGROUP id="A0" fromID="T0" fromText="situation" toID="M0"
toText="poor" orientation="negative"/>
<APPRAISALGROUP id="A1" fromID="M1" fromText="dark" toID="T1" toText="clouds
" orientation="negative"/>
<APPRAISALGROUP id="A2" fromID="M2" fromText="tense" toID="T2" toText="
    relationship" orientation="negative"/>
<MODIFIER id="M0" start="201" end="205" text="poor" attitude="appreciation"
    orientation="negative" force="normal" polarity="unmarked"/>
<MODIFIER id="M1" start="250" end="254" text="dark" attitude="appreciation"
    orientation="negative" force="normal" polarity="unmarked"/>
<MODIFIER id="M2" start="277" end="282" text="tense" attitude="appreciation"
    orientation="negative" force="normal" polarity="unmarked"/>
<TARGET id="T0" start="175" end="184" text="situation" type="thing" orientation="
    neutral"/>
<TARGET id="T1" start="255" end="261" text="clouds" type="thing" orientation="
    ambiguous"/>
<TARGET id="T2" start="283" end="295" text="relationship" type="thing" orientation="
    neutral"/>
```

OpinionMiningML example below annotated using the *OpinionMiningML* syntax:

```
<COMMENT id="1" ontologyreference="1">
<FRAGMENT id="1"> The U.S. State Department on Tuesday (KST) rated the human
    rights situation in North Korea "poor" </FRAGMENT>
<FRAGMENT id="2"> in its annual human rights report, casting dark clouds on the already
    tense relationship between Pyongyang and Washington.</FRAGMENT>
<APPRAISAL polarity="negative" intensity="medium">
    <FACETREFERENCE>1</FACETREFERENCE>
    <FRAGMENTREFERENCE>1</FRAGMENTREFERENCE>
    <FRAGMENTREFERENCE>2</FRAGMENTREFERENCE>
</APPRAISAL>
<APPRAISAL polarity="negative" intensity="medium">
    <FACETREFERENCE>2</FACETREFERENCE>
    <FRAGMENTREFERENCE>1</FRAGMENTREFERENCE>
    <FRAGMENTREFERENCE>2</FRAGMENTREFERENCE>
</APPRAISAL>
</COMMENT>
```

EmotionML example presented hereby an example annotated using the EmotionML syntax:

```
<emotionml xmlns="http://www.w3.org/2009/10/emotionml"
xmlns:meta="http://www.example.com/metadata"
category-set="http://www.w3.org/TR/emotion-voc/xml#occ-categories">
<info>  <meta:doc>Example taken from annotation of SentiML </meta:doc>  </info>
The U.S. State Department on Tuesday (KST)
<emotion>  < category   name="reproach"/>
   rated the human rights situation in North Korea "poor" </emotion> in its annual human
      rights report
<emotion>  <category name="disappointment"/>
   casting dark clouds </emotion>
 on the already <emotion>
   <category  name="disappointment"/>
   tense relationship between Pyongyang and Washington.
</emotion>
</emotionML>
```

2 Comparison

In this section we give a comparison of annotations schemes from different perspectives, summarized in Table 1. From this comparison, it can be concluded that SentiML has a larger scope and it is equipped with a more affordable vocabulary with respect to the previous work [1,4,6,8]. Hence, we find it the most suitable choice for our current work.

3 SentiML++

In this section, we provide an extension of *SentiML* considering the work of *Bing Liu* [3] as a reference and find out that most of the aspects defining an opinion seem to be missing (completely or partially). For example, *SentiML* works on sub-sentence level and hence leaves actual holder and target entities of sentiment of a sentence unmarked. As far as opinion orientation is concerned, it deals with prior polarities in a better way than the contextual ambiguities. It does not recognize the topic of a sentence, hence fails to identify topic-based contextual ambiguities. Similarly, the contexts defined by cultural phrases and emoticons cannot be identified using *SentiML*. Flexibility and completeness are important characteristics of an annotation scheme [7] and unfortunately, *SentiML* fails to have both of these characteristics. Identification of opinion words and their polarity with respect to a given topic could help resolving contextual ambiguities. Therefore, we propose to take topic identification into account in SentiML++ by proposing <TOPIC> element. A good share of the opinions generally found on the web are expressed informally. This includes the use of emoticons and sarcastic phrases or cultural expressions (e.g., "bored to death", "dressed to kill", etc.) that could invert the semantics of the text surrounding them. Identification of such contexts could aid the automated detection of such opinion inversions. In SentiML++, we deal with this problem using <INFORMAL> element.

Table 1. Comparison of annotation schemes

Scope	EmotionML, the W3C standard, is an effort to cover all aspects of emotions globally in all concerned fields while OpinionMiningML and SentiML limit themselves to domains of IR and NLP. In our view, SentiML has larger scope as compared to OpinionMiningML which limits itself only to feature-based sentiment analysis
Complexity	Because of its larger scope than the other two annotation schemes, EmotionML can be considered complex and less user-friendly. SentiML is much easier to use than OpinionMiningML because of the vocabulary of its annotation scheme which matches the vocabulary used in research work of this field (i.e. concepts like holder, target, modifier, etc.)
Vocabulary	EmotionML text annotation is equipped with new and broader vocabulary while targets of SentiML and OpinionMiningML are more specific. SentiML revolves around the concept of modifier and targets of the sentiments while OpinionMiningML's focus remains on sentiment relevant to features of the objects and equips itself with numerous meta-tags
Structure	The structure of all three annotation schemes follow XML based format but OpinionMiningML defines granularity better than the other annotation schemes by reaching up to the feature level
Contextual ambiguities	While all three annotation schemes focus on defining semantics of the expression types, such as appreciation, suggestion etc., SentiML also tackles the issue of contextual ambiguities which is a big research challenge in the field of opinion mining
Theoretical grounds	EmotionML is a W3C standard and has been recommended after years of discussion and debate between experts and stakeholders while SentiML is based on the Appraisal Framework, a strong linguistically-grounded theory. OpinionMiningML, in the contrary, has not been reported to have a theoretical basis
Granularity level	Another distinction that can be observed while comparing these annotation schemes is their granularity level. EmotionML is found to be operating on the sentence level while OpinionMiningML and SentiML are rather focusing on sub-sentence levels. While it is mandatory to analyze on a sub-sentence (or word level) to find correct sentiments, the sentence is however a more logical unit of discourse
Completeness	Completeness [7] is one of the most important features of annotation schemes. Completeness demands whether an annotation deals with all or most of the real world scenarios. Observing all of these annotations i.e. SentiML, EmotionML and OpinionMiningML in light of this particular characteristic, no annotation scheme seems to satisfy it. SentiML and EmotionML behave similarly by just annotating sentimental expressions while OpinionMiningML goes a step forward by targeting features of objects but fails to deal with contextual aspects of opinions, one of the major problems of opinion mining
Flexibility	EmotionML, knowing the challenges of different domains, gives freedom to use whatever vocabulary of emotional states suited to a particular domain. OpinionMiningML follows EmotionML in this regard and gives the choice of building a domain-based ontology as required, a possibility that SentiML lacks

SentiML++ Example. SentiML++ operates on both levels i.e. phrase as well as sentence level. In this section, we annotate the same sentence as an example using SentiML++. The annotation includes the introduction of sentence-level markups like <HOLDER>, <TARGET>, <ORIENTATION>, <TOPIC> and <INFORMAL> while only <HOLDER> is introduced on the sub-sentence level. All of these markups come under the main markup of <SENTENCE> while sub-sentence level annotation comes under <PHRASES>. The markup <SENTENCE> includes one attribute called "type" with possible values "general" or "informal". The value "general" is used for ordinary sentences while the value "informal" is only used when the whole identified sentence is an idiom, a metaphor or an emoticon. When the value "informal" is used, only the <INFORMAL> markup plays its role while other markups are discarded because they are rendered meaningless. The <HOLDER> markup was introduced on the sub-sentence level to identify the holders even at this smaller granularity, if needed.

```
<SENTENCE ID=0 type="general">
   <HOLDER id="H0" start="33" end="53" text="U.S. State Department" type="organization"
      orientation="neutral"/>
   <TARGET id="T0" start="108" end="117" text="North Korea" type="country" orientation="
      neutral"/>
   <ORIENTATION polarity="negative">
   <TOPIC id="1" ref="www.dmoz.org" chain="Society:Issues:Human Rights and Liberties">
   <PHRASES>
   <APPRAISALGROUP id="A0" fromID="T0" fromText="situation" toID="M0" toText="poor"
      Holder="H0" orientation="negative"/>
   <APPRAISALGROUP id="A1" fromID="M1" fromText="dark" toID="T1" toText="clouds"
      Holder="H1" orientation="negative"/>
   <APPRAISALGROUP id="A2" fromID="M2" fromText="tense" toID="T2" toText="relationship
      " Holder="H2" orientation="negative"/>
   <MODIFIER id="M0" start="201" end="205" text="poor" attitude="appreciation" orientation=
      "negative" force="normal" polarity="unmarked"/>
   <MODIFIER id="M1" start="250" end="254" text="dark" attitude="appreciation" orientation="
      negative" force="normal" polarity="unmarked"/>
   <MODIFIER id="M2" start="277" end="282" text="tense" attitude="appreciation" orientation=
      "negative" force="normal" polarity="unmarked"/>
   <TARGET id="T1" start="175" end="184" text="situation" type="thing" orientation="neutral"
      />
   <TARGET id="T2" start="255" end="261" text="clouds" type="thing" orientation="ambiguous
      "/>
   <TARGET id="T3" start="283" end="295" text="relationship" type="thing" orientation="
      neutral"/>
   <HOLDER id="H1" start="33" end="53" text="U.S. State Department" type="organization"
      orientation="neutral"/>
   <HOLDER id="H2" start="33" end="53" text="U.S. State Department" type="organization"
      orientation="neutral"/>
   <HOLDER id="H3" start="33" end="53" text="U.S. State Department" type="organization"
      orientation="neutral"/>
   </PHRASES>
</SENTENCE>
```

It must be noted that <APPRAISALGROUP> in SentiML++ links modifier, target and holder identified at the sub-sentence level. This is in contradiction with SentiML [2], where only modifier and target are linked. <Holder> and <Target> elements are found on both levels i.e. sentence and sub-sentence level. Natural language processing techniques such as syntactic parsing can be helpful in identifying these elements on both granularity levels.

4   Conclusions and Future Work

In this paper, we proposed *SentiML++*, an extension of SentiML. We proposed to add target (on sentence level), holder, topic and informal sentence identification as part of *SentiML++*. *SentiML++* adds flexibility to SentiML by giving freedom of choice for a taxonomy when annotating the topic of a sentence. As part of our future work, we plan to further enhance SentiML++ by modeling relations between its elements. The idea is to propose a more suitable model for the semantic web so that state-of-the-art semantic web tools can be leveraged to exploit its semantics.

References

1. Cambria, E., Schuller, B., Xia, Y., Havasi, C.: New avenues in opinion mining and sentiment analysis. IEEE Intell. Syst. **28**(2), 15–21 (2013)
2. Di Bari, M., Sharoff, S., Thomas, M.: Sentiml: Functional annotation for multilingual sentiment analysis. In: Proceedings of DH-CASE 2013, pp. 15:1–15:7. ACM, New York (2013). http://doi.acm.org/10.1145/2517978.2517994
3. Liu, B.: Sentiment analysis and subjectivity. In: Indurkhya, N., Damerau, F.J. (eds.) Handbook of Natural Language Processing, 2nd edn. Taylor and Francis, Boca Raton (2010)
4. Liu, B., Zhang, L.: A survey of opinion mining and sentiment analysis. In: Aggarwal, C.C., Zhai, C. (eds.) Mining Text Data, pp. 415–463. Springer, Berlin (2012)
5. Martin, J.R., White, P.R.R.: The language of evaluation, appraisal in English. Palgrave Macmillan, Basingstoke (2005)
6. Missen, M.M.S., Boughanem, M., Cabanac, G.: Opinion mining: reviewed from word to document level. Soc. Netw. Anal. Min. **3**(1), 107–125 (2013). doi:10.1007/s13278-012-0057-9
7. Oren, E., Möller, K., Scerri, S., Handschuh, S., Sintek, M.: What are semantic annotations? Technical report, DERI Galway (2006). http://www.siegfried-handschuh.net/pub/2006/whatissemannot2006.pdf
8. Pang, B., Lee, L.: Opinion mining and sentiment analysis. Found. Trends Inf. Retr. **2**(1–2), 1–135 (2008). doi:10.1561/1500000011
9. Robaldo, L., Caro, L.D.: Opinionmining-ml. Comput. Stan. Interfaces **35**(5), 454–469 (2013)
10. Schröder, M., Baggia, P., Burkhardt, F., Pelachaud, C., Peter, C., Zovato, E.: EmotionML – an upcoming standard for representing emotions and related states. In: D'Mello, S., Graesser, A., Schuller, B., Martin, J.-C. (eds.) ACII 2011, Part I. LNCS, vol. 6974, pp. 316–325. Springer, Heidelberg (2011)

Analysis of Companies' Non-financial Disclosures: Ontology Learning by Topic Modeling

Andy Moniz[1(✉)] and Franciska de Jong[1,2]

[1] Erasmus Studio, Erasmus University, Rotterdam, The Netherlands
moniz@rsm.nl, f.m.g.dejong@eshcc.eur.nl,
f.m.g.dejong@utwente.nl
[2] Human Media Interaction, University of Twente, Enschede, The Netherlands

Abstract. Prior studies highlight the merits of integrating Linked Data to aid investors' analyses of company financial disclosures. Non-financial disclosures, including reporting on a company's environmental footprint (*corporate sustainability*), remains an unexplored area of research. One reason cited by investors is the need for earth science knowledge to interpret such disclosures. To address this challenge, we propose an automated system which employs Latent Dirichlet Allocation (LDA) for the discovery of earth science topics in corporate sustainability text. The LDA model is seeded with a vocabulary generated by terms retrieved via a SPARQL endpoint. The terms are seeded as lexical priors into the LDA model. An ensemble tree combines the resulting topic probabilities and classifies the quality of sustainability disclosures using domain expert ratings published by Google Finance. From an applications stance, our results may be of interest to investors seeking to integrate corporate sustainability considerations into their investment decisions.

Keywords: Automated ontology learning · Topic modeling · LDA · Sustainability

1 Introduction

Prior studies [1, 2] highlight the benefits of employing Linked Data for investment analysis, by combining information from Dbpedia, stockmarket patterns and different taxonomy versions of companies' accounting statements. Increasingly, investors and regulators are demanding companies to disclose non-financial information, particularly firms' impacts on the environment (referred to as *sustainability*) [4]. The voluntary nature of corporate sustainability reporting has resulted in the publication of inconsistent and incomplete information [4]. This has inhibited the manual creation of ontologies [3, 8]. In this study, we employ an automated ontology learning system to overcome this challenge. The proposed system, labelled SPARQL LDA, employs Latent Dirichlet Allocation (LDA) [5] for the discovery of topics to represent ontology concepts [6–8].

The system works in three phases. The first phase employs a Naïve Bayesian model to categorize text in sustainability disclosures. The model detects text related to a firm's

© Springer International Publishing Switzerland 2015
F. Gandon et al. (Eds.): ESWC 2015, LNCS 9341, pp. 97–101, 2015.
DOI: 10.1007/978-3-319-25639-9_19

climate change impacts and aggregates sentences to create a composite document. The second phase employs a LDA topic model to detect contextual information in text. Topics are learned by retrieving terms via a SPARQL endpoint which are seeded as lexical priors into the LDA model. The final phase combines the LDA topic probabilities in an ensemble model and classifies the quality of corporate sustainability reporting using publically available disclosure ratings.

The rest of this study is structured as follows: Sect. 2 provides a brief overview of relevant sustainability datasets. In Sect. 3 we develop a system to evaluate the quality of corporates' sustainability disclosures. Section 4 provides an empirical evaluation of the proposed system. We conclude in Sect. 5.

2 Environmental Sustainability Datasets

Prior earth science literature has explored the benefits of incorporating Semantic Web technologies to predict the impacts of climate change [9–12]. To our knowledge, literature has not considered the implications for companies or government regulatory policy. To aid such analysis we highlight two publically available datasets. The US Global Change Research Act of 1990 requires a National Climate Assessment (NCA) report [13] on the impact of climate change and affected industries. This includes a Global Change Information System (GCIS) which stores climate change metadata. GCIS resources are exported into a triple store queryable through a public SPARQL interface. A second dataset, published under the "Key stats and ratios" section of Google Finance, provides ratings to evaluate the quality of firms' sustainability disclosures. These ratings are collected by the Carbon Disclosure Project (CDP), an initiative led by the United Nations, and are computed from annual surveys of domain experts. The highest CDP rating, 'A', corresponds to companies that are perceived to have published comprehensive climate change disclosures. The lowest rating, "E", corresponds to companies with poor quality disclosures.

3 Model of Corporate Sustainability

3.1 Climate Change Aspect Detection

The first phase of the system employs a Naïve Bayesian classifier to detect salient aspects in text. A pre-processing step selects classification features from Wikipedia's 'Carbon emissions reporting' page. The page provides an overview of corporate environmental reporting issues. We select the 10 most frequently occurring unigrams and bigrams as classification features: "climate", "climate change", "emissions", "emitters", "gas", "ghg", "greenhouse", "scope 1", "scope 2", "scope 3".

3.2 LDA Topic Model

The second phase of the system employs a LDA model [5] for the discovery of topics represented as ontology concepts [6–8, 16]. In LDA, a topic is modeled as a probability distribution over a set of words represented by a vocabulary and a document as a probability distribution over a set of topics. Our approach departs from a traditional LDA model [5] by seeding terms as lexical priors following the approach of [14]. Figure 1 displays the SPARQL query which retrieves the key recommendations from the latest NCA report using the GCIS interface (see Sect. 2). The unique terms (excluding stopwords) generated by the query form the LDA model's vocabulary.

```
1  PREFIX dcterms: <http://purl.org/dc/terms/>
2  PREFIX dbpedia: <http://dbpedia.org/resource/>
3  PREFIX xsd: <http://www.w3.org/2001/XMLSchema#>
4  SELECT str($statement) as $statement $finding
5  FROM <http://data.globalchange.gov>
6  WHERE {  $report dcterms:title "Climate Change Impacts in the United States: The Third National Climate Assessment"^^xsd:string .
7      $report gcis:hasChapter $chapter .
8      $finding gcis:isFindingOf $chapter .
9      $finding dcterms:description $statement . }
```

Fig. 1. SPARQL query used to retrieve a earth science terms

We implement standard settings for LDA hyperparameters with $\alpha = 50/K$ and $\beta = .01$ [15]. The number of topics, K, is set to five following a heuristic approach based on the number of climate change topics reported in the latest NCA report [13]. Table 1 displays the top terms associated with the topic clusters. Cluster labels are manually annotated to aid the reader's interpretation.

Table 1. Topic clusters and top words identified by SPARQL LDA

Footprint	Mitigation	Adaptation	Monitoring	Risks
Emissions	Processes	Systems	Monitoring	Risks
Impacts	Responses	Adaptation	Usage	Regulatory
Ocean	Plans	Goal	Volume	Reporting
Climates	Requirements	Thresholds	Percentile	Policymakers
Ecosystems	Reported	Technology	Stabilizing	Trends
Society	Estimates	Operational	Target	Economic
Reef	Measures	Achieving	Consumption	Shifts
Glacier	Mitigation	Improvements	Percent	Effects
Forest	Research	Target	Capacity	Changing

The outcome of the model is a finer-grained categorization of companies' disclosures based on topics discussed by the online scientific community. The probabilities associated with each topic cluster are included as components within the ensemble tree.

4   Ensemble Model

In this section we outline the evaluation of the ensemble classification tree, present the results and briefly conclude.

4.1   Data

Sustainability disclosures are reported annually on company websites. We retrieve a sample of 443 reports via the Google search query: "sustainability report type:pdf site:" followed by companies' urls obtained from DBpedia (dbpedia-owl:wikiPageExternalLink). Document text is extracted using PDFMiner. To evaluate the ensemble tree's classifications, we create a Boolean which takes a value of one if a company's CDP disclosure is 'A' rated and zero otherwise (see Sect. 2).

4.2   Experimental Setup

We design the evaluation by comparing two systems. The benchmark employs a traditional LDA model and infers topics using only the underlying collection of documents. The SPARQL LDA system incorporates lexical priors by seeding the SPARQL generated vocabulary (see Sect. 3.2). Any differences in classification between the two systems can be explained by the different approaches to topic learning. Experiments were validated using 10-fold cross validation. The performance is evaluated in terms of Precision, Recall, and F1-measure:

$$recall = \frac{TP}{TP+FN} \quad precision = \frac{TP}{TP+FP} \quad F1\,measure = \frac{precision * recall}{precision + recall}$$

The evaluation metrics are shown in Table 2.

Table 2. System evaluation

System	Precision	Recall	F1-measure
Benchmark	0.52	0.59	0.55
SPARQL LDA	0.69	0.65	0.67
%difference	32.7 %	10.2 %	21.8 %

Precision for the SPARQL LDA system improves by 33 % versus the traditional LDA approach.

5   Conclusion

The manual building of ontologies is a time-consuming and costly process particularly in fast evolving domains of knowledge such as earth science, where information is updated often. In this paper we employ a fully-automated method for learning ontologies to alleviate the need for manual approaches. Our findings point to the benefits of integrating Linked Data for investors' analyses of both financial and non-financial disclosures.

Acknowledgement. The research leading to these results has partially been supported by the Dutch national program COMMIT.

References

1. Kämpgen, B., Weller, T., O'Riain, S., Weber, C., Harth, A.: Accepting the XBRL challenge with linked data for financial data integration. In: Presutti, V., d'Amato, C., Gandon, F., d'Aquin, M., Staab, S., Tordai, A. (eds.) ESWC 2014. LNCS, vol. 8465, pp. 595–610. Springer, Heidelberg (2014)
2. Carretié, H., Torvisco, B., García, R., Carlos, J.: Using semantic web technologies to facilitate XBRL-based financial data comparability. In: FEOSW (2012)
3. O'Riain, S., Curry, E., Harth, A.: XBRL and open data for global financial ecosystems: a linked data approach. Int. J. Acc. Inf. Syst. **13**, 141–162 (2012)
4. Coburn, J., Cook, J.: Cool Response: The SEC & Corporate Climate Change Reporting. Ceres (2014)
5. Blei, D.M., Ng, A.Y., Jordan, M.I.: Latent Dirichlet allocation. J. Mach. Learn. Res. **3**, 993–1022 (2003)
6. Wong, W., Liu, W., Bennamoun, M.: Ontology Learning and Knowledge Discovery Using the Web: Challenges and Recent Advances. IGI Global, Hershey (2011)
7. Cimiano, P.: Ontology Learning and Population from Text: Algorithms, Evaluation and Applications. Springer-Verlag New York, Secaucus (2006)
8. Wei, W., Barnaghi, P., Bargiela, A.: Probabilistic topic models for learning terminological ontologies. IEEE Trans. Knowl. Data Eng. **22**, 1028–1040 (2009)
9. Pouchard, L., Branstetter, M., Cook, R., Devarakonda, R., Green, J., Palanisamy, G.: A linked science investigation: enhancing climate change data discovery with semantic technologies. Earth Sci. Inform. **63**, 175–185 (2013) (Oak Ridge National Laboratory)
10. Bozic, B., Peters-Anders, J., Schimak, G.: Ontology mapping in semantic time series processing and climate change prediction. In: 7th International Congress on Environmental Modelling (2014)
11. Emile-Geay, J., Eshleman, J.A.: Toward a semantic web of paleoclimatology. Goechem. Geophys. Geosyst. **14**, 457–469 (2013)
12. Tilmes, C., Fox, P., Ma, X., McGuinness, D.L., Privette, A.P., Smith, A., Waple, A., Zednik, S., Zheng, J.G.: Provenance representation for the national climate assessment in the global change information system. IEEE Trans. Geosci. Remote Sens. **51**, 5160–5168 (2013)
13. Melillo, J.M., Richmond, T.T., Yohe, G.W.: Climate Change Impacts in the United States: The Third National Climate Assessment. U.S. Global Change Research Program, Washington (2014)
14. Jagarlamudi, J., Daume III, H., Udupa, R.: Incorporating lexical priors into topic models. In: EACL (2012)
15. Griffiths, T., Steyvers, M.: A probabilistic approach to semantic representation. In: Conference of the Cognitive Science Society (2002)
16. Zavitsanos, E., Paliouras, G., Vouros, G.A., Petridis, S.: Discovering subsumption hierarchies of ontology concepts from text corpora. In: Proceedings of the International Conference on Web Intelligence (2007)

Curating a Document Collection via Crowdsourcing with Pundit 2.0

Christian Morbidoni[1]([✉]) and Alessio Piccioli[2]

[1] Università Politecnica delle Marche, Ancona, Italy
christian.morbidoni@gmail.com
[2] NET7 Internet Open Solutions, Pisa, Italy

Abstract. Pundit 2.0 is a semantic web annotation system that supports users in creating structured data on top of web pages. Annotations in Pundit are RDF triples that users build starting from web page elements, as text or images. Annotations can be made public and developers can access and combine them into RDF knowledge graphs, while authorship of each triple is always retrievable. In this demo we showcase Pundit 2.0 and demonstrate how it can be used to enhance a digital library, by providing a data crowdsourcing platform. Pundit enables users to annotate different kind of entities and to contribute to the collaborative creation of a knowledge graph. This, in turn, refines in real-time the exploration functionalities of the library's faceted search, providing an immediate added value out of the annotation effort. Ad-hoc configurations can be used to drive specific visualisations, like the timeline-map shown in this demo.

Keywords: Semantic annotation · Linked data · Faceted browsing · Digital humanities · Pundit

1 Introduction

Digital libraries need curated semantically structured data to provide meaningful exploration and search capabilities. However, while metadata, such as document title, authors and main topics, are usually present and well curated in digital libraries, there is a great amount of knowledge hidden in texts and that could be of great value to explore a corpus. Although automatic text annotation services are available and their performances greatly improved over the last years, there is still the need for human intervention to refine extracted data and to add information than can hardly be captured by automatic tools. Pundit[1] is a semantic annotation tool that combines powerful annotation functionalities, covering comments; tagging; semi-automatic entities markup and linking; composition of rich semantic statements by interlinking items in a web page - such as text or images - and resources from the LOD or from custom annotation vocabularies. Annotations in Pundit can be made public and then accessed - via REST

---

[1] http://thepund.it.

© Springer International Publishing Switzerland 2015
F. Gandon et al. (Eds.): ESWC 2015, LNCS 9341, pp. 102–106, 2015.
DOI: 10.1007/978-3-319-25639-9_20

APIS or SPARQL queries - and combined by developers to form RDF knowledge graphs. The tool adopts a flexible data model based on RDF and an extension of the Open Annotation model[2]. Pundit is the evolution of previous systems [1,2] and is designed as a configurable annotation service. It addresses online annotation communities by allowing customisation of both user interface - by activating/deactivating annotation functionalities - and annotation vocabularies, allowing community administrators to decide what properties and resources can be used in composing annotations. Domain specific annotation environments can be deployed and made available as bookmarklets or as REST services, making it easy to connect such environments to existing web sites. Pundit 2.0 has been recently released. It features a restyled graphical user interface and additional functionalities over the previous version [3,4], such as the preconfigured annotations templates that improves productivity when annotations with the same structure have to be repeatedly created. A paper describing Pundit 2.0 in detail is currently under review and is available online[3].

In this demo we show how Pundit 2.0 can enable the collaborative creation of a knowledge graph on top of a sample digital library. The demonstrative digital library showcased in this paper, allows users to freely annotate text documents, producing RDF triples and contributing in real time to the refinement of the faceted search/browsing functionalities of the library itself. Relevant entities discovered by users and annotated with Pundit are injected in the portal as facet values, thus producing immediate added value out of the annotation effort. Pundit APIs support both open crowdsourcing scenarios, where every user can annotate, and more controlled ones, where only those annotations from authorised users - or from their specific annotation collections - are imported.

2   Description of the Online Demo

The online demo can be accessed at http://purl.org/pundit/eswc2015. Different text documents from different authors in the area of philosophy and politics (including e.g. works from Antonio Gramsci[4] and correspondence from Jacob Burckhardt[5]) have been loaded into the portal to form a small sample digital library. A simple faceted browser is provided as the main exploration mean. Some of the facets reflect structural features of the documents, such as their provider or language. Other facets show different kind of entities that the documents talk about (e.g. persons, places). When users open a document they can perform different annotation tasks. The easiest one is probably that of marking relevant entities appearing in the text. By selecting the *suggestions* mode in the annotation side bar and clicking on *scan page*, users get automatic suggestions and can review results by approving or rejecting annotations. This feature is powered by DataTXT[6], an entity linking service based on the TAGME algorithm [5].

---

[2] http://www.openannotation.org/spec/core/.
[3] http://www.semantic-web-journal.net/content/pundit-20.
[4] http://dl.gramsciproject.org.
[5] http://burckhardtsource.org.
[6] https://dandelion.eu/products/datatxt/nex/demo.

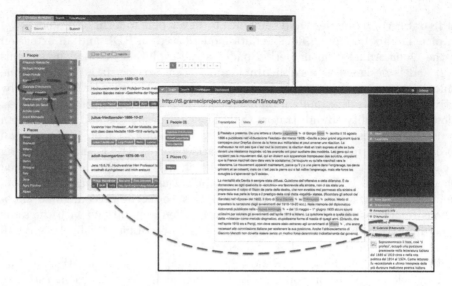

Fig. 1. A screenshot of the demo navigation portal. The facets browser (left) is populated from users annotations made on the text (right).

By annotating the documents, the user actively contribute to improve the browsing experience. For example, each time a user annotates an entity of type *place* or *person* this results in a new value appearing in the respective facet (Fig. 1). Note that for the purpose of this demo all users are entitled to do so and no quality check is performed. However, in a real world setting it would be possible to take into account annotations from trusted users only. An other way of adding annotations is by using the *annotation composer*. This allows expert users to freely compose triples. To do so, select a text in the page and choose *use as subject'*: the triple composer will appear. Complete the statement by choosing an object (e.g. searching on DBpedia or in custom vocabularies) and a predicate among the proposed ones (Fig. 2).

An alternative way of exploring the document collection is the one based on TimeMapper[7], an open-source tool developed by the Open Knowledge Labs[8]. This is an example of a possible specialised view on the document collection, where texts excerpts that identify a precise event are shown in a timeline along with the main person involved in the event and the place where it occurred. To contribute to such a view, users are required to create annotations with a precise structure. While it is possible to use the annotation composer to edit such annotations, a preconfigured annotations template is provided to make the task easier and to avoid errors. To activate the *template mode*, click on the pencil icon in the Pundit top bar and then choose the *PTP* template from the dropdown menu. Once this is activated, every time the user selects a text excerpt

---

[7] http://timemapper.okfnlabs.org/.

[8] http://okfnlabs.org/.

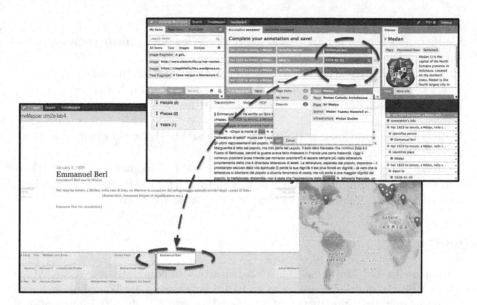

Fig. 2. An annotation created with the PTP template shows up as a new slide in the timeline view.

the annotation composer will be automatically populated with three statements. Users will then have to *fill the blanks*, by searching DBpedia or Freebase for the appropriate person and place and by entering a date. On save the annotation will be shown in the sidebar and a new item will appear in the timeline, as illustrated in Fig. 2.

3 Related Works

Semantic annotation systems have been reviewed and compared in literature [6] and formal models have been developed for annotations and annotation systems [3]. In this section we shortly mention some of the annotation systems we think are more related to Pundit. Annotea [8] is one of the first systems to implement RDF based annotation, providing both client and server APIs for storing structured data. Its semantic capabilities were limited to Dublin code fields. LORE (Literature Object Reuse and Exchange) [9] is a semantic annotation system providing a Mozilla plugin to annotate content. It implements the concept of compound object which is similar to semantic annotation in Pundit. Compound objects are basically set of inter-connected resources and can be linked to web content and created with a visual graph UI. Domeo [10] implements ontology-based annotation metadata on HTML or XML document targets, using the Annotation Ontology (AO) RDF model. Semantic Turkey [11] allows to capture knowledge from web pages by associating it to reference ontologies. To our knowledge, Pundit is the first annotation tool that combines:

- Semi-automatic linking of entities in text
- Configurable semantic annotation templates, allowing to create complex annotations in few steps
- Free composition of triples to link elements in web document (e.g. words, images, images parts) to LOD entities and among each other
- Configurable annotation vocabularies of entities and relations to be used in triples
- Delivery of annotations as RDF graphs via SPARQL or via open or authenticated REST API
- Delivery of the annotation environment as-a-service, so that web applications can make their content annotatable by calling a REST API (feed.thepund.it), as well as as a bookmarklet, or simply as a javascript library.

References

1. Tummarello, G., Morbidoni, C.: Collaboratively building structured knowledge with DBin: from del.icio.us tags to an RDFS Folksonomy. In: Workshop on Social and Collaborative Construction of Structured Knowledge, CKC 2007, International World Wide Web Conference, WWW 2007, Banff, AB, Canada (2007)
2. Tummarello, G., Morbidoni, C.: The DBin platform: a complete environment for semantic web communities. J. Web Semant. **6**(4), 257–265 (2008)
3. Grassi, M., Morbidoni, C., Nucci, M., Fonda, S., Piazza, F.: Pundit: augmenting web contents with semantics. Literary Linguis. Comput. **28**, 640–659 (2013)
4. Morbidoni, C., Grassi, M., Nucci, M., Fonda, S., Ledda, G.: Introducing the semlib project: semantic web tools for digital libraries. In: 1st International Workshop on Semantic Digital Archives, SDA 2011, Berlin, Germany (2011)
5. Ferragina, P., Scaiella, U.: TAGME: on-the-fly annotation of short text fragments (by wikipedia entities). In: Proceedings of the 19th ACM International Conference on Information and Knowledge Management, New York (2010)
6. Andrews, P., Zaihrayeu, I., Pane, J.: A classification of semantic annotation systems. Semant. Web J. **3**(3), 223–248 (2012). http://www.semantic-Web-journal.net/content/classification-semantic-annotation-systems
7. Agosti, M., Ferro, N.: A formal model of annotations of digital content. ACM Trans. Inf. Syst. (TOIS) **26**(1), 3 (2007). TOIS Homepage archive
8. Kahan, J., Koivunen, M.R.: Annotea: an open RDF infra-structure for shared web annotations. In: Proceedings of the 10th International Conference on World Wide Web (2001)
9. Gerber, A., Hunter, J.: Authoring, editing and visualizing compound objects for literary scholarship. J. Digit. Inf. **11**(1) (2010)
10. Ciccarese, P., Ocana, M., Clark, T.: DOMEO: a web-based tool for semantic annotation of online documents. In: Bio-Ontologies 2011 (2012)
11. Pazienza, M.T., Scarpato, N., Stellato, A., Turbati, A.: Semantic turkey: a browser-integrated environment for knowledge acquisition and management. Semant. Web J. **3**(3), 279–292 (2012)

SemNaaS: Add Semantic Dimension to the Network as a Service

Mohamed Morsey[1]([✉]), Hao Zhu[1], Isart Canyameres[2], and Paola Grosso[1]

[1] Informatics Institute, University of Amsterdam,
1098 XH Amsterdam, The Netherlands
{m.morsey,h.zhu,p.grosso}@uva.nl
[2] i2CAT Foundation, 08034 Barcelona, Spain
isart.canyameres@i2cat.net

Abstract. Cloud Computing has several provision models, e.g. Infrastructure as a service (IaaS). However, cloud users (tenants) have limited or no control over the underlying network resources. Network as a Service (NaaS) is emerging as a novel model to fill this gap. However, NaaS requires an approach capable of modeling the underlying network resources capabilities in abstracted and vendor-independent form. In this paper we elaborate on SemNaaS, a Semantic Web based approach for developing and supporting operations of NaaS systems. SemNaaS can work with any NaaS provider. We integrated it with the existing OpenNaaS framework. We propose Network Markup Language (NML) as the ontology for describing networking infrastructures.Based on that ontology, we develop a network modeling system and integrate with OpenNaaS. Furthermore, we demonstrate the capabilities that Semantic Web can add to the NaaS paradigm by applying SemNaaS operations to a specific NaaS use case.

1 Introduction

Cloud infrastructures and services are becoming the de facto architecture to support operations of large web infrastructures, to process Big Data and to provide users with ubiquitous and scalable computing and storage services. However, still there are many less explored challenges for an optimal operation: one of them being the delivery of tailored network services. The underlying network connecting (cloud) data center or within a single site is still less malleable and programmable than the other parts of the infrastructure. New frameworks are emerging to define and create such dynamic network services; they effectively provide easy APIs to define services at the network level. These frameworks in essence support Network as a Service (NaaS) operations.

The emerging NaaS software systems require powerful and rich vocabularies, such as the ones that can be provided by Semantic Web ontologies. Those vocabularies should hide the network implementation details from the user. Thus NaaS users can fully express their needs in terms of services, without having to know the details of the physical network devices. OWL ontologies have several

© Springer International Publishing Switzerland 2015
F. Gandon et al. (Eds.): ESWC 2015, LNCS 9341, pp. 107–111, 2015.
DOI: 10.1007/978-3-319-25639-9_21

advantages as models for NaaS; i.e. they are easy to extend, they allow for automatic validation of both requests and provisioned services, and they enhance network resource discovery.

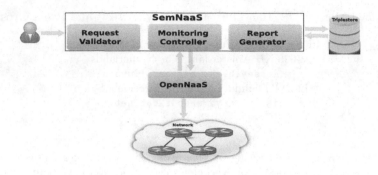

Fig. 1. The SemNaaS general system architecture.

2   SemNaaS Approach

SemNaaS[1] adds several potential improvements to OpenNaaS [2], namely (1) support of network request validation and network connectivity check; (2) system monitoring and failure condition detection; (3) capability of constructing distributed and interconnected OpenNaaS instances; (4) complex report generation.

2.1   Ontology

The ontology is at the core of the SemNaaS system, as it constitutes the main concepts required to create, define and link the various network nodes. We have reused and improved the Network Markup Language (NML) ontology [5]. NML constitutes the information model for describing and defining computer networks. In order to use NML in NaaS, we have devised more classes and properties, and enhanced the existing ones as well, in order to permit the creation of complex network topologies[2].

2.2   SemNaaS Architecture

The SemNaaS architecture is illustrated in Fig. 1. It consists basically of four components, which are (1) request validation and connectivity checking component; (2) OpenNaaS component, which is a pluggable component, that supports the network resources provisioning; (3) monitoring component; (4) report generation component.

---

[1] The source code is available at http://github.com/dana-i2cat/semnaas.
[2] The ontology is available at http://bitbucket.org/uva-sne/indl/src.

Request Generation and Validation. SemNaaS performs two levels of validation, namely request validation, and connectivity check. SemNaaS uses the Pellet reasoner [4] to validate the request against the NML ontology. In other words, it checks that the request adheres to the NML vocabulary, e.g. no component is declared as a port and as link at the same time, as those concepts are disjoint. The second level of validation, is the connectivity validation, in which SemNaaS utilizes SPARQL [1] to validate the request and detect if a network node is unreachable from another node. After a request is validated, it is passed to OpenNaaS for provisioning, and also its RDF data is stored in Virtuoso triplestore [3] for reporting.

Monitoring Component. Once the request is sent, OpenNaaS determines whether the requested resources can be granted immediately or the user should wait till those resources can be granted. During resource operation, it passes through several states, e.g. active or inactive. However, the resource may experience failure conditions as well, e.g. network connectivity failure. Whenever a change occurs in the resource status, SemNaaS tracks that change, thus it always reflects the most recent status of OpenNaaS resources.

Report Generation Component. SemNaaS empowers OpenNaaS to generate complex reports about the whole resource reservation process. Those reports enable the system administrator to identify the problematic resources of OpenNaaS, and monitor the resource failure conditions. Furthermore, a system administrator can view all network resources which have been reserved at a certain point of time and still active, in order to release them, and allow reallocation of them to other users.

Interconnection of Distributed NaaS Instances. One major challenge OpenNaaS has faced was how to maintain the uniqueness of the IDs assigned to the various network components. In other words, each network component, e.g. network node, has an ID that is only unique within the boundaries of the OpenNaaS instance in which it resides, e.g. host with ID "host1". Since we use the NML ontology to describe networks provisioned by OpenNaaS, we should assign a unique URI to each component. For example, http://ivi.fnwi.uva.nl/sne/resource/host1, and http://www.i2cat.net/resource/host1, are URIs for "host1" located in two remote NaaS instances.

3   Evaluation and Use Case

The best way to show how SemNaaS improves the functionality of network resource provisioning and path finding of OpenNaaS is to follow the system operations in two use cases: user request processing and implementation of Virtual Routing Function. This request passes several phases to get fulfilled: specifically (1) the user sends a request, formulated in NML, with the required details, e.g. source and destination nodes, as illustrated in Fig. 2(a); (2) SemNaaS receives the request, and validates it; (3) SemNaaS forwards the path finding request to

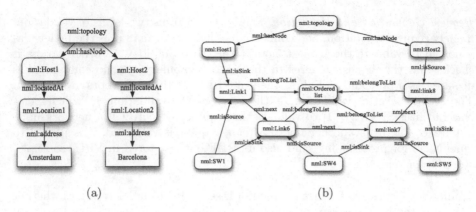

(a)   (b)

Fig. 2. An example request (a), and reply (b) in the virtual routing function use case.

OpenNaaS for fulfillment; (4) after OpenNaaS calculates the path between nodes, SemNaaS formulates the output response in NML as well.The Virtual Routing Function use case aims to implement inter-domain routing through OpenNaaS. The implementation of VRF is over an Openflow infrastructure. It extends the local routing of the Openflow controllers. VRF finds out a routing path according to the routing mode such as static, Dijkstra, and then invokes the controllers to dynamically create flow tables of the switches on the path. SemNaaS uses NML to describe resources in the request and reply of VRF. Figure 2(a) shows an example of a possible basic request in the VRF use case. The request contains a start host and a destination host, each one has different properties, e.g. IP address. Once the routing path is calculated and created, an understandable reply from OpenNaaS components is also important for user. As Fig. 2(b) shows the reply is described by NML as a routing path composed of a set of links and switches.

4   Conclusions

SemNaaS fuses Semantic Web with NaaS to develop an intelligent NaaS system, which improves NaaS systems with impressive features; e.g. connectivity checking.

References

1. SPARQL 1.1 Query Language. Technical report, W3C (2013)
2. Aznar, J.I., Jara, M., Rosello, A., Wilson, D., Figuerola, S.: OpenNaaS based management solution for inter-data centers connectivity. In: IEEE 5th International Conference on Cloud Computing Technology and Science, CloudCom, Bristol, United Kingdom (2013)
3. Erling, O., Mikhailov, I.: RDF Support in the virtuoso DBMS. In: Conference on social semantic web, vol. 113 of LNI, GI (2007)

4. Sirin, E., Parsia, B., Grau, B.C., Kalyanpur, A., Katz, Y.: Pellet: a practical OWL-DL reasoner. Web Semant. Sci. Serv. Agents World Wide Web **5**(2), 51–53 (2007)
5. van der Ham, J., Dijkstra, F., Łapacz, R., Zurawski, J.: The network markup language (NML) a standardized network topology abstraction for inter-domain and cross-layer network applications. In: Proceedings of the 13th Terena Networking Conference (2013)

LIDSEARCH: A SPARQL-Driven Framework for Searching Linked Data and Semantic Web Services

Mohamed Lamine Mouhoub[(✉)], Daniela Grigori, and Maude Manouvrier

PSL, Université Paris-Dauphine CNRS, LAMSADE UMR 7243, Paris Cedex 16, 75775 Colombes, France
{mohamed.mouhoub,daniela.grigori,maude.manouvrier}@dauphine.fr

Abstract. The Linked Open Data (LOD) cloud is a massive source of data in different domains. However, these data might be incomplete or outdated. Furthermore, there are still a lot of data that are not published as static linked data such as sensors data, on-demand data, and data with limited access patterns, that are in general available through web services. In order to use web services as complementary sources of data, we introduce LIDSEARCH (Linked Data and Services Search), a SPARQL-driven framework for searching linked data and relevant semantic web services with a single user query.

1 Introduction

The Linked Open Data cloud is a massive source of linked data in different domains. However, the data might be incomplete, missing or outdated in the LOD. Furthermore, there are still a lot of data that are not published as static linked data such as sensors data, on-demand data, and data with limited access patterns. Such data is in general available through web services. To overcome these issues and lacking potential, web services can be used as a complementary source of data [1].

Recently, a lot of research and standardization efforts (such as OWL-S[1], MSM[2] and iServe [2])has been carried to facilitate and automatize the discovery and composition of web services. These efforts involved the use of semantic web technologies, hence the emergence of Semantic Web Services [3].

Integrating LOD data with semantic web services (SWS) offer new perspectives for creating mashups, web and mobile applications, ETL operations, etc. However, users and developers must discover the relevant services first. This can only be done manually until now and requires a lot of prior knowledge and efforts from the users including: (a) an awareness of the existing public SWS repositories, (b) a knowledge of the different SWS description languages and (c) a knowledge of the service request vocabulary used by different repositories.

In this paper we present LIDSEARCH (Linked Data and Services Search), a prototype implementing the framework and approach introduced in [1].

---

[1] http://www.w3.org/Submission/OWL-S/.
[2] http://kmi.github.io/iserve/latest/data-model.html.

© Springer International Publishing Switzerland 2015
F. Gandon et al. (Eds.): ESWC 2015, LNCS 9341, pp. 112–117, 2015.
DOI: 10.1007/978-3-319-25639-9_22

2 Approach and Framework Overview

The goal of our framework is to search for both linked data and web services starting from a single query initially written by the user to search for data. Figure 1 shows an overview of our approach. When a SPARQL data query is submitted by a user through the Interface, two parallel search processes are launched:

1. Data search process: This process manages the execution of the data query in the distributed LOD sources which, for most, are accessible via SPARQL end-points. A SPARQL-federation approach along with the appropriate optimization and query rewriting techniques is used for this purpose. This process is delegated to FedX [4] and HiBISCuS [5] which are described further in the related works.
2. Service search process: This process aims to discover services that are relevant to the data query. The user's data query is rewritten to generate multiple service requests (for different service descriptions languages). These service requests are sent to service repositories on the LOD such as iServe. The rest of this section walks through this process with an example to give a brief overview of each step. The full details can be found in [1].

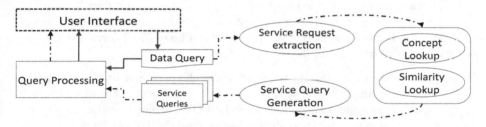

Fig. 1. An overview of the search processes of LIDSEARCH: [——] data search flow and [- - -] services search flow

Example Scenario. Let's consider the example data query in Listing 1.1. The user wants to know all the writers (dbpedia:Writer) born in Paris (dbpedia:Paris) and the books they authored. LIDSEARCH must provide data results from LOD as well as web services that provide or consume this data.

Service Request Extraction. The data query analysis aims to extract elements that can be used as inputs and outputs (I/O) for a service request. Service discovery is generally based on the matching of I/O types. The analysis relies on a set of rules that define the potential service request I/O that can be found in the data query. In general, Outputs are simply the selected variables of the query whereas Inputs are the bound values that appear in the triples of the query. In the example data query in Listing 1.1 ?person and ?book are identified as Outputs whilst :Paris is identified as an Input.

```
SELECT ?person ?book
WHERE {
?person rdf:type dbpedia-owl:Writer ;
dbpedia-owl:birthPlace dbpedia:Paris .
?book dbpedia-owl:author ?person ;
?book dbpedia-owl:isbn ?isbn .}
```

Listing 1.1. Example Data Query Q_D

```
SELECT  ?bookConcept FROM <http://dbpedia.org/ontology/> WHERE {
dbpedia-owl:author rdfs:domain
      ?bookConcept .
}
```

Listing 1.2. An example query of Concept Lookup in Ontology

Concept Lookup. The I/O elements from above need to have semantic concepts in order to be used in Service search. In general, concepts can either be declared by the user in the data query or can be found in an ontology or an RDF store in the LOD. The example query above contains already the concept of ?person declared in the triple `?person   rdf:type   dbpedia-owl:Writer`.

The concepts of `?book` and `dbpedia:Paris` are missing in the query. LID-SEARCH issues concept lookup queries for these elements and fetches the results from the LOD. The missing concept of an element can appear in an ontology as the `rdfs:domain` or `rdfs:range` of the predicates to used with it in the query triples. Listing 1.2 shows a concept lookup query that finds the concept of `?book`. The hosting ontologies of a property can be easily determined with an index/cache structure like in [5].

Similarity Lookup. To extend the service search space and find more results, we include the semantically similar concepts of every concept in the service search queries. Similar concepts can be found in the LOD ontologies either as super-/subclasses of the concepts or explicitly defined as similar concepts using the property `owl:equivalentClass`. They can also be inferred from the instances data based on the `owl:sameAs property`. The similarity lookup, like the concept lookup, is carried out using pure SPARQL generated queries and executed against the LOD sources.

Service Query Generation. Once all elements of the service request are gathered - i.e. I/O concepts and similar concepts, service discovery queries are generated in SPARQL using rewriting templates. Each Semantic Web Service description model, i.e. OWL-S, MSM, etc., has a dedicated template based on its ontology/model. These queries are sent to different Service Repositories that have SPARQL-endpoints such as iServe. In Fig. 2, a service query (in yellow) is generated for OWL-S and executed on two local service repositories.

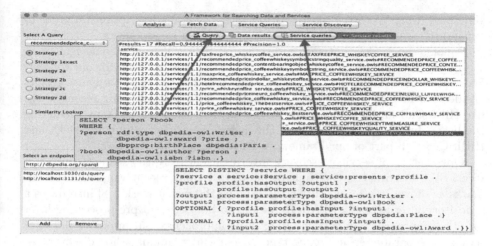

Fig. 2. A screenshot showing the results of a service discovery process

3   Implementation and Demonstration

We have implemented our framework in Java using Apache Jena[3] framework
to manage SPARQL queries and RDF. The demonstration materials can be
downloaded from the link bellow[4].

The framework GUI allows the user to write his query, add some SPARQL
endpoints of both data sources and service repositories, choose from a tight to a
loose service search strategy (see [1]) and activate/deactivate similarity lookup.

In Fig. 2, the user submits the data query in Listing 1.1 (green) through the
"Query Tab". The framework guides the user through the processes described in
Sect. 2. The query can be executed against the SPARQL-endpoints that the user
has selected and results will be displayed in the "Data Tab". On the other hand,
he can visualize the generated service queries in the "Service Queries Tab" and
adjust them to fit his needs if necessary then launch service discovery. Finally
the discovered services are returned to the user.

In Fig. 2 in the left panel, the user has selected Strategy#1. Therefore the
generated service query (in yellow) searches for services that should return the
data that the user is looking for as required by Strategy#1. The list in the
background shows the discovered services hosted in two local repositories.

4   Related Works

Our work is inspired by the work in [6] which aims to look for services that
are related to a given query based on keywords comparison between an SQL-
like query and a service ontology. This approach relies on semantic annotations

---

[3] https://jena.apache.org/.
[4] http://sites.google.com/site/lidsearch/.

generated using WordNet[5] on top of the classic service descriptions in order to expand the search area with the taxonomy provided by semantics.

Among the works that tackle distributed SPARQL query management in the LOD, SPARQL federation approaches are the most relevant for our context. FedX [4] is one of the most popular works that has good performance results besides the fact that the tool is available in open source. Some recent works like HiBISCuS [5] introduce some further optimization for FedX by predicting the best sources that might answer the query. We are actually using FedX and HiBISCuS as a part of our Framework for answering data queries.

Our context of service discovery involves exclusively the semantic web services. SWS discovery is the topic of interest of many recent works and benchmarks as shown in a recent survey [7]. Among the recent works, [8] introduces a repository filtering using SPARQL queries to be used as a pre-processing layer for other approaches. In contrast to existing approaches, our approach does not require a separate service request nor a particular language for discovery to search for services related to data. Instead, the service request is automatically derived from the user needs and adressed to service repositories such as iServe.

5   Conclusion and Perspectives

We present LIDSEARCH, a framework for searching data and relevant services in the LOD using a unique SPARQL query. This framework helps users to find services to build mashups, applications and integrate Linked and service data to create an added value. We plan to add more search capabilities and features to the framework such as Natural Language querying, cache-based optimization and automatic service composition (in case the framework doesn't find a relevant service that matches the user needs).

References

1. Mouhoub, M.L., Grigori, D., Manouvrier, M.: A framework for searching semantic data and services with SPARQL. In: Franch, X., Ghose, A.K., Lewis, G.A., Bhiri, S. (eds.) ICSOC 2014. LNCS, vol. 8831, pp. 123–138. Springer, Heidelberg (2014)
2. Pedrinaci, C., Liu, D., Maleshkova, M., Lambert, D., Kopecky, J., Domingue, J.: iserve: a linked services publishing platform. In: Ontology Repositories and Editors for the Semantic Web Workshop at the 7th Extended Semantic Web, Vol. 596, June 2010
3. Klusch, M.: Semantic web service description. In: CASCOM: Intelligent Service Coordination in the Semantic Web, pp. 31–57. Whitestein Series in Software Agent Technologies and Autonomic Computing. Birkhuser Basel (2008)
4. Schwarte, A., Haase, P., Hose, K., Schenkel, R., Schmidt, M.: FedX: optimization techniques for federated query processing on linked data. In: Aroyo, L., Welty, C., Alani, H., Taylor, J., Bernstein, A., Kagal, L., Noy, N., Blomqvist, E. (eds.) ISWC 2011, Part I. LNCS, vol. 7031, pp. 601–616. Springer, Heidelberg (2011)

---

[5] http://wordnet.princeton.edu/.

5. Saleem, M., Ngonga Ngomo, A.-C.: HiBISCuS: hypergraph-based source selection for SPARQL endpoint federation. In: Presutti, V., d'Amato, C., Gandon, F., d'Aquin, M., Staab, S., Tordai, A. (eds.) ESWC 2014. LNCS, vol. 8465, pp. 176–191. Springer, Heidelberg (2014)
6. Palmonari, M., Sala, A., Maurino, A., Guerra, F., Pasi, G., Frisoni, G.: Aggregated search of data and services. Information Systems **36**(2), 134–150 (2011). Special Issue: Semantic Integration of Data, Multimedia, and Services
7. Ngan, L.D., Kanagasabai, R.: Semantic web service discovery: state-of-the-art and research challenges. Pers. Ubiquit. Comput. **17**(8), 1741–1752 (2013)
8. García, J.M., Ruiz, D., Ruiz-Cortés, A.: Improving semantic web services discovery using sparql-based repository filtering. Web Semant. **17**, 12–24 (2012)

The Russian Museum Culture Cloud

Dmitry Mouromtsev[1]([✉]), Peter Haase[1,2], Eugene Cherny[1],
Dmitry Pavlov[1,3], Alexey Andreev[1], and Anna Spiridonova[1]

[1] ITMO University, St. Petersburg, Russia
mouromtsev@mail.ifmo.ru, eugene.cherny@niuitmo.ru,
aandreyev13@gmail.com, spiranna@list.ru
[2] Metaphacts GmbH, Walldorf, Germany
ph@metaphacts.com
[3] Vismart Ltd., St. Petersburg, Russia
dmitry.pavlov@vismart.biz

Abstract. We present an architecture and approach to publishing open linked data in the cultural heritage domain. We demonstrate our approach for building a system both for data publishing and consumption and show how user benefits can be achieved with semantic technologies. For domain knowledge representation the CIDOC-CRM ontology is used. As a main source of trusted data, we use the data of the web portal of the Russian Museum. For data enrichment we selected DBpedia and the published Linked Data of the British Museum. Our work can be reached at www.culturecloud.ru.

Keywords: Semantic web · Semantic data publishing · CIDOC-CRM · Open data · Cultural heritage

1 Introduction

This submitted demo is the result of the first steps in the direction of building the Russian Cultural Heritage Cloud, which is intended to make the heritage data available to anyone by means publishing the data as Linked Data as well as through implementation of end-user applications to work with the data [1]. Our long-term goal is to build the overall Russian Heritage Cloud that will integrate data from many data providers like museums, galleries, archives, libraries and other institutions and that will also have a powerful user interface equipped with a set of practical tools for data acquisition, modification and publishing. The pilot project was started in cooperation with the Russian Museum in St. Petersburg, which holds the largest collection of Russian art in the world. The primary goal of our research was to demonstrate the applicability and benefits of usage of semantic data to tackle the challenges of cultural heritage transfer in the digital era. The system is meant to deliver benefits to two different target groups: the museum art experts and museum visitors. These two groups greatly differ in their needs, but the system covers the interests of both of them.

© Springer International Publishing Switzerland 2015
F. Gandon et al. (Eds.): ESWC 2015, LNCS 9341, pp. 118–122, 2015.
DOI: 10.1007/978-3-319-25639-9_23

2   Overview of the System

The system has been built using the *metaphacts Knowledge Graph Workbench*, a platform for the development of semantic applications. The system architecture diagram is depicted in the Fig. 1.

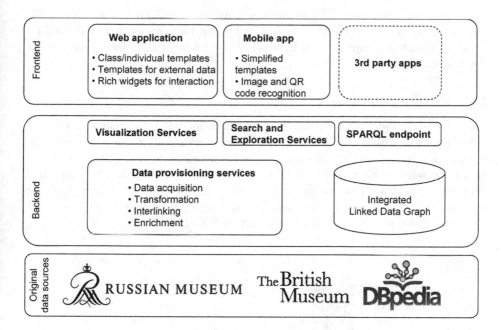

Fig. 1. Architecture of the system

Using the data provisioning services of the platform, the original data sources have been transformed, interlinked, enriched and finally ingested into a triple store (a Systap Blazegraph database), holding the integrated Linked Data graph. As described in detail in the subsequent section, Russian Museum relational data was transformed to RDF, represented using the CIDOC-CRM ontology. Where possible, links to DBpedia have been generated. The British Museum thesauri were used as genre and artwork type taxonomies. The resulting data in the triple store is published via a SPARQL endpoint, accessible at http://culturecloud.ru/sparql.

Using additional backend services of the platform, e.g. visualization, search and exploration services, two applications have been built: a web application and a mobile app, as described in detail in Sect. 3. The applications are accessible at http://culturecloud.ru/ On the frontend side we made use of the rich templating mechanism of the platform and created templates for the relevant CIDOC-CRM classes to visualize artworks and authors. Each template also includes data from linked DBpedia entities. The main purpose of the mobile application is to provide museum visitors with additional information about art objects. It has the ability to recognize the artwork by making photo of it or by scanning a QR code. Special simplified templates were developed for this use case.

3   Features of the End-User Applications

We created two end user applications for consuming the data: a website application and a mobile application. The website can be accessed from any mobile device or desktop computer web browser. The mobile application is created for the Android platform.

3.1   Website Application

The website provides a way to navigate through linked culture cloud data. The website is built using a wiki-based templating mechanism, where every concept of the underlying ontology is associated with a template that defines how the data is presented and which kind of interactions are possible. In the templates, rich widgets for the various data modalities are embedded, including widgets for exploring image collections, timelines for temporal data, maps for geo-spatial data, etc. Some screenshots of widgets can be found on Fig. 2.

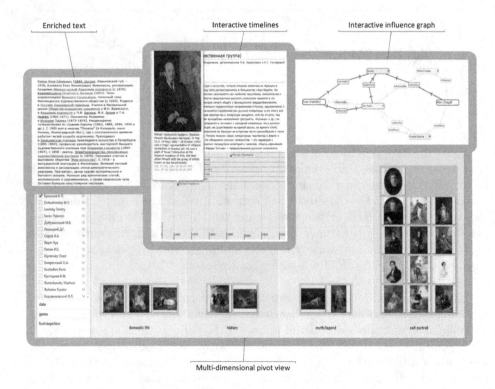

Fig. 2. Screenshots of the web application

The website also presents data in a number of traditional ways: text descriptions and illustrations of art works, hyperlinks connecting the web pages between each other, etc. At the same time the systems allows integration of more effective tools for data presentation, which provide a brighter use experience and prove to be more fruitful in a process of data exploration. Some of the widgets include:

Enriched text. Enriched text is a paragraph where some toponyms, personas and dates are linked against the semantic descriptions from external sources, in our case, these are: DBpedia and the British Museum. When the user clicks the link the article opens on same site. This delivers the additional context directly to the user and keeps him on site, while traditionally he would be forced to leave the original resource.

Interactive timelines. A Timeline widget enables additional visual demonstration of how long the process took place or in what sequence the events were occurring. For instance, our system employs timelines, when it demonstrates the artists lifetimes in relation to the art movement, to which the artists belong. The other use case for timelines is to place the art objects on artists life span to display his periods of activity and inactivity. This provides a means to learn and discover the facts interactively rather than reading long paragraphs of traditional text.

Interactive influence graph. The graph illustrates the influences of one artist on another. From this graph many intriguing conclusions could be made: who was the most influential artist in his time, who stands aside in the cultural art process, etc. The end-user can use such graph for finding other artists that can be of an interest to him based on the artists that he already knows. The art experts can construct more complicated graphs displaying connections between artists, art movements, countries, art school, etc.

Multi-dimensional Pivot widget. The Pivot widget enables to visual exploration of data by sorting and filtering it in multiple dimensions. For instance, one can select the artists of 1890 s that worked in the genres of portrait and sort their artworks by artists names. This is another exciting and interactive way to learn the content and make fascinating discoveries along the way. Such tool can simplify the routine work of an art expert when he is selecting the artworks for catalogues or when constructing the new exhibition.

Semantic search. A search widget allows to construct visually the structured, semantic queries against the fundamental relationships of the CIDOC-CRM ontology. The search widget provides auto-suggestions for search terms utilizing an entity index along with a suggestion of relationships that are applicable to a selected entity.

3.2   Mobile Application

The mobile applications is intended to make the visit to the museum more informative. It is done by enabling automatic identification of art work by taking snapshot with a mobile device. A typical scenario that will be demonstrated is the following:

- The user walks through the exposition in the museum. When the user feels compelled, he takes a snapshot of the artwork that the user wants to know more about.
- The artwork is automatically recognized and identified by the mobile application.
- The user can see the annotation and other details about this artwork on the screen of his mobile device.
- The user can also see the other works of the artist and where they are stored.
- The user can rank the selected artwork according to his likes or dislikes (5-star rating).
- The users ranks are stored and associated with his public social network profile.

The feedback that we acquired from museum proves that the mobile application lies in line with their task to achieve long tail effect and provide ways of interaction with expositions.The Russian museum currently uses QR-code tags positioned beneath the art-object to allow identification of artifacts by the museums mobile app, but all museum stakeholders agree that identification by photo is preferable because it eliminates the need to tag the artifacts and QR-codes look too gaudy in antique palace interiors.

4   Conclusions

The feedback acquired from two major museum in Russia – Russian Museum and Kunstkamera (Peter the Great Museum of Anthropology and Ethnology) – revealed a high demand for the flexible and extensible representation models for building applications that allow to get access to digital cultural heritage. Our system illustrates potentials of semantic technologies for creation of such solutions including semantic search and visualizations both for art experts and regular museum visitors. One of the features we achieved is to make data deliverable to end user in a more informative way in comparison with any data source provisioning our system. For example, the initial Russian Museum dataset does not contain much information about authors. Interlinking with external source allowed us to show user additional information about authors, such as date of birth or person they influenced and so on.

Reference

1. Mouromtsev, D., Haase, P., Cherny, E., Pavlov, D., Andreev, A., Spiridonova, A.: Towards the linked russian culture cloud: Data enrichment and publishing. In: Accepted at ESWC 2015 (2015) (to appear)

DataOps: Seamless End-to-End Anything-to-RDF Data Integration

Christoph Pinkel[(✉)], Andreas Schwarte, Johannes Trame,
Andriy Nikolov, Ana Sasa Bastinos, and Tobias Zeuch

Fluid Operations AG, Walldorf, Germany
{christoph.pinkel,andreas.schwarte,johannes.trame,
andriy.nikolov,ana.sasa,tobias.zeuch}@fluidops.com

Abstract. While individual components for semantic data integration are commonly available, end-to-end solutions are rare.

We demonstrate DataOps, a seamless Anything-to-RDF semantic data integration toolkit. DataOps supports the integration of both semantic and non-semantic data from an extensible host of different formats. Setting up data sources end-to-end works in three steps: (1) accessing the data from arbitrary locations in different formats, (2) specifying mappings depending on the data format (e.g., R2RML for relational data), and (3) consolidating new data with existing data instances (e.g., by establishing owl:sameAs links). All steps are supported through a fully integrated Web interface with configuration forms and different mapping editors. Visitors of the demo will be able to perform all three steps of the integration process.

1 Introduction

In recent years semantic data integration has evolved to an important application area in the industry: software eco systems in companies become more and more complex, produce large amounts of heterogenous information, and make it harder and harder to get a holistic view on the company's knowledge.

Traditionally, in such situations dedicated ETL-style systems are used for the analysis. Functionality is provided by large scale data warehouse systems or, more recently, by big data frameworks such as Hadoop YARN [1] that work as a *data operating systems* running a mix of data warehousing and other applications. Those systems share an important property for enterprise data analysis: available as ready solutions, they include everything - from assisted setup, a broad selection of access methods, over graphical configuration interfaces to a comprehensive documentation and support.

However, they come along with a downside: in classical data warehouses a dedicated, global warehousing schema must be designed, mappings must be constructed, and the resulting schema must be documented and communicated to users. For Hadoop-like systems, this is not necessarily the case, as a mix of relational and non-relational workloads are possible with different applications in the system. This comes at the price of either a very small set of supported

© Springer International Publishing Switzerland 2015
F. Gandon et al. (Eds.): ESWC 2015, LNCS 9341, pp. 123–127, 2015.
DOI: 10.1007/978-3-319-25692-9_24

queries and little flexibility, or involves even more initial effort for programming all the tasks and queries to be supported. Worse, with a number of data sources that quickly change in structure, maintenance of the resulting schema, mapping and queries can quickly become a nightmare in either case.

Often enough, the effort for setup and maintenance becomes unacceptable, especially if some data sources are complex in structure. This contributes to the current situation where enterprises are assumed to analyze less than one sixth of their potentially relevant data.[1] Semantic data integration, with its flexible graph model and vocabularies, is one possible and natural way to address this predicament.

To leverage the potential of semantic data integration in such cases, an integration environment needs to be fully functional and sufficiently usable, much the same as enterprise data warehousing solutions. While individual components for semantic data integration are commonly available, end-to-end solutions that fulfill all requirements are rare. Existing frameworks such as the Linked Data Integration Framework [3] focus on web-scale data rather than enterprise data. Similarly, many systems composed of loosely coupled special-purpose components (where setup or maintenance involve intense human effort) fail the one key requirement that motivates their use in the first place: to significantly reduce overall effort in configuration and maintenance.

With DataOps, we target the challenge of delivering an end-to-end solution for semantic ETL data integration that supports seamless setup and configuration as well as convenient maintenance procedures. DataOps delivers all primarily relevant components as a toolkit out of the box, fills any gaps between them and offers an integrated user interface, built on industry-proven platform technology.

We describe details about the DataOps demonstration in Sect. 2 before we discuss selected related systems in Sect. 3. Finally, we conclude with the contributions of our demo (Sect. 4).

2 DataOps Demo

We demonstrate DataOps, a seamless Anything-to-RDF semantic data integration toolkit. DataOps supports the integration of both semantic and non-semantic data from a host of different formats, including relational databases, CSV, Excel, XML, JSON, existing RDF graphs and others. Additional source formats can be integrated through an extension mechanism. We demonstrate this with a specialized data source that allows to directly access results from the statistical software R. In addition, each data source can be accessed from different locations within an organization, e.g., as local files, from network shares (which may optionally require authentication), from the Web through HTTP, or even through custom protocols.

---

[1] According to a recent study of business analysts [2], surveying several hundreds of enterprises.

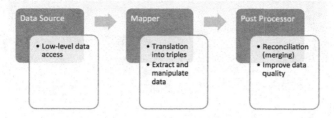

Fig. 1. DataOps process

As an integrated toolkit, DataOps supports all setup, configuration and maintenance steps through a fully integrated Web interface with configuration forms and different mapping editors. Setting up data sources end-to-end is implemented in a three-step process (Fig. 1):

1. Accessing the different data sources from arbitrary locations through different mechanisms (Fig. 2a).
2. Specifying mappings depending on the data source format (Fig. 2b).
3. Consolidating new data with existing data instances, e.g., by establishing owl:sameAs links (Fig. 2c).

For some of its features, DataOps makes use of established external components that are integrated in the backend. In particular, ETL extraction of relational databases currently relies on DB2Triples[2] and entity reconciliation uses Silk [4]. All modules are plug-able due to generic interfaces and standards. Post-processor modules can even be stacked as pipelines of sub components. For example, other standard R2RML mapping engines can be hooked in, if required. The interface used for editing relational-to-ontology mappings is a newer version of the prototype presented in [5].

DataOps builds on the technology of a semantic platform, Information Workbench [6]. Information Workbench is a platform for Linked Data application development, including flexible and extensible interfaces for semantic integration, visualization and collaboration. It provides features such as managed triple store connectivity, SPARQL federation [7], ontology management, or exploration and visualization of resulting data. More specific features for data integration and business analytics use cases can be installed as Apps (e.g., more advanced visualization components, or automatic mapping support [8]).

DataOps is available both under a commercial license and under Open Source terms, as part of the Information Workbench.[3]

Visitors of the demo will be able to perform all three steps of the integration process. In addition, visitors will be able to view and explore integrated data with widget provided by the platform.

---

[2] https://github.com/antidot/db2triples/.
[3] http://www.fluidops.com/en/company/training/open_source.

(a) Step 1: Configuration of Data Sources   (b) Step 2: Example of a Mapping Editor (R2RML)

(c) Step 3: Reconcilation Rules

Fig. 2. Setup/Configuration steps demonstrated

3   Related Work

Individual connector, extractor, translation and editor components that can be hooked together for disparate ETL style tasks are commonly available, including some of those used in DataOps (e.g., [4–6]). For end-to-end solutions, however, they are often hard to configure and to use, especially when disparate data sources (e.g., relational databases, XML, Excel, and RDF) each require different components in the setup.

There are recent approaches to target this heterogeneity challenge in semantic data integration, such as RML [9], a unified mapping language to translate different source formats into RDF. However, those (and similar) approaches are still isolated components when it comes to providing users with an end-to-end toolkit.

A few end-to-end semantic data integration platforms exist so far. However, they usually do not focus on the needs of enterprise data integration but rather on other use cases (e.g., on RDF data sources or on Web scale data rather than enterprise data). For instance, UnifiedViews [10] provides easy to use interfaces, however, focuses on processing of pre-existing RDF data. LDIF [3] provides an interface for some of the surrounding tasks but also has a focus on RDF data, even though relational data is also supported.

Some recent projects (e.g., the Optique platform [11]) aim at providing an integrated platform for large-scale enterprise data integration but at the same time focus to push on other limitations such as federated, virtualized scale-out or even streaming data.

4   Conclusion

We presented DataOps, a seamless Anything-to-RDF semantic data integration toolkit. In contrast to most existing frameworks, DataOps assumes data sources in any number of mostly non-semantic source data formats, available from different locations within one organization. DataOps also integrates all procedural and lifecycle aspects of setting up and providing integrated data in a single platform, offering a seamless user experience. It is thus novel as a targeted solution for semantic enterprise data integration with a focus on many different, heterogeneous data formats and ease of use.

In the demo, users can try all aspects of DataOps for themselves using both locally provided data and data accessible from the Web.

References

1. Vavilapalli, V.K., et al.: Apache Hadoop YARN: yet another resource negotiator. In: SOCC 2013 (2013)
2. Evelson, B., Kisker, H., Bennett, M., Christakis, S.: Benchmark your BI environment. Technical report, Forrester Research, Inc., October 2013
3. Schultz, A., Matteini, A., Isele, R., Bizer, C., Becker, C.: LDIF - linked data integration framework. In: COLD 2011 (2011)
4. Volz, J., Bizer, C., Gaedke, M., Kobilarov, G.: Discovering and maintaining links on the web of data. In: Bernstein, A., Karger, D.R., Heath, T., Feigenbaum, L., Maynard, D., Motta, E., Thirunarayan, K. (eds.) ISWC 2009. LNCS, vol. 5823, pp. 650–665. Springer, Heidelberg (2009)
5. Pinkel, C., Binnig, C., Haase, P., Martin, C., Sengupta, K., Trame, J.: How to best find a partner? An evaluation of editing approaches to construct R2RML mappings. In: Presutti, V., d'Amato, C., Gandon, F., d'Aquin, M., Staab, S., Tordai, A. (eds.) ESWC 2014. LNCS, vol. 8465, pp. 675–690. Springer, Heidelberg (2014)
6. Haase, P., Schmidt, M., Schwarte, A.: The information workbench as a self-service platform for linked data applications. In: COLD (2011)
7. Schwarte, A., Haase, P., Hose, K., Schenkel, R., Schmidt, M.: FedX: optimization techniques for federated query processing on linked data. In: Aroyo, L., Welty, C., Alani, H., Taylor, J., Bernstein, A., Kagal, L., Noy, N., Blomqvist, E. (eds.) ISWC 2011, Part I. LNCS, vol. 7031, pp. 601–616. Springer, Heidelberg (2011)
8. Pinkel, C., Binnig, C., Kharlamov, E., Haase, P.: IncMap: pay-as-you-go matching of relational schemata to OWL ontologies. In: OM (2013)
9. Dimou, A., Sande, M.V., Colpaert, P., Verborgh, R., Mannens, E., Walle, R.V.D.: RML: a generic language for integrated RDF mappings of heterogeneous data. In: LDOW (2014)
10. Knap, T., Kukhar, M., Macháč, B., Škoda, P., Tomeš, J., Vojt, J.: UnifiedViews: an ETL framework for sustainable RDF data processing. In: ESWC (Posters & Demos) (2014)
11. Kharlamov, E. et al.: Optique 1.0: semantic access to big data - the case of Norwegian petroleum directorate factpages. In: ISWC (Posters & Demos) (2013)

ABSTAT: Linked Data Summaries
with ABstraction and STATistics

Matteo Palmonari[1(✉)], Anisa Rula[1], Riccardo Porrini[1], Andrea Maurino[1],
Blerina Spahiu[1], and Vincenzo Ferme[2]

[1] University of Milano-Bicocca, Milan, Italy
{palmonari,rula,porrini,maurino,spahiu}@disco.unimib.it
[2] University of Lugano (USI), Lugano, Switzerland
vincenzo.ferme@usi.ch

Abstract. While much work has focused on continuously publishing
Linked Open Data, little work considers how to help consumers to better understand existing datasets. ABSTAT framework aims at providing
a better understanding of big and complex datasets by extracting summaries of linked data sets based on an ontology-driven data abstraction
model. Our ABSTAT framework takes as input a data set and an ontology and returns an ontology-driven data summary as output. The summary is exported into RDF and then made accessible through a SPARQL
endpoint and a web interface to support the navigation.

1 Introduction

As of April 2014 up to 1014 data sets have been published in the Linked Open
Data (LOD) cloud, a number that is constantly increasing[1]. However, for a user
interested in using available LOD, it is not easy to understand to what extent
a data set covers a domain of interest, how the knowledge is structured in the
data set, for example, to compare two data sets based on their content. To
this end, a data consumer should be able to answer to questions such as: what
types of resources are described in the data set? What properties are used to
describe the resources? What types of resources are linked and by means of what
properties? How many resources have a certain type and how frequent is the use
of a given property? Remarkably, difficulties in answering these questions have
several consequences for data consumption.

Linked data sets make use of ontologies to describe the semantics of their
data. However, answering the above questions by only looking at ontolologies is
not easy since ontologies may be large. For example, DBpedia uses a vocabulary consisting of 705 (local) concepts and 2,794 properties. Ontologies may be
underspecified to model a large amount of diverse data in a flexible way. For
example, either the domain or the range is unspecified for 585 properties of the
DBpedia Ontology. In addition, in relatively expressive ontologies like the Music
Ontology, some connections between types may be specified by means of OWL

---

[1] http://linkeddatacatalog.dws.informatik.uni-mannheim.de/state/.

© Springer International Publishing Switzerland 2015
F. Gandon et al. (Eds.): ESWC 2015, LNCS 9341, pp. 128–132, 2015.
DOI: 10.1007/978-3-319-25639-9_25

axioms, e.g., qualified range restrictions, which may be difficult to understand for many data practitioners. Finally, the ontology does not tell how frequently certain modelling patterns occur in the data set. Answers to the above questions can be collected with explorative queries, but at the price of a significant server overload and high response times.

In this paper we describe ABSTAT, a linked data summarization framework based on an ontology-based ABstraction model and on the computation of STATistics. ABSTAT extracts summaries that are represented in RDF and can be queried or navigated through a web interface, which demonstrates the contribution of our framework to answer questions like the ones listed at the beginning of this section. Although a summary contains several elements, as explained in the next section, the key feature of our approach is the extraction of Abstract Knowledge Patterns (AKPs) from the data with the help of the data ontology (we consider OWL and RDFS ontologies).

In our approach, a *type* is an ontology concept or a datatype. Observe that, differently from a literal, an ontology instance may have several types specified in the data, and most of them can be related by a subconcept relation. AKPs are triples having the form $<subjectType, pred, objectType>$, which represent the occurrence of triples $<sub, pred, obj>$ in the data, such that *subjectType* is a minimal type of *sub* and *objectType* is a minimal type of *obj*. By considering minimal types of resources, computed with the help of the data ontology, we exclude several redundant AKPs from the summary.

Our summarization framework introduces several novel contributions to mitigate the data set understanding problem. The AKPs that are extracted and represented with ABSTAT provide a richer characterisation of a data set, if compared to popular approaches based on metadata (e.g., using the DCAT vocabulary). Other approaches like Linked Open Vocabularies[2] and LODStats provide several statistics about the usage of vocabularies, types and properties [1] but they do not represent the connections between types. SchemeEx extracts interesting information for large data sets, by considering the co-occurrence of types and properties [3], but does not extract connections between types and does not represent the extracted information as a summary in RDF. Knowledge patterns have been extracted from RDF data in a previous work [4], but in the context of domain specific experiments and not with the purpose of defining a general linked data summarisation framework. ABSTAT's model can be applied to any data set that use a reference ontology and focuses on the representation of the summary. Another approach focuses on ranking patterns in the ontology (e.g., a subclass relation, or a property range restriction) based on their salience so as to present to the user a subset of significant axioms of the ontology [5], while we aim to provide an abstract but complete view of the data set. Another approach adopts bisimulation and contraction to find common patterns in data [2]. Their summaries are very different from the ones obtained with our abstraction model.

---

[2] http://lov.okfn.org/.

2 The ABSTAT Framework

Our ABSTAT framework takes as input a data set and an ontology (used by the data set) and returns an ontology-driven data summary. The summary is exported in RDF to support query and navigation.

A Linked Data Summary of a data set Δ that uses an ontology V consists of five components: (1) a Concept Graph, (2) a set of Abstract Knowledge Patterns (AKPs), (3) a set of Co-occurrence Patterns (CP), (4) a set of *Types* (concepts and datatypes) and *Properties*, and (5) a set *Stat* of functions that describe the occurrence of the other components in the data. AKPs are defined as in Sect. 1. CPs represent the co-occurrence of predicates and types and have the structure *<SubjectType,Property>* and *<Property,ObjectType>*. We explain the Concept Graph, the methods to extract the components, and their meaning here below.

Concept Graph. The Concept Graph represents the subconcept relation between concept types. It is extracted from V by traversing its subclass relation and considers also the ontologies directly imported by V (e.g., the Music Ontology, used in LinkedBrainz, imports other 7 ontologies). Every ontology concept that has no explicit superconcept is considered subconcept of `owl:Thing`.

AKPs and CPs. The dataset is partitioned in two sets of triples: one partition contains all the *typing statements*, i.e., all the triples where the predicate is `rdf:type`; the other partition contains *relation statements*, i.e., every other triple. We process all the typing statements to collect, for every instance x that occurs in some typing statement, its set of *minimal* types. This is done by traversing the subtype relation in the Concept Graph. An instance x may have one or more minimal types such that none of the minimal type is subtype of one another; although only one *minimum* type is often found. Then we scan every relation statement of the dataset (only once). For each triple *<sub,pred,obj>* we extract all the minimal types of *sub* and *obj*, denoted respectively by μ^{sub} and μ^{obj}, as follows. If x is a resource (in the subject or object position) we set μ^x as the set of minimal types found after scanning the typing statements; if x is untyped and no typing information was found, we define $\mu^x = \{$`owl:Thing`$\}$. If x is a typed literal, the minimal (and minimum) type is defined by its datatype. If x is an untyped literal, its minimal type is `rdfs:Literal`. An AKP $< t^{sub}, pred, t^{obj} >$ occurs in a triple *<sub,pred,obj>* iff $t^{sub} \in \mu^{sub}$ and $t^{obj} \in \mu^{obj}$. If an AKP occurring in a triple is present in the summary already, then we update the occurrence of the AKP. Else we add the AKP to the summary. When we scan a triple, we apply the above described method to extract CPs or update their occurrence.

Types and Properties. The set of Types and Properties of a dataset is defined by considering all the types, ontology concepts and datatypes, which occur in some AKP or in the ontology. Their occurrence stats are defined using the minimal type semantics used for AKPs.

To represent summaries in RDF we designed the *ld-summaries* ontology in OWL. We model AKPs and CPs through reified statements. Properties and types are represented with the lds:Property, skos:Concept and lds:Datatype concepts, respectively. The concept graph is represented by using the skos:broader property that connects the types. We represent URIs of properties and types by using the summary base (i.e., their local id in the summary) and link them to their global id from the source ontology with the rdfs:seeAlso property. This representation enables the linking between properties and types from both an intra-summary and inter-summary perspective. The data property lds:occurrence associates the occurrence statistic to AKPs, CPs, properties and types.

The extraction of the concept graph is implemented in JAVA and uses Jena to manipulate the ontologies. The rest of the summarisation framework is implemented in AWK[3], a scripting language specific for text processing and efficient when a large amount of triples have to be processed.

3 Demonstration

We now describe a practical use case of the ABSTAT framework. We showcase the benefits of using the ABSTAT framework for dataset understanding by means of a Web application (http://abstat.disco.unimib.it:8880), which supports the interactive visualization of the summaries. We store the summaries in a Virtuoso triple store instance so as to support querying and navigation.

Mike is a young entrepreneur who wants to create *MyMusicNow*, a new mobile app with music data. He wants to exploit one data set from the LOD cloud to semantically link news coming from twitter accounts of music artists. To realize his app Mike finds two datasets: DBpedia[4] and LinkedBrainz[5]. Mike does not know the semantic structure of the two datasets and their coverage in terms of instances. Hence, Mike uses ABSTAT to analyze the data sets and find answers to the following queries: (1) How are music artists/groups/songs described? (2) How many instances are covered? (3) Is there any incongruence in the data?

Figure 1 shows two screenshots of the main page of ABSTAT. After selecting the LinkedBrainz dataset, Mike visualizes the AKPs and their occurrences. He can either navigate the summary or filter out the AKPs by subject and/or object types, and/or by property and look at their occurrences. In the filter area, a self filling feature supports him in identifying the types of interests (e.g., mo:SoloMusicArtist, mo:MusicArtist, dbo:MusicalArtist or dbo:Band).

Mike easily finds that LinkedBrainz contains 237,464 mo:MusicArtist, while DBpedia contains 105,420 dbo:MusicalArtist, i.e., 60 % less than LinkedBrainz. On the other hand, musical artists are described in DBpedia with a richer and more diverse set of properties than in LinkedBrainz, as shown in Fig. 1. Mike also discovers potential errors in the two datasets. There is only one occurrence of the AKP <mo:MusicArtist,mo:member_of,mo:MusicArtist> in LinkedBrainz, which may depend on a mistyped instance. Several counterintuitive AKPs, such

---

[3] http://awk.info/.

[4] http://dbpedia.org.

[5] http://linkedbrainz.org/.

Fig. 1. The ABSTAT web interface.

as <dbo:Band,dbo:genre,dbo:Band> and <dbo:Band,dbo:instrument,dbo:Band>, which may reveal incorrect data, occur quite frequently also in DBpedia.

In order to gain a comparable level of understanding of the two datasets without the help of ABSTAT, Mike should have (1) manually inspected the two ontologies and understood their schemas, and (2) written many SPARQL queries to get the statistics about their number of instances. Getting answers for these queries may require a lot of time and even lead to timeouts in server responses. Finally, Mike could have hardly spotted the incongruences higlighted by ABSTAT, with the risk of developing unreliable services for his app.

Acknowledgements. This research has been supported in part by FP7/2013-2015 COMSODE (under contract number FP7-ICT-611358).

References

1. Auer, S., Demter, J., Martin, M., Lehmann, J.: LODStats – an extensible framework for high-performance dataset analytics. In: ten Teije, A., Völker, J., Handschuh, S., Stuckenschmidt, H., d'Acquin, M., Nikolov, A., Aussenac-Gilles, N., Hernandez, N. (eds.) EKAW 2012. LNCS, vol. 7603, pp. 353–362. Springer, Heidelberg (2012)
2. Khatchadourian, S., Consens, M.P.: ExpLOD: summary-based exploration of interlinking and RDF usage in the linked open data cloud. In: Aroyo, L., Antoniou, G., Hyvönen, E., ten Teije, A., Stuckenschmidt, H., Cabral, L., Tudorache, T. (eds.) ESWC 2010, Part II. LNCS, vol. 6089, pp. 272–287. Springer, Heidelberg (2010)
3. Konrath, M., Gottron, T., Staab, S., Scherp, A.: SchemEX - efficient construction of a data catalogue by stream-based indexing of linked data. J. Web Sem. **16**, 52–58 (2012)
4. Presutti, V., Aroyo, L., Adamou, A., Schopman, B.A.C., Gangemi, A., Schreiber, G.: Extracting core knowledge from linked data. In: COLD (2011)
5. Zhang, X., Cheng, G., Qu, Y.: Ontology summarization based on RDF sentence graph. In: WWW, pp. 707–716 (2007)

DaCENA: Serendipitous News Reading
with Data Contexts

Matteo Palmonari[1]($\boxtimes$), Giorgio Uboldi[2], Marco Cremaschi[1],
Daniele Ciminieri[2], and Federico Bianchi[1]

[1] Università degli Studi di Milano-Bicocca, Milano, Italy
{palmonari,cremaschi,f.bianchi}@disco.unimib.it
[2] Politecnico di Milano, Milano, Italy
{giorgio.uboldi,daniele.ciminieri}@gmail.com

Abstract. DaCENA (Data Context for News Articles) is a web application that showcases a new approach to reading online news articles with the support of a data context built from interlinked facts available on the Web of Data. Given a source article, a set of facts that are estimated to be more interesting for the readers are extracted from the Web and presented using tailored information visualization methods and an interactive user interface. By looking at this background factual knowledge, the reader is supported in the interpretation of the news content and is suggested connections to related topics that he/she can further explore.

1 Introduction

In this paper we present DaCENA (Data Context for News Articles), a web application that let a user read a news article while contextually exploring additional content extracted from a semantic Knowledge Base (KB). Like in other annotated corpora, a set of named entities of a KB is extracted from text using an entity linking tool. The key feature of DaCENA is the approach to model, organize, visualize and interact with the additional content presented to the reader: at the side of an article, we present several *semantic associations* [1], i.e., paths of connected facts extracted from a linked data source. The associations connect a main entity representing the article's topic with many other named entities found in the text. The set of extracted associations defines the *Data Context of the article*. For example, an article entitled "A Threat to Spanish Democracy" published in the New York Times on 7th, November 2014, discusses the threat of Catalan nationalism for Spanish democracy. *Catalonia* is deemed to be the main entity of the article, while other thirteen entities are found, including *Catalan nationalism*. The Data Context consists of 278 associations, among which we find that *Catalonia is birth place of Artur Mas I Gavarro, who is the president of Convergence and Union* (a party), *which has Catalan nationalism as ideology*.

The Data Context can be very large, e.g., up to dozens of thousands associations, and contain many uninteresting associations, e.g., *Barack Obama is born in America*. To rank and filter out the associations based on their expected

F. Gandon et al. (Eds.): ESWC 2015, LNCS 9341, pp. 133–137, 2015.
DOI: 10.1007/978-3-319-25639-9_26

interest for the reader, we evaluate every association using a novel *serendipity* measure. This measure considers the relevance of the association in relation to the news article and the unexpectedness of the association in the KB. The balance between relevance and serendipity can be determined by the user at run-time according to his/her preferences. A set of top-k serendipitous associations is presented to the reader, while more associations can be visualized on demand. DaCENA can be tested online on several articles extracted from the New York Times at the address http://dacena.densitydesign.org/.

DaCENA is targeted to two different kinds of users: readers who are interested in data-supported stories, in the vein of data journalism [3], and journalists in the newsroom. A reader can leverage the explored data to better understand the context of the story told in the article. For example, from the above mentioned association between *Catalonia* and *Catalan nationalism*, the reader discovers the name of a prominent politician (currently leading the Catalonia government) and of his party, which were not mentioned in the article. In addition he/she learns that such a party supports a nationalist vision. A journalist may use DaCENA to have inspiration for a new story. For example, in other associations found by DaCENA, e.g. the ones between *Catalonia* and *Autonomous countries of Spain*, he/she can find out about other autonomous communities. These findings may inspire a new story about the political landscape behind nationalist ideologies in Spain and a comparative analysis of different political movements in favour of autonomy. Ultimately, DaCENA aims to be a first steps towards data journalism based on the analysis of relational data.

The novelties introduced in DaCENA can be summarised as follows. (1) Data journalism initiatives has focused primarily on statistical data analysis and visualization [3]. Semantic technologies have been applied in the news domain mainly to connect articles based on the co-occurrences of named entities [7], or to extract relations among entities from large news corpora (e.g., in the News-Reader project[1]). We present a new application domain for semantic technologies, which could be defined as *relational data-journalism* because of its focus on relational data. (2) We introduce a measure to evaluate the serendipity of semantic associations in relation to an input text. (3) We introduce a novel interactive visualization interface, which combines text reading and data exploration.

2   DaCENA

The DaCENA framework consists of two main components. Text & Data Analyzer is a component responsible for processing and storing the information used to build the data context of an article. Contextual Explorer is an interactive user interface that let the user read the articles enriched with data contexts. The components exchange data in the JSON format via HTTP APIs. Processing the articles may require significant amount of time (up to thirty minutes) if

---

[1] http://www.newsreader-project.eu/.

semantic data are fetched by querying a SPARQL endpoint as we currently do[2]. Therefore, texts and data are processed off-line so as to make the interactive visualization features as much fluid as possible. The two components and the main features of DaCENA are explained here below.

Text and Data Analyzer. The data context extraction process is applied to any article scraped from a news source and consists of the following steps.

Entity linking and main topic extraction. The whole text of an article is passed to the DBpedia Spotlight service, which recognizes named entities in the text and links them to DBpedia. The confidence used by Spotlight to tune the precision vs recall of the algorithm is dynamically set based on the number of retrieved entities. When too many or too few entities are found, we dynamically adjust the confidence threshold (we use confidence values in the range $[0.20, 0.35]$). One of the entities recognized in the text, the one that is mentioned more frequently, is selected as main topic of the article.

Data Context Extraction. Given the main topic m, i.e., the main entity, we find every possible semantic associations between m and every other extracted entity e, which have a length equal or shorter than a given threshold (set to 3 in the current demo). A semantic association between two entities is defined as a semipath connecting the two entities, such that every other node in the path is also an entity. By considering only links between entities (we do not consider concepts or literals) we focus on sequences of relational facts. We traverse the graph in any possible directions when we search for the associations because the incoming links of an entity may represent unexpected connections, which are deemed valuable for the readers (e.g., *Catalonia is the birth place of Artur Mas I Gavarro*, in the example discussed in Sect. 1). The Data Context Graph of an article is the set of all the associations extracted from it. The Data Context Graph is retrieved by constructing and submitting a set of queries to the DBpedia SPARQL endpoint. Every extracted association is indexed and stored in a relational database to speed-up data fetching at runtime.

Data Context Evaluation. We evaluate each association of the Data Context Graph with measures that return values in the range $[0, 1]$, to ease their composition. The objective of DaCENA is to present serendipitous associations to readers. By referring to a previous definition [9], we can define serendipity as unexpected relevance of a finding. We propose to capture this definition by modeling *serendipity* as a linear combination of two measures: *relevance*, which estimates the degree of match between the topics covered by the article and the semantic associations, and *unexpectedness*, which estimates the level of surprise that associations can generate in the reader. We define a parametric serendipity measure applied to an article a and an association π as $s(\pi, a) = \alpha * r(\pi, a) + (1-\alpha) * u(\pi)$, where $r(\pi, a)$ is the relevance of π wrt the article a, $u(\pi)$ is the unexpectedness

---

[2] In our experiments with the DBpedia SPARQL endpoint, we observed that the time needed to process an article time is largely unpredictable and not correlated to the size of the data context.

of π, and α is a parameter in the interval $[0,1]$ that can be used to adjust the weight assigned to relevance and unexpectedness; for example, for $\alpha = 0.3$ the unexpectedness component of serendipity is emphasized, while for $\alpha = 0.7$ the relevance component of serendipity is emphasised. To capture unexpectedness we use a measure proposed in previous work [1], named Rarity, which evaluates how scarce the use of a property is in a dataset. In this way, rarity rewards those associations that use properties that are uncommon in the KB. Because we could not find a definition of *relevance of a semantic association wrt to a reference text*, we defined our own relevance measure inspired by Information Retrieval [5]. For each association (π) we concatenate the abstracts of each entity occurring in π so as to form a virtual document d^π, which is represented by a vector of weighted terms. Each term is weighted using TF-IDF [5], where IDF is computed over the collection of all the abstracts collected for an individual article. Analogously, we build a virtual document d^a for the article a. We then compute the relevance of π wrt a as the cosine similarity between the two documents d^π and d^a. Finally, before being combined into the serendipity measure, relevance and unexpectedness are normalised in the range $[0,1]$ using the min-max normalisation method, which preserves the relative distances between values [10]. We use Elastic Search[3] to process, index and match the virtual documents. The computation of serendipity s is very efficient if relevance r and unexpectedness u are available: r and u are computed for every association off-line, while serendipity is dynamically computed at run-time by letting users specify the parameter α, which determines the balance between relevance and unexpectedness. Serendipity is used to rank the associations in the Data Context Graph and select a set of top-k associations shown to the reader.

To the best of our knowledge, serendipity and relevance, defined for a semantic association in relation to an input text, are original contributions of our work, while unexpectedness has been taken from previous work [1]. The few computational definitions of serendipity that have been proposed, e.g., see [6,9], are not easily applicable to linked data because defined in very different contexts. Graph-based measures proposed to evaluate the relatedness between entities in semantic graphs [2,4] could be useful to enrich the definition of relevance. However, these measures do not consider a reference text as our relevance measure does, which is a key asset in our application scenario.

Contextual Explorer. The user interface of DaCena has been designed to offer the user an interactive environment to read the news article and visually explore the semantic associations simultaneously. The aim is to offer the user an innovative reading experience based on an exploration process characterized by the ?overview first, zoom and filter, details on demand? browsing model typical of information visualization interfaces [8]. The interface presents on the left side the news article formatted in order to guarantee a good readability of the text. The named entities found are highlighted in yellow in the article as the main entity, which is presented at the beginning of the section. On the right side we can find the interactive graph generated by the correlations between the main

---

[3] https://www.elastic.co/products/elasticsearch.

entity (the big yellow node), the other entities mentioned in the article (the small yellow nodes) and the entities that occur in the associations but not in the article (the grey nodes). Clicking on the entities, both through the visualization and the text on the left, the user can filter the network and explore in detail all the paths from the main entity to the selected one. In the upper part of the interface the user can access different parameters to filter or expand the graph.

3   The Demo

The demonstration showcases the concept and novel data exploration interface of DaCENA. Users can read several articles from within the interactive interface and personalize the data context view. They can dynamically change the number of displayed associations, filter out associations based on their length, and look associations between the main topic and one entity of interests in more details. In addition, users can dynamically tune serendipity to favor unexpectedness or relevance; their preferences will result in a quick adjustment of the shown graph.

Despite we developed DaCENA for the journalism domain, the main ideas presented in this paper can be virtually applied to any domain where it is useful to explore a (relational) data context related to a text of interest (for example, in the forensic or in the music domain). By exploring linked data with DaCENA in the context of reading tasks, we also experienced some limits in DBpedia, when this KB is challenged to provide interesting data for end-users. We believe that DaCENA can stimulate interesting discussions on topics such as data quality, data value, and content specialization in socio-political and economic domains.

References

1. Aleman-meza, B., Halaschek-wiener, C., Arpinar, I.B., Ramakrishnan, C., Sheth, A.: Ranking complex relationships on the semantic web. IEEE Internet Comput. **9**, 37–44 (2005)
2. De Vocht, L., Coppens, S., Verborgh, R., Vander Sande, M., Mannens, E., Van de Walle, R.: Discovering meaningful connections between resources in the web of data. In: 6th Workshop on Linked Data on the Web, p. 8 (2013)
3. Gray, J., Chambers, L., Bounegru, L. (eds.): The Data Journalism Handbook. O'Reilly, Sebastopol (2012)
4. Leal, J.P.: Using proximity to compute semantic relatedness in RDF graphs. Comput. Sci. Inf. Syst. **10**(4), 1727–1746 (2013)
5. Manning, C.D., Raghavan, P., Schütze, H.: Introduction to Information Retrieval, vol. 1. Cambridge University Press, Cambridge (2008)
6. Noda, Y., Kiyota, Y., Nakagawa, H.: Discovering serendipitous information from wikipedia by using its network structure. In: ICWSM (2010)
7. Raimond, Y., Ferne, T., Smethurst, M., Adams, G.: The BBC world service archive prototype. J. Web Sem. **27**, 2–9 (2014)
8. Shneiderman, B.: The eyes have it: a task by data type taxonomy for information visualizations. In: VL, pp. 336–343. IEEE Computer Society (1996)
9. Sun, T., Zhang, M., Mei, Q.: Unexpected relevance: an empirical study of serendipity in retweets. In: ICWSM (2013)
10. Tarique Ahmad, P.S.K.S.M., Haque, S.: Privacy preserving in data mining by normalization. Int. J. Comput. Appl. **95**(6), 14–18 (2014)

Visual Analysis of Statistical Data on Maps Using Linked Open Data

Petar Ristoski[✉] and Heiko Paulheim

University of Mannheim, Research Group Data and Web Science B6 26,
Mannheim, Germany
{petar.ristoski,heiko}@informatik.uni-mannheim.de

Abstract. When analyzing statistical data, one of the most basic and at the same time widely used techniques is analyzing correlations. As shown in previous works, Linked Open Data is a rich resource for discovering such correlations. In this demo, we show how statistical analysis and visualization on maps can be combined to facilitate a deeper understanding of the statistical findings.

Keywords: Linked Open Data · Visualization · Correlations · Statistical data

1 Introduction

Statistical datasets are widely spread and published on the Web. However, many users' information need is not the mere consumption of statistical data as such, but the search for patterns and explanations. As shown in previous works [3], information from the Linked Open Data (LOD) cloud can serve as background knowledge for interpreting statistical data, as it covers various domains, ranging from general purpose datasets to government and life science data [7].

In this paper, we present the Web-based tool *ViCoMap*[1], which allows automatic correlation analysis and visualizing statistical data on maps using Linked Open Data. The tool automatically enriches statistical datasets, imported from LOD, RDF datacubes, or local datasets, with information from Linked Open Data, and uses that background knowledge as a means to create possible interpretations as well as advanced map visualization of the statistical datasets. To visualize geospatial entities on a map, we use GADM[2], a LOD database of polygon shapes of the world's administrative areas.

So far, many tools for visualization of LOD and statistical data have been developed [4]. In particular, for RDF data cubes[3] exposing statistical data, different browsers have been developed, such as *CubeViz*[4] or *Payola*[5] [1]. The *CODE*

---

[1] The tool is available at http://vicomap.informatik.uni-mannheim.de/. Note: response times may vary according to the availability of the LOD sources used.
[2] http://gadm.geovocab.org/.
[3] http://www.w3.org/TR/vocab-data-cube/.
[4] http://aksw.org/Projects/CubeViz.html.
[5] http://live.payola.cz/.

© Springer International Publishing Switzerland 2015
F. Gandon et al. (Eds.): ESWC 2015, LNCS 9341, pp. 138–143, 2015.
DOI: 10.1007/978-3-319-25639-9_27

Visualisation Wizard[6] [2] also features different chart and map based visualizations. Tialhun et al. [8] have developed a LOD-based visualization system for healthcare data. The system visualizes different healthcare indicators per country on a map, and is able to perform correlation analysis between selected indicators, which can later be visualized as a chart.

The direct predecessor of *ViCoMap* is *Explain-a-LOD* [3], which is one of the first approaches for automatically generating hypothesis for explaining statistics using LOD. The tool enhances statistical datasets with background information from DBpedia[7], and uses correlation analysis and rule learning for producing hypothesis which are presented to the user.

ViCoMap, presented in this demo, combines map-based visualizations on the one hand side, and mining for correlations using background knowledge from LOD on the other. As such, it opens new ways of interpreting statistical data.

2   The ViCoMap Tool

The architecture of the ViCoMap tool consists of three main components, as shown in Fig. 1. The base component of the tool is the *RapidMiner Linked Open Data extension* [5]. The extension hooks into the powerful data mining platform *RapidMiner*[8], and offers operators for accessing LOD in RapidMiner, allowing for using it in sophisticated data analysis workflows using data from LOD. The extension allows for autonomously exploring the Web of Data by following links, thereby discovering relevant datasets on the fly, as well as for integrating redundant data found in dfferent datasets, and wraps additional services such as *DBpedia Lookup*[9] and *DBpedia Spotlight*[10].

All processes built within the RapidMiner platform can be exposed as Web services through the RapidMiner Server, which can be consumed in a user Web

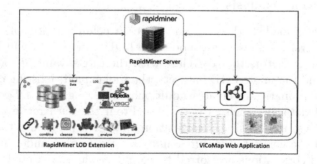

Fig. 1. ViCoMap architecture

---

[6] http://code.know-center.tugraz.at/search.
[7] http://dbpedia.org/.
[8] http://www.rapidminer.com.
[9] http://lookup.dbpedia.org.
[10] http://lookup.dbpedia.org.

application. We use such a setup to integrate the functionalities of the Rapid-Miner LOD extension, as well as the functionalities of RapidMiner built-in operators, in the ViCoMap Web application. The ViCoMap Web application offers three main functionalities to the end-user: *Data Import*, *Correlation Analysis*, and *Visualization on Maps*.

2.1   Data Import

There are three options to import data, i.e.,import a dataset published using the RDF Data Cube vocabulary, import data from a SPARQL endpoint, and import data from a local file.

Import RDF Data Cubes: To import a dataset published using the RDF Data Cube vocabulary, the user first needs to select the data publisher source, and a dataset that will be explored. Currently, we provide a static list of most used RDF Data Cube publishers, like WorldBank[11]. After selecting a data cube and the dimensions to be analyzed, the dataset is loaded into RapidMiner by the LOD extension.

SPARQL Data Import: To import data from a SPARQL endpoint, the user first needs to select a SPARQL endpoint and to provide a SPARQL query. The tool offers a SPARQL query builder assistant, which helps the user formulate queries such as *Select the number of universities per federal state in Germany*, by selecting a set of spatial entities (states in Germany) and a subject entity (universities).

Local Dataset Import: The user can import data from a local CSV file.

2.2   Correlation Analysis

Once the data is loaded, the user can select a column that will be used for correlation analysis. The user can choose the LOD sources that will be explored to find interesting factors that correlate with the target value at hand. To link the data at hand to remote LOD datasets, the tool exploits existing `owl:sameAs` links, and it automatically creates additional links, e.g., via *DBpedia Lookup* for non-linked datasets, such as CSV files. From the data retrieved from the additional LOD sources, a simple correlation analysis is performed to find simple correlations of the generated features and the target value under examination. The discovered correlations are sorted by confidence and presented to the user.

Visualization on Maps. After the correlation analysis is completed, the user can visualize any correlation on a map, using the Google Maps API[12] and displaying two maps for the correlated values side by side. The shape data of the

---

[11] http://worldbank.270a.info.
[12] https://developers.google.com/maps/.

geographical entities is retrieved from GADM. DBpedia provides external links to the GADM dataset, which were created using different heuristics based on the label and coordinates of geographical entities [6]. DBpedia 2014 contains 65, 616 links to the GADM dataset, for entities on different administration level, e.g., municipalities, regions, states, departments, countries, etc. Such links allow us to visualize spatial entities on any administrative level.

3 Use Case: Number of Universities per State in Germany

In this use case, we analyze which factors correlate with the number of universities per state in Germany[13]. To import the initial data we use the query builder assistant from the SPARQL data import tab (Fig. 2a). After executing the query, the data is presented in a table with two columns, i.e., the DBpedia URI for each state, and the number of universities per state (Fig. 2b). By pressing the button *Find Correlations*, we can select the LOD sources that will be included in the correlation analysis (Fig. 2c). Next, the discovered correlations are presented in a new table with two columns, i.e., a column with the factor label, and the a column with the correlation confidence (Fig. 2d).

We can see that in this case, as shown in Fig. 3, the highest positive correlation is the RnD expenses of the states (+0.84), which is retrieved from Eurostat. The highest negative correlation is the latitude of the states (−0.73), which is retrieved from GeoNames, which reflects the north-south gradient of the wealth distribution in Germany.[14]

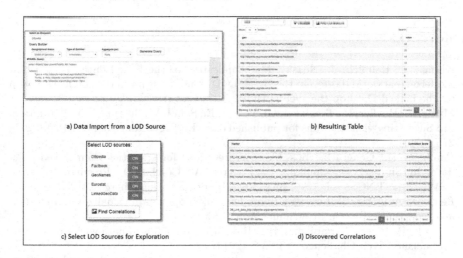

a) Data Import from a LOD Source

b) Resulting Table

c) Select LOD Sources for Exploration

d) Discovered Correlations

Fig. 2. German states use case workflow

---

[13] States of Germany: http://en.wikipedia.org/wiki/States_of_Germany.
[14] http://www.bundesbank.de/Redaktion/EN/Topics/2013/
2013_07_10_to_save_or_not_to_save_private_wealth_in_germany.html.

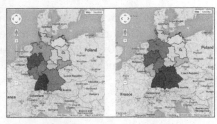 

(a) Positive correlation between #universities (left) and RnD expenses (right) per state

(b) Negative correlation between #universities (left) and latitude (right) per state

Fig. 3. Correlations visualized on a map using GADM geographical shape data

4   Conclusion

With this demo, we have introduced the web-based ViCoMap tool, which allows the users to analyze statistical data, and visualize it on maps using external knowledge from Linked Open Data. While at the moment, we use only literal data properties and types for finding correlations, we aim at a more intelligent exploration of the feature space, e.g., by automatically finding meaningful aggregations of different measures.

Acknowledgements. The work presented in this paper has been partly funded by the German Research Foundation (DFG) under grant number PA 2373/1-1 (Mine@LOD).

References

1. Klímek, J., Helmich, J., Neasky, M.: Application of the linked data visualization model on real world data from the Czech LOD cloud. In: 6th International Workshop on the Linked Data on the Web (LDOW 2014) (2014)
2. Mutlu, B., Hoefler, P., Tschinkel, G., Veas, E.E., Sabol, V., Stegmaier, F., Granitzer, M.: Suggesting visualisations for published data. In: Proceedings of IVAPP, pp. 267–275 (2014)
3. Paulheim, H.: Generating possible interpretations for statistics from linked open data. In: Simperl, E., Cimiano, P., Polleres, A., Corcho, O., Presutti, V. (eds.) ESWC 2012. LNCS, vol. 7295, pp. 560–574. Springer, Heidelberg (2012)
4. Peña, O., Aguilera, U., López-de Ipiña, D.: Linked open data visualization revisited: a survey. Under Review at Semant. Web J. (2015)
5. Ristoski, P., Bizer, C., Paulheim, H.: Mining the web of linked data with rapidminer. In: Semantic Web Challenge at ISWC (2014)
6. Ristoski, P., Paulheim, H.: Analyzing statistics with background knowledge from linked open data. In: Workshop on Semantic Statistics (2013)

7. Schmachtenberg, M., Bizer, C., Paulheim, H.: Adoption of the linked data best practices in different topical domains. In: Mika, P., et al. (eds.) ISWC 2014, Part I. LNCS, vol. 8796, pp. 245–260. Springer, Heidelberg (2014)
8. Tilahun, B., Kauppinen, T., Keßler, C., Fritz, F.: Design and development of a linked open data-based health information representation and visualization system: potentials and preliminary evaluation. JMIR Med. Inf. 2(2), 196–208 (2014)

Keyword Search on RDF Graphs: It Is More Than Just Searching for Keywords

Kostas Stefanidis[(✉)] and Irini Fundulaki

Institute of Computer Science, FORTH, Heraklion, Greece
{kstef,fundul}@ics.forth.gr

Abstract. In this paper, we propose a model for enabling users to search RDF data via keywords, thus, allowing them to discover relevant information without using complicated queries or knowing the underlying ontology or vocabulary. We aim at exploiting the characteristics of the RDF data to increase the quality of the ranked query results. We consider different dimensions for evaluating the value of results and achieving relevance, personalization and diversity.

1 Keyword Search on RDF Graphs

Typically, data in knowledge bases is represented using the RDF model. In RDF, everything we wish to describe is a *resource* that may be a person, an institution, a thing, a concept, or a relation between other resources. The building block of RDF is a *triple*, which is of the form (*subject, predicate, object*). The RDF Schema (RDFS) language is used to introduce useful semantics to RDF triples. It provides a built-in vocabulary for asserting user defined schemas within the RDF model. This vocabulary can be used to specify URIs as being of a specific type (*classes, properties* and *instances*), to denote special relationships between URIs. The flexibility of the RDF data model allows the representation of both schema and instance information in the form of RDF triples.

The traditional way to retrieve RDF data is through SPARQL, the W3C recommendation language for querying RDF datasets. SPARQL queries are built from *triple patterns* and determine the pattern to seek for; the answer is the part(s) of the set of RDF triples that matches this pattern. The correctness and completeness of answers of SPARQL queries are key research challenges. SPARQL is a structured query language that allows users to submit queries that may precisely identify their information needs, but require users to be familiar with the syntax, and the complex semantics of the language, as well as with the underlying schema or ontology. Moreover, this interaction mode assumes that users are to some extent familiar with the content of the knowledge base and also have a clear understanding of their information needs. On the other hand, today, there is a growing interest on a keyword-based search functionality to answer the search needs of users who are looking for specific information obtained by integrating numerous and heterogeneous sources. In addition, it is important for the user to be able to define different criteria on how all the resulting information could be ranked and returned to the user.

© Springer International Publishing Switzerland 2015
F. Gandon et al. (Eds.): ESWC 2015, LNCS 9341, pp. 144–148, 2015.
DOI: 10.1007/978-3-319-25639-9_28

2   Searching

A collection of RDF triples forms an *RDF graph* that is a *directed, edge and node labeled graph*, where nodes are subjects and objects of triples, and edges between nodes are predicates. An edge between a node corresponding to a subject s and a node corresponding to an object o exists only if a triple (s, p, o) exists in the triple set. Subjects, predicates and objects are URIs, while the latter could also be literals. [5] introduces a graph data model for representing RDF instance and schema information. Each RDF schema S defines a finite set of *class names C* and *property names P*. Properties are defined using class names or literal types, so that, for each property p, the domain of property p ($domain(p)$) is a class and the range of p ($range(p)$) is either a class or a literal. The model of [5] supports class and property hierarchies and denotes them as $H = (C \cup P, <)$.

A collection $\mathcal{A}$ of RDF triples forms a directed RDF graph $G(V, \lambda_V, \lambda_P, E)$, where: (i) $V = V_s \cup V_o$ represents a set of nodes; V_s and V_o contain a node for each subject and object, resp., in the triples of $\mathcal{A}$, (ii) $\lambda_v : V \to 2^C$ is a function that assigns to each node in G a set of class names from C, (iii) $\lambda_P : E \to P$ is a function that assigns to each edge in G one property name from P, and (iv) E represents a set of edges of the form $e(v_i, v_j)$ with $v_i \in V_s$, $v_j \in V_o$ and direction from v_i to v_j. Given that v_i, v_j, e correspond to a subject s, an object o and a predicate p, resp., the edge $e(v_i, v_j)$ exists in G, if and only if, $(s, p, o) \in \mathcal{A}$. The label of e is $\lambda_P(e) = p$, where $p \in P$.

A keyword query Q consists of a set of keywords $\{w_1, \ldots, w_m\}$. The result of Q is defined as a set of subgraphs H of G that are total, i.e., every keyword of Q is contained in at least one node n, one edge e, or their labels, $\lambda_V(n)$, $\lambda_P(e)$, resp., of H, and minimal, i.e., we cannot remove a node from H and get a total graph for Q. To process keyword queries over a graph G, we construct inverted indexes that store information about keyword occurrences in the RDF triples. Typically, after retrieving, for each keyword in Q, a list of matching elements, i.e., nodes, edges or labels, in G, we perform a bidirectional expansion search strategy to join elements from different lists.

3   Ranking

Given the abundance of available information, exploring the contents of a knowledge base is a complex process that may return a huge volume of data. Still, users would like to retrieve only a small piece of it, namely the most relevant to their interests. Previous approaches on querying RDF graphs mostly focus on the Boolean answer model, where query criteria are considered as hard by default and an answer is returned only if it satisfies all the criteria. In this context, a user can face the *too-many-answers problem*, where too many results match the query. Our focus in this work is on a keyword search model over RDF graphs, where users will be able to query the graph and be presented with a top-k result set by combining the *relevance* and the *diversity* of the results, and the *preferences* of the users.

Relevance. Relevance is an important and well-studied criterion for ranking the results $R(Q)$ of a keyword query Q. A natural characterization of the relevance of a subgraph $H \in R(Q)$ is its size, i.e., the number of its nodes: the smaller the size of the graph, the stronger the connection between the query keywords, thus the larger its relevance.

For XML documents, several approaches can be exploited for efficiently ranking keyword search results based on relevance (e.g., [8]). For RDF graphs, recently, [3] proposes ranking the resulting graphs of a query Q based on a statistical language-model. Specifically, this approach assigns a score to each graph $H \in R(Q)$ that reflects the probability of generating Q given the language-model of H. In this work, we intend *not to restrict* to a specific definition of relevance: we just assume that each individual subgraph is characterized by a degree of relevance *rel*, and combine relevance with preferences and diversity for performing top-k computations.

Preferences. For personalizing keyword queries results, we incorporate *user preferences* [7]. In general, preferences can be distinguished between *qualitative* and *quantitative* ones. In the former, a user specifies a binary preference relation $\mathcal{P}$, $\mathcal{P} = \{(w_i \succ w_j)\}$, where $w_i \succ w_j$ denotes that the user prefers keyword w_i over w_j. Given $\mathcal{P}$, we would like to rank the graphs in $R(Q)$ of a query Q. To do this, we use the fact that, for $w_i \succ w_j$, graphs containing w_i are preferred over graphs containing w_j. One way to assign preference scores to graphs is by using the winnow operator [2]. The intuition is to give the highest score to the most preferred graphs, that is, to the graphs for which there is no other graph in $R(Q)$ that is preferred over them. So, winnow at level 1 returns the most preferable graphs. An additional application of winnow, i.e., winnow at level 2, returns the next most preferred graphs, and so forth. In general, repeated applications of winnow result in ranking all graphs in $R(Q)$. We associate a preference score *pref* with each graph in $R(Q)$ based on the winnow level their keywords belong to. In the latter, instead of providing $\mathcal{P}$, users explicitly provide specific scores *pref* to interesting keywords. A higher score indicates a more important keyword. Then, scores to graphs are assigned with respect to the keywords they contain. Either qualitatively or quantitatively, preferences can be defined over the keywords of the nodes, edges and labels of the graph G. To impose an ordering of results when the results do not contain keywords in $\mathcal{P}$, we use the concept of *indirect dominance* [6]. Abstractly, a graph $H \in R(Q)$ that is related to a keyword w_i, not contained in H, is preferred over a graph $J \in R(Q)$ that is related to a keyword w_j, not contained in J, if $w_i \succ w_j$.

For structured queries, [1] focuses on personalizing XML search via qualitative preferences that target at: (i) expanding or restricting the original query result by adding, removing or replacing query predicates and (ii) specifying how to rank answers. Only recently, [4] sketches an IR methodology for training RDF-specific ranking functions.

Diversity. Top-results in $R(Q)$ are often very similar to each other, since they contain the same highly relevant and preferable piece of information. Caring for the quality of the result set as a whole, in our work, besides pure accuracy achieved by relevance and user preferences, we also consider retrieving results on a broader variety of topics, i.e., increasing the diversity of results. To achieve diversity, we target at avoiding the overlap among results, i.e., choosing graphs that are dissimilar to each other. For quantifying the overlap between two graphs, we use a Jaccard-like definition of distance, which measures dissimilarity between the keywords of the nodes that form these graphs. This objective is enhanced by taking into account the semantic similarity of classes and properties that can be inferred by the schema, or even OWL-like axioms[1] that define explicitly, for instance, disjointness of classes. Then, the diversity, *div*, of a set of graphs is computed with respect to their distances from each other.

Top-k selection. Given a budget k on the number of results for a keyword query Q, we would like to combine the order of results as indicated by the user preferences with the results relevance. Furthermore, to increase user satisfaction, we consider the results as a whole and aim at selecting those that differ from each other to achieve diversity.

This way, let f be a cost function that combines the above properties and maps a set of resulting graphs onto a score with respect to Q. If $|R(Q)| > k$, our goal is to select the subset of k results that maximizes f. Formally:

Definition 1. *Given an RDF graph G, a keyword query Q with results $R(Q)$ and a cost function f, the top-k results is the set B^* for which:* $B^* = argmax_{B \subseteq R(Q),\ |B|=k}$ $f(B)$.

4   Summary

In this paper, we have shown the growing importance of introducing new keyword search mechanisms for RDF data. The user experience in querying an RDF graph can be significantly improved by exploiting different criteria for ranking query answers towards meeting the users information needs. Criteria are oriented on ranking based on relevance, preferences, as well as on the diversity of the answer set as a whole. The problem of exploring how to combine such criteria is challenging. Research progress in this area does not necessarily demand working from scratch; a different point of view on how to employ or adapt existing algorithms and techniques should also be considered.

Acknowledgments. The work of the first author is partially supported by the project "IdeaGarden" funded by the Seventh Framework Programme under grand n° 318552.

References

1. Amer-Yahia, S., Fundulaki, I., Lakshmanan, L.V.S.: Personalizing xml search in pimento. In: ICDE (2007)

---

[1] http://www.w3.org/TR/owl2-profiles.

2. Chomicki, J.: Preference formulas in relational queries. ACM Trans. Database Syst. **28**(4), 427–466 (2003)
3. Elbassuoni, S., Blanco, R.: Keyword search over RDF graphs. In: CIKM (2011)
4. Giannopoulos, G., Biliri, E., Sellis, T.: Personalizing keyword search on RDF data. In: Aalberg, T., Papatheodorou, C., Dobreva, M., Tsakonas, G., Farrugia, C.J. (eds.) TPDL 2013. LNCS, vol. 8092, pp. 272–278. Springer, Heidelberg (2013)
5. Karvounarakis, G., Alexaki, S., Christophides, V., Plexousakis, D., Scholl, M.: RQL: a declarative query language for RDF. In: WWW (2002)
6. Stefanidis, K., Drosou, M., Pitoura, E.: Perk: personalized keyword search in relational databases through preferences. In: EDBT (2010)
7. Stefanidis, K., Koutrika, G., Pitoura, E.: A survey on representation, composition and application of preferences in database systems. ACM Trans. Database Syst. **36**(3), 19 (2011)
8. Tao, Y., Papadopoulos, S., Sheng, C., Stefanidis, K.: Nearest keyword search in XML documents. In: SIGMOD (2011)

Collaborative Development of Multilingual Thesauri with VocBench (System Description and Demonstrator)

Armando Stellato[1(✉)], Sachit Rajbhandari[2], Andrea Turbati[1],
Manuel Fiorelli[1], Caterina Caracciolo[2], Tiziano Lorenzetti[1],
Johannes Keizer[2], and Maria Teresa Pazienza[1]

[1] ART Group, Department of Enterprise Engineering, University of Rome,
Tor Vergata, Via Del Politecnico 1, 00133 Rome, Italy
{stellato, turbati, fiorelli, lorenzetti,
pazienza}@info.uniroma2.it
[2] Food and Agriculture Organization of the United Nations (FAO),
Viale delle Terme di Caracalla, 00153 Rome, Italy
{sachit.rajbhandari, caterina.caracciolo,
johannes.keizer}@fao.org

Abstract. VocBench is an open source web application for editing of SKOS and SKOS-XL thesauri, with a strong focus on collaboration, supported by workflow management for content validation and publication. Dedicated user roles provide a clean separation of competences, addressing different specificities ranging from management aspects to vertical competences on content editing, such as conceptualization versus terminology editing. Extensive support for scheme management allows editors to fully exploit the possibilities of the SKOS model, as well as to fulfill its integrity constraints. We describe here the main features of VocBench, which will be shown along the demo held at the ESWC15 conference.

Keywords: Collaborative thesaurus management · SKOS · SKOS-XL

1 Introduction

In 2008, the AIMS group of the Food and Agriculture Organization of the United Nations (FAO, http://www.fao.org/) fostered the development of a collaborative platform for managing the Agrovoc thesaurus [1]: the "Agrovoc Workbench". Later on, in the context of a joint collaboration between FAO and the ART group of the University of Tor Vergata in Rome (http://art.uniroma2.it), the system has been completely rethought as a fully-fledged collaborative platform for thesaurus management, available free of charge and open source: VocBench. With respect to its predecessor, VocBench complies with standard Semantic Web technologies, by relying on Semantic Turkey [2], an RDF management platform already developed and currently maintained by the ART team. In particular, VocBench natively supports the SKOS[1] W3C vocabulary for

---

[1] http://www.w3.org/TR/skos-reference/.

© Springer International Publishing Switzerland 2015
F. Gandon et al. (Eds.): ESWC 2015, LNCS 9341, pp. 149–153, 2015.
DOI: 10.1007/978-3-319-25639-9_29

representing thesauri and concept schemes, with its extension SKOS-XL[2] for extended labels (i.e. labels reified as RDF resources, which can be described in turn).

While providing a more thorough support for RDF, VocBench retains the focus on multilingualism, collaboration and on a structured content validation & publication workflow that characterized it yet from its infancy. The demo will provide a guided tour through all of VocBench features and will let the user experience the editorial process that accompanies the development of an authoritative resource.

2   A Quick Glance at VocBench Features

The feedback gathered from real thesaurus publishers guided the development of VocBench: FAO and its partners provided great support for shaping interaction and collaboration capabilities. Here follow the features that mostly characterize the system.

User Interface. VocBench has been conceived as a web application accessible through any modern browser, therefore disburdening end users from software installation and configuration. The user interface consists of multiple tabs, each one associated with specific information and functionalities. A quick exploration of the available tabs is sufficient to discover most of the VocBench functionalities. Figure 1 offers a typical view of VocBench, with the concept tree on the left, and the description of the selected concept on the right, centered on the term tab, listing all terms in the different languages available for the resource. Concepts in the tree may be shown through their labels in all of the selected languages for visualization. An option toggles between a view of preferred labels only, and all labels. The multilingual characteristics of VocBench are not limited to content management, as its interface is also localized in different languages, currently: English, Spanish, Dutch and Thai.

Role-Based Access Control. VocBench promotes the separation of responsibilities through a role-based access control mechanism, checking user privileges for requested functionalities through *roles* that users assume. A completely customizable access policy specifies roles and their assigned privileges. New roles can be created and existing ones can be modified. The default policy recognizes typical roles and their acknowledged responsibilities: *Administrators, Ontology editors, Term editors* (Terminologists), *Validators* and *Publishers*.

Formal Workflow and Recent Changes. Collaboration is essential for distributing effort and reaching consensus on the thesaurus being developed. To facilitate collaboration, VocBench provides an editorial workflow in which editors' changes are tracked and stored for approval by content validators. This workflow management is supported by role-based access control, by providing users with different roles so to enforce the separation between their responsibilities. In a collaborative environment, where users may proactively edit a shared resource, it is important to have means for monitoring the situation. Regarding this aspect, the ability to control recent changes to the thesaurus is

---

[2] http://www.w3.org/TR/skos-reference/skos-xl.html.

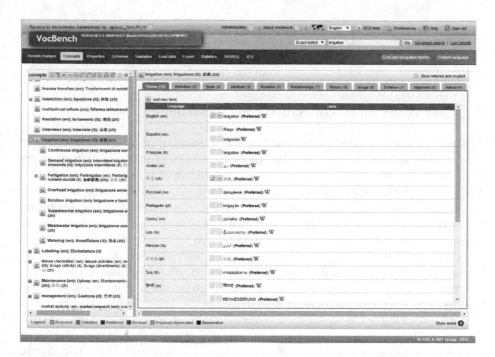

Fig. 1. VocBench User interface showing a fragment of the AGROVOC thesaurus

useful for detecting hot sections and coordinating with other editors. In VocBench, users can see recent changes both in the Web user interface and as an RSS feed.

Advanced Scheme Management. VocBench allows to manage thesauri organized around multiple concept schemes. Users can switch across schemes by selecting them through the relevant *Schemes* tab in the user interface. VocBench functionalities are well-behaved with respect to schemes, as actions that would generate *dangling* concepts (concepts not reachable through any tree-view) are forbidden, detailing the cause of the impediment to the users. In any case, since data can be loaded from pre-existing sources developed outside of VocBench, a fixing utility for dangling concept is available through the UI, and will be part of a larger section dedicated to Integrity Constraints Validation, especially thought for fixing violated SKOS constraints.

Metrics and SPARQL Querying. VocBench reports several metrics concerning the thesaurus itself and the collaborative workflow. In addition to statistics and visualizations provided by VocBench, users may formulate SPARQL 1.1 queries/updates to select precise information, perform custom analytical tasks or modify the thesaurus bypassing the standard editing functionalities. The SPARQL editor is based on the open source Flint SPARQL Editor (https://github.com/TSO-Openup/FlintSparqlEditor), which provides syntax highlighting and completion, and has been customized to be fed with information from the edited thesaurus.

Alignment. From version 2.3, VocBench supports alignments to other thesauri. Currently, the creation of alignments can either be performed manually, by inserting

URIs as values of the various SKOS mapping properties, or be assisted in case of mappings to other thesauri managed by the same instance of VocBench. In the latter case, a concept-tree browser with advanced search interfaces facilitates the identification of the best matching concepts from the targeted datasets.

3 Some Notes on Architecture and Technologies

Semantic Turkey, the RDF backbone of VocBench, offers an OSGi service-based layer for designing and developing OWL ontologies and SKOS(XL) thesauri. A lightweight Firefox interface is available for use as a desktop tool, which is now complemented by VocBench, mainly differentiating for its collaborative nature and its focus on thesauri.

VocBench has a layered architecture consisting of a presentation and multi-user management layer, a service layer and a data management layer. The first layer is implemented as a Web application, powered by GWT (Google Web Toolkit, http://www.gwtproject.org/). The other layers coincide with the Semantic Turkey RDF management platform, equipped with an extension providing additional services expressly developed for VocBench. VocBench is also in charge of user and workflow management, since these aspects are not covered by Semantic Turkey. User accounts and tracked changes are stored in a relational database accessed through a JDBC connector. The adoption of OSGi allows for plugging of extensions: in particular, other than realizing additional services, different connectors for specific RDF middleware and triple storage technologies can be provided. VocBench is currently shipped with a connector for Sesame2 [3], supporting all of its storage/connection possibilities: in memory, native, remote connection and their respective configurations. The remote connection is particularly useful, as it allows VocBench to connect to Sesame2 compliant triple stores (e.g. GraphDB [4]) without need for a dedicated connector. VocBench RDF API are based on OWL ART (http://art.uniroma2.it/owlart/), an abstraction layer supporting access to different triple stores. Different connectors can be implemented from scratch in terms of those API, or by reusing middleware already bridged through other existing connectors. For instance, the Virtuoso triplestore [5] is compatible with the Sesame API, but requires a dedicated client library: it thus needs to be introduced by a specific connector, though its implementation may be largely realized as an extension of the already existing Sesame connector. Finally, particular attention has been paid to system scalability, both on performance and maintenance aspects. To this end, information is provided to the frontend as much as possible in an incremental fashion (e.g. each level of the concept hierarchy, as nodes are expanded).

4 System Demo

In the demonstration, visitors will be guided through all of VocBench features, experiencing the editorial process that accompanies the development of an authoritative resource. The audience will initially be acquainted with the UI of the environment and learn how to browse the loaded dataset in order to explore its content. Later on, they will try the more common editing operations for creating, modifying and relating concepts and (SKOS-XL reified) labels. Interested people will go through the full editorial workflow, seeing how different roles will contribute to the evolution of the thesaurus.

The demo will be carried on real thesauri from a few of the large organizations that are already using VocBench for maintaining their resources. These thesauri include:

- Agrovoc (Food and Agriculture Organization)
- Eurovoc (EU Documentation Office)
- Unified Astronomy Thesaurus (Harvard-Smithsonian Center for Astrophysics)
- Teseo (Italian Senate)

5   More About VocBench

This paper accompanies the demo of VocBench being held at the 12th Extended Semantic Web Conference. More information about VocBench, an in-depth comparison with other systems, user evaluation, lessons learned and insights on the future of the system, can be found in [6], an article presented at the Research Track of this same conference.

5.1   Availability

VocBench is distributed as open-source under the Mozilla Public License (https://www.mozilla.org/MPL/2.0/).
VocBench home page: http://vocbench.uniroma2.it/
Source code on Bitbucket: https://bitbucket.org/art-uniroma2/vocbench
A sandbox server for testing VocBench capabilities is hosted by courtesy of the Malaysian research center MIMOS Berhad at: http://202.73.13.50:55481/vocbench/

References

1. Caracciolo, C., Stellato, A., Morshed, A., Johannsen, G., Rajbhandari, S., Jaques, Y., Keizer, J.: The AGROVOC linked dataset. Semant Web J. **4**(3), 341–348 (2013)
2. Pazienza, M.T., Scarpato, N., Stellato, A., Turbati, A.: Semantic Turkey: a browser-integrated environment for knowledge acquisition and management. Semant Web J. **3**(3), 279–292 (2012)
3. Broekstra, J., Kampman, A., van Harmelen, F.: Sesame: a generic architecture for storing and querying RDF and RDF schema. In: Horrocks, I., Hendler, J. (eds.) ISWC 2002. LNCS, vol. 2342, pp. 54–68. Springer, Heidelberg (2002)
4. Kiryakov, A., Ognyanov, D., Manov, D.: OWLIM – a pragmatic semantic repository for OWL. In: Int. Workshop on Scalable Semantic Web Knowledge Base Systems (SSWS 2005), WISE 2005, New York City, USA, 20 November 2005
5. Erling, O., Mikhailov, I.: RDF support in the virtuoso DBMS. In: Pellegrini, T., Auer, S., Tochterman, K., Schaffert, S. (eds.) Networked Knowledge - Networked Media. SCI, vol. 221, pp. 7–24. Springer, Heidelberg (2009)
6. Stellato, A., Rajbhandari, S., Turbati, A., Fiorelli, M., Caracciolo, C., Lorenzetti, T., Keizer, J., Pazienza, M.T.: VocBench: a web application for collaborative development of multilingual thesauri. In: Gandon, F., Sabou, M., Sack, H., d'Amato, C., Cudré-Mauroux, P., Zimmermann, A. (eds.) ESWC 2015. LNCS, vol. 9088, pp. 38–53. Springer, Heidelberg (2015)

Distributed Linked Data Business Communication Networks: The LUCID Endpoint

Sebastian Tramp[1]([✉]), Ruben Navarro Piris[1], Timofey Ermilov[1],
Niklas Petersen[2], and Marvin Frommhold[1], and Sören Auer[3]

[1] eccenca GmbH, Hainstr. 8, 04109 Leipzig, Germany
{sebastian.tramp,ruben.navarro.piris,timofey.ermilov}@eccenca.com
[2] Enterprise Information Systems (EIS) at the Institute for Applied Computer
Science at University of Bonn, Römerstr. 164, 53117 Bonn, Germany
petersen@cs.uni-bonn.de
[3] Fraunhofer Institute for Intelligent Analysis and Information Systems (IAIS),
Schloss Birlinghoven, 53757 Sankt Augustin, Germany
soeren.auer@iais.fraunhofer.de

Abstract. With the LUCID Endpoint, we demonstrate how companies
can utilize Linked Data technology to provide major data items for their
business partners in a timely manner, machine readable and with open
and extensible schemata. The main idea is to provide a Linked Data
infrastructure which enables all partners to fetch, as well as to clone
and to synchronize datasets from other partners over the network. This
concept allows for building of networks of business partners much like
as social network but in a distributed manner. It furthermore provides a
technical infrastructure for business communication acts such as supply
chain communication or master data management.

1 The LUCID Endpoint

The LUCID endpoint[1] provides the necessary technology stack to manage and
publish Linked Data, as well as to consume Linked Data from other LUCID
endpoints.

This includes authentication and authorization mechanisms to guarantee that
data consumers access only the data that the endpoint owner explicitly allows.
To ensure consumer authentication, OAuth2 [6] is used. Access control rules can
be defined on a named graph level.

Once a local graph was modified, the endpoint will notify its subscribers by
sending the latest change sets for inclusion[2]. An example of this approach is
depicted in Fig. 1. By sending only the modifications instead of the complete

---

[1] Which is based on the eccenca Linked Data Suite Backend.
[2] The overall process is compatible with the PubSubHubbub working draft v0.4 [4].
The specification of a more general architecture for this kind of distributed semantic
social networks is available as [8].

© Springer International Publishing Switzerland 2015
F. Gandon et al. (Eds.): ESWC 2015, LNCS 9341, pp. 154–158, 2015.
DOI: 10.1007/978-3-319-25639-9_30

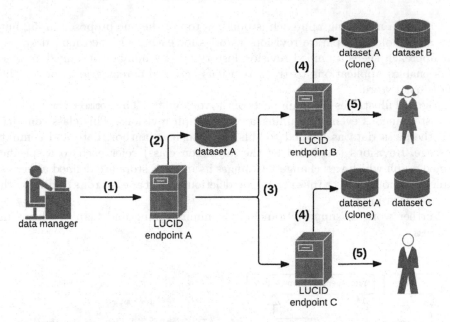

Fig. 1. The LUCID endpoint data management and publication process consists of the following steps: (**1**) modification of a dataset over SPARQL or a GUI (**2**) update of the dataset as well as revisioning (**3**) publication of the updates to all subscribers (**4**) application of the changes to the cloned datasets on subscriber site (**5**) user notification

new dataset, subscribers can easily recognize the changed triples without the need for calculation of expensive data diffs itself. Subscriber endpoints can then apply those modifications to their local dataset clones automatically. In order to describe these dataset changes, a vocabulary and exchange format is needed, which we will explain in the next section.

2 The Eccenca Revision Vocabulary

In order to both keep track of the modifications on the local quad store and notify subscribers of it about those modifications, we developed the eccenca Revision Vocabulary[3]. This vocabulary is modelled using OWL (OWL 2 DL profile) and extends as well as reuses several concepts of the PROV-O ontology [7].

Unlike other approaches, such as [1], which try to describe changes on higher semantic levels, our approach is based on triple (or rather quad) changes, where each revision or modification event (called commit) contains a diff representing the changed (either inserted and/or deleted) quads. This simple model enables applications to rebuild and revert each commit as well as to merge diverted evolution branches as explained in [3].

---

[3] The eccenca Revision Vocabulary is available at https://vocab.eccenca.com/revision/.

Our data modelling approach is build on top of the one proposed in [5], but instead of holding separate revision histories for each revisioned named graph, our approach keeps a unified revision history on any number of named graphs. This enables applications to track revisions across different graphs or for the whole quad store.

Figure 2 illustrates the main parts of the vocabulary: The Commit class defines an instantaneous event containing a set of graph revisions. This class contains also the meta data associated to this event such as author, date and commit message. Revisions (modelled as the Revision class) refer each to a specific named graph which was changed. Changes in an RDF store are defined either as triple insertions (deltaInsertion) or deletions (deltaDeletions) inline with the approach in [2].

Further work to support branching, commit signing and blank nodes is in progress.

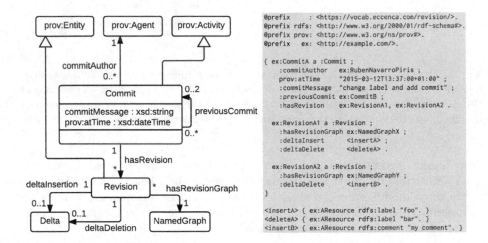

Fig. 2. LUCID revision vocabulary & example commit instance

3   Demonstration Use-Case: Master Data Management

Our setup for the demonstration of the LUCID endpoint deploys a very basic but pressing use case in business to business communication: master data management. Enterprise master data is the single source of basic business information used across all enterprise systems, applications and processes for an entire enterprise. This includes resources such as persons, company sites and subsidiaries as well as contact details.

Our proposed demo consists of the following parts:

– Publishing of master data datasets with a browser based user interface:
  A LUCID endpoint provides a dataset for each account. The account owner

is free to upload any data to this dataset. All resources from the dataset namespace are available as Linked Data and enabled for publish/subscribe as well as OAuth (in case the dataset is non-public). In addition to the generic access via SPARQL, the user can utilize a master data management application. This single page JavaScript application allows for creation of master data resources such as company subsidiaries and contact details. The RDF data model for these resources is based on the master data model from Odette International, a collaboration platform for the automotive supply chain.

- Versioning of the dataset changes on the SPARQL endpoint backend: All changes to the user dataset are logged as part of the internal LUCID endpoint triple store. The changed triples are calculated directly by the SPARQL query processor and added to the versioning store.
- Subscription to datasets of another LUCID endpoint by employing the dataset URL: All resources which are Linked Data accessible, are enabled for publish/subscribe activities as well. The user interface is able to manage subscriptions to other endpoints as well as to provide a preview for the incoming data.
- A publish/subscribe mechanism which uses commit push notifications based on the eccenca revision vocabulary described in Sect. 2: For each resource, a change log dataset is available, which provides the last `Commit` information. In addition to that, notifications with these `Commit` information as payload are pushed to all subscribers in case of a change. The subscribing endpoint adds the incoming data to its dataset clone as well as hold the change log in order to provide versioning information to the user.

Fig. 3. Screenshots of the master data management user interface: (left) Any user can subscribe to changes of other datasets by employing the subscription URL provided by the publisher. After committing the subscription process, the current version of the data model is fetched with an HTTP Linked Data request. (right) The publisher of a dataset is able to create its company master data which includes sites, contacts and other structures by using the master data manager. The master data manager is a browser-based user interface to an OAuth2 [6] enabled SPARQL endpoint.

Figure 3 depicts two screenshots of the master data management user interface which lies on top of the versioning and OAuth2 enabled SPARQL endpoint[4].

Acknowledgement. This work was partly supported by a grant from the German Federal Ministry of Education and Research (BMBF) in the IKT 2020 funding programme (GA no. 01IS14019) for the LUCID Project (http://lucid-project.org).

References

1. Auer, S., Herre, H.: A versioning and evolution framework for RDF knowledge bases. In: Proceedings of Ershov Memorial Conference (2006)
2. Berners-lee, T., Connolly, D.: Delta: an ontology for the distribution of differences between RDF graphs. Technical report, W3C (2004). http://www.w3.org/DesignIssues/lncs04/Diff.pdf
3. Cassidy, S., Ballantine, J.: Version control for RDF triple stores. In: Filipe, J., Shishkov, B., Helfert, M. (eds.) Proceedings of the Second International Conference on Software and Data Technologies, ICSOFT 2007, ISDM/EHST/DC, 22–25 July 2007, Barcelona, Spain, pp. 5–12. INSTICC Press (2007)
4. Fitzpatrick, B., Slatkin, B., Atkins, M., Genestoux, J.: PubSubHubbub Core 0.4. Working draft, PubSubHubbub W3C Community Group (2013). https://pubsubhubbub.googlecode.com/git/pubsubhubbub-core-0.4.html
5. Graube, M., Hensel, S., Urbas, L.: R43ples: revisions for triples - an approach for version control in the semantic web. In: Knuth, M., Kontokostas, D., Sack, H. (eds.) Proceedings of the 1st Workshop on Linked Data Quality Co-located with 10th International Conference on Semantic Systems, LDQ@SEMANTiCS 2014, 2nd September 2014, Leipzig, Germany, vol. 1215. CEUR Workshop Proceedings. CEUR-WS.org (2014)
6. Hardt, D.: The OAuth 2.0 Authorization Framework. RFC 6749, IETF, October 2012. https://tools.ietf.org/html/rfc6749
7. Lebo, T., Sahoo, S., McGuinness, D., Belhajjame, K., Cheney, J., Corsar, D., Garijo, D., Soiland-Reyes, S., Zednik, S., Zhao, J.: PROV-O: The PROV Ontology. W3C Recommendation, W3C, April 2013. http://www.w3.org/TR/prov-o/
8. Tramp, S., Frischmuth, P., Ermilov, T., Shekarpour, S., Auer, S.: An architecture of a distributed semantic social network. Semant. Web **5**(1), 77–95 (2014)

---

[4] An annotated demonstration video is available at http://downloads.eccenca.com/2015/03/13/eswc2015-lucid-demo.mp4.

Evaluating Entity Annotators Using GERBIL

Ricardo Usbeck^(✉), Michael Röder, and Axel-Cyrille Ngomo Ngonga

University of Leipzig, Leipzig, Germany
{usbeck,roeder,ngonga}@informatik.uni-leipzig.de

Abstract. The need to bridge between the unstructured data on the Document Web and the structured data on the Web of Data has led to the development of a considerable number of annotation tools. However, these tools are hard to compare due to the diversity of data sets and measures used for evaluation. We will demonstrate GERBIL, an evaluation framework for semantic entity annotation that provides developers, end users and researchers with easy-to-use interfaces for the agile, fine-grained and uniform evaluation of annotation tools on 11 different data sets within 6 different experimental settings on 6 different measures.

1 Introduction

The need for extracting structured data from text has led to the development of a large number of tools dedicated to the extraction of structured data from unstructured data (see [4] for an overview). In this demo, we present GERBIL, a framework for the evaluation of entity annotation frameworks. GERBIL provides a GUI that allows (1) configuring and running experiments, (2) assigning persistent URLs to experiments (better reproducibility and archiving), (3) exporting the results of the experiments in human- and machine-readable formats as well as (4) displaying the results w.r.t. the data sets and the features of the data sets on which the experiments were performed.

GERBIL is an open-source and extensible framework that allows evaluating tools against (currently) 9 different annotators on 11 different data sets within 6 different experiment types. To ensure that our framework is useful to both end users and tool developers, its architecture and interface were designed to allow (1) the easy integration of annotators through REST services, (2) the easy integration of data sets via DataHub[1], file uploads or direct source code integration, (3) the addition of new performance measures, (4) the provision of diagnostics for tool developers and (5) the portability of results. More information on GERBIL as well as a link to the online demo can be found at the project webpage at http://gerbil.aksw.org.

2 GERBIL in a Nutshell

An overview of GERBIL's architecture is given in Fig. 1. Based on this architecture, we will explain the features that we will present in the demonstration of the GERBIL framework.

---

[1] http://datahub.io.

© Springer International Publishing Switzerland 2015
F. Gandon et al. (Eds.): ESWC 2015, LNCS 9341, pp. 159–164, 2015.
DOI: 10.1007/978-3-319-25639-9_31

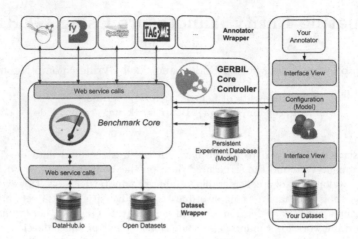

Fig. 1. Overview of GERBIL's abstract architecture. Interfaces to users and providers of data sets and annotators are marked in blue (Color figure online).

Feature 1: Experiment types. An experiment type defines the way used to solve a certain problem when extracting information. GERBIL extends the six experiments types provided by the BAT framework [1] (including entity recognition and disambiguation). With this extension, our framework can deal with gold standard data sets and annotators that link to any knowledge base, e.g., DBpedia, BabelNet [3] etc., as long as the necessary identifiers are URIs. During the demo, we will show how users can select the type of experiments in the interface (see Fig. 2) and explain the different types of experiments.

Fig. 2. Experiment configuration screen.

Feature 2: Matchings. GERBIL offers three types of matching between a gold standard and the results of annotation systems: a *strong entity matching* for URLs, as well as a *strong* and a *weak annotation matching* for entities. The selection and an explanation of the types of matching for given experiments will be part of the demo (see Fig. 2).

Feature 3: Metrics. Currently, GERBIL offers six measures subdivided into two groups: the micro- and the macro-group of precision, recall and f-measure. As shown in Fig. 3(a), these results are displayed using interactive spider diagrams

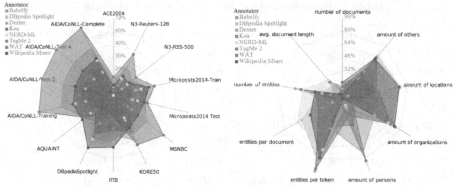

(a) Example spider diagram of recent A2KB experiments with weak annotation matching.

(b) Spider diagram of correlations between annotation results and data set features.

Fig. 3. Spider diagrams generated by the GERBIL interface.

that allow the user to easily (1) get an overview of the performance of single tools, (2) compare tools with each other and (3) gather information on the performance on tools on particular data sets. We will show how to interact with our spider diagrams during the demo.

Feature 4: Diagnostics. An important novel feature of our interface is that it displays the correlation between the features of data sets and the performance of tools (see Fig. 3(b)). By these means, we ensure that developers can easily gain an overview of the performance of tools w.r.t. a set of features and thus detect possible areas of improvement for future work.

Feature 5: Annotators. The main goal of GERBIL is to simplify the comparison of novel and existing entity annotation systems in a comprehensive and reproducible way. Therefore, GERBIL offers several ways to implement novel entity annotation frameworks. We will show how to integrate annotators into GERBIL by using a Java adapter as well as a *NIF-based Service* [2]. Currently, GERBIL offers 9 entity annotation systems with a variety of features, capabilities and experiments out-of-the-box, including Illinois Wikifier, DBpedia Spotlight, TagMe, AIDA, KEA, WAT, AGDISTIS, Babelfy, NERD-ML and Dexter [4].

Feature 6: Data sets. Table 1 shows the 11 sets data sets available via GERBIL. Thank to the large number of formats, topics and features of the datasets, GERBIL allows carrying out diverse experiments. During the demo, we will show how to add more data sets to GERBIL.

Feature 7: Output. GERBIL's main aim is to provide comprehensive, reproducible and publishable experiment results. Hence, GERBIL's experimental output is represented as a table containing the results, as well as embedded JSON-LD[2] RDF data. During the demo, we will show the output generated

---

[2] http://www.w3.org/TR/json-ld/.

Table 1. Features of the data sets and their documents.

Corpus	Topic	Format	Experiment	Size	Avg. Entity/Doc.
ACE2004	News	MSNBC	Sa2KB	57	4.44
AIDA/CoNLL	News	CoNLL	Sa2KB	1393	19.97
Aquaint	News	-	Sa2KB	50	14.54
IITB	Mixed	XML	Sa2KB	103	109.22
KORE 50	Mixed	NIF/RDF	Sa2KB	50	2.86
Meij	Tweets	TREC	Rc2KB	502	1.62
Microposts2014	Tweets	-	Sa2KB	3505	0.65
MSNBC	News	MSNBC	Sa2KB	20	32.50
N^3 Reuters-128	News	NIF/RDF	Sa2KB	128	4.85
N^3 RSS-500	RSS-feeds	NIF/RDF	Sa2KB	500	0.99
Spotlight Corpus	News	NIF/RDF	Sa2KB	58	5.69

by GERBIL for the different experiments implemented and show how the RDF
results can be used for the sake of archiving results. Moreover, we will show how
to retrieve experimental results using the permanent URI generated by GERBIL.

3   Evaluation

To ensure that GERBIL can be used in practical settings, we investigated the
effort needed to use GERBIL for the evaluation of novel annotators. To achieve
this goal, we surveyed the workload necessary to implement a novel annotator
into GERBIL compared to the implementation into previous diverse frameworks.
Our survey comprised five developers with expert-level programming skills in
Java. Each developer was asked to evaluate how much time he/she needed to
write the code necessary to evaluate his/her framework on a new data set. Further details pertaining to this evaluation are reported in the research paper to
this demo [4].

Overall, the developers reported that they needed between 1 and 4 h to
achieve this goal (4x 1-2 h, 1x 3-4 h), see Fig. 4(a). Importantly, all developers
reported that they needed either the same or even less time to integrate their
annotator into GERBIL. This result in itself is of high practical significance
as it means that by using GERBIL, developers can evaluate on (currently) 11
sets data sets using the same effort they needed for 1, which is a gain of more
than 1100 %. Moreover, all developers reported they felt comfortable—4 points
on average on a 5-point Likert scale between very uncomfortable (1) and very
comfortable (5)—implementing the annotator in GERBIL. Even though small,
this evaluation suggests that implementing against GERBIL does not lead to
any overhead. Furthermore, the interviewed developers represent a majority of
the active research and development community in the are of entity annotation
systems.

An interesting side-effect of having all these frameworks and data sets in a central framework is that we can now benchmark the different frameworks with respect to their runtimes within exactly the same experimental settings. For example, we evaluated the runtimes of the different approaches in GERBIL for the A2KB experiment type on the MSNBC data set, see Fig. 4(b).

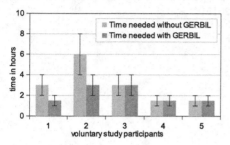
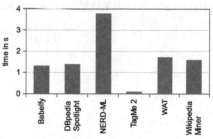

(a) Comparison of effort needed to implement an adapter for an annotation system.

(b) Runtime per document for the A2KB experiment type on the MSNBC data set.

Fig. 4. Overview of GERBIL evaluation results.

4   Conclusion and Future Work

In this paper, we presented a demo for GERBIL, a platform for the evaluation of annotation frameworks. We presented the different features that make the GERBIL interface easy to use and informative both for end users and developers. With GERBIL, we aim to push annotation system developers to better quality and wider use of their frameworks as well as include the provision of persistent URLs for reproducibility and archiving. GERBIL extends the state-of-the-art benchmarks by the capability of considering the influence of NIL attributes and the ability of dealing with data sets and annotators that link to different knowledge bases. In future work, we aim to provide a new theory for evaluating annotation systems and display this information in the GERBIL interface.

Acknowledgments. Parts of this work were supported by the FP7 project GeoKnow (GA No. 318159) and the BMWi project SAKE (GA No. 01MD15006E).

References

1. Cornolti, M., Ferragina, P., Ciaramita, M.: A framework for benchmarking entity-annotation systems. In: 22nd World Wide Web Conference (2013)
2. Hellmann, S., Lehmann, J., Auer, S., Brümmer, M.: Integrating NLP using linked data. In: Alani, H., et al. (eds.) ISWC 2013, Part II. LNCS, vol. 8219, pp. 98–113. Springer, Heidelberg (2013)

3. Navigli, R., Ponzetto, S.P.: BabelNet: the automatic construction, evaluation and application of a wide-coverage multilingual semantic network. Artif. Intell. **193**, 217–250 (2012)
4. Usbeck, R., Röder, M., Ngomo Ngonga, A.-C., Baron, C., Both, A., Brümmer, M., Ceccarelli, D., Cornolti, M., Cherix, D., Eickmann, B., Ferragina, P., Lemke, C., Moro, A., Navigli, R., Piccinno, F., Rizzo, G., Sack, H., Speck, R., Troncy, R., Waitelonis, J., Wesemann, L.: GERBIL - general entity annotation benchmark framework. In: 24th WWW Conference (2015)

Interactive Comparison of Triple Pattern Fragments Query Approaches

Joachim Van Herwegen[✉], Ruben Verborgh, Erik Mannens,
and Rik Van de Walle

Multimedia Lab – Ghent University – iMinds, Gaston Crommenlaan 8 Bus 201,
B-9050 Ledeberg-Ghent, Belgium
joachim.van.herwegen@ugent.be

Abstract. In order to reduce the server-side cost of publishing queryable Linked Data, Triple Pattern Fragments (TPF) were introduced as a simple interface to RDF triples. They allow for SPARQL query execution at low server cost, by partially shifting the load from servers to clients. The previously proposed query execution algorithm provides a solution that is highly inefficient, often requiring an amount of HTTP calls that is magnitudes larger than the optimal solution. We have proposed a new query execution algorithm with the aim to solve this problem. Our solution significantly improves on the current work by maintaining a complete overview of the query instead of just looking at local optima. In this paper, we describe a demo that allows a user to easily compare the results of both implementations. We show both query results and number of executed HTTP calls, proving a clear picture of the difference between the two algorithms.

Keywords: Linked data · SPARQL · Query execution · Query optimization · Demo

1 Introduction

In the past few years, there has been a steady increase of available RDF data [3]. If a publisher decides to provide live queryable access to datasets, the de-facto default choice is to offer a public SPARQL endpoint [2]. The downside of the flexibility of SPARQL is that some queries require significant processing power. Asking a lot of these complex queries can put a heavy load on the server, causing a significant delay or even downtime. Recently, Triple Pattern Fragments (TPF, [5]) were introduced as a way to reduce this load on the server by restricting the TPF server interface to more simple queries. Clients can then obtain answers to complex SPARQL queries by requesting multiple simple queries and combining the results locally. Concretely, a TPF server only replies to requests for a single triple pattern. The response of the server is then a list of matching triples, which can be paged in case the response would be too large. Furthermore, each TPF contains metadata and hypermedia controls to aid clients with query execution.

© Springer International Publishing Switzerland 2015
F. Gandon et al. (Eds.): ESWC 2015, LNCS 9341, pp. 165–168, 2015.
DOI: 10.1007/978-3-319-25639-9_32

The biggest challenge for the client is deciding which triple pattern queries result in the most efficient solution strategy. Since every subquery causes a new HTTP request to the server, minimizing the number of queries reduces the network load and improves the total response time. The algorithm proposed by Verborgh et al. [5] is greedy: at each decision point, clients choose the local optimum by executing the request that has the fewest results. This works fine for certain classes of queries, but others can perform quite badly.

In our paper at ESWC2015 [4] we propose a new algorithm that tries to minimize the number of HTTP requests. For our demo we have created an interface to compare the performance of both algorithms. This allows users to easily see the difference in HTTP calls and execution time for both implementations.

2   Related Work

The two most common ways to access linked data on the web currently are SPARQL endpoints and data dumps. Both of these have certain disadvantages.

SPARQL endpoints execute the complete query the client aims to solve. These queries can be quite complex and require a lot of computation power. This likely contributes to the low availability of public SPARQL endpoints [1].

An other solution is downloading a data dump from the server and then executing the query locally on the data dump. This entails a high cost for the client, and a major disadvantage is that data is not live: all changes that happen after the data was downloaded are not visible to the client. If the client wants an update, the entire dataset has to be downloaded again from the server.

Triple Pattern Fragments is a solution that proposes a middle ground between fully-fledged SPARQL endpoints and simple data dumps [5]. Server only answer single Basic Graph Pattern (BGP) queries which are combined client-side to answer complete SPARQL queries. This methodology has the live data advantage of SPARQL endpoints and the low server cost of data dumps.

3   Problem Statement

Because of the greedy implementation of the original algorithm [5], the performance varies highly between different SPARQL queries: for some queries the greedy solution might be optimal, while for others it is exponentially worse. We will exemplify this with such a worst-case query and show how our, more optimal, solution handles it.

```
SELECT ?person ?city WHERE {
   ?person a dbpedia-owl:Architect. # p₁ :              ±1,200 triples
   ?person dbpprop:birthplace ?city. # p₂ :           ±430,000 triples
   ?city dc:subject dbpedia:Capitals_in_Europe. # p₃ :      57 triples
}
```

Listing 1.1. SPARQL query to find European architects

We assume a page size of 100, i.e. a single server call returns 100 results for the corresponding triple pattern. Since the original implementation is greedy, it executes the query as follows:

1. Since p_3 has the least triples, download all corresponding ?city bindings.
2. Bind all the ?city values to p_2 and request all 57 patterns from the server, this requires a total of 430 calls since some cities have multiple pages of people and results in a total of 43,000 ?person bindings.
3. Bind all the ?person values to p_1 and request all 43,000 patterns from the server, requiring an additional 43,000 calls.

This results in a total of $\pm$ 43,431 HTTP calls. A more optimal solution would be the following:

1. Download all ?city bindings from p_3. (1 call)
2. Download all ?person bindings from p_2 after binding the values from the previous step. (430 calls)
3. Download all ?person bindings from p_1. (12 calls)
4. Locally compare the results from the previous two steps to find the final ?person bindings. (0 calls)

This solution only requires $\pm$ 443 calls, which is 100 times less than the greedy solution. Our algorithm [4] tries to solve queries in by checking which HTTP calls might provide the most efficient results. This is done by looking at the complete query all the time, not just the local bindings we got from the previous HTTP call.

4   Algorithm Comparison Demo

The demo which will be shown at the conference is an adaption of the Linked Data Fragments (LDF) web client found at http://client.linkeddatafragments. org/. It features an enhanced client which executes queries twice, for research purposes: once with the original algorithm and once with the optimized implementation. An example of this can be seen in Fig. 1. Besides just showing the results, we also show some statistics about how the algorithms operate, such as the number of HTTP calls executed so far and how many results they have found with these HTTP calls. This allows the user to see the immediate effect of our implementation. The greedy algorithm might execute its HTTP calls faster, since it requires less local processing, while still having found less results. As mentioned in our paper [4], the optimized algorithm is a lot better in some cases while only being equal or even worse in other cases. With our demo it will be easy to see the different results for all types of queries.

The optimized algorithm we propose has a more complex execution than the original algorithm. This demo allows a user to more easily follow the execution without having read or fully understood the original paper. This might help people who want to extend the implementation to allow for more advanced queries or to improve the existing parts.

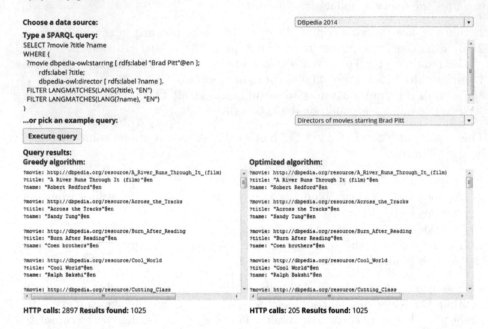

Fig. 1. The demonstrator shows live SPARQL query execution over the DBpedia fragments interface (http://fragments.dbpedia.org/). On the left-hand side are the results of the greedy algorithm; the right-hand side shows the optimized algorithm.

References

1. Buil-Aranda, C., Hogan, A., Umbrich, J., Vandenbussche, P.-Y.: SPARQL web-querying infrastructure: ready for action? In: Alani, H., et al. (eds.) ISWC 2013, Part II. LNCS, vol. 8219, pp. 277–293. Springer, Heidelberg (2013). http://link.springer.com/chapter/10.1007/978-3-642-41338-4_18

2. Harris, S., Seaborne, A.: SPARQL 1.1 query language. Recommendation, World Wide Web Consortium, March 2013. http://www.w3.org/TR/sparql11-query/

3. Schmachtenberg, M., Bizer, C., Paulheim, H.: Adoption of the linked data best practices in different topical domains. In: Mika, P., et al. (eds.) ISWC 2014, Part I. LNCS, vol. 8796, pp. 245–260. Springer, Heidelberg (2014). http://dx.doi.org/10.1007/978-3-319-11964-9_16

4. Van Herwegen, J., Verborgh, R., Mannens, E., Van de Walle, R.: Query execution optimization for clients of triple pattern fragments. In: Gandon, F., Sabou, M., Sack, H., d'Amato, C., Cudré-Mauroux, P., Zimmermann, A. (eds.) ESWC 2015. LNCS, vol. 9088, pp. 302–318. Springer, Heidelberg (2015)

5. Verborgh, R., Vander Sande, M., Colpaert, P., Coppens, S., Mannens, E., Van de Walle, R.: Web-scale querying through linked data fragments. In: Proceedings of the 7th Workshop on Linked Data on the Web, April 2014. http://events.linkeddata.org/ldow2014/papers/ldow2014_paper_04.pdf

Rubya: A Tool for Generating Rules for Incremental Maintenance of RDF Views

Vânia M.P. Vidal[1], Marco A. Casanova[2], Valéria M. Pequeno[3]([⊠]),
Narciso Arruda[1], Diego Sá[1], and José M. Monteiro[1]

[1] Federal University of Ceará, Fortaleza, CE, Brazil
{vvidal,narciso,diego,jmmfilho}@lia.ufc.br
[2] Pontifical Catholic University of Rio de Janeiro, Rio de Janeiro, RJ, Brazil
casanova@inf.puc-rio.br
[3] INESC-ID Lisbon, Porto Salvo, Portugal
vmp@inesc-id.pt

Abstract. We present *Rubya*, a tool that automatically generates the RDF view defined on top of relational data and all rules required for the incremental maintenance of the RDF view. Our approach relies on the designer to specify a mapping between the relational schema and a target ontology and results in a specification of how to represent relational schema concepts in terms of RDF classes and properties of the designers choice. Based on this mapping, the rules for incrementally maintenance of the RDF view are generated.

Keywords: RDF view maintenance · RDB-to-RDF · Linked data

1 Introduction

The Linked Data initiative [1] promotes the publication of previously isolated databases as interlinked RDF triple sets, creating a global scale dataspace known as the Web of Data. Since large volume of data is stored in relational data, making relational databases accessible to the Web of Data has special significance.

A general way to publish relational data in RDF format is to create RDF views of the relational data. The contents of views can be materialized to improve query performance and data availability. However, to be useful, a materialized view must be continuously maintained to reflect dynamic source updates.

In this demo, we show a framework named *RUBYA* (**R**ules **by** assertion), based on rules, for the incremental maintenance of external RDF views defined on top of relational data. *Rubya* has two main functionalities: (1) the generation of mappings between the relational schema and a target ontology; and (2) the generation of the rules required for the incremental maintenance of the view, based on the mapping initially generated. In Sect. 2, we further detail the *Rubya* tool.

The demo video is available at http://tiny.cc/rubya. First, the video shows, with the help of a real-world application, the process of defining the RDF view

© Springer International Publishing Switzerland 2015
F. Gandon et al. (Eds.): ESWC 2015, LNCS 9341, pp. 169–174, 2015.
DOI: 10.1007/978-3-319-25639-9_33

and generating the maintenance rules with *Rubya*. Then, it shows some practical examples of using the rules for incremental maintenance of a materialized RDF view. For more information see http://www.arida.ufc.br/ivmf/.

2   Generating Rules with *Rubya*

Figure 1 depicts the main components of the framework. Briefly, the administrator of a relational database, using *Rubya*, should create RDF views and define a set of rules using *Rubya* - Fig. 1(a). These rules are responsible for: (i) computing the view maintenance statements necessary to maintain a materialized view **V** with respect to base updates; and (ii) sending the view maintenance statements to the *view controller* of **V** - Fig. 1(b). The rules can be implemented using triggers. Hence, no middleware system is required. The *view controller* for the RDF view has the following functionality: (i) receives the view maintenance updates from the RDB server and (ii) applies the updates to the view accordingly.

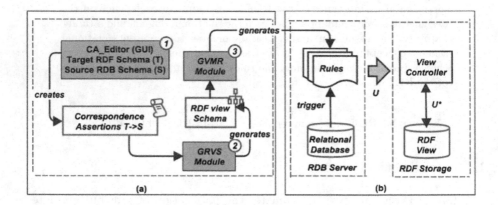

Fig. 1. Suggested framework.

The process of defining the RDF view and generating the maintenance rules with *Rubya* consists of three steps:

STEP 1 (Mapping specification): Using the correspondence assertions editor of *Rubya*, the user loads the source and target schema and then he can draw Correspondence Assertions (CAs) to specify the mapping between the target RDF schema and the source relational schema. The demo video shows how the *CA_Editor* helps the user graphically to define CAs.

A CA can be: (i) a class correspondence assertion (CCA), which matches a class and a relation schema; (ii) an object property correspondence assertion (OCA), which matches an object property with paths (list of foreign keys) of a relation schema; or (iii) a datatype property correspondence assertion (DCA), which matches a datatype property with attributes or paths of a relation schema.

CAs have a simple syntax and semantics and yet suffice to capture most of the subtleties of mapping relational schemas into RDF schemas. Figure 2 shows some examples of correspondence assertions between the relational schema *ISWC_REL* and the ontology *CONF_OWL*. CCA1 matches the class *foaf:Person* with the relation Persons. We refer the reader to [7] for the details and motivation of the mapping formalism.

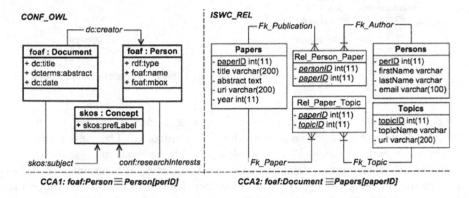

Fig. 2. *CONF_OWL* and *ISWC_REL* schemas and some examples of CAs.

STEP 2 (RDF view creation): The GRVS module automatically generates the RDF view schema, which is induced by the CAs defined in Step 1. The vocabulary of the RDF view schema contains all the elements of the target RDF schema that match an element of the source relational schema.

STEP 3 (Rule generation): The GVMR module automatically generates the set of rules required to maintain the RDF view defined in Step 2. The process of generating the rules for a view **V** consists of the following steps: (a) Obtain, based on the CAs of **V**, the set of all relations in the relational schema that are relevant to **V**. (b) For each relation R that is relevant to **V**, three rules are generated to account for insertions, deletions and updates on R.

Two procedures, *GVU_INSERTonR* and *GVU_DELETEonR*, are automatically generated, at view definition time, based on the CAs of **V** that are relevant to R. Note that an update is treated as a deletion followed by an insertion, as usual. *GVU_INSERTonR* takes as input a tuple r_{new} inserted in R and returns the updates necessary to maintain the view **V**. *GVU_DELETEonR* takes as input a tuple r_{old} deleted from R and returns the updates necessary to maintain the view **V**. In [7], we present the algorithms that compile *GVU_INSERTonR* and *GVU_DELETEonR* based on the CAs of **V** that are relevant to R.

Once the rules are created, they are used to incrementally maintain the materialized RDF view. For example, Fig. 3 shows the process to update a RDF view when an insertion occurs on the relation Papers. When an insertion occurs on

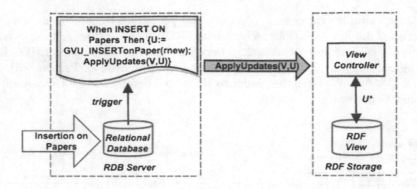

Fig. 3. Using the rules generated by *Rubya* when insertions occurs on Papers.

Papers, a corresponding trigger is fired. The trigger computes the view maintenance statements U, and sends it to the view controller. The view controller computes the view updates U*, and applies it to the view state.

Rubya was developed in Java. Actually, we use Oracle as the relational database system and Fuseki as RDF store. However, we can easily adapt *Rubya* for other relational database system and RDF store. Jena [2] is used for communication with Fuseki.

3   Related Work

There is significant work on reusing relational data in terms of RDF (see a survey in [5,6]). Karma [4], for example, is a tool to semi-automatically create mapping from a source to a target ontology. In our tool, the user defines mappings between a source and a target ontology using a GUI. The novelty of our proposal is that we generate rules to maintain the RDF views.

[3] proposes the R3M tool in order to maintain RDF views over RDF databases. In that work, there is not any difference between the structure of the view and the data source, i.e., the RDF view contains a subset of classes and properties of the data source. In this case, direct mappings are used to match the elements of the view and the data source and the process of the view maintenance is very simple. Our approach differs from [3] mainly in two aspects: (1) our data source are relational databases, while the above papers is RDF databases; (2) our tool deals with more complex types of mappings. For example, our tool can deal with situations such as, in the relational database the attributes *firstName* and *lastName* be mapped to the property *foaf:name*. We also can deal with mappings when the RDF view describes a property which the data source does not include, although the source can express it through a path which it possess. For example, consider the schemas in Fig. 2. The property *skos:subject* can be mapped to the path of Papers that includes the foreign keys *fk_Paper* and *fk_Topics*. For these cases involving complex mappings, simple view maintenance

approaches are not a solution, and other approaches are necessary in order to correctly translate updates from the data source into updates in the RDF view.

4   Conclusions

In this paper, we present *Rubya*, a tool for incremental maintenance of external RDF views defined on top of relational data. More details about the theoretical fundaments and algorithms used in *Rubya* can be found in [7]. A preliminary version of *Rubya* was presented, as poster, in [8].

Our approach is very effective for an externally maintained view because: the view maintenance rules are defined at view definition time; no access to the materialized view is required to compute the view maintenance statements propagated by the rules; and the application of the view maintenance statements by the *view controller* does not require any additional queries over the data source to maintain the view. This is important when the view is maintained externally [7], because accessing a remote data source may be too slow.

The use of rules is therefore an effective solution for the incremental maintenance of external views. However, creating rules that correctly maintain an RDF view can be a complex process, which calls for tools that automate the rule generation process, as *Rubya* does.

Acknowledgments. This work was partly funded by FCT with references UID/ CEC/50021/2013 and EXCL/EEI-ESS/0257/2012 (DataStorm) and grants SFRH/ BPD/76024/2011; by CNPq, under grants 442338/2014-7 and 303332/2013-1; and by FAPERJ, under grant E-26/201.337/2014.

References

1. Berners-Lee, T.: Design issues: Linked data (2006). http://www.w3.org/ DesignIssues/LinkedData.html
2. Carroll, J.J., Dickinson, I., Dollin, C., Reynolds, D., Seaborne, A., Wilkinson, K.: Jena: implementing the semantic web recommendations. In: WWW Alt 2004, pp. 74–83. ACM, New York (2004)
3. Deng, Y., Hung, E., Subrahmanian, V.: Maintaining RDF views. Technical report CS-TR-4612 (UMIACS-TR-2004-54), University of Maryland Institute for Advanced Computer Studies (2004)
4. Knoblock, C.A., et al.: Semi-automatically mapping structured sources into the semantic web. In: Simperl, E., Cimiano, P., Polleres, A., Corcho, O., Presutti, V. (eds.) ESWC 2012. LNCS, vol. 7295, pp. 375–390. Springer, Heidelberg (2012)
5. Michel, F., Montagnat, J., Faron-Zucker, C.: A survey of RDB to RDF translation approaches and tools. Research report, I3S (2014)
6. Spanos, D.E., Stavrou, P., Mitrou, N.: Bringing relational databases into the semantic web: a survey. Semant. Web J. **3**(2), 169–209 (2012)

7. Vidal, V.M.P., Casanova, M.A., Cardoso, D.S.: Incremental maintenance of RDF views of relational data. In: Meersman, R., Panetto, H., Dillon, T., Eder, J., Bellahsene, Z., Ritter, N., De Leenheer, P., Dou, D. (eds.) ODBASE 2013. LNCS, vol. 8185, pp. 572–587. Springer, Heidelberg (2013)
8. Vidal, V.M.P., Casanova, M.A., Monteiro, J.M., Arruda Jr., N.M., Cardoso, D.S., Pequeno, V.M.: A framework for incremental maintenance of RDF views of relational data. In: ISWC 2014 Posters & Demonstrations Track, pp. 321–324 (2014)

Time-Aware Entity Search in DBpedia

Lei Zhang[1]([✉]), Wentao Chen[1], Thanh Tran[2], and Achim Rettinger[1]

[1] Institute AIFB, Karlsruhe Institute of Technology (KIT), Karlsruhe, Germany
{l.zhang,rettinger}@kit.edu, wentao.chen@student.kit.edu
[2] San Jose State University, San Jose, USA
ducthanh.tran@sjsu.edu

Abstract. Searching for entities is a common user activity on the Web. There is an increasing effort in developing entity search techniques in the research community. Existing approaches are usually based on static measures that do not reflect the time-awareness, which is a factor that should be taken into account in entity search. In this paper, we propose a novel approach to time-aware entity search in DBpedia, which takes into account both popularity and temporality of entities. The experimental results show that our approach can significantly improve the performance of entity search with temporal focus compared with the baselines.

1 Introduction

The ever-increasing quantities of entities in large knowledge bases on the Web, such as Wikipedia, DBpedia and YAGO, pose new challenges but at the same time open up new opportunities of information access on the Web. In this regard, many research activities involving entities have emerged in recent years. Entity search has become a major area of interest because users often search for specific entities instead of documents, which helps users to directly find the intended information. On the other hand, time-awareness is a crucial factor in entity search due to the high dynamics of the underlying data.

In this paper, we address the problem of searching entities for a given user query in a time-aware setting. We formulate the *time-aware entity search* task as follows: given an entity collection $E = \{e_1, e_2, \cdots, e_N\}$[1], the input is a user query $q = \langle s, t \rangle$, which consists of an entity name s and a time range of contiguous days $t = \{d_1, d_2, \cdots, d_M\}$, where d_i represents a specific day, and the output is the intended entity matching s of particular interest within t. Our approach allows users to restrict their search interests to a time range. However, in a real-life search scenario, users usually do not specify the time range explicitly. In this case, our system can easily use the current day on which users issue the query and a certain period of time before it (e.g., one week) as the time range. Assuming that users search for the entity name *Irving* on *2014-02-21* and the intended entity is *Kyrie Irving*, who won the NBA All-Star Game MVP Award

---

[1] We use DBpedia as the entity collection, which extracts various kinds of structured information from Wikipedia and each DBpedia entity is tied to a Wikipedia article.

© Springer International Publishing Switzerland 2015
F. Gandon et al. (Eds.): ESWC 2015, LNCS 9341, pp. 175–179, 2015.
DOI: 10.1007/978-3-319-25639-9_34

on *2014-02-17*, the time range can be specified by our system as, for example, one week *from 2014-02-15 to 2014-02-21*.

The challenge of our entity search task is name ambiguity, i.e., a entity name could refer to different entities. For entity linking [1,2], where the goal is to link words or phrases in text documents with entities in knowledge bases, the entity disambiguation can be performed based on the context in documents. Without such contextual information in our entity search scenario, we propose a novel approach by taking into account both *popularity* and *temporality* of entities.

2   Approach

In this section, we present our approach to *time-aware entity search* in DBpedia, where each DBpedia entity corresponds to a Wikipedia article. In order to rank entities for a query $q = \langle s, t \rangle$, we calculate the score $\text{Score}(e, s, t)$ for each entity e based on different components, which will be discussed in the following.

Candidate Entity Generation. Given a query entity name s, we first generate a set of candidate entities matching s, denoted as E_s. For this, we need to extract the *surface forms* of each entity, i.e., words or phrases that can be used to refer to the corresponding entity. Wikipedia provides several structures that associate entities with their *surface forms*. Similar to [2], we make use of the following structures in Wikipedia: (1) *titles of articles*: the title of each Wikipedia article is generally the most common name for the entity; (2) *redirect pages*: a redirect page exists for each alternative name that can be used to refer to an entity; (3) *disambiguation pages*: when multiple entities could have the same name, a disambiguation page in Wikipedia containing the references to those entities is usually created; (4) *anchor texts of hyperlinks*: articles in Wikipedia often contain hyperlinks with anchor texts pointing to the mentioned entities, which provide a very useful source of surface forms of linked entities.

Given an entity name s, the probability $P(e|s) = \frac{C(e,s)}{\sum_{e_i \in E_s} C(e_i,s)}$, where $C(e, s)$ denotes the number of links pointing to e with anchor text s, has been widely used to model the likelihood of observing $e \in E_s$ [1,2]. However, we do not integrate this distribution into our approach since it would unduly favor entities with more links and might result in poor performance as shown in the experiments.

In order to rank the candidate entities in E_s w.r.t. the time range t, we calculate $\text{Score}(e, s, t)$ for each entity $e \in E_s$ as

$$\text{Score}(e, s, t) = \text{Score}_{popu}(e, s, t) \cdot \text{Score}_{temp}(e, s, t) \tag{1}$$

where $\text{Score}_{popu}(e, s, t)$ represents the popularity of e and $\text{Score}_{temp}(e, s, t)$ captures its temporality. Both scoring functions employ the page view statistics, which capture the number of times Wikipedia pages have been requested, and thus can be treated as a query log of entities.

Popularity Ranking. An entity well-known to most people usually gets more page views than others that are relatively obscure. For example, the NBA player

Michael Jeffrey Jordan get more page views than the Berkeley professor Michael I. Jordan. Based on that, we use the page view statistics within a long period of time T (e.g., one or several years) to calculate Score$_{popu}(e, s, t)$ as

$$\text{Score}_{popu}(e, s, t) = \sum_{d_i \in T} C(e, d_i) \tag{2}$$

where $C(e, d)$ denotes the number of page views of entity e on date d. We choose T as the union of the time range t and the recent year before t in our experiments, which makes our popularity ranking function also time-dependent. As shown in the experiments, our popularity ranking achieves better results than the approach based on the well-known PageRank algorithm.

Temporality Ranking. The score Score$_{temp}(e, s, t)$ is of particular interest in this work. The intuition is an entity will likely get more page views when an event about it takes place. For example, an Olympic athlete will get more page views when he has won a medal during the Olympics. Therefore, we use page views of each entity as a proxy for interest and equate page view spike with it.

In this regard, we track per-day page views and maintain a sliding window of n days (with $n = 10$ in our experiments) over the previous page view counts to compute the spikes for each entity e. We first compute the mean $\mu(e, d)$ and standard deviation $\sigma(e, d)$ of page views for entity e w.r.t. date d

$$\mu(e, d) = \frac{1}{n} \sum_{d_i = d-n}^{d-1} C(e, d_i) \tag{3}$$

$$\sigma(e, d) = \sqrt{\frac{1}{n} \sum_{d_i = d-n}^{d-1} (C(e, d_i) - \mu(e, d))^2} \tag{4}$$

Similar to [3], we then calculate the page view spike $S(e, d)$ as

$$S(e, d) = \begin{cases} \frac{C(e,d) - \mu(e,d)}{\sigma(e,d)} & \text{if } \frac{C(e,d) - \mu(e,d)}{\sigma(e,d)} > k, \\ 0 & \text{otherwise} \end{cases} \tag{5}$$

where only the page view count $C(e, d)$ that is large enough, i.e., $\frac{C(e,d) - \mu(e,d)}{\sigma(e,d)} > k$ (k is set as 0.5 in our experiments), is taken into account to make a contribution to the page view spike. Based on that, we calculate Score$_{temp}(e, s, t)$ as

$$\text{Score}_{temp}(e, s, t) = \sum_{d_i \in t} S(e, d) \tag{6}$$

3   Evaluation

Existing datasets for evaluating entity search usually only aim to quantify the degree to which the entities are relevant to the keyword query without involving time aspects, which makes these datasets unsuitable for our task. Therefore, we asked volunteers to provide queries consisting of the entity name and the time range along with the underlying information needs, i.e., the intended entities. By filtering out the unambiguous queries, for which there is only one candidate entity, it results in a final dataset containing 30 queries. As quality criteria, we consider recall at cutoff rank k (recall@k) and Mean Reciprocal Rank (MRR).

Table 1. The experimental results.

Methods	recall@1	recall@5	recall@10	recall@20	MRR
LinkProb	0.00	0.22	0.38	0.59	0.11
PageRank	0.31	0.75	0.87	0.96	0.49
Popu	0.56	0.91	0.97	0.97	0.69
Temp	0.72	0.94	0.97	0.97	0.81
Popu+Temp	**0.78**	**0.97**	**1.00**	**1.00**	**0.85**

We conducted the experiments with several approaches: (1) the baseline approach based on the link probability $P(e|s)$, as discussed in Sect. 2, denoted as *LinkProb*; (2) the baseline approach based on PageRank algorithm performed on Wikipedia link structures, denoted as *PageRank*; (3) our approach using only popularity ranking (Eq. 2), denoted as *Popu*; (4) our approach using only temporality ranking (Eq. 6), denoted as *Temp*; (5) our approach using both *Popu* and *Temp* ranking (Eq. 1), denoted as *Popu+Temp*.

The experimental results are shown in Table 1. It is observed that our approach with both popularity and temporality ranking yields the best results. Compared with the baselines, our approach achieves a significant performance improvement. While both ranking functions used in our approach contribute to the final performance improvement, temporality ranking contributes the most and achieves the best results among the individual ranking functions.

4   Conclusions

In this paper, we address the problem of time-aware entity search, where we believe that time-awareness is a very important issue. For this purpose, we defined a scoring function that aims to rank entities based on both popularity (for a long period of time) and temporality (regarding the user's time range of interest). We have experimentally shown that our approach achieves a significant improvement over the baselines in terms of recall@k and MRR.

Acknowledgments. This work is supported by the European Community's Seventh Framework Programme FP7-ICT-2013-10 (XLiMe, Grant 611346).

References

1. Milne, D.N., Witten, I.H.: Learning to link with Wikipedia. In: CIKM, pp. 509–518 (2008)
2. Shen, W., Wang, J., Luo, P., Wang, M.: LINDEN: linking named entities with knowledge base via semantic knowledge. In: WWW, pp. 449 458 (2012)
3. Osborne, M., Petrović, S., Mccreadie, R., Macdonald, C., Ounis, I.: Bieber no more: first story detection using Twitter and Wikipedia. In: #TAIA (2012)

ESWC2015 Developers Workshop

Templating the Semantic Web via RSLT

Silvio Peroni[1,2][✉] and Fabio Vitali[1]

[1] Department of Computer Science and Engineering,
University of Bologna, Bologna, Italy
silvio.peroni@unibo.it, fabio@cs.unibo.it
[2] STLab-ISTC, Consiglio Nazionale Delle Ricerche, Rome, Italy

Abstract. In this paper we introduce *RSLT*, a simple transformation language for RDF data. RSLT organises the rendering of RDF statements as transformation templates associated to properties or resource types and producing HTML. A prototype based on *AngularJs* is presented and we also discuss some implementation details and examples.

Keywords: RDF dataset visualisation · RSLT · Templates

1 Introduction

Works introducing methods and tools for creating visual representations of RDF data exist, e.g., [2,3,5–7], and of course some visualisation interfaces are supported in existing triplestores such as Virtuoso[1]. Nonetheless, visualisation tools for RDF data are still far less sophisticated than reporting tools for other data types, e.g., for traditional databases. For instance, most of such tools display triplestore content as simple tabular data, provide little or no way to prioritise differently identificative, descriptive and secondary properties, or even to customise or reorganise the order in which properties are displayed; often, related entities are presented as an opaque IRI rather than some textual description of the nature and feature of the entity, so that readability is basically absent.

In order to determine the characteristics of adequate tools for readable representations of RDF datasets for the general public, we believe that some basic guidelines should be followed:

- the tool should be easy to integrate in a web-based application;
- it should be possible (even to non-Semantic Web people, e.g., practitioners of traditional web-based technologies such as HTML and XML) to represent convoluted OWL entities more or less as easily as individual RDF statements;
- related entities should be meant to be represented with readable and meaningful text or other representations rather than as the IRI they are represented by – but their IRI should still be available for special rendering needs (e.g., as destinations for links and HTML anchors);
- complex representations of main resources should be built by composition, i.e. by combining simple representations of lesser entities and properties.

---

[1] http://virtuoso.openlinksw.com/.

© Springer International Publishing Switzerland 2015
F. Gandon et al. (Eds.): ESWC 2015, LNCS 9341, pp. 183–189, 2015.
DOI: 10.1007/978-3-319-25639-9_35

Traditional reporting software tools have limitations, such as the complexity to integrate them in web-based architectures or the variety and complexity of approaches in generating and delivering the reports. Yet, we found XSLT [4] a fairly natural and sophisticated approach to provide presentation support to XML documents, and sought to provide something similar for RDF data.

In this paper we introduce *RSLT (RDF Stylesheet Language Transformations,* pronounced *result),* a simple transformation language for RDF data. RSLT organises rendering as transformation templates associated to resources, properties or resource types, produces HTML and can recursively call other templates. A browser-based prototype based on the *AngularJs* library has been created that allows client-based presentations of SPARQL constructs, and soon of Turtle datasets as well. The rest of the paper is organised as follows: in Sect. 2 we introduce the main constructs of RSLT. In Sect. 3 we introduce some implementation details of RSLT and few examples, and in Sect. 4 we conclude the paper by sketching out some future works.

2   RSLT

RDF Stylesheet Language Transformations (RSLT)[2], pronounced *result,* is a direct and trivial translation of (some parts of) the XSLT language into the RDF domain. Similarly to its noble ancestor, an RSLT document contains a number of templates that create fragments of output in some displayable format (e.g., HTML) when navigating through a graph of RDF statements. The fact that RDF graphs, differently than XML documents, lack a natural hierarchy in its internal organisation and that no obvious selector language for RDF exists[3] provide for some interesting complications of the original design, though.

Thus, while XSLT always starts transforming the root of an XML document, no such concept exists for RDF graphs, which therefore require a starting template such as the following one:

```
<template match='$start'>
  <div class="container">
    <applyTemplates select="??person foaf:familyName 'Horrocks'.">
    </applyTemplates></div></template>
```

The above template will be fired at the beginning of the process and will create an HTML `div` element, and will first select all entities whose `foaf:familyName` is "Horrocks", and then look for a reasonable template for each of them.

The lack of a correspondence for XPath forced us to invent a new syntax for `<applyTemplates>` selectors, liberally derived from the SPARQL query syntax, that allow templates to distinguish statements from entities. Thus, the selector "?person foaf:familyName 'Horrocks'." with a *single question mark (SQM)*

---

[2] RSLT is available on GitHub: https://github.com/fvitali/rslt. The tool as well as all the additional scripts are distributed under an ISC License, while the other related files such as HTML documents are distributed under a CC-BY 4.0 License.

[3] SPARQL cannot be considered as a pure selector language for RDF as XPath, used by XSLT, is. Rather, it is a full-featured query language, similar to XQuery for XML.

in the variable selects all *RDF statements* whose predicate is `foaf:familyName` and whose object equals "Horrocks". On the other hand, the selector "`??person foaf:familyName 'Horrocks'.`" with *double question marks (DQM)* selects a list of *RSLT entities*, where each RSLT entity is defined as the set of available statements that share the same subject. The DQM selector above can be converted as follows in SPARQL 1.1:

```
SELECT DISTINCT ?s ?p ?o WHERE {
  ?person foaf:familyName "Horrocks". { bind(?person as ?s) ?s ?p ?o. } }
```

RSLT templates can be either associated to RDF statements (by matching a triple with one or more unbound SQM variables), to a specific resource (by matching the IRI of the resource) or to resources of a particular type (by using a special syntax), as described in the following excerpts:

```
<!-- RSLT templates for RDF statements -->
<template match='?person foaf:familyName "Horrocks"'> ... </template>
<template match='?person foaf:familyName ?string'> ... </template>
<!-- RSLT templates for a particular resource -->
<template match='http://www.semanticlancet.eu/resource/person/ian-horrocks'>
    ... </template>
<!-- RSLT templates for resources of a particular type -->
<template match="?person -> foaf:Person"> ... </template>
```

Within a template all unbound variables are bounded to the relevant RLST entities and all associated properties are available for presentation. Any markup or content can be placed inside templates, and RSLT constructs can be specified to refer to literals or other resources associated to the bounded entities. Values in literal statements can be rendered immediately through `<valueOf>` elements, while values of resource statements are additional RSLT entities, and therefore are rendered through additional templates. For instance, the following is a complete template of a class:

```
<template match="?person -> foaf:Person">
  <p>Found <valueOf select="count(?person pro:holdsRoleInTime ?r)"></valueOf>
    papers authored by <valueOf select="?person foaf:givenName ?g"></valueOf>
    <valueOf select="?person foaf:familyName ?f"></valueOf>:</p>
  <ul><applyTemplates select='?person pro:holdsRoleInTime /
    pro:relatesToDocument ??work'></applyTemplates></ul></template>
```

Whenever the rendering engine comes across an entity of type `foaf:Person`, this template is triggered, creating an HTML fragment with a `<p>` element containing text and the values of data properties `foaf:givenName` and `foaf:family` `Name`, then an `<ul>` element containing the rendering recursively produced by selecting all entities `??work` related to `?person` through the chain of properties `pro:holdsRoleInTime / pro:relatedToDocument`. This rendering is generated by looking for and executing the templates that match the `??work` entities just selected. In order to avoid circularity in the selection of templates, a simple approach is taken to consider the template as *spent* when applied in a recursion, so it cannot be chosen and applied again inside itself. Once all relevant templates have been spent, if a template for a specific entity is needed again, a default one is applied that does not recurse, thus halting any potential circularity.

Given the strong dependance of the current implementation of RSLT to the AngularJS framework, a shorter syntax exists that uses the classical double brackets of the framework. Additionally, since all entities are in fact Javascript objects and the colon ":" is a forbidden character in Javascript variables, Javascript's dot notation is used and the underscore is used instead:

```
<template match="?person -> foaf:Person">
  <p>Found {{ count(person.pro_holdsRoleInTime) }} papers authored
    by {{person.foaf_givenName}} {{person.foaf_familyName}}:</p>
  <ul><applyTemplates select='?person pro_holdsRoleInTime /
    pro_relatesToDocument ??work'></applyTemplates></ul></template>
```

In addition to `<template>`, `<applyTemplates>` and `<valueOf>`, at the moment the RSLT language inherits from XSLT also constructs such as `<callTemplate>` and `<forEach>`, that have similar behaviour as their XSLT counterparts. Also, the template element inherits the `mode` and `priority` attributes, with similar functions to XSLT. Finally, the `<rslt>` element allows the specification of a triple store through the `triplestore` attribute, and element `<prefix>` allows the specification of prefixes for selectors and property names.

When executing `<applyTemplates>` and `<forEach>` instructions, RSLT verifies whether the requested entities are already locally available, and if not it proceeds to execute another SPARQL query to the triplestore. However, in order to avoid to run a large number of queries every time RSLT templates will match, RSLT implements a mechanism to preload (through the attribute `preload`) as many entities as needed, so that no further queries (or many less queries) need to be executed. In the following listing we show how this works, loading additional entities specified by the DQM variables in the `preload` attribute:

```
<template match='$start'>
  <applyTemplates select="??person foaf:familyName'Horrocks'."
    preload="?person pro:holdsRoleInTime ??role.
      ?role pro:relatesToDocument ??work."></applyTemplates></template>
```

In conclusion, RSLT is rather similar to its ancestor, XSLT, but for a few key differences, such as the specification of a different selector language, and the efficiency requirement that led us to include the *preload* attribute. The selector language is in itself just a subset of the SPARQL language, similarly to how the selector language XPath is but a subset of the query language XQuery, and for similar reasons. Would it be possible to just use an existing implementation of XSLT? Unfortunately, the requirements for non-circularity in template matching and the effort to adapt a new selector language to existing code probably makes this endeavour excessive and not worthy. We have rather reimplemented a few key commands of the language relying on a few peculiarities of AngularJs directives, as explained in the next section.

3   An Implementation of RSLT

A working implementation of the RSLT engine has been developed to run as an AngularJS module. In its simplest incarnation, a simple specification of the libraries and one line of Javascript is enough to have a full working instance of RSLT in the browser, as shown in the following listing:

```
<html ng-app="simplestRSLT">
  <head><script src="angular.js"> </script><script src="rslt.js"> </script>
    <script>var app = angular.module('simplestRSLT', ['rslt']);</script>
  </head>
  <body><rslt> ... </rslt></body>
</html>
```

The **ng-app** attribute of element **<html>** is required by AngularJs to create
an Angular application (named **'simplestRSLT'**), which corresponds to an empty
AngularJs module that simply includes and uses the RSLT library. Anywhere in
the body of the HTML document the **<rslt>** element creates the rendering of
the entities selected in its $start template.

Each element of the RSLT language is defined as an AngularJs directive,
which allows HTML to be extended with new markup and new element names.
AngularJs directives create nested contexts where only selected objects are accessible. This is a very easy mechanism for managing context entities in templates:
namely, each template can only access the entities that correspond to variables
in the match attribute, thereby ensuring clean and controlled processing of entities and properties. Each variable name is in fact bound bidirectionally to a
Javascript object that contains all triples of the corresponding entity, with the
additional precaution of converting into underscores all colons separating the
prefix from the actual name of the property. For instance, **foaf:familyName**
of the DQM variable **??person** is always available as **person.foaf_familyName**
within all directives/factories/filters in the current scope.

A little note on the RSLT syntax used in the current implementation: in
AngularJs a normalisation takes place for all directive names, where colons,
dashes and underscores are removed and converted into camelCase. This means
that **<apply-templates>**, **<apply:templates>** and **<apply_templates>** are all
equivalent to **<applyTemplates>**. The standard Angular recommendation is to
"use name-with-dashes for attribute names and camelCase for the corresponding
directive name", so in all our examples we are uing **<applyTemplates>** instead
of **<apply-templates>** as XSLT introduced. The same goes for **<forEach>** and
<valueOf> instead of **<for-each>** and **<value-of>**. They are all equivalent.

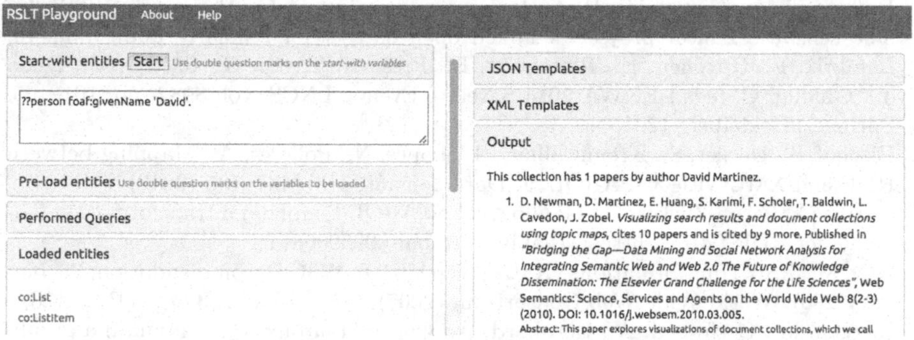

Fig. 1. The RSLT playground with a working presentation.

At the address http://www.fabiovitali.it/rslt/ it is possible to find four working examples of RSLT, all using as data source the Semantic Lancet Triplestore [1]. The first and the second examples are identical and show the simplest RSLT document accessing and rendering entities and properties across seven different classes – the only difference being in the rendering speed (which in example 1 is lacks any preload instruction in the queries).

The third example is a simple and straightforward reimplementation of the Lancet Data Browser (http://www.semanticlancet.eu/browser) already presented in [1], whose source code becomes incredibly simpler and more straightforward through the use of the RSLT library. Finally, example 4 (see Fig. 1) is a tool for the RSLT programmer that supports the interactive specifications of triplestores, start-with RSLT entities, pre-loaded RSLT entities, and templates (both in XML as described in this paper as well as in an experimental JSON format not yet documented) as well as checks the output of the RSLT transformation, the actual SPARQL queries sent to the triplestore and the list of entities that have been downloaded client-side by the full sequence of SPARQL queries generated through the execution of the RSLT templates.

4   Conclusions

In this paper we have introduced *RSLT*, i.e., a simple transformation language for RDF data. RSLT organises rendering of RDF statements in a triplestore through transformation templates recursively producing HTML. A prototype based on the *AngularJs* library has been presented. In the future, there are ongoing plans to integrate support for the management of Turtle and JSON-LD files, to extend the language to supporting more features of the XSLT language and of the query language. Finally, our plan is to study the requirements for providing support of the language on the server as well.

References

1. Bagnacani, A., Ciancarini, P., Di Iorio, A., Nuzzolese, A.G., Peroni, S., Vitali, F.: The semantic Lancet project: a linked open dataset for scholarly publishing. In: Lambrix, P., Hyvönen, E., Blomqvist, E., Presutti, V., Qi, G., Sattler, U., Ding, Y., Ghidini, C. (eds.) EKWA 2014 Satellite Events. LNCS, vol. 8982, pp. 101–105. Springer, Heidelberg (2015)
2. Bischof, S., Decker, S., Krennwallner, T., Lopes, N., Polleres, A.: Mapping between RDF and XML with XSPARQL. J. Data Semant. **1**(3), 147–185 (2012)
3. Corby, O., Faron-Zucker, C., Gandon, F.: SPARQL template: a transformation language for RDF (2014). https://hal.inria.fr/hal-00969068v1
4. Kay, M.: XSL Transformations (XSLT) Version 2.0. W3C Recommendation, 23 January 2007. World Wide Web Consortium (2007). http://www.w3.org/TR/xslt20/
5. Luggen, M., Gschwend, A., Bernhard, A., Cudré-Mauroux, P.: Uduvudu: a graph-aware and adaptive UI engine for linked data. In: Proceedings of LDOW 2015 (2015)

6. Pietriga, E., Bizer, C., Karger, D.R., Lee, R.: Fresnel: a browser-independent pre-sentation vocabulary for RDF. In: Cruz, I., Decker, S., Allemang, D., Preist, C., Schwabe, D., Mika, P., Uschold, M., Aroyo, L.M. (eds.) ISWC 2006. LNCS, vol. 4273, pp. 158–171. Springer, Heidelberg (2006)
7. Skjveland, M.G.: Sgvizler: a javascript wrapper for easy visualization of SPARQL result sets. In: Proceedings of the Workshops and Demo tracks of ESWC 2012 (2012)

Developing a Sustainable Platform for Entity Annotation Benchmarks

Michael Röder[(⊠)], Ricardo Usbeck, and Axel-Cyrille Ngonga Ngomo

University of Leipzig, Leipzig, Germany
{roeder,usbeck,ngonga}@informatik.uni-leipzig.de

Abstract. The existing entity annotation systems that drive the extraction of RDF from unstructured data are hard to compare as their evaluation relies on different data sets and measures. We developed GERBIL, an evaluation framework for semantic entity annotation that provides developers, end users and researchers with easy-to-use interfaces for the agile, fine-grained and uniform evaluation of 9 annotation tools on 11 different data sets within 6 different experimental settings on 6 different measures. In this paper, we present the developed interfaces, data flows and data structures. Moreover, we show how GERBIL supports a better reproducibility and archiving of experimental results.

1 Introduction

The need for extracting structured data from text has led to the development of a large number of tools dedicated to the extraction of structured data from unstructured data (see [6] for an overview). While these tools do provide evaluation results, these results are rarely fully comparable as they commonly rely on different data sets or different measures. This is partly due to data preparation being a tedious problem in the annotation domain due to the different formats of the gold standards as well as the different data representations across reference data sets. Recently, benchmarking frameworks such as the BAT-framework [3] or NERD-ML [5] for entity annotation systems have began addressing the problem on reproducible experiments for entity annotation. With GERBIL[1] we aim to unify experiment setups, ease implementation and testing effort as well as contribute to an open, repeatable, publishable and archivable open science area to foster an active community of entity annotation tool developers.

GERBIL goes beyond the state of the art by extending the BAT-framework [3] as well as Nerd-ML [5] in several dimensions. In particular we provide fine-grained diagnostics for annotation tools, enhanced reproducibility through archiving experiments and assigning URIs to them, easily publishable results by providing results both as RDF (for machines) and tables (for humans). Overall, we provide the following features:

Feature 1: Extensible experiment types. An experiment type defines the way used to solve a certain problem when extracting information. GERBIL

---

[1] More information and a demo can be found at http://gerbil.aksw.org.

© Springer International Publishing Switzerland 2015
F. Gandon et al. (Eds.): ESWC 2015, LNCS 9341, pp. 190–196, 2015.
DOI: 10.1007/978-3-319-25639-9_36

extends the six experiment types provided by the BAT framework [3] (including entity recognition and disambiguation) towards more general, URI based experiments. With this extension, our framework can deal with gold standard data sets and annotators that link to any knowledge base as long as the necessary identifiers are URIs.

Feature 2: Matchings. GERBIL offers three types of matching between a gold standard and the results of annotation systems: a *strong entity matching* for URIs, as well as a *strong* and a *weak annotation matching* for entities.

Feature 3: Measures. Currently, GERBIL offers six measures subdivided into two groups: the micro- and the macro-group of precision, recall and f-measure. As shown in Fig. 1(a), these results are displayed using interactive spider diagrams that allow the user to easily (1) get an overview of the performance of single tools and (2) compare tools.

Explicit definitions can be found in Usbeck et al. [6].

Feature 4: Diagnostics. An important novel feature of our interface is that it displays the correlation between the features of data sets and the performance of tools (see Fig. 1(b)). By these means, we ensure that developers can easily gain an fine-grained overview of the performance of tools and thus detect possible areas of improvement for future work.

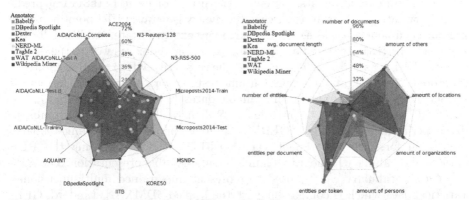

(a) Example spider diagram of recent A2KB experiments with weak annotation matching. (b) Spider diagram of correlations between annotation results and data set features.

Fig. 1. Spider diagrams generated by the GERBIL interface.

Feature 5: Annotators. Currently, GERBIL offers 9 entity annotation systems with a variety of features, capabilities and experiments out-of-the-box.

Feature 6: Data sets. The latest version of GERBIL offers 11 data sets. Thanks to the large number of formats, topics and features of the data sets, GERBIL allows carrying out diverse experiments.

Feature 7: Output. GERBIL's experimental output is represented as a table containing the results, as well as embedded JSON-LD[2] RDF data for the sake of archiving experiment results and additional information, e.g., the version of GERBIL that has been used. Moreover, GERBIL generates a permanent URI for each experimental result.

In this paper, we will give a detailed explanation of the different RDF data structures underlying GERBIL's architecture. We will explain the internal workflow of GERBIL and argue why it simplifies the implementation of further experiments, annotators, data sets, matchings and measures. We conclude by pointing at future work.

2   GERBIL's Interfaces, Dataflow, Structure

2.1   Datastructures

GERBIL unifies the different formats used by existing datasets and annotators. To this end, GERBIL's interfaces are mainly based on the *NLP Interchange Format* (NIF). This is a RDF-based Linked Data serialization which provides several advantages such as interoperability by standardization or query-ability. The *NIF-standard* assigns each document an URI as starting point and generates another Linked Data resource per semantic entity. Each document is a resource of type `nif:Context` and its content is the literal of its `nif:isString` predicate. Every entity is an own resource with a newly generated URI pointing to the original document via the `nif:referenceContext` predicate. Additionally the begin (`nif:beginIndex`) and end position (`nif:endIndex`) as well as the disambiguated URI (`itsrdf:taIdentRef`) and the respective KB (`itsrdf:taSource`) are stored. NIF's paramount position amongst corpora serialisation formats is evident by the growing number of available datasets [6].[3]

GERBIL's main aim is to provide comprehensive, reproducible and publishable experiment results. Thus, GERBIL enforces the use of a machine-readable description for each experiment via JSON-LD[4] RDF data using the RDF DataCube vocabulary [4] next to a human-readable table presentation. The *RDF DataCube* vocabulary can be used to represent fine-grained multidimensional, statistical data which is compatible with the Linked SDMX [2] standard. GERBIL models each experiment as `qb:Dataset` containing `qb:Observations` for each individual run of a annotator on a dataset. Each observation features the `qb:Dimensions` experiment type, matching type, annotator, corpus, and time. The evaluation measures and an error count are expressed as `qb:Measures`.[5]

GERBIL relies on the DataID ontology [1] to represent further metadata as well as annotator and corpus information. Besides metadata properties like

---

[2] http://www.w3.org/TR/json-ld/.

[3] The prefix `nif` stands for http://persistence.uni-leipzig.org/nlp2rdf/ontologies/ nif-core# while `itsrdf` is short for http://www.w3.org/2005/11/its/rdf#.

[4] http://www.w3.org/TR/json-ld/.

[5] `qb` is a prefix for for http://purl.org/linked-data/cube#.

titles, descriptions and authors, the source files of the open datasets themselves are linked as `dcat:Distributions`, allowing direct access to the evaluation corpora. Furthermore, ODRL license specifications in RDF are linked via `dc:license`, potentially facilitating automatically adjusted processing of licensed data by NLP tools. Licenses are further specified via `dc:rights`, including citations of the relevant publications.[6] To describe annotators in a similar fashion, we extended DataID for services. The class `Service`, to be described with the same basic properties as dataset, was introduced. To link an instance of a `Service` to its distribution the `datid:distribution` property was introduced as super property of `dcat:distribution`, i.e., the specific URI the service can be queried at. Furthermore, Services can have a number of `datid:Parameters` and `datid:Configurations`. Datasets can be linked via `datid:input` or `datid:output`.[7] An example JSON-LD for an archived experiment can be found below.

```
{
    "@graph" : [ {
        "@id" : "http://gerbil.aksw.org/gerbil/experiment?id=...#experiment_...",
        "@type" : [ "gerbil:Experiment", "qb:Dataset" ],
        "experimentType" : "gerbil:A2KB",
        "matching" : "gerbil:WeakAnnoMatch",
        "structure" : "gerbil:dsd",
        "label" : "Experiment 201503160001"
    }, {
        "@id" : "http://gerbil.aksw.org/gerbil/experiment?id=...#experiment_..._task_0",
        "@type" : "qb:Observation",
        "annotator" : "http://gerbil.aksw.org/gerbil/dataId/corpora/Babelfy",
        "dataset" : "http://gerbil.aksw.org/gerbil/dataId/annotators/ACE2004",
        "statusCode" : "-1",
        "timestamp" : "2015-03-16T12:31:52.469Z"
    } ],
    "@context" : {
        ...
    }
}
```

2.2   Workflow

Figure 2 shows the architecture of GERBIL with the data sets at the bottom, the annotators in the top and the user interface as well as user defined annotator and data set at the right. A GERBIL session starts at the configuration screen with which a user defines the experiment he is interested in. Each experiment is divided into tasks. A task comprises the evaluation of a single annotator using a single data set, is encapsulated into fault-tolerant classes and runs inside an own thread. Our fault-tolerance classes at two types of errors: (1) an annotator may return error codes for single documents, e.g., because of the missing ability to handle special characters. While other evaluation frameworks tend to cancel the experiments after an exception thrown by the annotator, GERBIL counts these smaller errors and reports them as part of the evaluation result. The second type of fault tolerance aims at (2) larger errors, e.g., the data set couldn't be loaded or the annotator is unreachable via its Web service. These run-time errors

---

[6] The prefix `dcat` stands for http://www.w3.org/ns/dcat# while `dc` is short for http://purl.org/dc/elements/1.1/.

[7] `datid` is a prefix for for http://dataid.dbpedia.org/ns/core#.

194   M. Röder et al.

are handled by storing one of the predefined error codes inside the experiment database. Therewith, we ensure that the user gets instant feedback if some parts of the experiment couldn't be performed as expected.

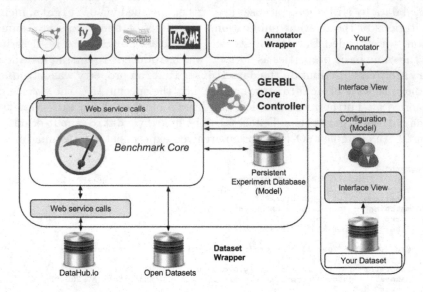

Fig. 2. Overview of GERBIL's abstract architecture. Interfaces to users and providers of data sets and annotators are marked in blue (Color figure online).

During a task, the single documents of a data set are sent to the annotator. After finishing the last document, the responses are evaluated. Currently, the evaluation is focused on the quality, i.e., precision, recall, F1-score and error counts, but can be extended. Moreover, a runtime is also available [6]. For some experiment types, e.g., the entity-linking tasks, the evaluation needs additional information. GERBIL is able to search for owl:sameAs links to close the gap between data sets and annotators that are based on different knowledge bases. Currently, this search is mainly based on the information inside the data set and retrieval of the entity mentioned by the annotator. The search could be extended by using local search indexes that contain mappings between well-known knowledge bases, e.g., DBpedia and Freebase. The results are currently written to an HSQL database[8].

2.3 Extensible Interfaces

The workflow of GERBIL is very general. An experiment has a certain experiment type, a matching, and a couple of datasets and annotators. Thus, it is easily possible to add new experiment types to GERBIL that are not part of

---

[8] http://hsqldb.org/.

the system, e.g., word sense disambiguation. One major advantage towards this form of extensibility is the usage of NIF for transferring the single documents. Since NIF is based on RDF the documents sent and received by the system as well as the datasets can be enriched with further information that can be used for the experiments. Thus, it is easy to add a new experiment type even if the type needs information that cannot be expressed with NIF, e.g., the entity typing task defined in the Open Knowledge Extraction Challenge 2015[9]. For this challenge, an adapted version of GERBIL has been developed[10]. In this version, an annotator that is able to identify the type of a new, unknown entity adds this type to the RDF model of its response. This information can't be understood directly by the response handling, but is kept and made available to the evaluation component of GERBIL. Thus, this type information can be used to evaluate the typing performance of an annotator.

3   Conclusion and Future Work

In this paper, we presented GERBIL, a platform for the evaluation, publishing and archiving of semantic entity annotation experiments. GERBIL extends the state-of-the-art benchmarks by dealing with data sets and annotators that link to different knowledge bases. Furthermore it offers extensible interfaces, reliable experiment descriptions as well as diagnostics and decision support. Our future work will comprise a better experiment task scheduling to achieve a higher efficiency. Another task is the improvement of the user interface towards a better intelligibility. Finally, we will devise a solution to ensure that GERBIL remains available to the community for the years to come.

Acknowledgments. Parts of this work were supported by the FP7 project GeoKnow (GA No. 318159) and the BMWi project SAKE (GA No. 01MD15006E).

References

1. Brümmer, M., Baron, C., Ermilov, I., Freudenberg, M., Kontokostas, D., Hellmann, S.: DataID: towards semantically rich metadata for complex datasets. In: I-SEMANTICS (2014)
2. Capadisli, S., Auer, S., Ngomo, A.-C.N.: Linked SDMX data. Semant. Web J. **5**, 1–8 (2013)
3. Cornolti, M., Ferragina, P., Ciaramita, M.: A framework for benchmarking entity-annotation systems. In: 22nd World Wide Web Conference (2013)
4. Cyganiak, R., Reynolds, D., Tennison, J.: The RDF Data Cube Vocabulary (2014). http://www.w3.org/TR/vocab-data-cube/

---

[9] http://2015.eswc-conferences.org/important-dates/call-OKEC.
[10] https://github.com/AKSW/gerbil/releases/tag/OKE2015.

5. Rizzo, G., van Erp, M., Troncy, R.: Benchmarking the extraction and disambiguation of named entities on the semantic web. In: 9th LREC (2014)
6. Usbeck, R., Röder, M., Ngomo, A.-C.N., Baron, C., Both, A., Brümmer, M., Ceccarelli, D., Cornolti, M., Cherix, D., Eickmann, B., Ferragina, P., Lemke, C., Moro, A., Navigli, R., Piccinno, F., Rizzo, G., Sack, H., Speck, R., Troncy, R., Waitelonis, J., Wesemann, L.: GERBIL - general entity annotation benchmark framework. In: 24th WWW Conference (2015)

Managing the Evolution and Preservation of the Data Web - First Diachron Workshop

A Diagnosis and Repair Framework for DL-LiteA KBs

Michalis Chortis and Giorgos Flouris[✉]

ICS-FORTH, Heraklion, Greece
{mhortis,fgeo}@ics.forth.gr

Abstract. Several logical formalisms have been proposed in the literature for expressing structural and semantic integrity constraints of Linked Open Data (LOD). Still, the integrity of the datasets published in the LOD cloud needs to be improved, as published data often violate such constraints, jeopardising the value of applications consuming linked data in an automatic way. In this work, we propose a novel, fully automatic framework for detecting and repairing violations of integrity constraints, by considering both explicit and implicit ontological knowledge. Our framework relies on the ontology language $DL\text{-}Lite_A$ for expressing several useful types of constraints, while maintaining good computational properties. The experimental evaluation shows that our framework is scalable for large datasets and numbers of invalidities exhibited in reality by reference linked datasets (e.g., DBpedia).

Keywords: Repairing · Diagnosis · $DL\text{-}Lite_A$ · Integrity constraints

1 Introduction

Linked Open Data (LOD) published on the Web of Data are often associated with various structural (e.g., primary key) and semantic (e.g., disjointness) integrity constraints. These constraints are usually expressed in ontological [19,22] or database [10] logic frameworks. However, LOD sources do not impose such constraints a priori, when data are created, so violations of integrity constraints must be detected and repaired a posteriori. As reported in [15], reference LOD sources, such as DBpedia[1] or LinkedGeoData[2], exhibit millions of violations (this is also verified by our own experiments – see Table 3).

In most of the cases, LOD are manually repaired by their curators or by their consuming applications, using, at best, diagnosis approaches or tools (e.g., [16,19,22], Stardog[3], QUONTO [1] etc.) for detecting violations of various types of integrity constraints. Obviously, the manual repair of millions of violations is a time-consuming and error-prone task, a fact that seriously limits the data quality of the available LOD sources. Thus, a major challenge is to automatically

---

[1] http://dbpedia.org.
[2] http://linkedgeodata.org.
[3] http://stardog.com/.

© Springer International Publishing Switzerland 2015
F. Gandon et al. (Eds.): ESWC 2015, LNCS 9341, pp. 199–214, 2015.
DOI: 10.1007/978-3-319-25639-9_37

detect and repair violations of both structural and semantic integrity constraints, especially when ontology reasoning is involved (i.e., detect and repair violations of constraints like disjointness, functional constraints etc., taking into account logical inference and its interaction with those constraints).

In this work, we propose a novel *automatic framework* for assisting curators in the arduous task of enforcing integrity constraints in large datasets. We provide an efficient methodology for detecting invalidities (*diagnosis*), as well as for automatically resolving them (*repairing*), in a manner that has minimal impact in terms of lost knowledge on the Knowledge Base (KB), according to the principles set out in earlier works [2,8].

We consider detecting and repairing of invalidities attributed to constraints of a purely logical nature (e.g., class disjointness). Constraints are expressed in the language $DL\text{-}Lite_A$ [4], which belongs to the $DL\text{-}Lite$ family of ontology languages that forms the foundation of the popular $OWL\ 2\ QL^4$ language. The choice of $DL\text{-}Lite_A$ was motivated by the fact that it is arguably rich enough to capture several useful types of integrity constraints that are used in practice in LOD datasets, and their interaction with implicit knowledge, while at the same time supporting efficient query answering [4].

The main contributions of our work are the following:

- We propose a framework for detecting and automatically repairing invalidities, for constraints that are expressed in $DL\text{-}Lite_A$, namely: concept/property disjointness constraints, property domain/range disjointness constraints and functional constraints. Diagnosis of invalidities related to both explicit and inferred constraints can be performed in linear time with respect to the dataset size, whereas repairing can be performed in polynomial time with respect to the number of invalidities.
- We have implemented an operational repairing system for real-world applications. Our implementation is modular, allowing each component to be implemented in a manner independent to the other components. This way, we managed to reuse off-the-shelf, state-of-the-art tools for many of the components, such as reasoning, storage, query answering, etc.
- We have experimentally evaluated the scalability and performance of our algorithms, using real and synthetic datasets. The main conclusion drawn is that our framework can scale for very large datasets, such as DBpedia, as well as for large numbers (millions) of invalidities.

The rest of the paper is structured as follows: in Sect. 2, we motivate the use of the $DL\text{-}Lite_A$ language for this problem and explain its features; in Sect. 3, we describe our framework and explain how we address the problems of detecting and resolving invalidities; Sect. 4 describes our algorithms for diagnosis and repairing; in Sect. 5, we describe our experimental evaluation and report on the main conclusions drawn; finally, Sect. 6 compares our contributions to the related work and Sect. 7 concludes.

---

[4] http://www.w3.org/TR/owl2-profiles/#OWL_2_QL.

2   Preliminaries

In $DL\text{-}Lite_{\mathcal{A}}$ [4], concept expressions, hereafter expressed by the letter C, and role expressions, denoting binary relations between concepts and hereafter expressed by the letter R, are formed according to the following syntax, where A denotes an atomic concept and P denotes an atomic role:

$$C \longrightarrow A \mid \exists R \qquad\qquad R \longrightarrow P \mid P^-$$

A $DL\text{-}Lite_{\mathcal{A}}$ TBox consists of axioms of the following form:

$$C_1 \sqsubseteq C_2 \qquad C_1 \sqsubseteq \neg C_2 \qquad R_1 \sqsubseteq R_2 \qquad R_1 \sqsubseteq \neg R_2 \qquad (\text{funct } R)$$

A $DL\text{-}Lite_{\mathcal{A}}$ ABox is a finite set of assertions of the following form:

$$A(x) \qquad\qquad P(x,y)$$

In order to guarantee good complexity results for reasoning tasks like consistency checking, $DL\text{-}Lite_{\mathcal{A}}$ imposes a limitation in the TBox, namely that a functional role cannot be specialized by using it in the right-hand side of a role inclusion assertion. This means that if a $DL\text{-}Lite_{\mathcal{A}}$ TBox contains an axiom of the form $R' \sqsubseteq R$, then it cannot contain (funct R) or (funct R^-) [5]. Note that $DL\text{-}Lite_{\mathcal{A}}$ assertions can be also expressed in OWL syntax.

$DL\text{-}Lite_{\mathcal{A}}$ follows the standard reasoning semantics of DLs [4–6]. A $DL\text{-}Lite_{\mathcal{A}}$ KB $\mathcal{K} = \langle \mathcal{T}, \mathcal{A} \rangle$ is called *inconsistent* iff $\mathcal{T} \cup \mathcal{A}$ is inconsistent (in the standard logical sense). It is called *consistent* otherwise.

With respect to performance, $DL\text{-}Lite_{\mathcal{A}}$ has the important property of *FOL-Reducibility* [5], which essentially means that one can reduce the process of inconsistency checking and query answering to the evaluation of First-Order Logic (FOL) queries over the ABox, considered as a database; this makes both tasks tractable (in LOGSPACE with respect to the data) [5].

3   Diagnosis and Repair

3.1   Constraints in $DL\text{-}Lite_{\mathcal{A}}$

For the purposes of diagnosis and repair, we can distinguish three different types of $DL\text{-}Lite_{\mathcal{A}}$ TBox axioms, namely *positive inclusions* (of the form $C_1 \sqsubseteq C_2$, $R_1 \sqsubseteq R_2$), *negative inclusions* (of the form $C_1 \sqsubseteq \neg C_2$, $R_1 \sqsubseteq \neg R_2$) and *functionality assertions* (of the form (funct R)). This distinction is important for diagnosis and repair due to the fact that the ABox is viewed under the Open World Assumption (OWA), which is considered for Description Logics and the ontology languages of the Semantic Web in general (such as OWL – but see [22] for an effort to understand OWL under the Closed World Assumption, and the NRL language[5] for a similar analysis). Due to the OWA, a TBox consisting of

---
[5] http://www.semanticdesktop.org/ontologies/2007/08/15/nrl.

positive inclusions only can never lead to an inconsistent KB; therefore, the only interesting (from the diagnosis perspective) constraints are the negative inclusions and the functionality assertions. In the following, the term *constraint* will be used to refer to negative TBox inclusions and functionality assertions.

Despite that, positive inclusions are still relevant for the diagnosis process, because they may generate inferred information that should be taken into account. As an example, assume that the TBox contains the constraint $A_1 \sqsubseteq \neg A_3$ and the axiom $A_2 \sqsubseteq A_3$ (where A_1, A_2, A_3 are atomic concepts), and suppose that the ABox contains both $A_1(x)$ and $A_2(x)$ for some x. Even though no constraint is explicitly violated, the combination of the ABox contents with the aforementioned TBox would lead to inferring both $A_3(x)$ and $\neg A_3(x)$, i.e., an invalidity. Note that the positive inclusion $A_2 \sqsubseteq A_3$, albeit not violated itself, plays a critical role in creating this invalidity.

Rather than capturing such invalidities via the obvious method of computing the closure of the ABox, it is more efficient to identify the constraints implied by the explicitly declared constraints and the positive inclusions in the TBox. In our example, we could identify that the constraint $A_1 \sqsubseteq \neg A_2$ is a consequence of the two explicit axioms in the TBox, so the presence of $A_1(x)$ and $A_2(x)$ violates this implicit constraint.

This process amounts to computing all explicit and implicit constraints of the TBox (denoted by $cln(\mathcal{T})$) [5], i.e., the set of all the functionality assertions and the explicit and implicit negative inclusions present in the TBox. In fact, it has been proven that, in order to check the consistency of a $DL\text{-}Lite_{\mathcal{A}}$ KB, one has to take into account only the constraints in $cln(\mathcal{T})$ [6]. More formally, a $DL\text{-}Lite_{\mathcal{A}}$ KB $\mathcal{K} = \langle \mathcal{T}, \mathcal{A} \rangle$ is inconsistent iff there is a constraint $c \in cln(\mathcal{T})$ and a pair of assertions $a_1, a_2 \in \mathcal{A}$ such that the $DL\text{-}Lite_{\mathcal{A}}$ KB $\mathcal{K}' = \langle \{c\}, \{a_1, a_2\} \rangle$ is inconsistent [6]. Note that if $\mathcal{T}$ is incoherent [11], then it could be the case that $a_1 = a_2$. In the following, the triple (a_1, a_2, c) will be called an *invalidity* of $\mathcal{K}$. It is obvious by the above result that in order to render a KB consistent, for each invalidity (a_1, a_2, c), one of a_1, a_2 has to be removed from the ABox.

Example 1. Consider the following $DL\text{-}Lite_{\mathcal{A}}$ KB $\mathcal{K} = \langle \mathcal{T}, \mathcal{A} \rangle$:

$$\mathcal{T} = \{(\text{funct } P_1),\ A_1 \sqsubseteq \neg A_2,\ \exists P_2 \sqsubseteq A_1\}$$
$$\mathcal{A} = \{A_1(x_1),\ A_2(x_1),\ P_2(x_1, y_1),\ P_1(x_3, y_2),\ P_1(x_3, y_3),\ P_1(x_3, y_4)\}$$

The closure of negative inclusions and functionality assertions of $\mathcal{T}$ ($cln(\mathcal{T})$), computed in the way that was presented in [6], is the following:

$$cln(\mathcal{T}) = \{(\text{funct } P_1),\ A_1 \sqsubseteq \neg A_2,\ \exists P_2 \sqsubseteq \neg A_2\}$$

We conclude that $(A_1(x_1), A_2(x_1), A_1 \sqsubseteq \neg A_2)$ is an invalidity of the KB.   □

3.2   Approach for Diagnosis and Repair

Diagnosis amounts to identifying the invalidities, i.e., the data assertion(s) and the (possibly implicit) constraint that are involved in an invalidity. Using the property of FOL-Reducibility, the identification of invalidities in a $DL\text{-}Lite_{\mathcal{A}}$

KB can be reduced to the execution of adequately defined FOL queries over a database [5] – see also Table 1. Exploiting this property, diagnosis is performed by simply executing the queries corresponding to the constraints in $cln(\mathcal{T})$, to get all the invalidities of the KB under question.

Repairing is based on the aforementioned property that restoring consistency requires eliminating all invalidities from a KB via removing either one of the two data assertions that take part in each invalidity; formally:

Definition 1. *Given a DL-Lite$_\mathcal{A}$ KB $\mathcal{K} = \langle \mathcal{T}, \mathcal{A} \rangle$ a repairing delta of $\mathcal{K}$ is a selection of data assertions RD, such that $\mathcal{K}' = \langle \mathcal{T}, \mathcal{A} \setminus RD \rangle$ is consistent. A repairing delta RD is called minimal iff there is no repairing delta RD', such that $RD' \subset RD$.* □

The notion of minimality is important, as many authors have proposed the identification of *minimal* repairing deltas (under different forms of minimality) as one of the main concerns during repairing [2,8]; as is obvious by Definition 1, minimal repairing deltas correspond to *subset repairs* in the terminology of [2].

Identifying the minimal repairing delta(s) is not trivial. The computation of such delta(s) is based on the fact that constraints expressed in *DL-Lite$_\mathcal{A}$* allow the presence of interrelated invalidities, i.e., data assertions being involved in more than one invalidities. This implies that potential resolutions of such invalidities coincide, and that there exist resolutions which resolve more than one invalidity at the same time.

To help in the process of identifying the minimal repairing delta, the diagnosed invalidities are organized into an *interdependency graph*, which is used to identify assertions involved in multiple invalidities. Formally:

Definition 2. *The interdependency graph of a DL-Lite$_\mathcal{A}$ KB $\mathcal{K} = \langle \mathcal{T}, \mathcal{A} \rangle$ is an undirected labelled graph $IG(\mathcal{K}) = (V, E)$ such that $V = \{a \mid (a_1, a_2, c)$ is an invalidity of $\mathcal{K}$ and $a = a_1$ or $a = a_2\}$ and $E = \{(a_1, a_2, c) \mid (a_1, a_2, c)$ is an invalidity of $\mathcal{K}\}$.* □

The use of the interdependency graph as a structure to represent the invalidities that are diagnosed in the KB gives the ability to get a better grasp of the form and complexity of the invalidities and their interrelationships, as well as to use methods and tools that come from graph theory in order to facilitate the repairing process. Note that an interdependency graph is different from a conflict-graph [9], as the interdependency graph does not contain every assertion in the ABox, having an obvious impact in the algorithm time-cost.

In terms of the interdependency graph, resolving an invalidity amounts to removing one of the two vertices that are connected by the edge representing this invalidity. Therefore, a minimal repairing delta is essentially the minimal *vertex cover* of the corresponding interdependency graph, which reduces the problem of repairing to the well-known problem of VERTEX COVER [20]. This fact forms the basis of our algorithms presented in the next section.

4 Algorithms for Diagnosis and Repairing

4.1 Diagnosis Algorithm

The diagnosis algorithm is used to detect all the invalidities in a KB, and provide them as output in the form of an interdependency graph. The steps needed to perform diagnosis are illustrated in Algorithm 1.

Algorithm 1. Diagnosis($\mathcal{K}$)

Input: A $DL\text{-}Lite_A$ KB $\mathcal{K} = \langle \mathcal{T}, \mathcal{A} \rangle$
Output: The interdependency graph of $\mathcal{K}$, $IG(\mathcal{K}) = (V, E)$
1: $V, E \leftarrow \emptyset$
2: Compute the $cln(\mathcal{T})$
3: **for all** $c \in cln(\mathcal{T})$ **do**
4:     $q_c \leftarrow \delta(c)$
5:     $Ans_{q_c} \leftarrow q_c^{\mathcal{A}}$
6:     **for all** $\langle a_1, a_2 \rangle \in Ans_{q_c}$ **do**
7:         $V \leftarrow V \cup \{a_1, a_2\}$
8:         $E \leftarrow E \cup \{(a_1, a_2, c)\}$
9:     **end for**
10: **end for**
11: **return** $IG(\mathcal{K}) = (V, E)$

The diagnosis algorithm starts by computing the closure $cln(\mathcal{T})$ of negative inclusions and functionality assertions of the TBox (line 2 of Algorithm 1), in order to get the full set of constraints that need to be checked over the ABox. Each of the constraints in $cln(\mathcal{T})$ is then transformed to a FOL query (line 4) using predefined patterns, as defined in Table 1 (see also [5]), whose answers determine the invalidities. These queries are executed over the ABox in line 5 (Ans_{q_c} contains pairs $\langle a_1, a_2 \rangle$ such that (a_1, a_2, c) is an invalidity). Note that these FOL queries can be easily expressed as SPARQL queries over an ABox stored in a triple store, so that off-the-shelf, optimized tools can be used for query answering. The last step of the algorithm encodes the invalidities in the form of an interdependency graph (lines 6–9) as specified in Definition 2.

The following example illustrates the diagnosis algorithm in action:

Example 2. Consider the KB $\mathcal{K}$ and the $cln(\mathcal{T})$ of Example 1. The corresponding FOL queries to check for invalidities, according to Table 1 are:

$$q_1(x) \leftarrow P_1(x, y) \land P_1(x, z) \land y \neq z$$
$$q_2(x) \leftarrow A_1(x) \land A_2(x)$$
$$q_3(x) \leftarrow P_2(x, y) \land A_2(x)$$

Table 1. Transformation of $DL\text{-}Lite_A$ constraints to FOL queries.

Constraint (c)	Transformation $(\delta(c))$
$c = A_1 \sqsubseteq \neg A_2$	$\delta(c) = q(x) \leftarrow A_1(x), A_2(x)$
$c = A_1 \sqsubseteq \neg \exists P_1$ (or $c = \exists P_1 \sqsubseteq \neg A_1$)	$\delta(c) = q(x) \leftarrow A_1(x), P_1(x,y)$
$c = A_1 \sqsubseteq \neg \exists P_1^-$ (or $c = \exists P_1^- \sqsubseteq \neg A_1$)	$\delta(c) = q(x) \leftarrow A_1(x), P_1(y,x)$
$c = \exists P_1 \sqsubseteq \neg \exists P_2$	$\delta(c) = q(x) \leftarrow P_1(x,y_1), P_2(x,y_2)$
$c = \exists P_1^- \sqsubseteq \neg \exists P_2^-$	$\delta(c) = q(x) \leftarrow P_1(y_1,x), P_2(y_2,x)$
$c = \exists P_1 \sqsubseteq \neg \exists P_2^-$	$\delta(c) = q(x) \leftarrow P_1(x,y_1), P_2(y_2,x)$
$c = P_1 \sqsubseteq \neg P_2$ (or $c = P_1^- \sqsubseteq \neg P_2^-$)	$\delta(c) = q(x,y) \leftarrow P_1(x,y), P_2(x,y)$
$c = P_1 \sqsubseteq \neg P_2^-$	$\delta(c) = q(x,y) \leftarrow P_1(x,y), P_2(y,x)$
$c =$(funct P)	$\delta(c) = q(x) \leftarrow P(x,y_1), P(x,y_2)$
$c =$(funct P^-)	$\delta(c) = q(x) \leftarrow P(y_1,x), P(y_2,x)$

From the execution of the above three queries over the ABox of Example 1, we get the following answers (each of which corresponds to an invalidity):

$$Ans_{q_1} = \{\langle P_1(x_3,y_2), P_1(x_3,y_3) \rangle,$$
$$\langle P_1(x_3,y_2), P_1(x_3,y_4) \rangle,$$
$$\langle P_1(x_3,y_3), P_1(x_3,y_4) \rangle\}$$
$$Ans_{q_2} = \{\langle A_1(x_1), A_2(x_1) \rangle\}$$
$$Ans_{q_3} = \{\langle A_2(x_1), P_2(x_1,y_1) \rangle\}$$

Figure 1 shows the corresponding interdependency graph.   □

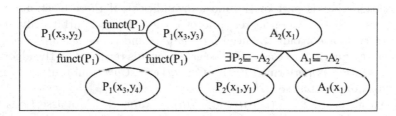

Fig. 1. Example of an interdependency graph.

As already mentioned, computing $cln(\mathcal{T})$ (line 2) is in LOGSPACE with respect to the data [5], whereas the remaining steps of the algorithm are linear with respect to the number of invalidities and the number of constraints in $cln(\mathcal{T})$.

4.2 Repairing Algorithm

The repairing algorithm (Algorithm 2) takes as input the interdependency graph and is responsible for automatically repairing the KB. As explained in Sect. 3.2, the main idea behind the repairing algorithm is the computation of the vertex cover of the interdependency graph.

To do so, the repairing algorithm first breaks the interdependency graph $IG(\mathcal{K})$ into the set of its connected components (line 2). Note that the computation of the vertex cover for each of the connected components is independent to the others, and can be parallelized for better performance.

This computation (vertex cover) is performed in lines 3–5. Recall that VERTEX COVER is a well-known NP-COMPLETE problem [20], but many approximation algorithms have been proposed, such as the *2-approximation* algorithm [20], or the approximation algorithm presented in [14].

Algorithm 2. Repair($IG(\mathcal{K}), \mathcal{A}$)

Input: An interdependency graph $IG(\mathcal{K})$ and a *DL-Lite$_\mathcal{A}$* ABox $\mathcal{A}$
Output: $\mathcal{K}$ in a consistent state
1: *repairing_delta* $\leftarrow \emptyset$
2: $CC \leftarrow ConnectedComponents(IG(\mathcal{K}))$
3: **for all** $cc \in CC$ **do**
4:       *repairing_delta* $\leftarrow$ *repairing_delta* $\cup$ *GreedyVertexCover(cc)*
5: **end for**
6: $\mathcal{A} \leftarrow \mathcal{A} \setminus$ *repairing_delta*

For our implementation and experiments below, we chose (for efficiency) to compute the vertex cover in a greedy manner, as presented in [20] (but any other algorithm for VERTEX COVER could be used instead). Greedy means that, in each step of the computation, the vertex that is chosen to be included in the cover is the vertex with the highest degree (in other words, the invalid data assertion that is part of the most invalidities). If there exist more than one vertices with the same degree, one of those vertices is arbitrarily chosen; this arbitrary choice avoids the need for complex and time-consuming selection conditions and guarantees that a single vertex cover is returned by the algorithm. This computation is performed in the *GreedyVertexCover* subroutine, which is omitted for brevity (but see [20]).

The output of lines 3–5 (*repairing_delta*) contains the data assertions to be removed from the dataset in order to render it valid. The actual repairing is performed in line 6, through a single SPARQL-Update statement[6] requesting the deletion of all the assertions in the repairing delta.

The correctness of our algorithms is guaranteed by our analysis in Sect. 3 and the results in [6]. The computational complexity of Algorithm 2 is dominated by the computation of the vertex cover, which is proven to achieve $O(\log n)$ approximation of the optimal solution (where n is the number of vertices of the graph), with a time complexity of $O(n \log n)$ [20].

---

[6] http://www.w3.org/TR/2013/REC-sparql11-update-20130321/.

The following concludes the running example for our framework:

Example 3. Consider the interdependency graph of Fig. 1. The repairing algorithm will compute the following repairing delta:

$$repairing\_delta = \{A_2(x_1), P_1(x_3, y_2), P_1(x_3, y_3)\}$$

After the application of the repairing delta, the ABox $\mathcal{A}$ is in the following state:

$$\mathcal{A} = \{A_1(x_1), P_2(x_1, y_1), P_1(x_3, y_4)\}$$

which can be easily verified to be a consistent KB with respect to $\mathcal{T}$.   □

5 Experimental Evaluation

5.1 Overview of Experimental Evaluation

We have implemented our framework as a Java web application. More specifically, we have created a system that uses a triple store, which lies on a Virtuoso Open-Source Edition Server[7] version 07.10, as a storage for the ABox instances and as an endpoint for query answering. For storing the set of constraints, we used a main memory model, which, along with the communication with the Virtuoso Server, are handled by the Apache Jena[8] framework. Apache Jena is also used for the various reasoning tasks (e.g., computation of $cln(\mathcal{T})$). The system used for the experiments was an AMD Opteron 3280, 8-core CPU with 24 GB RAM (we allocated 8 GB for the JVM), running Ubuntu Server 12.04.

We have performed several experiments in order to measure the performance and scalability of our framework, as well as to determine the decisive factors for the performance of the different phases of the process. More specifically, we performed three sets of experiments: (*i*) the first set verified that our framework can handle millions of violations in real-world ABoxes that scale up to more than 2 billion triples, considering hundreds of thousands of constraints; (*ii*) the second set of experiments quantified the impact of ABox size on performance, by using real Tboxes with constraints and synthetic ABoxes of varying sizes; and, (*iii*) the third set quantified the impact of the number of invalid data assertions on performance, by using real TBoxes with constraints and synthetic ABoxes with varying number of invalid data assertions.

In all of the above sets of experiments, we measured the time needed to run the diagnosis algorithm and produce the interdependency graph (*diagnosis time*), the time needed by the repairing algorithm to compute the repairing delta (*repair computation time*) and the time needed to apply this repairing delta on the dataset, using a SPARQL-Update query (*repair application time*). All of our experiments were run in sets of 5 hot runs and the average times were taken.

---

[7] http://virtuoso.openlinksw.com/dataspace/doc/dav/wiki/Main/.
[8] http://jena.apache.org/.

5.2   Real and Synthetic Datasets Used

For the TBox, we used two versions (3.6, 3.9) of the DBpedia ontology, which is a reference dataset for LOD, already containing different amounts and types of constraints; this is illustrated in Table 2, which shows information on how many functional and (concept/domain/range) disjointness constraints exist in the original TBox, as well as how many of these exist in the closure of negative inclusions $(cln(\mathcal{T}))$[9], and how many queries need to be executed for diagnosis. Property disjointness is the only type of constraint supported by $DL\text{-}Lite_{\mathcal{A}}$ that was not considered in our experiments, because we were unable to find any real TBoxes with this constraint (so it seems irrelevant for practical applications).

For running our experiments, we used the above TBoxes, together with both real and synthetic ABoxes. Real ABoxes were used to evaluate our system in realistic conditions, whereas synthetic ABoxes allow controlling the important factors for the performance of our algorithm, such as size and number of invalidities, and the appropriate evaluation of their effect on performance.

Table 2. Constraints in DBpedia versions 3.6 and 3.9.

TBox version	Constraints		Constraints in $cln(\mathcal{T})$		Queries
	Functional	Disjointness	Functional	Disjointness	
DBpedia 3.6	18	0	18	0	18
DBpedia 3.9	26	17	26	323.389	323.415

Real ABoxes were taken by the two DBpedia versions corresponding to the two aforementioned TBoxes, stored in a local Virtuoso instance. The DBpedia 3.6 ABox contains around 541 million triples, whereas the DBpedia 3.9 ABox contains more than 2 billion triples.

To generate synthetic ABoxes, we started from each TBox and an empty ABox, and added data and property instances of the classes/properties of the corresponding TBox, making sure to include some invalid pairs of assertions as well (taking into account the constraints). For the first set of generated ABoxes we created a fixed number of invalid data assertions (10 K) and a varying ABox size (500 K–5 M triples, with a step of 500 K triples). The second set of ABoxes had a fixed size (10 M triples) and a varying number of invalid data assertions (50 K–500 K, with a step of 50 K). The above two sets of ABoxes were used in the second and third set of experiments respectively.

5.3   Scalability and Performance Evaluation

The first set of experiments aimed at verifying the scalability of our framework in real-world settings, with ABoxes of billions of triples and with large numbers

---

[9] The big difference in the amount of disjointness constraints between the original DBpedia 3.9 and its closure is caused by the many positive inclusions and their interaction with the negative inclusions during the computation of the closure.

of constraints (up to hundreds of thousands). For this purpose, we used DBpedia versions 3.6 and 3.9 (TBox and real ABox). For each version, we measured the diagnosis time (identifying invalidities and creating the interdependency graph), the repair computation time (computing the repairing delta), the repair application time (applying the repairing delta) and the total time (sum of the above). We also measured the number of invalid data assertions that appear in the datasets, to see how well our framework scales with respect to that, as well as the size of the repairing delta, to verify that a manual repair by the curator would be infeasible in this context.

The results of this set of experiments are illustrated in Table 3. In the table, IDA denotes the number of invalid data assertions, Delta is the size of the repairing delta (in triples), t_d denotes the diagnosis time, $t_{r.c.}$ the repair computation time, $t_{r.a.}$ the repair application time and t_t the total time needed for diagnosis and repairing. All times are in milliseconds.

Table 3. Experiments performed on real datasets.

Version	Triples	IDA	Delta	t_d	$t_{r.c.}$	$t_{r.a.}$	t_t
DBpedia 3.6	541 M	1.109	749	2.440	402	219	3.061
DBpedia 3.9	>2 B	1.020.199	717.798	9.610.319	27.190.191	1.415.329	38.215.839

The results show that our framework is scalable, for both large datasets and big numbers of invalid data assertions, and that it can be applied in real-world settings. It also proves that already deployed and massively used reference KBs, such as DBpedia, don't have sufficient mechanisms for preventing the introduction of invalid data or for detecting and repairing such invalid data. Moreover, our experiments illustrate that the number of invalid data assertions and the size of the repairing delta would be prohibitive for manual repairing.

Our second set of experiments evaluated the effect of ABox size on performance using synthetic ABoxes of varying sizes and a fixed number of invalid data assertions. The results of this set of experiments appear in Fig. 2. Note that some of the curves in the graphs are difficult to distinguish, either because they are too close to the start of the x-axis (e.g., the repair computation time and the repair application time in the left figure), or because they are too close with another curve (e.g., the diagnosis time and the total time in the right figure).

From the results of this set of experiments, we conclude that diagnosis time grows linearly with respect to the ABox size and that it is the dominating factor of the total time, when the number of invalid data assertions is fixed. This is an important conclusion because it shows that, overall, our framework scales linearly with respect to the dataset size.

The third set of experiments evaluated the effect of the number of invalidities using ABoxes of fixed size, but with a varying number of invalid data assertions. The results of this set of experiments are illustrated in Fig. 3.

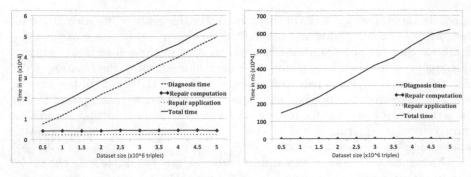

Fig. 2. Performance for DBpedia 3.6 (left) and 3.9 (right) with 10 K invalidities.

From these results, we can conclude that the number of invalid data assertions has no immediate impact on the diagnosis time. On the contrary, it is the main impact factor of the repair computation time. That was an expected behaviour, as the repair computation is done by computing the vertex cover of the interdependency graph. A bigger number of invalid data assertions leads to a bigger graph and this leads to a more costly computation of the vertex cover.

Another significant impact factor of the repair computation time is the amount of interdependencies in the interdependency graph. We can see that the repair computation time increases with a higher rate in the left graph of Fig. 3 than in the right one, which can be explained by the fact that the DBpedia 3.6 TBox contains only functional constraints, which form cliques in the interdependency graph (thus, more interdependencies), whereas the DBpedia 3.9 TBox contains mainly disjointness constraints, which cause less interdependencies, therefore less "touching" edges in the interdependency graph.

Moreover, the repair application time seems to be negligible in all of the experiments. This is due to the fact that the repair application is performed by executing a single SPARQL-Update query requesting the deletion of all the triples in the repairing delta, which is very efficient due to the optimizations for batch operations of Virtuoso.

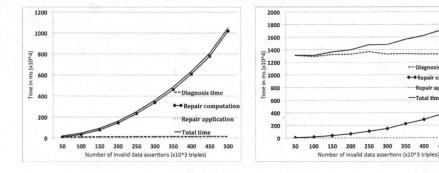

Fig. 3. Performance for DBpedia 3.6 (left) and 3.9 (right) with 10M triples.

The last significant conclusion comes from the comparison of the times measured for the two different DBpedia TBox versions. We see that the diagnosis times for version 3.9 are two orders of magnitude higher compared to the respective times of version 3.6. This is due to the fact that the closure of version 3.9 contains 323.415 constraints, whereas the closure of version 3.6 only 18; more constraints require the generation of more queries to be executed by the diagnosis algorithm, eventually causing this big difference in the measurements.

The following main conclusions can be distilled from our evaluation:

- Diagnosis can be performed in linear time with respect to the ABox size.
- Repair computation can be performed in polynomial time with respect to the number of invalid data assertions that appear in the dataset.
- Our implementation enjoys a decent performance in real-world settings with large datasets, numbers of constraints and invalidities, being able to repair the huge DBpedia 3.9 (>2 B triples) in about 10 hours, which is a reasonable amount of time, given that repairing is expected to be an offline process.

It should be noted that the experimental evaluation of the only other work in the literature that performs automated repairing of inconsistent DL-$Lite_A$ KBs ([18] – see Sect. 6), only considers datasets of size up to 30.000 triples, whereas we consider datasets of up to 5 orders of magnitude larger; thus, the results are not comparable.

6   Related Work

The problem of inconsistencies appearing in KBs can be tackled either by providing the ability to query inconsistent data and get consistent answers (*Consistent Query Answering - CQA*) [3], or by actually *repairing* the KB, which leads to a consistent version of it [12]. Both these approaches have attracted researchers' attention, mostly in the context of relational databases and, lately, in the context of linked data and ontology languages as well.

In the context of relational databases, CQA has been studied in various works dealing with different classes of conjunctive queries and denial constraints, mainly key constraints (e.g., [13,23]). These works underline the main advantages of using First-Order query rewriting for the validation of integrity constraints. Note that CQA techniques systematically drop all information involved in a constraint violation, whereas repairing techniques, like ours, make explicit decisions on what to keep and what to drop, in accordance with the principles set out in [2], that require preserving as much information as possible.

Different semantics have been studied for the repairing of inconsistent relational databases, considering different kinds of constraints. For example, [9] studied the problem of repairing by allowing only tuple deletions and, in this way, resolving violations of denial constraints and inclusion dependencies, which is a more expressive set of constraints than the one we consider in this work. However, as proven in [9], the unrestricted combination of those constraints leads to intractability issues.

In the context of linked data and the corresponding languages and technologies, there has been research on the topic of using ontological languages to encode integrity constraints (ICs) that must be checked over a dataset. In [22], the authors present a way to integrate ICs in OWL and they show that IC validation can be reduced to query answering, for integrity constraints that fall into the $\mathcal{SROI}$ DL fragment. A similar approach has been followed in [19]. In [16], the presented approach integrates constraints that come from the relational world (primary-key, foreign-key) into RDF and provides a way to validate these constraints. IC validation is also an important part of some of the current OWL reasoners, such as Stardog[10]. The above approaches address, essentially, only the KB satisfiability problem and do not consider detection and repairing of invalidities.

In the field of diagnosis for *DL-Lite* KBs, there has been some work regarding inconsistency checking. The $DL\text{-}Lite_{\mathcal{A}}$ reasoner QUONTO [1] has the ability to check the satisfiability of a $DL\text{-}Lite_{\mathcal{A}}$ KB. However, it does not detect the invalid data assertions in the ABox, neither repairs it. A problem very similar to repairing (but in a different setting) is addressed in the context of *DL-Lite* KB evolution (e.g., [7,21]), where the objective is to identify the minimal set of assertions to remove in order to render a *DL-Lite* KB consistent during evolution.

Recently, there has also been some research on CQA for inconsistent knowledge bases expressed in Description Logic languages, using query rewriting techniques. For example, [17] deals with different variants of inconsistency-tolerant semantics to reach a good compromise between expressive power of the semantics and computational complexity of inconsistency-tolerant query answering.

Finally, [18] is (to our knowledge) the only work addressing the automatic repairing of an inconsistent $DL\text{-}Lite_{\mathcal{A}}$ KB, and thus the closest to our work. It is based on the inconsistency-tolerant semantics studied in [17] and resolves each invalidity by removing both data assertions that take part in it. On the contrary, our repairing algorithm considers the removal of only one of two involved data assertions. Thus, [18] removes more information than necessary from the original KB. In addition, the work of [18] has only been evaluated with datasets that are unrealistically small (up to 30.000 triples).

7   Conclusion and Future Work

We presented a novel, fully automatic and modular diagnosis and repairing framework, which can be used on top of already deployed datasets to assist curators in the task of enforcing the validity of logical integrity constraints, taking into account logical inference, in order to maintaining their consistency. Our experimental evaluation showed that our framework is scalable for large dataset sizes, often found in real reference linked datasets such as DBpedia.

As future work, we will try to improve the scalability properties of our algorithms, possibly using a parallel implementation relying on the MapReduce

---

[10] http://stardog.com/.

model. In addition, we will consider different models of interaction with the curator, to allow him to influence the repairing process (e.g., via user guidelines or preferences) without being overwhelmed with the complete set of invalidities; the ultimate goal is to develop an interactive repairing process that will combine the quality of manual curation with the efficiency of automatic repairing. Another possible extension is to experiment with more LOD datasets, and provide a comprehensive study of the number and types of violations that exist in different popular datasets.

Acknowledgement. This work was partially supported by the EU project DIACHRON (ICT-2011.4.3, #601043), and by the State Scholarships Foundation.

References

1. Acciarri, A., Calvanese, D., De Giacomo, G., Lembo, D., Lenzerini, M., Palmieri, M., Rosati, R.: QUONTO: querying ontologies. In: AAAI, vol. 5 (2005)
2. Afrati, F., Kolaitis, P.: Repair checking in inconsistent databases: algorithms and complexity. In: ICDT (2009)
3. Arenas, M., Bertossi, L., Chomicki, J.: Consistent query answers in inconsistent databases. In: PODS (1999)
4. Calvanese, D., De Giacomo, G., Lembo, D., Lenzerini, M., Poggi, A., Rosati, R.: Linking data to ontologies: the description logic DL-Lite$_A$. In: OWLED (2006)
5. Calvanese, D., De Giacomo, G., Lembo, D., Lenzerini, M., Rosati, R.: Tractable reasoning and efficient query answering in Description Logics: the DL-Lite family. J. Autom. Reasoning **39**(3), 385–429 (2007)
6. Calvanese, D., De Giacomo, G., Lembo, D., Lenzerini, M., Poggi, A., Rodriguez-Muro, M., Rosati, R.: Ontologies and databases: the DL-Lite approach. In: Reasoning Web (2009)
7. Calvanese, D., Kharlamov, E., Nutt, W., Zheleznyakov, D.: Evolution of DL-Lite knowledge bases. In: ISWC (2010)
8. Chomicki, J., Marcinkowski, J.: On the computational complexity of minimal-change integrity maintenance in relational databases. Inconsist, Toler (2005)
9. Chomicki, J., Marcinkowski, J.: Minimal-change integrity maintenance using tuple deletions. Inf. Comput. **197**(1), 90–121 (2005)
10. Deutsch, A.: FOL modeling of integrity constraints (dependencies). In: Encyclopedia of Database Systems. Springer (2009)
11. Flouris, G., Huang, Z., Pan, J.Z., Plexousakis, D., Wache, H.: Inconsistencies, negations and changes in ontologies. In: AAAI 2006 (2006)
12. Greco, G., Greco, S., Zumpano, E.: A logical framework for querying and repairing inconsistent databases. IEEE TKDE **15**(6), 1389–1408 (2003)
13. Grieco, L., Lembo, D., Rosati, R., Ruzzi, M.: Consistent query answering under key and exclusion dependencies: algorithms and experiments. In: CIKM (2005)
14. Karakostas, G.: A better approximation ratio for the vertex cover problem. In: Caires, L., Italiano, G.F., Monteiro, L., Palamidessi, C., Yung, M. (eds.) ICALP 2005. LNCS, vol. 3580, pp. 1043–1050. Springer, Heidelberg (2005)
15. Kontokostas, D., Westphal, P., Auer, S., Hellmann, S., Lehmann, J., Cornelissen, R.: Databugger: a test-driven framework for debugging the web of data. In: WWW (Companion Volume) (2014)

16. Lausen, G., Meier, M., Schmidt, M.: SPARQLing constraints for RDF. In: EDBT (2008)
17. Lembo, D., Lenzerini, M., Rosati, R., Ruzzi, M., Savo, D.F.: Query rewriting for inconsistent DL-Lite ontologies. In: Rudolph, S., Gutierrez, C. (eds.) RR 2011. LNCS, vol. 6902, pp. 155–169. Springer, Heidelberg (2011)
18. Masotti, G., Rosati, R., Ruzzi, M.: Practical ABox cleaning in DL-Lite (progress report). In: Description Logics (2011)
19. Motik, B., Horrocks, I., Sattler, U.: Bridging the gap between OWL and relational databases. In: WWW (2007)
20. Papadimitriou, C., Steiglitz, K.: Combinatorial optimization: algorithms and complexity. Courier Dover Publications (1998)
21. Qi, G., Wang, Z., Wang, K., Fu, X., Zhuang, Z.: Approximating model-based ABox revision in DL-Lite: Theory and practice. In: AAAI (2015)
22. Tao, J., Sirin, E., Bao, J., McGuinness, D.: Integrity constraints in OWL. In: AAAI (2010)
23. Wijsen, J.: Consistent query answering under primary keys: a characterization of tractable queries. In: ICDT (2009)

4th Workshop on Knowledge Discovery and Data Mining Meets Linked Open Data (Know@LOD)

Sorted Neighborhood for Schema-Free RDF Data

Mayank Kejriwal[(✉)] and Daniel P. Miranker

University of Texas at Austin, Austin, USA
{kejriwal,miranker}@cs.utexas.edu

Abstract. Entity Resolution (ER) concerns identifying pairs of entities that refer to the same underlying entity. To avoid $O(n^2)$ pairwise
comparison of n entities, blocking methods are used. Sorted Neighborhood is an established blocking method for Relational Databases. It has
not been applied to schema-free Resource Description Framework (RDF)
data sources widely prevalent in the Linked Data ecosystem. This paper
presents a Sorted Neighborhood workflow that may be applied to schema-
free RDF data. The workflow is modular and makes minimal assumptions about its inputs. Empirical evaluations of the proposed algorithm
on five real-world benchmarks demonstrate its utility compared to two
state-of-the-art blocking baselines.

Keywords: Entity resolution · Sorted neighborhood · Schema-free RDF

1 Introduction

Entity Resolution (ER) is the problem of identifying pairs of entities across
databases that refer to the same *underlying* entity. An example is illustrated
in Fig. 1. The problem goes by many names in the data mining and knowledge
discovery communities, examples being *deduplication* [5], *record linkage* [4], *link
discovery* [15] and *coreference resolution* [13], to name just a few. Instances of
the problem have been documented for structured [5], semistructured [17], as
well as unstructured data models [13].

Given n entities and a boolean *link specification* function that determines
whether two entities are equivalent, a naïve ER application would run in time
$O(n^2)$. Scalability indicates a two-step approach [5]. The first step is called *blocking*. Blocking uses a many-many clustering function called a *blocking key* to
assign entities in near-linear time into one or more *blocks*, where each block represents a cluster [4]. In the second *similarity* step, only entities sharing a block
are paired and evaluated by the (expensive) link specification function [8,15].

In the Relational Database (RDB) community, a state-of-the-art blocking
algorithm is *Sorted Neighborhood* (SN) [6]. The classic SN version accepts a
rigidly structured tabular database as input, and sorts the table by using the
blocking key as a *sorting key*. A window of constant size is then slid over the
records, and records sharing a window are paired and become candidates for

© Springer International Publishing Switzerland 2015
F. Gandon et al. (Eds.): ESWC 2015, LNCS 9341, pp. 217–229, 2015.
DOI: 10.1007/978-3-319-25639-9_38

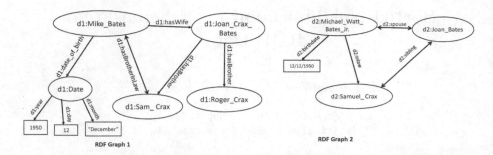

Fig. 1. An instance of the Entity Resolution (ER) problem on two RDF graphs. Various entities between the two graphs need to be interlinked using *owl:sameAs* edges

the second ER step. In several studies, the RDB version of SN was verified to have excellent theoretical run-time guarantees and good empirical performance [4,6]. To the best of our knowledge, an SN algorithm has never been proposed for *schema-free* RDF data sources despite its success. Such data sources are common on Linked Open Data (LOD), which has continued to grow since its inception in 2007 with just 12 datasets [20]. According to a recently concluded study, LOD currently contains over 1000 datasets and tens of billions of triples[1].

Typical blocking systems such as Silk and Limes in the Semantic Web community assume that the link specification function is known *a priori* [8,15]. Using the properties of the link specification function, these systems partition the space of entities into blocks. In contrast, Sorted Neighborhood does not assume any knowledge of the link specification function [6]. In practice, employing an *agnostic* blocking method such as Sorted Neighborhood enables an ER practitioner to *decouple* the two ER steps in terms of implementation and execution.

This paper presents a Sorted Neighborhood workflow that processes schema-free RDF data and accommodates a range of practical options (Sect. 3). The described algorithm is evaluated on five real-world test cases against two established baselines (Sect. 4). Preliminary results show that the method is a promising blocking procedure for schema-free RDF datasets.

2   Related Work

Entity Resolution is an old problem [14], and is methodologically surveyed by Elmagarmid et al. [5]. The blocking step is surveyed separately by Christen [4], who has also written a book synthesizing recent trends in ER research [3]. We note that traditionally, blocking has not been given as much importance as the second ER step, but this changed in the mid-90's, with large databases increasingly accessible over the Web [4]. Hernàndez and Stolfo published the Sorted Neighborhood work [6], and extended it to include parallel implementations [7]. Recent work has adapted the method to XML data, but under the assumption

---

[1] http://linkeddata.org.

that the XML data sources possess the *same schema*, possibly after a *schema matching* step [17]. To the best of our knowledge, the method has not been adapted yet to *schema-free* semi-structured data.

The advent of Linked Open Data has brought renewed focus on the RDF-based version of Entity Resolution, which is commonly denoted as *instance matching* or *link discovery* in the Linked Data community [15,18]. The fourth Linked Data principle states that data must not exist in silos, but must be inter-linked to maximize value [2]. Linked Open Data (LOD) is currently known to contain over eight million entities [20], many of which are believed to refer to the same underlying entity. Silk and Limes are two popular ER frameworks that have sought to address the issue of discovering these entity pairs [8,15]. Another example of a Semantic Web-based ER system is RDF-AI, which offers customizable packages, similar to the proposed workflow [19]. The survey by Scharffe et al. provides more details on recently developed ER systems in the Linked Data community [18]. While these systems represent significant advances, the blocking methods that they employ are typically not agnostic of the link specification function. In contrast, the Sorted Neighborhood workflow proposed in this paper is completely independent of the second ER step, and operates on schema-free RDF data. Additionally, the proposed workflow offers options for both batch and online data access settings.

3   The Workflow

Figure 2 illustrates a Sorted Neighborhood workflow for schema-free RDF data. At a high level, the workflow accepts two inputs, namely the pair of RDF graphs G_1 and G_2 containing entities that need to be interlinked, as well as corresponding blocking keys B_1 and B_2. The final output is a set of entity-entity pairs (denoted as the *candidate set*), which is piped to the second ER step and evaluated by an unknown link specification function. As earlier noted, an advantage of Sorted Neighborhood is that it is agnostic of the link specification function.

3.1   Blocking Keys

The quality of the workflow in Fig. 2 depends directly on the quality of blocking keys B_1 and B_2. There are several methods in the literature on both defining and learning appropriate blocking keys for schema-free data [9,16]. One of the earliest solutions for this problem was to use a simple token-based distance measure (e.g. cosine similarity) to cluster entities, and to ignore all structural information [12]. This token-based algorithm, called *Canopy Clustering* [12], was found to have good performance on many test cases, but has been outperformed by more sophisticated learning algorithms in recent years [1,9].

Two classes of viable learning algorithms (for blocking keys) have emerged as state-of-the-art. The first is the Attribute Clustering (AC) algorithm [16]. AC is an unsupervised procedure that groups properties (or *attributes*) after

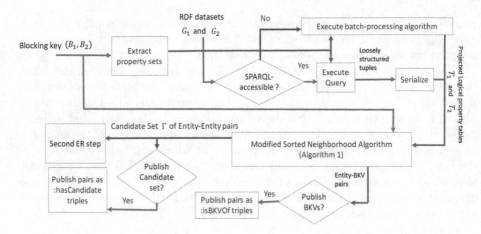

Fig. 2. A modular Sorted Neighborhood workflow for schema-free RDF graphs

computing the overlap between the properties' object value-sets using a trigram-based similarity score. Two entities share a block if they share tokens in any two properties that were grouped together. The main advantage of AC is that it does not require *property alignments* to be computed between the input RDF graphs, and is simple and effective to implement. Empirically, the learned blocking keys were found to be competitive when evaluated by a variety of blocking methods [16]. Note that the Sorted Neighborhood method was not proposed or considered in that paper. In Sect. 4, we use a high-performing blocking method called *block purging* from the original AC paper as a baseline for evaluating the proposed Sorted Neighborhood workflow.

The second class of learnable blocking keys, called the Disjunctive Normal Form (DNF) blocking keys, are currently considered state-of-the-art in the Relational Database community [1,9]. The learning procedure for these keys is adaptive, in that training samples are used by a machine learning algorithm to learn the key. In recent work, we extended DNF blocking keys to operate on schema-free RDF data [10,11]. A potential disadvantage of this method is that tractably learning these keys requires some form of property alignment between the schema-free datasets. Recent research has proposed some reliable methods for automatic property alignment, making the class of DNF blocking keys a promising unsupervised alternative to the AC class.

In summary, a practitioner has several viable options for acquiring blocking keys. In this paper, the only requirement that is imposed on the blocking key is that it must not rely on the existence of a schema or type information. In practice, this implies that the blocking key will be defined either in terms of the properties in the input RDF graphs or the subject URIs in the triples (or both). An even simpler alternative is to use the Canopy Clustering algorithm and block entities based on their degree of token overlap [12]. We consider this option as a baseline in Sect. 4.

3.2 Projected Logical Property Table

As mentioned in Sect. 3.1, the blocking keys $B_{1,2}$ will be defined[2] in terms of the properties in the RDF graphs $G_{1,2}$, since schema information cannot be assumed. Let the set of properties used in the construction of B_i be denoted as the *property set* P_i of the blocking key B_i ($i = 1, 2$).

Example 1. Consider Fig. 1, and let the blocking keys B_1 and B_2 be given by the respective expressions[3] *Tokens(subject)* $\cup$ *Tokens(d1:hasBrother)* and *Tokens(subject)* $\cup$ *Tokens(d2:sibling)*, where *subject* indicates the subject URI of the entity to which the blocking key is applied. The property sets P_1 and P_2 are respectively {d1:hasBrother} and {d2:sibling}. *subject* is not included in the sets since it is not technically a property.

Given B_1 and B_2, the property sets P_1 and P_2 are first constructed. The goal of extracting the property sets is to construct a *projected logical property table*. A logical property table representation of an RDF graph G_i is defined by the schema {*subject*} $\cup \mathcal{P}_i$, where $\mathcal{P}_i$ is the set of *all* property URIs occurring in G_i [11]. The *subject* column essentially serves as the key for the table. Two special cases need to be borne in mind when populating a property table. First, there may be subjects that do not have object values for a given property. For example, in graph G_1 in Fig. 1, d1:Sam_Crax does not have an object value for the property d1:hasBrother. For such cases, a reserved keyword (e.g. *null*) is inserted in the corresponding table cell[4] The second special case is that an entity may have *mutliple* object values for a given property. Again, an example can be found in graph G_1 in Fig. 1, with d1:Joan_Crax_Bates having two object values for the property d1:hasBrother. For such cases, a reserved delimiter (e.g. ;) is used to collect multiple object values in a single table cell.

A projected logical property table with respect to a property set P is a table that contains only the *subject* column and the properties in P. In other words, the columns $\mathcal{P} - P$ are projected out from the schema of the logical property table. As with the logical property table, the projected table also always has the *subject* column as its key.

The advantages of this tabular serialization (of an RDF graph) are subsequently described. At present, we note that, if an RDF graph G_i is accessible as a *batch* file (e.g. in N-triples format), devising a linear-time batch-processing algorithm for scanning the triples and populating the table in two passes is straightforward [11]. In a first pass, the triples would be scanned and the property set P_i would be populated, along with an index with the subject URIs as keys. In the second pass, the rows of the initialized table would be populated. The index ensures that updates and inserts into the table are near-constant.

---

[2] $B_{1,2}$ is shorthand for the phrase 'B_1 and B_2'; similarly for other quantities.

[3] *Tokens* is a function that tokenizes a string into a set of words, based on a given set of delimiters. The set of tokens generated by the blocking key is precisely the set of blocking key values (BKVs) assigned to that entity.

[4] Located in the row of subject d1:Sam_Crax and column d1:hasBrother.

If the graph is accessible through a SPARQL endpoint, an efficient procedure is less straightforward. A naïve option would be to use a SELECT * style query to download the entire graph as a batch dump and then run the linear-time algorithm mentioned above. In an online setting, bandwidth is a precious resource. If $|P| << |\mathcal{P}|$, obtaining a full batch dump is clearly not efficient.

Instead, we deploy the following query on the SPARQL endpoint to obtain a table of *loosely structured tuples*:

SELECT ?entity $?o_1 \ldots ?o_d$
WHERE{
{SELECT DISTINCT ?entity WHERE ?entity ?p ?o.
FILTER (?p = $< p_1 >$ ||$\ldots$|| ?p = $< p_d >$}}
OPTIONAL {?entity $< p_1 >$ $?o_1$}
$\ldots$
OPTIONAL {?entity $< p_n >$ $?o_d$}
}

Subject	d1:hasBrother
d1:Mike_Bates	
d1:Joan_Crax_Bates	d1:Sam_Crax
d1:Joan_Crax_Bates	d1:Roger_Crax
d1:Date	
d1:Sam_Crax	

(a)

Subject	d1:hasBrother
d1:Mike_Bates	*null*
d1:Joan_Crax_Bates	d1:Sam_Crax; d1:Roger_Crax
d1:Date	*null*
d1:Sam_Crax	*null*

(b)

Fig. 3. (a) is the table of loosely structured tuples obtained when the given SPARQL query is executed on graph G_1 in Fig. 1, assuming property set $P_1 = \{d1 : hasBrother\}$. (b) is the projected logical property table serialization of G_1 w.r.t P_1

Here, $< p_i >$ (for $i \in \{1 \ldots d\}$) is a placeholder for a property URI in P. In the nested query, the triples are filtered by the properties in P. As earlier mentioned, an RDF entity is not guaranteed to have an object value for a property in P. The *Optional* clause (for each property) provides a safeguard for this possibility.

Example 2. Consider again the first graph in Fig. 1. Assuming the blocking key *Tokens(subject)* ∪ *Tokens(d1:hasBrother)* defined in the example earlier, the loosely structured tuples generated by executing the query are shown in Fig. 3(a). Figure 3(b) shows the projected logical property table serialization of graph G_1 given the property set $P_1 = \{d1 : hasBrother\}$.

These tuples are denoted as *loosely-structured* for two reasons. First, the table is not guaranteed to contain a column that serves as a key. Secondly, there may be empty table cells. In order to impose structure on this table, therefore, the table is serialized into a projected logical property table.

We note that an advantage of employing the property table, instead of inventing a serialization, is that it already has a *physical* implementation in triple

---

Algorithm 1. Modified Sorted Neighborhood

Input: Blocking keys $B_{1,2}$, projected logical property tables $T_{1,2}$, windowing parameter w

Output: Candidate set Γ of entity-entity pairs

1. Initialize Γ to be an empty set
2. Apply B_1 (B_2) to each tuple in T_1 (T_2) to obtain *multimaps* $\Pi_1 = \{< bkv, R >\}$ ($\Pi_2 = \{< bkv, S >\}$), with bkv in each key-value set pair referring to a blocking key value string and R (S), denoted as a *block*, being a set of subject URIs in T_1 (T_2)
3. Join Π_1 and Π_2 on their keys to obtain joined map $\Pi_{map} = \{< bkv, < R, S >\}$, where $keySet[\Pi_{map}] = keySet[\Pi_1] \cap keySet[\Pi_2]$, and the larger of R and S in each pair in Π_{map} is truncated so that $|R| = |S|$
4. Sort Π_{map} into a list L with columns BKV, $subject_1$ and $subject_2$, using the keys in Π_{map} (or the BKV column) as sorting keys
5. For each tuple $< bkv, s_1, s_2 >$ in L, emit pairs $< s_1, bkv >$ and $< s_2, bkv >$ as entity-BKV pairs (Fig. 2)
6. Slide a window of size w over tuples in L (Fig. 4)
7. Add entity-entity pair $< e_1, e_2 >$ to Γ, where e_1 (e_2) is a subject URI from column $subject_1$ ($subject_2$) and e_1 and e_2 are in (not necessarily the same) tuples that fall within a common window
8. **return** Γ

---

stores such as Jena [21]. The primary advantage of the physical table is that it allows storing RDF files in back-end Relational Database infrastructure and significantly speeds up self-joins on properties for certain SPARQL queries. This paper proposes yet another use-case for this table; namely, realizing the Sorted Neighborhood algorithm for schema-free RDF data.

3.3 Candidate Set Generation

Given two projected logical property tables $T_{1,2}$ derived from graphs $G_{1,2}$, the blocking keys $B_{1,2}$, and the windowing parameter w, Algorithm 1 performs Sorted Neighborhood (SN) on $T_{1,2}$. Note that the original Sorted Neighborhood cannot be used, since it assumes either a single dataset (adhering to a single schema) or two datasets that have been individually cleansed of duplicates and then merged into a single dataset. Also, the original SN method assumes that each entity has at most one blocking key value [6]. In the heterogeneous space of RDF datasets, these assumptions are too restrictive [16]. Algorithm 1 performs the SN procedure without making these assumptions.

First, the algorithm applies the blocking keys to each tuple in the projected property tables and obtains two *multimaps* $\Pi_{1,2}$ of *blocks* indexed by a blocking key value (BKV), with each block essentially being a set of subject URIs. Considering the blocking key $B_1 = Tokens(subject) \cup Tokens(d1:hasBrother)$ in Example 1, one example of a generated block (on the first dataset in Fig. 1) would be $\{d1 : Mike\_Bates, d1 : Joan\_Crax\_Bates\}$, indexed by the BKV $Bates$, since

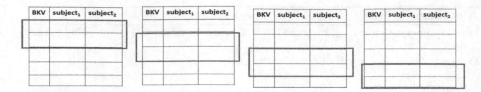

Fig. 4. The window sliding procedure on the sorted three-column list L, with $w = 2$

the two entities share a common token in their subject URIs. Note that an entity may have multiple BKVs and may occur in several blocks. Next, the algorithm joins Π_1 and Π_2 into a map Π_{map} by using the keysets (the BKVs) as the join keys. Thus, blocks in Π_1 that do not have a corresponding[5] block in Π_2 are discarded; similarly for blocks in Π_2. Also, for any two blocks R and S (from Π_1 and Π_2 respectively), we truncate the larger block by randomly removing elements till $|R| = |S|$. In line 4, Algorithm 1 sorts Π_{map} into a three-column sorted list by using the BKVs as sorting keys. This is similar to the sorting step in the original SN algorithm [6]. Finally, a window of size w is slid over the tuples in L and two entities (from columns $subject_1$ and $subject_2$ respectively) sharing a window are added to Γ (Fig. 4).

Algorithm 1 (and also, the last part of the workflow) allows the user to make operational decisions on whether the candidate set or the BKVs of entities (or both) should be *published* as sets of triples using two specially defined properties *:hasCandidate* and *:IsBKVOf* with *equivalence class* and *inverse function* semantics respectively. These triples can be published by third-party sources on dedicated servers and be made accessible as business services, similar to Relational Database cloud-based data matching[6] services.

4 Experimental Analysis

4.1 Test Cases, Metrics and Setup

The system is evaluated on five publicly available benchmarks, four of which (*Persons 1*, *Persons 2*, *Film* and *Restaurants*) were published as part of the 2010 *instance matching* track of OAEI[7], which is an annual Semantic Web initiative, and one of which (*IM-Similarity*) is a multilingual, crowdsourced dataset describing books and was released as part of OAEI 2014. These datasets, summarized in Table 1, span several domains and offer a variety of qualitative challenges.

---

[5] That is, indexed by the same blocking key value (BKV).

[6] An example is the D&B Business Insight service: https://datamarket.azure.com/dataset/dnb/businessinsight.

[7] Ontology Alignment Evaluation Initiative: http://oaei.ontologymatching.org/2010/#instance.

Table 1. Details of evaluation benchmarks. Each benchmark is a *pair* of RDF files with the notation (where applicable) being (first dataset) /× (second dataset)

ID	Name	Triples	Entity pairs	Matching entities
1	Persons 1	9000/7000	2000 × 1000 = 2 million	500
2	Persons 2	10,800/5600	2400 × 800 ≈ 1.92 million	400
3	Restaurants	1130/7520	339 × 2256 = 764,784	89
4	IM-Similarity	2204/2184	181 × 180 = 32,580	496
5	Film	9995/8979	1549 × 519 = 803,931	412

The blocking step[8] is typically evaluated by computing *efficiency* and *effectiveness* metrics for the candidate set Γ of entity-entity pairs generated by the blocking method. Let the number of *matching* (or ground-truth) entity pairs in Γ be denoted by the symbol Γ_m. Similarly, let Ω denote the full set (the Cartesian product) of entity pairs, and Ω_m denote the ground-truth set of matching entity pairs. With this terminology, the efficiency metric, *Reduction Ratio* (RR), and the effectiveness metric, *Pairs Completeness* (PC), are defined below:

$$RR = \frac{1 - |\Gamma|}{|\Omega|} \tag{1}$$

$$PC = \frac{|\Gamma_m|}{|\Omega_m|} \tag{2}$$

We capture the tradeoff between RR and PC by computing their harmonic mean or their F-score[9]:

$$F\text{-}score = \frac{2 \times RR \times PC}{(RR + PC)} \tag{3}$$

Note that, for all three metrics (PC, RR and the F-score), higher values indicate better performance.

We discovered the blocking key for each dataset in the five test cases by employing the trigrams-based Attribute Clustering (AC) algorithm that was described briefly in Sect. 3.1; complete details are provided in the original paper by Papadakis et al. [16]. In general, the learning algorithm leads to a blocking key that considers tokens of multiple properties (or 'attributes') and the name of the entity (its subject URI) as blocking key values. Brief examples were earlier provided. Once learned, Algorithm 1 is executed with w varied from 2 to 50. For each value of w, PC, RR and F-score values are recorded, with values corresponding to the highest-achieved F-score reported.

---

[8] This includes both the blocking key learning and the subsequent blocking method (such as the Sorted Neighborhood method presented in this paper).

[9] This is different from the F-score employed in Information Retrieval, where it is typically the harmonic mean of *precision* and *recall*.

4.2   Baselines and Implementation

Two baseline blocking methods are used to gauge the performance of Algorithm 1 on the five test cases. The first baseline is the *block purging* method that was used with the AC blocking key in the original paper along with a variety of other blocking methods, many of which made assumptions that are not applicable to this work [16]. Block purging was the least restrictive in terms of assumptions, simple to implement and execute (but with excellent empirical performance), and similar to the proposed method, involved a single parameter $maxPairs$. For these reasons, we employ it as a baseline to test the proposed system. Similar to lines 1–3 of Algorithm 1, block purging first generates a map of joined blocks Π_{map} (but without truncating larger blocks). Rather than employing a sliding window, the method discards an entry $< bkv, < R, S >>$ from Π_{map} if $|R||S| > maxPairs$. Among surviving entries, all entity-entity pairs in $R \times S$ are added to the candidate set Γ.

We also employed the classic *Canopy Clustering* (CC) blocking method as a second baseline [12]. CC is a generic clustering method that relies on an inexpensive similarity function such as cosine similarity, and is known to perform well on tabular datasets [4]. Given a single threshold parameter $thresh = [0, 1]$, the algorithm operates by locating for every tuple t in the *first* dataset, all tuples s in the *second* dataset such that the tuple pair $< t, s >$ has similarity at least $thresh$, and adds $< t, s >$ to the candidate set Γ. Note that CC does not rely on a blocking key, but uses all tokens in the tuples to compute the cosine similarity. We execute CC on the full[10] logical property table representations of the input RDF datasets. Similar to w in Algorithm 1 and $maxPairs$ in the block purging method, $thresh$ is varied and only the highest-achieved F-score values are reported. For a *fixed* value of the thresholds, note that the algorithms are deterministic and only need to be run once. Finally, we restricted parameter tuning (per test case) to a maximum of fifty iterations. In terms of run-time, all algorithms (for a given setting of the parameters) ran within a minute per dataset, making them roughly equal in that respect.

Finally, all programs were implemented serially in Java on a 32-bit Ubuntu virtual machine with 3385 MB of RAM and a 2.40 GHz Intel 4700MQ i7 processor. We have released datasets and ground-truth files on a project website[11].

4.3   Results and Discussion

Table 2 shows the highest F-scores obtained by the proposed method and the block purging baseline, along with corresponding PC and RR values. The results show that, on three of the five test cases, the modified SN procedure outperforms the block purging algorithm. On the RR metric, SN outperforms block purging by over 6 % and on the F-score metric by over 3.5 %. On the PC metric, block purging does better by about 1.7 %. Overall, the results show that the modified

---

[10] Since there is no blocking key (and no property set), projection does not take place.
[11] https://sites.google.com/a/utexas.edu/mayank-kejriwal/projects/
    sorted-neighborhood.

Table 2. Comparative results of Algorithm 1 and the block purging baseline. Both methods used the same blocking key, learned through Attribute Clustering [16]. *Count* tabulates number of test cases on which a method performs *equal/better/worse*

Test Case	Sorted Neighborhood			Block Purging		
	PC	RR	F-score	PC	RR	F-score
1 Persons 1	100.00 %	99.26 %	**99.63 %**	100.00 %	98.86 %	99.43 %
2 Persons 2	91.25 %	89.77 %	90.50 %	99.75 %	99.02 %	**99.38 %**
3 Restaurants	100.00 %	99.41 %	99.70 %	100.00 %	99.57 %	**99.79 %**
4 IM-Similarity	100.00 %	84.73 %	**91.73 %**	100.00 %	62.79 %	77.14 %
5 Film	97.33 %	92.10 %	**94.64 %**	97.33 %	73.09 %	83.49 %
Average	*97.72 %*	**93.05 %**	**95.24 %**	**99.42 %**	*86.67 %*	*91.85 %*
Count	*4/0/1*	*0/3/2*	*0/3/2*	*4/1/0*	*0/2/3*	*0/2/3*

SN algorithm is a promising blocking candidate. We note that, on the RR metric in particular, the SN algorithm is more *stable*, with block purging achieving less than 75 % on at least two datasets. As earlier authors have noted [4], even small variations in RR can have a large impact on the run-time of a full ER workflow, since RR is quadratic in the number of input entities (Eq. 1). Thus, SN may be a more reliable method than block purging under resource-constrained settings.

Although not tabulated here due to space constraints, the average (on the five test cases) highest F-score and corresponding PC and RR results obtained by the Canopy Clustering (CC) baseline are 84.74 %, 80.39 % and 96.58 % respectively. Both the block purging and proposed method outperform CC on both PC and F-score by a large margin, demonstrating that on schema-free RDF data, simple token-based blocking techniques are rarely sufficient.

5   Conclusion and Future Work

In this paper, we proposed a Sorted Neighborhood workflow for schema-free RDF data, implemented as a sequence of relatively independent modules. All workflow steps can be operationalized using existing Semantic Web technology. Evaluations on five test cases show that the proposed algorithm is competitive with established blocking techniques for schema-free RDF data.

Future work will aim to deploy the system as a Linked Data service in a distributed paradigm, and to evaluate it on large-scale datasets. Given certain assumptions about the input datasets, a promising theoretical avenue is to automatically determine the optimal value of w for the inputs.

References

1. Bilenko, M., Kamath, B., Mooney, R.J.: Adaptive blocking: learning to scale up record linkage. In: Sixth International Conference on Data Mining, 2006. ICDM 2006, pp. 87–96. IEEE (2006)
2. Bizer, C., Heath, T., Berners-Lee, T.: Linked data-the story so far. Int. J. semant. Web Inf. Syst. **5**(3), 1–22 (2009)
3. Christen, P.: Further topics and research directions. In: Christen, P. (ed.) Data Matching, pp. 209–228. Springer, Heidelberg (2012)
4. Christen, P.: A survey of indexing techniques for scalable record linkage and deduplication. IEEE Trans. Knowl. Data Eng. **24**(9), 1537–1555 (2012)
5. Elmagarmid, A.K., Ipeirotis, P.G., Verykios, V.S.: Duplicate record detection: a survey. IEEE Trans. Knowl. Data Eng. **19**(1), 1–16 (2007)
6. Hernández, M.A., Stolfo, S.J.: The merge/purge problem for large databases. In: ACM SIGMOD Record, vol. 24, pp. 127–138. ACM (1995)
7. Hernández, M.A., Stolfo, S.J.: Real-world data is dirty: data cleansing and the merge/purge problem. Data Min. Knowl. Disc. **2**(1), 9–37 (1998)
8. Isele, R., Jentzsch, A., Bizer, C.: Efficient multidimensional blocking for link discovery without losing recall. In: WebDB (2011)
9. Kejriwal, M., Miranker, D.P.: An unsupervised algorithm for learning blocking schemes. In: Thirteenth International Conference on Data Mining, ICDM 2013. IEEE (2013)
10. Kejriwal, M., Miranker, D.P.: A two-step blocking scheme learner for scalable link discovery. In: Thirteenth International Semantic Web Conference on Ontology Matching Workshop, ISWC 2014 (2014)
11. Kejriwal, M., Miranker, D.P.: A dnf blocking scheme learner for heterogeneous datasets (2015). arXiv preprint arXiv:1501.01694
12. McCallum, A., Nigam, K., Ungar, L.H.: Efficient clustering of high-dimensional data sets with application to reference matching. In: Proceedings of the Sixth ACM SIGKDD International Conference on Knowledge Discovery and Data Mining, pp. 169–178. ACM (2000)
13. McCarthy, J.F., Lehnert, W.G.: Using decision trees for coreference resolution (1995). arXiv preprint cmp-lg/9505043
14. Newcombe, H., Kennedy, J., Axford, S., James, A.: Automatic linkage of vital records (1959)
15. Ngomo, A.-C.N.: A time-efficient hybrid approach to link discovery. In: Ontology Matching, p. 1 (2011)
16. Papadakis, G., Ioannou, E., Niederée, C., Fankhauser, P.: Efficient entity resolution for large heterogeneous information spaces. In: Proceedings of the Fourth ACM International Conference on Web Search and Data Mining, pp. 535–544. ACM (2011)
17. Puhlmann, S., Weis, M., Naumann, F.: XML duplicate detection using sorted neighborhoods. In: Ioannidis, Y., Scholl, M.H., Schmidt, J.W., Matthes, F., Hatzopoulos, M., Böhm, K., Kemper, A., Grust, T., Böhm, C. (eds.) EDBT 2006. LNCS, vol. 3896, pp. 773–791. Springer, Heidelberg (2006)
18. Scharffe, F., Ferrara, A., Nikolov, A., et al.: Data linking for the semantic web. Int. J. Seman. Web Inf. Syst. **7**(3), 46–76 (2011)
19. Scharffe, F., Liu, Y., Zhou, C.: RDF-AI: an architecture for RDF datasets matching, fusion and interlink. In: Proceedings of the IJCAI 2009 workshop on Identity, reference, and knowledge representation (IR-KR), Pasadena (CA US) (2009)

20. Schmachtenberg, M., Bizer, C., Paulheim, H.: Adoption of the linked data best practices in different topical domains. In: Mika, P., et al. (eds.) ISWC 2014, Part I. LNCS, vol. 8796, pp. 245–260. Springer, Heidelberg (2014)
21. Wilkinson, K., Sayers, C., Kuno, H.A., Reynolds, D., et al.: Efficient RDF storage and retrieval in Jena2. SWDB **3**, 131–150 (2003)

The Triplex Approach for Recognizing Semantic Relations from Noun Phrases, Appositions, and Adjectives

Seyed Iman Mirrezaei[1]([✉]), Bruno Martins[2],
and Isabel F. Cruz[1]

[1] ADVIS Lab, Department of Computer Science,
University of Illinois at Chicago, Chicago, USA
smirre2@uic.edu, ifc@cs.uic.edu
[2] Instituto Superior Técnico and INESC-ID,
Universidade de Lisboa, Lisbon, Portugal
bruno.g.martins@tecnico.ulisboa.pt

Abstract. Discovering knowledge from textual sources and subsequently expanding the coverage of knowledge bases like DBpedia or Freebase currently requires either extensive manual work or carefully designed information extractors. Information extractors capture triples from textual sentences. Each triple consists of a subject, a predicate/property, and an object. Triples can be mediated via verbs, nouns, adjectives, and appositions. We propose TRIPLEX, an information extractor that complements previous efforts, concentrating on noun-mediated triples related to nouns, adjectives, and appositions. TRIPLEX automatically constructs templates expressing noun-mediated triples from a bootstrapping set. The bootstrapping set is constructed without manual intervention by creating templates that include syntactic, semantic, and lexical constraints. We report on an automatic evaluation method to examine the output of information extractors both with and without the TRIPLEX approach. Our experimental study indicates that TRIPLEX is a promising approach for extracting noun-mediated triples.

Keywords: Open domain information extraction · Relation extraction · Noun-mediated relation triples · Compound nouns · Appositions

1 Introduction

Deriving useful knowledge from unstructured text is a challenging task. Nowadays, knowledge needs to be extracted almost instantaneously and automatically from continuous streams of information such as those generated by news agencies or published by individuals on the social web to enrich properties related to people, places, and organizations in existing large-scale knowledge bases, such as Freebase [3], DBpedia [1], or Google's Knowledge Graph [11]. Subsequently these values can be used by search engines to provide answers for user queries

© Springer International Publishing Switzerland 2015
F. Gandon et al. (Eds.): ESWC 2015, LNCS 9341, pp. 230–243, 2015.
DOI: 10.1007/978-3-319-25639-9_39

(e.g., the resignation date of a given politician, or the ownership after a company acquisition). For many natural language processing (NLP) applications, including question answering, information retrieval, machine translation, and information extraction, it is important to extract facts from text. For example, a question answering system may need to find the location of the *Microsoft Visitor Center* in the sentence *The video features the Microsoft Visitor Center, located in Redmond.*

Open Information Extractors (OIE) aim to extract triples from text, with each triple consisting of a subject, a predicate/property, and an object. These triples can be expressed via verbs, nouns, adjectives, and appositions. Most OIE systems described in the literature, such as TextRunner [2], WOE [12], or ReVerb [7], focus on the extraction of verb-mediated triples. Other OIE systems, such as OLLIE [9], ClauseIE [6], Xavier and Lima's system [14], or ReNoun [15], may also, or only, extract noun-mediated triples from text. OLLIE was the first approach for simultaneously extracting verb-mediated and noun-mediated triples, although it can only capture noun-meditated triples that are expressed in verb-mediated formats. For example, OLLIE can extract the triple <Bill Gates; be co-founder of; Microsoft> from the sentence *Microsoft co-founder Bill Gates spoke at a conference* but it cannot extract a triple <Microsoft; headquarter; Redmond> from the sentence *Microsoft is an American corporation headquartered in Redmond.* ClauseIE extracts noun-mediated triples from appositions and possessives based upon a predefined set of rules. ReNoun uses seeds (i.e., examples gathered through manually crafted rules) and an ontology to learn patterns for extracting noun-mediated triples.

The OIE system that we have built is named Triplex. It is designed specifically to extract triples from noun phrases, adjectives, and appositions. Systems like OLLIE, which can only extract triples corresponding to relations expressed through verb phrases, can be assisted by Triplex, which extracts triples from grammatical dependency relations involving noun phrases and modifiers that correspond to adjectives and appositions. Triplex recognizes templates that express noun-mediated triples during its automatic bootstrapping process. The bootstrapping process finds sentences that express noun-mediated triples using Wikipedia pages. Then, it constructs templates from sentences in the bootstrapping set. The templates express how noun-mediated triples occur in sentences and they allow for information to be extracted relating to different levels of text analysis, from lexical (i.e., word tokens) and shallow syntactic features (i.e., part-of-speech tags), to features resulting from a deeper syntactic analysis (i.e., features derived from dependency parsing). In addition, semantic constraints may be included in some templates to obtain more precise extractions. Templates are then generalized to broaden their coverage (i.e., those with similar constraints are merged together). Finally, the templates can be used to extract triples from previously unseen text. We evaluated Triplex according to the automated framework of Bronzi et al. [4], extending it to assess noun-mediated triples.

The remainder of this paper is organized as follows: In Sect. 2, we briefly summarize related work in the area of open-domain information extraction. The TRIPLEX pipeline is presented in Sect. 3. Section 4 describes our experiments, ending with a discussion of the obtained results. Finally, Sect. 5 concludes the paper, summarizing the main aspects and presenting possible directions for future work.

2 Related Work

OIE systems are used to extract triples from text and they can be classified into two major groups. The first group includes systems that extract verb-mediated triples (i.e., TextRunner [2], WOE [12], ReVerb [7], or OLLIE [9]). The second group includes systems that extract noun-mediated triples (i.e., OLLIE [9], ClauseIE [6], Xavier and Lima's system [14], and ReNoun [15]).

In the first group, the earliest proposed OIE system was TextRunner. This system first detects pairs of noun phrases and it then finds a sequence of words as a potential relation (i.e., predicate) between each pair of noun phrases. In a similar way, WOE uses a dependency parser to find the shortest dependency path between two noun phrases. All of the approaches in the first group assume that the object occurs after the subject.

OLLIE, which is a member of both the first and the second groups, was the first approach to extract both noun-mediated and verb-mediated triples. It uses high confidence triples extracted by ReVerb as a bootstrapping set to learn patterns. These patterns, mostly based on dependency parse trees, indicate different ways of expressing triples in textual sources. It is important to note that OLLIE only extracts noun-mediated triples that can be expressed via verb-mediated formats. Therefore, it only covers a limited group of noun-mediated triples. In comparison, TRIPLEX only extracts triples from compound nouns, adjectives, and appositions. ClauseIE uses knowledge about the English grammar to detect clauses based on the dependency parse trees of sentences [6]. Subsequently, triples are generated depending on the type of those clauses. ClauseIE has predefined rules to extract triples from dependency parse trees and it is able to generate both verb-mediated triples from clauses and noun-mediated triples from possessives and appositions. In contrast, TRIPLEX automatically learns rules that extract triples during its bootstrapping process.

Xavier and Lima use a boosting approach to expand the training set for information extractors so as to cover an increased variety of noun-mediated triples [14]. They find verb interpretations for noun and adjective based phrases. Then, the verb interpretations are transformed into verb-mediated triples to enrich the training set. Still, these verb interpretations can create long and ambiguous sentences. Therefore, filtering unrelated interpretations is essential before adding the inferred verb interpretations to the training set of information extractors. TRIPLEX does not depend on verb patterns to extract noun-mediated triples, thereby making such filtering unnecessary. Closer to our work is ReNoun, a system that uses an ontology of noun attributes and a manually crafted set of extraction rules, to extract seeds [15]. The seeds are then used to learn dependency parse patterns for extracting triples. In contrast, TRIPLEX uses data from Wikipedia during its bootstrapping process without requiring manual intervention.

3   Triplex

OIE systems extract triples from an input sentence according to the format `<subject; relation;object>`. In these triples, a relation phrase (i.e., a predicate or property) expresses a semantic relation between the subject and the object. The subject and the object are noun phrases and the relation phrase is a textual fragment that indicates a semantic relation between two noun phrases. The semantic relation can be verb-mediated or noun-mediated. For example, an extractor may find the triples `<Kevin Systrom;profession;cofounder>` and `<KevinSystrom;appears on; NBC News>` in the sentence *Instagram cofounder Kevin Systrom appears on NBC News.* The first triple is noun-mediated and the second one is verb-mediated.

The TRIPLEX approach focuses on noun-mediated triples from noun phrases, adjectives, and appositions. First, it finds sentences that express noun-mediated triples. These sentences are detected by using a dependency parser to find grammatical relations between nouns, adjectives, and appositions. Second, it automatically extracts templates from the sentences. Finally, these templates are used to extract noun-mediated triples from previously unseen text.

The TRIPLEX pipeline uses the Stanford NLP toolkit[1] to parse sentences, extract dependencies, label tokens with named entity (NE) and with part-of-speech (POS) information, and perform coreference resolution. The coreference resolution module is used to replace in all the sentences pronouns and other coreferential mentions with the corresponding entity spans prior to subsequent processing. The dependency parser discovers the syntactic structure of input sentences. A dependency parse of a sentence is a directed graph whose vertices are words and whose edges are syntactic relations between the words. Each dependency corresponds to a binary grammatical relation between a governor and a dependent [5]. For example, the dependency relations `nsubj<went,Obama>` and `prep-to<went,Denver>` can be found in the sentence *Obama went to Denver.* In the dependency relation `prep-to<went,Denver>`, the word `went` is the governor and the word `Denver` is the dependent. The part-of-speech tagger assigns a morpho-syntactic class to each word, such as noun, verb, or adjective. The Named Entity Recognition (NER) model[2] labels sequences of words according to pre-defined entity categories: *Person, Organization, Location,* and *Date.*

The other components of the pipeline are a noun phrase chunker, which complements the POS, NER, and dependency parsing modules from the Stanford NLP toolkit, WordNet synsets, and Wikipedia synsets. The noun phrase chunker extracts noun phrases from sentences. WordNet is a lexical database that categorizes English words into sets of synonyms called synsets. WordNet synsets

---

[1] http://nlp.stanford.edu/software/corenlp.shtml.
[2] http://nlp.stanford.edu/software/CRF-NER.shtml.

are used to recognize entities within each sentence according to the pre-defined categories, complementing the Stanford NER system. Several synsets are also built for each Wikipedia page. There are different mentions for a Wikipedia page (e.g., redirects and alternative names) and also in the hypertext anchors that point to a Wikipedia page. For example, in the Wikipedia page for the *University of Illinois at Chicago*, the word *UIC* is extensively used to refer to the university. Synsets of Wikipedia pages are constructed automatically by using redirection page links, backward links, and hypertext anchors. These links are retrieved using the Java-based Wikipedia Library[3].

TRIPLEX uses infobox properties and infobox values of Wikipedia during its bootstrapping process. We use a Wikipedia English dump[4] to extract all Wikipedia pages and we query Freebase and DBpedia according to the Wikipedia page ID to determine the type of the page. Wikipedia pages are categorized under the following types: *Person, Organization,* or *Location.* Additionally, we perform coreference resolution on the extracted Wikipedia pages to identify words that refer to the same Wikipedia page subject. We then use these words to enrich synsets of the respective Wikipedia page. We now describe the TRIPLEX approach for extracting templates, starting with the generation of the bootstrapping set of sentences.

3.1 Bootstrapping Set Creation

Following ideas from the OLLIE system, which leverages bootstrapping [9], our first goal is to construct automatically a bootstrapping set that expresses in multiple ways how the information in noun phrases, adjectives, and appositions is encapsulated. The bootstrapping set is created by processing the extracted Wikipedia pages and their corresponding infoboxes.

Wikipedia pages without infobox templates are ignored during sentence extraction, while the other pages are converted into sets of sentences. Finally, we perform preprocessing on the sentences from the extracted Wikipedia pages and we use custom templates (i.e., regular expressions) to identify infobox values from the text. We also convert dates to strings. For instance, the infobox with value 1961|8|4 is translated to August 4, 1961. We begin template extraction by processing 3,061,956 sentences from the extracted Wikipedia pages that are matched with infobox values.

The sentence extractor automatically constructs a bootstrapping set by matching infobox values of the extracted Wikipedia pages with phrases from the text of the corresponding Wikipedia pages. If in a sentence there exists a dependency path between the current infobox value and the synset of the page name, and if this dependency path only contains nouns, adjectives, and appositions, then the sentence is extracted. For instance, given the page for *Barack Obama*, the extractor matches the infobox value *August 4, 1961* with the sentence *Barack Hussein Obama II (born August 4, 1961).* This process is repeated for all infobox values of a Wikipedia page.

---

[3] https://code.google.com/p/jwpl/.
[4] http://dumps.wikimedia.org/backup-index.html.

In order to match complete names with abbreviations such as *UIC*, the extractor uses a set of heuristics that was originally proposed in WOE [12], named *full match*, *synset match*, and *partial match*. The full match heuristic is used when the page name is found within a sentence of the page. The synset match heuristic is used when one member of the synset for the page name is discovered within a sentence. The partial match heuristic is used when a prefix or suffix of a member of the synset is used in a sentence. Finally, a template is created by marking an infobox value and a synset member in the dependency path of a selected sentence. We apply a constraint on the length of the dependency path between a synset member and an infobox value to reduce bootstrapping errors. This constraint sets the maximum length of the dependency path to 6, a value which was determined experimentally by checking the quality of our bootstrapping set. Specifically, we randomly selected 100 sentences for manual examination; of these, 90 % satisfied the dependency path length constraint.

After creating the bootstrapping set, the next step is to automatically create templates from dependency paths that express noun-mediated triples. Templates describe how noun-mediated triples can occur in textual sentences. Each template results from a dependency path between a synset member (a subject) and an infobox value (an object). We annotate these paths with POS tags, named entities, and WordNet synsets. In the template, to each infobox value we add the name of the infobox. In addition, a template includes a template type, based on the types of the Wikipedia page where the sentence occurred. The types of dependencies between synset members and infobox values are also attached to the template. If there is a copular verb or a verbal modifier in the dependency path, we will add them as a lexical constraint to the template. For example, *headquartered* is a verbal modifier added as a lexical constraint to the corresponding template for the sentence: *Microsoft is an American corporation headquartered in Redmond* (see Fig. 1). *Born* is another lexical constraint for templates related to nationality, as in the sentence *The Italian-born Antonio Verrio was frequently commissioned*. We merge templates if the only differences among them relate to lexical constraints. We keep one template and a list of lexical constraints for the merged templates. Finally, we process all templates and remove redundant ones.

Infobox values may occur before or after synset members of the page name in sentences. If there exists a dependency path between these values independently of their position, the related template is extracted. For example, the infobox value occurs before the synset member in the sentence *Instagram co-founder Kevin Systrom announced a hiring spree*. In this example, *co-founder* is the infobox value and *Steve Hafner* is the synset member of the Wikipedia page. The infobox value may also occur after the synset member, as shown in the sentence *Microsoft is an American corporation headquartered in Redmond*. In this case, *corporation* is the synset member and *Redmond* is the infobox value (see Fig. 1).

The noun phrase chunker is finally used to search dependency paths and merge words that are part of the same noun phrase chunk. In addition, we do

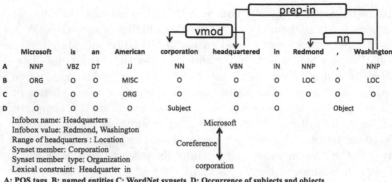

Fig. 1. An example sentence annotated with the corresponding dependency relations, the POS tags for the word tokens, named entities, WordNet synsets, and occurrences of the synset member of the Wikipedia page (subjects) and the infobox values (objects).

not apply the noun phrase chunker if a synset member and the infobox value occur in the same chunk.

3.2 Template Matching

This section describes how we use the dependency paths of a sentence together with the extracted templates to detect noun-mediated triples. First, named entities and WordNet synsets are used to recognize the candidate subjects of a sentence together with their types. Then, dependency paths between candidate subjects and all potential objects are identified and annotated by the NLP pipeline. Finally, candidate infobox names (which are properties in DBpedia) are assigned to a candidate subject and a candidate object, derived from matching templates with subject types, dependency types, WordNet synsets, POS tags, and named entity annotations. If there are lexical constraints in a template, the words in the dependency path between a subject and an object must be matched with one of the phrases in the lexical constraint list. We also consider the semantic similarity between the words and the member of the lexical constraint list, using Jiang and Conrath's approach to calculate the semantic similarity between words [8].

When there is a specific range (*Person, Organization, Location*, or *Date*) for an infobox name (property) of a triple, and when the object type of a triple is unknown, a previously trained confidence function is used to adjust the confidence score of the triple. A logistic regression classifier is used in this confidence function after it is trained using 500 triples extracted from Wikipedia pages. Our confidence function is an extension of the confidence function proposed for OLLIE [9] and for ReVerb [7]. A set of features (i.e., frequency of the extraction template, existence of particular lexical features in templates, range of properties, and semantic object type) are computed for each extracted triple. The confidence score is assigned the probability computed by the classifier.

Finally, each candidate triple has an infobox name that is mapped to a DBpedia property and the object type of a candidate triple should be matched with the range of that property. When the range of a property is a literal, all possible values of the property are retrieved from DBpedia and compared with the candidate object. If their values are not matched, the candidate triple is discarded.

4   Evaluation

We conducted a comprehensive set of experiments to compare the outputs of TRIPLEX, OLLIE, and ReVerb based upon the approach by Bronzi et al. [4]. These authors introduced an approach to evaluate verb-mediated information extractors automatically. We improve on their approach by expanding it to the evaluation of noun-mediated triples. Additionally, we compare TRIPLEX, OLLIE, and ReVerb using a manually constructed gold standard. Finally, we compare the various information extractors according to the quality of their extracted triples.

We first created a dataset by taking 1000 random sentences from Wikipedia that have not been used during the bootstrapping process. Each sentence in the test dataset has a corresponding Wikipedia page ID. All extracted facts gathered by information extractors from these sentences needed to be verified. We recall that a fact is a triple `<subject;predicate;object>` that expresses a relation between a subject and an object. A fact is correct if its corresponding triple has been found in the Freebase or DBpedia knowledge bases or if there is a significant association between the entities (subjects and objects) and its predicate [4] according to Eq. 2. In order to estimate the precision of an information extractor, we use the following formula:

$$Precision = \frac{|a| + |b|}{|S|} \qquad (1)$$

In Eq. 1, $|b|$ is the number of extracted facts from Freebase and DBpedia, $|S|$ is the total number of facts extracted by the system, and $|a|$ is the number of correct facts returned by the information extractor, which have been validated by using the pointwise mutual information (PMI), as defined in Eq. 2. Since values of properties in Freebase and DBpedia are not completely filled, Bronzi et al. [4] compute the PMI to verify a fact. The PMI of a fact measures the likelihood of observing the fact given that we observed its subject ($subj$) and object (obj), independently of the predicate ($pred$):

$$\text{PMI}(subj, pred, obj) = \frac{\text{Count}(subj \wedge pred \wedge obj)}{\text{Count}(subj \wedge obj)} \qquad (2)$$

When verifying the extracted facts, we use the corresponding Wikipedia ID of each sentence to retrieve all possible properties and their values from Freebase or DBpedia. These values are then used to verify extracted facts from sentences. The semantic similarity between the properties of those knowledge bases and the predicate of a fact are calculated [8]. The semantic similarity measure uses Word-Net together with corpus statistics to calculate the semantic similarity between phrases. If the semantic similarity is above a predetermined threshold and if the entities corresponding to the subject and object also match the knowledge base properties, then the fact is deemed correct [4].

The function Count(q) returns the number of results retrieved by the Google search engine for query q, where the elements of the query occur within the maximum distance of 4 words. The range of the PMI function is between 0 and 1. The higher the PMI value, the more likely that the fact is correct. Specifically, a fact is deemed correct if its PMI value is above the threshold of 10^{-3}, which was determined experimentally. We also use the method in Eq. 3 to estimate recall [4]:

$$Recall = \frac{|a| + |b|}{|a| + |b| + |c| + |d|} \tag{3}$$

The parameters $|a|$ and $|b|$ are computed as in Eq. 1. We now describe how $|c|$ and $|d|$ are computed. First, all correct facts within sentences of the dataset are identified. Each fact contains two entities and a relation. All possible entities of a sentence are detected by the Stanford NER and from the WordNet synsets. Furthermore, we use the Stanford CoreNLP toolkit to detect all verbs (predicates) in a sentence. Finally, we expand the set of predicates from sentences by adding DBpedia and Freebase properties.

We use three sets S, P, and O to create all the possible facts, which are respectively the set of recognized subjects, predicates, and objects in the sentences. All possible facts are produced by the Cartesian product of these three sets, $G = (S \times P \times O)$. Assuming that D is the set of all the facts in Freebase and in DBpedia, $|c|$ is computed as follows:

$$|c| = |D \cap G| - |b| \tag{4}$$

Finally, $|d|$ is determined by subtracting $|a|$ from the size of the set of all facts in G that are not in D, which have been validated using PMI (that is, those whose PMI is above the threshold).

We further select 50 sentences from the dataset of 1000 sentences, and a human judge extracts all of the correct facts. Then, we use the method by Bronzi et al. [4] to compute the agreement between the automatic and manual evaluations. The agreement is defined as the ratio between the number of facts where the human and automatic evaluators agree and the total number of facts. This agreement was found to be 0.71. With this information, we are able to determine the precision and recall of our information extractors.

We ran OLLIE, ReVerb, and TRIPLEX individually and then we combine TRIPLEX with OLLIE and with ReVerb. Table 1 shows the results in terms of precision, recall, and F_1 (harmonic mean of precision and recall).

ReVerb only generates verb-mediated triples and OLLIE extracts verb-mediated triples and also noun-mediated triples, if they are expressed in verb-mediated styles. TRIPLEX generates noun-mediated triples and it can complement the results of OLLIE and ReVerb. OLLIE, ReVerb, and TRIPLEX all assign a confidence score to each extracted triple. In these experiments, the extracted triples are only considered if their confidence scores are above a threshold of 0.2. TRIPLEX shows an improvement in Table 1 when using the manual evaluation instead of the automatic evaluation because extracted facts with very low PMI are considered false in the automatic evaluation. However, these facts are often evaluated as true by a human judge. We analyze the errors made by TRIPLEX in the gold standard dataset that was manually annotated. The errors made by TRIPLEX can be classified into two groups: false positives and false negatives. In the gold standard, 65 % of the triples are related to verb-mediated triples, which are not extracted by TRIPLEX.

Table 1. Automatic and manual evaluation of information extractors. OLLIE * only generates noun-mediated triples. The confidence scores of all extracted triples are above 0.2.

	Automatic evaluation			Manual evaluation		
	Precision	Recall	F1	Precision	Recall	F1
ReVerb	0.61	0.15	0.24	0.55	0.11	0.18
OLLIE	**0.64**	0.30	0.40	**0.65**	0.32	0.42
OLLIE*	0.62	0.10	0.17	0.63	0.11	0.18
TRIPLEX	0.55	0.17	0.25	0.62	0.22	0.32
TRIPLEX + OLLIE	0.57	**0.40**	**0.47**	0.63	**0.44**	**0.51**
TRIPLEX + ReVerb	0.58	0.32	0.41	0.55	0.35	0.42

Table 2 shows the results associated with the triples in the gold standard that are not extracted by TRIPLEX. Of those, 10 % obtain low confidence scores (false negatives) because the NER module and WordNet could not find the semantic type for the objects. We penalize the confidence score of a candidate triple if its predicate has one particular property type and if no type is detected for the triple's object. For example, the range of the *nationality* property in DBpedia is a *Location* constraint but neither the NER module nor WordNet can recognize a type in the phrase *Swedish writer* or *Polish-American scientist*. Also, 12 % of the errors are related to the dependency parser, specifically when the parser could not detect a correct grammatical relation between the words in a sentence. Another 7 % of the errors occur when the coreferencing module did not properly resolve coreferential expressions during template extraction. This problem is alleviated by assigning low confidence scores to this group of templates. Finally, 6 % of the errors are caused by over-generalized templates. During template generalization, POS tags are substituted by universal POS tags [10]. Since some templates only extract triples for proper nouns, nouns, or personal pronouns, generalizing and merging these templates together did not produce correct triples.

Approximately 20 % of the false positives are in fact correct triples. This stems from the fact that there are few Google search results for queries that

Table 2. Percentage of the gold standard triples missed by TRIPLEX.

	Missed extractions
10 %	No semantic types
12 %	Dependency parser problems
7 %	Coreferencing errors
6 %	Over generalized templates
65 %	Verb-mediated triples (outside the of scope for TRIPLEX)

contain the subjects of these triples, thus impacting the computation of the PMI scores. Applying the same PMI threshold as used for prominent subjects proved to be ineffective. For example, triples extracted by TRIPLEX are judged incorrect in the sentence, *Alexey Arkhipovich Leonov (born 30 May 1934 in Listvyanka, Kemerovo Oblast, Soviet Union) is a retired Soviet/Russian cosmonaut.* These triples include information about birth date, birth place, origin, and profession, but are not available in the gold standard. Other false positives are due to problems resulting from dependency parsing, named entity recognition, chunking, and over generalized templates.

OIE systems such as ReVerb and OLLIE usually fail to extract triples from compound nouns, adjectives, conjunctions, reduced clauses, parenthetical phrases, and appositions. TRIPLEX only covers noun-mediated triples in sentences.

Table 3. Distribution of correctly extracted triples for TRIPLEX + OLLIE based on their categories. The confidence score of extracted triples by TRIPLEX and OLLIE is above 0.2.

	Distribution	Triple category
Noun-mediated	12 %	Conjunctions, adjectives and noun phrases
	9 %	Appositions and parenthetical phrases
	6 %	Titles or professions
	8 %	Templates with lexicon
Verb-mediated	65 %	Verb-mediated triples

We also examine the output of TRIPLEX with respect to the gold standard, as shown in Table 3. The table shows that 12 % of the noun-mediated triples are related to conjunctions, adjectives, and noun phrases, meaning that TRIPLEX is also able to extract noun-mediated triples from noun conjunctions. For example, TRIPLEX extracts triples about Rye Barcott's professions from the sentences *Rye Barcott is author of It Happened on the Way to War and he is a former U.S. Marine and cofounder of Carolina for Kibera.* Moreover, TRIPLEX is able to extract triples from appositions and parenthetical phrases, and 9 % of the extracted triples are contained within the triple category of appositions and parenthetical phrases. For example, extracted triples from *Michelle LaVaughn Robinson Obama (born January 17, 1964), an American lawyer and writer, is the wife of the current president of the United States* contain Michelle Obama's two professions, birth date, and nationality. We saw that 6 % of the triples are related to titles or professions, such as *Sir Herbert Lethington Maitland, Film director Ingmar Bergman,* and *Microsoft co-founder Bill Gates*. OLLIE is similarly able to capture this kind of triples because they are expressed in a verb-mediated style. However, TRIPLEX does so without using a verb-mediated format. The final fraction of 8 % is for noun-mediated triples that rely on the lexicon of noun-mediated templates. For example, the *headquarters* of Microsoft is extracted from the sentence, *Microsoft is an American multinational corporation headquartered in Redmond, Washington*. Finally, 65 % of the extracted triples are verb-mediated triples. Both ReVerb and OLLIE generate verb-mediated triples from sentences. The majority of errors produced by OLLIE and ReVerb are due to incorrectly identifying subjects or objects. ReVerb first locates verbs in a sentence and then looks for noun phrases to the left and right of the verbs. ReVerb's heuristics sometimes fail to find correct subjects and objects because of compound nouns, appositions, reduced clauses, or conjunctions. OLLIE relies on extracted triples from ReVerb for its bootstrapping process and learning patterns. Although OLLIE produces noun-meditated triples if they can be expressed with verb-mediated formats, it does not cover all formats of noun-mediated triples.

Finally, we analyze some sentences to figure out why different information extractors are not able to produce all of the triples in the gold standard. The first reason is that there may not be sufficient information in a sentence to extract triples. For example, TRIPLEX can find the triple <Antonio;nationality;Italian> but it cannot find the triple <Antonio;nationality;England> in the sentence *The Italian-born Antonio Verrio was responsible for introducing Baroque mural painting into England*. Second, OLLIE and ReVerb cannot successfully extract verb-mediated triples from sentences that contain compound nouns, appositions, parentheses, conjunctions, or reduced clauses. When OLLIE and ReVerb cannot yield verb-mediated triples, recall will be affected because verb-mediated triples are outside of the scope of TRIPLEX. Improvements to OLLIE and ReVerb could substantially lead to better results in TRIPLEX. Also, improvements to the different NLP components can lead to better precision and recall for information extractors that rely heavily on them.

5   Conclusions and Future Work

This paper presented TRIPLEX, an information extractor to generate triples from noun phrases, adjectives, and appositions. First, a bootstrapping set is automatically constructed from infoboxes in Wikipedia pages. Then, templates with semantic, syntactic, and lexical constraints are constructed automatically to capture triples. Our experiments found that TRIPLEX complements the output of verb-mediated information extractors by capturing noun-mediated triples. The extracted triples can for instance be used to populate Wikipedia pages with missing infobox attribute values or to assist authors in the task of annotating Wikipedia pages. We also extended an automated evaluation method to include noun-mediated triples.

In future work, we plan to improve upon the generation of extraction templates by considering numerical values and their units (e.g., meter, square meter). We would also like to enrich the bootstrapping set generation process by using a probabilistic knowledge base (e.g., Probase [13]), as it may broaden the coverage of the bootstrapping set and support the construction of more templates.

Acknowledgments. We would like to thank Matteo Palmonari for useful discussions. Cruz and Mirrezaei were partially supported by NSF Awards CCF-1331800, IIS-1213013, and IIS-1143926. Cruz was also supported by a Great Cities Institute scholarship. Martins was supported by the Portuguese FCT through the project grants EXCL/EEI-ESS/0257/2012 (DataStorm Research Line of Excellence) and PEst-OE/EEI/LA0021/2013 (INESC-ID's Associate Laboratory multi-annual funding).

References

1. Auer, S., Bizer, C., Kobilarov, G., Lehmann, J., Cyganiak, R., Ives, Z.G.: DBpedia: a nucleus for a web of open data. In: Aberer, K., et al. (eds.) ASWC 2007 and ISWC 2007. LNCS, vol. 4825, pp. 722–735. Springer, Heidelberg (2007)
2. Banko, M., Cafarella, M.J., Soderland, S., Broadhead, M., Etzioni, O.: Open information extraction for the web. In: International Joint Conference on Artificial Intelligence (IJCAI), pp. 2670–2676 (2007)
3. Bollacker, K., Evans, C., Paritosh, P., Sturge, T., Taylor, J.: Freebase: a collaboratively created graph database for structuring human knowledge. In: ACM SIGMOD International Conference on Management of Data, pp. 1247–1250 (2008)
4. Bronzi, M., Guo, Z., Mesquita, F., Barbosa, D., Merialdo, P.: Automatic evaluation of relation extraction systems on large-scale. In: NAACL-HLT Joint Workshop on Automatic Knowledge Base Construction and Web-scale Knowledge Extraction (AKBC-WEKEX), pp. 19–24 (2012)
5. De Marneffe, M.C., Manning, C.D.: Stanford typed dependencies manual (2008). http://nlp.stanford.edu/software/dependencies_manual.pdf
6. Del Corro, L., Gemulla, R.: ClausIE: Clause-based open information extraction. In: International World Wide Web Conference (WWW), pp. 355–366 (2013)
7. Fader, A., Soderland, S., Etzioni, O.: Identifying relations for open information extraction. In: Conference on Empirical Methods on Natural Language Processing (EMNLP), pp. 1535–1545 (2011)
8. Jiang, J., Conrath, D.: Semantic similarity based on corpus statistics and lexical taxonomy. In: International Conference Research on Computational Linguistics (ROCLING), pp. 19–33 (1997)
9. Mausam, S.M., Bart, R., Soderland, S., Etzioni, O.: Open language learning for information extraction. In: Joint Conference on Empirical Methods in Natural Language Processing and Computational Natural Language Learning (EMNLP-CoNLL), pp. 523–534 (2012)

10. Petrov, S., Das, D., McDonald, R.: A universal part-of-speech tagset. In: International Conference on Language Resources and Evaluation (LREC), pp. 2089–2096 (2011)
11. Singhal, A.: Introducing the Knowledge Graph: Things. Not Strings, Official Google Blog, May 2012
12. Wu, F., Weld, D.S.: Open information extraction using wikipedia. In: Annual Meeting of the Association for Computational Linguistics (ACL), pp. 118–127 (2010)
13. Wu, W., Li, H., Wang, H., Zhu, K.Q.: Probase: a probabilistic taxonomy for text understanding. In: ACM SIGMOD International Conference on Management of Data, pp. 481–492 (2012)
14. Xavier, C., Lima, V.: Boosting open information extraction with noun-based relations. In: International Conference on Language Resources and Evaluation (LREC), pp. 96–100 (2014)
15. Yahya, M., Whang, S.E., Gupta, R., Halevy, A.: Renoun: fact extraction for nominal attributes. In: Conference on Empirical Methods on Natural Language Processing (EMNLP), pp. 325–335 (2014)

LDQ: 2nd Workshop on Linked Data Quality

What's up LOD Cloud?
Observing the State of Linked Open Data Cloud Metadata

Ahmad Assaf[1,2]([✉]), Raphaël Troncy[1],
and Aline Senart[2]

[1] EURECOM, Sophia Antipolis, France
{ahmad.assaf,raphael.troncy}@eurecom.fr
[2] SAP Labs France, Mougins, France
aline.senart@sap.com

Abstract. Linked Open Data (LOD) has emerged as one of the largest collections of interlinked datasets on the web. In order to benefit from this mine of data, one needs to access descriptive information about each dataset (or metadata). However, the heterogeneous nature of data sources reflects directly on the data quality as these sources often contain inconsistent as well as misinterpreted and incomplete metadata information. Considering the significant variation in size, the languages used and the freshness of the data, one realizes that finding useful datasets without prior knowledge is increasingly complicated. We have developed Roomba, a tool that enables to validate, correct and generate dataset metadata. In this paper, we present the results of running this tool on parts of the LOD cloud accessible via the datahub.io API. The results demonstrate that the general state of the datasets needs more attention as most of them suffers from bad quality metadata and lacking some informative metrics that are needed to facilitate dataset search. We also show that the automatic corrections done by Roomba increase the overall quality of the datasets metadata and we highlight the need for manual efforts to correct some important missing information.

Keywords: Dataset profile · Metadata · Data quality · Data portal

1 Introduction

The Linked Open Data (LOD) cloud[1] has grown significantly in the past years, offering various datasets covering a broad set of domains from life sciences to media and government data [3]. To maintain high quality data, publishers should comply with a set of best practices detailed in [2]. Metadata provisioning is one of those best practices requiring publishers to attach metadata needed to effectively understand and use datasets.

Data portals expose metadata via various models. A model should contain the minimum amount of information that conveys to the inquirer the nature

---

[1] The datahub.io view of the LOD cloud is at http://datahub.io/dataset?tags=lod.

© Springer International Publishing Switzerland 2015
F. Gandon et al. (Eds.): ESWC 2015, LNCS 9341, pp. 247–254, 2015.
DOI: 10.1007/978-3-319-25639-9_40

and content of its resources [9]. It should contain information to enable data discovery, exploration and exploitation. We divided the metadata information into the following types:

- **General information:** General information about the dataset (e.g. title, description, ID). This general information is manually filled by the dataset owner. In addition to that, tags and group information is required for classification and enhancing dataset discoverability.
- **Access information:** Information about accessing and using the dataset. This includes the dataset URL, some license information (i.e. license title and URL) and information about the datasets resources. Each resource has generally a set of attached metadata (e.g. resource name, URL, format, size).
- **Ownership information:** Information about the ownership of the dataset (e.g. organization details, maintainer details, author). The existence of this information is important to identify the authority on which the generated report and the newly corrected profile will be sent to.
- **Provenance information:** Temporal and historical information on the dataset and its resources (e.g. creation and update dates, version information, version number). Most of this information can be automatically filled and tracked.

Data portals are datasets' access points providing tools to facilitate data publishing, sharing, searching and visualization. CKAN[2] is the world's leading open-source data portal platform powering web sites like the Datahub which hosts the LOD cloud metadata.

We have created Roomba [1], a tool that automatically validates, corrects and generates dataset metadata for CKAN portals. The datasets are validated against the CKAN standard metadata model[3]. The model describes four main sections in addition to the core dataset's properties. These sections are:

- **Resources:** The actual accessible raw data. They can come in various formats (JSON, XML, RDF, etc.) and can be downloaded or accessed directly (REST API, SPARQL endpoint).
- **Tags:** Provide descriptive knowledge on the dataset content and structure.
- **Groups:** Used to cluster or a curate datasets based on shared themes or semantics.
- **Organizations:** Organizations describe datasets solely on their association to a specific administrative party.

The results demonstrate that the general state of the examined datasets needs much more attention as most of the datasets suffers from bad quality metadata and lacking some informative metrics needed that would facilitate dataset search. The noisiest metadata values were access information such as licensing information and resource descriptions in addition to large numbers of resource reachability problems. We also show that the automatic corrections of the tool

---

[2] http://ckan.org.

[3] http://demo.ckan.org/api/3/action/package_show?id=adur_district_spending.

increase the overall quality of the datasets metadata and highlight the need for manual efforts to correct some important missing information.

2   Related Work

The Data Catalog Vocabulary (DCAT) [8] and the Vocabulary of Interlinked Datasets (VoID) [5] are models for representing RDF datasets metadata. There exist several tools aiming at exposing dataset metadata using these vocabularies such as [4]. Few approaches tackle the issue of examining datasets metadata. The Project Open Data Dashboard[4] validator analyzes machine readable files for automated metrics to check their alignment with the Open Data principles. Similarly on the LOD cloud, the Datahub LOD Validator[5] checks a dataset compliance for inclusion in the LOD cloud. However, it lacks the ability to give detailed insights about the completeness of the metadata and an overview on the state of the entire LOD cloud group.

The *State of the LOD Cloud Report* [7] measures the adoption of Linked Data best practices back in 2011. More recently, the authors in [10] used LDSpider [6] to crawl and analyze 1014 different datasets in the web of Linked Data in 2014. While these reports expose important information about datasets like provenance, licensing and accessibility, they do not cover the entire spectrum of metadata categories as presented in [11].

3   Experiments and Evaluation

In this section, we describe our experiments when running the Roomba tool on the LOD cloud. All the experiments are reproducible by our tool and their results are available on its Github repository at https://github.com/ahmadassaf/opendata-checker.

3.1   Experimental Setup

The current state of the LOD cloud report [10] indicates that there are more than 1014 datasets available. These datasets have been harvested by the LDSpider crawler [6] seeded with 560 thousands URIs. However, since Roomba requires the datasets metadata to be hosted in a data portal where either the dataset publisher or the portal administrator can attach relevant metadata to it, we rely on the information provided by the Datahub CKAN API. We consider two possible groups: the first one tagged with "lodcloud" returns 259 datasets, while the second one tagged with "lod" returns only 75 datasets. We manually inspect these two lists and find out that the API result for the tag "lodcloud" is the correct one. The 259 datasets contain a total of 1068 resources. We run the instance and resource extractor from Roomba in order to cache the metadata

---

[4] http://labs.data.gov/dashboard/.
[5] http://validator.lod-cloud.net/.

files for these datasets locally and we launch the validation process which takes around two and a half hours on a 2.6 Ghz Intel Core i7 processor with 16 GB of DDR3 memory machine.

3.2 Results and Evaluation

CKAN dataset metadata includes three main sections in addition to the core dataset's properties. Those are the **groups**, **tags** and **resources**. Each section contains a set of metadata corresponding to one or more metadata type. For example, a dataset resource will have general information such as the resource name, access information such as the resource url and provenance information such as creation date. The framework generates a report aggregating all the problems in all these sections, fixing field values when possible. Errors can be the result of missing metadata fields, undefined field values or field value errors (e.g. unreachable URL or syntactically incorrect email addresses).

Figures 1 and 2 show the percentage of errors found in metadata fields by section and by information type respectively. We observe that the most erroneous information for the dataset core information is related to ownership since this information is missing or undefined for 41 % of the datasets. Datasets resources have the poorest metadata. 64 % of the general metadata, all the access information and 80 % of the provenance information contain missing or undefined values. Table 1 shows the top metadata fields errors for each metadata information type.

We notice that 42.85 % of the top metadata problems shown in Table 1 can be fixed automatically. Among them, 44.44 % of these problems can be fixed by our tool while the others can be fixed by tools that should be plugged into the data portal. We further present and discuss the results grouped by metadata information type in the following sub-sections.

3.3 General Information

34 datasets (13.13 %) do not have valid `notes` values. `tags` information for the datasets are complete except for the `vocabulary_id` as this is missing from all the datasets' metadata. All the datasets `groups` information are missing `display_name`, `description`, `title`, `image_display_url`, `id`, `name`. After manual examination, we observe a clear overlap between group and organization information. Many datasets like `event-media` use the organization field to show group related information (being in the LOD Cloud) instead of the publishers details.

3.4 Access Information

25 % of the datasets access information (being the dataset URL and any URL defined in its groups) have issues: generally missing or unreachable URLs. 3 datasets (1.15 %) do not have a URL defined (tip, uniprotdatabases, uniprot-citations) while 45 datasets (17.3 %) defined URLs are not accessible at the time

Table 1. Top metadata fields error % by information type

Metadata field		Error %	Section	Error type	Auto fix
General	group	100 %	Dataset	Missing	-
	vocabulary_id	100 %	Tag	Undefined	-
	url-type	96.82 %	Resource	Missing	-
	mimetype_inner	95.88 %	Resource	Undefined	Yes
	hash	95.51 %	Resource	Undefined	Yes
	size	81.55 %	Resource	Undefined	Yes
Access	cache_url	96.9 %	Resource	Undefined	-
	webstore_url	91.29 %	Resource	Undefined	-
	license_url	54.44 %	Dataset	Missing	Yes
	url	30.89 %	Resource	Unreachable	-
	license_title	16.6 %	Dataset	Undefined	Yes
Provenance	cache_last_updated	96.91 %	Resource	Undefined	Yes
	webstore_last_updated	95.88 %	Resource	Undefined	Yes
	created	86.8 %	Resource	Missing	Yes
	last_modified	79.87 %	Resource	Undefined	Yes
	version	60.23 %	Dataset	Undefined	-
Ownership	maintainer_email	55.21 %	Dataset	Undefined	-
	maintainer	51.35 %	Dataset	Undefined	-
	author_email	15.06 %	Dataset	Undefined	-
	organization_image_url	10.81 %	Dataset	Undefined	-
	author	2.32 %	Dataset	Undefined	-

of writing this paper. One dataset does not have resources information (bio2rdf-chebi) while the other datasets have a total of 1068 defined resources.

On the datasets resources level, we notice wrong or inconsistent values in the size and mimetype fields. However, 44 datasets have valid size field values and 54 have valid mimetype field values but they were not reachable, thus providing incorrect information. 15 fields (68 %) of all the other access metadata are missing or have undefined values. Looking closely, we notice that most of these problems can be easily fixed automatically by tools that can be plugged to the data portal. For example, the top six missing fields are the cache_last_updated, cache_url, urltype, webstore_last_updated, mimetype_inner and hash which can be computed and filled automatically. However, the most important missing information which require manual entry are the dataset's name and description which are missing from 817 (76.49 %) and 98 (9.17 %) resources respectively. A total of 334 resources (31.27 %) URLs were not reachable, thus affecting highly the availability of these datasets. CKAN resources can be of various predefined types (*file, file.upload, api, visualization, codeanddocumentation*). Roomba also breaks down these unreachable resources according to their types:

211 (63.17%) resources do not have valid `resource_type`, 112 (33.53%) are files, 8 (2.39%) a re metadata and one (0.029%) are example and documentation types.

To have more details about the resources URL types, we created a *key* : *objectmeta − fieldvalues* group level report on the LOD cloud with `resources>format:title`. This will aggregate the resources format information for each dataset. We observe that only 161 (62.16%) of the datasets valid URLs have SPARQL endpoints defined using the `api/sparql` resource format. 92.27% provided RDF example links and 56.3% provided direct links to RDF down-loadable dumps.

The noisiest part of the access metadata is about license information. A total of 43 datasets (16.6%) does not have a defined `license_title` and `license_id` fields, where 141 (54.44%) have missing `license_url` field.

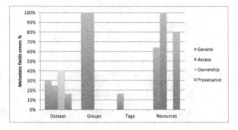

Fig. 1. Error % by section   **Fig. 2.** Error % by information type

3.5 Ownership Information

Ownership information is divided into direct ownership (author and maintainer) and organization information. Four fields (66.66%) of the direct ownership information are missing or undefined. The breakdown for the missing information is: 55.21% `maintainer_email`, 51.35% `maintainer`, 15.06% `author_email`, 2.32% `author`. Moreover, our framework performs checks to validate existing email values. 11 (0.05%) and 6 (0.05%) of the defined `author_email` and `maintainer_email` fields are not valid email addresses respectively. For the organization information, two field values (16.6%) were missing or undefined. 1.16% of the `organization_description` and 10.81% of the `organization_image_url` information with two out of these URLs are unreachable.

3.6 Provenance Information

80% of the resources provenance information are missing or undefined. However, most of the provenance information (e.g. `metadata_created`, `metadata_modified`) can be computed automatically by tools plugged into the data portal. The only field requiring manual entry is the `version` field which was found to be missing in 60.23% of the datasets.

3.7   Enriched Profiles

Roomba can automatically fix, when possible, the license information (title, url and id) as well as the resources mimetype and size.

20 resources (1.87 %) have incorrect `mimetype` defined, while 52 resources (4.82 %) have incorrect `size` values. These values have been automatically fixed based on the values defined in the HTTP response header.

We have noticed that most of the issues surrounding license information are related to ambiguous entries. To resolve that, we manually created a mapping file[6] standardizing the set of possible license names and urls using the open source and knowledge license information[7]. As a result, we managed to normalize 123 (47.49 %) of the datasets' license information.

To check the impact of the corrected fields, we seeded Roomba with the enriched profiles. Since Roomba uses file based cache system, we simply replaced all the datasets `json` files in the `\cache\datahub.io\datasets` folder with those generated in `\cache\datahub.io\enriched`. After running Roomba again on the enriched profiles, we observe that the errors percentage for missing `size` fields decreased by 32.02 % and for `mimetype` fields by 50.93 %. We also notice that the error percentage for missing `license_urls` decreased by 2.32 %.

4   Conclusion and Future Work

In this paper, we presented the results of running Roomba over the LOD cloud group hosted in the Datahub. We discovered that the general state of the examined datasets needs attention as most of them lack informative access information and their resources suffer low availability. These two metrics are of high importance for enterprises looking to integrate and use external linked data. We found out that the most erroneous information for the dataset core information are ownership related since this information is missing or undefined for 41 % of the datasets. Datasets resources have the poorest metadata: 64 % of the general metadata, all the access information and 80 % of the provenance information contained missing or undefined values.

We also show that the automatic correction process can effectively enhance the quality of some information. We believe there is a need to have a community effort to manually correct missing important information like ownership information (maintainer, author, and maintainer and author emails). As part of our future work, we plan to run Roomba on various data portals and perform a detailed comparison to check the metadata health of LOD datasets against those in other prominent data portals.

Acknowledgments. This research has been partially funded by the European Union's 7th Framework Programme via the project Apps4EU (GA No. 325090).

---

[6] https://github.com/ahmadassaf/opendata-checker/blob/master/util/
licenseMappings.json.

[7] https://github.com/okfn/licenses.

References

1. Assaf, A., Sénart, A., Troncy, R.: Roomba: automatic validation, correction and generation of dataset metadata. In: 24th World Wide Web Conference (WWW), Demos Track, Florence, Italy (2015)
2. Bizer, C.: Evolving the web into a global data space. In: Fernandes, A.A.A., Gray, A.J.G., Belhajjame, K. (eds.) BNCOD 2011. LNCS, vol. 7051, p. 1. Springer, Heidelberg (2011)
3. Bizer, C., Heath, T., Berners-Lee, T.: Linked data - the story so far. Int. J. Semant. Web Inf. Syst. (IJSWIS) **5**, 1–22 (2009)
4. BöHm, C., Lorey, J., Naumann, F.: Creating VoID descriptions for web-scale data. J. Web Semant. **9**(3), 339–345 (2011)
5. Cyganiak, R., Zhao, J., Hausenblas, M., Alexander, K.: Describing Linked Datasets with the VoID Vocabulary. W3C Note (2011). http://www.w3.org/TR/void/
6. Isele, R., Umbrich, J., Bizer, C., Harth, A.: LDspider: an open-source crawling framework for the web of linked data. In: 9th International Semantic Web Conference (ISWC), Posters & Demos Track (2010)
7. Jentzsch, A., Cygania, R., Bizer, C.: State of the lod cloud. http://lod-cloud.net/state/
8. Maali, F., Erickson, J.: Data Catalog Vocabulary (DCAT). W3C Recommendation (2014). http://www.w3.org/TR/vocab-dcat/
9. Nebert, D.: Developing Spatial Data Infrastructures: The SDI Cookbook (2004). http://www.gsdi.org/docs2004/Cookbook/cookbookV2.0.pdf
10. Schmachtenberg, M., Bizer, C., Paulheim, H.: Adoption of the linked data best practices in different topical domains. In: Mika, P., Tudorache, T., Bernstein, A., Welty, C., Knoblock, C., Vrandečić, D., Groth, P., Noy, N., Janowicz, K., Goble, C. (eds.) ISWC 2014, Part I. LNCS, vol. 8796, pp. 245–260. Springer, Heidelberg (2014)
11. Zaveri, A., Rula, A., Maurino, A., Pietrobon, R., Lehmann, J., Auer, S.: Quality assessment methodologies for linked open data. Semant. Web J. (2012)

2015 Workshop on Legal Domain and Semantic Web Applications

A Bottom-Up Approach for Licences Classification and Selection

Enrico Daga[1]([⊠]), Mathieu d'Aquin[1], Enrico Motta[1],
and Aldo Gangemi[2,3]

[1] Knowledge Media Institute, The Open University, Walton Hall, Milton Keynes, UK
{enrico.daga,mathieu.daquin,enrico.motta}@open.ac.uk
http://kmi.open.ac.uk
[2] Université Paris13, Sorbonne Cité CNRS UMR7030, Paris, France
[3] Istitute of Cognitive Sciences and Technologies - CNR,
Via S. Martino Della Battaglia 44, 00185 Rome, RM, Italy
aldo.gangemi@{univ-paris13.fr,cnr.it}
http://www.univ-paris13.fr
http://istc.cnr.it

Abstract. Licences are a crucial aspect of the information publishing process in the web of (linked) data. Recent work on modeling of policies with semantic web languages (RDF, ODRL) gives the opportunity to formally describe licences and reason upon them. However, choosing the right licence is still challenging. Particularly, understanding the number of features - permissions, prohibitions and obligations - constitute a steep learning process for the data provider, who has to check them individually and compare the licences in order to pick the one that better fits her needs. The objective of the work presented in this paper is to reduce the effort required for licence selection. We argue that an ontology of licences, organized by their relevant features, can help providing support to the user. Developing an ontology with a bottom-up approach based on Formal Concept Analysis, we show how the process of licence selection can be simplified significantly and reduced to answering an average of three/five key questions.

Keywords: RDF · Licences and linked data · Formal Concept Analysis

1 Introduction

Licence specification is an important part of the data publishing process on the web. Recently, a part of the Semantic Web and Linked Data community has been focusing on providing support to the expression of policies on the semantic web. The Open Digital Rights Language (ODRL) provides an ontology for representing policies in the semantic web, and it is used and extended to formally express permissions, prohibitions and duties that licences include[1]. The

---

[1] http://www.w3.org/ns/odrl/2/ODRL21.

© Springer International Publishing Switzerland 2015
F. Gandon et al. (Eds.): ESWC 2015, LNCS 9341, pp. 257–267, 2015.
DOI: 10.1007/978-3-319-25639-9_41

RDF Licenses database[2] is a first notable attempt at developing a knowledge base of licences described following ODRL. However, identifying suitable licences is still not a trivial task for a data publisher. In the current version, ODRL identifies more than fifty possible actions to be used as permissions, prohibitions or obligations, and there are ontologies that extend ODRL adding even more fine grained policies (e.g. LDR[3]). Therefore, not only are there many licences that can be applied, but each might include any subset of the many possible features (permitted, prohibited and required actions), that need to be explored in order to obtain a small selection of comparable licences to choose from.

The question that this paper aims to answer is: *How can we reduce the effort for licence identification and selection?* We advance the hypothesis that an ontology defining relevant classes of licences, formed on the basis of the *key features* of the instances, should facilitate the selection and identification of a suitable licence. The methodology applied relies on a bottom-up approach to ontology construction based on Formal Concept Analysis (FCA). We developed a tool, Contento, with the purpose of analysing data about licences using FCA, in order to generate a concept lattice. This concept lattice is used as a draft taxonomy of licence classes that, once properly annotated and pruned, can be exported as an OWL ontology and curated with existing ontology editors. We applied this approach to the use case of licence identification, and created a service to support data providers in licence selection by asking a few key questions about their requirements. We show that, with this service, we can reduce the selection of licences from comparing more than fifty possible licence features, to answering on average three to five questions.

The next section surveys related work. Section 3 describes the process of building the ontology, the Contento tool and the modeling choices that have been made. In Sect. 4 we report on the application of the ontology in a service for identification of suitable licences for data providers. Ultimately, we discuss some future work in the concluding Sect. 5.

2   Related Work

Licence recommendation is very common on the web, particularly for software. Services like http://choosealicense.com/ are usually based on common and well known concerns, and recommend a restricted number of trusted solutions. The Creative Commons Choose service[4] shares with our approach a workflow based on few questions. However, it is an ad-hoc tool which focuses on selecting a Creative Commons licence. Differently, we are interested in applying a knowledge-based approach, where the way information about licences and requirements is modelled guides the path to the solution.

The Open Digital Rights Language (ODRL) is a rights expression language formalised as an XML Schema[5]. Recently, an alternative representation based

---

[2] http://datahub.io/dataset/rdflicense.
[3] http://oeg-dev.dia.fi.upm.es/licensius/static/ldr/.
[4] https://creativecommons.org/choose/.
[5] http://www.w3.org/TR/odrl/.

on RDF/OWL has been identified as the backbone for representing policies in the semantic web [1]. The RDF Licenses database [2] includes the description of licences in RDF[6]. We used this database as starting point for the present work. However, population and curation of such knowledge base is clearly a necessary step for licence recommendation systems. For example, the descriptions do not specify the types of assets a licence is eligible for (and we don't cover this aspect in the present paper). The enrichment of the possible terms to express policies will contribute to increase the precision and quality of the descriptions (see LiMO[7], L4LOD[8] and ODRS[9]). Applying natural language processing techniques, like the ones proposed in [3], can facilitate the process of data acquisition.

Licentia [4] is a tool for supporting users in choosing a licence for the web of data. Similarly to our approach, it is based on the RDF licence database. The user selects possible permissions, obligations and duties extracted from the licence descriptions, in order to specify her requirements. The system applies reasoning over the databases of licences, proposing a list of compatible ones to choose from. With this approach the user needs to perform an action for each of its requirements. Our approach restricts the number of questions through the inferences implied by the classification of licences in a hierarchy (e.g.: any "share alike" licence allows distribution) and only suggests the ones for which a solution actually exists.

The approach proposed in this paper relies on an ontology of licences as a means for licence selection. Such an ontology has been created following a bottom-up approach. Bottom-up approaches for ontology design have been commonly applied in knowledge engineering [5] and we use here one particular method based on Formal Concept Analysis (FCA) [6]. FCA has been succesfully used in the context of recommender systems [7,8]. Moreover, FCA has been proposed in the past to support ontology design and other ontology engineering tasks [9,10]. In the present work we use FCA as a learning technique to boost the early stage of the ontology design.

3   Building the Ontology

Our hypothesis is that an ontology can help on orienting the user in the complex set of existing licences and policies. The RDF Licenses database contains 139 licences expressed in RDF/ODRL. Our idea is therefore to start from the data to create the ontology. The reason for choosing a bottom-up approach to ontology construction is also that the data will include only policies that are relevant.

In order to support the production of the ontology we implemented a bottom-up ontology construction tool called Contento, which relies on FCA. FCA has the capability of classifying collections of objects depending on their *features*. The input of a FCA algorithm is a *formal context* - being a binary matrix having

---

[6] http://purl.org/NET/rdflicense.
[7] http://data.opendataday.it/LiMo.
[8] http://ns.inria.fr/l4lod/v2/l4lodv2.htm.
[9] http://schema.theodi.org/odrs/.

the full set of objects as rows and the full set of attributes as columns. Objects and attributes are analysed and clustered in *closed concepts* by FCA. In FCA, a concept consists of a pair of sets - objects and attributes: the objects being the extent of the concept and the attributes its intent.

For the mathematical definition, FCA introduces the derivation operator $'$. For a set of objects X, we define X' as the set of attributes all shared by the objects in X. Similarly, for a set of attributes Y, Y' is the set of objects that share all attributes in Y. A *closed concept* is a pair of objects and attributes (X, Y) so that $X' = Y$ and $X = Y'$. It is possible to derive a close concept (also called *formal concept*) from a set of objects using a simple routine:

1. Select a set of objects X.
2. Derive the set of attributes X'.
3. Derive in the same way the related objects $(X')'$.
4. (X'', X') is a close concept.

The same process can be performed starting from a set of attributes. A subsumption relation can be enstablished between formal concepts in order to define an order on the set of formal concepts in a formal context. As a result, formal concepts are organized in a hierarchy, starting from a top concept (e.g., *Any*), including all objects and an empty set of attributes, towards a bottom concept (e.g., *None*), with an empty set of objects. Moreover, this ordered set forms a mathematical structure: the concept *lattice*.

The objective of the Contento tool is to support the user in the generation and curation of concept lattices from formal contexts (binary matrixes) and to use them as drafts of semantic web ontologies.

3.1   Contento

Contento[10] has been developed to create, populate and curate FCA formal contexts and associated lattices, also interpreted as taxonomies of concepts. Formal contexts can be created and populated from scratch. Sets of items can be managed with a number of features in the *Collections* section. The user can assign the role of objects' set and attributes' set to two collections, thus to generate a formal context. Figure 1 presents the formal context browser of *Contento*. Each context is represented as a list of relations between one object and one attribute and a *hold* status: *yes, no* or *undefined*. The *undefined* status has been included to indicate that the relation has not been supervised yet. The user can then incrementally populate the formal context by chosing whether each object/attribute association occurs or not. This can be done conveniently thanks to a set of filtering options that can reduce the list to only a subset of the context to be analysed. Data can be filtered in different ways:

- by object name (or all that have a given attribute)
- by attribute name (or all that have a given object)
- by status (holds, does not hold, to be decided).

---

[10] http://bit.ly/contento-tool.

Therefore, the user can display only the relations that need to be checked (the ones with status *undefined*), focus on the extent of a specific attribute or on the intent of an object. Moreover, she can display the set of relations having for object any that include a specific attribute (or vice versa). Eventually, the user can set all filtered relations to a given state in bulk, if meaningful. With this interface, the binary matrix can be incrementally populated to constitute a proper input for a FCA algorithm.

Fig. 1. Contento: formal context browser and editor. In this example, we have fixed the object in order to review its relations with the attributes.

In many cases, however, a ready made binary matrix can be imported from pre-existing data. In this case the formal context is created directly from that, ready to be used to generate the concept lattice with the procedure provided by Contento.

Contento implements the Chein algorithm [11] to compute concept lattices. The result of the algorithm is stored as a *taxonomy*. A taxonomy can be navigated as an ordered list of concepts, from the top to the bottom, each of them including the extent, the intent and links to upper and lower concept bounds in the hierarchy (see Fig. 2). In addition, the tool shows which objects and attributes are *proper* to the concept, i.e. do not exist in any of the upper (for attributes) or lower (for objects) concepts.

Moreover, it can be visualized and explored as a concept lattice (Fig. 3). The lattice can be navigated by clicking on the nodes. Focusing on a single node, the respective upper and lower branches are highlighted, to facilitate the navigation to the user. Similarly, objects and attributes from the focused node can be selected, thus highlighting all nodes in the hierarchy sharing all of the selected features (in orange in Fig. 3). Contento supports the user on the curation of the concept hierarchy, to transform it from a concept lattice to a draft ontology taxonomy, through the annotation of each concept with a label and a comment, and the pruning of unwanted concepts. This last operation implies an adjustment of the hierarchy, by building links between lower and upper bounds of the deleted node (only if no other path to the counterpart exists). As a result, relevant concepts can be qualified, and concepts that are not relevant for the task at end can be removed.

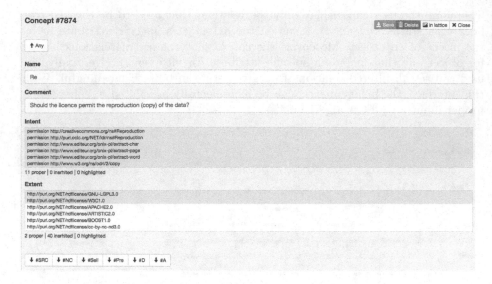

Fig. 2. Contento: each concept is presented showing the extent, the intent and links to upper and lower concept bounds in the hierarchy. The portion of the intent not included in any of the upper concepts (called *proper*) is highlighted, as well as any objects not appearing in lower concepts. Concepts can be annotated and deleted.

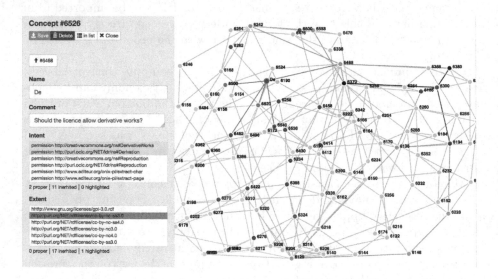

Fig. 3. Contento: the lattice explorer for annotation and pruning. The branching of the current concept is presented in the lattice in green (on the left side of the picture). The user can still point to other nodes to inspect the branching of other concepts (on the right side of the picture, the lower branch being displayed in blue and the upper in red). By selecting one or more items in the extent or intent of the concept, all the nodes sharing the same are bolded in orange (Colour figure online).

Taxonomies can be translated into OWL ontologies. The user can decide how to represent the taxonomy in RDF, what terms to use to link concepts, objects and attributes, and whether items need to be represented as URIs or literals. Ultimately, these export configurations can be shared and reused. For example, Contento offers a default profile, using example terms, or a SKOS profile.

3.2   The Ontology

For the use case at hand, we used Contento to support the creation of the Licence Picker Ontology (LiPiO)[11], starting from data in the RDF Licenses database. The data has been preprocessed in order to produce a binary matrix to be imported in Contento. The preprocessing included reasoning on SKOS-like relations between ODRL actions[12]. Moreover, we reduced the number of licences from the initial 139 to 48 by removing localized versions (for instance Creative Commons CC-BY-SA 3.0 Portugal). In this case, the licences are the objects of the matrix, while the set of attributes represent the policies, expressed as ODRL permissions, prohibitions or duties. Below is an example taken from the input CSV:

```
http://purl.org/NET/rdflicense/cc-by4.0,permission http://www.w3.org/ns/odrl/2/copy,1
http://purl.org/NET/rdflicense/allrightsreserved,prohibition http://www.w3.org/ns/odrl/2/copy,1
http://purl.org/NET/rdflicense/MOZILLA2.0,duty http://www.w3.org/ns/odrl/2/shareAlike,0
```

In the above excerpt, the "CC-BY" licence permits to *copy*, the "All rights reserved" policy prohibits it, and the "Mozilla 2.0" licence does not include a *share-alike* requirement.

The CSV has been imported in the Contento tool that created the formal context automatically. After that, a concept lattice was generated. The lattice included 103 concepts organized in a hierarchy, the top concept representing *All* the licences, while the bottom concept, *None*, includes all the attributes, and no licence. Figure 3 shows the lattice as it looked like at this stage of the process. In this phase, the objective is to inspect the concepts and, for each one of them, to perform one of the following actions:

– If the concept is meaningful, name it and annotate it with a relevant question (e.g. "should others be allowed to distribute the work?") in the comment field;
– If the concept is not meaningful or useful, it can be deleted (with the lattice being automatically adjusted).

We judged the meaningfulness of a concept by observing its intent (set of features). If the concept was introducing new features with respect to the upper concepts, then it is kept in the lattice, given a name and annotated with a question. In the case its intent does not include new features (it is a union of the intents of the respective upper concepts), then it is deleted, because the

---

[11] http://bit.ly/licence-picker-ontology.
[12] We also introduced some changes in the original descriptions, that will be contributed to evolve the RDF Licence database itself.

respective licences will necessarily be present in (at least one of) the upper concepts, and no new question need to be asked to identify them. With this process the lattice has been reduced significantly, and proper names and questions have been attached to the remaining concepts (almost 20 % of the initial lattice). Figure 4 displays the resulting lattice, labels being synthetic names referring to policies/attributes that have been introduced in that point of the hierarchy; i.e. according to the *key features* that define the concept in relation to its parents.

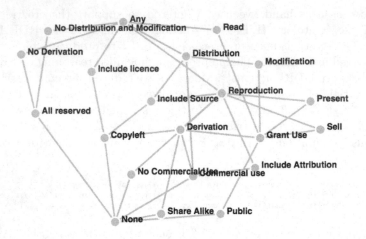

Fig. 4. Contento: the annotated and pruned concept lattice.

The resulting annotated taxonomy has been exported as OWL ontology as the initial draft of the the Licence Picker Ontology. The draft included a sound hierarchy of concepts. Both concepts (classes) and licences were annotated with the respective set of policies. Because the policies were expressed as plain literal on a generic *has* property (the data being manipulated as object/attribute pairs by the FCA based tool), a small refactoring permitted to reintroduce the RDF based descriptions with ODRL. The Licence Picker ontology[13] currently contains 21 classes linked to 45 licences with a is-A relation. Each class is associated with a relevant question to be asked that makes explicit the key feature of the included set of licences. The ontology embeds annotations on the classes about the policies included in all the licences of a given concept, and a ODRL based description of permissions, prohibitions and duties of each instance.

4   Pick the Licence

The Licence Picker Ontology has been designed to support data providers in choosing the right policy under which to publish their data. In order to evaluate this ontology we applied it in a service for licence selection. The Licence Picker

---

[13] http://bit.ly/licence-picker-ontology.

Webapp is an ontology driven web application[14]. The user is engaged in answering questions regarding her requirements to reach a small set of suitable licences to compare, like in the following guide example. We consider a scenario, inspired from our work on smart cities data hubs [12], in which sensors are installed in a city to detect how busy different areas are at different times, as information to be provided to local retailers, restaurants, etc. This information is collected in a data store and offers access to statistics through a number of web-based services. The managers of the data store needs to choose a license to attach to the data in order to limit their exploitation to the expected uses. They want (a) the data to be accessible and copied for analysis, but (b) to not be modified or redistributed to third parties. In addition, (c) commercial uses should be allowed, but (d) the data consumers should attribute the source of the data to the owner of the data store.

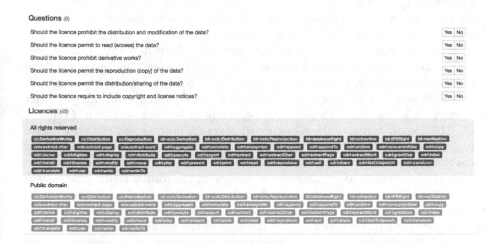

Fig. 5. Licence Picker Webapp: the user is engaged in answering questions.

The Licence Picker Webapp welcomes the user with forty-five possible licences and a first set of questions, as show in Fig. 5. One of them catches the eye of the user: *Should the licence prohibit derivative works?* She promptly answers *Yes*. The set of possible licences is reduced to five, and the system propose a single question: *Should the licence prohibit any kind of use (All rights reserved)?* This time the user answers *No*, because they want the users to use the information to boost the activities in the data store. As a result, the system proposes to pick one of four licences. The user notices that all of them require an attribution statement and prohibit to produce derivative works. Two of them also prohibit the use for commercial purposes, so the user decides to choose the *Creative Commons CC-BY-ND 4.0* licence.

---

[14] http://bit.ly/licence-picker-webapp.

The example above shows an important property of the approach presented in the paper. As the licences are classified by the mean of their features, and the classes organized in a hierarchy, we can notably reduce the number of actions to be taken to obtain a short list of comparable licences. The user had four requirements to fullfill, more then fifty existed in the database, and she could get an easy comparable number of licences with only two steps.

5   Conclusions and Future Work

Licences are an important part of the data publishing process, and choosing the right licence may be challenging. By applying the Licence Picker Ontology (LiPiO), this task is reduced to answering an average of three to five questions (five being the height of the class taxonomy in LiPiO) and assessing the best licence from a small set of choices. We showed how our approach reduces significantly the effort of selecting licences in contrast with approaches based on feature exploration. In addition, a bottom-up approach on ontology building in this scenario opens new interesting challenges. The RDF description of licences is an ongoing work, modeling issues are not entirely solved and we expect the data to evolve in time, including eventually new licences and new types of policies. For example, in our use case the data has been curated in advance in order to obtain an harmonized knowledge base, ready to be bridged to the *Contento* tool. This clearly impacts the ontology contruction process and the application relying on it, as different data will lead to different classes and questions. This gives the opportunity to explore methods to automate some of the curation tasks (especially pruning) and to integretate changes in the formal context incrementally, to support the ontology designer in the adaptation of the ontology to the changes performed in the source knowledge base. Such evolutions do not impact the Licence Picker Webapp, because changes in the ontology will be automatically reflected in the tool. We foresee that the description of licences will be extended including other relevant properties - like the type of assets a licence can be applied to. The advantage of the proposed methodology is that it can be applied to any kind of licence feature, not only policies.

The Contento tool was designed to support the task at the center of the present work. However, the software itself is domain independent, and we plan to apply the same approach to other domains. Ultimately, we want to compare Contento to other similar tools, for example ToscanaJ [13], and perform a user based evaluation.

References

1. Steyskal, S., Polleres, A.: Defining expressive access policies for linked data using the ODRL ontology 2.0. In: Sack, H., et al. (eds.) Proceedings of the 10th International Conference on Semantic Systems (SEMANTiCS 2014). ACM, New York (2014)

2. Rodríguez-Doncel, V., Villata, S., Gómez-Pérez, A.: A dataset of RDF licenses. In: Hoekstra, H. (ed.) Legal Knowledge and Information Systems. JURIX 2014: The Twenty-Seventh Annual Conference. IOS Press, Amsterdam (2014)
3. Cabrio, E., Palmero Aprosio, A., Villata, S.: These are your rights. In: Presutti, V., d'Amato, C., Gandon, F., d'Aquin, M., Staab, S., Tordai, A. (eds.) ESWC 2014. LNCS, vol. 8465, pp. 255–269. Springer, Heidelberg (2014)
4. Cardellino, C., Villata, S., Gandon, F., et al.: Licentia: a tool for supporting users in data licensing on the web of data. In: Horridge, M., Rospocher, M., van Ossenbruggen, J. (eds.) Proceedings of the ISWC 2014 Posters Demonstrations Track, a Track within the 13th International Semantic Web Conference (ISWC 2014), Riva del Garda, Italy, 21 October 2014
5. Van Der Vet, P.E., Mars, N.J.I.: Bottom-up construction of ontologies. IEEE Trans. Knowl. Data Eng. 10(4), 513–526 (1998)
6. Ganter, B., Stumme, G., Wille, R. (eds.): Formal Concept Analysis, Foundations and Applications. LNCS (LNAI), vol. 3626. Springer, Heidelberg (2005)
7. du Boucher-Ryan, P., Bridge, D.: Collaborative recommending using formal concept analysis. Knowl.-Based Syst. 19(5), 309–315 (2006)
8. Li, X., Murata, T.: A knowledge-based recommendation model utilizing formal concept analysis and association. In: 2010 the 2nd International Conference on Computer and Automation Engineering (ICCAE), vol. 4, pp. 221–226. IEEE (2010)
9. Cimiano, P., Hotho, A., Stumme, G., Tane, J.: Conceptual knowledge processing with formal concept analysis and ontologies. In: Eklund, P. (ed.) ICFCA 2004. LNCS (LNAI), vol. 2961, pp. 189–207. Springer, Heidelberg (2004)
10. Obitko, M., Snasel, V., Smid, J., Snasel, V.: Ontology design with formal concept analysis. In: CLA, vol. 110 (2004)
11. Chein, M.: Algorithme de recherche des sous-matrices premieres dune matrice. Bull. Math. Soc. Sci. Math. RS Roumanie 13(61), 21–25 (1969)
12. d'Aquin, M., Adamou, A., Daga, E., et al.: Dealing with diversity in a smart-city datahub. In: Omitola, T., Breslin, J., Barnaghi, P. (eds.) Proceedings of the Fifth Workshop on Semantics for Smarter Cities, a Workshop at the 13th International Semantic Web Conference (ISWC 2014), Riva del Garda, Italy, 19 October 2014. CEUR-WS.org
13. Becker, P., Correia, J.H.: The ToscanaJ Suite for implementing conceptual information systems. In: Ganter, B., Stumme, G., Wille, R. (eds.) Formal Concept Analysis. LNCS (LNAI), vol. 3626, pp. 324–348. Springer, Heidelberg (2005)

4th Workshop on the Multilingual Semantic Web

One Ontology to Bind Them All:
The META-SHARE OWL Ontology
for the Interoperability of Linguistic Datasets
on the Web

John P. McCrae[1], Penny Labropoulou[3], Jorge Gracia[2]([✉]), Marta Villegas[4],
Víctor Rodríguez-Doncel[2], and Philipp Cimiano[1]

[1] Cognitive Interaction Technology, Excellence Cluster,
Bielefeld University, Bielefeld, Germany
{cimiano,jmccrae}@cit-ec.uni-bielefeld.de
[2] Ontology Engineering Group, Universidad Politécnica de Madrid, Madrid, Spain
{jgracia,vrodriguez}@fi.upm.es
[3] CILSP/"Athena" RC, Athens, Greece
penny@ilsp.athena-innovation.gr
[4] University Pompeu Fabra, Barcelona, Spain
marta.villegas@upf.edu

Abstract. META-SHARE is an infrastructure for sharing Language
Resources (LRs) where significant effort has been made into providing
carefully curated metadata about LRs. However, in the face of the flood
of data that is used in computational linguistics, a manual approach
cannot suffice. We present the development of the META-SHARE ontology, which transforms the metadata schema used by META-SHARE into
ontology in the Web Ontology Language (OWL) that can better handle
the diversity of metadata found in legacy and crowd-sourced resources.
We show how this model can interface with other more general purpose
vocabularies for online datasets and licensing, and apply this model to
the CLARIN VLO, a large source of legacy metadata about LRs. Furthermore, we demonstrate the usefulness of this approach in two public
metadata portals for information about language resources.

Keywords: Language resources and evaluation · Metadata · Ontologies · Harmonization

1 Introduction

The study of language and the development of natural language processing
(NLP) applications requires access to language resources (LRs). Recently, several
digital repositories that index metadata for LRs have emerged, supporting the
discovery and reuse of LRs. One of the most notable of such initiatives is META-
SHARE[1] [18], an open, integrated, secure and interoperable exchange infrastruc-

---

[1] http://www.meta-share.eu.

© Springer International Publishing Switzerland 2015
F. Gandon et al. (Eds.): ESWC 2015, LNCS 9341, pp. 271–282, 2015.
DOI: 10.1007/978-3-319-25639-9_42

ture where LRs are documented, uploaded, stored, catalogued, announced, downloaded, exchanged and discussed, aiming to support reuse of LRs. Towards this end, META-SHARE has developed a rich metadata schema that allows aspects of LRs accounting for their whole lifecycle from their production to their usage to be described. The schema has been implemented as an XML Schema Definition (XSD)[2] and descriptions of specific LRs are available as XML documents.

Yet, META-SHARE is not the only source for discovering LRs and their descriptions; other sources include the catalogs of agencies dedicated to the promotion and distribution of LRs, such as ELRA[3] and LDC[4], other infrastructures such as the CLARIN Virtual Language Observatory (VLO)[5] [2], the Language Grid[6] and Alveo[7], the Open Language Archives Community (OLAC)[8], catalogs with crowd-sourced metadata, such as the LREMap[9] [5], and, more recently, repositories coming from various communities (e.g. OpenAire[10], EUDAT[11] etc.). The metadata schemes of all these sources vary with respect to their coverage and the set of specific metadata captured. Currently, it is not possible to query all these sources in an integrated and uniform fashion. The Web of Data is a natural scenario for exposing LRs metadata in order to allow their automated discovery, share and reuse by humans or software agents. The benefits of this model including interoperability, federation, expressivity and dynamicity were laid out by Chiarcos et al. [7].

In this paper we contribute to the interoperability of these repositories by developing an ontology in the Web Ontology Language (OWL) [17] that allows us to represent the metadata schemes of these repositories under an extensible, open-world model.[12] The proposed ontology is based on the ontology developed by Villegas et al. [22] for the University Pompeu Fabra's (UPF) META-SHARE node (covering part of the original schema), which is extended to the complete schema (in order to cover all relevant LRs) and incorporates the consensus reached in the context of the W3C Linked Data for Language Technologies (LD4LT) Community Group[13]. We show how this model interacts with the DCAT [16] vocabulary as well as the most prominent models in the CLARIN VLO data. Further, we describe the application of the model in two portals, firstly the IULA LOD catalogue and secondly *Linghub*[14].

---

[2] https://github.com/metashare/META-SHARE/tree/master/misc/schema/v3.0.
[3] http://www.elra.info/en.
[4] https://www.ldc.upenn.edu/.
[5] http://catalog.clarin.eu/vlo/?1.
[6] http://langrid.org/en/index.html.
[7] http://alveo.edu.au.
[8] http://www.language-archives.org.
[9] http://www.resourcebook.eu/searchll.php.
[10] https://www.openaire.eu/.
[11] http://eudat.eu.
[12] http://purl.org/net/def/metashare.
[13] https://www.w3.org/community/ld4lt.
[14] http://linghub.org/.

The remainder of this paper is structured as follows: in Sect. 2 we will describe the related work in the fields of LR metadata harmonization. The development of the META-SHARE ontology is described in Sect. 3 and its application in Sect. 4. Finally, in Sect. 5 we consider the broader impact of this ontology as a tool for computational linguists and as a method to realize an architecture of (linked) data-aware services.

2   Related Work

The task of finding common vocabularies for linguistics is of wide interest and several general ontologies for linguistics have been proposed. The General Ontology for Linguistic Description [9, GOLD] was proposed as a common model for linguistic data, but its relatively limited scope and low coherence has not led to wide-spread adoption. An alternative approach that has been proposed is to use ontologies to create coherence among the resources, in particular by using ontologies to align different linguistic schemas [6].

This lack of consensus resides also in the description of LRs, even for non-linguistic concepts. In fact, there are as many metadata schemas for their descriptions as catalogs and repositories for their presentation (e.g. those used by ELRA and the LDC) and communities describing them (e.g. TEI [14] or CES [13]). The most widely used schema for the exchange of LRs is the one suggested by the Open Language Archives Community [1, OLAC], which builds on the Dublin Core metadata and has been criticized as being too reductionistic. Differences between the schemas lie in the range of features used and their labels and datatypes.

An important effort to harmonize metadata has been the ISO Data Category Registry (ISOcat DCR) [15], intended as a registry where metadata providers can register their concepts (Data Categories) and link them to those of other providers. A subset thereof was selected by metadata experts as the core elements for the description of LRs ("Athens Core"). The Component Metadata Infrastructure [4] proposed by CLARIN extends this principle of a common registry to include "components" and "profiles"; "components" consist of semantically close elements to be shared among different communities when producing "profiles" for specific LR types. However, as we observe in Sect. 3.5, this has in practice merely resulted in each contributing institute using its own scheme, with very little commonality between different institutes. To improve this situation it was recently proposed that the conversion of these CMDI schemas to RDF would enable better interoperability [21].

A different approach was taken for the design of the META-SHARE schema [11], which was based on a comparative study of the most widespread metadata schemas and catalog descriptions, analysis of user needs and discussions with metadata providers and experts in order to arrive at a common schema, taking into account previous initiatives and recommendations (cf. [8,20]).

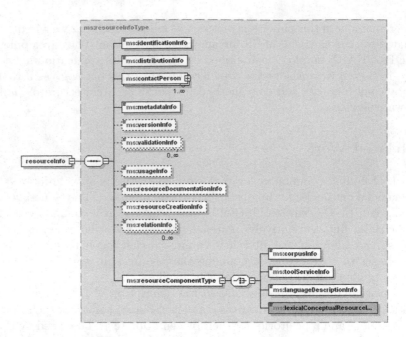

Fig. 1. The core of the META-SHARE model

3   The META-SHARE OWL Ontology

3.1   Original MS XSD Schema

The META-SHARE schema [11] has been designed not only as an aid for LR search and retrieval, but also as a means to foster their production, use and re-use by bringing together knowledge about LRs and related objects and processes, thus encoding information about the whole lifecycle of the LR from production to usage. The central entity of the META-SHARE schema is the LR *per se*, which encompasses both **data sets** (e.g., textual, audio and multimodal/multimedia corpora, lexical data, ontologies, terminologies, computational grammars, language models) and **technologies** (e.g., tools, services) used for their processing. In addition to the central entity, other entities are also documented in the schema; these are reference documents related to the LR (papers, reports, manuals etc.), persons/organizations involved in its creation and use (creators, distributors etc.), related projects and activities (funding projects, activities of usage etc.), accompanying licenses, etc., all described with metadata taken as far as possible from relevant schemas and guidelines (e.g. BibTex for bibliographical references). The META-SHARE schema proposes a set of elements to encode specific descriptive features of each of these entities and relations holding between them, taking as a starting point the LR. Following the CMDI approach, these elements are grouped together into "components". The core of the schema is the `resourceInfo` component (Fig. 1), which subsumes:

- administrative components relevant to all LRs, e.g. `identificationInfo` (name, description and identifiers), `distributionInfo` (licensing and intellectual property rights information), `usageInfo` (information about the intended and actual use of the LR).
- components specific to the resource type (corpus, lexical/conceptual resource, language model, tool/service) and media type (text, audio, video, image), which support the encoding of information relevant to resource/media combinations, e.g. text or audio parts of corpora, lexical/conceptual resources etc., such as language, formats, classification.

The META-SHARE schema recognises obligatory elements (minimal version) and recommended and optional elements (maximal version). An integrated environment supports the description of LRs, either from scratch or through uploading of XML files adhering to the META-SHARE metadata schema, as well as browsing, searching and viewing of the LRs.

3.2 Formal Modelling and Mapping Issues

In the META-SHARE XSD schema, *elements* are formalized as simple elements whereas *components* are formalized as complex-type elements. When mapping the XSD schema to RDF, *elements* can be naturally understood as properties (e.g. name, gender, etc.). *Components* (i.e. complex-type elements), however, deserve a careful analysis. General mapping rules from XSD to RDF establish that a local element with complex type translates into an object property and a class. We observed that the straightforward application of such a principle may derive unnecessarily verbose graphs. Thus, following Villegas et al. [22], we identified potentially removable nodes before undertaking the actual RDFication process. Embedded complex elements with cardinality of exactly one are identified as potentially removable, provided they contain neither text nor attributes. This allows for a simplification of the model, for example in the chain `resourceInfo ∘ identificationInfo ∘ resourceName`, the `identificationInfo` property is not needed. Interestingly enough, the removal of the superfluous wrapping elements has also led to a change of philosophy in the schema and a need for restructuring in order to ensure that properties are attached to the most appropriate node, as exemplified and discussed in Sect. 3.4. Beyond this, we made extensions to our mapping strategy in order to improve the ontology, such as the following:

- Removal of the `Info` suffix from the names of wrapping elements of components.
- Improvement of names that created confusion, as already noted by the META-SHARE group and/or the LD4LT group; thus, `resourceInfo` was renamed `LanguageResource`, `restrictionsOfUse` became `conditionsOfUse`.
- Generalization of concepts, e.g. `notAvailableThroughMetashare` with `availableThroughOtherDistributor`;
- Development of novel classes based on existing values, for example: `Corpus ≡ ∃resourceType.corpus`

– Grouping similar elements under novel superclasses, e.g. `annotationType` and `genre` values are structured in classes and subclasses better reflecting the relation between them. Indicatively, the superclass `SemanticAnnotation` can be used to bring together semantic annotation types, such as semantic roles, named entities, polarity, and semantic relations.
– Extension of existing classes with new values and new properties (e.g. `licenseCategory` for licences).

The actual mapping was achieved by means of a custom domain-specific language called LIXR [?].

```
<> a dcat:Dataset ;
  dc:description "Cette base de donnes..."@fr
  dc:language "tur" ;
  dc:source "META-SHARE" ;
  ms:corpusInfo <#corpusInfo> ;
  ms:distributionInfo <#distributionInfo> ;
  rdfs:seeAlso <http://metashare.elda.org/reposit...ac770/> .

<#corpusInfo> a ms:CorpusInfo , ms:CorpusAudioInfo ;
  dc:language "tur" ;
  ms:languageName "Turkish" ;
  ms:mediaType ms:audio .
```

Fig. 2. An abridged example of a metadata entry represented with common metadata properties from DCAT and Dublin Core and novel properties from the META-SHARE ontology.

3.3   Interface with DCAT and Other Vocabularies

The META-SHARE model can be considered broadly similar to DCAT in that there are classes that are nearly an exact match to the ones in DCAT for three out of four classes. DCAT's `dataset` corresponds nearly exactly to the `resourceInfo` tag and, similarly, `distributions` are similar to `distributionInfo` classes and `catalogRecord` is similar to `metadataInfo`. Thus, we introduced *equivalent class* relations between these elements. The fourth main class, `catalog` covers a level not modelled by META-SHARE. DCAT uses Dublin Core properties for many parts of the metadata, and often these properties are found deeply nested in the META-SHARE description. For example, language is found in several places deeply nested under six tags[15]. In META-SHARE this allows different media types in the resource to have different languages, e.g., the dialogues and the scripts of a video may be in English, whereas the subtitles can be in French and

---

[15] e.g., `resourceInfo` ∘ `resourceComponentType` ∘ `corpus` ∘ `corpusMediaType` ∘ `corpusVideoInfo` ∘ `languageInfo` → `dc:language`.

German. We still include this fine-grained metadata but also add the property at the resource level to indicate if any part of the resource is in the stated language. Similarly, it is also the case that some Dublin Core properties are not directly specified in the META-SHARE model, but can be inferred from related properties, e.g., Dublin Core's 'contributor' follows (by means of a property chain) from people indicated as 'annotators', 'evaluators', 'recorders' or 'validators'. Furthermore, several DCAT specific-properties, such as 'download URL', are nearly exactly equivalent to those in META-SHARE but occur in places that do not fit the domain and range of the properties. In this particular case, it was a simple fix to move the property to the enclosing `DistributionInfo` class. Inevitably, several properties from DCAT did not have equivalences in META-SHARE, notably 'keyword'. Figure 2 shows a simplified example of a META-SHARE metadata entry.

In addition to DCAT, we used also other vocabularies to establish equivalences to parts of the model. In particular, we mapped to the Friend of a Friend (FOAF) ontology to describe people and organizations and the Semantic Web for Research Communities (SWRC) ontology to describe scientific publications.

3.4 Licensing Module

A specific area where we made a significant effort to improve the modelling was in the licensing information in order to allow the formulation of a clear and concise rights information of the LRs. Some languages already exist for this purpose and, among them, ODRL 2.1 (Open Digital Rights Language) was chosen and extended. ODRL is a policy and rights expression language specified by the W3C ODRL Community Group[16], which defines a model for representing permissions, prohibitions and duties. The most common licenses (for software, data or general works) have been already expressed in ODRL in the RDF License dataset[17] [19] and can be pointed to when an LR is licensed with any of these. Extensions to the ODRL vocabulary have been made to represent some of the specificities of the LR domain. The specification also suggested changes, some of them structural, to the previous META-SHARE modelling, and to this extent we combined the existing META-SHARE licensing vocabulary with ODRL. In addition, we extended the model by adding some new properties and individuals based on requirements from the LD4LT community group[18]. In particular, the generic *conditions-of-use* values of the META-SHARE schema have been exploited for creating RDF codes for non-standard licenses and are mapped to ODRL actions (e.g. the duty to attribute), and included in an RDF document, as shown in Fig. 3. This module has been published both as independent module[19] and as part of the META-SHARE ontology.

---

[16] https://www.w3.org/community/odrl/.
[17] http://purl.org/NET/rdflicense.
[18] https://www.w3.org/community/ld4lt/wiki/Metashare_vocabulary_for_licenses.
[19] http://purl.org/NET/ms-rights.

```
<#distributionInfo> a ms:DistributionInfo , dcat:Distribution ;
  dct:license <http://purl.org/NET/rdflicense/ms-c-nored-ff> ;
  dcat:accessURL <http://catalog.elra...> .
```

Fig. 3. An example of the modelling of licenses in a record

3.5   Harmonizing Other Resources with META-SHARE

While a basic level of interoperability can be established by using standard vocabularies such as DCAT and Dublin Core, this can only be done by sacrificing completeness and ignoring all metadata particular to language resources. For this reason, we use the META-SHARE model to represent and harmonize the metadata relating specifically to the domain of linguistics and language resources. As a proof-of-concept, we show how the META-SHARE ontology supports the harmonization of data from the CLARIN VLO. The CLARIN repository describes its resources using a small common set of metadata and a larger description defined by the Component Metadata Infrastructure [4, CMDI]. These metadata schemes are extremely diverse as shown in Table 1. We will focus on the top five of these types for which we have created corresponding mappings. Two of these schemes are only Dublin Core properties and so do not have specific language resource metadata. The most frequent tag 'Song' is used to describe records of a database consisting of musical recordings. While many of the properties used by this tag (e.g., 'number of stanzas') have no correspondence in Dublin Core, they can be described with respect to existing elements of the META-SHARE Ontology. The `Session` tag is used to provide IMDI metadata [3], and has a very loose correspondence to META-SHARE. For instance, there are no corresponding properties to describe the participants of a media recording. This highlights the advantage of taking an open world, ontological approach as opposed to a fixed schema, in that we can easily introduce new properties while still reusing the META-SHARE properties where they are appropriate. The MODS metadata scheme [10] is in fact a general domain metadata framework. We found that 28 entities from META-SHARE corresponded to elements used in the 'Sing' metadata of the Meertens Institute collection, and 37 to the IMDI metadata, although there was only minor overlap with the MODS scheme (in particular 4 entities used to describe language) as this scheme is not specific to language resources.

4   Applications

4.1   IULA LOD Catalogue

The IULA-UPF CLARIN Competence Centre[20] aims to promote and support the use of technology and text analysis tools in the Humanities and Social Sciences research. The centre includes a Catalogue[21] with information on language

---

[20] http://www.clarin-es-lab.org/index-en.html.
[21] http://lod.iula.upf.edu/.

Table 1. The top 10 most frequent component types in CLARIN and the institutes that use them. Abbreviations: MI = Meertens Institute (KNAW), MPI = Max Planck Insitute (Nijmegen), BeG = Netherlands Institute for Sound and Vision, HI = Huygens Institute (KNAW), BBAW = Berlin-Brandenburg Academy of Sciences

Component root tag	Institutes	Frequency
Song	1 (MI)	155,403
Session	1 (MPI)	128,673
OLAC-DcmiTerms	39	95,370
MODS	1 (Utrecht)	64,632
DcmiTerms	2 (BeG,HI)	46,160
SongScan	1 (MI)	28,448
media-session-profile	1 (Munich)	22,405
SourceScan	1 (MI)	21,256
Source	1 (MI)	16,519
teiHeader	2 (BBAW, Copenhagen)	15,998

resources and technology. The Catalogue is based on the initial linked open data (LOD) version of the META-SHARE model as described in [22] and the original data generated from the UPF META-SHARE node[22]. The source XML records were converted into RDF and augmented with service descriptions (not included in the UPF META-SHARE node) and relevant documentation (appropriate articles, documentation, sample data and results, illustrative experiments, examples from outstanding projects, illustrative use cases, etc.) to encourage potential users to embrace digital tools. Finally, the data was enriched with internal and external links. The resulting linked data maximised the information contained in the original repository and enabled data mashup techniques that get relevant data from the DBpedia and the DBLP[23]. The catalogue demonstrates the benefits of the LOD framework and how this can be easily used as the basis for a web browser application that maximizes information and helps users to navigate throughout the datasets in a comprehensive way.

4.2   Linghub

Linghub is a portal designed to allow common querying of metadata from multiple highly heterogeneous repositories. Currently, it draws not only from META-SHARE, but also from the LRE-Map [5], the CLARIN VLO [2] and DataHub, and is regularly updated with new/changed information. The repository is based on the DCAT and Dublin Core vocabularies. However, these models do not capture any specific linguistic information. For this reason, the ontology described in this paper has been integrated into the system to allow users to

---

[22] http://metashare.upf.edu.
[23] http://dblp.uni-trier.de/db/index.html.

use META-SHARE as the basic vocabulary for querying linguistic information about language resources, and the mappings previously described have already been applied to data from LRE-Map and the CLARIN VLO. Linghub supports browsing and querying by several means, including faceted browsing, full-text search, SPARQL querying and related item search. As such, we believe that the portal, while not a direct collector of metadata, will enable users to find more language resources and do so more easily. See Fig. 4 for a screenshot of the Linghub web interface.

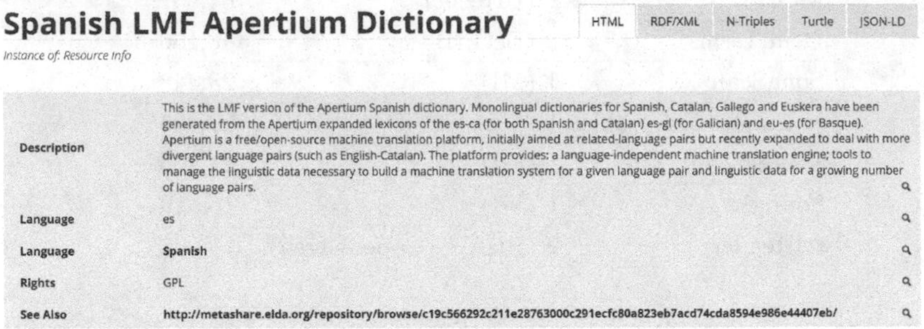

Fig. 4. META-SHARE data as displayed within the Linghub interface

The Linghub portal is thus a proof-of-concept for the level of harmonization that the use of a common ontology provides, as metadata originating from different repositories can be uniformly queried in Linghub in an integrated fashion. We adhere to an open architecture in which not only Linghub but other discovery services that aggregate and index data could potentially be developed.

5   Conclusion

This work represents only a first starting point for the harmonization of language resources by providing a standard ontology that can be used in the description of metadata of linguistic resources and there are still a number of challenges ahead of us to be addressed. Firstly, the next step would be to make sure that not only metadata, but the actual data is available on the Web in open web standards such as RDF so that data can be automatically crawled and analyzed. Secondly, it should be required that linguistic data published on the Web should ideally follow the same format (e.g. RDF) so that it can be easily integrated and data can be queried across datasets. This presupposes the agreement on best practices for data publication and formats, and the Natural Language Processing Interchange Format (NIF) [12] is an obvious candidate for that. Thirdly, harmonization should be extended to the description of NLP services so that NLP services can be distributed across providers and repositories. The mechanisms for description of the functionality of NLP services should be extremely lightweight. Finally, input and output formats for services should be standardized and homogenized so that services can be easily composed to realize more complex workflows, without relying on too much parametrization. Workflows of services should be easily executable 'on the cloud'. In order to scale, services should support parallelization, streaming and non-centralized processing. We believe that the development of common vocabularies such as the one presented in this paper should enable the emergence of a new paradigm supporting the discovery and exploitation of linguistic data and services across repositories.

Acknowledgments. We are very grateful to the members of the W3C Linked Data for Language Technologies (LD4LT) for all the useful feedback received and for allowing this initiative to be developed as an activity of the group. This work is supported by the FP7 European project LIDER (610782), by the Spanish Ministry of Economy and Competitiveness (project TIN2013-46238-C4-2-R and a Juan de la Cierva grant), the Greek CLARIN Attiki project (MIS 441451) and the H2020 project CRACKER (645357).

References

1. Bird, S., Simons, G.: The OLAC metadata set and controlled vocabularies. In: Proceedings of the ACL 2001 Workshop on Sharing Tools and Resources, vol. 15, pp. 7–18. Association for Computational Linguistics (2001)
2. Broeder, D., Kemps-Snijders, M., Van Uytvanck, D., Windhouwer, M., Withers, P., Wittenburg, P., Zinn, C.: A data category registry-and component-based metadata framework. In: Proceedings of the Seventh Conference on International Language Resources and Evaluation, pp. 43–47 (2010)
3. Broeder, D., Offenga, F., Willems, D., Wittenburg, P.: The IMDI metadata set, its tools and accessible linguistic databases. In: Proceedings of the IRCS Workshop on Linguistic Databases, pp. 11–13 (2001)
4. Broeder, D., Windhouwer, M., Van Uytvanck, D., Goosen, T., Trippel, T.: CMDI: a component metadata infrastructure. In: Describing LRs with Metadata: Towards Flexibility and Interoperability in the Documentation of LR, pp. 1–4 (2012)
5. Calzolari, N., Del Gratta, R., Francopoulo, G., Mariani, J., Rubino, F., Russo, I., Soria, C.: The LRE map. Harmonising community descriptions of resources. In: Proceedings of the Eighth Conference on International Language Resources and Evaluation, pp. 1084–1089 (2012)
6. Chiarcos, C.: Ontologies of linguistic annotation: Survey and perspectives. In: Proceedings of the Eighth International Conference on Language Resources and Evaluation, pp. 303–310 (2012)
7. Chiarcos, C., McCrae, J., Cimiano, P., Fellbaum, C.: Towards open data for linguistics: linguistic linked data. In: Oltramari, A., Vossen, P., Qin, L., Hovy, E. (eds.) New Trends of Research in Ontologies and Lexical Resources: Ideas, Projects, Systems, pp. 7–25. Springer, Heidelberg (2013)
8. Cieri, C., Choukri, K., Calzolari, N., Langendoen, D.T., Leveling, J., Palmer, M., Ide, N., Pustejovsky, J.: A road map for interoperable language resource metadata. In: Chair, N.C.C., Choukri, K., Maegaard, B., Mariani, J., Odijk, J., Piperidis, S., Rosner, M., Tapias, D. (eds.) Proceedings of the Seventh International Conference on Language Resources and Evaluation (LREC'10). European Language Resources Association (ELRA), Valletta, Malta, May 2010

9. Farrar, S., Lewis, W., Langendoen, T.: A common ontology for linguistic concepts. In: Proceedings of the Knowledge Technologies Conference, pp. 10–13 (2002)
10. Gartner, R.: MODS: Metadata object description schema. JISC Techwatch report TSW, pp. 3–6 (2003)
11. Gavrilidou, M., Labropoulou, P., Desipri, E., Piperidis, S., Papageorgiou, H., Monachini, M., Frontini, F., Declerck, T., Francopoulo, G., Arranz, V., Mapelli, V.: The META-SHARE metadata schema for the description of language resources. In: Proceedings of the Eighth International Conference on Language Resources and Evaluation, pp. 1090–1097 (2012)
12. Hellmann, S., Lehmann, J., Auer, S., Brümmer, M.: Integrating NLP using linked data. In: Alani, H., et al. (eds.) The Semantic Web – ISWC 2013. LNCS, vol. 8219, pp. 98–113. Springer, Heidelberg (2013)
13. Ide, N.: Corpus encoding standard: SGML guidelines for encoding linguistic corpora. In: Proceedings of the First International Language Resources and Evaluation Conference, pp. 463–470 (1998)
14. Ide, N., Véronis, J. (eds.): Text Encoding Initiative: Background and Contexts. Springer, Heidelberg (1995)
15. Kemps-Snijders, M., Windhouwer, M., Wittenburg, P., Wright, S.E.: ISOcat: corralling data categories in the wild. In: Proceedings of the Seventh Conference on International Language Resources and Evaluation (2008)
16. Maali, F., Erickson, J., Archer, P.: Data catalog vocabulary (DCAT). W3C recommendation, The World Wide Web Consortium (2014)
17. Motik, B., Patel-Schneider, P.F., Parsia, B., Bock, C., Fokoue, A., Haase, P., Hoekstra, R., Horrocks, I., Ruttenberg, A., Sattler, U., Smith, M.: OWL 2 web ontology language structural specification and functional-style syntax. W3C recommendation, The World Wide Web Consortium (2012)
18. Piperidis, S.: The META-SHARE language resources sharing infrastructure: principles, challenges, solutions. In: Proceedings of the Eighth Conference on International Language Resources and Evaluation, pp. 36–42 (2012)
19. Rodriguez-Doncel, V., Villata, S., Gomez-Perez, A.: A dataset of RDF licenses. In: Proceedings of the 27th International Conference on Legal Knowledge and Information System (JURIX), pp. 187–189 (2014)
20. Soria, C., Calzolari, N., Monachini, M., Quochi, V., Bel, N., Choukri, K., Mariani, J., Odijk, J., Piperidis, S.: The language resource strategic agenda: the flarenet synthesis of community recommendations. Lang. Resour. Eval. **48**(4), 753–775 (2014). http://dx.doi.org/10.1007/s10579-014-9279-y
21. Ďurčo, M., Windhouwer, M.: From CLARIN component metadata to linked open data. In: Proceedings of the 3rd Workshop on Linked Data in Linguistics, pp. 13–17 (2014)
22. Villegas, M., Melero, M., Bel, N.: Metadata as linked open data: mapping disparate XML metadata registries into one RDF/OWL registry. In: Proceedings of the Ninth International Conference on Language Resources and Evaluation, pp. 393–400 (2014)

Applying the OntoLex Model to a Multilingual Terminological Resource

Julia Bosque-Gil[✉], Jorge Gracia, Guadalupe Aguado-de-Cea,
and Elena Montiel-Ponsoda

Ontology Engineering Group, Universidad Politécnica de Madrid,
Campus de Montegancedo, Boadilla Del Monte, 28660 Madrid, Spain
{jbosque,jgracia,lupe,emontiel}@fi.upm.es

Abstract. Terminesp is a multilingual terminological resource with terms from a range of specialized domains. Along with definitions, notes, scientific denominations and provenance information, it includes translations from Spanish into a variety of languages. A linked data resource with these features would represent a potentially relevant source of knowledge for NLP-based applications. In this contribution we show that Terminesp constitutes an appropriate validating test bench for OntoLex and its **vartrans** module, a newly developed model which evolves the *lemon* model to represent the lexicon-ontology interface. We present a first showcase of this module to account for variation across entries, while highlighting the modeling problems we encountered in this effort. Furthermore, we extend the resource with part-of-speech and syntactic information which was not explicitly declared in the original data with the aim of exploring its future use in NLP applications.

Keywords: Ontolex · Variation · Translation · Terminological resource

1 Introduction

Recent years have seen growing interest in the publication of language resources (LRs) as linked data, and the presence of machine readable dictionaries, lexicons, and thesauri in the Linguistic Linked Open Data (LLOD) cloud[1] continues to increase. Linking language resources not only enables humans and software agents easier access and querying of structured data collections, but linked multilingual LRs represent a potentially relevant source of knowledge for NLP-based applications developed in the fields of machine translation, content analytics, multilingual information extraction, word sense disambiguation or ontology localization. The inclusion of terminological knowledge from different domains into the LLOD cloud has already been explored with the creation and publication of thesauri, vocabularies and terminology repositories, especially in the environmental and geological domain [1,2,11], as well as in the financial [10] and linguistics [3,4,7] fields. Converting and publishing terminological dictionaries as linked data opens new doors

---

[1] http://linguistic-lod.org/.

© Springer International Publishing Switzerland 2015
F. Gandon et al. (Eds.): ESWC 2015, LNCS 9341, pp. 283–294, 2015.
DOI: 10.1007/978-3-319-25639-9_43

to the reuse of these resources in domain specific NLP applications and machine translation. A new approach has been suggested to migrate terminologies in TBX format to RDF on the basis of the *OntoLex* model (see below), linking them to one another and to BabelNet[2] concepts [5].

Aimed originally at bridging the gap between lexical and conceptual information, the *lemon* model (LExicon Model for ONtologies) [8] is now a widespread representation model for the publication of lexical resources as linked data which has been gradually expanded to include new modules under the umbrella of the W3C Ontology-Lexica Community Group[3], resulting in the newly developed model *OntoLex/lemon*.[4] An extension to *lemon* that accounts for translation relations among lexical senses from the same or different data sets was also developed [6]. In such effort, the Terminesp[5] data served as a validating example of a terminological LR to which the translation module would apply.

Our contribution builds on such previous work [6] and describes a first showcase of the `vartrans` module of OntoLex in order to account for terminological variation and translation relations among entries. In addition to showcasing the `vartrans` module, we extend the resource further by adding components to represent definitions and terminological norms of Terminesp entries. The entries themselves range from simple nouns and adjectives to complex nominal, prepositional and adjectival phrases, which led us to include part-of-speech information for each entry and turn to LexInfo [4] classes to account for that mixed nature as well. We also draw attention to the modeling problems to which these prepositional phrases give rise and which will be tackled in future work.

The structure of this paper is as follows: Sect. 2 briefly explains the OntoLex `vartrans` module, with special focus on the terminological variation aspects not addressed in previous work. Section 3 introduces the Terminesp database and provides an example of the structure of its data. Section 4 dwells on previous work with Terminesp and describes our approach to model the entries, including definitions and syntactic information, among other aspects. Following, we showcase the `vartrans` module to represent scientific denominations. Lastly, Sect. 5 discusses some conclusions and future lines of work.

2   The OntoLex `vartrans` Module

OntoLex is the resulting work of the continued efforts made by the W3C Ontology Lexica Community Group during the past three years to build a rich model to represent the lexicon-ontology interface. It is largely based on the *lemon* model [8] and, along with the extensions to it, integrates work of the various Community members.

---

[2] http://babelnet.org/.

[3] https://www.w3.org/community/ontolex/.

[4] See http://www.w3.org/community/ontolex/wiki/Final_Model_Specification. We will refer to it as *OntoLex* in the rest of this paper.

[5] http://www.wikilengua.org/index.php/Wikilengua:Terminesp.

Broadly, each entry in the lexical database belonging to an `ontolex:Lexicon` is modeled as an `ontolex:LexicalEntry` and mapped to its respective ontology entity. The mappings are established at the sense level through the property `ontolex:reference` and the class `ontolex:LexicalSense`, thereby capturing the fact that a single lexical entry may have different senses, each one referring to a different ontology entity and evoking a particular lexical concept. However, information regarding the realization of a lexical entry (e.g. inflection, pronunciation, etc.) is recorded at the lexical form level via `ontolex:Form`.

The OntoLex `vartrans` module was developed to record variation relations across entries in the same or different languages. The intuition behind it is to capture two kinds of relations: those among senses and those among lexical entries and/or forms. Variation relations among senses are of semantic nature and include terminological relations (dialectal, register, chronological, discursive, and dimensional variation)[6] and translation relations. In contrast, relations among lexical entries and/or forms concern the surface form of a term and encode morphological and orthographical variation, among other aspects. This last kind of relations are not considered semantic in nature; grammatical meaning encoded in morphological affixes is thus represented at a different layer than lexical meaning (senses), and variation in orthography is thought as a relation between two similar forms (e.g. *analyze, analyse*), in contrast to synonymy and antonymy relations between two senses (e.g. *shut, close*) in which the surface forms are not involved. In this paper we only focus on the first kind of relations, variation relations among senses, to represent translations and register (also called *diaphasic*) relations between a term and its scientific denomination.

2.1 Translations

The OntoLex `vartrans` module frames translation relations as a special type of lexico-semantic variation across the entries of different lexica, more specifically, as relations that hold among senses. The translation component goes back to the *lemon* Translation module. In this view, the `vartrans` module turns to a pivot class `vartrans:Translation` to represent translations among lexical entries as relations among `ontolex:LexicalSenses` that point to the same ontology concept. One of the main differences between the OntoLex and the *lemon* translation modules is the conception of a class to encompass variation relations, the `vartrans:LexicoSemanticRelation` class. Its subclasses denote relations that hold among lexical entries (`vartrans:LexicalRelation`) and relations that hold among lexical senses (`vartrans:SenseRelation`). The pivot class `vartrans:Translation` mentioned before is thus a `vartrans:SenseRelation`, and so are the relations among terminological variants as well (`vartrans:TerminologicalVariant`). The Terminesp database contains translation relations of the *directEquivalent* category, but other translation categories (e.g. *culturalEquivalent*, for culture-dependent concepts; *lexicalEquivalent*, for literal translations of the source term, etc.) are supported as well and can be included from

---

[6] http://www.w3.org/community/ontolex/wiki/Specification_of_Requirements/
Properties-and-Relations-of-Entries.

an external ontology [6]. In addition to translation relations among their senses, lexical entries in different languages can be directly related through the property vartrans:translatableAs.

2.2 Terminological Variants in the Same Language

Terminological variants in the same language are modeled as relations among senses, too. The vartrans module allows for the encoding of dialectal (diatopic), register (diaphasic), chronological (diachronic), stylistical (diastratic) as well as dimensional variation among entries. In this way and in the same fashion as translations, two lexical entries are mapped to their respective lexical senses, and these are related through the pivot class vartrans:TerminologicalVariant, with the property vartrans:category allowing for the specific type of terminological variation at hand to be included as well. For cases in which there is not any directionality involved, that is, there is not any source or target term, the property vartrans:relates (similar to the former tr:translationSense in *lemon*) links the two senses to the element acting as pivot. In the following example, there is a diachronic variation between the terms *phthisis* and *tuberculosis*, being the latter one the one used nowadays. This shift is captured by representing the two senses as source and target respectively.

```
@prefix ontolex: <http://www.w3.org/ns/lemon/ontolex#> .
@prefix vartrans: <http://www.w3.org/ns/lemon/vartrans#> .
@prefix dct: <http://purl.org/dc/terms/>.

:tuberculosis a ontolex:LexicalEntry ;
      ontolex:lexicalForm :tuberculosis_form ;
      ontolex:sense :tuberculosis_sense.
:tuberculosis_form ontolex:writtenRep "tuberculosis"@en .
:tuberculosis_sense ontolex:reference
   <http://dbpedia.org/resource/Tuberculosis>.
:phthisis a ontolex:LexicalEntry ;
      ontolex:lexicalForm :phthisis_form ;
      ontolex:sense :phthisis_sense.
:phthisis_form ontolex:writtenRep "phthisis"@en .
:phtisis_sense ontolex:reference
   <http://dbpedia.org/resource/Tuberculosis>;
              dct:subject
                 <http://dbpedia/resource/Medicine> .
:phtisis_diachronic_var a vartrans:TerminologicalVariant;
   vartrans:source :phthisis_sense ;
   vartrans:target :tuberculosis_sense ;
   vartrans:category isocat:diachronic.
```

3 The Terminesp Database

The Terminesp terminological database was created by the *Asociación Española de Terminología* (Spanish Association for Terminology, AETER) by extracting the terminological data from the UNE ('*Una Norma Española*' a Spanish norm) documents produced by AENOR (*Asociación Española de Normalización y Certificación*). It contains the terms and definitions used in the UNE Spanish technological norms (standards) and amounts to more than thirty thousand terms with equivalences in other languages whenever they are available. These norms, similar to the ISO standards, have been elaborated by Spanish committees composed of experts in different fields. The norms are defined over a range of domains, from aeronautics and electro-technical engineering to fruit nomenclature. An entry in Terminesp consists of the definition of the term, the norm from which the term is extracted, the norm title, and, if available, the translation of the term to one or several different languages, namely German, French, Italian, Swedish, and/or English. A Terminesp entry is presented in Table 1.[7]

Table 1. Terminesp entry for the Spanish term *admitancia cinética*

Norm	UNE_21302-801
Norm title	Vocabulario electrotecnico: capítulo 801. Acústica y electroacústica
Spanish term	**admitancia cinética**
German term	Bewegungsadmittanz
English term	motional admittance
French term	admittance cinétique, admittance motionnelle
Definition	En un transductor, diferencia entre la admitancia eléctrica en carga y su admitancia eléctrica cuando está mecánicamente bloqueado.
Note	NOTA - Esta definición es válida principalmente para transductores con acoplamiento por transformador

4   Migrating Terminesp to Linked Data

In this contribution we renew the previous work with Terminesp [6] in order to (1) detect errors and inconsistencies in the data before linking the data set to other lexical resources (i.e. LexInfo), (2) provide a validating example of the OntoLex *vartrans* module to account for variation across entries, with emphasis on scientific naming, (3) extend the LD resource with definitions, norms, and part-of-speech categories, and (4) create a database of nominal, prepositional, and adjectival phrases with highly specialized content (not covered by other LRs) to be used by NLP applications. Since we have built upon previous work [6] with

---

[7] En. *Norm*: Electrotechnical vocabulary: Chap. 801. Acoustics and electroacoustics. *Definition*: Referred to a transducer, the difference between the electrical admittance on charge and its electrical admittance when it is mechanically locked. *Note*: NOTE - This definition applies mainly to transducers with transformer coupling.

the lexical database, we have stuck to the resource structure and URI naming strategy that the authors followed in their approach.[8] Being OntoLex still under development, the RDF files resulting from our tests with Terminesp are not published as linked data yet, but they are open and accessible online.[9]

As in [6], we instantiate a skos:Concept for any given Terminesp entry in order to ground the terms conceptually. A Terminesp entry, in turn, is modeled as an ontolex:LexicalEntry whose ontolex:LexicalSense points to the appropriate skos:Concept. Translations are included by instantiating a vartrans: Translation element with the properties source and target linking the two translation senses, one for each language. The senses are attached to the vartrans: Translation by an additional property too, vartrans:relates.

4.1   Definitions, Notes, and Norms

In addition to the available translations for a given entry that were captured in the previous *lemon* version [6], definitions, notes, norm codes, norm titles and provenance were added as linked data as well.

Specifically, definitions are attached to the skos:Concept the ontolex:Lexi calSense is mapped to. This is done through the property skos:definition. Moreover, some of these definitions include a note that provides additional information about the definition content, use cases, etc. and, in order to distinguish this from the definition itself, we use rdfs:comment to relate the skos:Concept to the string acting as note. In *lemon*, the class lemon:SenseDefinition allowed to treat the definition of a term as an object whose property lemon:value pointed to the definition string itself. This was particularly well-suited for capturing elements that were not definitions but which were nonetheless related to them, as in the case of notes to definitions, as we have in Terminesp. The class lemon:SenseDefinition is not included in OntoLex, in fact, definitions are not encoded at the sense, but at the ontolex:LexicalConcept level with the property ontolex:definition. A lexical concept in OntoLex aims to reify the concept one or several senses evoke and lexicalize, resembling a *synset* in WordNet. In our view, the approach based on the skos:definition property appeared more suitable for the task. That is, an account of Terminesp definitions in terms of LexicalConcept definitions would imply instantiating a lexical concept for any Terminesp entry, which, along with the lexical sense, would bring unnecessary complexity to the representation.

Terminesp entries are all extracted from Spanish UNE documents and, in addition to definitions, the database provides norms and norm code information. The norm each entry comes from is thus captured by dc:title, and the norm code included with an instantiation of the dc:source property.

---

[8] e.g. http://linguistic.linkeddata.es/data/terminesp/lexiconES.
[9] http://dx.doi.org/10.6084/m9.figshare.1344810.

4.2   Part-of-speech Tags and Syntactic Phrases

Part-of-speech (POS) tags were not provided in the original data. In order to link each entry to its corresponding syntactic category through `lexinfo:partOf-Speech` at the `ontolex:LexicalEntry` level, TreeTagger[10] was used. The initial idea was to tag the Spanish data in order to obtain part-of-speech information that holds for translations to different languages as well. In other words, given that the terms are highly specialized, a mechanical term in Spanish that is a noun is likely to have a corresponding translation in English or German that is a noun as well. However, the nature of Terminesp entries is mixed: the data set is made up of adjectives, verbs and nouns, along with complex noun phrases (NP), prepositional phrases (PP) and adjective phrases (AP). In order to represent this, we linked multi-word Terminesp entries to `lexinfo:NounPhrase`, `lexinfo:AdjectivePhrase` and `lexinfo:PrepositionPhrase` accordingly. In this way we are encoding the syntax of a prepositional phrase and also stating that it may function as an adjective or as an adverb (via `lexinfo:partOfSpeech`), for instance. Table 2 shows the distribution of the different part of speech tags, and which of them involve a complex phrase structure (NPs, PPs, APs).

Table 2. Distribution of part-of-speech categories and syntactic phrases in Terminesp Spanish entries. The tag *simple* is included here for contrastive purposes: it refers to those entries that do not involve a complex constituent structure.

lexinfo:PartOfSpeech	Synt.Phrase	# Entries
noun	simple	13777
	NP	18552
verb	simple	69
adjective	simple	31
	PP	56
	AP	4
adverb	PP	2
Total		32491

Interestingly, the PPs are regarded here as independent entries and there is not any information pointing to their syntactic governor, even though there are complex NPs in the data that are formed by a noun and a PP that occurs as lexical entry too. Thus, we find a PP such as *en reposo* 'idle' as a Terminesp entry and other entries (NPs) with that same PP as constituent: *masa en reposo, tinta en reposo, pasador en reposo*. However, the PP and the NP entries are not related in the data. Not only does this contrast with conventional dictionaries, where the preposition is usually accessed through its NP complement (**reposo**, en –)

---

[10] http://www.cis.uni-muenchen.de/~schmid/tools/TreeTagger/.

or the whole PP is accessed through its syntactic governor (**masa**, – en reposo), but it also prevents us from using OntoLex's syntax and semantics module to encode syntactic behavior, since we cannot access the syntactic governor of the PP or the syntactic frame in which the PP would be fit as argument. Moreover, some of these PPs can also accompany a verb (*estar en reposo*, 'to be idle'; *funcionar en reposo*, 'to work idle'), so that the type of syntactic frame we are dealing with is not always inferable from the PP alone.

Most entries in Terminesp are actually NPs (see Table 2): e.g. *potencia isótropa radiada equivalente* 'equivalent isotropically radiated power'. With an initial random test set of 500 entries, TreeTagger achieved 0.997 precision and 0.995 recall. The reason behind this is the high number of nouns. In cases in which the entry was a complex phrase, TreeTagger tagged every element in it, which allowed us to identify prepositional phrases. The remaining multi-word entries were initially tagged as nouns. An analysis of the errors revealed that deverbal adjectives were used as nouns throughout the data, and that some multi-word entries included their tag (*capacitivo, adj.*, 'capacitive') or even a disambiguation note: *funcionar (para los relés elementales)*, 'function (for elemental relays)'. The tags for the scarce adjectives and verbs were checked and corrected manually, and PPs were tagged as adjectives or adverbs according to their definition and sample uses, if the latter were available.

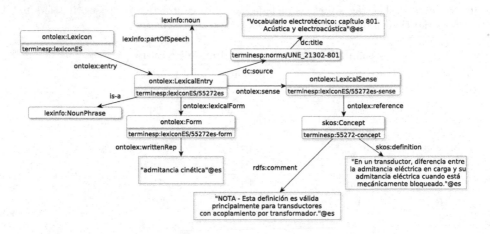

Fig. 1. A Terminesp entry modeled with OntoLex

It is worth mentioning, however, that PPs pose modeling problems still. There seem to be different degrees of lexicalization among them: some of them are fixed both in the specialized domain and in the general language (*en reposo*); others, e.g. *a circuito abierto* 'open-circuited', may admit a certain degree of variation and are not even regarded as a set phrase outside the specialized domain. Being the meaning of these entries compositional (to a certain degree), they could not be considered *idioms* according to the definition of `lexinfo:idiom`, nor are they collocations in the sense of `olia:Collocation`,[11] and they do not correspond either to the category of prepositional constructions as, for instance, composite prepositions (*in front of*) or prepositional adverbs (*outside*), which are accounted for in linguistic terminology repositories. Furthermore, translations from the Spanish entry (a PP) into other language may be in the form of PPs as well, adjectives, or adverbs, depending on the target language. The part-of-speech that we assigned to the Spanish entry itself is subject to change given that we do not have the syntactic context in which the entry occurs: some of them are eligible for both adjectival and adverbial use. Capturing these nuances, however, was outside the scope of this paper but will be considered for future work on terminological data.

Figure 1 is included as an example of a Terminesp entry in OntoLex with information about the definition, the norm code, the norm title, the part-of-speech category and the syntactic phrase. Translations are not included in this figure, but we refer the reader to Fig. 2.

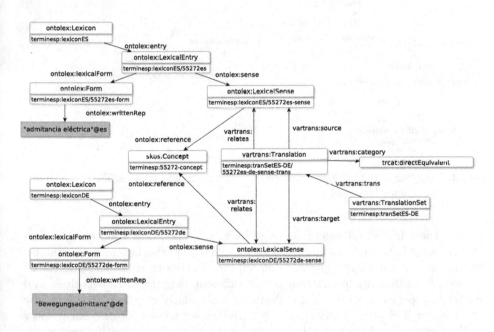

Fig. 2. Modeling of the German translation of the Spanish entry *admitancia cinética* 'motional admittance', *Bewegungsadmittanz*.

4.3   Scientific Denominations

Another important issue is the scientific naming of Terminesp terms. The entries that provide a Latin term come mainly from the botanical domain, denoting

---

[11] http://purl.org/olia/olia.owl#Collocation.

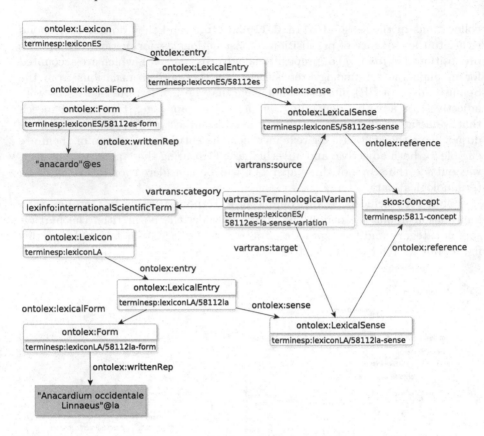

Fig. 3. Modeling of the Spanish entry *anacardo* 'cashew' and its scientific name, *Anacardium occidentale Linnaeus*.

most of them fruits and vegetables. e.g. Sp. *uva* 'grape', Lat. *Vitis vinifera Linnaeus*. These Latin terms could have been modeled as translations from Spanish into Latin, following the approach adopted for all other translations, since, after all, we are dealing with variation across different languages. Nonetheless, and inspired by previous work on this domain, particularly on the LIR (Linguistic Information Repository) model [9], we have decided to identify the Latin entry as the international scientific denomination. In this sense, scientific names are considered a specific type of terminological variants subject to domain and register rather than to any other factor. Also, they are internationally accepted over scientific communities and can appear in texts written in any language, provided that the register and the domain are adequate for their use. Taking this into account, Latin terms are thought here as terminological variants (see Fig. 3) and, more specifically, as lexinfo:InternationalScientificTerm(-s). Relations among the Latin term and the entries in other languages are not included, since the Spanish lexicon is taken to be the core of the resource, but we do not discard adding them in future versions. The language tag of Latin entries remains Latin, even though this results in a relation between two senses in different languages that does not use a `vartrans:Translation` element.

Our approach, however, might be regarded as limited by some terminologists. The relation between scientific and common terms could be viewed as a special case of synonymy [13] or could be captured by `sameAs` properties (which might be refined into `hasScientificTaxonomicName` and `isScientificTaxonomic-NameOf` [12]), for instance. It is worth mentioning, however, that Terminesp is not conceived as a taxonomic terminological database and in that respect its data lack the richness we find in AGROVOC [2]. A proposal for restructuring scientific names in AGROVOC to allow for a better identification of an organism through its various denominations has been suggested [12]. The authors distinguish between the different scientific names of a term and the most common accepted one of them, and also address relations between a term a taxa concept (order, family) to allow for the modeling of the taxonomy via properties such as `hasSpecies`. In contrast, our proposal deems appropriate for terminological databases that contain Latin denominations but are not aimed at representing taxonomic knowledge. As such, we focus on the intuition that a Latin term is just another lexicalization of a concept and turn to the fact that scientific denominations are used as terminological variants in different registers and domains than common terms.

5   Conclusions and Future Work

Terminesp has proved to be a suitable testing bench for the OntoLex core and the `vartrans` module. Since OntoLex is still under development, migrating Terminesp to RDF allowed us to carry out a first application of the model on a multilingual and terminological data set to check for any gaps or incongruities in the representation approach. On the one hand, the multilingual nature of Terminesp provided an appropriate use case of the `vartrans` module to account for translations, and on the other hand, the scientific denominations available in some Terminesp entries proved suitable to encode register variation as well. However, we missed the inclusion of a class or property in OntoLex to capture sense definitions or notes to them, since just modeling in terms of `ontolex:LexicalConcept`(-s) would overly complicate the task and did not seem to fit for this particular resource. Lastly, we draw attention to the modeling problems that entries with varying degrees of lexicalization might give rise to in future efforts with terminological data.

As a first future step, the data set will be published as linked data as soon as the OntoLex model is released. This contribution not only aims to report on the first results of applying the model, but the Terminesp RDF data set promises to be a potential significant resource for NLP-based applications. It provides terminological information in several languages, some of them currently under-represented in the LLOD cloud (e.g. Swedish), and translations among the different languages are accessible through the Spanish terms acting as interlingua elements. We will also explore the use of the pool of syntactic phrases discussed in Sect. 4.2 in multilingual information extraction and language generation tasks.

Acknowledgments. We are very thankful to the participants of the MSW'15 workshop (where a previous version of this paper was presented) for the feedback received, which we have incorporated into this version. This work is supported by the FP7 European project LIDER (610782) and by the Spanish Ministry of Economy and Competitiveness (project TIN2013-46238-C4-2-R).

References

1. Albertoni, R., Martino, M.D., Franco, S.D., Santis, V.D., Plini, P.: EARTh: an environmental application reference thesaurus in the linked open data cloud. Seman. Web **5**(2), 165–171 (2014)
2. Caracciolo, C., Stellato, A., Morshed, A., Johannsen, G., Rajbhandari, S., Jaques, Y., Keizer, J.: The AGROVOC linked dataset. Seman. Web **4**(3), 341–348 (2013)
3. Chiarcos, C., Sukhareva, M.: OLiA - ontologies of linguistic annotation. Seman. Web **6**(4), 379–386 (2015)
4. Cimiano, P., Buitelaar, P., McCrae, J., Sintek, M.: LexInfo: a declarative model for the lexicon-ontology interface. Web Seman.: Sci. Serv. Agents World Wide Web **9**(1), 29–51 (2011)
5. Cimiano, P., McCrae, J.P., Rodríguez-Doncel, V., Gornostay, T., Gómez-Pérez, A., Siemoneit, B., Lagzdins, A.: Linked terminology: applying linked data principles to terminological resources. In: Proceedings of eLex 2015, Sussex, UK (2015)
6. Gracia, J., Montiel-Ponsoda, E., Vila-Suero, D., Aguado-de Cea, G.: Enabling language resources to expose translations as linked data on the web. In: Proceedings of 9th Language Resources and Evaluation Conference (LREC 2014), Reykjavik (Iceland), pp. 409–413. European Language Resources Association (ELRA), May 2014
7. Kemps-Snijders, M., Windhouwer, M., Wittenburg, P., Wright, S.E.: ISOcat: corralling data categories in the wild. In: Calzolari, N., Choukri, K., Maegaard, B., Mariani, J., Odijk, J., Piperidis, S., Tapias, D. (eds.) Proceedings of the Sixth International Conference on Language Resources and Evaluation (LREC 2008). European Language Resources Association (ELRA), Marrakech, Morocco, May 2008. http://www.lrec-conf.org/proceedings/lrec2008/
8. McCrae, J., Aguado-de Cea, G., Buitelaar, P., Cimiano, P., Declerck, T., Gómez-Pérez, A., Gracia, J., Hollink, L., Montiel-Ponsoda, E., Spohr, D.: Interchanging lexical resources on the semantic web. Lang. Resour. Eval. **46**(4), 701–719 (2012)
9. Montiel-Ponsoda, E., Aguado-de Cea, G., Gómez-Pérez, A., Peters, W.: Enriching ontologies with multilingual information. Nat. Lang. Eng. **17**(3), 283–309 (2010)
10. Neubert, J.: Bringing the "Thesaurus for Economics" on to the web of linked data. In: Bizer, C., Heath, T., Berners-Lee, T., Idehen, K. (eds.) LDOW. CEUR Workshop Proceedings, vol. 538. CEUR-WS.org (2009)
11. Rüther, M., Fock, J., Bandholtz, T., Schulte-Coerne, T.: Linked environment data. In: Gerlinde Knetsch, K.J. (ed.) Umweltbundesamt, pp. 89–92. Umweltbundesamt (2010). ISSN:1862–4804
12. Sini, M., Soergel, D., Johannsen, G.: Proposal for restructuring Scientific Names and Common Names of Organisms in AGROVOC (2009)
13. Soergel, D., Lauser, B., Liang, A., Fisseha, F., Keizer, J., Katz, S.: Reengineering thesauri for new applications: the AGROVOC example. J. Digit. Inf. **4**(4), 1–23 (2006)

NoISE: Workshop on Negative or Inconclusive rEsults in Semantic Web

What SPARQL Query Logs Tell and Do Not Tell About Semantic Relatedness in LOD
Or: The Unsuccessful Attempt to Improve the Browsing Experience of DBpedia by Exploiting Query Logs

Jochen Huelss and Heiko Paulheim[(✉)]

Research Group Data and Web Science,
University of Mannheim, Mannheim, Germany
`jochen@huelss.de, heiko@dwslab.de`

Abstract. Linked Open Data browsers nowadays usually list facts about entities, but they typically do not respect the relatedness of those facts. At the same time, query logs from LOD datasets hold information about which facts are typically queried in conjunction, and should thus provide a notion of intra-fact relatedness. In this paper, we examine the hypothesis how query logs can be used to improve the display of information from DBpedia, by grouping presumably related facts together. The basic assumption is that properties which frequently co-occur in SPARQL queries are highly semantically related, so that co-occurence in query logs can be used for visual grouping of statements in a Linked Data browser. A user study, however, shows that the grouped display is not significantly better than simple baselines, such as the alphabetical ordering used by the standard DBpedia Linked Data interface. A deeper analysis shows that the basic assumption can be proven wrong, i.e., co-occurrence in query logs is actually *not* a good proxy for semantic relatedness of statements.

Keywords: Semantic relatedness · Linked Open Data · Linked data browsers · Query log mining · DBpedia

1 Motivation

Usefulness is considered as one of the key challenges to human users who attempt to benefit from the immense knowledge graph of semantic web [13]. This challenge implies that the user experience and visual presentation of linked data is currently not tangible for human users. Back in 2006, this lack of a tool which enables a curated, grouped, and sorted browsing experience of semantic data describing real-world entities was also mentioned by Sir Tim Bernes Lee in a talk on the *Future of the Web* at University of Oxford[1]. With the web of Linked Data having grown to more than 1,000 datasets [15], and the emergence of central

---

[1] http://webcast.oii.ox.ac.uk/?view=Webcast&ID=20060314.

© Springer International Publishing Switzerland 2015
F. Gandon et al. (Eds.): ESWC 2015, LNCS 9341, pp. 297–308, 2015.
DOI: 10.1007/978-3-319-25639-9_44

hubs in the semantic web such as DBpedia, the semantic web research community has put a lot of effort into the fields of browsing and interacting with linked data [4,8] and summarizing important properties of a semantic entity. However, these problems persist since all major semantic web databases and browsers still present their linked data as an unordered or lexicographically ordered list to their users.

Traditionally, web usage logs are mined for behavioral patterns to cluster items of common interest and recommend them to users. Our approach applies web usage mining on SPARQL query logs and looks for patterns that relate equally interesting properties of semantic entities. Thus, our general hypothesis is that, in a data set of SPARQL queries, it should be possible to mine information about the semantic relatedness of statements. Such information again can be exploited to form coherent groups of properties which are beneficial for the human browsing experience of the semantic web.

2   Related Work

Although much work has been devoted to the creation of browsers for Linked Open Data, most of them essentially present facts about entities as lists, in which the facts have no relation among each other [4]. Examples for such classic browsers are *DISCO*[2] and *Tabulator* [2]. A semantic grouping of facts, as proposed in this paper, has been rarely proposed so far.

Some browsers, such as *Zitgist*[3], provide domain-specific templates that order information which uses popular ontologies, such as FOAF[4] or the Music Ontology[5]. While there is a trend towards reusing popular vocabularies for LOD, there is, at the same time, a trend towards using *multiple* vocabularies in parallel [15], which, in turn, creates new challenges for such template-based approaches.

A slightly different, yet related problem is the ranking and filtering of semantic web statements into more and less relevant ones. Here, some works have been proposed in the past, e.g., [3,5,6,9,17].

In [16], we have presented a first domain-independent attempt of creating a semantic grouping of facts. Here, we try mapping predicates to WordNet synsets, and measure the similarity among predicates in WordNet. Similar predicates are grouped together, with the labels for synsets of common ancestors being used as group headings. Like the work presented in this paper, no statistical significant improvements over baseline orderings of facts could be reported.

3   Approach

In this paper, we present an approach for semantically grouping semantic web statements, based on SPARQL query logs. Those logs are read once and pre-processed into a database schema including basic statistics, as shown in Fig. 1.

---

[2] http://wifo5-03.informatik.uni-mannheim.de/bizer/ng4j/disco/.
[3] Meanwhile offline.
[4] http://www.foaf-project.org/.
[5] http://musicontology.com/.

Given that a user requests a URI, such as http://dbpedia.org/resource/ Mannheim, the system first reads the corresponding set of triples, then uses the preprocessed database to create a grouping, with different possible algorithms (see below). The result of grouped statements is delivered to the user through the modular semantic web browser *MoB4LOD*[6].

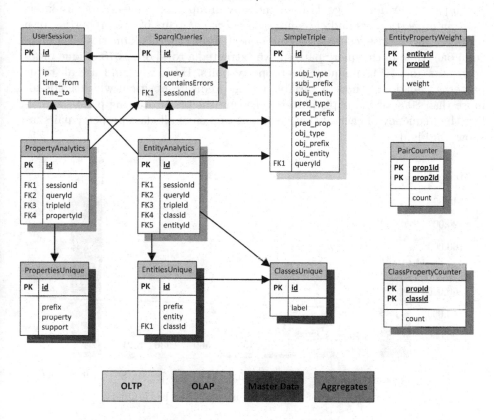

Fig. 1. DB schema for storing and analyzing SPARQL queries

3.1 Dataset and Preprocessing

The basis of our experiments is the UseWOD 2014 SPARQL dataset [1], which collects 300k SPARQL queries for the public DBpedia endpoint[7] over the period 06/12/2013 – 01/27/2014, out of which 249 k are *valid* SPARQL queries, the vast majority (more than 98 %) being SELECT queries.[8] The dataset is fully anonymized.

---

[6] http://www.ke.tu-darmstadt.de/resources/mob4lod.

[7] http://dbpedia.org/sparql.

[8] Note that the approach is not limited to DBpedia, but could be applied to any dataset for which such a logfile exists.

From those SPARQL queries, we extract *triple patterns* for further analysis. Figure 2 depicts the distribution of the number of triple patterns over the dataset, showing that most of the datasets have only one triple pattern, while there is an anomaly at nine triple patterns, caused by a bot posing almost the same query repeatedly.

In particular, for our goal of semantically grouping statements, we are interested in *property pairs* and *class-property pairs*, i.e., pairs of two properties, or a property and a class, co-occurring in a query. From the 171 k queries with more than one triple in the query pattern, we extracted a total of 12,078 unique property pairs and 1,141 unique class-property pairs. Here, we could use all triple patterns that do not have a variable in the predicate position, which holds for more than 80 % of the triple patterns. During the pre-processing phase, we collect the frequency of each of those pairs, as well as of all class-property pairs, as shown in Fig. 1.

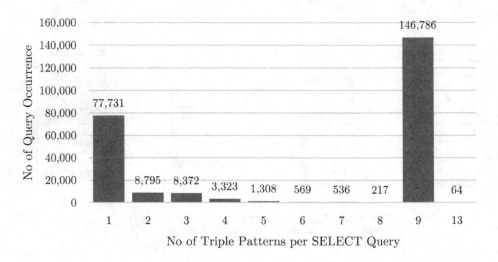

Fig. 2. Distribution of number of triple patterns per query

3.2 Approaches for Grouping Statements

For displaying results, we use two baseline approaches, as well as three approaches based on clustering statements together that have predicates often requested together.

Baseline 1: Lexicographic. The first baseline follows the approach of traditional semantic web browsers, ordering facts about an entity lexicographically by their predicate. Groups are created by starting letters of the properties (A-F, G-K etc.).

Baseline 2: Counting. The second baseline simply orders properties by their frequency in the SPARQL log for the class the retrieved resource belongs to. No grouping is made.

Approaches Based on Clustering. To create groupings of statements for properties that co-occur frequently, we use three different clustering algorithms: DBSCAN [7], hierarchical clustering [18], and Partitioning Around Medoids (PAM), an implementation of k-medoids [10]. For the latter, we chose to use $k = 7$, so that seven groups of statements are produced, following the widespread paradigm that humans can perceive roughly seven items at once [12].

For all clustering algorithms, we use the implementation in *WEKA* [19] with the following distance function between two properties:

$$distance(p_1, p_2) = \frac{1}{count_{p_1, p_2} + \omega} \tag{1}$$

With this formula, the distance between two properties is the larger the more often they are queried together. ω is used as a smoothing factor which prevents a division by zero for pairs of properties that never occur together, and that influences the steepness of the curve between 0 and 1 co-occurences.

In our experiments, we have used $\omega = 5$. Furthermore, the following settings were used: (1) the top-7 properties showing the highest support count in the UseWOD queries were excluded from clustering since they are merely general purpose properties, such as `rdf:type` and `owl:sameAs`, and (2) properties not occurring at all in UseWOD data set were also excluded. The clusters shaped were ranked descendingly based on the median value for support of the properties assigned to a cluster. The employment of a median was anticipated to be better than an average function because it is not prone to very high or low outliers within the clusters.

4   Evaluation

We have evaluated the three different grouping options of our approach against the two baselines in an end-user study. In that study, users were presented an entity from DBpedia with the statements grouped according to one of the five approaches, and had to answer a question about the entity.

4.1   Setup

The study was conducted as an online experiment using the *MoB4LOD* semantic web browser introduced above. A sample screenshot for the property grouping for the DBpedia entity *Cambridge* is shown in Fig. 3. The hypotheses of this study are derived from studies conducted by [5, 14, 16]:

H1 A participant finds a required fact significantly faster with a grouping based on our approach than with a baseline.

H2 The participant's subjective assessment of a grouping based on our approach
is significantly better than the sorting of baseline.

H3 A participant is significantly more accurate in finding a required fact with a
grouping based on our approach than with a baseline.

All of these hypotheses share the underlying assumption that the more coherent, i.e. semantically-related groups of statements are, the easier it becomes for
humans to consume semantic web data and satisfy their information needs.

For investigating these hypotheses, the online experiment employed a 5×5
within-subject design with five questions and five groupings (i.e. five tasks) for
each participant. For each data sample, we measured the completion time of
a task (in seconds), the subjective assessment of a task (5-point Likert-type
scale), and the accuracy of an answer of a task (true / false). These data items
are the dependent variables for the study's independent variables which are the
five sortings. The two baselines and the three groupings of our approach were
exposed to a participant in a randomized manner that ensured that each tasks
was answered equally often using one of the five sortings. Table 1 depicts the
average number of groups and group sizes for each approach.

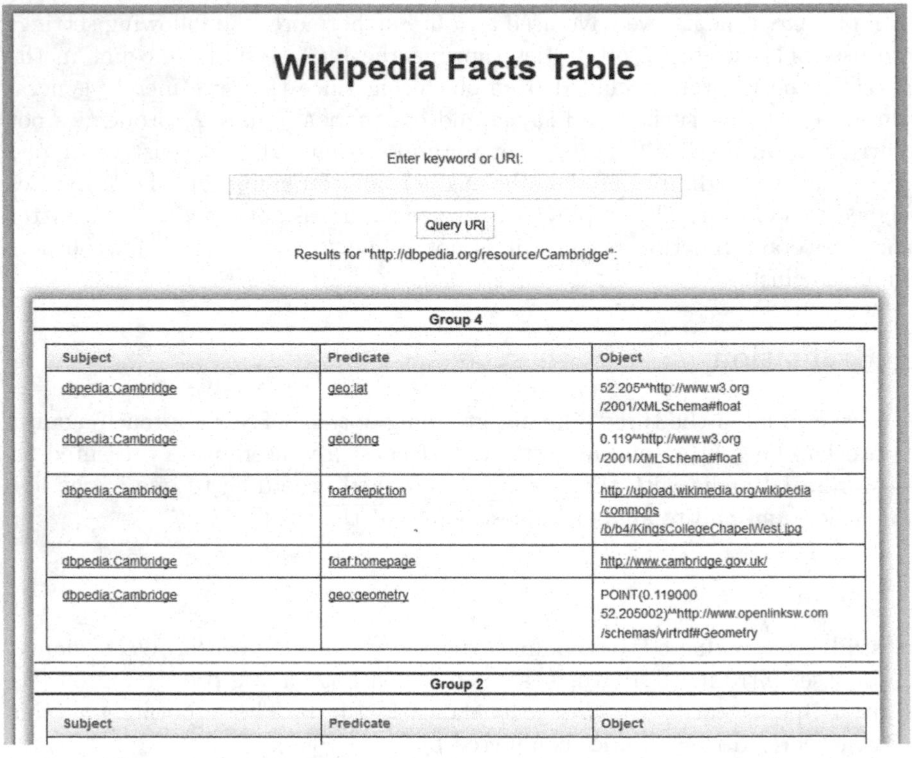

Fig. 3. Screenshot of MoB4LOD browser with groups of RDF triples for DBpedia
entity *Cambridge*

Table 1. Average number and size of groups produced by the different approaches

Characteristic	Lexicographic	DBSCAN	Hierarchical Clustering	PAM
Avg. # Groups	3.0	4.33	6.00	7.00
Avg. Elem. / Group	8.2	5.68	9.20	7.88

4.2   Tasks and Users

Each task of the online experiment consisted of a question and a grouped list of semantically related properties of a specified DBpedia entity. The five different sortings were the actual stimulus material for evaluating our approach. For the questions, entities from five DBpedia classes were employed (*Settlement, Film, Office Holder, Country, Musical Artist*). The chosen questions were intended to not be answerable based on the participants' general knowledge. A sample question of a task is: *What is the elevation of the city of Mannheim?* After each question, the participants were asked for their subjective assessment of a listing.[9]

80 participants from Germany completed the experiment. They were recruited by convenience sampling via social network sites, e-mailing, and other online channels. To remove obvious outliers, we removed all experiment data from participants who did not answer all questions, as well as those with a completion time outside of a 3σ confidence interval, i.e., extremely low or high processing times. After data cleansing, the sample consisted of *65* participants, which means that each question was solved 13 times with each sorting, on average. Exactly 40 % of the participants reported to be familiar with the concepts of semantic web.

4.3   Results

For all hypotheses, the independent variable was the set of the five sortings and the hypotheses are individually analyzed on task level. An overall determination of the best sorting is impossible because the equality of all tasks' level of difficulty cannot be assumed. Table 2 exposes the descriptive statistics (i.e. means of the dependent variables) of our experiment to the readers.

For the recorded completion times T1-5, the analysis of the means does not lead to a conclusive picture. For three out of five tasks, the best mean completion is even taken by one of the baselines. A one-way ANOVA investigates pair-wise significant differences between the three groupings and the two baselines in case of H1 and H2. For H1, only Task 1 depicted significant pair-wise differences. A Bonferroni posthoc test indicated that the hierarchical clustering grouping had a significant difference with the simple count baseline ($p < .05$). Therefore, H1 cannot be confirmed consistently across the tasks.

---

[9] The questionnaire is available at http://dws.informatik.uni-mannheim.de/en/research/noise-2015-accompanying-material.

Regarding the subjective assessment of the groupings, Table 2 shows the average assessment for each grouping. The best assessment is given to the PAM grouping which is contradictive to the completion time findings. The executed one-way ANOVA does not reveal any significant pair-wise differences between any of the cluster groupings and either one of the baselines. Therefore, also H2 cannot be confirmed for all tasks.

The results of the experiment also show that the percentage of correctly answered tasks exceeds 92 % for all sortings (see Table 2). H3 cannot be validated with an ANOVA since it is measured as a nominal variable. It can be accepted or refused by using frequency scales partitioned by the different sortings. However, these frequency scales revealed only non-significant differences between the groupings and the baselines. Thus, H3 cannot be confirmed either.

Table 2. Descriptive statistics for H1-3, mean time in seconds (shorter is better), mean assesment as intervall [1,5] (higher is better) and mean accuracy as percentage of correctly given answers (in %)

Dep. Variable	Lexic. Baseline	Count. Baseline	DBSCAN	Hier. Clustering	PAM
Time T1	30.9	42.4	24.6	**21.8**	39.2
Time T2	28.3	**26.2**	38.5	44.2	38.5
Time T3	24.7	26.5	35.9	**23.7**	23.9
Time T4	**33.0**	38.9	38.4	58.1	39.4
Time T5	40.2	**22.7**	30.5	33.2	38.6
Assessment	3.66	3.57	3.66	3.57	**3.69**
Accuracy	94.0	**98.0**	94.7	92.7	96.7

To support the assumption of the previous section that an overall evaluation of the hypotheses is impossible, Table 3 shows the mean working time and mean assessment of all tasks. Time has got a range of 15.52 s. This indicates that the different levels of difficulty led to varying answering times. Moreover, the table shows that the mean time and the mean assessment of the individual questions correlate negatively using Pearson's correlation ($\rho = -0.88$). The longer the time, the more negative the assessment. This finding is significant for Tasks 3-5. Table 3 also shows that, for the chosen ontology classes, the number of property pairs found in our database is small compared to the total amount of triples retrieved for the DBpedia entities.

5   Discussion

The experiments presented in the previous section have shown that the hypotheses formulated for this research work could not be confirmed, at least not for DBpedia. In particular, the assumption that the visual grouping of properties co-occurring in SPARQL logs leads to an improved human consumption of semantic

Table 3. Effect of time and assessment of all sortings on task level (mean), a correlation of longer time and more negative assessment is revealed, $n = 65$, $**p < .01$

	T1	T2	T3	T4	T5
Ontology Class	Settlement	Film	OfficeHolder	Country	MusicalArtist
Pairs found	98	29	123	92	133
Total Triples	2,242	225	257	4,248	337
Time	31.76(16.94)	35.09(17.59)	26.42(12.79)	41.94(21.77)	32.47(18.24)
Assessment	3.65(1.268)	3.52(1.200)	3.98(1.192)	3.46(1.187)	3.57(1.274)
Correlation	-0.162	-0.170	-0.321**	-0.369**	-0.276**

web data is proven wrong. Since three different clustering algorithms were tried in the experiments, the cause is most likely not a shortcoming of the clustering method, but the approach itself.

The main weak point about the assumption is that SPARQL queries and LOD interfaces serve the same information needs. First of all, a large fraction of SPARQL queries are posed by machine agents, while Linked Data interfaces are used by humans. Second, seasoned semantic web experts will be able to use SPARQL as well as Linked Data interfaces, and choose among them given the specific characteristics of their problem. These differences make the overall assumption problematic.

In the following, we will analyze this result in more detail. We exemplify potential problems both with the approach as well as the evaluation methodology.

5.1 Problems of the Approach

An a posteriori analysis revealed that one central problem of the approach presented in this paper is the coverage of the log file used for the experiments. According to DBpedia mapping statistics[10], there are currently 6,126 different DBpedia ontology properties. In the UseWOD data set we found 488 pairs consisting of DBpedia's ontology properties. Thus, the recall of class-property pairs is 7.96 % (given all of those pairs that appear for at least one entity in DBpedia). For the property pairs generated from UseWOD, the recall is even lower at 1.9 % (again given all such pairs that appear for at least one entity in DBpedia). This, in turn, means that the distance function for the majority of pairs is mostly uniform (i.e., $\frac{1}{\omega}$), with meaningful distances only assigned to a minority of pairs.

Another problem we observed was that redundant properties (such as `dbo:birthPlace`, `dbp:birthPlace`, and `dbp:placeOfBirth`) were rarely grouped into the same cluster by any of the clustering based approaches. At second glance, this is actually a built-in problem of the approach: when a user poses a query against DBpedia, he or she will likely pick one of the properties, and not use them in conjunction – for example, there are 2,687 using at least one of the

---

[10] http://mappings.dbpedia.org/server/statistics/en/?show=100000.

three aforementioned properties, but only 41 (i.e., 1.53%) use at least two of those. This shows that redundant properties – which have the highest semantic relatedness! – are unlikely to frequently co-occur in queries, and hence, are likely not to end up in the same cluster.

In informal feedback, many users complained that the groupings of statements we created had only generic titles, which are essentially the cluster names (*group 1*, *group 2*, etc.). Furthermore, DBSCAN identifies "noise points" which do not belong to any cluster, that were displayed under the headline *noise*, which lead to additional confusion. This shows that the assignment of meaningful headlines to groups of statements is a desirable – if not required – property of an approach like the one presented in this paper. This claim can be formulated even more strongly, stating that grouping without assigning headlines is pointless, since a user will have to scan each group for the desired piece of information, and will thus not perceive any usability advantage. Assigning headlines to groups, however, is a hard research problem in itself and was out of scope of the research work.

5.2   Problems of the Methodology

Using lexicographic sorting as a baseline is a straightforward idea. Especially since many tools use that ordering, it is also necessary to show that a significant advancement can be made over that ordering in order to prove the utility of the approach.

However, in our case, the baseline is rather strong due to some particular characteristics of DBpedia. DBpedia has two major namespaces – i.e., http:// dbpedia.org/ontology/ holds all the higher quality properties mapped against the DBpedia ontology, while http://dbpedia.org/property/ contains the lower-quality, raw extraction from the Wikipedia infoboxes [11]. The information conveyed by the former usually contains all the major information about an entity. In lexicographic ordering by property URI, the properties from the DBpedia ontology namespace are all listed before those from the raw extraction namespace, which leads to the major facts presented way up in the list.

Moreover, the properties that were required to answer the questions might have a different perceived importance (comparing, e.g., the elevation of a city to the governor of a state). Thus, users may implicitly search for properties they deem more important further up on the list. Since this importance is also partly reflected by the overall number of occurrences in DBpedia, this strategy may be successful on the counting baseline, which may explain why this is also a very strong baseline.

When analyzing the results in more detail, we found that there is a significant negative correlation between task completion time and assessment of the presentation. At the same time, the presented entities had significantly different sizes of the statement sets, which may furthermore influence both the completion time and the assessment. A more balanced selection of entities w.r.t. the number of statement displayed may have lead to more conclusive results.

6   Conclusion

In this paper, we have analyzed how SPARQL query logs can be used for creating meaningful groupings of statements for semantic web browsers. The analysis of the results show that this is not possible for various reasons, including the coverage of the SPARQL log files and blind spots of the approach, such as redundant properties.

In particular, it has been shown that co-occurence of properties in SPARQL queries is not a suitable proxy to determine semantic relatedness of those properties. This is best illustrated with the case of redundant properties, which are maximally semantically related, but extremely unlikely to co-occur in a query.

Many of the problems leading to the insignificant results – e.g., the problem of redundant properties or the strength of certain baselines – are specific to one dataset, in our case: DBpedia. For other datasets with different characteristics, those problem may or may not hold. Thus, evaluations on other datasets than DBpedia before eventually discarding the approach.

Still, we think that finding ways to create semantically coherent, visually appealing ways to present semantic web statements is a desirable property of Linked Open Data browsers. We hope that the results presented in this paper inspire future researchers to explore different ways of achieving that goal.

References

1. Berendt, B., Hollink, L., Hollink, V., Luczak-Rösch, M., Möller, K., Vallet, D.: Usage analysis and the web of data. In: ACM SIGIR Forum. vol. 45, pp. 63–69. ACM (2011)
2. Berners-Lee, T., Chen, Y., Chilton, L., Connolly, D., Dhanaraj, R., Hollenbach, J., Lerer, A., Sheets, D.: Tabulator: exploring and analyzing linked data on the semantic web. In: Proceedings of the 3rd International Semantic Web User Interaction Workshop (SWUI2006) at the 5th ISWC Conference, Athens, USA (2006)
3. Cheng, G., Tran, T., Qu, Y.: RELIN: relatedness and informativeness-based centrality for entity summarization. In: Aroyo, L., Welty, C., Alani, H., Taylor, J., Bernstein, A., Kagal, L., Noy, N., Blomqvist, E. (eds.) ISWC 2011, Part I. LNCS, vol. 7031, pp. 114–129. Springer, Heidelberg (2011)
4. Dadzie, A.S., Rowe, M.: Approaches to visualising linked data: a survey. Semant. Web 2(2), 89–124 (2011)
5. Delbru, R., Toupikov, N., Catasta, M., Tummarello, G., Decker, S.: Hierarchical link analysis for ranking web data. In: Aroyo, L., Antoniou, G., Hyvönen, E., ten Teije, A., Stuckenschmidt, H., Cabral, L., Tudorache, T. (eds.) ESWC 2010, Part II. LNCS, vol. 6089, pp. 225–239. Springer, Heidelberg (2010)
6. Ding, L., Pan, R., Finin, T.W., Joshi, A., Peng, Y., Kolari, P.: Finding and ranking knowledge on the semantic web. In: Gil, Y., Motta, E., Benjamins, V.R., Musen, M.A. (eds.) ISWC 2005. LNCS, vol. 3729, pp. 156–170. Springer, Heidelberg (2005)
7. Ester, M., Kriegel, H.P., Sander, J., Xu, X.: A density-based algorithm for discovering clusters in large spatial databases with noise. In: Proceedings of the 2nd International Conference on Knowledge Discovery and Data Mining, pp. 226–231, Portland, USA (1996)

8. García, R., Paulheim, H., Di Maio, P.: Special issue on semantic web interfaces. Semant. Web **6**(8), 213–214 (2015)
9. Kirchberg, M., Ko, R., Lee, B.S.: From linked data to relevant data - time is the essence. In: Proceedings of the 1st International Workshop on Usage Analysis and the Web of Data (USEWOD2011) at the 20th WWW Conference, Hyderabad, India (2011)
10. Van der Laan, M., Pollard, K., Bryan, J.: A new partitioning around medoids algorithm. J. Stat. Comput. Simul. **73**(8), 575–584 (2003)
11. Lehmann, J., Isele, R., Jakob, M., Jentzsch, A., Kontokostas, D., Mendes, P.N., Hellmann, S., Morsey, M., van Kleef, P., Auer, S., et al.: Dbpedia-a large-scale, multilingual knowledge base extracted from wikipedia. Semant. Web **6**(2), 167–195 (2015)
12. Miller, G.A.: The magical number seven, plus or minus two: some limits on our capacity for processing information. Psychol. Rev. **63**(2), 81 (1956)
13. Möller, K., Hausenblas, M., Cyganiak, R., Handschuh, S.: Learning from linked open data usage: patterns & metrics. In: Proceedings of the 2nd Web Science Conference (WebSci10), Raleigh, USA (2010)
14. Paulheim, H.: Improving the usability of integrated applications by using interactive visualizations of linked data. In: Proceedings of the ACM International Conference on Web Intelligence, Mining and Semantics, Sogndal, Norway (2011)
15. Schmachtenberg, M., Bizer, C., Paulheim, H.: Adoption of the linked data best practices in different topical domains. In: Mika, P., Tudorache, T., Bernstein, A., Welty, C., Knoblock, C., Vrandečić, D., Groth, P., Noy, N., Janowicz, K., Goble, C. (eds.) ISWC 2014, Part I. LNCS, vol. 8796, pp. 245–260. Springer, Heidelberg (2014)
16. Seeliger, A., Paulheim, H.: A semantic browser for linked open data. In: Proceedings of the Semantic Web Challenge at the 11th ISWC Conference, Boston, USA (2012)
17. Thalhammer, A., Toma, I., Roa-Valverde, A., Fensel, D.: Leveraging usage data for linked data movie entity summarization. In: Proceedings of the 2nd International Workshop on Usage Analysis and the Web of Data (USEWOD2012) at the 21st WWW Conference, Lyon, France (2012)
18. Ward Jr., J.H.: Hierarchical grouping to optimize an objective function. J. Am. Stat. Assoc. **58**(301), 236–244 (1963)
19. Witten, I., Frank, E., Hall, M.: Data Mining: Practical Machine Learning Tools and Techniques, 3rd edn. Morgan Kaufmann, San Francisco (2011)

PhiloWeb 2015

The "Peer-to-Peer" Economy and Social Ontology: Legal Issues and Theoretical Perspectives

Federico Costantini[✉]

Dipartimento di Scienze Giuridiche,
Università Degli Studi di Udine, Udine, Italy
federico.costantini@uniud.it

Abstract. Several business models based on the use of web platforms have recently become more widespread. These are generally called "peer-to-peer" models, and are much disputed because of their impact on the traditional economy. In this paper, an analysis of the legal concerns – which are briefly presented by assessing a recent Italian court case – introduces the main problem, which is the manipulation of economic and social processes through the control of the information generated by these models. The definition of these issues within a philosophical framework – given by the contrast between a "realistic" perspective and a "naturalistic" vision of "social ontology" – allows directions for future research to be suggested.

Keywords: Peer-to-peer economy · Social ontology · Philosophy of law · Collaborative consumption · Legal issues

1 Introduction

This paper addresses the issues arising from the use of semantic web technologies as the intermediary in economic and financial transactions among users in what is called "sharing", or "collaborative consumption", or the "peer-to-peer" economy. This business model is emerging as a result of the exploitation of the Internet as a conceptual framework and as a tool for the marketing and distribution of products and services. I do not intend to investigate the economic reasons for its success here, nor to describe the technologies employed, but to focus, from a theoretical perspective, on the legal concerns that are emerging, in order to assess the compatibility between the "peer-to-peer" economy and the structure of economic and social relations, namely "social ontology".

In order to pursue this purpose, I will: (1) explain a court case – the first of its kind concluded in favour of the plaintiff in Italy[1] – concerning Uber, a well-known system

---

[1] There have been other cases involving Uber, but some of the appeals were declared inadmissible and therefore those proceedings did not reach a final judgment. As a result of two of the judgments, six vehicles have recently been confiscated in Milan from their owners, who were also Uber's partners. http://milano.repubblica.it/cronaca/2015/03/03/news/milano_dopo_i_sequestri_scattano_le_confische_linea_dura_della_prefettura_contro_uberpop-108598862/.

© Springer International Publishing Switzerland 2015
F. Gandon et al. (Eds.): ESWC 2015, LNCS 9341, pp. 311–322, 2015.
DOI: 10.1007/978-3-319-25639-9_45

of sharing and exchange in car transport, and outline the background legal issues; (2) identify from a theoretical perspective the legal concerns that emerge in the entire field of the "peer-to-peer" economy; (3) focus on the main underlying philosophical problems concerning the control of information in society; and (4) set out an evaluation and suggest some paths of research that can be undertaken in the future.

2 The First Italian "Uber Case": Explanation and Legal Assessment

On February 14, 2015, an honorary judge in Genoa (Italy) – in Italian a *Giudice di pace* – upheld the appeal brought by a "driver" affiliated with Uber against a punishment imposed for the infringement of the provisions governing public transport services. In order to understand the implications of the case, I will: (1) describe briefly what Uber is, the services that are offered, and how the services are provided; (2) identify what features of the service were argued before the judge, and on what grounds; and (3) suggest some preliminary observations in order to identify the underlying problem and proceed with the discussion.

2.1 What Uber Is and How It Works

Uber is a company headquartered in San Francisco, California (USA) that was founded in March 2009 by Travis Kalanick and Garrett Camp. In 2010 it started to spread its services through a web platform, using mobile applications in particular.[2] In 2012, it began to expand its business internationally and, in 2014, it extended the range of services provided. Over these years, Uber has grown very fast, obtaining huge amounts of funding from many investors.[3]

Through its web platform, Uber aims to support service transport provided by third parties, as an intermediary between demand and supply, arranging trip reservations and managing payments and reimbursements.[4] We could say that Uber makes an information platform available that is used to provide four kinds of service: (1) a traditional taxi service (UberTAXI); (2) chauffeur-driven luxury vehicles (UberBLACK, Uber-SUV and UberLUX);[5] (3) trips provided by private drivers in their everyday vehicles

---

[2] www.uber.com.

[3] http://en.wikipedia.org/wiki/Uber_%28company%29.

[4] https://www.uber.com/it/legal/ita/terms.

[5] In New York, from 2013 onwards, helicopter rides (UberCHOPPER) have been offered, too.

(UberX, UberXL and UberPOP);[6] and (4) the sharing of fares among Uber users on UberX trips (UberPOOL)[7].

In this paper, I focus on the third kind of service (UberX, UberPOP) in which owners of private cars pick up Uber users and drive them to their chosen destination, with the fare having been already paid by credit card to Uber.

2.2   The Judgment and the Legal Framework

The judgment of the Genoa court mentioned above is grounded in the Italian transport services regulations, and specifically in the law governing taxi and chauffeur services.[8] These rules state that enterprises wishing to engage in such activities have to fulfil precise requirements – covering the personal qualities of the driver and the technical specification of the vehicle – that allow them to obtain a licence. Those who do not respect these provisions are severely punished in accordance with the traffic regulations. To be precise, the absence of a licence results in an expensive fine, the suspension of the driver's driving licence and the confiscation of the vehicle.[9]

These legal proceedings began with an action brought by a private driver against a penalty imposed by the municipal police under these rules. The judge upheld the appeal and revoked the punishment, arguing that there was no unlawfulness in the conduct of the applicant, because his activities constituted not the unauthorized practice of a regulated profession, but a simple sharing of his vehicle with Uber users.

Since the full decision has not yet been published, scholars have not had the opportunity to discuss the grounds for it in depth. Therefore, it must be said that the case described here is not the only one, and nor will it be the last. Indeed, similar proceedings are reported to be taking place in other Italian cities where the service has

---

[6] Drivers decide not only whether or not to join the service, but also whether to accept each request made by a user. The fare is established by Uber, and may vary – or even increase greatly (surge) – depending on the time and location of the posted travel request.

[7] It seems appropriate to highlight some concerns related to the terms of service provided in Italy: (1) Uber asks the user, under a contract termination clause, to act in accordance with Italian law – literally "*di rispettare tutte le leggi vigenti in materia nel proprio Paese o nella Nazione, Stato e/o città in cui si trova al momento dell'utilizzo dell'Applicazione o del Servizio*" – but this provision is not so explicit for the supplier of transport services; (2) each party is entitled to terminate the contract – literally "*diritto di rescindere*" – but the legal concept cannot be the one to which the terms of the contract refer – the "*rescissione*" of the contract (Art. 1447 and Art. 1448 Italian Civil Code) – but must be that of a termination clause – "*clausola risolutiva espressa*" – (Art. 1456 Italian Civil Code) or a unilateral withdrawal – in Italian "*recesso unilaterale*" – (Art. 1373 Italian Civil Code); (3) pursuant to Art. 1341 paragraph 2 Italian Civil Code, the right to unilateral withdrawal would require a specific written consent, which obviously cannot be expressed via the web; and (4) the contract gives the court in Amsterdam jurisdiction over any dispute arising between the parties, since the European subsidiary has its headquarters in Amsterdam, but this provision, which would also require written consent, is not permitted by consumer law in the European Union.

[8] Law 15th January 1992, n. 21, "*Legge quadro per il trasporto di persone mediante autoservizi pubblici non di linea*", in Official Journal n. 18 of 23rd January 1992.

[9] Art. 86, Legislative Decree 30th April 1992, n. 285 "*Nuovo codice della strada*", in Official Journal n. 114 of 18th May 1992, Ordinary Supplement n. 74.

been introduced,[10] and it is known that disputes and controversies have accompanied Uber from the beginning of its expansion in the European Union[11] and all over the world.[12]

2.3 Preliminary Findings

The key concept is that the business of a public transport service in the Member States of the European Union – but, in fact, the same question arises everywhere – is based upon a licence, in order to protect the public interest. Indeed, on the one hand, a good driver must be under the influence of neither drugs nor alcohol, must not be suffering from physical or mental distress, and must not be socially dangerous; on the other hand, a suitable vehicle must be reliable, safe and clean.

The main issue is not just the freedom of doing business without licences or permits, but is how to assess whether and under what terms the safety of workers and the security of passengers, cyclists and pedestrians should be left in the hands of "amateur" drivers, and – in the end – whether these values can be traded by private people through a website.

3   Legal Concerns in the "Peer-to-Peer" Economy

Uber is not the only web platform of this kind, as other businesses have adopted the same model in different fields.[13] For example, AirBnB[14] finds accommodation in private houses, without the need to make a reservation in a hotel, hostel, or bed and breakfast accommodation. TaskRabbit[15] allows people to delegate household activities that are commonly considered annoying, such as home maintenance, and also other tasks that may have a certain economic worth (for example, carpentry work or plumbing or electrical repairs). Amazon Mechanical Turk[16] is a marketplace for a mass workforce, where Human Intelligence Tasks (HIT) placed by certain users – such as

---

[10] On 10th October 2014, the administrative regional court of Lombardy – in Italian the *Tribunale Amministrativo Regionale*, suspended – as a precautionary measure – the effects of an order of the Municipality of Milan, or, more precisely, the *"Determinazione dirigenziale"* n. 209 of 29th July 2013 that prescribed strict boundaries for the activity of chauffeurs, to restrict the use of smartphone applications, one of which is evidently Uber.

[11] Uber has filed two complaints against a French law, the first in December 2014 and the second in February 2015. On 22nd January 2015 the CEO of Uber, Travis Kalanick, was received by the European Commissioner Violeta Bulc. On 1st April 2015 Uber filed other complaints, against a German and a Spanish law, with the European Commission.

[12] Given the aggressive commercial policy of Uber, various legal systems have reacted to limit its business. For a quick appraisal, see: http://en.wikipedia.org/wiki/Legal_status_of_Uber%27s_ service.

[13] www.blablacar.it, in Italy, promotes car sharing among users.

[14] www.airbnb.com.

[15] www.taskrabbit.com.

[16] www.mturk.com.

labelling images, writing the description of products, or finding the email addresses of given people – are performed online by other users for a certain price. In Italy, Supermercato24[17] acts as an intermediary between users who shop from the website and others who deliver the goods they have purchased to their home.

From a technical standpoint, these platforms have the same basic idea: they create a marketplace in which supply and demand can meet easily, transactions can take place safely, costs are cut to the bone and profits are made from infinitesimal commissions on a large number of transactions. In this section, I focus on common legal issues in order to reach a deeper understanding. To this intent, I will: (1) provide a brief overview of the economic model defined as "peer-to-peer"; (2) outline the main legal issues that affect the parties involved in these exchanges; and (3) make an overall assessment and identify some key points in order to proceed with the discussion.

3.1 Overview of the "Peer-to-Peer" Economy

Around the year 2000, scholars began to discuss a "lattice" vision of an economy. The common purpose was to encourage the sharing of economic resources, as a historical necessity (at that time a greater awareness of the limits of the planet's natural resources was emerging), or as a business opportunity (the increasing use of the Internet made people realize that the sharing of information increases the value of the goods or services to which it refers), or as a kind of moral duty (on the basis that sharing knowledge allowed an open – and thus better – society to be built) [1–3].

In this context, it was believed that the traditional concept of the market could be taken over by a new paradigm in which the demand and the supply of goods and services could balance each other – pervasively, continuously and directly – among customers through information technology. The idea of "collaborative consumption", introduced in the 1970s [4], was redrafted as a collective strategy for a sustainable economy centred on the use of the Internet [5, 6]. For some scholars it represented the hope of an alternative economy, and was addressed precisely as "anti-consumption" [7].

The core concept of this model, we can say, is that information technology is crucial, since it allows the economic processes to be controlled in order to increase efficiency by reducing waste and lowering costs. The key factor is the participation of all users, because the sharing of resources is the result of their spontaneous organization, which is ultimately the effect of the interaction between them and the system collecting their data [8].

It is important to focus on a shift in this model that occurs once the information system reaches a higher level of complexity, and specifically when the goal for which the community is gathering and the users are aggregating data, namely the purpose for which the resources are organized, is no longer the sharing of information, but the control of information. This leads to the emergence of a relationship of dependence on the technological platform by each individual user, who becomes, as a result of being

---

[17] www.supermercato24.it.

the beneficiary of the information shared by others, a simple tool for collecting and processing data.

If technology platforms are developed for profit, this change is remarkable. In fact, precisely because the shared information acquires value, there are several ways in which the provider of the technology platform can use this to his advantage: for example, by charging – even a small amount – for any request for access to data, or by creating additional services and selling them for a fee. Here the information asymmetry is increased – and no longer bridged – by the sharing of information, generating more inequality among users [9]. It is noteworthy that, since the platform owner takes advantage of every little transaction, the sharing economy has also very tellingly been defined as the "skimming economy" [10].

This revolution finds empirical confirmation when the sharing of information relates to economic resources that belong to the real world. Users end up performing duties just because the system cannot do them autonomously, because the tasks they require are too complicated: driving a car, accommodating a guest in a room, delivering a package to someone's home, fixing a sink, or babysitting are all quite simple for a human being to perform, but are still impossible for a computer.

To put it simply, in this kind of "peer-to-peer" economy users expect to receive services at a cost lower than the market price, and those who carry out such activities are willing to perform them despite the low cost. The difference between the agreed remuneration and the normal cost forms part of the profit that the platform owner receives for doing nothing other than collecting the information that the users themselves provide. Since there is this mark-up, it is quite difficult to conclude that this is truly an economy based on "sharing" or "cooperation".

3.2   Evaluation of Legal Issues Arising from a For-profit Peer-to-Peer Platform

Below I will investigate the phenomenon previously outlined through a brief analysis of the general legal issues that may arise in a peer-to-peer for-profit platform on which information about services carried out by humans in the real world is shared. I will consider three types of relationship: (1) the relationship between the system and the user who performs the task requested through the platform; (2) the relationship between the user who requests goods or services and the user who performs or produces them on behalf of the platform; and (3) relationships with third parties who may become involved by accident. I will provide some examples relating to transport services, since I began this paper with a case from this field.

1. *"Working" as a peer.* Since the person who accepts the obligation to perform is a private individual, it is difficult to define, in legal terms, his relationship with the owner of the platform. The main issue is whether or not it is an employment relationship. If it is, there would have to be – at least in countries still relying on the principles of the welfare state – some rights given to the employee: working and rest hours, health care and accident insurance, and social security. If not, it would have to be recognized that the services had been supplied with complete independence –

meaning that this was a business venture – and so – among other aspects – there should be fair competition, and proper taxes should be paid. Therefore, can we argue that an "amateur" driver is "working"? The answer lies not so much in the – quite inadequate, at least in the Italian version – words of the terms for the services provided by the website, but in what actually happens in real life and in the way in which the activity is carried out: we realize that an "amateur" driver has none of the rights of an employee, but has all the risks of a business enterprise. It is obvious that if under the law he could be seen as either an underpaid employee or an unprejudiced entrepreneur, very sensitive issues emerge, involving, on the one hand, the user as a person (the undeniable fact that humans can become ill, grow old and die), and, on the other hand, the context in which the system is located, namely society, with its needs (even just the maintenance and cleaning of the roads), which are likewise unavoidable. In their "Terms and Conditions", these platforms usually declare that they just "intermediaries" for information, and this is true: in fact, they take into account neither the first nor the second of these concerns.

2. *Anonymous delegation among peers.* Within a "peer-to-peer" economy, it is difficult to define in legal terms the relationship between those who request services or goods on the platform and those who perform or provide the goods or services on behalf of the platform. I can outline two possibilities, depending on whether the order is considered to be addressed to the platform or to the person who is willing to execute it. In the first case, there has to be a legal bond between the platform and the individual who actually performs the assignment: here the issues explained in the first profile re-emerge. Under the second hypothesis, in contrast, it has to be said that the legal bond lies directly between the users, so tasks are assigned to someone whose identity is unknown to the delegator. This is not acceptable, for example, in certain types of contract in which personal trust is a key feature.

3. *Liability and third parties.* Third parties are not directly involved in peer-to-peer exchanges, but they are inevitably affected by them. The problem mainly exists when it comes to imputing liability with respect to a tort committed by a user who performs a service on behalf of the platform. Let us consider the case where, while carrying a passenger, an "amateur" driver causes a car crash, injuring a pedestrian. Who should be held liable as a matter of civil law? Theoretically, three possibilities can be identified: (1) assuming that the driver is an employee of the platform owner, the responsibility should be ascribed to the latter; (2) if the driver qualifies as an independent contractor, he – and nobody else – should bear the damage caused by him doing his business; and (3) if it is argued that the driver is working on behalf of the passenger, then at least a *pro rata* obligation to compensate should be ascribed to the latter, as the for having contributed to the damage. The first and the second possibilities again raise the issues mentioned in the previous two paragraphs, but the last – as difficult as it may be to sustain from a strictly legal standpoint – seems to be promising, since it is more consistent with a peer-to-peer pattern. The result, in this last case, is quite odd, because the passenger would find himself to be held liable for any wrongdoing committed by the driver, almost as if he had signed a personal guarantee at the same time as he arranged the transport.

3.3 Key Findings

The "peer-to-peer" economy has been described as a new theoretical paradigm, and it really is this, in some ways. We can argue that its newness can be seen not so much in the shape of the relationship between the economic agents, or even by the "sharing" of information on the resources traded – such aspects could indeed also be found in the traditional economy – but in the fact that the value of goods and services is transfigured in terms of information.

The result is a comprehensive vision of the economic processes that can be defined as a synthesis of the two extreme positions in contemporary thought – individualistic liberalism [11] and a socialist central-planned economy [12] – and is based on the belief that the spontaneous sharing of information might lead to a balance between demand and supply for goods or services. However, we have seen that this belief is a utopia, at least in for-profit platforms, as the system tends to take advantage of the information asymmetries of users, imposing on them worse economic conditions than those that could be negotiated in the traditional market.[18]

I have outlined the legal issues that arise from the influence of the control of information on the relationships between the system, the users and third parties. The peer-to-peer structure tends to dismantle the relationship between the enterprise and the market, and thus to blur the distinction between professionals and consumers that, not only in the European Union, is one of the pillars in the regulation of commerce. Consequently, it is difficult to understand whether the people involved are entitled to claim any rights, because it is not clear – recalling the example of the transport service – if the driver is an employee or a contractor, if the passenger is a client, or if the injured pedestrian is entitled to be compensated just by the driver, as an individual, or by the platform owner, or by the passenger.

4 Theoretical Perspectives on the Problem of Control in the "Peer-to-Peer" Economy

Two of the observations made above deserve to be deepened: (1) the transition from simple sharing to control of information causes a sort of dependence – at least from an economic point of view – of the user on the platform; and (2) the difficulty in describing in legal terms the new figure – the "user" – who results from a blending of the concepts of "professional" and "consumer".

To understand such issues better, we should acknowledge that the concept of control is not just a pragmatic solution, since it expresses an overall epistemological approach that has been proposed as a further advancement of modern scientific thought. This "bottom-up" perspective is intended to overlap with the former "top-down" vision in different areas, such as in network technologies, where peer-to-peer systems would prevail over the most common "server/client" architecture, or in political science, where the "governance" model would overcome the pairing of state and subject, or – as

---

[18] For reasons of space, I cannot discuss here when and how sharing becomes control, or what the causes of such a phenomenon are.

we have seen – in economics, where "collaborative consumption" would solve the conflict between wealth and labour, or in commercial regulation, where the "user" would resolve the opposition between professionals and consumers.

At this point, it seems crucial to deepen the meaning of control of information in order to provide a theoretical perspective on the issues raised above. Therefore, below I will: (1) identify the basis of the theoretical concept of control and briefly describe the features that can be found in a "peer-to-peer" economy; (2) reassess from this perspective the issues that have been previously identified, highlighting the problems that affect the structure of social relations.

4.1   The Meaning of Control in the "Peer-to-Peer" Economy

The idea of control used herein finds its philosophical framework in what is called "naturalism", which can be interpreted as an effort to explain what is actually experienced without admitting the existence of transcendent entities or claiming "a priori" concepts: in a nutshell, *juxta propria principia* [13].

This perspective is expressed in twentieth century thought by cybernetics [14], which aims to formulate a scientific representation suitable not only for describing but also for manipulating natural, physical and organic processes. Scholars pursued their initial pioneering investigations, addressing the study of the self-organization of dynamic systems [15], and achieved the definition of autopoiesis, namely the specific quality of systems that are able to appear, preserve, defend and reproduce themselves [16].

The subject of cybernetics is control, and precisely how control can feature in anything – things, living creatures, social relations, the bodies and souls of men – for any purpose. To enable or disable certain processes, to gauge their intensity, to steer their flow: this is, essentially, to have control over something. It has to be emphasized that the concept of control, in this perspective, has very specific properties: (1) it is absolute, since its power has no intrinsic limitations; (2) it is exclusive, as it is not divisible; (3) it is teleonomic, since it cannot have a further or extrinsic purpose; and (4) the exercise of its power is self-exculpatory, as it does not admit the concept of error, but only that of anomaly.

The tool of control is information. Through a process of abstraction, cybernetics translates whatever is existing in the flow of data from which connections are obtained ("syntactic information", or "information as reality"), meaning ("semantic information", or "information about reality") and organization ("pragmatic information", or "information for reality") [17, 18]. What matters is that the control, namely the manipulation of the elements of the experience, is exercised by interaction with this ontological dimension; some scholars envisage this to be properly a unified vision of mind and nature [19], which has many enthusiasts because of its spiritual consequences [20].

Therefore, I could argue that this sort of control also lies in the "peer-to-peer" economy. In fact, we can observe that, in this model, the demand and the supply of goods or services do not meet naturally or spontaneously, as would seem to be the case at first glance, but they meet because of the artificial process performed by the intermediary. The platform owner, to sum up, controls the flow of economic transactions through the information processes.

4.2   Issues of "Social Ontology" in the "Peer-to-Peer" Economy

The conceptual tools of cybernetics have also been used to provide a theoretical representation of social relations [21, 22], and with this perspective very recent studies have produced a conception of "social ontology" from a naturalistic point of view [23].[19]

Hereinafter I intend to define three issues relating to the "peer-to-peer" economy – precisely, relating to its profitable business model – that can be discussed using the legal concerns described above.[20] I will focus on: (1) the extreme flexibility of the connections among users; (2) the anonymity and depersonalization of their contact; and (3) the pervasiveness of the trade exchanges.

1. *Social connections: control or politics.* In the "peer-to-peer" model, human relations are considered to be unstable and flexible, since there are no constraints that cannot be untied if others offer more efficiency in the system. Hence, relationships are instrumental to the purpose as a whole and, in the end, are controlled – in the sense specified above – by those who own the platform. From concrete experience we should acknowledge that the links between human beings are likely to be consolidated and may establish social structures. Moreover, precisely because of the absence of control, institutions can be erected and the political sphere – in the traditional sense – can emerge.

2. *Users: anonymous agents or human beings.* In the "peer-to-peer" model, what matters, as we have seen, is that every transaction is carried out in the most efficient way, not that it is fulfilled by a specific person, or even by a human "agent" [24] [21]. Indeed, since all performances should be uniform and standardized, they should be deprived of their human component, as this generates uncertainty and instability [25]. Conversely, in the real economy, people invest their working energies to promote their name and to communicate their personal qualities – motivation, style – that differentiate them from their competitors. I can argue that, in the "peer-to-peer" economy, human trust would be replaced with brand loyalty.

3. *Performances: for profit or for free.* In the "peer-to-peer" economy, the value of the performance of each task is measured exclusively in economic terms and is controlled – directly or indirectly – by the owner of the platform. In real life, activities are done free of charge – for genuine solidarity or in simple courtesy – and it is

---

[19] Here "social ontology" could be defined – generically – as the structure of human relations holding a social community as a unity that is balanced inwards and outwards.

[20] I do not intend to claim that these three aspects are side-effects from an economic perspective, as this is outside my competence. Instead, I will emphasize that there could be great incompatibility from a theoretical standpoint. This is much more significant, in my opinion, as the practical difficulties can be resolved, while the others cannot be overcome.

[21] It is not just the identity of the person who performs the task – the fact that he is one person rather than another – but also the human aspect of the performance – the fact that there is actually a human being behind it – that becomes irrelevant, because what matters is just that, through the platform and directly or indirectly, there should be a change in the state of the facts – the "difference that makes the difference", called "information"– for which payment has been made.

important to emphasize that these are precisely the main unifying elements of a community.

5 The Issue of Social Ontology in the "Peer-to-Peer" Economy: Conclusions and Future Research

Let us consider the "Flash mob".[22] Although this could seem to be a spontaneous event to an external observer, it is actually the result of a plan. Indeed, it creates a strong contrast between the state of people and places before and after the event and their state during the time when the performance is carried out. Ordinary life looks to be chaotic, since the synchronization of movement within a "Flash mob" shows an order that, for a glimmer of time, has an aesthetical and ethical perfection. For just one moment, it is likely that each participant wonders if his entire life could be a never-ending "Flash mob", in which his existence merges with that of others in a collective consciousness. Thus, I may argue that a "Flash mob" is not so much an expression of joyous vitality, or natural spontaneity, or youthful exuberance, but an expression of the power of information, which can take control of human actions, artificially creating the conditions in which the social ties that naturally link individuals are wiped away.

In the "peer-to-peer" economy, we can find the same theoretical opposition between a "naturalistic" and a "realistic" vision of "social ontology". The first – which can be represented as a "lattice" pattern lying on a horizontal surface – flattens interpersonal relationships to information exchanges among intentional agents, while, in the second, different features such as political values, legal principles and even mere courtesy are taken into proper account, so it may be seen as a "molecular" multi-dimensional structure.

The study of legal issues has led to the identification of problems that are not only practical, but that have a theoretical relevance in contemporary social experience, particularly in the use of the Internet. In the future, it would seem to be useful to proceed in this direction, following three lines of research: (1) exploring the "social ontology", by deepening the contrast between the realistic – or "molecular" – and the naturalistic – or "lattice" – visions; (2) identifying the features – if any – that have to be considered intangible, from the perspective of the philosophy of law; and (3) verifying, under these premises, whether Internet business models – such as the "peer-to-peer" economy – are radically irreconcilable or whether and how they can be adapted to the human "social ontology".

---

[22] In recent years a social phenomenon called "Flash mob" has become widespread. This is basically an event organized by users on the Internet – normally, through social networks – who gather at a specific place and time to perform a given action, which can be a political protest, a musical show, an artistic performance, or anything else. These events cause a great sensation among those who witness them, because they begin and finish abruptly. They usually happen in crowded places – squares, stations – so that participants hide themselves among innocent passers-by until they unexpectedly reveal, through their actions, the real reason why they are there.

References

1. Benkler, Y.: Coase's penguin, or, Linux and "the nature of the firm". Yale Law J. **112**, 369–446 (2002)
2. Benkler, Y.: The Wealth of Networks: How Social Production Transforms Markets and Freedom. Yale University Press, New Haven (2006)
3. Lessig, L.: The Future of Ideas: The Fate of the Commons in a Connected World. Random House, New York (2001)
4. Felson, M., Spaeth, J.L.: Community structure and collaborative consumption: a routine activity approach. Am. Behav. Sci. **21**, 614–624 (1978)
5. Botsman, R., Rogers, R.: What's Mine Is Yours: How Collaborative Consumption Is Changing the Way We Live. Collins, London (2011)
6. Belk, R.: You are what you can access: sharing and collaborative consumption online. J. Bus. Res. **67**, 1595–1600 (2014)
7. Albinsson, P.A., Yasanthi Perera, B.: Alternative marketplaces in the 21st century: building community through sharing events. J. Consum. Behav. **11**, 303–315 (2012)
8. Law, E., von Ahn, L.: Human Computation. Morgan and Claypool Publishers, San Rafael (2011)
9. Clarkson, G., Jacobsen, T.E., Batcheller, A.L.: Information asymmetry and information sharing. Gov. Inf. Quart. **24**, 827–839 (2007)
10. Malhotra, A., Van Alstyne, M.: The dark side of the sharing economy … and how to lighten it. Commun. ACM **57**, 24–27 (2014)
11. von Hayek, F.A.: Law, Legislation and Liberty: A New Statement of the Liberal Principles of Justice and Political Economy. University of Chicago Press, Chicago (1973)
12. Medina, E.: Cybernetic Revolutionaries: Technology and Politics in Allende's Chile. MIT Press, Cambridge (2011)
13. Telesio, B.: De rerum natura iuxta propria principia. Casa del libro, Cosenza (1965–1971)
14. Wiener, N.: Cybernetics or Control and Communications in the Animal and the Machine. Hermann and Cie – The Technology Press, Paris – Cambridge (1948)
15. Ashby, W.R.: Principles of the self-organizing dynamic system. J. Gen. Psychol. **37**, 125–128 (1947)
16. Maturana, H.R., Stafford Beer, A., Varela, F.J.: Autopoiesis and cognition: The realization of the living. D. Reidel Pub. Co., Dordrecht (1972)
17. Boekee, D.E., van der Lubbe, J.C.A.: Informatietheorie. Delftse U.M, Delft (1988)
18. Floridi, L.: The Philosophy of Information. Oxford University Press, Oxford (2013)
19. Bateson, G.: Mind and Nature: A Necessary Unity. Dutton, New York (1979)
20. Haker, H., Borgmann, E., van Erp, S.: Introduction: Cyberspace – Cyberethics – Cybertheology. Concilium **40**, 7–11 (2005)
21. Parsons, T.: The Social System: Outlines of a Conceptual Scheme for the Analysis of Structure and Process in Social Systems. Tavistock Publ, London (1952)
22. Luhmann, N.: Soziale Systeme: Grundriss einer allgemeinen Theorie. Suhrkamp, Frankfurt am Main (1984)
23. Tuomela, R.: Social Ontology: Collective Intentionality and Group Agents. Oxford University Press, Oxford (2013)
24. Bateson, G.: Steps to an Ecology of Mind. Ballantine Books Inc, New York (1972)
25. Breton, P.: L'utopie de la communication: L'émergence de "l'homme sans intérieur". Éditions La Découverte, Paris (1992)

PROFILES'15: 2nd International Workshop on Dataset PROFIling and fEderated Search for Linked Data

Roomba: An Extensible Framework to Validate and Build Dataset Profiles

Ahmad Assaf[1,2]([⊠]), Raphaël Troncy[1],
and Aline Senart[2]

[1] EURECOM, Sophia Antipolis, France
{ahmad.assaf,raphael.troncy}@eurecom.fr
[2] SAP Labs France, Mougins, France
aline.senart@sap.com

Abstract. Linked Open Data (LOD) has emerged as one of the largest collections of interlinked datasets on the web. In order to benefit from this mine of data, one needs to access to descriptive information about each dataset (or metadata). This information can be used to delay data entropy, enhance dataset discovery, exploration and reuse as well as helping data portal administrators in detecting and eliminating spam. However, such metadata information is currently very limited to a few data portals where they are usually provided manually, thus being often incomplete and inconsistent in terms of quality. To address these issues, we propose a scalable automatic approach for extracting, validating, correcting and generating descriptive linked dataset profiles. This approach applies several techniques in order to check the validity of the metadata provided and to generate descriptive and statistical information for a particular dataset or for an entire data portal.

Keywords: Linked data · Dataset profile · Metadata · Data quality

1 Introduction

From 12 datasets cataloged in 2007, the Linked Open Data cloud has grown to nearly 1000 datasets containing more than 82 billion triples[1] [4]. Data is being published by both the public and private sectors and covers a diverse set of domains from life sciences to media or government data. The Linked Open Data cloud is potentially a gold mine for organizations and individuals who are trying to leverage external data sources in order to produce more informed business decisions [8].

Dataset discovery can be done through public data portals like Datahub.io and publicdata.eu or private ones like quandl.com and enigma.io. Private portals harness manually curated data from various sources and expose them to users either freely or through paid plans. Similarly, in some public data portals, administrators manually review datasets information, validate, correct and

---

[1] http://datahub.io/dataset?tags=lod.

© Springer International Publishing Switzerland 2015
F. Gandon et al. (Eds.): ESWC 2015, LNCS 9341, pp. 325–339, 2015.
DOI: 10.1007/978-3-319-25639-9_46

attach suitable metadata information. This information is mainly in the form of predefined tags such as *media, geography, life sciences* for organization and clustering purposes. However, the diversity of those datasets makes it harder to classify them in a fixed number of predefined tags that can be subjectively assigned without capturing the essence and breadth of the dataset [21]. Furthermore, the increasing number of datasets available makes the metadata review and curation process unsustainable even when outsourced to communities.

There are several Data Management Systems (DMS) that power public data portals. CKAN[2] is the world's leading open-source data portal platform powering web sites like DataHub, Europe's Public Data and the U.S Government's open data. Modeled on CKAN, DKAN[3] is a standalone Drupal distribution that is used in various public data portals as well. Socrata[4] helps public sector organizations improve data-driven decision making by providing a set of solutions including an open data portal. In addition to these tradition data portals, there is a set of tools that allow exposing data directly as RESTful APIs like thedatatank.com.

Metadata provisioning is one of the Linked Data publishing best practices mentioned in [3]. Datasets should contain the metadata needed to effectively understand and use them. This information includes the dataset's license, provenance, context, structure and accessibility. The ability to automatically check this metadata helps in:

- **Delaying data entropy:** *Information entropy* refers to the degradation or loss limiting the information content in raw or metadata. As a consequence of information entropy, data complexity and dynamicity, the life span of data can be very short. Even when the raw data is properly maintained, it is often rendered useless when the attached metadata is missing, incomplete or unavailable. Comprehensive high quality metadata can counteract these factors and increase dataset longevity [20].
- **Enhancing data discovery, exploration and reuse:** Users who are unfamiliar with a dataset require detailed metadata to interpret and analyze accurately unfamiliar datasets. A study conducted by the European Union commission [29] found that both business and users are facing difficulties in discovering, exploring and reusing public data due to missing or inconsistent metadata information.
- **Enhancing spam detection:** Portals hosting public open data like Datahub allow anyone to freely publish datasets. Even with security measures like captchas and anti-spam devices, detecting spam is increasingly difficult. In addition to that, the increasing number of datasets hinders the scalability of this process, affecting the correct and efficient spotting of datasets spam.

Data profiling is the process of creating descriptive information and collect statistics about that data. It is a cardinal activity when facing an unfamiliar

---

[2] http://ckan.org.
[3] http://nucivic.com/dkan/.
[4] http://www.socrata.com.

dataset [24]. Data profiles reflect the importance of datasets without the need for detailed inspection of the raw data. It also helps in assessing the importance of the dataset, improving users' ability to search and reuse part of the dataset and in detecting irregularities to improve its quality. Data profiling includes typically several tasks:

- **Metadata profiling:** Provides general information on the dataset (dataset description, release and update dates), legal information (license information, openness), practical information (access points, data dumps), etc.
- **Statistical profiling:** Provides statistical information about data types and patterns in the dataset (e.g. properties distribution, number of entities and RDF triples).
- **Topical profiling:** Provides descriptive knowledge on the dataset content and structure. This can be in form of tags and categories used to facilitate search and reuse.

In this work, we address the challenges of automatic validation and generation of descriptive dataset profile. This paper proposes Roomba, an extensible framework consisting of a processing pipeline that combines techniques for data portals identification, datasets crawling and a set of pluggable modules combining several profiling tasks. The framework validates the provided dataset metadata against an aggregated standard set of information. Metadata fields are automatically corrected when possible (e.g. adding a missing license URL reference). Moreover, a report describing all the issues highlighting those that cannot be automatically fixed is created to be sent by email to the dataset's maintainer. There exist various statistical and topical profiling tools for both relational and Linked Data. The architecture of the framework allows to easily add them as additional profiling tasks. However, in this paper, we focus on the task of dataset metadata profiling. We validate our framework against a manually created set of profiles and manually check its accuracy by examining the results of running it on various CKAN-based data portals.

The remainder of the paper is structured as follows. In Sect. 2, we review relevant related work. In Sect. 3, we describe our proposed framework's architecture and components that validate and generate dataset profiles. In Sect. 4, we evaluate the framework and we finally conclude and outline some future work in Sect. 5.

2   Related Work

Data Catalog Vocabulary (DCAT) [25] and the Vocabulary of Interlinked Datasets (VoID) [11] are concerned with metadata about RDF datasets. There exist several tools aiming at exposing dataset metadata using these vocabularies. In [6], the authors generate VoID descriptions limited to a subset of properties that can be automatically deduced from resources within the dataset. However, it still provides data consumers with interesting insights. Flemming's Data Quality Assessment Tool[5] provides basic metadata assessment as it computes data

---

[5] http://linkeddata.informatik.hu-berlin.de/LDSrcAss/datenquelle.php.

quality scores based on manual user input. The user assigns weights to the pre-defined quality metrics and answers a series of questions regarding the dataset. These include, for example, the use of obsolete classes and properties by defining the number of described entities that are assigned disjoint classes, the usage of stable URIs and whether the publisher provides a mailing list for the dataset. The ODI certificate[6], on the other hand, provides a description of the published data quality in plain English. It aspires to act as a mark of approval that helps publishers understand how to publish good open data and users how to use it. It gives publishers the ability to provide assurance and support on their data while encouraging further improvements through an ascending scale. ODI comes as an online and free questionnaire for data publishers focusing on certain characteristics about their data.

Metadata Profiling: The Project Open Data Dashboard[7] tracks and measures how US government web sites implement the Open Data principles to understand the progress and current status of their public data listings. A validator analyzes machine readable files: e.g. JSON files for automated metrics like the resolved URLs, HTTP status and content-type. However, deep schema information about the metadata is missing like description, license information or tags. Similarly on the LOD cloud, the Datahub LOD Validator[8] gives an overview of Linked Data sources cataloged on the Datahub. It offers a step-by-step validator guidance to check a dataset completeness level for inclusion in the LOD cloud. The results are divided into four different compliance levels from basic to reviewed and included in the LOD cloud. Although it is an excellent tool to monitor LOD compliance, it still lacks the ability to give detailed insights about the completeness of the metadata and overview on the state of the entire LOD cloud group and it is very specific to the LOD cloud group rules and regulations.

Statistical Profiling: Calculating statistical information on datasets is vital to applications dealing with query optimization and answering, data cleansing, schema induction and data mining [14,17,21]. Semantic sitemaps [10] and RDF-Stats [22] are one of the first to deal with RDF data statistics and summaries. ExpLOD [19] creates statistics on the interlinking between datasets based on `owl:sameAs` links. In [24], the author introduces a tool that induces the actual schema of the data and gather corresponding statistics accordingly. LODStats [2] is a stream-based approach that calculates more general dataset statistics. Pro-LOD++ [1] is a Web-based tool that allows LOD analysis via automatically computed hierarchical clustering [7]. Aether [26] generates VoID statistical descriptions of RDF datasets. It also provides a Web interface to view and compare VoID descriptions. LODOP [13] is a MapReduce framework to compute, optimize and benchmark dataset profiles. The main target for this framework is to optimize the runtime costs for Linked Data profiling. In [18] authors calculate

---

[6] https://certificates.theodi.org/.
[7] http://labs.data.gov/dashboard/.
[8] http://validator.lod-cloud.net/.

certain statistical information for the purpose of observing the dynamic changes in datasets.

Topical Profiling: Topical and categorical information facilitates dataset search and reuse. Topical profiling focuses on content-wise analysis at the instances and ontological levels. GERBIL [28] is a general entity annotation framework that provides machine processable output allowing efficient querying. In addition, there exist several entity annotation tools and frameworks [9] but none of those systems are designed specifically for dataset annotation. In [15], the authors created a semantic portal to manually annotate and publish metadata about both LOD and non-RDF datasets. In [21], the authors automatically assigned Freebase domains to extracted instance labels of some of the LOD Cloud datasets. The goal was to provide automatic domain identification, thus enabling improving datasets clustering and categorization. In [5], the authors extracted dataset topics by exploiting the graph structure and ontological information, thus removing the dependency on textual labels. In [12], the authors generate VoID and VoL descriptions via a processing pipeline that extracts dataset topic models ranked on graphical models of selected DBpedia categories.

Although the above mentioned tools are able to provide various types of information about a dataset, there exists no approach that aggregates this information and is extensible to combine additional profiling tasks. To the best of our knowledge, this is the first effort towards extensible automatic validation and generation of descriptive dataset profiles.

3 Profiling Data Portals

In this section, we provide an overview of Roomba's architecture and the processing steps for validating and generating dataset profiles. Figure 1 shows the main steps which are the following: (i) data portal identification; (ii) metadata extraction; (iii) instance and resource extraction; (iv) profile validation (v) profile and report generation.

Roomba is built as a Command Line Interface (CLI) application using Node.js. Instructions on installing and running the framework are available on its public Github repository[9]. The various steps are explained in detail below.

3.1 Data Portal Identification

Roomba should be extensible to any data portal that exposes its functionalities via an external accessible API. Since every portal ca have its own data model, identifying the software powering data portals is a vital first step. We rely on several Web scraping techniques in the identification process which includes a combination of the following:

– **URL inspection:** Various CKAN based portals are hosted on subdomains of the http://ckan.net. For example, CKAN Brazil (http://br.ckan.net). Checking the existence of certain URL patterns can detect such cases.

---

[9] https://github.com/ahmadassaf/opendata-checker

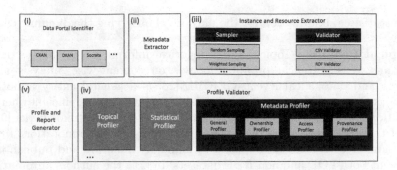

Fig. 1. Processing pipeline for validating and generating dataset profiles

- **Meta tags inspection:** The `<meta>` tag provides metadata about the HTML document. They are used to specify page description, keywords, author, etc. Inspecting the `content` attribute can indicate the type of the data portal. We use CSS selectors to check the existence of these meta tags. An example of a query selector is `meta[content*=''ckan'']` (all meta tags with the attribute content containing the string $CKAN$). This selector can identify CKAN portals whereas the `meta[content*=''Drupal'']` can identify DKAN portals.
- **Document Object Model (DOM) inspection:** Similar to the meta tags inspection, we check the existence of certain DOM elements or properties. For example, CKAN powered portals will have DOM elements with class names like `ckan-icon` or `ckan-footer-logo`. A CSS selector like `.ckan-icon` will be able to check if a DOM element with the class name `ckan-icon` exists. The list of elements and properties to inspect is stored in a separate configurable object for each portal. This allows the addition and removal of elements as deemed necessary.

The identification process for each portal can be easily customized by overriding the default function. Moreover, adding or removing steps from the identification process can be easily configured.

After those preliminary checks, we query one of the portal's API endpoints. For example, DataHub is identified as CKAN, so we will query the API endpoint on http://datahub.io/api/action/package_list. A successful request will list the names of the site's datasets, whereas a failing request will signal a possible failure of the identification process.

3.2   Metadata Extraction

Data portals expose a set of information about each dataset as metadata. The model used varies across portals. However, a standard model should contain information about the dataset's title, description, maintainer email, update and creation date, etc. We divided the metadata information into the following types:

General Information: General information about the dataset. e.g., title, description, ID, etc. This general information is manually filled by the dataset owner. In addition to that, tags and group information is required for classification and enhancing dataset discoverability. This information can be entered manually or inferred modules plugged into the topical profiler.

Access Information: Information about accessing and using the dataset. This includes the dataset URL, license information i.e., license title and URL and information about the dataset's resources. Each resource has as well a set of attached metadata e.g., resource name, URL, format, size.

Ownership Information: Information about the ownership of the dataset. e.g., organization details, maintainer details, author. The existence of this information is important to identify the authority on which the generated report and the newly corrected profile will be sent to.

Provenance Information: Temporal and historical information on the dataset and its resources. For example, creation and update dates, version information, version, etc. Most of this information can be automatically filled and tracked.

Building a standard metadata model is not the scope of this paper, and since we focus on CKAN-based portals, we validate the extracted metadata against the CKAN standard model[10].

After identifying the underlying portal software, we perform iterative queries to the API in order to fetch datasets metadata and persist them in a file-based cache system. Depending on the portal software, we can issue specific extraction jobs. For example, in CKAN-based portals, we are able to crawl and extract the metadata of a specific dataset, all the datasets in a specific group (e.g. LOD cloud) or all the datasets in the portal.

3.3   Instance and Resource Extraction

From the extracted metadata we are able to identify all the resources associated with that dataset. They can have various types like a SPARQL endpoint, API, file, visualization, etc. However, before extracting the resource instance(s) we perform the following steps:

– **Resource metadata validation and enrichment:** Check the resource attached metadata values. Similar to the dataset metadata, each resource should include information about its mimetype, name, description, format, valid de-referenceable URL, size, type and provenance. The validation process issues an HTTP request to the resource and automatically fills up various missing information when possible, like the mimetype and size by extracting them from the HTTP response header. However, missing fields like name and description that needs manual input are marked as missing and will appear in the generated summary report.

---

[10] http://demo.ckan.org/api/3/action/package_show?id=adur_district_spending.

- **Format validation:** Validate specific resource formats against a liter or a validator. For example, node-csv[11] for CSV files and n3[12] to validate N3 and Turtle RDF serializations.

Considering that certain datasets contain large amounts of resources and the limited computation power of some machines on which the framework might run on, a sampler module can be introduced to execute various sample-based strategies detailed as they were found to generate accurate results even with comparably small sample size of 10 %. These strategies introduced in [12] are:

- **Random Sampling:** Randomly selects resource instances.
- **Weighted Sampling:** Weighs each resources as the ratio of the number of datatype properties used to define a resource over the maximum number of datatype properties over all the datasets resources.
- **Resource Centrality Sampling:** Weighs each resource as the ration of the number of resource types used to describe a particular resource divided by the total number of resource types in the dataset. This is specific and important to RDF datasets where important concepts tend to be more structured and linked to other concepts.

However, the sampler is not restricted only to these strategies. Strategies like those introduced in [23] can be configured and plugged in the processing pipeline.

3.4   Profile Validation

A dataset profile should include descriptive information about the data examined. In our framework, we have identified three main categories of profiling information. However, the extensibility of our framework allows for additional profiling techniques to be plugged in easily (i.e. a quality profiling module reflecting the dataset quality). In this paper, we focus on the task of metadata profiling.

Metadata validation process identifies missing information and the ability to automatically correct them. Each set of metadata (general, access, ownership and provenance) is validated and corrected automatically when possible. Each profiler task has a set of metadata fields to check against. The validation process check if each field is defined and if the value assigned is valid.

There exist many special validation steps for various fields. For example, the email addresses and urls should be validated to ensure that the value entered is syntactically correct. In addition to that, for urls, we issue an HTTP HEAD request in order to check if that URL is reachable. We also use the information contained in a valid `content-header` response to extract, compare and correct some resources metadata values like `mimetype` and `size`.

From our experiments, we found out that datasets' license information is noisy. The license names if found are not standardized. For example, Creative

---

[11] https://github.com/wdavidw/node-csv.
[12] https://github.com/RubenVerborgh/N3.js.

Commons CCZero can be also CC0 or CCZero. Moreover, the license URI if found and if de-referenceable can point to different reference knowledge bases e.g., http://opendefinition.org. To overcome this issue, we have manually created a mapping file standardizing the set of possible license names and the reference knowledge base[13]. In addition, we have also used the open source and knowledge license information[14] to normalize the license information and add extra metadata like the domain, maintainer and open data conformance.

```
{
  "license_id": ["ODC-PDDL-1.0"],
  "disambiguations": ["Open Data Commons Public Domain Dedication and License (PDDL)
    "]
},
{
  "license_id": ["CC-BY-SA-4.0","CC-BY-SA-3.0"],
  "disambiguations": ["cc-by-sa","CC BY-SA","Creative Commons Attribution Share-
    Alike"]
}
```

Listing 1.1. License mapping file sample

3.5   Profile and Report Generation

The validation process highlights the missing information and presents them in a human readable report. The report can be automatically sent to the dataset maintainer email if exists in the metadata. In addition to the generated report, the enhanced profiles are represented in JSON using the CKAN data model and are publicly available[15].

Data portal administrators need an overall knowledge of the portal datasets and their properties. Our framework has the ability to generate numerous reports of all the datasets by passing formatted queries. There are two main sets of aggregation tasks that can be run:

- **Aggregating meta-field values:** Passing a string that corresponds to a valid field in the metadata. The field can be flat like `license_title` (aggregates all the license titles used in the portal or in a specific group) or nested like `resource>resource_type` (aggregates all the resources types for all the datasets). Such reports are important to have an overview of the possible values used for each metadata field.
- **Aggregating key:object meta-field values:** Passing two meta-field values separated by a colon : e.g., `resources>resource_type:resources>name`. These reports are important as you can aggregate the information needed when also having the set of values associated to it printed.

For example, the meta-field value query `resource>resource_type` run against the LODCloud group will result in an array containing [$file, api, documentation...$] values. These are all the resource types used to

---

[13] https://github.com/ahmadassaf/opendata-checker/blob/master/util/ licenseMappings.json.
[14] https://github.com/okfn/licenses.
[15] https://github.com/ahmadassaf/opendata-checker/tree/master/results.

describe all the datasets of the group. However, to be able to know also what
are the datasets containing resources corresponding to each type, we issue a
key:object meta-field query `resource>resource_type:name`. The result will be
a JSON object having the `resource_type` as the key and an array of corresponding datasets titles that has a resource of that type.

```
                        Metadata Report

group information is missing. Check organization information as they
     can be mixed sometimes
organization_image_url field exists but there is no value defined

                        Tag Statistics

There is a total of: 21 [undefined] vocabulary_id fields    100.00

                        License Report

License information has been normalized !

                    Resource Statistics

There is a total of: 10 [missing] url-type fields    100.00
There is a total of: 9 [missing] created fields    90.00
There is a total of: 10 [undefined] cache_last_updated fields    100.00
There is a total of: 10 [undefined] size fields    100.00
There is a total of: 10 [undefined] hash fields    100.00
There is a total of: 10 [undefined] mimetype_inner fields    100.00
There is a total of: 7 [undefined] mimetype fields    70.00
There is a total of: 10 [undefined] cache_url fields    100.00
There is a total of: 6 [undefined] name fields    60.00
There is a total of: 9 [undefined] webstore_url fields    90.00
There is a total of: 9 [undefined] last_modified fields    90.00
There is one [undefined] format field    10.00

                Resource Connectivity Issues

There are 2 connectivity issues with the following URLs:
  - \url{http://dbpedia.org/void/Dataset}

                Un-Reachable URLs Types

There are: 1 unreachable URLs of type [file]
```

Listing 1.2. Excerpt of the DBpedia validation report

4   Experiments and Evaluation

In this section, we provide the experiments and evaluation of the proposed framework. All the experiments are reproducible by our tool and their results are available in its Github repository. A CKAN dataset metadata describes four main
sections in addition to the core dataset's properties. These sections are:

- **Resources:** The distributable parts containing the actual raw data. They can
  come in various formats (JSON, XML, RDF, etc.) and can be downloaded or
  accessed directly (REST API, SPARQL endpoint).
- **Tags:** Provide descriptive knowledge on the dataset content and structure.
  They are used mainly to facilitate search and reuse.

– **Groups:** A dataset can belong to one or more group that share common semantics. A group can be seen as a cluster or a curation of datasets based on shared categories or themes.
– **Organizations:** A dataset can belong to one or more organization controlled by a set of users. Organizations are different from groups as they are not constructed by shared semantics or properties, but solely on their association to a specific administration party.

Each of these sections contains a set of metadata corresponding to one or more type (general, access, ownership and provenance). For example, a dataset resource will have general information such as the resource name, access information such as the resource url and provenance information such as creation date. The framework generates a report aggregating all the problems in all these sections, fixing field values when possible. Errors can be the result of missing metadata fields, undefined field values or field value errors (e.g. unreachable URL or incorrect email addresses).

4.1 Experimental Setup

We ran our tool on two CKAN-based data portals. The first one is datahub.io targeting specifically the LOD cloud group. The current state of the LOD cloud report [27] indicates that the LOD cloud contains 1014 datasets. They were harvested via a LDSpider crawler [16] seeded with 560 thousands URIs. Roomba, on the other hand, fetches datasets hosted in data portals where datasets have attached relevant metadata. As a result, we relied on the information provided by the Datahub CKAN API. Examining the tags available, we found two candidate groups. The first one tagged with "lodcloud" returned 259 datasets, while the second one tagged with "lod" returned only 75 datasets. After manually examining the two lists, we found out the datasets grouped with the tag "lodcloud" are the correct ones. To qualify other CKAN-based portals for the experiments, we use http://dataportals.org/ which contains a comprehensive list of Open Data portals from around the world. In the end, we chose the Amsterdam data portal[16]. The portal was commissioned in 2012 by the Amsterdam Economic Board Open Data Exchange (ODE) and covers a wide range of information domains (energy, economy, education, urban development, etc.) about Amsterdam metropolitan region.

We ran the Roomba instance and resource extractors in order to cache the metadata files for these datasets locally and ran the validation process. The experiments were executed on a 2.6 Ghz Intel Core i7 processor with 16 GB of DDR3 memory machine. The approximate execution time alongside the summary of the datasets' properties are presented in Table 1.

In our evaluation, we focused on two aspects: (i) *profiling correctness* which manually assesses the validity of the errors generated in the report, and (ii) *profiling completeness* which assesses if the profilers cover all the errors in the datasets metadata.

---

[16] http://data.amsterdamopendata.nl/.

Table 1. Summary of the experiments details

Data portal	No. datasets	No. groups	No. resources	Processing time
LOD cloud	259	N/A	1068	140 mins
Amsterdam open data	172	18	480	35 mins

4.2 Profiling Correctness

To measure profile correctness, we need to make sure that the issues reported by Roomba are valid on the dataset, group and portal levels.

On the dataset level, we choose three datasets from both the LOD Cloud and the Amsterdam data portal. The datasets details are shown in Table 2.

To measure the profiling correctness on the groups level, we selected four groups from the Amsterdam data portal containing a total of 25 datasets. The choice was made to cover groups in various domains that contain a moderate number of datasets that can be checked manually (between 3–9 datasets). Table 3 summarizes the groups chosen for the evaluation.

After running Roomba and examining the results on the selected datasets and groups, we found out that our framework provides 100 % correct results on the individual dataset level and on the aggregation level over groups. Since our portal level aggregation is extended from the group aggregation, we can infer that the portal level aggregation also produces complete correct profiles. However, the lack of a standard way to create and manage collections of datasets was the source of some errors when comparing the results from these two portals.

Table 2. Datasets chosen for the correctness evaluation

Dataset name	Data portal	Group ID	Resources	Tags
dbpedia	Datahub	lodcloud	10	21
event-media	Datahub	lodcloud	9	15
bbc-music	Datahub	lodcloud	2	14
bevolking_cijfers_amsterdam	Amsterdam	bevolking	6	12
bevolking-prognoses-amsterdam	Amsterdam	bevolking	1	3
religieuze_samenkomstlocaties	Amsterdam	bevolking	1	8

Table 3. Groups chosen for the correctness evaluation

Group name	Domain	Datasets	Resources	Tags
bestuur-en-organisatie	Management	9	45	101
bevolking	Population	3	8	23
geografie	Geography	8	16	56
openbare-orde-veiligheid	Public Order & Safety	5	19	34

For example, in Datahub, we noticed that all the datasets `groups` information were missing, while in the Amsterdam Open Data portal, all the `organisation` information was missing. Although the error detection is correct, the overlap in the usage of group and organization can give a false indication about the metadata quality.

4.3   Profiling Completeness

We analyzed the completeness of our framework by manually constructing a set of profiles that act as a golden standard. These profiles cover the range of uncommon problems that can occur in a certain dataset[17]. These errors are:

- Incorrect `mimetype` or `size` for resources;
- Invalid number of tags or resources defined;
- Check if the license information can be normalized via the `license_id` or the `license_title` as well as the normalization result;
- Syntactically invalid `author_email` or `maintainer_email`.

After running our framework at each of these profiles, we measured the completeness and correctness of the results. We found out that our framework covers indeed all the metadata problems that can be found in a CKAN standard model correctly.

5   Conclusion and Future Work

In this paper, we proposed a scalable automatic approach for extracting, validating, correcting and generating descriptive linked dataset profiles. This approach applies several techniques in order to check the validity of the metadata provided and to generate descriptive and statistical information for a particular dataset or for an entire data portal. Based on our experiments running the tool on the LOD cloud, we discovered that the general state of the datasets needs attention as most of them lack informative access information and their resources suffer low availability. These two metrics are of high importance for enterprises looking to integrate and use external linked data.

It has been noticed that the issues surrounding metadata quality affect directly dataset search as data portals rely on such information to power their search index. We noted the need for tools that are able to identify various issues in this metadata and correct them automatically. We evaluated our framework manually against two prominent data portals and proved that we can automatically scale the validation of datasets metadata profiles completely and correctly.

As part of our future work, we plan to introduce workflows that will be able to correct the rest of the metadata either automatically or through intuitive manually-driven interfaces. We also plan to integrate statistical and topical profilers to be able to generate full comprehensive profiles. We also intend to suggest a ranked standard metadata model that will help generate more accurate

---

[17] https://github.com/ahmadassaf/opendata-checker/tree/master/test.

and scored metadata quality profiles. We also plan to run this tool on various CKAN-based data portals, schedule periodic reports to monitor the evolvement of datasets metadata. Finally, at some stage, we plan to extend this tool for other data portal types like DKAN and Socrata.

Acknowledgments. This research has been partially funded by the European Union's 7th Framework Programme via the project Apps4EU (GA No. 325090).

References

1. Abedjan, Z., Gruetze, T., Jentzsch, A., Naumann, F.: Profiling and mining RDF data with ProLOD++. In: 30th IEEE International Conference on Data Engineering (ICDE), pp. 1198–1201 (2014)
2. Auer, S., Demter, J., Martin, M., Lehmann, J.: LODStats – an extensible framework for high-performance dataset analytics. In: ten Teije, A., Völker, J., Handschuh, S., Stuckenschmidt, H., d'Acquin, M., Nikolov, A., Aussenac-Gilles, N., Hernandez, N. (eds.) EKAW 2012. LNCS, vol. 7603, pp. 353–362. Springer, Heidelberg (2012)
3. Bizer, C.: Evolving the web into a global data space. In: Fernandes, A.A.A., Gray, A.J.G., Belhajjame, K. (eds.) BNCOD 2011. LNCS, vol. 7051, pp. 1–1. Springer, Heidelberg (2011)
4. Bizer, C., Berners-Lee, T.H.T.: Linked data - the story so far. Int. J. Semant. Web Inf. Syst. (IJSWIS) **5**(3), 1–22 (2009)
5. Böhm, C., Kasneci, G., Naumann, F.: Latent topics in graph-structured data. In: 21st ACM International Conference on Information and Knowledge Management (CIKM), Maui, Hawaii, USA, pp. 2663–2666 (2012)
6. BöHm, C., Lorey, J., Naumann, F.: Creating voiD descriptions for web-scale data. J. Web Semant. **9**(3), 339–345 (2011)
7. Bohm, C., Naumann, F., Abedjan, Z., Fenz, D., Grutze, T., Hefenbrock, D., Pohl, M., Sonnabend, D.: Profiling linked open data with ProLOD. In: 26th International Conference on Data Engineering Workshops (ICDEW) (2010)
8. Boyd, D., Crawford, K.: Six provocations for big data. In: A Decade in Internet Time: Symposium on the Dynamics of the Internet and Society (2011)
9. Cornolti, M., Ferragina, P., Ciaramita, M.: A framework for benchmarking entity-annotation systems. In: 22nd World Wide Web Conference (WWW) (2013)
10. Cyganiak, R., Stenzhorn, H., Delbru, R., Decker, S., Tummarello, G.: Semantic sitemaps: efficient and flexible access to datasets on the semantic web. In: Bechhofer, S., Hauswirth, M., Hoffmann, J., Koubarakis, M. (eds.) ESWC 2008. LNCS, vol. 5021, pp. 690–704. Springer, Heidelberg (2008)
11. Cyganiak, R., Zhao, J., Hausenblas, M., Alexander, K.: Describing linked datasets with the VoID vocabulary. W3C Note (2011). http://www.w3.org/TR/void/
12. Fetahu, B., Dietze, S., Pereira Nunes, B., Antonio Casanova, M., Taibi, D., Nejdl, W.: A scalable approach for efficiently generating structured dataset topic profiles. In: Presutti, V., d'Amato, C., Gandon, F., d'Aquin, M., Staab, S., Tordai, A. (eds.) ESWC 2014. LNCS, vol. 8465, pp. 519–534. Springer, Heidelberg (2014)
13. Forchhammer, B., Jentzsch, A., Naumann, F.: LODOP - multi-query optimization for linked data profiling queries. In: International Workshop on Dataset PROFIling and fEderated Search for Linked Data (PROFILES), Heraklion, Greece (2014)

14. Frosterus, M., Hyvönen, E., Laitio, J.: Creating and publishing semantic metadata about linked and open datasets. In: Wood, D. (ed.) Linking Government Data, pp. 95–112. Springer, New York (2011)
15. Frosterus, M., Hyvönen, E., Laitio, J.: DataFinland—a semantic portal for open and linked datasets. In: Antoniou, G., Grobelnik, M., Simperl, E., Parsia, B., Plexousakis, D., De Leenheer, P., Pan, J. (eds.) ESWC 2011, Part II. LNCS, vol. 6644, pp. 243–254. Springer, Heidelberg (2011)
16. Isele, R., Umbrich, J., Bizer, C., Harth, A.: LDspider: an open-source crawling framework for the web of linked data. In: 9th International Semantic Web Conference (ISWC), Posters and Demos Track (2010)
17. Jentzsch, A.: Profiling the web of data. In: 13th International Semantic Web Conference (ISWC), Doctoral Consortium, Trentino, Italy (2014)
18. Käfer, T., Abdelrahman, A., Umbrich, J., O'Byrne, P., Hogan, A.: Observing linked data dynamics. In: Cimiano, P., Corcho, O., Presutti, V., Hollink, L., Rudolph, S. (eds.) ESWC 2013. LNCS, vol. 7882, pp. 213–227. Springer, Heidelberg (2013)
19. Khatchadourian, S., Consens, M.P.: ExpLOD: summary-based exploration of inter-linking and rdf usage in the linked open data cloud. In: Aroyo, L., Antoniou, G., Hyvönen, E., ten Teije, A., Stuckenschmidt, H., Cabral, L., Tudorache, T. (eds.) ESWC 2010, Part II. LNCS, vol. 6089, pp. 272–287. Springer, Heidelberg (2010)
20. Kovács-Láng. Global terrestrial observing system. Technical report, GTOS Central and Eastern European Terrestrial Data Management and Accessibility Workshop (2000)
21. Lalithsena, S., Hitzler, P., Sheth, A., Jain, P.: Automatic domain identification for linked open data. In: IEEE/WIC/ACM International Joint Conferences on Web Intelligence (WI) and Intelligent Agent Technologies (IAT), pp. 205–212 (2013)
22. Langegger, A., Woss, W.: RDFStats - an extensible RDF statistics generator and library. In: 20th International Workshop on Database and Expert Systems Application (DEXA), pp. 79–83 (2009)
23. Leskovec, J., Faloutsos, C.: Sampling from large graphs. In: 12th ACM International Conference on Knowledge Discovery and Data Mining (KDD'12) (2006)
24. Li, H.: Data profiling for semantic web data. In: Wang, F.L., Lei, J., Gong, Z., Luo, X. (eds.) WISM 2012. LNCS, vol. 7529, pp. 472–479. Springer, Heidelberg (2012)
25. Maali, F., Erickson, J.: Data catalog vocabulary (DCAT). W3C Recommendation (2014). http://www.w3.org/TR/vocab-dcat/
26. Mäkelä, E.: Aether – generating and viewing extended void statistical descriptions of rdf datasets. In: Presutti, V., Blomqvist, E., Troncy, R., Sack, H., Papadakis, I., Tordai, A. (eds.) ESWC Satellite Events 2014. LNCS, vol. 8798, pp. 429–433. Springer, Heidelberg (2014)
27. Schmachtenberg, M., Bizer, C., Paulheim, H.: Adoption of the linked data best practices in different topical domains. In: Mika, P., et al. (eds.) ISWC 2014, Part I. LNCS, vol. 8796, pp. 245–260. Springer, Heidelberg (2014)
28. Usbeck, R., Röder, M., Ngonga-Ngomo, A.-C., Baron, C., Both, A., Brümmer, M., Ceccarelli, D., Cornolti, M., Cherix, D., Eickmann, B., Ferragina, P., Lemke, C., Moro, A., Navigli, R., Piccinno, F., Rizzo, G., Sack, H., Speck, R., Troncy, R., Waitelonis, J., Wesemann, L.: GERBIL - general entity annotation benchmark framework. In: 24th World Wide Web Conference (WWW) (2015)
29. Vickery, G.: Review of recent studies on PSI-use and related market developments. Technical report, EC DG Information Society (2011)

RDF Stream Processing Workshop

The Role of RDF Stream Processing
in an Smart City ICT Infrastructure -
The Aspern Smart City Use Case

Josiane Xavier Parreira[✉], Deepak Dhungana,
and Gerhard Engelbrecht

Siemens AG Österreich, Vienna, Austria
{josiane.parreira,deepak.dhungana,gerhard.engelbrecht}@siemens.com

Abstract. In this paper we discuss the opportunities of adopting RDF stream processing in the context of smart cities. As a concrete example we take the Aspern Smart City Research project – one of the largest smart city projects in Europe – which aims at overcoming silos in smart grid and smart building domains. We present the envisioned smart ICT infrastructure and identify how RDF Stream processing can be explored in the different interactions among data sources, storage centers and applications/services.

Keywords: RDF stream processing · Semantic web · Smart cities · Aspern urban lakeside district

1 Introduction

The Aspern Smart City Research (ASCR)[1], is a joint initiative between Siemens AG Österreich, Wiener Netze (a Power Grid operator), Wien Energie (an energy supplier), Wirtschaftsagentur Wien, and Wien 3420 Aspern Development AG. Started in October 2013, with an expected duration of 5 years and a budget of almost 40 million Euros, the project will have as testbed a "living laboratory" which is being created in the urban-lake-side district of Aspern, one of the largest urban development projects in Europe[2]. This area will include apartments, offices, and a business, science, research, and education quarter. Altogether, it will cover around 240 hectares. Fifty percent of the space is reserved for public areas – plazas, parks, and recreation areas. Step by step, between now and 2030, the district will evolve into an intelligent city of the future, with 20,000 residents and 20,000 additional jobs.

The Aspern project represents an opportunity to develop a long-term integrated concept for an energy-optimized city district, using appropriate technologies, products, and solutions in a real-world infrastructure. The overall goal is to make the whole system "smarter", by having power supplies, building systems,

---

[1] http://www.ascr.at/.
[2] http://www.aspern-seestadt.at/en.

© Springer International Publishing Switzerland 2015
F. Gandon et al. (Eds.): ESWC 2015, LNCS 9341, pp. 343–352, 2015.
DOI: 10.1007/978-3-319-25639-9_47

intelligent power grids, and information and communication technologies (ICT) interacting in an optimal manner. For example, part of the project involves connecting buildings that have different functions, i.e. offices and apartments, to the low-voltage distribution network. This will allow efficient management of the energy exchange between buildings and optimization of the local energy consumption. This offers building operators the possibility to participate actively on the energy markets. To this end, data from the different domains will be combined and used by different applications and services.

The project envisions a Smart ICT platform at the core of the interaction between the different players in a smart city. The Smart ICT platform is responsible for, among other things, mediating the interaction between data owners/publishers and applications/services. Data owners can make their data available via the ICT platform – either directly or via a data publisher – which are then stored locally. Application and services developers can access the stored data via the platform to create new applications, which in turn can be made available to end users also via the platform. The ICT platform supports different other functionality such as access control, policy enforcement, billing, monitoring and discovery.

We have identified different opportunities in the Smart ICT platform in which RDF Stream processing can aid delivering efficient and scalable data integration and analytics solutions for heterogeneous domains. For example, RDF Stream processing can be integrated in existing ETL tools to deliver semantically annotated and aggregated information from the raw data sources, which is then stored and combined with existing knowledge bases (e.g. buildings' layouts), before being delivered to third party applications and services. Real time log data from applications/services can, in turn, be analyzed to optimize the data acquisition process.

Next we describe the ASCR's infrastructure and its main components, in particular the Smart ICT platform. We then identify where RDF Stream processing can be explored by the Smart ICT platform in the different interactions among data sources, storage and applications/services, followed by a deeper discussion about its benefits.

2   The ASCR Infrastructure

The overall goal of Aspern is to deliver "smarter" solutions for energy utilization, by having power supplies, building systems, intelligent power grids, and information and communication technologies (ICT) interacting in an optimal manner. To this end, the ASCR infrastructure is responsible for the integration, interaction, analysis and provisioning of data coming from smart grids and smart buildings (e.g. temperature, energy consumption, water consumption, power demand), as well as external data sources (e.g. weather, city events, energy market, traffic reports). It is clear that the success of the infrastructure will depend in efficient solutions for handling heterogeneous data. The combination of data from different domains will not only lead to better forecast models, but it will also enable exploratory analysis to discover new correlations among the data, thus improving even further the optimization measures. In addition, the infrastructure also serves as a tool to aggregate and compare data at different levels, e.g., whole city, districts and building complexes.

Access to the data and analytical tools is limited to grids and building management systems. Smart citizens should be able to access data relevant to them and to also contribute by providing services to other users. For that, they will take the role of application developers, and applications can be made available via the ICT infrastructure. Figure 1 shows the ASCR Infrastructure and its main components.

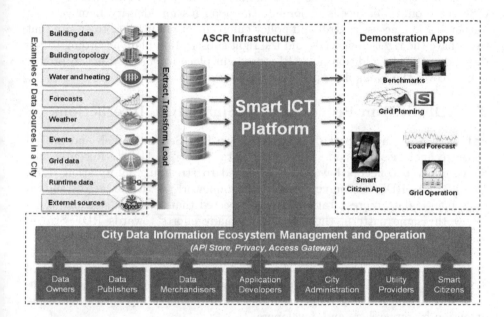

Fig. 1. The ICT infrastructure as a backbone for applications in Aspern [9]

Data from different sources in the city go over Extract, Transformation, Load (ETL) processes before being stored locally. The Smart ICT platform then performs different data analyses in the stored data, for instance [9]:

- **Benchmarking** of the different aspects of the ecosystem, in order to assess the performance of the optimization measures in the buildings and grid operation.
- **Load forecast,** by improving existing models with additional data from external sources.
- **Grid planning,** by early detection of anomalies or threshold violations in the low voltage network and identification of possible causes.

The platform delivers both the data and the data analysis to different applications, in order to provide the smart citizens with useful services. For example, mobile applications can be developed to give energy saving advices to citizens, based on their energy consumption, preferences, schedule and other external factors (e.g. weather). Citizens are encouraged to actively contribute to the platform, by developing applications on top of the available data and services. Allowing data access to third party users fosters a rapid increase of the number of functionalities offered by the platform, thus increasing its uptake they the community.

Different stakeholders are part of this complex ecosystem – data owners, data publishers, smart citizens, city administrators, etc. – and they all have different profiles and needs. Therefore, mechanisms for identity management, authentication, access control and policy enforcement are in place to ensure that users have the right credentials and the right subscription plan, according to the data source(s). In addition, an API store is in place to enable users to browse and discover the available applications and services.

3   RDF Stream Processing for Smart ICT Interactions

Extensive work in the past decade has shown how Semantic Web and Linked Data technologies can aid overcoming data silos [2,6,11,23]. Recently, the Semantic Web concepts have been extended to streaming information [7,15, 18,19,22]. As RDF (Resource Description Framework) is the de facto standard for semantic data representation, it was expected that semantic streams would follow the same pattern, thus leading to many efforts towards RDF Stream processing (RSP) [1,5,8,13]. RDF Stream processing enables data integration – not only among heterogeneous stream data sources, but also with other, possibly heterogeneous, existing sources. The advent of concepts such as of Internet of Things [24], Web of Things [20], and Industry 4.0 [16] – where integration of sensory information is at the core – also make RSP a timely topic with increasing attention by researchers and developers.

The RSP paradigm is well aligned with the requirements of the ASCR Smart ICT platform. A lot of the data that goes into the platform comes from sensor sources, for example, energy meters, room occupancy, temperature, and they need to be integrated with other knowledge bases, like building layout and grid topology. Moreover, data stored in the platform needs to be deliver to the applications on demand, and its often the case that they are streamed into the different applications. At last, application log streams are fed into the system for monitoring and performance improvement.

Based on this analysis, we have identified three different stages of the Smart ICT data pipeline, as shown in Fig. 2 – from data sources to local storage, from local storage to applications, and from applications back to data sources. RDF Stream processing can be explored in all these stages, in different ways. These are discussed in detail in the following sections. For some cases, existing work in RDF Stream processing tools and techniques already fulfills the requirements, while some are still open challenges for the RSP community.

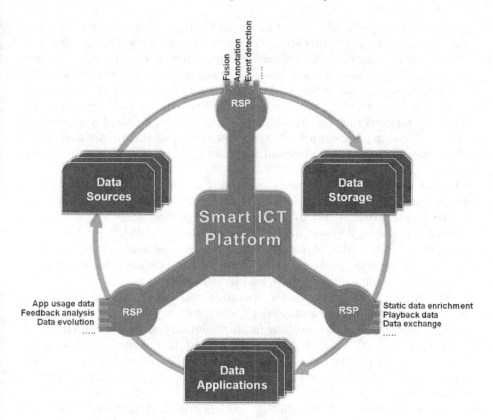

Fig. 2. RDF stream processing in the smart ICT platform.

3.1   From Data Sources to Data Storage

Heterogeneous data streams from diverse application domains (e.g., energy, traffic, event calendars, and environmental sensors for pollution or weather warnings, GIS databases) are at the heart of any smart city – as the data from these sources and their timely analysis can highly impact the smartness of the city. While data integration is paramount, not all data sources and not all data from these sources are relevant for decision makers, or citizens of the city. The dilemma for data-infrastructure engineers and data scientists is clear: what part of the data should be stored, how it should be stored and for how long? Here, RDF stream processing tools and techniques can be used to continuously monitor the data sources and perform pre-processing, filtering and integration, in order to store only the relevant parts of the data streams. For example, in the case of the Aspern project, RSP tools and techniques could be used for:

– **Data annotation:** Different RSP platforms, such as the Linked Stream Middleware [15], Graph of Things[3] and BOTTARI [4], provide the so-called wrap-

---

[3] http://graphofthings.org/.

pers, which can take different input formats and produce semantically annotate content. This is the first step to enable semantic integration and it can be
tailored to capture different relevant information that goes beyond the measures themselves, such as provenance and accuracy. In Aspern, information
about ownership is an example of an important data feature that should be
kept through all the data pipeline, and RDF Streams can easily provide modeling abstractions that fits the different requirements. Existing wrappers still
require initial manual configuration so that the input is correctly mapped to
the semantic description. Automatic semantic annotation of stream data is
still an open challenge.

- **Stream storage:** The platforms mentioned in the item above also support
  storing and querying historical stream data. Efficient encoding solutions for
  RDF already exist [10,17] to reduce the storage size, while still allowing a
  limited set of query operations. These could be extended to deal with the
  temporal aspect of RDF Streams. In addition, in cases where there is no need
  to store the original input data, RSP engines can provide data filtering and
  aggregation which can potentially lead to storage savings.
- **Data fusion:** RSP engines offer operators and functions similar to those
  found in relational database systems (RDBS), such as joins, unions, and aggregation, therefore supporting data fusion. Solutions such as C-SPARQL [5],
  SPARQL$_{Stream}$ [8], CQELS [13] and EP-SPARQL [1] have been extensively
  benchmark and results can be found at [14,25]. The benchmark frameworks
  can aid the choice of the most adequate RSP engine, given a specific set of
  requirements.
- **Event detection:** A large number services within Aspern relies on event
  detection, for example, grid planning. While most of the RSP engines are
  based on the Stream Data Management Systems (DSMS) paradigm, some of
  the existing work, such as EP-SPARQL, takes an Complex Event Processing (CEP) approach. EP-SPARQL's support of Allens temporal relationships
  enables event detection on RDF streams. RDF Stream Reasoning is also
  gained popularity [21]. While a few works already support it, further research
  is still needed to address scalability issues due to the complexity of reasoning
  tasks.

3.2 From Data Storage to Data Applications

One of the key issues with streaming data sources is that the data may not be
available when it is needed, as sensors might be faulty. Many applications relying
on streaming data sources however assume that the data is always accessible and
available. In order to deal with this issue, the Aspern project stores the data
locally in a big data processing infrastructure and passes these to the applications
as required in a controlled manner. Nevertheless, many applications still expect
streaming data, simply due to the very nature of some data points in the city. In
order to deal with this, RSP tools and techniques could be used. In the Aspern
project, this use case has many facets, which gives several opportunities to apply
RSP.

– **Playback data to applications:** Most of RSP solutions follow the query
  semantics defined by the Continuous Query Language (CQL) [3]. One class of
  operators is the "relation-to-stream" operators that produce a stream from a
  relation. That enables stored data to be delivered to application as streams.
– **Integration of static information:** Similar to the data fusion task described
  in Sect. 3.1, data integration is one of the main reasons for adopting RSP in
  the Aspern project. As mentioned earlier, Semantic Web can help overcoming
  silos, by promising seamless way of integration data. The benefits of using
  semantic technologies go beyond the ASCR project and can further facilitate
  the integration of other city data providers. Furthermore, it can easily be
  extended to other applications where heterogeneous devices must cooperate,
  for example, in the Industry 4.0 vision. All the solutions mentioned in Sect. 3.1
  can be explored for data integration tasks.
– **Semantic streams as a data exchange format:** Different serializations
  formats available for RDF are also supported by RSP engines, such as Turtle[4], N-triples[5], JSON-LD[6]. However, they might not be suitable for cases
  involving constrained devices or when the communication is over channels
  with low transfer rates, for example, mobile applications communicating via
  3G networks. Binary representations, similar to the ones used for compressing,
  and compact representations (e.g. EXI [12]) are currently being considered by
  ongoing research.

3.3 From Data Applications to Data Sources

Different applications used by the citizens and decision makers in the context of
a smart city are themselves generators of data. They represent a very valuable
data sources, as they can give a lot of insights into how the applications are
being used, whether the applications themselves are of any value to the users
and how these can be improved. The events generated by the applications, the
data browsing "behavior patterns" of the users, and the direct feedback that
comes from the users, annotated with the contextual information – all of these
data points come as streaming sources– which can be treated as yet another
data sources in the smart city context. In the context of the Aspern project,
such data could be collected, analyzed and stored using RDF stream processing
tools and techniques.

– **Feedback analysis:** Data analysis in general is crucial in many applications,
  for example benchmarking and load forecast, and as such it is not limited to
  feedback data logs. Nevertheless, feedback analysis concerns the overall performance of the platform, and it therefore deserves special attention. How
  the performance is perceived is highly dependent of the user needs and usage
  behavior. Therefore, we expect different user groups to behave differently (e.g.

---

[4] http://www.w3.org/TR/turtle/.
[5] http://www.w3.org/TR/n-triples/.
[6] http://www.w3.org/TR/json-ld/.

data publishers vs. app developers). By identifying these patterns we would be able to identify groups of users and automatically adapt the platform to their needs. Feedback analysis is also important to monitor and predict the performance of the overall infrastructure in order to maintain high performance and reduce down times.

Feedback analysis can be quite complex and might involved a number of steps. Complex event processing and reasoning over RDF streams can provide the first step for identifying meaningful patterns. An interesting, still unsolved challenge, would be how to combined RSP methods with traditional machine learning approaches to enable dynamic and complex data analysis.

4   Conclusion

Semantic Web technologies provide a schema-free data abstraction that fosters data reuse and integration, across different domains. RDF Stream Processing brings the Semantic Web paradigm to streaming information, thus bridging the gap between stream resources and knowledge bases. The Aspern project represents an opportunity to apply RSP solutions in a real-world infrastructure with the goal of developing a long-term integrated concept for an energy-optimized city district. In this paper we have consider the Smart ICT infrastructure from Aspern to demonstrate the benefits of RSP. We have looked at concrete functionalities in the platform and discussed how RSP can be applied.

Despite being a recent topic, research on RDF Stream Processing has already made considerable progress towards supporting tools and methods. Nevertheless there are still a large number of open challenges.

One very important step to foster the development and uptake of RSP technologies was the creation of the W3C RDF Stream Processing community group[7]. In this group, which was created in 2013, researchers in the area of RSP have joint forces to define common models for producing, transmitting and continuously querying RDF Streams. The expected outcome is a set of specifications for RDF extensions for streaming data – including modeling, querying, syntax, semantics, and service interfaces – to be adopted by future solutions.

References

1. Anicic, D., Fodor, P., Rudolph, S., Stojanovic, N.: EP-SPARQL: a unified language for event processing and stream reasoning. In: WWW, pp. 635–644. ACM (2011)
2. Antoniou, G., van Harmelen, F.: A Semantic Web Primer, 2nd edn. The MIT Press, Cambridge (2008)
3. Arasu, A., Babu, S., Widom, J.: The CQL continuous query language: semantic foundations and query execution. VLDB J. **15**(2), 121–142 (2006)
4. Balduini, M., Celino, I., DellAglio, D., Valle, E.D., Huang, Y., Lee, T., Kim, S.-H., Tresp, V.: BOTTARI: an augmented reality mobile application to deliver personalized and location-based recommendations by continuous analysis of social media streams. Web Semant. Sci. Serv. Agents World Wide Web **16**(5), 33–41 (2012)

---

[7] https://www.w3.org/community/rsp/.

5. Barbieri, D.F., Braga, D., Ceri, S., Valle, E.D., Grossniklaus, M.: C-SPARQL: a continuous query language for RDF data streams. Int. J. Semant. Comput. **4**(1), 3–25 (2010)
6. Bizer, C., Heath, T., Berners-lee, T.: Linked data - the story so far. Int. J. Semant. Web Inf. Syst. **5**, 1–22 (2009)
7. Bouillet, E., Feblowitz, M., Liu, Z., Ranganathan, A., Riabov, A.V., Ye, F.: A semantics-based middleware for utilizing heterogeneous sensor networks. In: Aspnes, J., Scheideler, C., Arora, A., Madden, S. (eds.) DCOSS 2007. LNCS, vol. 4549, pp. 174–188. Springer, Heidelberg (2007)
8. Calbimonte, J.-P., Corcho, O., Gray, A.J.G.: Enabling ontology-based access to streaming data sources. In: Patel-Schneider, P.F., Pan, Y., Hitzler, P., Mika, P., Zhang, L., Pan, J.Z., Horrocks, I., Glimm, B. (eds.) ISWC 2010, Part I. LNCS, vol. 6496, pp. 96–111. Springer, Heidelberg (2010)
9. Engelbrecht, G., Dhungana, D., Parreira, J.X.: Smart ICT in der seestadt aspern (poster). In: Smart Grids Week (2015)
10. Arias Gallego, M., Corcho, O., Fernández, J.D., Martínez-Prieto, M.A., Suárez-Figueroa, M.C.: Compressing semantic metadata for efficient multimedia retrieval. In: Bielza, C., Salmerón, A., Alonso-Betanzos, A., Hidalgo, J.I., Martínez, L., Troncoso, A., Corchado, E., Corchado, J.M. (eds.) CAEPIA 2013. LNCS, vol. 8109, pp. 12–21. Springer, Heidelberg (2013)
11. Hitzler, P., Krötzsch, M., Rudolph, S.: Foundations of Semantic Web Technologies. Chapman and Hall/CRC, London (2009)
12. Käbisch, S., Peintner, D., Anicic, D.: Standardized and efficient RDF encoding for constrained embedded networks. In: Gandon, F., Sabou, M., Sack, H., d'Amato, C., Cudré-Mauroux, P., Zimmermann, A. (eds.) ESWC 2015. LNCS, vol. 9088, pp. 437–452. Springer, Heidelberg (2015)
13. Le-Phuoc, D., Dao-Tran, M., Xavier Parreira, J., Hauswirth, M.: A native and adaptive approach for unified processing of linked streams and linked data. In: Aroyo, L., Welty, C., Alani, H., Taylor, J., Bernstein, A., Kagal, L., Noy, N., Blomqvist, E. (eds.) ISWC 2011, Part I. LNCS, vol. 7031, pp. 370–388. Springer, Heidelberg (2011)
14. Le-Phuoc, D., Dao-Tran, M., Pham, M.-D., Boncz, P., Eiter, T., Fink, M.: Linked stream data processing engines: facts and figures. In: Cudré-Mauroux, P., et al. (eds.) ISWC 2012, Part II. LNCS, vol. 7650, pp. 300–312. Springer, Heidelberg (2012)
15. Le-Phuoc, D., Nguyen-Mau, H.-Q., Parreira, J.-X., Hauswirth, M.: A middleware framework for scalable management of linked streams. Web Semant. Sci. Serv. Agents World Wide Web **16**(5), 42–51 (2012)
16. Lee, J., Lapira, E., Bagheri, B., Kao, H.: Recent advances and trends in predictive manufacturing systems in big data environment. Manuf. Lett. **1**(1), 38–41 (2013)
17. Owens, A., Seaborne, A., Gibbins, N., Schraefel, m.c.: A clustered triple store for jena, Clustered TDB (2008)
18. Sequeda, J.F., Corcho, O.: Linked stream data: a position paper. In: SSN (2009)
19. Sheth, A., Henson, C., Sahoo, S.S.: Semantic sensor web. IEEE Internet Comput. **12**, 78–83 (2008)
20. Uckelmann, D., Harrison, M., Michahelles, F.: Architecting the Internet of Things, 1st edn. Springer, Heidelberg (2011)
21. Valle, E.-D., Ceri, S., van Harmelen, F., Fensel, D.: It's a streaming world! reasoning upon rapidly changing information. IEEE Intell. Syst. **24**, 83–89 (2009)

22. Whitehouse, K., Zhao, F., Liu, J.: Semantic streams: a framework for composable semantic interpretation of sensor data. In: Römer, K., Karl, H., Mattern, F. (eds.) EWSN 2006. LNCS, vol. 3868, pp. 5–20. Springer, Heidelberg (2006)
23. Wood, D.: Linking Enterprise Data, 1st edn. Springer, New York (2010)
24. Zanella, A., Bui, N., Castellani, A.-P., Vangelista, L., Zorzi, M.: Internet of things for smart cities. IEEE Internet Things J. $1(1)$, 22–32 (2014)
25. Zhang, Y., Duc, P.M., Corcho, O., Calbimonte, J.-P.: SRBench: a streaming RDF/SPARQL benchmark. In: Cudré-Mauroux, P., et al. (eds.) ISWC 2012, Part I. LNCS, vol. 7649, pp. 641–657. Springer, Heidelberg (2012)

Towards a Unified Language for RDF Stream Query Processing

Daniele Dell'Aglio[1]([⊠]), Jean-Paul Calbimonte[2]([⊠]), Emanuele Della Valle[1],
and Oscar Corcho[3]

[1] DEIB, Politecnico of Milano, Milano, Italy
{daniele.dellaglio,emanuele.dellavalle}@polimi.it
[2] EPFL, Lausanne, Switzerland
jean-paul.calbimonte@epfl.ch
[3] Ontology Engineering Group, Universidad Politécnica de Madrid, Madrid, Spain
ocorcho@fi.upm.es

Abstract. In recent years, several RDF Stream Processing (RSP) systems have emerged, which allow querying RDF streams using extensions of SPARQL that include operators to take into account the velocity of this data. These systems are heterogeneous in terms of syntax, capabilities and evaluation semantics. Recently, the W3C RSP Group started to work on a common model for representing and querying RDF streams. The emergence of such a model and its accompanying query language is expected to take the most representative, significant and important features of previous efforts, but will also require a careful design and definition of its semantics. In this work, we present a proposal for the query semantics of the W3C RSP query language, and we discuss how it can capture the semantics of existing engines (CQELS, C-SPARQL, SPARQL$_{stream}$), explaining and motivating their differences. Then, we use RSP-QL to analyze the current version of the W3C RSP Query Language proposal.

1 Introduction

RDF Stream Processing (RSP) systems allow querying streams of RDF data, extending the SPARQL language with operators that can handle the highly dynamic and volatile nature of these data sources [1,3,6,10]. These systems are heterogeneous in terms of syntax and capabilities, due to the choice of operators and syntax selected to extend SPARQL. In addition, they implement different evaluation semantics for a set of constructs that may look similar in principle. However, these engines have different assumptions on how the query processing and delivery of results take place, which makes it difficult to describe, compare, understand and evaluate their behavior.

Initiatives have started with the goal of proposing a common model and query language for processing RDF Streams, converging in the RSP Community Group of the W3C[1]. The emergence of such a model is expected to take the

---

[1] W3C RSP Group: http://www.w3.org/community/rsp.

© Springer International Publishing Switzerland 2015
F. Gandon et al. (Eds.): ESWC 2015, LNCS 9341, pp. 353–363, 2015.
DOI: 10.1007/978-3-319-25639-9_48

most representative, significant and important features of previous efforts, but will also require a careful design and definition of its semantics. In this context, it is essential to lay down the foundations of formal semantics for the standardized RSP query model, such that we consider beforehand the notions of correctness, continuous evaluation, evaluation time, and operational semantics, to name a few.

To address this challenge, we have previously proposed RSP-QL [9], a unifying formal model for representing and querying RDF streams, that reflects the different semantics of existing RSP systems. RSP-QL extends the SPARQL model and also takes into account two existing models coming from the streaming data world: CQL [2] and SECRET [4]. This model, which already explains the heterogeneous semantics of existing RSP systems, can be used as a basis for the current RSP Group standardization effort. In this paper, we show that the new language proposed in the RSP Group are covered by the RSP-QL model, therefore providing a well-founded semantics for it. We also show that this new language allows covering cases that previous RSP languages are unable or partially able to address.

As running example, consider a social network micro-blogging stream, which contains microposts emitted by users on different topics. Such stream contains timestamped sets of RDF triples that represent posts, their authors, topics, etc., as in the following RDF stream snippet:

```
1   :post12 sioc:has_creator :susan [10]
2   :post12 sioc:topic :rsp2015 [10]
3   :post12 sioc:content ''Workshop just started" [10]
```

Listing 1. RDF stream elements: each RDF stream is enriched with a time instant representing its validity time.

The task we aim at solving is the search of the emerging topics on this stream. One way of characterizing emerging topics is by finding out those which are frequently appearing lately, and less before. This apparently simple query contains some interesting elements that reveal differences among existing RSP languages, and challenge some of their capabilities. This is first, due to the fact that it requires looking at the same stream from two different perspectives: in the one hand it needs to keep track of very recent topics, while on the other hand needs to be aware of a longer time span, so that it can make sure that the new topics were not present before. Moreover, as we will see later, current RSP languages have implicit assumptions on how the results of a continuous query are streamed out, and how they react to changes on the sliding windows. We showed previously [9] that the RSP-SQL model is capable of covering these cases, while – as we will see next – current systems cannot. We also show that existing RSP languages present limitations that are partially solved by the current proposed language of the RSP Group, and that the latter is also covered by the RSP-QL model.

The remainder of this paper is structured as follows. We introduce the RSP-QL model in Sect. 2, including its main definitions. In Sect. 3, we provide a summary of the main semantic differences between existing RSP languages. Afterwards, we compare the syntactical limitations of these languages, compared to RSP-QL model, in Sect. 4. Section 5 is dedicated to explaining how the language proposed by the W3C RSP Group covers some of these limitations, and we show that it is also covered by the RSP-QL model. Finally, we conclude and provide final remarks on Sect. 6.

2   RSP-QL Semantics

The main difference between RDF Stream Processing and traditional RDF/S-PARQL processing is given by the time dimension. In RSP, time plays a main role, and it has to be taken into account in both the data and query models. In the following, we present extensions of those models, and we will use them in the remaining of the paper to analyze existing languages.

Data Model. The RDF data model does not take into account the time, as stated in the RDF 1.1 recommendation [13]:

> The RDF data model is atemporal: RDF graphs are static snapshots of information.

For this reason, the RDF data model has to be extended to take into account the time dimension. We propose two different extensions, that bring data to be roughly classified in two classes: *RDF stream* and *background data*.

An **RDF stream** is a sequence of timestamped data items (d_i, t_i), where each d_i is a RDF statement[2] and t_i is the time instant associated to d_i:

$$S = ((d_1, t_1), (d_2, t_2), \ldots, (d_n, t_n), \ldots)$$

Given a RDF stream S, the time stamps are in a non-decreasing order (i.e. for each i, $t_i \leq t_{i+1}$). Consumers usually access RDF streams through push paradigms: they register themselves to the RDF stream producers, and they start to receive the new streamed data.

Background data identifies the data that does not change (static) or changes very slowly w.r.t. data stream rate (quasi-static), and it is usually used to solve more complex queries (e.g., combining a stream of micro-posts with the graphs of authors) [7]. Background data includes RDF data stored in SPARQL endpoints, RDF repositories and sets of RDF data (that are usually fetched by the query processor). In this case, the time dimension is pushed through the notions of **time-varying** and **instantaneous** graphs. The former captures the dynamic evolution of a RDF graph over time: a time-varying graph G is a function that maps time instants to RDF graphs

$$G : T \rightarrow \{g|g \text{ is an RDF graph}\}$$

---

[2] In this work we consider the case where data items are RDF statements.

The latter is the value of G at a fixed time instant t: the instantaneous graph $G(t)$ identifies an RDF graph.

Query Model. The time dimension also affects the query model, moving the evaluation from one-time paradigm to a continuous one. While SPARQL allows to issue queries that are evaluated once, RSP-QL allows to register continuous queries (i.e. issued once) and evaluated multiple times. The answer of a continuous query is composed by listing the results of each evaluation iteration. We define RSP-QL queries as extension of SPARQL queries, in order to maintain backward compatibility with the SPARQL query model. The intuition behind this choice is that the continuous evaluation can be viewed as a sequence of instantaneous evaluations, so, fixed a time instant, the operators can work in a time-agnostic way.

A SPARQL query [12] is defined through a triple (E, DS, QF), where E is the algebraic expression, DS is the data set and QF is the query form. We extend this definition for RSP-QL: a RSP-QL query is defined through a quadruple (SE, SDS, ET, QF), where SE is an RSP-QL algebraic expression, SDS is an RSP-QL dataset, ET is the sequence of time instants on which the evaluation occurs, and QF is the Query Form. While the Query Form values are the same of SPARQL (i.e. SELECT, CONSTRUCT, DESCRIBE and ASK), dataset and algebraic expression are extended to take into account the time dimension.

ET is the set of time instants on which the evaluation occurs. This notion is useful for modelling the RSP-QL query, but it is worth to note that it is hard to use it in practice when designing the RSP-QL syntax or implementing the RSP engines. In fact, the ET sequence is potentially infinite, so the syntax needs a compact representation of this set. Moreover, ET could be unknown when the query is issued: the time instants on which the query has to be evaluated can depend on the data in the RDF stream, e.g. the query should be evaluated every time the window content changes. For this reason, we relate ET to policies, as defined in SECRET [4]. Policies allow to determine when the query has to be evaluated, e.g. evaluation can be periodical or can depend on the status of window content.

A dataset represents the data against which the algebraic expression is evaluated. Given that we moved from RDF graphs to time-varying graphs and RDF streams, the notion of dataset as in SPARQL needs to be extended accordingly. In particular, fixed an evaluation time instant $t \in ET$, we aim at having a SPARQL-compliant data set. That is, we need a way to move from time-varying graphs and RDF streams to RDF graphs. Regarding the former, we already introduced the notion of instantaneous graph, that identifies an RDF graph at time t; regarding the latter, we use the notion of sliding window to determine a subset of the RDF stream to be taken into account at time t. A **time-based sliding window** $\mathbb{W}$ takes as input a stream S and produces a time-varying graph $G_{\mathbb{W}}$. $\mathbb{W}$ is defined through a set of parameters (α, β, t_0), where: α is the width parameter, β is the slide parameter, t_0 is the time instant on which $\mathbb{W}$ starts to operate. A sliding window generates a sequence of windows, i.e., portions of data items in the stream that can be queried as RDF graphs. We can finally define a RSP-QL dataset SDS as a set composed by an optional default graph G_0, n named graphs (u_i, G_i) and m named sliding windows over $o \leq m$ streams $(w_i, \mathbb{W}_i(S_j))$:

$$
\begin{aligned}
SDS = \{G_0, \\
(u_1, G_1), \ldots, (u_n, G_n), \\
(w_1, \mathbb{W}_1(S_1)), \ldots, (w_j, \mathbb{W}_j(S_1)), \\
(w_{j+1}, \mathbb{W}_{j+1}(S_2)), \ldots, (w_k, \mathbb{W}_k(S_2)), \\
\ldots \\
(w_l, \mathbb{W}_l(S_o)), \ldots, (w_m, \mathbb{W}_m(S_o))\}
\end{aligned}
$$

An RSP-QL expression uses all the SPARQL operators. As explained above, fixed an evaluation time t, the RSP-QL dataset SDS can be converted in a SPARQL dataset, and consequently the SPARQL operators can be used in order to process it (additional details on the evaluation semantics can be found in [9]). Additionally, a new class of *streaming operators is introduced: they transform sequences of solution mappings in sequences of timestamped solution mappings. Those operators are required to prepare the part of the answer to be appended to the output stream. These operators have been first introduced in [2], and are named Rstream, IStream and Dstream. **Rstream** streams out the computed set of mappings at each step; its answers can be verbose as the same mapping could be in different portions of the output stream computed at different steps. It is suitable when it is important to have the whole SPARQL query answer at each step, e.g., discover popular topics in the last time period in a social network. **Istream** streams out the difference between the current set of solution mappings and the one computed at the previous step. In this case, answers are usually shorter than Rstream ones (they contain only the difference) and consequently this operator is used when data exchange is expensive. Finally, **Dstream** does the opposite of Istream: it streams out the difference between the solution mappings computed at the previous step and the current one.

3 Heterogeneity in RSP Engines

Existing RSP query languages have different underlying semantics, and even if their syntax is similar, these differences have fundamental consequences at query evaluation time. This analysis involves the query models of C-SPARQL, SPARQL$_{stream}$ and CQELS, as well as their query language syntaxes. In the case of C-SPARQL [3], the stream processor is built on top of Esper[3] and Jena, combining them to process windows over streams with the first, and SPARQL execution with the second. CQELS [10] has a completely native implementation aimed at achieving higher performance. Finally, SPARQL$_{stream}$ [5] adopts an ontology-based data access to stream processing engines through query rewriting.

---

[3] Esper: http://esper.codehaus.org/.

All these systems support a subset of SPARQL 1.1 operators [14] and they are heterogeneous in the way they process the RDF streams and report the results.

Some of the differences in RSP engines are reflected in how the query dataset is constructed and how the windows are declared. For instance, CQELS associates a named (time-varying) graph to each window in the query, and the window content is accessed with the STREAM clause, analogous to the GRAPH in SPARQL. However, it is not possible to declare the sliding window in such a way that its content is included in the default graph of the dataset. On the contrary, C-SPARQL does not allow to name the time-varying graphs computed by the sliding windows, but all the graphs computed by the sliding windows are merged and set as the default graph. Similarly, in SPARQL$_{stream}$ named stream graphs can be declared but not used inside the query body. This allows writing simpler queries in C-SPARQL and SPARQL$_{stream}$, as all sliding windows are declared before the WHERE clause and the data from the streams is available in the default graph. Nevertheless, this does not allow defining more complex queries, such as those with multiple sliding windows over the same stream, which is possible in CQELS.

Regarding the evaluation time of windows, the query models of C-SPARQL, SPARQL$_{stream}$ and CQELS allow controlling the width and slide of windows. However, they provide no way to determine the time when the first window opens (known as t^0 in [8]), as this parameter is managed internally by the systems. Another important but diverging aspect in available RSP systems, is related to the report policy and strategy, which are implementation-dependent. This is a major source of heterogeneity, as these systems do not allow explicitly specifying control policies and strategies in the query syntax. As analyzed in [8], C-SPARQL and SPARQL$_{stream}$ adopt a Window Close and Non-empty Content policy to the windows of the query, while CQELS implements the Content-Change policy, evaluating the query every time new statements enter the window. Finally, another important feature that is supported differently is the streaming operator, i.e. Rstream, Istream and Dstream. Only SPARQL$_{stream}$ actually supports them in its syntax. C-SPARQL implicitly uses only the Rstream operator, streaming out the whole output at each evaluation, while CQELS works only in Istream mode. As a result, C-SPARQL answers can be more verbose, as the same solutions can be present in the output stream, computed at different evaluation times. Conversely, CQELS streams out the difference between the set of mappings computed at the last and previous evaluation steps.

4   Syntactical Limitations in RSP Languages

The heterogeneity of existing RSP engines described previously is reflected by their syntaxes. Their different design choices brought differences in the RSP engines and in their execution models. In this section, we use the RSP-QL model and the running example described above to highlight those differences. The task we want to solve is the identification of all the most emerging topics in the last 10 min. Emerging topics are identified as those that appear at least a certain amount of times in the latest 10 min, and sensibly less in a longer time span of 120 min.

CQELS. First, we analyze CQELS. In Listing 2, we report the CQELS-QL query that models the task described above in the running example.

```
1   CONSTRUCT {?topic a :EmergingTopic}
2   WHERE{
3     STREAM :in [RANGE 120m STEP 10m] {
4       SELECT ?topic (COUNT(*) AS ?totalLong)
5       WHERE { ?m1 sioc:topic ?topic.}
6       GROUP BY ?tlong}
7     STREAM :in [RANGE 10m STEP 10m] {
8       SELECT ?topic (COUNT(*) AS ?totalShort)
9       WHERE { ?m2 sioc:topic ?topic. }
10      GROUP BY ?tshort}
11    FILTER (totalShort-totalLong/12 > threshold)
12  }
```

Listing 2. CQELS query to find the emerging topics

The query declares two sliding windows over the same input stream :in: the first, $\mathbb{W}_l^{CQ}$ (Line 3), has width $\alpha_l = 120\,\mathrm{min}$ and slide $\beta_l = 10\,\mathrm{min}$; the second, $\mathbb{W}_s^{CQ}$ (Line 7), has width and slide $\alpha_s = \beta_s = 10\,\mathrm{min}$ (it is a *tumbling window*). Each sliding window contains a subquery to compute the topics and the total number of their appearances (respectively ?totalLong and ?totalShort). The emerging value is computed at Line 11: if this value is greater than a threshold value, then the topic is selected as emergent, and it is streamed out according to the CONSTRUCT clause at Line 1. The RSP-QL dataset of this query is the following:

$$SDS^{CQ} = \{(w_l, \mathbb{W}_l^{CQ}(\text{:in})), (w_s, \mathbb{W}_s^{CQ}(\text{:in}))\}$$

The syntax of CQELS-QL brings to assign an implicit name to each sliding windows (in the example, $\mathbb{W}_l^{CQ}$ and $\mathbb{W}_s^{CQ}$). In other words, it is not possible to assign explicit identifiers to the sliding windows. In this way, the language gains in usability, but it forbids to add sliding windows contents to the default graph.

Another limit of CQELS is given by the *streaming operator: as explained above, CQELS uses an Istream operator to produce the output. That is, it cannot produce an Rstream with the whole result of each operator. In other words, the algebraic expressions of CQELS-QL always assume Istream as outer element of the algebraic expression.

C-SPARQL. The example query cannot be written in one C-SPARQL query, as the syntax of C-SPARQL does not allow to distinguish among multiple windows defined over the same stream. Let us consider the query in Listing 3, the RSP-QL dataset built by the query is the following:

$$SDS^{CS} = \{G_0 = \{\mathbb{W}_l^{CS}(\text{:in}), \mathbb{W}_s^{CQ}(\text{:in})\}$$

The dataset SDS^{CS} has the two sliding windows in the default graph position, i.e., the graphs produced by the sliding windows are merged in the default graph. In fact, C-SPARQL does not allow to name the sliding windows, and consequently, the generated windows.

```
1   REGISTER STREAM :out AS
2   CONSTRUCT {?tshort a :EmergingTopic}
3   FROM STREAM :in [RANGE 120m STEP 10m]
4   FROM STREAM :in [RANGE 10m STEP 10m]
5   WHERE{
6     ?m sioc:topic ?topic.
7   }
```

Listing 3. C-SPARQL Query: the triple pattern is evaluated against the union of the two sliding windows

It is actually possible to solve the running example task through a network of three C-SPARQL queries. First, Q_1^{CS} and Q_2^{CS} process the input stream :in in order to process the number of topics in the long and in the short windows. Listings 4 shows Q_1^{CS}.

```
1   REGISTER STREAM :longStream AS
2   CONSTRUCT {?topic :totalLong ?totalLong}
3   FROM STREAM :in [RANGE 120m STEP 10m]
4   WHERE{
5     SELECT ?topic ((COUNT(?topic) AS ?totalLong)
6     WHERE{ ?m1 sioc:topic ?topic. }
7     GROUP BY ?topic
8   }
```

Listing 4. C-SPARQL Query Q_1^{CS}: it counts the number of topics in the previous 120 min

The query builds a stream :longStream, that brings the topics and the number of appearance of the topics in the last 120 min (according to the sliding window definition at Line 3). Similarly, query Q_2^{CS} (we omit it for brevity, but it is similar to Q_1^{CS} – it changes the window size, the name of the output stream and the property name in the CONSTRUCT close) builds a stream :shortStream with the topics and their number of appearance in the previous 10 min. Those streams are the input of query Q_3^{CS}, reported in Listing 5, which computes the trending value of the topics, and add the topic in the output stream :out if the emerging value is greater than the threshold one (Line 7). In this case, the output contains the whole list of topics, as C-SPARQL uses Rstream as *streaming operator.

```
1   REGISTER STREAM :out AS
2   CONSTRUCT {?tshort a :EmergingTopic}
3   FROM STREAM :longStream [RANGE 10m STEP 10m]
4   FROM STREAM :shortStream [RANGE 10m STEP 10m]
5   WHERE{
6     ?topic :countLong ?totalLong; :countShort ?totalShort.
7     FILTER (?totalShort-?totalLong/12 > threshold)
8   }
```

Listing 5. C-SPARQL Query Q_3^{CS}: computation of the trending topics

SPARQL$_{stream}$. The case of SPARQL$_{stream}$, is similar to the one of C-SPARQL. Named stream graphs can be declared but the names cannot be used inside the query body. Therefore, graphs derived by sliding windows are logically merged in the default graph of the query dataset. As stated before, the Rstream operator can be explicitly indicated in the query.

5 Analysis of the W3C RSP Query Language Proposal

In this section, we briefly analyze the language under development by the W3C RDF Stream Processing community group[4]. Listing 6 shows the query that captures the running example task.

```
1   REGISTER STREAM :out
2   AS CONSTRUCT RSTREAM{ ?tshort a :EmergingTopic }
3   FROM NAMED WINDOW :lwin ON :in [RANGE PT120M STEP PT10M]
4   FROM NAMED WINDOW :swin ON :in [RANGE PT10M STEP PT10M]
5   WHERE{
6     WINDOW :lwin{
7       SELECT ?topic (COUNT(*) AS totalLong)
8       WHERE { ?m1 sioc:topic ?topic. }
9       GROUP BY ?topic }
10    WINDOW :swin{
11      SELECT ?topic (COUNT(*) AS totalShort)
12      WHERE { ?m2 sioc:topic ?tshort. }
13      GROUP BY ?topic }
14    FILTER(?totalShort-?totalLong)/12 > threshold)
15  }
```

Listing 6. The running example modelled through the W3C RSP Query Language

Observing the query, it is possible to note that the new language puts together the features of C-SPARQL, CQELS and SPARQL$_{stream}$ in order to overcome some of the limits highlighted in the previous sections.

First, the new language allows to declare the *streaming operator (Rstream, at Line 2). Moreover, the new language allows to build both CQELS and C-SPARQL data sets: it is possible due to the sliding windows declarations in the FROM clause, combined with the use of the NAMED keyword (Lines 3 and 5). Next, in the WHERE clause, the WINDOW keyword is used to refer to the content of the named sliding windows (similarly to the GRAPH keyword in SPARQL). The RSP-QL dataset built by the query is:

$$SDS^{RSP} = \{(:\text{lwin}, \mathbb{W}_l^{RSP}(:\text{in})), (:\text{swin}, \mathbb{W}_s^{RSP}(:\text{in}))\}$$

Nevertheless, this syntax is not enough to determine a unique query following th RSP-QL model. As we explained in Sect. 3, there is no explicit information to determine which is the report policy and when the sliding windows start to

---

[4] We refer at the version of the language available at July 2015.

work (i.e., the t^0 value). A possible solution for the latter problem can be the introduction of a STARTING AT command to express the t^0 value. Alternatively, the language could allow to define a pattern to express the t^0 value.

6   Conclusions

In this paper, we presented RSP-QL, a formal query model that extends SPARQL for evaluating continuous queries over RDF streams. We first used the model to inspect the query languages of three RSP engines, namely C-SPARQL, CQELS and SPARQL$_{stream}$. As we discussed, RSP-QL can capture the semantics of those different engines and languages. Having well-defined RSP engine models would enable interoperability through common query interfaces, even if the implementations architectural approaches.

We then used RSP-QL to discuss the language under development at the W3C RSP Community Group. On the one hand, we provided evidence that the new language overcomes some limitations of C-SPARQL, CQELS-QL and SPARQL$_{stream}$; on the other hand, it still lacks some features that could lead in misinterpretations and in different implementations. We strongly believe that those aspects need to be addressed at a syntactic or and semantic level, in order to guarantee that a query is associated to one RSP-QL query. This would guarantee the possibility of determining a unique answer given the query and the data. In this sense, RSP-QL aims at constituting a contribution to ongoing efforts in the Semantic Web community to provide standardized and agreed definition of extensions to RDF and SPARQL for managing data streams.

The RSP-QL model can be used, not only to characterize and define new RDF stream query languages, but also to define and develop new tools and optimizations in RSP systems. As an example, in [8] we use RSP-QL to provide foundations for defining RSP benchmarks that take into account the often disregarded problem of correctness in stream processing. RSP-QL can also be used to understand the behavior and capabilities of RSP engines, from theoretical to practical perspectives.

Several challenges are in the scope of future works around the RSP-QL model. The current version of the model focuses on window-based continuous query languages, but other paradigms can also be studied, such as those inspired in Complex Event Processing [1]. This may include the need for studying intervals on RDF streams and additional operators such as sequences. Furthermore, it might be worth considering the possibility of implementing an engine that follows RSP-QL, and validate the execution model. We also foresee to include stream reasoning in RSP-QL, currently absent in the model, which is one of the key features of Semantic Web systems [11]. We are convinced that a well-defined and unified RSP query language will contribute to the overall goal of establishing a model that is both well-founded and applicable in real RSP systems.

Acknowledgments. This research is partially supported by the IBM Ph.D. Fellowship Award 2014 granted to D. Dell'Aglio.

References

1. Anicic, D., Fodor, P., Rudolph, S., Stojanovic, N.: EP-SPARQL: a unified language for event processing and stream reasoning. In: Proceedings of 20th International Conference on World Wide Web WWW 2011, pp. 635–644 (2011)
2. Arasu, A., Babu, S., Widom, J.: The CQL continuous query language : semantic foundations. VLDB J. **15**(2), 121–142 (2006)
3. Barbieri, D.F., Braga, D., Ceri, S., Della Valle, E., Grossniklaus, M.: C-SPARQL: a continuous query language for RDF data streams. IJSC **4**(1), 3–25 (2010)
4. Botan, I., Derakhshan, R., Dindar, N., Haas, L., Miller, R.J., Tatbul, N.: Secret: a model for analysis of the execution semantics of stream processing systems. PVLDB **3**(1), 232–243 (2010)
5. Calbimonte, J.-P., Corcho, O., Gray, A.J.G.: Enabling ontology-based access to streaming data sources. In: Patel-Schneider, P.F., Pan, Y., Hitzler, P., Mika, P., Zhang, L., Pan, J.Z., Horrocks, I., Glimm, B. (eds.) ISWC 2010, Part I. LNCS, vol. 6496, pp. 96–111. Springer, Heidelberg (2010)
6. Calbimonte, J.P., Jeung, H., Corcho, O., Aberer, K.: Enabling query technologies for the semantic sensor web. IJSWIS **8**(1), 43–63 (2012)
7. Dehghanzadeh, S., Dell'Aglio, D., Gao, S., Della Valle, E., Mileo, A., Bernstein, A.: Approximate continuous query answering over streams and dynamic linked data sets. In: Cimiano, P., Frasincar, F., Houben, G.-J., Schwabe, D. (eds.) ICWE 2015. LNCS, vol. 9114, pp. 307–325. Springer, Heidelberg (2015)
8. Dell'Aglio, D., Calbimonte, J.-P., Balduini, M., Corcho, O., Della Valle, E.: On correctness in RDF stream processor benchmarking. In: Alani, H., Kagal, L., Fokoue, A., Groth, P., Biemann, C., Parreira, J.X., Aroyo, L., Noy, N., Welty, C., Janowicz, K. (eds.) ISWC 2013, Part II. LNCS, vol. 8219, pp. 326–342. Springer, Heidelberg (2013)
9. Dell'Aglio, D., Della Valle, E., Calbimonte, J.P., Corcho, O.: RSP-QL semantics: a unifying query model to explain heterogeneity of RDF stream processing systems. IJSWIS **10**(4), 17–44 (2015)
10. Le-Phuoc, D., Dao-Tran, M., Xavier Parreira, J., Hauswirth, M.: A native and adaptive approach for unified processing of linked streams and linked data. In: Aroyo, L., Welty, C., Alani, H., Taylor, J., Bernstein, A., Kagal, L., Noy, N., Blomqvist, E. (eds.) ISWC 2011, Part I. LNCS, vol. 7031, pp. 370–388. Springer, Heidelberg (2011)
11. Margara, A., Urbani, J., van Harmelen, F., Bal, H.E.: Streaming the web: reasoning over dynamic data. J. Web Sem. **25**, 24–44 (2014)
12. Prud'hommeaux, E., Harris, S., Seaborne, A.: SPARQL 1.1 Query Language, March 2013. http://www.w3.org/TR/sparql11-query
13. Wood, D., Lanthaler, M., Cyganiak, R.: RDF 1.1 concepts and abstract syntax, February 2014. http://www.w3.org/TR/rdf11-concepts/
14. Zhang, Y., Duc, P.M., Corcho, O., Calbimonte, J.-P.: SRBench: a streaming RDF/SPARQL benchmark. In: Cudré-Mauroux, P., et al. (eds.) ISWC 2012, Part I. LNCS, vol. 7649, pp. 641–657. Springer, Heidelberg (2012)

SALAD Services and Applications over Linked APIs and Dat

Web API Management Meets
the Internet of Things

Paul Fremantle[✉], Jacek Kopecký,
and Benjamin Aziz

University of Portsmouth, Portsmouth PO1 3HE, UK
{paul.fremantle,jacek.kopecky,benjamin.aziz}@port.ac.uk

Abstract. In this paper we outline the challenges of Web API management in Internet of Things (IoT) projects. Web API management is a key
aspect of service-oriented systems that includes the following elements:
metadata publishing, access control and key management, monitoring
and monetization of interactions, as well as usage control and throttling.
We look at how Web API management principles, including some of the
above elements, translate into a world of connected devices (IoT). In
particular, we present and evaluate a prototype that addresses the issue
of managing authentication with millions of insecure low-power devices
communicating with non-HTTP protocols. With this first step, we are
only beginning to investigate IoT API management, therefore we also
discuss necessary future work.

1 Introduction

Web APIs are capabilities offered across the web that are designed to be accessed
by software rather than people. Unlike traditional APIs, Web APIs are inher-
ently public or semi-public in that they are designed to be used over the public
Internet and not solely over private networks or VPNs. The public nature of
Web APIs poses a number of challenges addressed by the emerging area of *API
Management.*

The Internet of Things is the name given to the systems that connect the real
world to the Internet. This includes both sensors that measure the world around
us (including pollution sensors, weather monitors, car parking space sensors,
baby monitors and many others) and actuators that affect the world (including
automated lighting systems, internet-connected door locks, and many others).
Complex devices such as Connected Cars, Connected Homes, and so forth, combine multiple sensors and actuators. Due to their low power, IoT devices often
employ non-HTTP protocols such as MQ Telemetry Transport (MQTT) and
Constrained Application Protocol (CoAP).

Inevitably the Internet of Things will need to engage with Web APIs. For
now, most IoT devices connect to services that are created by the provider of
the hardware, and so are using private APIs. Public APIs are an increasingly
important factor. There are a set of companies that are providing common cloud
services and corresponding APIs for IoT (such as Xively [20]), and there are

F. Gandon et al. (Eds.): ESWC 2015, LNCS 9341, pp. 367–375, 2015.
DOI: 10.1007/978-3-319-25639-9_49

emerging API standards for IoT communication (such as HyperCat [11]). Much of the envisioned strength of the IoT will emerge when data from multiple sources can be aggregated, analysed and acted upon. This will increase the demand for IoT devices to communicate with open Web APIs.

Our work addresses the new problem of adapting the principles and technologies of Web API management to the landscape of the IoT, which poses challenges stemming from the great numbers and low power of IoT devices, compared to typical full-fledged clients for Web APIs. The problems we are addressing can be clearly stated:

- What is the impact of the Internet of Things onto Web APIs and Web API Management
- How do IoT devices identify themselves to Web APIs over IoT protocols? *
- How can we add IoT protocol support to existing Web API Management systems?
- What is the impact of adding identity, usage control and analytics to existing IoT protocol interactions?

This paper provides three clear contributions: firstly, the identification of new challenges that emerge from the use of Web APIs from IoT devices, especially those around authentication, usage control and analytics. Secondly, we have implemented a prototype which we believe is the first of its kind to add support for IoT specific protocols to API management systems. In addition, the prototype demonstrates the use of an extension to the OAuth2 protocol called *Dynamic Client Registration (DCR)* [16], which is an important approach for IoT. Finally we provide early experimental data on the performance of this prototype.

The rest of the paper is laid out as follows. In the next section, we look more closely at the area of Web API Management. We then we review related work that gives us a basis for defining in Sect. 4 the unique challenges of Web API management for the IoT, especially in connection with binary protocols such as MQ Telemetry Transport (MQTT) or the Constrained Application Protocol (CoAP). Section 5 introduces our prototype, a messaging gateway we call IGNITE, designed to allow us to evaluate the viability and performance of our approach; in Sect. 6 we present the design and results of our performance experiments. We conclude the paper in Sect. 7 with a summary and a discussion of further work we expect in this open research area.

2   Web API Management

There is no universal definition of this space, and little academic research as yet, but the authors' industrial experience in this area, together with a review of [8,10,18] identifies a set of key areas to be addressed:

- Publishing details of the APIs, documentation, SDKs and other human- and machine-readable material in a portal aimed at developers.
- Allowing developers to sign up, define application clients, test out Web APIs, and subscribe to them.

- Managing access control and authentication of API clients using "API keys" or tokens.
- Usage control and throttling of traffic to specific clients based on a Service Level Agreement (SLA) or other factors.
- Monitoring the usage of specific clients in order to be able to limit access or charge for API usage.

One of the key aims of API Management is a desire to manage these aspects *orthogonally* from the creation of the API itself. This is a major benefit to developers or organizations that wish to expose APIs, because these capabilities can be added in a standard way to their systems without requiring custom development that is specific to the application or business logic.

This is often achieved by the use of a pattern called a "reverse proxy", where the client believes it is connecting to the API itself, but the reverse proxy intercepts these calls, and acts upon them before passing them onto the "target" API. This pattern of infrastructure is also often known as a server-side gateway.

3 Related Work

While there is a great deal of industrial effort and research on Web API management, the academic literature is sparse. In the industrial sector, much of the literature is provided by vendors. However, the report by Forrester [8] provides a good overview. In the academic literature, Raivio et al. [14] explore the business models around Open APIs for the telecommunications industry, and we discuss in [9] the challenges and approaches of managing Web APIs.

In the IoT space, there are a number of efforts around creating open APIs for IoT: for instance, HyperCat [11] is a JSON-based catalogue format for exposing IoT information over the web, developed by a consortium of academic and industrial partners, and ZettaJS [21] is an open source Web API for IoT devices.

There are a number of existing IoT gateways, including [2,4,22], that deal with the problem of connecting wireless devices to the wider Internet. They typically bridge multiple low-power devices in a house or factory into a traditional Internet connection. However, our literature search did not identify any server-side gateways/reverse proxies specifically designed for IoT.

We identified two significant gaps in the current literature and existing work in this space. Firstly, most of the work on using APIs with IoT are very limited: there is a common assumption that devices will only communicate with a single API, and there is no discussion of management of these APIs beyond access control. In the access control space, there is a reliance on using outdated models of authentication and authorization (passwords and/or client-side certificates) that are not suitable for device-to-server communication. Two papers address this with token-based authentication schemes: in [7], we addressed the use of OAuth2 with MQTT, and in IOT-OAS [3], Cirani et al. address the use of OAuth2 with CoAP. However, neither of these publications deal with the wider issues around API Management including monitoring, usage control, simplicity of key issuing, developer portals, and monetisation. Furthermore, neither of these works suggests the use of DCR as a means of ensuring the uniqueness of tokens stored on hardware.

Secondly, when looking at the API Management related work, we found no research that addresses how API Management techniques can be used in the face of IoT specific challenges, especially when using IoT-friendly binary protocols such as MQTT and CoAP. These protocols are important for IoT because of the lower requirements for energy and the lower cost of components required to support them.

4   Challenges for the Internet of Things and Web APIs

There is no accurate number of connected devices, but the best estimates all agree that there are more devices currently than humans on the planet. Cisco forecasts that there will be 50 billion connected devices by 2020 [6].

From our experience working with commercial customers of Web API management software, we find that most Web APIs have tens, hundreds or maybe thousands of known clients. These clients act as machine-to-machine systems where one Web server connects to another Web server.

Most new Web APIs are working with the OAuth2 [5] standard and utilising the "Bearer Token" as the API Key. One of the challenges of moving from a model where the API clients are themselves Web servers to a more diverse model where the clients are devices is that the security of these devices is typically much easier to compromise than the security of Web servers. This problem has become apparent with mobile devices. Mobile application developers must embed the OAuth2 credentials into their mobile apps, and because those mobile devices can be "rooted", these credentials can be stolen. There are solutions to this such as Samsung Knox [17], but these are proprietary and only suitable for high-end devices. This rules them out for many IoT devices.

Therefore we envisage that IoT devices will be more likely to need their own OAuth2 credentials per device. It is impractical to think that these client keys will be issued manually to the IoT devices: this process must be automated. DCR is the API that automates the process that a developer would go through on the API portal to gain OAuth2 credentials on behalf of their API client. We therefore intend to use our prototype to explore the use of DCR in IoT scenarios. We think this is an important contribution of this paper.

We are not aware of any API yet in production where millions of devices each have their own API key, their own set of throttling measures, etc. It can therefore be seen that API management systems will need to evolve to support very large numbers of keys, with millions or even tens of millions of concurrently connected devices.

Another challenge is that IoT devices are often low-powered and reliant on low energy usage. Protocols such as MQTT and CoAP are lower in bandwidth which has a direct effect on energy usage, especially in wireless transmission scenarios. Nicholas [13] shows that MQTT uses considerably less energy that

HTTPS in comparative scenarios. This is particularly true in scenarios where notifications need to be sent to devices ("push" scenarios). The traditional way to do this in Web APIs was to require the client to poll the server on a regular basis for updates, which is very expensive in energy and bandwidth usage.

In summary, our work is addressing how to adapt the existing Web API management capabilities to support:

– Large numbers of clients, each with their own credential, issued via DCR.
– Devices communicating with public APIs via binary and low-energy protocols such as MQTT and CoAP.
– Usage control, access control, throttling and other API management techniques applied to IoT scenarios.
– How to apply these capabilities orthogonally to existing systems.

5   IGNITE - An API Gateway for IoT Protocols

To solve these issues we are building a system that allows using the capabilities of existing API management solutions with IoT protocols. We call the system IGNITE (Intelligent Gateway for Network IoT Events)[1]. Our initial work focuses on the MQTT protocol, but in future we intend to extend this to CoAP.

For our proof-of-concept prototype, we extended three major existing open source projects:

– The WSO2 API Manager [19] project provides the main capabilities for Web API Management including a developer portal, subscription management system, key server, API gateway, access control, throttling, monitoring and analytics system;
– The MITREid-Connect project implements of OAuth2 and OpenID Connect [15] and includes new capabilities such as Dynamic Client Registation and Token Introspection.
– The Mosquitto MQTT broker provides an open source messaging broker for the MQTT protocol.

As of March 2015, upcoming releases of both the WSO2 API Manager and the MITREid-Connect projects plan to support using these two projects in conjunction with each other. Both projects are written in Java.

In conjunction with these projects we have created an API management gateway for IoT — a reverse proxy for IoT protocols that plugs into the existing key server architecture and monitoring capabilities.

We currently have built a first prototype of this gateway in Python and we are porting it to Java to improve performance. Figure 1 shows the overall architecture with the capabilities of the existing projects plus our added capabilities.

The IGNITE component implements the following logic: On a **CONNECT** packet arriving, it extracts the OAuth2 Bearer token from the username field

---

[1] The source code is available at https://github.com/pzfreo/ignite.

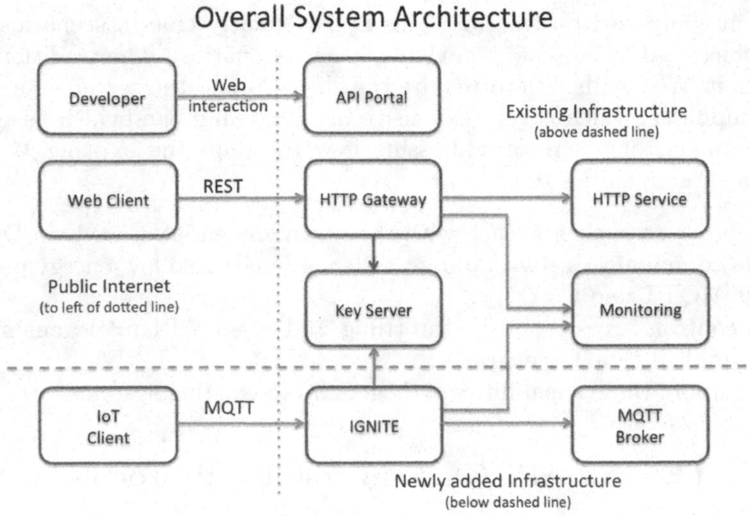

Overall System Architecture

Fig. 1. System architecture

in the packet. It then invokes the Token Introspection service on the MITREid-Connect server to validate the token. If the token is valid, the gateway replaces the token in the request with the userid returned from the introspection call, and forwards the request on to the existing MQTT Broker, which may implement its own validation checks as well. If the token is invalid or no longer active, the IGNITE responds to the client with a packet that indicates that the credential was invalid (a CONNACK packet with ReturnCode=5).

The monitoring and usage control/throttling aspects of IGNITE are still in development.

6 Results

To test the system, we evaluated the performance of this system compared to a direct call to the MQTT broker. In this case, the MQTT broker was not running any authentication of its own, so the comparison is not completely like-for-like. Figure 2 shows the architecture of the test set-up.

We used the open source Mosquitto [12] broker as the backend of the tests and ensured that there was a subscriber attached so that the messages would require delivery. For the tests we sampled two flows: A CONNECT flow and a PUBLISH flow. For PUBLISH we tested all three levels of QoS: fire-and-forget (QoS0), at least once (QoS1) and exactly-once (QoS2). QoS1 and QoS2 involve multiple packets transferring between the client and the server.

The tests were all run on a single machine[2] using the localhost networking. The gateway tests include both the more functional Python prototype of IGNITE

---

[2] Mac OS/X 10.10 running on a 3Ghz Intel Core i7 with 16Gb RAM and SSD storage.

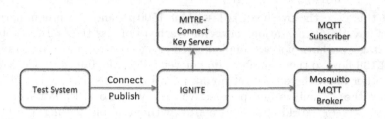

Fig. 2. Test architecture

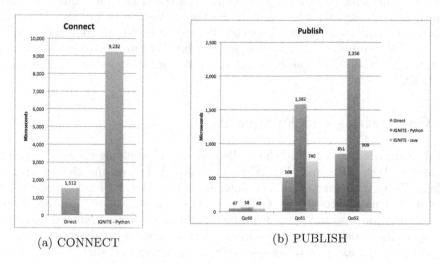

(a) CONNECT   (b) PUBLISH

Fig. 3. Performance results

and an early prototype of the Java version. The tests show the average result over 1,000 CONNECT/CONNACK messages and 10,000 PUBLISH messages, in both cases giving the system time to warm up before capturing timing data. The QoS 1 and 2 tests inherently capture the use of PUBACK, PUBREC, PUBREL, and PUBCOMP messages. The focus on connection was because the authentication step during connection is where the most work takes place, and on publication because this is the most used flow in MQTT, as subscriptions are rare compared to publication.

The CONNECT results are shown in Fig. 3a. The results show that the overhead of using the Python IGNITE for CONNECT is around 7,700µs per request. Given that this includes a HTTP REST call to the key server this is not unexpected. In the WSO2 API Manager this overhead has been reduced by implementing a binary key validation protocol instead of HTTP. However given that MQTT is a persistent connection compared to existing Web API gateways and HTTP where each request needs to be validated we feel this is a very effective result. We did not (yet) implement caching of token introspection results which could improve this considerably.

The PUBLISH numbers (Fig. 3b) show a much lower overhead. For QoS0 the overhead of going through the IGNITE is around 11 µs. The QoS2 case has a significant higher overhead due to considerably more complex message flow.

Even in this case the overhead is less than 1500 µs and the preliminary data from the Java implementation shows an overhead of less than 60 µs. Note that at this stage we have not yet implemented usage control and monitoring into the PUBLISH flow so these numbers do not yet reflect the full workload required. On the other hand there is as yet no optimisation of this prototype code.

To put these numbers into perspective, the typical overhead of such a gateway in the HTTP world is around 500 µs without implementing any OAuth2 token introspection [1]. In addition, these numbers are all likely to be dwarfed by average internet latencies. For example, the speed of light requires a minimum latency of 40,000 µs between the East and West Coasts of the USA, and typical real-world latencies are twice this. Even with prototype code and no optimization, these numbers are respectable and would fit into the tolerance of many existing IoT projects. Therefore we can conclude that this approach is eminently practicable.

7   Conclusions and Further Work

In this paper we have outlined the challenges around applying the newly emerging area of Web APIs and Web API to connected devices and the Internet of Things. We outline our model of enhancing existing Web API management systems with a new gateway — IGNITE — that focuses on IoT protocols and demonstrates how protocols such as MQTT can be integrated into existing API Management models with some success, in a completely orthogonal manner. We have also demonstrated the use of DCR to ensure that each device has its own credentials. In addition, the model of the server-side IoT gateway that we have introduced with IGNITE offers a considerable number of possibilities for managing usage control, access control, monitoring, etc.

We have identified a number of areas for future research. There is work on improving the IGNITE: to support CoAP, to optimize performance; to integrate into the monitoring framework; and to support throttling of traffic. In addition we believe there is considerable scope for research to be done on description languages for using MQTT and CoAP for IoT Web APIs.

Finally we present preliminary data on performance which shows that the overheads of such approaches are reasonable even before optimisation, caching and other techniques are introduced.

Acknowledgements. The travel expenses of presenting this research paper were funded by the University of Portsmouth, Faculty of Technology Research Capital Investment Fund (RCIF) number 46175.

References

1. Abeyruwan, D.: ESB Performance Round 6.5 — WSO2 Inc. http://wso2.com/library/articles/2013/01/esb-performance-65/#latency. Accessed 24 March 2015

2. Chen, H., Jia, X., Li, H.: A brief introduction to IoT gateway. In: IET International Conference on Communication Technology and Application (ICCTA 2011), pp. 610–613 (2011)
3. Cirani, S., Picone, M., Gonizzi, P., Veltri, L., Ferrari, G.: Iot-oas: an oauth-based authorization service architecture for secure services in iot scenarios. IEEE Sens. J. **15**(2), 1224–1234 (2015)
4. Datta, S.K., Bonnet, C., Nikaein, N.: An IoT gateway centric architecture to provide novel M2M services. In: 2014 IEEE World Forum on Internet of Things (WF-IoT), pp. 514–519. IEEE (2014)
5. Hardt, D. (ed.): The OAuth 2.0 Authorization Framework. RFC 6749, IETF, October 2012. http://www.rfc-editor.org/rfc/rfc6749.txt
6. Evans, D.: The internet of things. How the Next Evolution of the Internet is Changing Everything, Whitepaper, Cisco Internet Business Solutions Group (IBSG) (2011)
7. Fremantle, P., Aziz, B., Scott, P., Kopecky, J.: Federated identity and access management for the internet of things. In: 3rd International Workshop on the Secure IoT (2014)
8. Heffner, R.: The Forrester Wave^{TM}: API Management Solutions, Q3 2014 (2014)
9. Kopecky, J., Fremantle, P., Boakes, R.: A history and future of Web APIs. Inf. Technol. **56**, 90–97 (2014)
10. Lane, K.: API Evangelist Blog. http://apievangelist.com/blog/ Accessed 24 March 2015
11. Lea, R.: HyperCat: an IoT interoperability specification (2013)
12. Mosquitto: An Open Source MQTT v3.1 Broker. http://mosquitto.org/. Accessed 13 November 2013
13. Nicholas, S.: Power Profiling: HTTPS Long Polling vs. MQTT with SSL, on Android. http://stephendnicholas.com/archives/1217. Accessed 04 June 2013
14. Raivio, Y., Luukkainen, S., Seppala, S.: Towards open telco-business models of API management providers. In: 2011 44th Hawaii International Conference on System Sciences (HICSS), pp. 1–11. IEEE (2011)
15. Richer, J., Greenwood, D., Bakis, B.: Componentization of security principles. In: Symposium on Usable Privacy and Security (SOUPS) (2014)
16. Sakimura, N., Bradley, J., Jones, M.: Final: OpenID Connect Dynamic Client Registration 1.0 incorporating errata set 1. http://openid.net/specs/openid-connect-registration-1_0.html
17. Samsung: Mobile Enterprise Security — Samsung KNOX. https://www.samsungknox.com/en (2015). Accessed 24 March 2015
18. Williams, A.: 5 Rules For API Management — TechCrunch. http://techcrunch.com/2012/11/11/5-rules-for-api-management/, Accessed 24 March 2015
19. WSO2: WSO2 API Manager - 100% Open Source API Management Platform — WSO2 Inc. http://wso2.com/products/api-manager/
20. Xively: Xively by LogMeIn - Business Solutions for the Internet of Things. https://xively.com/
21. ZettaJS: Zetta - An API-First Internet of Things (IoT) Platform - Free and Open Source Software. http://www.zettajs.org/
22. Zhu, Q., Wang, R., Chen, Q., Liu, Y., Qin, W.: IoT gateway: bridging wireless sensor networks into internet of things. In: 2010 IEEE/IFIP 8th International Conference on Embedded and Ubiquitous Computing (EUC), pp. 347–352. IEEE (2010)

A RESTful Approach for Developing Medical Decision Support Systems

Tobias Weller[1]([✉]), Maria Maleshkova[1], Keno März[2],
and Lena Maier-Hein[2]

[1] AIFB, Karlsruhe Institute of Technology (KIT), Karlsruhe, Germany
{tobias.weller,maria.maleshkova}@kit.edu
[2] German Cancer Research Center, Heidelberg, Germany
{k.maerz,l.maier-hein}@dkfz.de

Abstract. Current developments in the medical sector are witnessing the growing digitalization of data in terms of patient tests, records and trials, use of sensors for monitoring and recording procedures, and employing digital imagery. Besides the increasing number of published guidelines and studies, it has been shown that clinicians are often unable to observe these guidelines correctly during the actual care process. [1] The increasing number of guidelines and studies, and also the fact that physicians are often unable to observe these guidelines correctly provide the foundation for this paper. We will tackle these problems by developing a medical assistance system which processes the gathered and integrated data from different sources, and assists the physicians in making decisions, preparing treatment plans, and even guide surgeons during invasive procedures. In this paper we demonstrate how a RESTful architecture combined with applying Linked Data principles for data storage and exchange can effectively be used for developing medical decision support systems. We propose different autonomous subsystems that automatically process data relevant to their purpose. These so-called "Cognitive Apps" provide RESTful interfaces and perform tasks such as converting and uploading data and deducing medical knowledge by using inference rules. The result is an adaptive decision support system, based on distributed decoupled Cognitive Apps, which can preprocess data in advance but also support real-time scenarios. We demonstrate the practical applicability of our approach by providing an implementation of a system for processing patients with liver tumors. Finally, we evaluate the system in terms of knowledge deduction and performance.

1 Introduction

The growing use of sensors in the medical domain, designated devices for recording patient data, and the digitalization of medical knowledge in terms of recording trials or medical guidelines result in large data volumes, which are hard to process and manage by individual physicians. Nowadays, most of the patient data is stored in semi-structured document formats such as spreadsheets, while the results of clinical trials are published directly as text in papers. At the same

© Springer International Publishing Switzerland 2015
F. Gandon et al. (Eds.): ESWC 2015, LNCS 9341, pp. 376–384, 2015.
DOI: 10.1007/978-3-319-25639-9_50

time more and more sensors are being used to observe patients, resulting in large data volumes. As a consequence, not only is it difficult to benefit from all available data in order to solve a particular medical case, it also becomes unfeasible for a physician to mentally process all the patient data according to current clinical studies and keep track of new studies at the same time. To alleviate this situation, we have presented a concept to support clinical decision making using holistic data analysis [3]. This paper shows the realization of this vision using a RESTful architecture for medical decision support systems, which supports physicians at a decision. In particular, we advocate a solution based on formally modeling patient data with RDF and applying Linked Data principles to publish and interlink individual records [3]. Furthermore, we incorporate studies by describing them as formalized rules in RDF.

These rules are interpreted and executed by multiple Cognitive Apps, which are accessible via a RESTful interface and consume and produce Linked Data. This provides flexible and adaptive composition of the system. In summary, this paper makes the following contributions:

1. We describe a rule-based decision system built up from individual Cognitive Apps.
2. We introduce an exemplary Cognitive App for processing medical guidelines, with a RESTful interface and described in Linked Data.
3. We provide a specific implementation for a use case scenario and demonstrate the added value in terms of automatically deduced additional patient knowledge.
4. We show the suitability of the rule-based decision support system for real-time scenarios, while dealing with large data volumes.

This paper is structured as follows: the following section introduces our medical scenario. Section 3 describes our approach toward designing a decoupled REST-based decision support system, while Sect. 4 provides the specific implementation details. We demonstrate the practical applicability of our solution by realizing a specific medical use case and evaluating the added value to the decision support. We evaluate the system in terms of its suitability of supporting real-time scenarios, in cases where physicians need data usable within intraoperative situations (Sect. 5). In addition, we will show how many new facts were generated by applying the inference rules to the patient data. Finally, related work is described in Sect. 6, and we summarize our contributions and provide some conclusions in Sect. 7.

2   Motivation Scenario

Despite the abundance of medical data, currently, the choice of treatment is usually not obvious, as it depends on a wide range of factors. In a previous publication, we defined three concepts [3]:

(i) Patient data represents all data that can be acquired for a patient for whom the treatment plan is prepared. This information can be extracted from images, laboratory reports or other sources of information (e.g. clinical reports,

hospital databases etc.). It can be related to the disease, the organ anatomy and function or general information (e.g. age, habits etc.). *(ii) Factual knowledge* is written down in quotable sources (e.g. clinical guidelines, studies). This allows the physician to make predictions about the morbidity and mortality of the disease and the possible interventions. Guidelines give more specific directions on treatment options for a specific patient. However, they typically merely give rough directions, taking into account only a fraction of the patient individual parameters (e.g. size and number of tumors), while detailed treatment decisions remain to the surgeon *(iii) Practical knowledge* results from experience. It comprises case knowledge that encompasses the ability to interpret patient data, form a prognosis and deduce implications for the treatment, as well as expert knowledge about treatment options and their respective strengths and weaknesses.

The challenges of diagnosing and providing patient individual treatment plans, can be summarized as follows: (i) collect and integrate patient data so that it can be processed and interpreted in a unified manner; (ii) capture factual knowledge given in the form of medical guidelines by formalizing it in terms of rules; (iii) compensate for the lack of observing the factual knowledge. We address all challenges, focusing especially on the last one, by developing an approach for automatically deducing further patient knowledge in the form of mortality probabilities, procedure level of suitability, etc. by applying the rules from (ii) on the patient knowledge base (i), thus compensating for the lack of observing factual knowledge (iii).

3   Developing a Decision Support System

In the following, we describe in detail our design for realizing a decision support system capable of supporting this scenario, as well as being flexible enough for enabling further medical scenarios.

Figure 1 shows a high-level overview of a decision support system for deducing additional patient knowledge. We adopt a classical three-tier architecture including – Data tier, Business-logic tier, and Client tier.

Data tier – semantic knowledge base consisting of distributed interlinked repositories: (1) a central file storage (**XNAT**), which is used to store data generated by users and other systems, and make this data accessible within the knowledge base. (2) a semantic Wiki (**Surgipedia**), which is the data hub in the system and allows modelling metadata and linking it to all knowledge base relevant data instances. For example, Surgipedia contains links to files stored in XNAT or other external data sources. Furthermore, it provides support for annotating the medical guidelines with metadata. (3) a repository for storing **Patient data** where all patient test results are saved, based on a formally specified patient model. (4) a repository for storing factual knowledge in the form of medical guidelines and studies (**Rules**). Rules are formally defined in N3 format, so that they can directly be applied to the patient data. (5) a repository for commonly used data models (**Onto 1**). Data in the knowledge base is published using the Linked Data principles. In this way, the interoperability between the

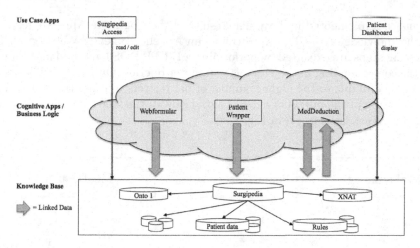

Fig. 1. High-Level overview of the decision support system for deducing patient knowledge

components of the system, the integration of new data into the knowledge base and the ability to interpret this data is realized and guaranteed.

Business-logic tier – implemented via distributed reusable RESTful processing blocks in the form of Cognitive Apps. The communication and interaction between the knowledge base and the Cognitive Apps is based on RESTful interfaces. Cognitive Apps are Web APIs, which also have a semantic description based on the Linked Data principles. The RESTful architecture and the semantic description allows interpreters like Data-Fu [4] to automatically execute Cognitive Apps. This particular scenario includes the following Cognitive Apps – the **PatientWrapper** automatically converts the patient test results into a shared patient model and stores them in the knowledge base. The **Webformular** provides a semi-automated support for converting the medical guidelines into formalised rules in RDF. It takes as input the published studies and the manually composed guidelines via an input GUI and generates corresponding rules. Finally, **MedDeduction** uses the patient data and the rules in order to automatically generate new patient knowledge via deduction and thus provide more data for supporting a better decision.

Client tier – implemented via individual Use Case Apps supporting specific physician decision tasks. For this particular scenario, we have implemented a Use Case App for inputting medical guidelines, in order to assist the process of extracting formalized rules. Another Use Case App provides a user interface for displaying the deduced patient knowledge, including predictions for the morbidity and mortality of a certain intervention (Hepatectomy).

4   Patient Knowledge Deductive System

In this section we describe the implementation of the decision support system, which consists of four Cognitive Apps (PatientWrapper, MedDeduction, Patient-Generator and WebFormular) and the Knowledge Base. These components of the system are implemented in Java. The results of the Cognitive Apps are fed back into the knowledge base. The Apps run on an Apache Tomcat 7 Web Server. The processing steps are executed by performing a HTTP POST method and submitting the corresponding parameters as parameter queries. Only the WebFormular is not RESTful due to the higher number of parameters that are transferred during processing of the inference rules. An overview of the steps of each component in the business tier is given in Fig. 2.

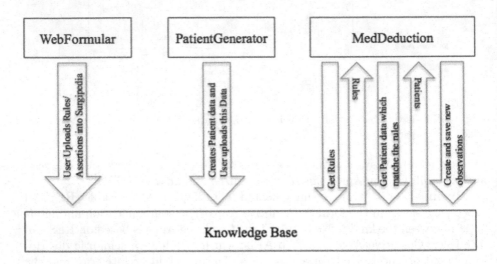

Fig. 2. Overview of the steps of each component in the business tier

The **WebFormular**[1] is a HTML page for entering the medical guidelines in the form of rules. It is divided in two parts – the condition part of the inference rule and the conclusions. An example rule is {hasHepatectomy ∧ hasHCC ∧ Albumin < 40} → {Death due to progression after 1 Year is 0.1336} (**Rule ID: 423**). The preprocessing of the entered conditions and implications will be done within a .jsp file. A servlet converts the preprocessed data into the inference rule in N3 format and provides it for downloading. Thereby the user receives the inference rule in RDF and proceeds to upload it into Surgipedia and link it to a wiki page. In addition, the user can enter metadata about the rule. In this way medical guidelines from publications can be stored and described in the knowledge base.

Due to privacy constraints real patient data cannot be used for testing our system implementation. Evaluation has been performed in [3] with a smaller amount of real patient data. This paper validates the technical concept on a large scale by using a large number of patients. Therefore, the **PatientGenerator**[2], which is a Cognitive App that generates patient data for testing the correctness

---

[1] https://github.com/TobiasWeller/Webformular.

[2] https://github.com/TobiasWeller/Patientgenerator.

and performance of the implementation, as well as for evaluating the knowledge deduction process helps by generating a large number of patients. For example, we generated the Patient 4.899960.7 with an Albumin value of 32.1483 g/dL. The parameters for this patient fit one of the rules. So later on, it will be deduced that this patient has Hepatectomy and HCC.

The **Patient Wrapper**[3] performs a HTTP POST request and takes as input the patient data (in a spreadsheet format) and the predefined patient model. The patient data is then transformed into RDF and uploaded to the knowledge base.

Once the rules and the patient data are in the system, we can deduce additional medical knowledge. In order to do this, the **MedDeduction**[4] retrieves the rules from the knowledge base, checks if patients matches the conditions of the rules, and inserts the corresponding deduced new triples. In total it provides four functions. The first function is for deducing all inference rules for all patients. The second deduces one inference rule for all patients. The third tries to deduce all inference rules for one patient. The fourth is for deducing one inference rule for one patient. The Cognitive App can be executed by performing a HTTP POST request and transmitting the corresponding parameters. The HTTP POST request for executing the deducing process is the following:

```
curl POST http://aifb-ls3-vm2.aifb.kit.edu:8080/MedDeduction/
Executer/AllRuleAllPatient
```

Our approach towards implementing the decision support system provides a very flexible distributed solution, where new processing components, i.e. Cognitive Apps, can be integrated on demand, while alternatives providing the same functionality can be used to optimize the results.

5 Evaluation

We evaluate the implemented decision support system based on two criteria – knowledge deduction and performance evaluation. For the knowledge deduction we show that there was new knowledge deduced by applying the formalized rules. For the performance evaluation we show that the system supports real-time scenarios and we compare the results to a local execution of the system. In order to conduct the experiments, we generated 1,000 patients with the help of the Patient Generator. The values for the corresponding factors were randomly generated according to a given range. We used 60 rules, which were taken from studies , and converted with the help of the Webformular. **Knowledge Deduction** In total there were 18,444 new facts generated or rather 129,108 new triples (one fact consists of 7 triples). There were no new patients generated. There was no new knowledge deduced for 4 out of the 1,000 patients, because no rule fit to these patients. The rule that generated most new facts was the following: `{MilanCriteriaFulfilled = True} → {hasHepatectomy = True}`

---

[3] https://github.com/TobiasWeller/PatientWrapper.
[4] https://github.com/TobiasWeller/MedDeducter.

In total this rule took 9.141 s on the server and was performed for 861 Patients. The rule that took the shortest time was: {ColorectalCarcinoma = True ∧ hasHepatectomy = True} → {Probability of 2 YearDisease Free Survival = 0.37}
In total, this rule took 0.09 s on the server and did not result in new facts or triples. We looked up among others observations created by these two rules to comprehend the results. The deduction was performed correctly and did not lead to flawed observations.

Performance Evaluation. We compared the performance between execution on a local and on a remote system. The first experiment runs the deduction process locally on a workstation and communicates with the knowledge base over the Web (**Local**). The second experiment runs the deduction process on a remote virtual machine (**Remote**). However, the virtual machine is on the same system as the knowledge base. The local machine has 4 Cores at 2.93 Ghz with 8 GB memory. The virtual machine has 4 Cores at 2.6 Ghz with 16 GB memory.

We compared for each rule the number of new facts that were generated. Both, the local and the remote experiment used the same inference rules and patient data, and produced the same number of facts. All results were valid and the number of facts, generated by both experiments, were the same. Naturally, the runtimes were different. Table 1 contains the measured results. We measured the total runtime for deducing all 60 rules, the shortest time for deducing a rule and the longest time, as well as the average time for deducing one rule.

Table 1. Evaluation local vs. remote deployment

Experiment	Total runtime	Min time p. rule	Max time p. rule	Avg. time p. rule
Local	20.575 min	0.337 sec (0 Facts)	80.31 sec (855 Facts)	0.067 sec
Remote	3.843 min	0.09 sec (0 Facts)	13.066 sec (0 Facts)	0.013 sec

It can be clearly seen that the remote system has and advantage against the local solution. However, this is based on the fact that the deductive system runs on the same machine as knowledge base. Therefore, no long transmission time is needed to transfer the data. In three cases, the experiment on the remote server took longer than the local experiment. However, these rules had not generated new observations.

In total 18,444 new observations were created during a total runtime of 3.843 min for the remote experiment. This leads to 0.013 facts and rule per second. Since in average the deduction of a fact for one rule takes 0.013 s, we can assume that for 1,000 rules the deduction for one patient sums up to 13 s. This makes the decision support system suitable for real-time use cases, where the physician can immediately take the additional knowledge into consideration for making a decision and planning an appropriate treatment.

6   Related Work

IBM Research developed in collaboration with the Cleveland Clinic Lerner College of Medicine of Case Western Reserve University a medical domain expert system. This cognitive computing technology, called WatsonPaths, supports clinical reasoning by exploring a complex scenario and drawing conclusions. It pulls its knowledge from reference materials, clinical guidelines and medical journals in real-time. On the base of this knowledge, it disproves a set of hypotheses to generate new factors in order to support diagnosis and treatment options.[5]

Another development is the FM-Ultranet [5,6]. This is a decision support system using case-based reasoning in the ultrasonography sector. This decision support system exploits image analysis and pattern recognition techniques to improve and train ultrasound scans interpretation and diagnosis of foetus malformations and abnormalities. Thereby it uses past similar ultrasound scans, stored in the database, for interpreting and diagnosing the actual scans.

CARE-PARTNER is a computerised medical knowledge-support assistance that offers its functionality on the web [2]. It proposes case-based and rules-based reasoning and information retrieval methods to provide useful knowledge to physicians. The system is implemented on the concept of evidence-based medical practice.

7   Conclusions

The increasing digitalization of medical data calls for new solutions that support physicians in planning a treatment strategy. To this end, we introduced a rule-based medical decision support system based on a decoupled distributed RESTful architecture. We combined REST with Linked Data to present a novel approach that has not been previously tested in the medical domain. The system consists of multiple Cognitive Apps that process the medical data. The so implemented system successfully derives additional knowledge about patients, thus assisting the physicians in making decisions. As shown in the valuation section, the system is also suitable for real-time scenarios.

The future work includes the integration of further information sources in order to enlarge the number of inference rules. A significant contribution, therefore, would be the automated extraction of inference rules from studies and guidelines.

Acknowledgments. This work was carried out with the support of the German Research Foundation (DFG) as part of project A02, I01, and S01, SFB/TRR 125 Cognition-Guided Surgery. We would particularly like to thank Patrick Philipp, Mohammadreza Hafezi, Arianeb Mehrabi and Marco Nolden. All of the authors state no conflict of interests. All studies have been approved and performed in accordance with ethical standards. Patient data were gathered and evaluated under informed consent only.

---

[5] http://www.research.ibm.com/cognitive-computing/watson/watsonpaths.shtml.

References

1. De Clercq, P., Kaiser, K., Hasman, A.: Computer-interpretable guideline formalisms. Stud. Health Technol. Inform. **139**, 22–43 (2008)
2. Bichindaritz, I., Kansu, E., Sullivan, K.M.: Case-based reasoning in CARE-PARTNER: gathering evidence for evidence-based medical practice. In: Smyth, B., Cunningham, P. (eds.) EWCBR 1998. LNCS (LNAI), vol. 1488, p. 334. Springer, Heidelberg (2006)
3. März, K., Hafezi, M., Weller, T., Saffari, A., Nolden, M., Fard, N., Majlesara, A., Zelzer, S., Maleshkova, M., Volovyk, M., Gharabaghi, N., Wagner, M., Emami, G., Engelhardt, S., Fetzer, A., Kenngott, H., Rezai, N., Rettinger, A., Studer, R., Mehrabi, A., Maier-Hein, L.: Toward knowledge-based liver surgery: holistic information processing for surgical decision support. Int. J. Comput. Assist. Radiol. Surg. **10**, 749–759 (2015)
4. Stadtmüller, S., Speiser, S., Harth, A., Studer, R.: Data-Fu: a language and an interpreter for interaction with read/write linked data. In: International World Wide Web Conferences Steering Committee, pp. 1225–1236 (2013)
5. Balaa, Z.E., Strauss, A., Maximini, K.: Fm-ultranet: a decision support system using case-based reasoning, applied to ultrasonography. In: Workshop on CBR in the Health Sciences, p. 3 (2003)
6. Balaa, Z.E., Traphoener, R.: Case-based decision support and experience management for ultrasonography. In: German Workshop on Experience Management, GWEM 2003, pp. 277–278 (2003)

3rd International Workshop on Human Semantic Web Interaction (HSWI)

QueryVOWL: A Visual Query Notation
for Linked Data

Florian Haag(✉), Steffen Lohmann, Stephan Siek,
and Thomas Ertl

Institute for Visualization and Interactive Systems, University of Stuttgart,
Universitätsstraße 38, 70569 Stuttgart, Germany
{florian.haag,steffen.lohmann,thomas.ertl}@vis.uni-stuttgart.de

Abstract. In order to enable users without any knowledge of RDF and
SPARQL to query Linked Data, visual approaches can be helpful by providing graphical support for query building. We present QueryVOWL,
a visual query language that is based upon the ontology visualization
VOWL and defines mappings to SPARQL. We aim for a language that
is intuitive and easy to use, while remaining flexible and preserving
most of the expressiveness of SPARQL. In contrast to related work, the
queries can be created entirely with visual elements, taking into account
RDFS and OWL concepts often used to structure Linked Data. This
paper is a revised version of a workshop paper where we first introduced
QueryVOWL. We present the query notation, some example queries, and
two prototypical implementations of QueryVOWL. Also, we report on a
qualitative user study that indicates lay users are able to construct and
interpret QueryVOWL graphs.

Keywords: Visual querying · VOWL · QueryVOWL · Visualization ·
Linked Data · SPARQL · RDF · OWL · Semantic Web

1   Introduction

An increasing amount of Linked Data is being published and ready for consumption [4,12]. The data is not only of interest to the Semantic Web community but
first and foremost to lay users and domain experts from different areas [17]. A
large portion of Linked Data is available in RDF format and can be queried using
the standardized query language SPARQL [6,12]. However, writing SPARQL
queries is not an easy task and requires technical knowledge on RDF, HTTP,
and IRIs, among others. Lay users cannot be expected to have this knowledge,
but visual interfaces can provide graphical support for querying Linked Data.
The interfaces must enable the flexible creation of queries without any knowledge
of RDF, SPARQL, and related Semantic Web technologies.

Experience from relational databases and SQL querying can only partly be
reused, as the data is organized in fixed table structures in those databases.
Linked Data, by contrast, is often represented as an RDF graph, which is more

© Springer International Publishing Switzerland 2015
F. Gandon et al. (Eds.): ESWC 2015, LNCS 9341, pp. 387–402, 2015.
DOI: 10.1007/978-3-319-25639-9_51

related to the representation of data in graph databases, and SPARQL is used to retrieve information from this graph-based data. Appropriate solutions must therefore address the unique specifics of SPARQL and Linked Data, such as the schema-independent description of resources and the use of IRIs for global identification.

This paper presents QueryVOWL, a novel approach for visual querying that reuses graphical elements from the Visual Notation for OWL Ontologies (VOWL) [28] and defines SPARQL mappings for them. The paper is a revised and extended version of our paper for the HSWI workshop [21], where we first introduced QueryVOWL.

2   Related Work

Several approaches to support the querying of Linked Data have been proposed in the last couple of years. A popular paradigm is form-based querying, where the queries are composed by entering variables, identifiers, and other query components using form elements, such as text boxes with auto-completion features, drop-down lists, and radio buttons. Examples of form-based querying include SPARQLViz [14], Konduit VQB [7], PepeSearch [22], or DBpedia's Graph Pattern Builder [8]. While form-based querying can be very usable, it offers a rather linear way of query building that is less flexible than other querying paradigms. Furthermore, most of the available approaches are not designed for lay users but for people who have at least some knowledge of RDF and SPARQL and are familiar with the triple representation.

Graph-based querying usually provides more flexibility than the form-based paradigm by using node-link diagrams to create arbitrary SPARQL query patterns. Examples for such approaches include NITELIGHT [31], iSPARQL [5], RDF-GL [25], and LUPOSDATE [18]. However, the visual query languages used in these tools are still very close to the RDF and SPARQL syntax: Although the triples are visually combined to node-link diagrams, they strictly follow the subject-predicate-object notation from RDF instead of providing a higher degree of abstraction. While this is fine for expert users, lay users are known to have problems with the low-level semantics of RDF graphs [17].

The same holds true for many works that visualize queries on a slightly higher degree of abstraction. One such approach supports the composition of SPARQL queries with UML-based diagrams [9]. These diagrams can further reduce the challenges of querying Linked Data, but they are still comparatively difficult to use for lay users [29].

Other approaches completely depart from the SPARQL syntax. For instance, SparqlFilterFlow [19] supports the visual composition of SPARQL queries by letting users create filters connected by flows. However, edges in SparqlFilterFlow represent logical connections between filter criteria rather than property links between classes or individuals. Thus, the focus is on the logical combination of filter criteria, whereas object relations made explicit in QueryVOWL are not directly displayed.

Furthermore, Linked Data can be queried as part of the browsing process by generating and sending SPARQL queries in the background. Examples of such Linked Data browsers include Tabulator [11], Disco [2], and gFacet [24], among others [17]. These browsers are comparatively easy to use, but rely on particular patterns of queries and are therefore limited in their flexibility and expressiveness. Similar constraints apply to visual approaches that query Linked Data for specific purposes, such as relationship discovery [23] or to explore context information about locations [10].

QueryVOWL is related to visual querying approaches for graph databases, such as qGraph [13], or a visual graph-based system for genomics data [16]. In contrast to those attempts, QueryVOWL specifically addresses RDF and SPARQL that Linked Data is usually based on, and defines reusable mappings for the visual language. It is therefore related to open web standards and the well-specified VOWL notation. This is different from visual querying approaches in the context of graph databases, which often use underspecified or proprietary languages supported only by specific graph databases.

3   QueryVOWL

We decided to base the visual query language on the VOWL notation, which has proven to be comparatively intuitive and understandable, also and especially to lay users [28,29]. Furthermore, it provides the degree of abstraction we consider helpful to ease the query building, as VOWL has been designed for RDFS and OWL, and concepts from these vocabularies are often used to structure Linked Data.

3.1   VOWL

VOWL defines mappings of OWL language constructs to graphical elements that are combined to node-link diagrams. Figure 1 shows the VOWL visualization of a small ontology created with WebVOWL 0.4 [27]. Classes are represented by circles that contain the class name, whereas datatypes are displayed as rectangles with a border. Property names are shown inside borderless rectangles that are complemented by arrow lines indicating the direction of the properties. Some language constructs are expressed in a different way, such as subclass relations or special OWL classes.

In addition, VOWL comes with a set of colors that are defined in an abstract way according to their function in order to allow for custom color schemes. This leaves the freedom to use custom color schemes beside the default scheme recommended by the specification. For each visual element, the applicable colors are specified in abstract terms. For instance, classes can have the "general", "deprecated", or "external" color, datatypes and resources are always shown in their respective fixed color, and a "highlight" color is used to dynamically display certain features of elements in interactive contexts. Shapes and textual labels in VOWL have, however, been chosen in a way so no essential information

Table 1. Visual elements of QueryVOWL and their translation into SPARQL.

QueryVOWL Element	SPARQL Mapping
The VOWL class notation is used to represent sets of individuals. The label indicates the class the individuals are restricted to. If no label is set, the class of the individuals is not restricted. Similar to VOWL, the size of the circle may be used to roughly indicate the number of matching individuals. The exact number is additionally displayed.	Each set of individuals is represented by a unique variable. If the class of the individuals is restricted, that restriction is added as a triple: `?x a dbpo:Volcano .` The number of individuals is retrieved with the `count` function.
The VOWL notation for RDFS classes is used to represent a single individual.	Single individuals are represented by their IRI: `dbpr:Aracar`
The VOWL property notation is used to represent properties that connect sets of individuals and/or single individuals. Like in VOWL, the arrow line indicates the direction of the property.	Properties are represented as predicates in the triples: `?x a dbpo:Album .` `?x dbpp:artist` `dbpr:Vangelis .`
If the VOWL property notation is used without an arrowhead, matching properties can point in both directions.	`?y a dbpo:Politician .` `{ ?x dbpo:child ?y . }` `UNION` `{ ?y dbpo:child ?x . }`
The VOWL literal notation is also used in QueryVOWL. It can be restricted either by using specific values or by applying filters, such as range or pattern restrictions. Literals can be connected to more than one property to define that they shall have the same value as range.	Each literal is represented by a unique variable used in all triples and filters that refer to that literal: `?x a dbpo:Astronaut .` `?y a dbpo:Cyclist .` `?x foaf:surname ?v .` `?y foaf:surname ?v .`
The VOWL notation for disjointedness is used to define that the individuals in different sets are disjoint.	`?x a dbpo:Painter .` `?y a dbpo:Architect .` `FILTER(?x != ?y).`
The VOWL union notation is used to represent the set of individuals that are contained in *at least one* of the connected nodes.	`?x a dbpo:Bird .` `?y a dbpo:Fish .` `{ ?s a dbpo:Bird . }` `UNION` `{ ?s a dbpo:Fish . }`
The VOWL intersection notation is used to represent the set of individuals that are contained in *all* connected nodes.	`?x a dbpo:Painter .` `?y a dbpo:Poet .` `?s a dbpo:Painter ;` `    a dbpo:Poet ;` `    foaf:surname ?n .`

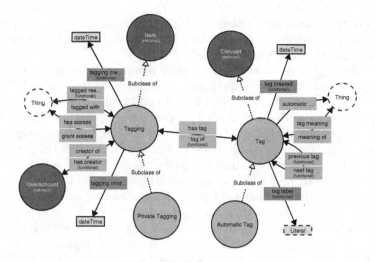

Fig. 1. Small ontology (MUTO [26]) visualized with WebVOWL 0.4 [27].

is lost if the colors are absent [28]. All elements and visual attributes of VOWL are precisely defined in a specification document [30].

3.2 Visual Elements

In contrast to VOWL, which has been designed to visualize complete ontologies, the purpose of QueryVOWL is to express user-defined filter criteria for searching for specific RDF graphs in Linked Data. The basic idea is to visually model a partial graph that is presumed to exist in a dataset. The graph defines certain restrictions, with some of its elements being placeholders. This mimics SPARQL, which allows to define graph patterns where some elements are variables.

When a QueryVOWL graph is applied to a given RDF dataset, all subgraphs from the dataset that match the query are retrieved, as with a SPARQL query. One difference is that the SPARQL query explicitly specifies the format and selection of results (for instance, as a list of table columns), and so do visual queries in related query visualizations [18,31]. In contrast, QueryVOWL enables users to dynamically explore the matches for parts of the graph: QueryVOWL users can select any of the visual query elements to retrieve the set of matching resources. Visualization approaches outside the scope of QueryVOWL can then be used to display the results in a user-friendly way, for instance, on a map or timeline as in NITELIGHT [31] and similar tools.

We started out from the VOWL specification and reused elements and definitions as appropriate for building query graphs. In contrast to VOWL, where each visual element represents a particular conceptual element from the TBox of an ontology [28], visual elements in QueryVOWL can also act as placeholders that are not fully specified on a TBox level, and for which restrictions can be added by the user. Therefore, some VOWL elements had to be adapted to indicate the variability of the IRIs or values they represent, and to provide for the interaction options that users require to specify their query. Unlike other notations [25,31], users do not get in touch with variable names.

The VOWL property notation is used to represent properties that connect specific individuals or sets of individuals, analogously to related work [5,24,25]. Different from VOWL, QueryVOWL allows to add properties without specifying the direction. In these cases, matching properties can point in either direction. It also permits empty property labels, in which case all matching properties are considered. This is related to the idea of the RelFinder [23], in particular, if properties and classes are combined to chains.

Literal nodes can be connected to several datatype properties (also of different objects) to enforce that only individuals with the same value for these properties are found, like in other approaches [18].

Table 1 (above) outlines the visual elements that QueryVOWL consists of, as well as their mappings to SPARQL query fragments. Figure 2 shows a small QueryVOWL graph assembled from the visual elements, along with the SPARQL query that results from the graph based on the selected element.

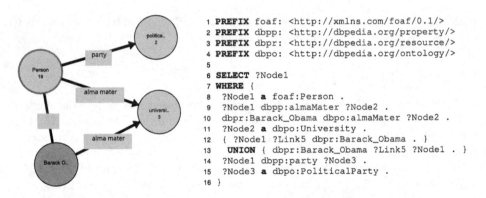

```
 1 PREFIX foaf: <http://xmlns.com/foaf/0.1/>
 2 PREFIX dbpp: <http://dbpedia.org/property/>
 3 PREFIX dbpr: <http://dbpedia.org/resource/>
 4 PREFIX dbpo: <http://dbpedia.org/ontology/>
 5
 6 SELECT ?Node1
 7 WHERE {
 8   ?Node1 a foaf:Person .
 9   ?Node1 dbpp:almaMater ?Node2 .
10   dbpr:Barack_Obama dbpo:almaMater ?Node2 .
11   ?Node2 a dbpo:University .
12   { ?Node1 ?Link5 dbpr:Barack_Obama . }
13     UNION { dbpr:Barack_Obama ?Link5 ?Node1 . }
14   ?Node1 dbpp:party ?Node3 .
15   ?Node3 a dbpo:PoliticalParty .
16 }
```

Fig. 2. Example of a QueryVOWL graph, along with the SPARQL query resulting from that graph (when class *Person* is focused, as indicated by the red border) (Color figure online).

3.3   Interactive Editing

WYSIWYG editing of the query graph can be allowed by adding interactive features to the aforementioned elements. The following four functions are required:

Delete: All visual elements contain a delete button so that they can be removed.
Connect: Properties can be added as links, either as unspecified properties or by choosing from a list of available properties.
Substitute: Any class, individual, and property can be replaced by another class, individual, or property, based on a list of available choices.

Edit: Restrictions on classes, properties, and literal values can be set or removed.

These interactive features may remain hidden unless the elements are pointed at (Fig. 3). In that case, additional information (e.g., IRIs or long labels) or interactive elements that would otherwise not have enough display space may also be shown.

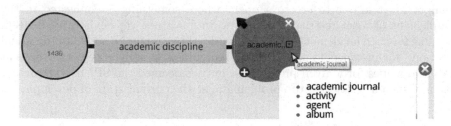

Fig. 3. Interaction elements are usually hidden and only appear on demand.

Whenever the graph structure or restrictions are modified, any connected class nodes will dynamically update their counts. This helps users immediately recognize the effects of their changes and provides them with a way to estimate whether further extensions or restrictions are required to retrieve a meaningful result. Some nodes can be excluded from this update process to reduce server load: Subgraphs that are *exclusively* connected via nodes restricted to specific individuals are only included in the SPARQL query if they contain the focused element. To retrieve all that information, as well as the final result set, the internally generated SPARQL queries are sent to a SPARQL endpoint that can be chosen as a backend in the visualization.

Generation of the SPARQL queries requires only a negligible amount of time, as this merely requires an iteration over all elements found in the query graph, while the statements expressed by these graphical elements are added to the resulting SPARQL query step-by-step. For a QueryVOWL graph that consists only of n class and/or individual nodes and m edges, time complexity of this SPARQL query generation remains within $\mathcal{O}(n \cdot m)$. Depending on the SPARQL engine and the triple store running on the server, the processing time for the query may vary significantly, though.

3.4   Language Limitations

QueryVOWL covers a part of the SPARQL query language, but, to date, also omits some elements. Literal nodes can be restricted based on constant values, and they can be used to express that several individuals are connected to the same property value. A visual representation for other types of relationships, such as inequality or asymmetric relationships (greater than, less than, etc.), has not yet been defined. Furthermore, we focused on a straightforward setup where a query is sent to the default graph of a dedicated endpoint. Federated queries or named graphs are currently not included in QueryVOWL, although it should be noted that implementations might support such features as a part of their backend configuration, without any explicit indication in the QueryVOWL visualization.

There are also some OWL concepts represented by graphical elements in VOWL, for which we did not define related QueryVOWL elements yet. While it might be desirable to create a query where something is connected to the complement of a set restricted by filters, we have not yet devised a SPARQL mapping for such an element. Likewise, cardinalities might be added to the visual notation—for instance, to search for all individuals of a given type that have at most two values for a given property—, but we deemed the SPARQL representation of such a restriction too problematic at the current state of development.

4   Exemplary Queries

The following examples illustrate how the visual elements of QueryVOWL can be assembled to query graphs. As QueryVOWL is independent of any particular dataset, we are using different datasets in the examples, all accessed by their SPARQL endpoints.

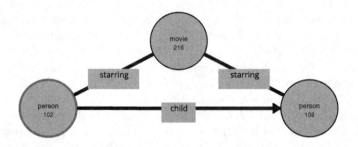

Fig. 4. DBpedia knows about 102 persons who starred in movies together with at least one of their children.

Who *starred* in a *movie* together with his or her *child*? Figure 4 shows a QueryVOWL graph based on DBpedia for retrieving any movies along with two of their actors, one of whom must be the child of the other. The latter actor is focused, as the graph is used to identify the elder actor of the two (according to the direction of the property *child*).

Which *authors* published on both conferences *ESWC* and *WWW* in the same *year*? The QueryVOWL graph created for the Faceted DBLP dataset [3] is depicted in Fig. 5a. It asked for authors of two works, which are linked via the year of issue to indicate that they were published in the same year (any same year). One of the works should belong to the series *ESWC*, the other one to the series *WWW*.

Which *countries* have at least two different *industries* and participate in the *World Health Organization*? This query is shown in Fig. 5b, based on the CIA World Factbook [1]. A *disjoint* edge is used to indicate that the two *Industry* nodes are supposed to map to different individuals in each result. WHO is represented by an individual node.

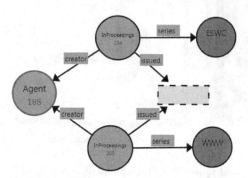
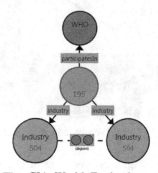

(a) There are 188 authors who published at ESWC and WWW in the same year according to Faceted DBLP.

(b) The CIA World Factbook contains data on 195 countries that have at least two different industries and participate in the World Health Organization.

Fig. 5. Examplary QueryVOWL graphs.

5   Evaluation

We have evaluated the applicability and usability of the approach by implementing it in two interactive prototypes and by conducting a qualitative user study.

5.1   Implementations

The two prototypes are based on different technologies to verify various aspects of the approach and to get an idea of how well it can be implemented with different frameworks and development techniques.

Web-Based Implementation. The web-based prototype (Fig. 6a) implements the main elements of the visual query language and provides an opportunity to try the look and feel of an interactive QueryVOWL implementation.[1] It is based

---

[1] The web-based prototype is available at http://queryvowl.visualdataweb.org.
  A demo of that prototype has been presented at ESWC 2015 [20].

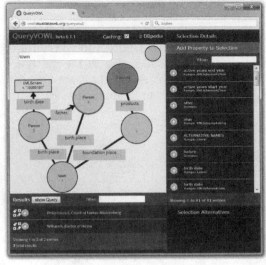 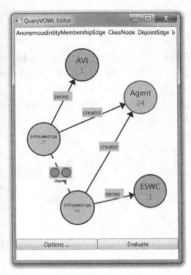

(a) Web-based implementation.   (b) C# implementation.

Fig. 6. Screenshots of two prototypical QueryVOWL implementations.

on open web standards (HTML, JavaScript, CSS, SVG) and integrates some JavaScript libraries, most importantly D3 [15] for the visualization of the query graph.

Users can create and modify QueryVOWL graphs by adding and removing visual elements as well as positioning nodes with drag-and-drop. Restricted and unrestricted class nodes, properties (both directed and undirected), individuals, and literal nodes with filters for some ordinal types are supported. The union, intersection, and disjointedness operators, as well as the mapping of result set sizes to class node radii, have not yet been included. Query building is supported by automatic updates upon changes to the graph, asynchronous loading of lists of resources compliant with the current selection, and configuration options that are displayed upon hovering over elements.

A sidebar provides information about the selected element, as well as options to modify its filter restrictions and to add linked elements. A result list at the bottom shows individuals that are valid replacements for the selected node.

Stand-Alone Desktop Application. The desktop application (Fig. 6b) runs on the Microsoft .NET Framework and was created in C# with the Windows Presentation Foundation (WPF) user interface toolkit. It is intended as a show-case for the object-oriented implementation of the QueryVOWL elements that uses polymorphism for the generation of SPARQL query strings based on the rules outlined in Table 1.

All elements listed in the table are implemented in this prototype, but inter-activity is limited. The prototype supports drag-and-drop, dynamic node scaling, and the insertion of IRIs from the system clipboard. As in the web implementation, SPARQL queries are automatically generated and sent to a given SPARQL endpoint. Once the requests are answered, the retrieved result counts are displayed and nodes are scaled accordingly.

5.2 User Study

We have conducted a qualitative user study to gather further insight into the comprehensibility of QueryVOWL, the usability of our interactive implementation, and some general comments on the visual query language.

Tasks. We prepared a total of eight tasks based on data from the DBpedia dataset. While the study was conducted in German, much of the structural information in the DBpedia dataset uses English. Therefore, all tasks were provided bilingually, to help participants bridge any possible gaps in their English knowledge.

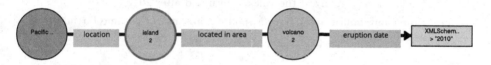

Fig. 7. One of the query graphs that participants of the user study had to construct. It can be used to answer the question "How many islands contain a volcano and are located in the Pacific Ocean?"

Seven tasks consisted of a natural language question, and possibly some more specific sub-questions. Users were asked to construct a QueryVOWL graph that represents the question with our web-based prototype (like the one in Fig. 7) and to select the appropriate element in the graph to find an answer to the question. Answering the question meant showing the graph and explaining briefly where on the screen the response to the question can be found. The full set of construction questions is listed in Table 2.

The eighth task was a comprehension task, in which a QueryVOWL graph with a selected node was shown (Fig. 8). Users were asked to express the query represented by the graph as a natural language question.

In all, the tasks in the study made use of the QueryVOWL features available in the web-based implementation. They made use of labeled and unlabeled class nodes, individuals, directed and undirected property edges, as well as literal values.

Material. A MacBook Air with a 13.3 in. display, a screen resolution of 1440 × 900 pixels, and an external mouse was used during the study. The QueryVOWL implementation was executed in a Mozilla Firefox 31 browser in full-screen mode.

Table 2. English text of the construction tasks from the user study. For tasks split up by forward slashes (/) in this table, participants had to incrementally assemble the query in a stepwise manner.

#	Question
1	How many films did Bruce Willis star in? / Does anyone appear together with his or her child in any of these films? / What film and which child?
2	How many persons / wrote a song / and are connected to a band in some way / that Freddie Mercury used to belong to? / How many bands are there?
3	How many persons / are spouses of a senator / and have any children born in or after 1935? / How many children are there?
4	How many mountains are there in Madagascar? / How many rivers / originate from one of those mountains / and flow into the Indian Ocean?
5	How many bridges are there in Pittsburgh? / How many of them span a river? / How many of them span the Ohio River?
6	How many islands / contain a volcano / and are located in the Pacific Ocean? / How many of the volcanos erupted after 2010?
7	How many politicians / have a spouse / and have the same birthdate as their spouse?

All on-screen activity was captured by a screen recording software to ease the analysis.

The tasks, as well as a questionnaire on demographic data and the participants' impression of QueryVOWL, were printed on paper. An introductory video with a runtime of approximately 4.5 min was prepared. It explained QueryVOWL by constructing an exemplary query step by step.

Participants. Six participants (3 female, 3 male) between the age of 22 and 43 (median: 26) took part in the user study. All of them had different professions, none of them from the field of information technology. None of the participants had any prior experience with ontologies or the Semantic Web. Therefore, we could ensure that participants did not bring any prior knowledge on querying Linked Data, which might bias the results.

Procedure. The study was conducted in a closed room, with one participant at a time. Participants were first shown the introductory video and were asked to complete a training task to get to know the visualization and the user interface. Subsequently, the sheet with the questions was handed out, and screen recording was started.

After reading each of the tasks, participants were given an opportunity to ask questions in the case of doubts about the tasks. Participants would then start solving the tasks, while the interaction steps were noted down.

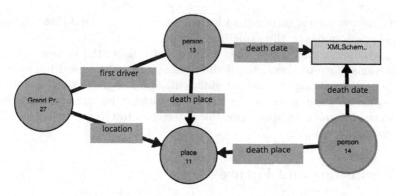

Fig. 8. The query graph shown to the participants of the user study. Participants had to recognize that this graph can be used to find people who passed away on the same date and at the same place as the first driver of a Grand Prix.

Finally, participants were asked to complete the questionnaire to gather information on which parts of the visualization caused confusion and which elements were helpful for understanding the queries.

Results. Participants could solve most of the tasks. Some adapted their initial query to reach a correct solution. There was a noticeable preference for elements and features that had been presented during the introductory video. Moreover, when constructing QueryVOWL graphs, participants followed the provided questions very closely and used exactly the words and the order of words found in the questions.

In general, the use of class nodes and properties was clear. Participants could understand the basic graph structure and correctly identify which graph element represented the entity searched for. Likewise, five of the six participants could easily read the visualized query in the comprehension task. The only difficulty seemed to be the distinction between class nodes and individual nodes, whose difference in color was either not understood or not even consciously noticed by participants.

In a few cases, participants got confused during the composition tasks over the distinction between classes and properties. While they correctly identified *spouse* as a relationship between two persons, they expected a class *child* rather than a *child* property. Moreover, when participants were aware they had to use a property, participants sometimes were unsure about its direction, for example, whether the *child* property points from the parent to the child ("has the child") or vice-versa ("is child of").

Participants could flawlessly understand and use the literal node for single property values, even though it had not been shown in the introductory video. The only difficulty arose when two persons with the same birth date had to be found. Almost all participants expected to make the comparison explicit by two connected literal nodes, rather than by simply linking the *birthDate* property of the two *Person* nodes to the same literal node.

All participants stated that they could imagine using the approach in everyday situations. Two of them stated the technique could be used in cases where conventional search engines are not sufficient, and two more participants could also imagine browsing data in QueryVOWL without having a specific goal in mind, as the information about possible extensions to the query is accessible in the interactive graph.

6   Conclusions and Future Work

We have built upon the ontology visualization VOWL to create QueryVOWL, a visual query language for Linked Data. Visual elements of VOWL were reused and adapted, and we have defined how the resulting graphs map to SPARQL queries. By using our web-based prototype, we have conducted a qualitative user study where we found that lay users could handle the basic query structure well, except for some more specific aspects of the visualization that were not immediately clear to the study participants.

Based on the user study, we believe that a brief but complete introduction to the visual notation is an efficient way to teach previously untrained users how to use QueryVOWL. Furthermore, user comments suggest that dynamically displayed explanations, and possibly a natural language representation of the query or parts thereof, may further support comprehension. We consider including these features in future versions.

Other suggestions referred to interaction features of the web-based implementation. Some interactive elements, such as the property direction toggle button, might be placed so as to avoid accidental clicking. Also, literal nodes could signal in a more obvious way that they can be connected to more than one class or individual node at a time.

Overall, QueryVOWL covers many concepts found in Linked Data. As the general approach appears to be usable, we would like to consider more advanced features, such as functions to process or transform property values for filtering. Likewise, enforcing comparison relationships between property values of two or more individuals beside equality could be desirable. Introducing existential or universal quantifiers as well as disjunctions between alternative filter restrictions could make QueryVOWL even more powerful, if appropriate ways of visualizing the concepts and mapping them to SPARQL can be found. Finally, the selection of new query elements currently happens primarily through lists of identifiers found in the SPARQL endpoint. Integrating an ontology or dataset overview visualization such as VOWL to select elements from might render the creation of QueryVOWL queries on unknown datasets more intuitive.

References

1. CIA world fact book in DAML. http://www.daml.org/2001/12/factbook/
2. Disco. http://www4.wiwiss.fu-berlin.de/bizer/ng4j/disco/
3. Faceted DBLP. http://dblp.l3s.de
4. Linked data. http://linkeddata.org
5. OpenLink iSPARQL. http://oat.openlinksw.com/isparql/
6. SPARQL endpoints status. http://sparqles.okfn.org
7. Ambrus, O., Möller, K., Handschuh, S.: Konduit VQB: a visual query builder for SPARQL on the social semantic desktop. In: VISSW 2010, vol. 565. CEUR-WS (2010)
8. Auer, S., Bizer, C., Kobilarov, G., Lehmann, J., Cyganiak, R., Ives, Z.G.: DBpedia: a nucleus for a web of open data. In: Aberer, K., et al. (eds.) ASWC 2007 and ISWC 2007. LNCS, vol. 4825, pp. 722–735. Springer, Heidelberg (2007)
9. Bārzdiņš, G., Rikačovs, S., Zviedris, M.: Graphical query language as SPARQL frontend. In: ABDIS 2009, Workshops and DC, pp. 93–107. Riga Technical University (2009)
10. Becker, C., Bizer, C.: Exploring the geospatial semantic web with DBpedia Mobile. Web Semant. **7**(4), 278–286 (2009)
11. Berners-Lee, T., Chen, Y., Chilton, L., Connolly, D., Dhanaraj, R., Hollenbach, J., Lerer, A., Sheets, D.: Tabulator: exploring and analyzing linked data on the semantic web. In: SWUI 2006 (2006)
12. Bizer, C., Heath, T., Berners-Lee, T.: Linked data - the story so far. Int. J. Semant. Web Inf. Syst. **5**(3), 1–22 (2009)
13. Blau, H., Immerman, N., Jensen, D.: A visual query language for relational knowledge discovery. Computer Science Department Faculty Publication Series 105, University of Massachusetts-Amherst (2001)
14. Borsje, J., Embregts, H.: Graphical query composition and natural language processing in an RDF visualization interface. Bachelor's thesis, Erasmus University Rotterdam (2006)
15. Bostock, M., Ogievetsky, V., Heer, J.: D3 data-driven documents. IEEE Trans. Visual Comput. Graphics **17**(12), 2301–2309 (2011)
16. Bulter, G., Wang, G., Wang, Y., Zou, L.: A graph database with visual queries for genomics. In: Proceedings of the APBC 2005, pp. 31–40. Imperial College Press (2005)
17. Dadzie, A.S., Rowe, M.: Approaches to visualising linked data: a survey. Semant. Web **2**(2), 89–124 (2011)
18. Groppe, J., Groppe, S., Schleifer, A.: Visual query system for analyzing social semantic web. In: WWW 2011, pp. 217–220. ACM (2011)
19. Haag, F., Lohmann, S., Ertl, T.: SparqlFilterFlow: SPARQL query composition for everyone. In: Presutti, V., Blomqvist, E., Troncy, R., Sack, H., Papadakis, I., Tordai, A. (eds.) ESWC Satellite Events 2014. LNCS, vol. 8798, pp. 362–367. Springer, Heidelberg (2014)
20. Haag, F., Lohmann, S., Siek, S., Ertl, T.: QueryVOWL: Visual composition of SPARQL queries. In: Gandon, F., Guéret, C., Villata, S., Breslin, J., Faron-Zucker, C., Zimmermann, A. (eds.) ESWC Satellite Events 2015. LNCS, vol. 9341, pp. 62–66. Springer (2015)
21. Haag, F., Lohmann, S., Siek, S., Ertl, T.: Visual querying of linked data with QueryVOWL. In: Joint Proceedings of SumPre 2015 and HSWI 2014-15. CEUR-WS (to appear)

22. Heggestøyl, S., Vega-Gorgojo, G., Giese, M.: Visual query formulation for linked open data: the norwegian entity registry case. In: 27th Norsk Informatikkonferanse (NIK 2014). Bibsys Open Journal Systems (2014)
23. Heim, P., Lohmann, S., Stegemann, T.: Interactive relationship discovery via the semantic web. In: Aroyo, L., Antoniou, G., Hyvönen, E., ten Teije, A., Stuckenschmidt, H., Cabral, L., Tudorache, T. (eds.) ESWC 2010, Part I. LNCS, vol. 6088, pp. 303–317. Springer, Heidelberg (2010)
24. Heim, P., Ziegler, J., Lohmann, S.: gFacet: a browser for the web of data. In: IMC-SSW 2008, vol. 417, pp. 49–58. CEUR-WS (2008)
25. Hogenboom, F., Milea, V., Frasincar, F., Kaymak, U.: RDF-GL: a SPARQL-based graphical query language for RDF. In: Chbeir, R., Badr, Y., Abraham, A., Hassanien, A.-E. (eds.) Emergent Web Intelligence: Advanced Information Retrieval. Advanced Information and Knowledge Processing, pp. 87–116. Springer, London (2010)
26. Lohmann, S., Díaz, P., Aedo, I.: MUTO: the modular unified tagging ontology. In: I-SEMANTICS 2011, pp. 95–104. ACM (2011)
27. Lohmann, S., Link, V., Marbach, E., Negru, S.: WebVOWL: web-based visualization of ontologies. In: Lambrix, P., Hyvönen, E., Blomqvist, E., Presutti, V., Qi, G., Sattler, U., Ding, Y., Ghidini, C. (eds.) EKAW 2014 Satellite Events. LNCS, vol. 8982, pp. 154–158. Springer, Heidelberg (2015)
28. Lohmann, S., Negru, S., Haag, F., Ertl, T.: VOWL 2: user-oriented visualization of ontologies. In: Janowicz, K., Schlobach, S., Lambrix, P., Hyvönen, E. (eds.) EKAW 2014. LNCS, vol. 8876, pp. 266–281. Springer, Heidelberg (2014)
29. Negru, S., Haag, F., Lohmann, S.: Towards a unified visual notation for OWL ontologies: insights from a comparative user study. In: Proceedings of the 9th International Conference on Semantic Systems, I-SEMANTICS 2013, pp. 73–80. ACM (2013)
30. Negru, S., Lohmann, S., Haag, F.: VOWL: visual notation for OWL ontologies (2014). http://purl.org/vowl/
31. Russell, A., Smart, P., Braines, D., Shadbolt, N.: NITELIGHT: a graphical tool for semantic query construction. In: SWUI 2008, vol. 543. CEUR-WS (2008)

Semantic Web for Scientific Heritage

Studying the History of Pre-modern Zoology by Extracting Linked Zoological Data from Mediaeval Texts and Reasoning on It

Molka Tounsi[1], Catherine Faron Zucker[1(✉)], Arnaud Zucker[1], Serena Villata[2], and Elena Cabrio[2]

[1] University of Nice Sophia Antipolis, Sophia Antipolis, France
tounsi.molka@etu.unice.fr, {faron,zucker}@unice.fr
[2] Inria Sophia Antipolis Méditerranée, Sophia Antipolis, France
{serena.villata,elena.cabrio}@inria.fr

Abstract. In this paper we first present the international multidisciplinary research network Zoomathia, which aims at studying the transmission of zoological knowledge from Antiquity to Middle Ages through varied resources, and considers especially textual information, including compilation literature such as encyclopaedias. We then present a preliminary work in the context of Zoomathia consisting in (i) extracting pertinent knowledge from mediaeval texts using Natural Language Processing (NLP) methods, (ii) semantically enriching semi-structured zoological data and publishing it as an RDF dataset and its vocabulary, linked to other relevant Linked Data sources, and (iii) reasoning on this linked RDF data to help epistemologists, historians and philologists in their analysis of these ancient texts. This paper is an extended and updated version of [13].

Keywords: History of zoology · Semantic analysis of mediaeval compilations · Linked data and vocabularies

1 Introduction

Scholars concerned with cultural issues in Antiquity or Middle Ages have to deal with a huge documentation. The literary material is a significant part of this material, but the commonly used technology supporting these researches is to date far from satisfactory. In spite of pioneering undertakings in digitization since the 70's, historians and philologists still have access to few tools to operate on texts, mostly limited to lexical searches. Therefore they stand in need for more intelligent tools, in order to overcome this word-dependency, to access the semantics of texts and to achieve more elaborated investigations.

The Semantic Web has an increasing role to play in this process of providing new methodological implements in cultural studies. During the last decade, several works addressed the semantic annotation and search in Cultural Heritage collections and Digital Library systems. They focus on producing Cultural Heritage RDF datasets [2,5], aligning these data and their vocabularies on

© Springer International Publishing Switzerland 2015
F. Gandon et al. (Eds.): ESWC 2015, LNCS 9341, pp. 405–415, 2015.
DOI: 10.1007/978-3-319-25639-9_52

the Linked Data cloud [3,9], and exploring and searching among heterogenous semantic data stores [4,7,8,12]. In [2,3] the authors describe how they created a five stars dataset for the entire collection of the Amsterdam Museum. They present an approach and a tool to create linked cultural datasets for Cultural Heritage institutes, based on the Europeana Data Model (EDM), and they stress on the prime importance of the vocabulary supporting the modeling and the reuse LOD vocabularies. The E-culture project investigates the use of Semantic Web technologies to integrate heterogenous cultural datasets from multiple museum collections and support the semantic annotation and exploration of these collections [7,12]. In addition, in [4], the authors address the problem of diversying search results when searching Cultural Heritage collections.

The Pleiades[1] project aims to collaboratively create and share historical geographic information about the ancient world in digital form. It publishes geospatial data in RDF, aligned with the Geonames dataset [5]. The SPAN[2] project addresses the problem of aligning existing datasets from the classical world on persons, names and person-like entities in Greco-Roman antiquity and publish it as Linked Data [9]. The PELAGIOS[3] project aims to help introduce Linked Open Data into online resources that refer to places in the historic past, with the goal of providing new modes of discovery and visualization [8]. The *Linked Ancient World Data Institute* (LAWDI) proceedings[4] are a survey of current initiatives or expressions of interest on the use of Linked Open Data (LOD) in the study of the ancient world. Most of them consider the first step of making publicly available online the data of digital libraries or of projects working on ancient texts.

The international research network Zoomathia[5] has been set up to address this challenge of adopting a LOD-based methodological approach in the area of History of Science. Zoomathia primarily focuses on the transmission of zoological knowledge from Antiquity to Middle Ages, through textual resources and considers compilation literature such as encyclopaedias. It aims to develop interconnected researches on History of Zoology in pre-modern times and to raise collaborative work involving philologists, historians, naturalists and researchers in Knowledge Engineering and Semantic Web.

In this context, we conducted a preliminary work, first presented in [13] and updated and extended in this paper. It focuses on the fourth book of the late mediaeval encyclopaedia *Hortus Sanitatis* (15th century), written in Latin, which compiles ancient texts on fishes. Each chapter of this book is dedicated to one fish, with possible references to other fishes. In this work we aim at *(i)* automating information extraction from these texts, such as zoonyms, zoological sub-discipline (ethology, anatomy, medicinal properties, etc.); *(ii)* building an RDF dataset and its vocabulary representing the extracted knowledge,

---

[1] http://pleiades.stoa.org/home.
[2] http://snapdrgn.net/.
[3] http://pelagios-project.blogspot.fr/.
[4] http://dlib.nyu.edu/awdl/isaw/isaw-papers/7/.
[5] http://www.cepam.cnrs.fr/zoomathia/.

and link them to the Linked Data; and finally, at *(iii)* reasoning on this linked data to produce new expert knowledge. We build upon the results of two previous French research projects on structuring mediaeval encyclopaedias in XML according to the TEI model and manualy annotating author sources (SourceEncyMe project[6]) and zoonyms (Ichtya project[7]).

This paper is organized as follows: Sect. 2 presents the challenges addressed within Zoomathia and its general goals. Section 3 presents our work on knowledge extraction from the mediaeval encyclopaedia *Hortus Sanitatis*, while Sect. 4 describes the publication of a linked RDF dataset and its vocabularies. Section 5 presents preliminary work on the exploitation of these data to support the study of the history of pre-modern zoology, and Sect. 6 concludes the paper.

2   The Zoomathia Research Network

Zoomathia primarily focuses on the transmission of zoological knowledge from Antiquity to Middle Ages. The intellectual challenge is to go beyond the classical Quellenforschung, only focused on the analysis of the discontinuous transmission of specific information. We aim at operating methodically on a set of five representative works distant from each other of approximatively five centuries through two millenaries of zoological discourse: Aristotles Historia Animalium (4 BC), Plinys Historia naturalis (1 CE), Isidorus Etymologies (7 CE), Vincent of Beauvais Speculum Naturale (13 CE), and Hortus sanitatis (15 CE). Historians of zoology traditionally regard biological ambition as suffering a decline after Aristotle, if not a disappearance. [10] We should rather consider that a lasting shift in intellectual interest and cultural involvement with animals occurs in the Alexandrine and Roman period. Which animals are worth to take into account and to comment? What is worth to examine in them? What is worth to say about them?

The automatic annotation of the selected texts and the systematic identification of the topics and subjects of all their units will enable an accurate evaluation and interpretation of the development of the zoological knowledge. Manual search and computing on ancient and mediaeval texts enable to some extend to address the quantitative dimension of data but fail to answer the epistemological demands, which concern the scientific relevancy and the diachronic features of the documentation. A large range of investigations on specific topics is inaccessible through simple lexical queries and requires a rich, scientific and semantic annotation. When investigating, for example, on ethological issues (such as animal breeding, intraspecific communication or technical skills) or on pharmaceutical properties of animal products, we have to face a scattered documentation and a changing terminology hampering a direct access to and a synthetic grasp of the topics studied. An automatic and semantic-based process will help to link and cluster together the related data, compare evidences in a

---

[6] http://atelier-vincent-de-beauvais.irht.cnrs.fr/encyclopedisme-medieval/
   programme-sourcencyme-corpus-et-sources-des-encyclopedies-medievales.
[7] http://www.unicaen.fr/recherche/mrsh/document_numerique/projets/ichtya.

diachronic approach and to figure out the major trends of the cultural representations of animal life and behaviour.

In this network, we aim at *(i)* identifying a corpus of zoology-related historical
data, in order to progressively encompass the whole known documentation, and
(ii) producing a common thesaurus operating on heterogeneous resources (icono-
graphic, archaeological and literary). This thesaurus should enable to represent
different kinds of knowledge: zoonyms; historical period; geographical area; literary genre; economical context; zoological sub-discipline (ethology, anatomy,
physiology, psychology, animal breeding, etc.). The difficulty of the task lies in
the extreme variety of the expresions used to refer to each of these subjects. The
ultimate goal is to synthesize the available cultural data on zoological matters
and to crosscheck them with a synchronic perspective. This would enable to
reach the crucial concern, i.e. to precisely assess the transmission of zoological
knowledge along the period and the evolution of the human-animal relations.
Finally, this thesaurus should be published on the Linked Data and linked to
modern reference sources (biological and ecological) to appraise the relevance of
the historical documentation.

3 Knowledge Extraction from Historians and Texts

3.1 Interviews with Historians

We conducted several interviews with three Historians participating in
Zoomathia to explicit a list of major knowledge elements which would be useful
in the study of the transmission of ancient zoological knowledge in mediaeval
texts. Among them, let us cite the presence (or absence) of zoonyms in the corpus texts, variant names or name alternatives given to an animal (polyonymy),
the relative volume of textual records devoted to a given zoonym, references
to a zoonym and frequency of occurrences related to it out of their dedicated
chapter, geographical location of the described animals, numerical data in the
text (size, longevity, fertility, etc.) and other animal properties related to zoological sub-disciplines (ethology, anatomy, physiology, psychology, animal breeding,
etc.).

3.2 Extraction of Zoonyms and Animal Properties from Texts

We processed two versions of book 4 of *Hortus Sanitatis*, the original Latin
text and its translation in French. We used the XML structured version of these
texts, identifying the 106 chapters of the book, divided in paragraphs, themselves
including 753 citations. We used TreeTagger to parse Latin and French texts and
determine the lemmas and part of speech (PoS) of each word in the text.

Extraction of Zoonyms. We searched for the resources available to support
the knowledge extraction process. A lexicon of fish names in French and in Latin
has been provided by the Ichtya project and we — Knowledge Engineers and

Historians — collaboratively built a thesaurus of zoological sub-disciplines and concepts involved in the descriptions relative to these sub-disciplines. Then we defined two sets of patterns (i.e. syntactic rules) for French and Latin to recognize zoonyms from the lexicon of fish names among the lemmas identified in the texts. For instance, the rule $SN+SADJ$ (noun + adjective) applies to zoonym *Vitulus marinus* or *Testudo lutaria*. As a result, we extracted 736 zoonyms from the 106 chapters of book 4 of *Hortus Sanitatis*.

Extraction of Animal Properties. We conducted a second processing of the same two texts to extract zoological sub-disciplines and animal properties. We focused on these seven topics: reproduction, fishing, therapeutic, cooking, anatomy, diet, longevity. The process consists in the following steps: For each sub-discipline, we constructed a list of semantically related terms based on EXtended WordNet Domains[8] (XWND) and BabelNet[9]. WordNet[10] is a large lexical database in English, where nouns, verbs, adjectives and adverbs are grouped into sets of cognitive synonyms (synsets), each expressing a distinct concept; synsets are interlinked by conceptual and lexical relations. WordNet Domains (WND) is a lexical resource where synsets have been semi-automatically annotated with one or more domain labels from a set of 170 hierarchically organized domains, thus reducing the problem of word polysemy. eXtended WordNet Domains (XWND) [6] is an ongoing work aiming to automatically improve WordNet Domains. BabelNet is a very large multilingual ontology and semantic network created by linking the largest multilingual Web encyclopedia — Wikipedia — to the most popular computational lexicon — WordNet. The integration is performed via an automatic mapping and by filling in lexical gaps in resource-poor languages based on machine translation. The result is an "encyclopedic dictionary that provides babel synsets, i.e., concepts and named entities lexicalized in many languages and connected with large amounts of semantic relations [11]. Each list of semantically related terms is constructed as follows: (i) If the sub-discipline exists as an XWDM domain, we extract the offset of all the WordNet synset from this domain and we translate the terms in French via BabelNet based on the WordNet Offset. (ii) If the sub-discipline is not an XWND domain, we use BabelNet to extract all the terms in the network representing a specific domain. (iii) Finally, we apply a manual processing step to reduce the number of terms in each set associated to a zoological discipline (while keeping the more relevant). The list of semantically related terms in Latin is the translation of the French terms; this has been manually done by a philologist. As a result, the networks representing the cooking, therapeutic and fishing topics in French or in Latin comprise about 100 terms. For instance the Latin verbs *medeor* (heal) or *cura* (cure) are used to identify the therapeutic topic; the verbs *epulor* or *edo* (eat) are used to identify the diet topic. There are between 20 and 50 terms for the others topics.

---

[8] http://adimen.si.ehu.es/web/XWND.
[9] http://babelnet.org/.
[10] https://wordnet.princeton.edu/.

Evaluation. The analysis of the results of the automatic annotation process was conducted by knowledge engineers and validated by two philologists involved in the manual annotation. For the evaluation of the extraction of zoonyms we considered Chaps. 1 to 53 of book 4 of *Hortus Sanitatis*. We compared the results of the automatic annotation with those of the manual annotation of zoonyms conducted within the past Ichtya project. F-measure equals to 0.93 for both the annotation of the Latin text and the French text. Most missing annotations are due to the fact that the parsing tool is unable to deduce the exact lemma of some words, especially for Latin words. Among 65 missing annotations, 51 (rare) fish names were not annotated because TreeTagger does not recognize them (e.g., *loligo*). Other missing annotations concern composed names and are due to a mismatch between the complete fish name in the reference lexicon and the short name used in the text to be annotated (e.g. *locusta* instead of *locusta marina*). Conversely, most annotation errors are due to ambiguities between marine animal names and terrestrial animals. For instance, lemma *lupus* (wolf) is present in the provided lexicon of fish names (*wolffish*) and there are some comparisons in the text with the (terrestrial) wolf[11].

For the evaluation of the automatic extraction of animal properties, we considered for the test set the 25 first chapters of *Hortus Sanitatis*, consisting in 142 citations. These citations have been manually annotated by two philologists to build a reference version. They considered the same seven topics as in the automatic annotation process. Most of them were declared relative to anatomy (62) and therapeutics (44). Then, we compared the result of our automatic annotation process with this reference version. F-measure is above 0.5 for the French text and 0.4 for the Latin text. Considering that the segments we annotate are relatively short texts, we did not expect a high value for this metrics. However this should be improved. These results are clearly those of an ongoing work. Most wrong annotations are related to the therapeutics topic which semantic network of terms intersects the networks of other topics, especially anatomy and diet. There texts dealing with the therapeutic power of some animal on a human organ, and therefore annotated with the anatomy topic instead of therapeutics. Also the question of considering the diet topic as a sub-topic of therapeutics is currently discussed by the philologists involved in the project. More generally, the choice of the topics should be further studied. We will iteratively conduct further experimentations by revising the semantic networks representing the topics and the targeted topics as well.

4   From Structured Data to Linked Data

The extracted knowledge has first been used to enrich the available XML annotation of *Hortus Sanitatis*. Then we translated the whole XML annotation (text structure, source authors, zoonyms and animal properties) into an RDF dataset and vocabularies and exploited it with SPARQL queries.

---

[11] "And although this is the case for all fishes, it is however more obvious in him (*wolffish*), as it is also for the wolf and the dog among the beasts".

4.1 Zoomathia RDF Dataset

An RDF dataset describing *Hortus Sanitatis* has been automatically generated by writing an XSL stylesheet to be applied to its XML annotation. Listing 1.1 presents an extract of it describing quotation 4 of paragraph 3 of Chap. 20. It is a citation of Aristotle, refering to the *crocodile* zoonym and addressing the *therapeutics* and *anatomy* topics.

```
<http://zoomathia.unice.fr/HortusSanitatis/FR.hs.4.25.3/cit4>
  a tei:Citation;
  tei:hasHead"FR.hs.4.25.3.cit4";
  tei:hasBibliography [ a tei:Bibliography;
    tei:hasAuthor <http://zoomathia.unice.fr/auteurs/Aristote>;
    tei:hasReference
      <http://zoomathia.unice.fr/oeuvres/612_a_21-25N_MS>. ];
  tei:hasCitationText "...";
  zoo:hasZoonym <http://zoomathia.unice.fr/Crocodile>;
  dcterms:subject
    <http://zoomathia.unice.fr/subject/therapeutique>,
    <http://zoomathia.unice.fr/subject/anatomie>. ] ].
```

Listing 1.1. RDF annotation of an Aristotle's citation on crocodiles

4.2 Zoomathia Vocabulary

Thesaurus of Zoonyms. Based on the lexicon initially provided by Historians involved in the Ichtya project, we built a SKOS thesaurus of 137 concepts representing zoonyms and we aligned it with both the cross-domain DBpedia ontology and the Agrovoc thesaurus specialized for Food and Agriculture[12]. Listing 1.2 presents an extract of the thesaurus describing taxon *Garfish*.

```
<http://zoomathia.org/Orphie> a skos:Concept ;
  skos:prefLabel "orphie"@fr ;
  skos:closeMatch <http://fr.dbpedia.org/resource/Orphie> ;
  skos:closeMatch <http://dbpedia.org/resource/Garfish> ;
  skos:closeMatch <http://aims.fao.org/aos/agrovoc/c_5102> ;
  skos:altLabel "gwich" .
```

Listing 1.2. Extract of the Zoomathia thesaurus of zoonyms

Thesaurus of Animal Properties. We built an RDFS vocabulary of zoology-related sub-disciplines and animal properties, based on the results of interviews with Historians and the properties extracted from texts. It comprises 49 classes and we chose seven of them for the topic detection. This is a preliminary modelisation which has to be further developed.

---

[12] http://aims.fao.org/vest-registry/vocabularies/agrovoc-multilingual-agricultural-thesaurus.

5   Reasoning on Historical Zoological RDF Data

In order to exploit the extracted RDF knowledge base, we built a set of SPARQL queries enabling to answer questions such as "What are the zoonyms studied in this text?", "What are the topics covered in this text?", "Where can we find these topics?", "What are the zoonym properties (in which chapter or paragraph or citation)?". Let us note that it is the semantics captured in the constructed vocabularies which make it possible to answer these queries: multiple labels associated with a taxon in the thesaurus of zoonyms, hierarchy of zoology-related sub-disciplines, denoted by various terms.

We went a step further in the exploitation of the RDF dataset by writing SPARQL queries of the CONSTRUCT form to construct new RDF graphs capturing synthetic knowledge. When graphically visualized, they support the analytical reasoning of historians on texts. For instance, Fig. 1 presents an RDF graph capturing the relative importance of zoonyms in the *Hortus Sanitatis* and their location in it. At a glance, it shows that dolphins, whales and eels occupy a predominant place in this text, far ahead of other animals. Figure 2 presents the RDF graph capturing the relative importance of zoology-related sub-disciplines in the *Hortus Sanitatis* and their location in it. At a glance, it shows that anatomy occupies a predominant place in this text, far ahead of therapeutics and fishing.

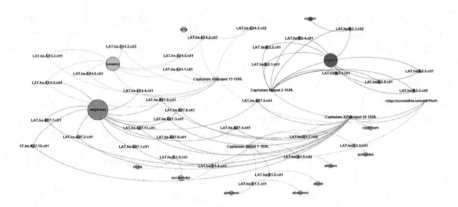

Fig. 1. Relative importance of zoonyms in *Hortus Sanitatis*

These are preliminary results, but yet showing the potentiality of using Semantic Web technologies to support the analysis of ancient and mediaeval zoological knowledge from texts. They are the starting point of an iterative process which will be collaboratively conducted with researchers in Humanities and in Knowledge Engineering.

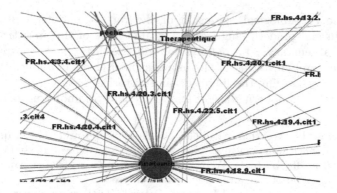

Fig. 2. Relative importance of zoological topics in *Hortus Sanitatis*

6   Conclusion and Future Work

We presented a preliminary work conducted in the context of the Zoomathia network, on the zoological mediaeval encyclopaedia *Hortus Sanitatis*. This work combines NLP techniques to extract knowledge from texts, and knowledge engineering and semantic web methods to build a linked RDF dataset of zoological annotations of this scientific text. It exploits this dataset to support the analysis of the Ancient zoological knowledge compiled in the encyclopaedia.

We are currently working on applying the knowledge extraction process presented in this paper on a classical Latin book on fishes (Pliny, *Historia Naturalis*, book 9, 1st century AD), which is a major, though indirect, source of the *Hortus Sanitatis*. We want to deal with the historical perspective of zoology, by comparing the knowledge extracted from these two texts, and appraising the density of the transmission and the evolution of the zoological knowledge on an epistemological point of view. We intend to systematically compare the two texts, with the aim of evaluating the loss, distortion or enrichment of information, and comparing the relative importance in the books of the different zoological perspectives (anatomical, ethological, geographical, etc.) and of the different animal species. Reasoning on the extracted knowledge will enable to identifiy for both texts a "typological profile", shaped by the relative proportions of text devoted to each of the zoological specialities (or scientific perspectives). By extending the corpus this method will enable a progressive assess of the epistemological evolution of the zoological discourse.

In a near future we will align the Zoomathia thesaurus of zoonyms with the TAXREF taxonomy specialized in Conservation Biology and integrating Archaeozoological data[13], thus enabling to support the integration of heterogenous datasets in order to crosscheck the zoological evidences extracted from texts with archaeozoological and iconographical datasets. We are currently working on the formalisation and publication of a SKOS thesaurus from the JSON output format of TAXREF [1].

---

[13] http://inpn.mnhn.fr/programme/referentiel-taxonomique-taxref?lg=en.

Given the chronological extension of the corpus and its multilingualism (Greek, Latin and modern languages) a related issue of this investigation concerns historical semantics. This affects not only the theoretical concepts but also the distinction and clustering of the animals themselves. It implies to build up a vocabulary both saving the linguistic and historical meaning of concepts and linking them to the modern state of knowledge and common terminology.

Acknowledgments. We thank Isabelle Draelants and Catherine Jacquemard we interviewed to explicit philological and historical questions to be addressed when studying ancient and mediaeval texts. We thank Irene Pajòn Leyra for her participation to the manual evaluation of the automatic extraction process.

Zoomathia is an International Research Group (GDRI) supported by the French National Scientific Research Center (CNRS).

References

1. Callou, C., Michel, F., Faron-Zucker, C., Martin, C., Montagnat, J.: Towards a shared reference thesaurus for studies on history of zoology, archaeozoology and conservation biology. In: Proceedings of the First International Workshop Semantic Web for Scientific Heritage, ESWC 2015, Portorož, Slovenia, 2015. CEUR-WS.org (2015)
2. de Boer, V., Wielemaker, J., van Gent, J., Hildebrand, M., Isaac, A., van Ossenbruggen, J., Schreiber, G.: Supporting linked data production for cultural heritage institutes: the Amsterdammuseum case study. In: Simperl, E., Cimiano, P., Polleres, A., Corcho, O., Presutti, V. (eds.) ESWC 2012. LNCS, vol. 7295, pp. 733–747. Springer, Heidelberg (2012)
3. de Boer, V., Wielemaker, J., van Gent, J., Oosterbroek, M., Hildebrand, M., Isaac, A., van Ossenbruggen, J., Schreiber, G.: Amsterdam museum linked open data. Semant. Web 4(3), 237–243 (2013)
4. Dijkshoorn, C., Aroyo, L., Schreiber, G., Wielemaker, J., Jongma, L.: Using linked data to diversify search results a case study in cultural heritage. In: Janowicz, K., Schlobach, S., Lambrix, P., Hyvönen, E. (eds.) EKAW 2014. LNCS, vol. 8876, pp. 109–120. Springer, Heidelberg (2014)
5. Elliott, T., Gillies, S.: Digital geography and classics. Digital Humanities Quarterly 3(1) (2009)
6. González, A., Rigau, G., Castillo, M.: A graph-based method to improve WordNet domains. In: Gelbukh, A. (ed.) CICLing 2012, Part I. LNCS, vol. 7181, pp. 17–28. Springer, Heidelberg (2012)
7. Hildebrand, M.: Interactive exploration of heterogeneous cultural heritage collections. In: Sheth, A.P., Staab, S., Dean, M., Paolucci, M., Maynard, D., Finin, T., Thirunarayan, K. (eds.) ISWC 2008. LNCS, vol. 5318, pp. 914–919. Springer, Heidelberg (2008)
8. Isaksen, L., Simon, R., Barker, E.T.E., de Soto Cañamares, P.: Pelagios and the emerging graph of ancient world data. In: ACM Web Science Conference, WebSci 2014, Bloomington, IN, USA. ACM (2014)
9. Jackson, M., Antonioletti, M., Hume, A.C., Blanke, T., Bodard, G., Hedges, M., Rajbhandari, S.: Building bridges between islands of data - an investigation into distributed data management in the humanities. In: Fifth International Conference on e-Science, e-Science 2009, Oxford, UK. IEEE Computer Society (2009)

10. Lennox, J.G.: The disappearance of aristotles biology: a hellenistic mystery. Apeiron **27**(4), 7–24 (1994)
11. Navigli, R.: A quick tour of BabelNet 1.1. In: Gelbukh, A. (ed.) CICLing 2013, Part I. LNCS, vol. 7816, pp. 25–37. Springer, Heidelberg (2013)
12. Schreiber, G., Amin, A.K., Aroyo, L., van Assem, M., de Boer, V., Hardman, L., Hildebrand, M., Omelayenko, B., van Ossenbruggen, J., Tordai, A., Wielemaker, J., Wielinga, B.J.: Semantic annotation and search of cultural-heritage collections: the MultimediaN E-culture demonstrator. J. Web Sem. **6**(4), 243–249 (2008)
13. Tounsi, M., Faron-Zucker, C., Zucker, A., Villata, S., Cabrio, E.: Studying the history of pre-modern zoology with linked data and vocabularies. In: Proceedings of the First International Workshop Semantic Web for Scientific Heritage, ESWC 2015, Portorož, Slovenia. CEUR-WS.org (2015)

SemanticHPST: Applying Semantic Web Principles and Technologies to the History and Philosophy of Science and Technology

Olivier Bruneau[1](✉), Serge Garlatti[2], Muriel Guedj[3], Sylvain Laubé[4], and Jean Lieber[5]

[1] LHSP-AHP, University of Lorraine, 91 avenue de la Libération,
BP 454, 54001 Nancy Cedex, France
olivier.bruneau@univ-lorraine.fr
[2] LabSTICC, Telecom-Bretagne, CS 83818, 29238 Brest Cedex 3, France
[3] LIRDEF, University of Montpellier 2, 2 place Marcel Godechot,
BP 4152, 34092 Montpellier Cedex 5, France
[4] University of Bretagne Occidentale, Centre François Viète (EA 1161),
20, rue Duquesne, CS 98837, 29238 Brest Cedex 3, France
[5] University of Lorraine, LORIA, Campus scientifique,
BP 239, 54506 Vandoeuvre-lès-Nancy Cedex, France

Abstract. SemanticHPST is a project in which interacts ICT (especially Semantic Web) with history and philosophy of science and technology (HPST). Main difficulties in HPST are the large diversity of sources and points of view and a large volume of data. So, HPST scholars need to use new tools devoted to digital humanities based on semantic web. To ensure a certain level of genericity, this project is initially based on three sub-projects: the first one to the port-arsenal of Brest, the second one is dedicated to the correspondence of Henri Poincaré and the third one to the concept of energy. The aim of this paper is to present the project, its issues and goals and the first results and objectives in the field of harvesting distributed corpora, in advanced search in HPST corpora. Finally, we want to point out some issues about epistemological aspects about this project.

Keywords: HPST (history and philosophy of science and technology) · Modern history · Semantic web · RDFS annotations · HPST ontologies · Exact search · Approximate search · Harvesting distributed corpora · Epistemology

1 Introduction

The application of computer science to research in history has existed for a long time [5,22] though it can be noticed that the recent research domain of "Digital Humanities" (DH) is growing as result of a digital "revolution" at work that impacts the whole society at the international level. In France, tools and utilities dedicated to DH like the very large facility Huma-Num (http://www.humanum.fr)

© Springer International Publishing Switzerland 2015
F. Gandon et al. (Eds.): ESWC 2015, LNCS 9341, pp. 416–427, 2015.
DOI: 10.1007/978-3-319-25639-9_53

have been created in order to favor "the coordination of the collective production of corpora of sources (scientific recommendations, technological best practices)." It also provides research teams in the human and social sciences with a range of utilities to facilitate the processing, access, storage and interoperability of various types of digital data." The *Dacos and Mounier report* [10] shows that the French research is active, however the authors recommend the creation of "Centers of Digital Humanities". The research network SemanticHPST is based on a strong coupling of laboratories in History and Philosophy of Science and Technology (HPST) and in Computer Science (LHSP–AHP, LORIA in Nancy) and (CFV, LabSTIIC in Brest) with research questions about the use of semantic web for HPST. The SemanticHPST project takes part in the emerging issues at the French and international levels in the domain of HPST.[1] Actually, the Semantic Web technology appears as efficient in order to generate tools adapted to the need of production and diffusion of distributed "intelligent digital" corpus in history [19]. The objectives of the project are: (i) to integrate the existing technologies to manipulate digital contents of large volume by modeling knowledge as ontologies (annotation, request) for History and Philosophy of Science and Technology; (ii) to extent these technologies. The goal of this paper is to present the SemanticHPST project: its history, its objectives, the first results according to the information retrieval aspect and some epistemological issues. Because the methods in History of science and Technology are covering some elements of others domains in humanities (for example in history or in archeology), another goal of the SemanticHPST group is to share questions and results with the scientific community.

The paper is organized as follows. Section 2 presents the main goals of the SemanticHPST project and its three French HPST sub-projects for which semantic web technologies are useful. Section 3 presents some requirements and corresponding tools supporting different resource retrieval processes according to the researchers' practices. Section 4 presents some issues from an epistemological viewpoint. Section 5 concludes the paper.

2   The SemanticHPST Project

In November 2010, the main topic of a European workshop was the uses of ICT and history of science and technology in education.[2] To improve research in HPST on one hand, and to promote dissemination of the HPST in the field of education on the other hand, some participants were convinced by the necessity to use new ICT tools [7,8,11,13].

---

[1] See the 18th session organised by some authors of this paper during the last meeting of SFHST (French society for history of science and technology), April 2014 (http://sfhst2014lyon.sciencesconf.org/resource/page/id/5), and the last meeting of the international consortium DigitalHPS at Nancy, September 2014, (http://dhps2014.sciencesconf.org).

[2] After this workshop, an extensive book written by participants and others has been published in 2012 [6].

In 2012, some historians of science and technology and computer scientists have created a consortium called SemanticHPST.[3]

The main goal of SemanticHPST project is to enrich the practices of researchers and communities in HPST. According to the specificity of the practice as historians of science, three main issues were tackled:

1. The management of large quantities of data especially for the most recent periods (XIXth, XXth centuries up to the present day). Knowing that the historical approach involves to integrate relevant elements from the context of production of these data into metadata.
2. The heterogeneity of sources and corpora constituted from these sources.
3. The production of new relevant digital corpora from several available digital historical collections.

To address our main goal and the three previous issues, our project is based on the Semantic Web principles and technologies. Thus, it has three main sub-goals: (i) Building intelligent digital corpora, that is to say corpora with primary and secondary sources having semantic metadata and their corresponding ontologies; (ii) Designing tools to access and enrich existing corpora and to create new ones; (iii) Evaluating the resulting practices and building an epistemological viewpoint about the use of TIC in HPST.

To achieve these goals, it is necessary to ensure a certain level of genericity for metadata, ontology, computer-based tools and practices.

To deal with genericity and the diversity of sources, the project is applied in three different use cases or sub-projects with the aim to cover different methods and approaches that are typical in the domain of HPST. Those approaches are covering only partially the methods used in history and archaeology. These sub-projects are described in the following paragraph.

2.1   The Port-Arsenal of Brest

This sub-project takes part in the research programs "History of marine science and technology" and "Digital Humanities for History of Science and Technology" developed in Brest in the Centre F. Viète. One topic concerns the comprehension of the scientific and technological evolution of the port-arsenal in Brest (France) on a large period (XVIIth to XXth century) with a methodological approach considering this military-industrial complex dedicated to shipbuilding as a large technological system [14]. The objectives are:

1. To compose and publish a digital library (based on semantic web) about the material culture of the port-arsenal of Brest associated to several projects

---

[3] Participants at this consortium came initially from LaB-STICC (Telecom Bretagne, Brest), Centre François Viète (University of Brest), LIRDEF (University of Montpellier), LHSP-Archives Poincaré (University of Lorraine, Nancy) and later LORIA (University of Lorraine, Nancy). During the years 2012–2014, the INSHS (a French national institute of human and social sciences), the national network of Maisons des Sciences de l'Homme and University of Lorraine supported this consortium.

about 3D replications of artifacts and to cultural mediations dedicated to science and technology heritage.
2. To develop digital tools (based on semantic web) dedicated to a comparative history of science and technology of the port on a large area and a large period (since ancient times until now).

The hypothesis is to consider the large technological system of the port-arsenal as a large spatiotemporal and multi-scale artifact which is possible to decompose in elements of smaller scale (which are also artifacts) like industrial workshops, shipbuilding areas, storage areas, etc. Each of these elements are themselves composed by elements/artifact of smaller scale. The system has to be seen as the sum of all these artifacts and of all the relationships between them. The research in Brest [16,17] has shown the interest to propose an historical evolution model of the port (inspired by works in geography [3]) where "simple" artifact like cranes, quays, dry docks are efficient indicators to characterize the cycle of evolution of the port-arsenal during a large period. This method is used in a comparative research [18] between Brest (France) and Mar del Plata (Argentine) in a thesis in progress by B. Rohou (directed by S. Garlatti and S. Laubé).[4] From these works, the contribution in the SemanticHPST group is to produce a methodology and a knowledge model efficient to produce a generic ontology where an artifact is a material object (made by human beings) associated to a "life cycle" with at least three steps:

1 design and construction of the artifact;
2 the artifact in use;
3 the disappearance of the artifact.

That "life cycle" involves the elaboration of fives categories of entities: time entities, actors (individuals or social groups), concepts/theories, location and artifacts. The analysis of the important ontology in the domain of cultural heritage named CIDOC-CRM (that "provides definitions and a formal structure for describing the implicit and explicit concepts and relationships used in cultural heritage documentation")[5] shows that this ontology could be a first reference to help and build our own ontologies because some concepts and relationships about "temporal entities" and "actors" can be reused. But if the concept of "Thing" exists in the CIDOC-CRM, we consider that the concept of "Artifact" and the associated relationships have to be elaborated first from our historical model and by considering of course the possibility of equivalent concepts in the CIDOC-CRM. A work is in progress in Brest about this topic from concrete examples of artifact as crane, quays and seawalls. A second step will be to examine others methods to produce ontologies well-adapted to our HPST problems in the domain of marine history [4].

This work is coupled with examples of typical requests (when and where were positioned all the cranes in the port of Brest since 1650 until 1970? In the

---

[4] See http://brmdp.hypotheses.org/.
[5] http://www.cidoc-crm.org/.

port of Mar del Plata? Which firms were in charge of the construction of the quays/cranes in the port of Brest since 1800 until 1900? What are the engine power of all cranes in the world since 1850 until 1970? Etc.).

2.2 Henri Poincaré's Correspondence

The Platform Henri Poincaré Papers. In 1992, the laboratory of history of science and philosophy Archives Henri Poincaré was created to promote Henri Poincaré's manuscripts and to publish his correspondence. For more than 20 years, this long-term project has produced three volumes of letters: the first one is devoted to the Poincaré - Mittag-Leffler letters [20], the second one is on the correspondence with physicists, chemists and engineers [23], the third one is with astronomers and, in particular, geodesists [24]. Two other volumes are in preparation, one devoted to the letters from or of mathematicians and the other one consists of administrative and personnal correspondences.[6]

The corpus consists of more than 2000 letters, 1046 sent by Henri Poincaré and 949 received by him.[7] All known letters are digitalized[8] and around 50 % of them are in plain text (in LaTeX and XML versions). Lots of letters contain mathematical and physical formulae. In Henri Poincaré Papers website,[9] the correspondence is available. In this platform, each known letter is indexed with Dublin Core extended metadata.[10] This enables to query the corpus by e.g.

$Q_1 = $ "Letters sent by Henri Poincaré in 1885"
$Q_2 = $ "Letters received by Eugénie Launois between 1882 and 1894"

There is also the possibility of plain text search for the letters already transcribed.

Towards More HPST-Adapted Search. Now, consider the following queries:

$Q_3 = $ "Letters from an astronomer"
$Q_4 = $ "Letters in reply to a letter of Mittag-Leffler"
$Q_5 = $ "Letters about the n-body problem"
$Q_6 = $ "Letters of the late XIXth century"

These queries cannot be executed in the current platform. They require additional data and knowledge:

---

[6] This correspondence is partly online http://henripoincarepapers.univ-lorraine.fr.

[7] About 50 % of this letters are with scientists. Original letters come from 63 different archive centers and libraries from 14 countries.

[8] Due to copyright laws, some are not available online.

[9] http://henripoincarepapers.univ-lorraine.fr.

[10] It exists different projects devoted to scientific correspondences for example the CKCC project (http://ckcc.huygens.knaw.nl) [25] or Mapping the Republic of Letters (http://republicofletters.stanford.edu).

- Q_3 requires to know that an individual is an astronomer, possibly using deduction (for instance, Rodolphe Radau was a geodesist and every geodesist is an astronomer).
- Q_4 requires to know relationships between letters (including lost letters).
- Q_5 requires semantic annotations about the content of the letters (Poincaré worked on the three-boby problem).
- Q_6 raises the problem of modeling "late XIXth century": the boundaries of interval of time are imprecise.

The possibility to take into account such queries using semantic web principles and technologies, are examined in the SemanticHPST consortium.

2.3   The Concept of Energy

One part of the SemanticHPST project is dedicated to the concept of energy. Our aim is to create an ontology of energy for researchers working in the field of HPST as well as for science teachers.

For researchers, the ontology aims at making available a methodical body of knowledge that allows previously unseen connections to be made. For example, correspondence between two authors or the presence of a specific term or concept in a text will allow researchers to put forward hypotheses regarding the emergence of an idea or the cross-fertilization of ideas.

For teachers, the ontology aims at acting as a resource, allowing educators to find historical information relevant to school curricula as well as ideas for specific activities to carry out in the classroom.

The content consists of reference texts in the field of HPST, contemporary scientific texts and a database of historic scientific instruments and documents. This content is currently being selected and developed and will be enhanced as the research progresses.

To date, the following three steps have been undertaken on the project:

- The first step was to identify the presumed ways the ontology will be used, for example, the type of requests that a researcher or teacher might make in a search. To this end, one 'persona' for a researcher and one for a teacher have been created. Analyzing the theoretical queries from these two personas helps in the selection of a relevant body of work and is also a useful guide for indexing.
- The second step was to begin indexing the reference texts. Duhem, Poincaré, Mach and Meyerson have been selected for a first approach in order to produce keywords and common references and to outline an embryonic model. Using the shared scientific knowledge of the physicists involved in the project, a sort of 'cloud' of concepts related to describing energy was defined and classified. These elements led to the structure of an initial mind map.
- Finally, based on this mind map (created with Docear), we used Protégé software to create a first draft overview of the project. The next steps require documenting these three steps in detail to refine the data and then build the ontology.

During the stages of the project carried out so far, various problems have been identified that must be resolved. One of the main problems concerns the modeling of time. How can an event be modeled? Moreover, how can knowledge be modeled in a way that avoids immobilizing the knowledge? How should knowledge be contextualized? What approach should be adopted when modeling concerns a concept or an object? How can a coherent and logical body of content be created and how can its coherence be assessed? It is clear that the question of time as well as how to approach the treatment of objects and works are issues to be investigated in the semanticHPST project.

3   The SemanticHPST Tools and Requirements

According to the three described sub-projects, the main goals of researchers in HPST are to access and retrieve relevant resources in existing primary and secondary sources or corpora, to produce new resources in existing corpora, to enrich existing digital corpora or to create new ones, for answering research questions in the history of science and technology. Existing digital corpora come from libraries, information holdings, digital libraries or others like Gallica (http://gallica.bnf.fr), Internet Archive (http://archive.org), Google Books (http://books.google.com), etc., and CMS (Content Management System) (blogs, wikis, Drupal, Omeka, etc. more generally social media tools) have been used by the community[11] and digital AHP (http://www.ahp-numerique.fr/). Some heritage and bibliographic resources have already been described by several institutions, associations and/or project (BNF, Gallica, British Museum, Europeana, Amsterdam Museum, LODLAM, ...). The creation of new corpora or resources can be made on social media tools distributed on Internet (as well as other digital corpora).

The design of tools for HPST researchers has to integrate and/or aggregate the existing heterogeneous tools and to ensure interoperability among them. Thus, the goal is not to build a single new environment, but to design a platform which integrates existing tools selected for their relevance according to the practices of researchers and provide an agile architecture able to model and/or support the processes involved in the research work and enrichment.

This platform will be mainly based on the Semantic Web and Linked Data approaches (RDF Triple Store, ontologies, OWL 2, RDFS, SPARQL, etc.). Nevertheless, the platform will also provide access to non-semantic resources. A network of ontologies dedicated to HPST will be designed to meet the interoperability and open access requirements for corpora. Some existing ontologies and standards will be reused and integrated in the ontology network, like CIDOC-CRM, FRBRoo, FRSAD, Dublin Core, etc. and those available at LOV (http://lov.okfn.org/dataset/lov/).

In this paper, we focus our attention on the resource retrieval problem that we can divide into two different aspects : advanced search in HPST corpora and

---

[11] The *alambic numérique* (http://alambic.hypotheses.org/4924) is based on Omeka.

harvesting distributed corpora. The former focuses on advanced search functionalities in a single corpus. The latter studies the resource retrieval on distributed
corpora. These two aspects will be integrated.

3.1 Advanced Search in HPST Corpora

In order to perform advanced searches in a HPST corpus, we have to build
intelligent digital corpus: corpus with primary and secondary sources having
semantic metadata (RDF Triples) and their corresponding ontologies using a
fragment of OWL (actually, RDFS will be sufficient for the following examples).
These ontologies are domain ontologies related to the corpus. A domain ontology
for Henri Poincaré letters has already been designed. Finally, some tools will have
to be developed for answering some of the queries.

This section presents the advanced search using the query examples Q_3–Q_6
introduced in Sect. 2.2.

Q_3 requires some additional data and knowledge to get satisfactory answers,
as stated in Sect. 2.2. In particular, if the annotation file contains the following
RDFS triples:

> (letter1 isSentBy rodolphe_radau)
>
> (rodolphe_radau rdf:type Geodesist)
>
> (Geodesist rdfs:subClassOf Astronomer)

then the execution of the following SPARQL query on an engine supporting
RDFS

$Q_3 = $ SELECT $?\ell$ WHERE $\{?\ell$ isSentBy $?a$. $?a$ rdf:type Astronomer$\}$

will return letter1.

Q_4, similarly, can be answered by a SPARQL engine supporting RDFS with
the following query:

$Q_4 = $ SELECT $?\ell$ WHERE $\left\{ \begin{array}{l} ?\ell \text{ isAnAnswerTo } ?\ell2 \text{ .} \\ ?\ell2 \text{ isSentBy mittag-leffler} \end{array} \right\}$

It can be noticed that this query can give a letter of the corpus that answers a
lost letter: the missing letter cannot be found, but its answer can.

Q_5, for being executed, requires the use of annotations about the scientific
content of the letter:

$Q_5 = $ SELECT $?\ell$ WHERE $\left\{ \begin{array}{l} ?\ell \text{ hasForTopic } ?t \text{ .} \\ ?t \text{ rdf:type N-body-problem} \end{array} \right\}$

The n-body problem is a topic having sub-topics, in particular, the 3-body problem is a problem more specific than the n-body problem. For this reason, we have

chosen to model these two problems by two classes, the former being more general than the latter. Therefore, a letter of the corpus about the 3-body problem will be returned by the execution of this query.[12]

Q_6 can be modeled by a SPARQL query based on the assumption that "the late XIXth century" corresponds to the interval 1881–1900:

$$Q_6 = \text{SELECT } ?\ell \text{ WHERE } \left\{ \begin{array}{l} ?\ell \texttt{ sentDuringYear ?y .} \\ \texttt{FILTER(?y >= 1881 \&\& ?y <= 1900)} \end{array} \right\}$$

However, this solution is debatable: the modeling of the fuzzy period of time by a crisp interval raises the problem of the choice of the boundaries. Indeed, some events before 1881 or after 1900 can be considered by historians to be related to the end of the XIXth century. In order to address this issue, some approximate search is planned. How to put this idea in practice is an ongoing work.

3.2 Harvesting Distributed Corpora

Harvesting distributed corpora at semantic level (according to Linked Data principles) require to solve two different problems. The first one is to queries several triple store by means of federated queries to linked distributed sources. The second one is to get RDF triples from social media tools.

Most of social media applications are data silos. In other words, data are unavailable on the web. Only people may have access to data, not computers. Reuse and exchange of data among social media tools are only possible by means of API – that is to say manually by mean of one API per tool. Some social media tools like Drupal, Semantic media wiki may have their own triple store exposing data to others.

A toolkit, called SMOOPLE for Semantic Massive Open Online Pervasive Learning Environment, has been designed to solve these two problems. It was firstly dedicated to the technology-enhanced learning domain [12]. The core part of the toolkit can be reused for HPST. It fulfills the needs of researchers in HPST, that is to say it enables us to federate distributed sources and tools.

SMOOPLE has semantic services which are in charge of managing incorporated semantic models, extracting and storing the data produced on social media tools, making and answering to semantic queries against one or several distributed sources (federated queries). The Semantic Web server (semantic services) is based on Jena 2. When the social media tools do not have a triple store and a SPARQL endpoint, content and corresponding semantic metadata can be extracted on the fly from social media applications, by means of plugin (similar to sioc_export) and stored in a RDF repository. Several light ontologies (SIOC, FOAF, DC, RDF, RDFS, etc.) are used to acquire semantic metadata

---

[12] We could also have chosen to model the 3-body problem as an instance of the n-body problem, but first, it is more homogeneous to consider every topic as a class, second, this way, it is always possible to consider a more specific topic, e.g., the restricted 3-body problem for which the mass of one of the 3 bodies in considered to be negligible.

automatically. It will be necessary to define the interlinkage among distributed sources (triple stores) to support federated queries.

4   Epistemological Aspects

An aim of the SemanticHPST project is to focus on the epistemological issues raised by the development of these new tools based on semantic web. This work in progress takes part to epistemological questions in the domain of Digital Humanities.[13] A first series of questions concerns the modeling of knowledge, the main step in building ontologies so that researchers can easily identify and apprehend knowledge. Therefore the creation of effective ontologies requires defining concepts and elucidating certain tacit or implicit knowledge. So the initial questions are: How to approach these definitions? How to ensure that indexing does not immobilize knowledge? How can the modeling anticipate how it will be used in order to ensure that the knowledge generated is contextualized to avoid anachronism and misinterpretation? Moreover, the wide range of works in the collection, including texts (manuscripts, books, letters, web pages), multimedia documents, 3D archaeological or historical objects and media from a variety of sources (photographs, original texts, maps, etc.), necessitate different approaches. This raises the question: How to approach a photograph, a scientific instrument or a text and still obtain a unified ontology? How can the modeling enable relationships between objects yet avoid the pitfalls described above?

In the field of HPST, the issue of modeling time is central and particularly tricky. Modeling a long period of time, an event, a succession of events or events that are juxtaposed requires making decisions that should be taken collectively. Indeed, this emerging issue is shared by historians [9,15,21] and should serve to feed into theoretical discussions between researchers from different disciplines.

A second series of questions concerns the researcher's environment, which has significantly changed with the rise of digitized data. Whatever the works considered or their origin (libraries, archives, etc.), the massive volume of data, its diversity and location are all part of this change. Yet this radical shift is not exclusively the result of the accumulation of a large amount of data. The fact that data can be 'analyzed as well as communicated, represented, reused – in short, mobilized for research – in a quantity and with an ease incomparable with previous periods' [10] is a major transformation that needs to be taken into account. This raises new questions for researchers:

– How does one build and define a body of content that is coherent and complete? Whereas 'traditional' methods created collections using identified, bounded, localized archives, with the question of consistency limited in most cases to the cross-fertilization of archives as regards the historical context, the accessibility of multiple documents today requires a reexamination of the very concept of a collection of works.

---

[13] See thematical issue "la numérisation du patrimoine" of [1] or the issue "Le métier d'historien à l'ére numérique : nouveaux outils, nouvelle épistémologie ?" of [2].

– How does one evaluate a body of work; in other words, how does one recognize its relevance?
– In this context, the type of source and its references must be specified. Does the wide range of sources used require more refined classification than the standard usage of primary and secondary sources? Would a new typology be pertinent given this broad diversity? Should the references to these sources, particularly information concerning digital archives, lead to new codification that allows, for example, multiple identifications for the considered source, improving its accessibility?

5   Conclusion

The aim of this proposal is to contribute to the development of the research in the domain of digital humanities. Based on the Semantic Web principles and technologies, the SemanticHPST group proposes new methodologies in History and Philosophy of Science and Technology in the framework of a strong collaboration between labs working in the area of computer science and humanities (here HPST). The main goal is to enrich the practices of researcher and communities in HPST as well in science and technology heritage. To deal with such a goal, the project has to: (i) Build intelligent digital corpora, that is to say corpora with primary and secondary sources having semantic metadata and their corresponding ontologies; (ii) Design tools to access and enrich existing corpora and to create new ones; (iii) Evaluate the resulting evolution of practices in historical science and build an epistemological viewpoint about the impact of new tools and practices in humanities based on knowledge modeling and semantic web.

Another important issue is to deal with the reuse of intelligent digital corpora. Thus, it is necessary to build representations of the entities, people and processes involved in producing the digital corpora. The "PROV Model Primer" from W3C (http://www.w3.org/TR/prov-primer/) can be used to address this issue.

References

1. Documents pour l'Histoire des Techniques, vol. 18-2 (2009)
2. Revue d'histoire moderne et contemporaine, vol. 58–4bis (2011)
3. Bird, J.: The Major Seaports of the United Kingdom. Hutchinson, London (1963)
4. de Boer, V., van Rossum, M., Leinenga, J., Hoekstra, R.: Dutch ships and sailors linked data. In: Mika, P., Tudorache, T., Bernstein, A., Welty, C., Knoblock, C., Vrandečić, D., Groth, P., Noy, N., Janowicz, K., Goble, C. (eds.) ISWC 2014, Part I. LNCS, vol. 8796, pp. 229–244. Springer, Heidelberg (2014)
5. Boonstra, O., Breure, L., Doorn, P.: Past, present and future of historical information science. Historical Inf. Sci. **29**(2), 4–132 (2004)
6. Bruneau, O., Grapi, P., Peter, H., Laubé, S., Massa-Esteve, M.R., De Vittori, T.: History of Science and Technology. ICT and Inquiry Based Science Teaching. Frank-Timme, Berlin (2012)
7. Bruneau, O., Laubé, S.: Inquiry based Science teaching and History of Science. In: [6], pp. 13–28 (2012)

8. Bruneau, O., Laubé, S., de Vittori, T.: ICT and History of mathematics in the case of IBST. In: [6], pp. 145–160 (2012)
9. Corda, I., Bennett, B., Dimitrova, V.: A logical model of an event ontology for exploring connections in historical domains. In: Tenth International Semantic Web Conference (ISWC) Workshop on Detection, Representation and Exploitation of Events in Semantic Web (Derive 2011) (2011)
10. Dacos, M., Mounier, P.: Humanités numériques. rapport commandé, Institut Français, Ministére des Affaires étrangères, Paris (2014)
11. Gilliot, J.M., Pham, N.C., Garlatti, S., Rebaï, I., Laubé, S.: Tackling mobile & pervasive learning in IBST. In: [6], pp. 181–201 (2012)
12. Gilliot, J.M., Garlatti, S., Rebaï, I., Pham Nguyen, C.: A Mobile Learning Scenario improvement for HST Inquiry Based learning. In: Workshop Emerging Web Technologies, Facing the Future of Education (2012). workshop in conjunction with www2012 conference
13. Guedj, M., Bachtold, M.: Towards a new strategy for teaching energy based on the history and philosophy of the concept of energy. In: [6] (2012)
14. Hughes, T.P.: The Evolution of Large Technological Systems. In: Bijker, W., Hughes, T.P., Pinch, T.J. (eds.) The Social Construction of Technological Systems, pp. 51–82. MIT Press, Cambridge (1987)
15. Hyvönen, E., Lindquist, T., Törnroos, J., Mäkelä, E.: History on the semantic web as linked data–an event gazetteer and timeline for the world war i. In: Proceedings of CIDOC (2012)
16. Laubé, S.: Culture matérielle du port arsenal de Brest au XVIIIème siècle : approche systémique. In: [16] (To be published in 2015)
17. Laubé, S.: Les grues de l'arsenal en tant que marqueurs de l'évolution scientifique et technologique du port arsenal de Brest. In: [16] (To be published in 2015)
18. Laubé, S., Rohou, B., Garlatti, S.: Humanités numériques et web sémantique. De l'intérêt de la modélisation des connaissances en histoire des sciences et des techniques pour une histoire comparée des ports de Brest (France) et Mar del Plata (Argentine). In: Digital Intelligence 2014, 17–19 September 2014
19. Meroño-Peñuela, A., Ashkpour, A., van Erp, M., Mandemakers, K., Breure, L., Scharnhorst, A., Schlobach, S., van Harmelen, F.: Semantic technologies for historical research: A survey. Semant. Web J. 1–27 (2015). http://iospress.metapress.com/content/A842V11135QK5055
20. Nabonnand, P. (ed.): La correspondance entre Henri Poincaré et Gösta Mittag-Leffler. Birkhäuser, Basel (1998)
21. Neelameghan, A., Narayana, G.J.: Concept and expression of time: Cultural variations and impact on knowledge organization: PART 7: Ontology and representation of time in knowledge organization tools used in information systems1. Inf. Stud. 19(2), 105–131 (2013)
22. Ustinov, V.A.: Les calculateurs électroniques appliqués à la sciencehistorique. Annales Économies, Sociétés, Civilisations 18(2), 263–294 (1963)
23. Walter, S., Bolmont, E., Coré, A. (eds.): La correspondance entre Henri Poincaré et les physiciens, chimistes et ingénieurs. Birkhäuser, Basel (2007)
24. Walter, S., Krömer, R., Schiavon, M. (eds.): La correspondance entre Henri Poincaré avec les astronomes et les géodésiens. Birkhäuser, Basel (2014)
25. Wittek, P., Ravenek, W.: Supporting the exploration of a corpus of 17th-century scholarly correspondences by topic modeling. In: Maegaard, B. (ed.) Supporting Digital Humanities 2011: Answering the unaskable, Copenhagen, Denmark (2011)

5th International USEWOD Workshop: Using the Web in the Age of Data

DBpedia's Triple Pattern Fragments: Usage Patterns and Insights

Ruben Verborgh[(✉)]

Ghent University – iMinds, Ghent, Belgium
ruben.verborgh@ugent.be

Abstract. Queryable Linked Data is published through several interfaces, including SPARQL endpoints and Linked Data documents. In October 2014, the DBpedia Association announced an official Triple Pattern Fragments interface to its popular DBpedia dataset. This interface proposes to improve the availability of live queryable data by dividing query execution between clients and servers. In this paper, we present a usage analysis between November 2014 and July 2015. In 9 months time, the interface had an average availability of 99.99%, handling 16,776,170 requests, 43.0% of which were served from cache. These numbers provide promising evidence that low-cost Triple Pattern Fragments interfaces provide a viable strategy for live applications on top of public, queryable datasets.

Keywords: Linked Data · Linked Data Fragments · DBpedia

1 Introduction

DBpedia [2] is currently the most well-known dataset within the Semantic Web community. It consists of hundreds of millions of RDF triples automatically generated from the free Wikipedia encyclopedia. Such large Linked Datasets come with important challenges – most prominently: *how do we provide scalable queryable access to them?* The traditional answer has been to set up a public SPARQL endpoint [4], but such endpoints suffer from low availability rates [3]. Yet reliable access is a prerequisite to build applications on top of a queryable DBpedia interface.

Mid-October 2014, the DBpedia community opened a Triple Pattern Fragments interface[1] [14] maintained by the author of this paper. This interface is designed to allow high availability on the server side, while still enabling live querying on the client side. Queries take more time and bandwidth, because they are mostly executed by the client, but the timings are consistent so that building applications on top of a public DBpedia interface becomes realistic.

In this paper, we discuss the analysis of the first 9 full months of usage data of the English DBpedia Triple Pattern Fragments interface, as well as availability statistics measured by an independent party.

---

[1] Available at http://fragments.dbpedia.org/2014/en.

© Springer International Publishing Switzerland 2015
F. Gandon et al. (Eds.): ESWC 2015, LNCS 9341, pp. 431–442, 2015.
DOI: 10.1007/978-3-319-25639-9_54

The remainder of this paper is structured as follows. First, we discuss interfaces to Linked Data in Sect. 2. We then discuss the hardware and software setup of the server and analysis in Sect. 3. Next, Sect. 4 formulates and answers usage questions with log data. Finally, we conclude in Sect. 5.

2   Related Work

In this section, we summarize existing Web APIS to publish Linked Datasets. *Linked Data Fragments* (LDF, [14,16]) were introduced as a uniform view to capture the characteristics of any Linked Data Web API. The common aspect of all interfaces is that, in one way or another, they offer specific parts of a dataset. Each part is referred to as a *Linked Data Fragment*, consisting of:

data the triples of the dataset that match an interface-specific *selector*;
metadata triples to describe the fragment itself;
controls hyperlinks and/or hypermedia forms that lead to other fragments.

File-Based Datasets. So-called *data dumps* are conceptually the most simple APIS: the *data* consists of all triples in the dataset. They are combined into a (usually compressed) archive and published at a single URL. Sometimes the archive contains *metadata*, but *controls*–with the possible exception of HTTP URIs in RDF triples–are not present.

Linked Data Documents. Datasets published through the Linked Data principles [1] are available as individual documents per subject, which can be retrieved by performing an HTTP GET request on the subject's URL *("dereferencing")*. Each such document is a fragment, in which the *data* consists of triples related to that subject, the *metadata* set might contain properties such as author and publication data, and the *controls* consist of links to other Linked Data documents. Querying is possible through strategies such as link traversal [7].

SPARQL Endpoints. SPARQL endpoints [4] allow executing SPARQL queries [6] on a dataset through HTTP. A SPARQL fragment's *data* consists of triples matching the query (assuming the CONSTRUCT form); the *metadata* and *control* sets are empty. Query execution is performed entirely by the server, and because each client can ask highly individualized requests, the reusability of fragments is low. This, combined with complexity of SPARQL query execution, likely contributes to the low availability of public SPARQL endpoints [3].

Triple Pattern Fragments. The Triple Pattern Fragments interface has been designed to minimize server-side processing, while at the same time enabling efficient live querying on the client side [11,14]. A fragment's *data* consists of all triples that match a specific triple pattern, and can possibly be paged. Each fragment page mentions the estimated total number of matches as metadata, and contains *hypermedia controls* to find all other Triple Pattern Fragments of the same dataset. Since requests are less individualized, fragments are more likely to be reused across clients, which increases the benefits of caching [14].

3   Deployment and Analysis Setup

3.1   Server Specifications

Hardware. The official DBpedia Triple Pattern Fragments interface is hosted on a virtual machine from the Amazon Elastic Compute Cloud (EC2). We opted for a c3.2xlarge machine configuration, which has the following characteristics:

virtual cpus	8 (Intel Xeon E5-2680 v2)
memory	15 GB
hard disk space	2 × 80 GB
price	$ 0.478 per hour

We would like to stress that the above specifications are actually too high for our purpose; as a result, the server is currently mostly idle. The issue is, however, that Amazon does not allow customization of machines. While lighter configurations exist, they come with lower disk throughput and/or bandwidth.

Software. The machine has been configured with the following open-source software packages and versions:

operating system	Ubuntu Linux 14.04 LTS
Web server	nginx 1.4.6
application server	LDF server[2] 1.1.4 on top of Node.js 0.10.36

The nginx server acts as a reverse proxy and cache. All requests first reach nginx, which checks whether a response is present in the cache based on a unique identifier consisting of the request URI and the value of the HTTP Accept header. If so, it is sent to the client; if not, the request is forwarded to the application server. The application server then parses the request, and retrieves the DBpedia data from an HDT file [5] that is loaded into memory. It is then serialized in a format according to the Accept header, sent to the client, and stored in the cache.

3.2   Analysis Setup

All incoming requests are logged line by line in a file by the nginx Web server. Note that logging does *not* happen on the application server, as this server only receives those requests that are not handled by the cache. The resulting access logs are hosted publicly.[3] Each log line contains the following fields:

1. the client's IP address;
2. the URI requested by the client;
3. value of the client's Accept header;
4. value of the client's Referer header;
5. value of the client's User-Agent header;
6. the server's local time;

---

[2] Source code available at https://github.com/LinkedDataFragments/Server.js.
[3] Available at http://fragments.dbpedia.org/logs/.

7. the server's response size;
8. the server's response cache status;
9. the server's response HTTP status code.

Additionally, the availability of the HTTP interface is monitored by the independent third-party service Pingdom, because public availability—by definition—cannot reliably be monitored by the Web server under consideration. Pingdom performs an HTTP request once every minute for the ?s rdf:type ?o fragment and notes whether a response was successfully received. If no timely response arrives, the interface is assumed to be unavailable.

4   Usage Analysis

In this section, we will search for answers to the following usage questions:

1. How many requests were issued?
2. Which clients made these requests?
3. What types of content were those clients interested in?
4. Where did the requests originate from?
5. What kind of triple patterns were requested?
6. How effective has the cache been?
7. What part of time was the server (un-)available?

We focused on requests with an HTTP 200 OK response only, in order to remove (very minimal) noise from the 0.19 % invalid requests against the interface.

4.1   Number of Requests

The server logs reveal a total of 16,776,170 requests for Triple Pattern Fragments of the English DBpedia version[4], or an average of 1,864,019 requests per month during the 9 considered months (November 2014–July 2015). Large outliers skew this average, so perhaps the median of 486,045 (obtained in March) is a more meaningful number. Figure 1 visualizes the number of requests per month.

April 2015 had a strong traffic peak with over 10 million requests. While we have no concrete evidence, we assume there is a connection with the submission deadline of the International Semantic Web Conference 2015: main track papers were due April 30, 2015, so perhaps one or more research groups were running experiments against the interface.

4.2   User Agents

Figure 2 shows the proportion of user agents per requested fragment. The majority of requests were issued by clients that identified themselves as Triple Pattern

---

[4] URLs starting with http://fragments.dbpedia.org/2014/en.

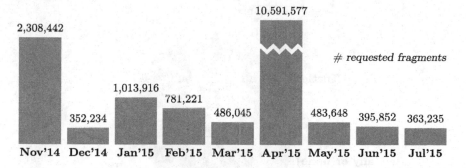

Fig. 1. April had an exceptionally high consumption of fragments, followed by November. The median is 486,045, which was obtained in March.

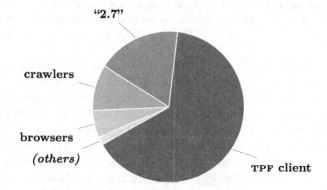

Fig. 2. The Triple Pattern Fragments client is by far the most common client, followed by an unknown client, crawlers, and finally browsers. Some minorities (command-line utilities, other languages...) are marginally represented.

Fragment (TPF) clients. This is the identification sent by the JavaScript client-side library,[5] which can either be used as standalone utility from the command-line or as a library inside of other applications (which thus cannot be distinguished by default). If the library runs inside of a browser application, the user agent will be that of the browser, so these usages are counted in that category.

The second-most popular client identifies itself with "User-Agent: 2.7", which requested approximately 3 million requests, all of which originated from Germany. This seems to be an error, as "2.7" does not follow a conventional format for user agent strings. We could not determine the identify of this client more precisely. There might be a connection with Python 2.7 (which is a common version), but other Python clients identified themselves in a more conventional way (e.g., "python-requests/2.7.0").

Crawlers requested a large portion of DBpedia fragments. This is especially remarkable because such usage contrasts with SPARQL endpoints, which belong

---

[5] Source code available at https://github.com/LinkedDataFragments/Client.js.

436   R. Verborgh

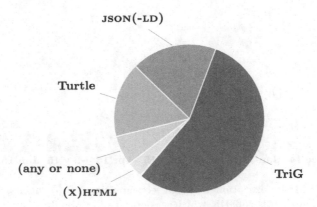

Fig. 3. The quad-based TriG and JSON-LD formats were most popular, followed by the triple-based format Turtle. Over a million requests did not carry a preference.

to the so-called "deep Web": in order to access data, a user must write a SPARQL query in an HTML form. The only SPARQL endpoint resources that are accessible on the Web are SPARQL queries that are explicitly linked from another page. While the Triple Pattern Fragments specification only demands the presence of a hypermedia form (which would thus also hide fragments in the deep Web), the used server implementation explicitly links to relevant fragments. For instance, the fragment "subjects born in Slovenia" links to fragments for the birthplace predicate, and all individual subjects born in Slovenia. This allows people and crawlers to browse the interface similar to how Linked Data documents are navigated. An added value of Triple Pattern Fragments is that *all* resources can be followed within the interface, not only those resources that share the URI space of the current document (as is the cases with Linked Data documents [16]).

Finally, browser consumption accounted for almost a million requests, the majority of which (840,006) appear to be performed by client-side scripts. This latter number was determined by looking for non-human-targeted content types such as Turtle or JSON, which we discuss in more detail in the next section.

4.3   Requested Content Types

Figure 3 shows the preferred content type indicated in the `Accept` header of the request. Given that the TPF client made most of the requests (Fig. 2), this client's preferred content type TriG is also the most popular. Previous versions of the TPF client consumed Turtle, which partly accounts for the popularity of this format in Fig. 3. The drawback of triple-based formats such as Turtle is that they do not allow a clean separation of data and metadata, while quad-based formats like TriG do [14]. In a previous analysis, we predicted the increased popularity of TriG because of this changed client preference [15]. The popularity of JSON(-LD) might come as a surprise for the Linked Data community, but perhaps less so for JavaScript developers, who employ JSON as a native format.

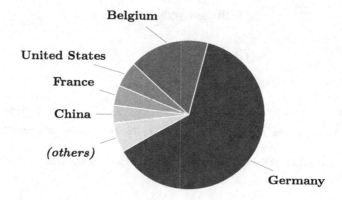

Fig. 4. Germany requested most fragments, followed by Belgium. Automated crawlers strongly influence consumption from the United States (Google) and China (Baidu).

Only a minority of clients did not indicate a specific preference, either by explicitly accepting */* or not sending an Accept header at all. These clients received an HTML representation from the server.

4.4 Geographic Location

The majority of requests originated from Germany, as visualized in Fig. 4. On the second place is Belgium; most Belgian requests were generated by our team at Ghent University – iMinds, which coordinates the DBpedia Triple Pattern Fragments server. Requests from the United States and China were largely made by respectively the Google and Baidu crawlers.

In total, requests arrived from 80 different countries. While determining more detailed locations is possible (e.g., city level), we decided not to do so out of privacy concerns.

4.5 Requested Triple Patterns

SPARQL endpoints typically receive highly specific queries that provide an insight into a concrete question. If Triple Pattern Fragments interfaces are used to evaluate SPARQL queries, only triple patterns arrive at the server. Such individual patterns only provide a limited idea of what clients were doing, which could be enhanced by analyzing series of requests made by particular clients. However, there is no guarantee that clients are actually executing SPARQL queries (except perhaps if the user agent is "TPF Client"), since the interface can be used in many different ways. For example, crawlers do not evaluate complex queries.

Figure 5 shows the four most requested kinds of patterns:

1. *"Subjects of a specific type"* fragments (?s rdf:type <o> for specific <o>) are most common. We expect such patterns to occur frequently in SPARQL queries.

Ruben Verborgh

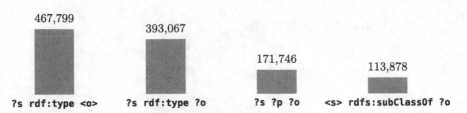

Fig. 5. Type and subclass selections were popular, as well as the generic "all" fragment.

2. The pattern *"subjects that have a type"* (`?s rdf:type ?o`) is highly popular. The main reason for this is that the Pingdom service (see Sect. 4.7) requests this fragment to measure availability.
3. The *"all"* fragment (`?s ?p ?o`), which is the most generic fragment of the dataset and thus a natural starting point, was requested 171,746 times. Query evaluations typically start from this fragment (but this is by no means an obligation). This number might thus be a vague indication for the number of executed SPARQL queries.
4. *"Subclasses of a specific subject"* fragments (`<s> rdf:type ?o` for specific `<s>`) were also represented significantly in the total number.

The information these patterns yield is quite limited. While this is positive for privacy on the one hand, it restricts the possibilities for analysis on the other hand. In Sect. 5, we review possible strategies to circumvent this obstacle.

4.6   Cache Effectiveness

A premise of the Triple Pattern Fragments interface is that clients partly reuse the same fragments to achieve different but similar goals. With SPARQL endpoints, clients instead send highly specialized requests; overlapping information between them cannot be reused on the HTTP interface level. With Triple Pattern Fragments, the number of *unique* requests is relatively smaller, so regular HTTP caches function more effectively.

The nginx reverse proxy server has been configured to cache requested fragments for a maximum time of 1 h. Uniqueness of requests is determined by a combination of URL and `Accept` header. As such, the Triple Pattern Fragments server generates each unique response at most once per hour; all subsequent requests are handled by the cache. Furthermore, the proxy server sets the expiration date of responses to 7 days in the future. Clients that have a built-in cache themselves, such as browsers, are thereby suggested to only repeat a request for a resource after a week. Note that the standalone TPF client does not have a persistent cache; each invocation of that client results in new resource accesses.

As Fig. 6 shows, 43.0 % of responses were served directly from the nginx cache; another 16.5 % were present but had been so for longer than the expiration time.

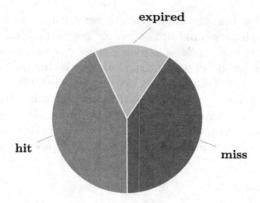

Fig. 6. 59.5 % of requested fragments was already present in the cache; 16.5 % had expired, but 43.0 % could be reused. The remaining 40.5 % was not cached.

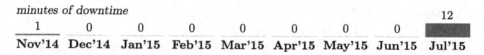

Fig. 7. Most months had 100 % uptime. The total downtime was limited to 13 min in the 9 full months the interface has been available so far.

In other words, roughly two fifths of all responses were needed again by the same client or other clients within the hour. Finally, a few requests (3,054) explicitly asked to bypass the cache. So while 57.0 % of requests were not served by the cache, the caching mechanism was able to reduce the load on the application server by 43.0 %. Since the dataset in this case is static, and the number of fragments finite, we could set a higher (of even infinite) cache timeout. At the moment, however, there was no necessity to do so.

4.7 Availability

One of the main goals of the Triple Pattern Fragments interface is to maximize availability, in order to allow building applications on public, live queryable Linked Data sources. During the period of November 2014 to July 2015, a fragment was retrieved from the server every minute to verify availability. This amounts to a total of 273 days × 1, 440 min per day = 393, 120 min. The results are available in an online interface[6] and summarized in Fig. 7.

The results reveal that the interface had 100 % uptime in 7 months out of 9. There were three separate downtime incidents during which ping requests did not result in a timely response: one in November (1 min) and two in July (1 min and 11 min). In all of these cases, the Pingdom requests did not even reach the nginx server, as evidenced by a lack of log entries during those periods.

---

[6] Available at http://stats.pingdom.com/tpb64v451f9p/1382520.

There is no indication that the application server was unavailable or overloaded. The cause of the incidents could unfortunately not be determined.

In any case, these observations allow a precise calculation of the availability during the observed period of 9 months. Dividing the minutes of availability by the total number of minutes gives $393,107/393,120 \approx 99.9967\%$. This amounts to an availability level of "4 nines", which can only be achieved with an average maximum of 4 min of downtime per month, which was met in all months except July. The next availability level ("5 nines") would restrict downtime to 26 seconds per month, which was met in all months except November and July.

5   Conclusions

When the official Triple Pattern Fragments interface for DBpedia was released, we mostly heard three types of questions:

- Will this interface be used?
- If so, how will clients use it?
- Will the availability of this interface be sufficient for live application usage?

The analysis in this paper allows us to formulate a preliminary answer to all three of them.

First of all, the interface has indeed been used, as evidenced by more than 16 million requests in the course of its first 9 months. Most of this usage came from the client-side SPARQL query executor we built for the Triple Pattern Fragments interface, while can serve as a library for many types of applications. Search engine crawlers also consumed many fragments of the interface. Relatively few people browsed the interface directly, as it is primarily targeted at machines. It does raise the question whether it makes sense to improve accessibility for people. Client IP addresses from 80 countries (as opposed to 47 in a previous analysis [15]) show that usage is spreading geographically.

Second, while the analysis provides us with some insights about how the interface is used, more high-level patterns are absent. On the one hand, this is a blessing for privacy: clients only ask generic questions, and they themselves can combine this to answers for more complex questions in any way they see fit. On the other hand, it makes it harder to understand what kind of usage is popular, and for which use cases we could or might need to optimize. This process could be facilitated if we explicitly ask clients to provide feedback [13]. For now, we are in the dark as to precisely what SPARQL queries–and other tasks–clients have executed. Having more information would allow us to compare this with, for instance, the logs of the public DBpedia SPARQL endpoint. At the same time, we should realize that not all clients of Triple Pattern Fragments interfaces necessarily have the evaluation of SPARQL queries as a task or subtask.

Third, the average availability of 99.99% of the server (100% in 7 months out of 9) removes any doubt that the Triple Pattern Fragments interface is sufficiently reliable for live applications. We must, however, remark two things here. While 16.8 million requests is a large quantity for a young interface, it is still nowhere near full capacity. The server is still mostly idling, so in order to really find out its limits, more requests are necessary. Also, the number of requests cannot be compared to that of a SPARQL endpoint, as in many cases, more requests are necessary to achieve the same goal. When talking about availability, we therefore need to mention expressivity too. The goal of the Triple Pattern Fragments interface is to reliably balance both.

In the future, we should consider experimenting with more expressive interfaces. For instance, we could provide extra functionality such as substring searches [10], which enable faster evaluation of SPARQL queries with certain FILTER clauses. It could also drive specific tools and applications such as auto-completion widgets or linking and reconciliation tasks [8]. To improve query performance, the incorporation of additional metadata in responses can be beneficial [12].

Our conclusion is that applications now have a reliable interface to query the public DBpedia dataset. Therefore, we seem to have overcome one of the main obstacles that could hold developers from building applications on top of live Linked Data. An important question remains: *is this enough?* Now that reliable access is possible, what excuses remain for not building intelligent Linked Data clients? It seems the next move should be made by application developers, given that the data and the tools are now *really* there, 99.99 % of time. We should keep our eyes, ears, and minds open to the demands of this community to help evolve the concept of Semantic Web applications from vision to reality. Furthermore, the DBpedia use case can act as an inspiration for others who want to publish queryable Linked Data at low cost – or even for free [9].

Acknowledgements. Ruben Verborgh is a Postdoctoral Fellow of the Research Foundation Flanders.

Pingdom (https://www.pingdom.com/) graciously provided us with availability monitoring. The geographic analysis was performed using GeoLite data created by Max d. Special thanks to Dimitris Kontokostas from the DBpedia Association for giving us the opportunity to host DBpedia as Triple Pattern Fragments.

References

1. Bizer, C., Heath, T., Berners-Lee, T.: Linked Data - the story so far. Int. J. Semant. Web Inf. Syst. **5**(3), 1–22 (2009). http://tomheath.com/papers/bizer-heath-berners-lee-ijswis-linked-data.pdf
2. Bizer, C., Lehmann, J., Kobilarov, G., Auer, S., Becker, C., Cyganiak, R., Hellmann, S.: DBpedia - a crystallization point for the Web of Data. J. Web Semant. **7**(3), 154–165 (2009). http://www.sciencedirect.com/science/article/pii/S1570826809000225
3. Buil-Aranda, C., Hogan, A., Umbrich, J., Vandenbussche, P.Y.: SPARQL Web-querying infrastructure: ready for action?. In: Proceedings of the 12th International Semantic Web Conference, November 2013. http://link.springer.com/chapter/10.1007/978-3-642-41338-4_18

4. Feigenbaum, L., Williams, G.T., Clark, K.G., Torres, E.: SPARQL 1.1 protocol. Recommendation, World Wide Web Consortium, March 2013. http://www.w3. org/TR/sparql11-protocol/
5. Fernández, J.D., Martínez-Prieto, M.A., Gutiérrez, C., Polleres, A.: Binary RDF representation for publication and exchange (HDT). J. Web Semant. **19**, 22–41 (2013)
6. Harris, S., Seaborne, A.: SPARQL 1.1 query language. Recommendation, World Wide Web Consortium, March 2013. http://www.w3.org/TR/sparql11-query/
7. Hartig, O.: An overview on execution strategies for Linked Data queries. Datenbank-Spektrum **13**(2), 89–99 (2013). http://dx.doi.org/10.1007/s13222-013-0122-1
8. van Hooland, S., Verborgh, R., De Wilde, M., Hercher, J., Mannens, E., Van de Walle, R.: Evaluating the success of vocabulary reconciliation for cultural heritage collections. J. Am. Soc. Inform. Sci. Technol. **64**(3), 464–479 (2013). http://freeyourmetadata.org/publications/freeyourmetadata.pdf
9. Matteis, L., Verborgh, R.: Hosting queryable and highly available Linked Data for free. In: Proceedings of the ISWC Developers Workshop, October 2014. http://ceur-ws.org/Vol-1268/paper3.pdf
10. Van Herwegen, J., De Vocht, L., Verborgh, R., Mannens, E., Van de Walle, R.: Substring filtering for low-cost Linked Data interfaces. In: Proceedings of the 14th International Semantic Web Conference, October 2015. http://linkeddatafragments.org/publications/iswc2015-substring.pdf
11. Van Herwegen, J., Verborgh, R., Mannens, E., Van de Walle, R.: Query execution optimization for clients of Triple Pattern Fragments. In: Proceedings of the 12th Extended Semantic Web Conference, June 2015. http://linkeddatafragments.org/publications/eswc2015.pdf
12. Vander Sande, M., Verborgh, R., Van Herwegen, J., Mannens, E., Van de Walle, R.: Opportunistic Linked Data querying through approximate membership metadata. In: Proceedings of the 14th International Semantic Web Conference, October 2015. http://linkeddatafragments.org/publications/iswc2015-amf.pdf
13. Verborgh, R.: The lonesome LOD cloud. In: Proceedings of the 4th USEWOD Workshop on Usage Analysis and the Web of Data (May 2014), http://people.cs. kuleuven.be/bettina.berendt/USEWOD2014/verborgh_usewod2014.pdf
14. Verborgh, R., et al.: Querying datasets on the web with high availability. In: Mika, P., et al. (eds.) ISWC 2014, Part I. LNCS, vol. 8796, pp. 180–196. Springer, Heidelberg (2014). http://linkeddatafragments.org/publications/iswc2014.pdf
15. Verborgh, R., Mannens, E., Van de Walle, R.: Initial usage analysis of DBpedia's Triple Pattern Fragments. In: Proceedings of the 5th USEWOD Workshop on Usage Analysis and the Web of Data, June 2015. http://linkeddatafragments.org/publications/usewod2015.pdf
16. Verborgh, R., Vander Sande, M., Colpaert, P., Coppens, S., Mannens, E., Van de Walle, R.: Web-scale querying through Linked Data Fragments. In: Proceedings of the 7th Workshop on Linked Data on the Web, April 2014. http://events. linkeddata.org/ldow2014/papers/ldow2014_paper_04.pdf

WaSABi: 3rd Workshop on Semantic Web Enterprise Adoption and Best Practice

Applying Semantic Technology to Film Production

Jos Lehmann[1]([⊠]), Sarah Atkinson[1], and Roger Evans[2]

[1] School of Art, Design and Media, University of Brighton, Brighton, UK
jos.lehmann@gmail.com, s.a.atkinson@brighton.ac.uk
[2] School of Computing, Engineering and Mathematics, University of Brighton,
Brighton, UK
r.p.evans@brighton.ac.uk

Abstract. Film production is an information- and knowledge-intensive industrial process which is undergoing dramatic changes in response to evolving digital technology. The Deep Film Access Project (DFAP) has been researching the potential role of semantic technology in film production, focussing on how a semantic infrastructure could contribute to the integration of the data and metadata generated during the film production lifecycle. This paper reports on the preliminary development of a knowledge framework to support the automatic management of feature film digital assets, based on a workflow analysis supported by an OWL ontology. We discuss the challenges of building on previous work and present examples of ontological modelling of key film production concepts in a semantically rich hybrid ontological framework.

1 Introduction

Film production is an information- and knowledge-intensive industrial process, spanning several phases from development to archiving to re-purposing, which is undergoing dramatic changes in response to evolving digital technology. In this context the Deep Film Access Project (DFAP)[2] has been focussing on the potential role of semantic technology in film production, in particular on how a semantic infrastructure could contribute to the integration of the data and metadata generated during the film production lifecycle.

An important research objective of DFAP is the development of a knowledge framework, consisting of a workflow analysis and an ontology, to support the automatic management of feature film digital assets. To facilitiate this, the project has benefited from the consultation with the independent film production company, Adventure Pictures Ltd., who provided access to a full set of digital assets for their recent production *Ginger & Rosa* (Dir. Sally Potter, 2012), their

---

A previous version of this paper appeared at http://2015.wasabi-ws.org/papers/wasabi15_3.pdf and https://www.academia.edu/12293840/Applying_Semantic_Technology_to_Film_Production.

© Springer International Publishing Switzerland 2015
F. Gandon et al. (Eds.): ESWC 2015, LNCS 9341, pp. 445–453, 2015.
DOI: 10.1007/978-3-319-25639-9_55

interactive film production website SP-ARK[1], and discussions with key practioners involved in the production process. This data, metadata and expertise were analysed to develop a preliminary understanding of the knowledge underlying the film production process, which was then represented as a workflow chart and coded as an extension of pre-existing foundational and core ontologies in the Web Ontology Language (OWL)[2] using the ontology editor Protégé [3].

This process offered insights into a number of issues that need to be taken into account when automating a business process such as film production using semantic technology. It became apparent how eliciting knowledge from practioners and coding such elicited knowledge into a pre-existing ontology both raise issues of meaning negotiation. But it also has begun to reveal the benefits that more precise modelling can bring to the management, re-use and archiving of digital assets.

This paper presents results of these research activities. Section 2 describes related work for both the description of the process of producing a film and the semantic technology that may have an impact on film production. Section 3 presents a reduced version of the DFAP workflow chart that is being developed. Section 4 presents examples of modelling concepts that are relevant to film production in the DFAP ontology. Section 5 draws conclusions about the process so far and future work.

2   Related Work

In defining the area of semantic technology for film production we have elicited knowledge and researched the literature from two perspectives:

1. Process description: what happens to (digital and other) film production assets throughout the film production process?
2. Relevance of semantic technology: which results in semantic technology research offer solutions that can meet industry expectations in terms of improving the film production process?

As mentioned in Sect. 1, in order to address question 1, above, the assessment of the state of the art in the Film Industry was based on knowledge elicitation from professional film practice. An initial description of the process of film production was provided by the taxonomy of SP-ARK. This was then enriched with categories and populated with data generated during the production of *Ginger & Rosa*. In addition, the professional film practioners were interviewed; these interviews supported the negotiation of meaning with practioners as well of the temporal and functional ordering of process components.

To address question 2, a review of projects concerned with the automation of various aspects of film production was undertaken. Some proposals concentrate on supporting workflow automation, others on supporting the automation

---

[1] http://www.sp-ark.org.
[2] http://www.w3.org/TR/owl2-overview/.
[3] http://protege.stanford.edu/.

of content analysis. Three projects were particularly relevant to the focus of this paper. The *Loculus System* [5] is "an ontology-based information management framework for the Motion Picture Industry". It takes a perspective-based approach to modelling two industry timelines: the Production Cycle Timeline and the Life Stage Timeline (which includes activities beyond production, such as re-purposing). Exploration of Loculus showed that the ontology is quite flat and the production-related branches are not very well developed. However the terminology is very extended and two additional contributions of Loculus are a rule-based relatedeness metric between the various parts of the ontology and the discussion of information extraction techniques that may apply to the production process. *OntoFilm* [4] is a core ontology for Film Production, which conceptualizes the domain and workflows of the film production process. The ontology uses Semantic Web Rule Language (SWRL) rules to express classification conditions. *COMM* [1] is a core ontology for multimedia annotation. Implemented with the purposes of explaining how a media object is composed and what its parts represent, it conveys the semantics of multimedia files (e.g. MPEG-7) by incorporating a foundational ontology (DOLCE) to support conceptual clarity, soundness and extensibility. Wrapping the multimedia ontology in a foundational ontology makes it easier to model the distinction and the relationship between what is represented and the representation. However, the philosophical and terminological overload of the chosen foundational ontology can make use by non-experts rather difficult. Also, despite providing a deeply structured hierarchy, the definitions of the foundational OWL classes are mostly quite shallow or even empty.

Based on the overall results of the literature review, the project decided to adopt an integration and extension approach of existing proposals. In particular the initial DFAP ontology imported both Loculus (for film production terminology) and COMM (for multimedia and foundational terminology). But, as this first version of the DFAP Ontology grew, with more classes using parent classes and properties defined in Loculus and COMM, the imported ontologies became more entangled, which seemed to cause ever growing efficiency problems in reasoning. Loculus was therefore dropped and part of it remodelled directly in the next version of the DFAP ontology. Besides COMM the DFAP Ontology also imports an implementation of Allen's Interval Algebra as SWRL rules created as part of the scene interpretation system SCENIOR [3] which enhances the expressivity of COMM and supports the representation of non-reified temporal and identity constraints within and across classes.

3   The DFAP Workflow

Figure 1 shows part of the current state of the (ongoing) activity of charting the Film Production process as a workflow, using five main categories (i.e., Process, Phase, Operation, Agent or Agent Role, Product). These categories are akin to classes commonly used in Business Process Modelling or Planning (e.g. Process, Activity, Task etc.).

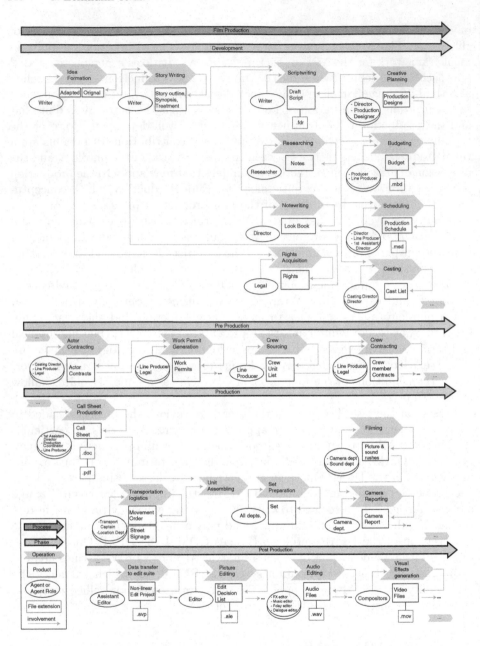

Fig. 1. Fragment of the preliminary DFAP Workflow.

In very general terms, the relations between these categories should be under-stood as temporal part-of relations: a process comprises phases, which in turn comprise operations, which involve agents, often indicated by the role they have, and products. More accurate definitions of these relations depend on the adopted foundational ontology, which is discussed in Sect. 4.

In defining the workflow, the transition from the source material (e.g. existing taxonomies, data, specialist knowledge etc.) had several aims: avoiding ambiguity (when for instance the name of a product was used for the operation that produces that product); finding the right temporal order; finding the right functional order (i.e. the output of which operation is the input of which later operation). The entire workflow consists of seven main phases (Development, Pre-production, Production, Post-production, Delivery, Marketing Distribution and Reception, Archiving).

4   The DFAP Ontology

As mentioned, the DFAP Ontology[4] is based on an integration and extension approach of existing proposals. Figure 2 shows the present import structure of the DFAP ontology: on the right side the COMM multimedia ontology and its imports[5], the names of which mostly convey the type of knowledge coded in the .owl file (e.g. *spatial-relations*-very-lite.owl); on the left hand side, the SWRL-rule representation of Allen's Interval Algebra.

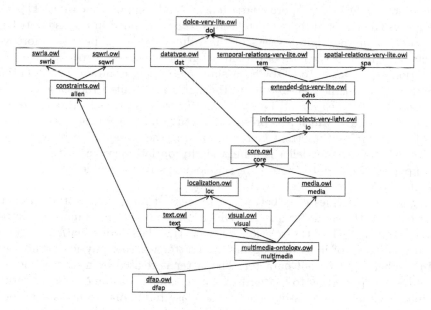

Fig. 2. DFAP Ontology import structure.

Figures 3, 4 and 5 provide examples of how to give a semantics to the notions employed in the Workflow chart show in Fig. 1. Figure 3 models the temporal

[4] http://dfap.dame.org.uk/dfap-ontology/dfap.owl.
[5] http://www.uni-koblenz.de/FB4/Institutes/IFI/AGStaab/Research/comm/ Ontology/.

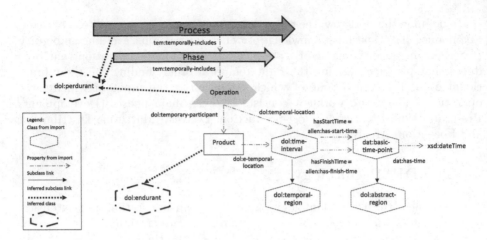

Fig. 3. Pattern for temporal relations

parthood relations between Process, Phase, Operation and Product in terms of temporal inclusion, temporal participation and temporal location. This further allows the adopted temporal relations to be grounded in the xsd:dateTime data present in the digital assets of the Film Production process. Moreover, the classifier returns the correct classification for the classes Process, Phase and Operation with respect to DOLCE, as subtypes of dol:perdurant, i.e., as entities that take place in their entirety only through time, while Product is classified as a subtype of dol:endurant, i.e., as an entity that is present in its entirety at each unit of time at which it is present. Although not surprising, such results of classification are an important factor in guiding the modelling process, as they confirm whether the modeller is using the appropriate relations with respect to the imported ontology to express the ontological structure underlying his or her domain of reference.

Figure 4 exemplifies even better the process of meaning negotiation taking place between the modeller and the DFAP ontology and its imports. The pattern shows a model of the relation between the class IndividualAgent (which includes all types of individual agents, no matter whether physical or fictional) and its subclass FictionalCharacter. The latter is related by means of the relation edns:interpreted-by to the former. The classifier, on the one hand, returns the intuitively correct classification of the class IndividualAgent as subtype of dol:endurant by virtue of temporal participation in an operation and similarly to Product in Fig. 3. On the other hand, FictionalCharacter is also classified as an edns:information-object, i.e., as something like the content of a document, which is an interesting option for the modeller – indeed a fictional character should at least implicitly have some of the properties of a agent, even of a physical agent (e.g. weight), as well as the properties of a non physical information object (e.g. the contents of a book) as it inherently needs to be interpreted by an individual agent. This type of consequences force the modeller to think through his or her

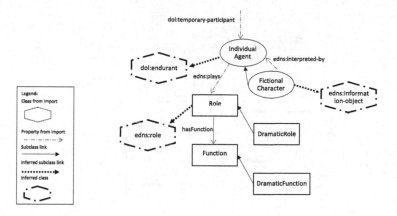

Fig. 4. Pattern for fictional characters

modelling choices, as well as about how much the imported ontologies she or he is using are sufficiently developed.

Figure 5 illustrates an initial model for the class Scene, its relation to the classes Text, Video and Sound, entities which during most phases of the Film Production process are stored in different types of files that need to be synchronized to achieve semantic integration. Similarly to the previous example for the class FictionalCharacter, Scene is correctly classified as a dol:non-physical-endurant with respect to the imports.

5   Conclusion

The DFAP workflow and ontology presented here are still preliminary, but their development has already offered insights into a number of issues for automating the process of film production using semantic technology, and indeed the practical application of semantic technology more generally. While working on the workflow and the ontology, it has become apparent how the activity of eliciting knowledge from film production specialists and the activity of coding such elicited knowledge into a pre-existing ontology pose similar issues of meaning negotiation. On the one hand, when practitioners are interviewed about their activities, they need to be guided through an analytical process of simplification of what they know about their field. On the other hand, when the elicited knowledge is coded into a pre-exiting foundational or core ontology, the knowledge modeller needs to keep testing whether the consequences drawn by the reasoner about the newly inserted knowledge are compatible with the elicited domain knowledge.

From the ontologist's perspective, these two aspects require a range of skills. Working with practitioners is essential to keep the modelling process grounded, but expectation management is also important: comprehensive coverage is an ambitious target and needs to be achieve through milestones which can be

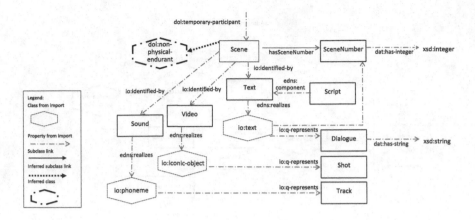

Fig. 5. Pattern for scenes

demonstrably useful, without being perfect. From a technical perspective, development needs to be focused, but designed with scalability and maintainability in mind, and based on a disciplined methodology, borrowing from software engineering quite precise notions of module and interface (between ontologies – cf. [6]) and testing methodologies (such as the ontological equivalent of unit testing).

Once these things are established, the full power of semantic reasoning will be available to support advanced semantic inference over film assets. Our long term aim is to show what impact semantic technology could have on the film industry, for example by improving ease of access to film assets, increasing the depth and value of access, providing new methods of processing data sets for digital film production, and extending metadata protocols within film archival practices.

References

1. Arndt, R., Troncy, R., Staab, S., Hardman, L.: COMM: a core ontology for multimedia annotation. In: Staab, S., Studer, R. (eds.) Handbook on Ontologies, pp. 403–421. Springer, Heidelberg (2009)
2. Atkinson, S., Lehmann, J., Evans, R.: The Deep Film Access Project: Ontology and metadata design for digital film production assets. In: IEEE International Conference on Big Data, Big Data 2014, Washington, DC, October 27–30, 2014, pp. 1–4 (2014)
3. Bohlken, W., Koopmann, P., Hotz, L., Neumann, B.: Towards ontology-based real-time behaviour interpretation. In: Guesgen, H.W., Marsland, S. (eds.) Human Behavior Recognition Technologies: Intelligent Applications for Monitoring and Security, IGI Global, pp. 33–64 (2013)
4. Chakravarthy, A., Beales, R., Matskanis, N., Yang, X.: OntoFilm: a core ontology for film production. In: Chua, T.-S., Kompatsiaris, Y., Mérialdo, B., Haas, W., Thallinger, G., Bailer, W. (eds.) SAMT 2009. LNCS, vol. 5887, pp. 177–181. Springer, Heidelberg (2009)

5. Choudhury, S.T.: Loculus : an ontology-based information management framework for the motion picture industry. PhD thesis, Queensland University of Technology (2010)
6. Ensan, F., Du, W.: A modular approach to scalable ontology development. In: Du, W., Ensan, F. (eds.) Canadian Semantic Web, pp. 79–103. Springer, US (2010). doi:10.1007/978-1-4419-7335-14. ISBN 978-1-4419-7334-4

4th International Workshop on Detection, Representation, and Exploitation of Events in the Semantic Web (DeRiVE 2015)

Reactive Processing of RDF Streams of Events

Jean-Paul Calbimonte[✉] and Karl Aberer

Faculty of Computer Science and Communication Systems, EPFL,
Lausanne, Switzerland
{jean-paul.calbimonte,karl.aberer}@epfl.ch

Abstract. Events on the Web are increasingly being produced in the
form of data streams, and are present in many different scenarios and
applications such as health monitoring, environmental sensing or social
networks. The heterogeneity of event streams has raised the challenges of
integrating, interpreting and processing them coherently. Semantic technologies have shown to provide both a formal and practical framework
to address some of these challenges, producing standards for representation and querying, such as RDF and SPARQL. However, these standards are not suitable for dealing with streams for events, as they do not
include the concpets of streaming and continuous processing. The idea
of RDF stream processing (RSP) has emerged in recent years to fill this
gap, and the research community has produced prototype engines that
cover aspects including complex event processing and stream reasoning
to varying degrees. However, these existing prototypes often overlook
key principles of reactive systems, regarding the event-driven processing,
responsiveness, resiliency and scalability. In this paper we present a reactive model for implementing RSP systems, based on the Actor model,
which relies on asynchronous message passing of events. Furthermore,
we study the responsiveness property of RSP systems, in particular for
the delivery of streaming results.

1 Introduction

Processing streams of events is challenging task in a large number of systems
in the Web. Events can encode different types of information at different levels,
e.g. concerts, financial patterns, traffic events, sensor alerts, etc., generating large
and dynamic volumes of streaming data. Needless to say, the diversity and the
heterogeneity of the information that they produce would make it impossible to
interpret and integrate these data, without the appropriate tools. Semantic Web
standards such as RDF[1] and SPARQL[2] provide a way to address these challenges, and guidelines exist to produce and consume what we know as Linked
Data. While these principles and standards have already gained a certain degree
of maturity and adoption, they are not always suitable for dealing with data
streams. The lack of order and time in RDF, and its stored and bounded characteristics contrast with the inherently dynamic and potentially infinite nature

---

[1] RDF 1.1 Primer http://www.w3.org/TR/rdf11-primer/.
[2] SPARQL 1.1 http://www.w3.org/TR/sparql11-query/.

© Springer International Publishing Switzerland 2015
F. Gandon et al. (Eds.): ESWC 2015, LNCS 9341, pp. 457–468, 2015.
DOI: 10.1007/978-3-319-25639-9_56

of the time-ordered streams. Furthermore, SPARQL is governed by one-time semantics as opposed to the continuous semantics of a stream event processor. It is in this context that it is important to ask *How can streaming events can be modeled and queried in the Semantic Web?*. Several approaches have been proposed in the last years, advocating for extensions to RDF and SPARQL for querying streams of RDF events. Examples of these RDF stream processing (RSP) engines include C-SPARQL [4], SPARQL$_{stream}$ [6], EP-SPARQL [3] or CQELS [11], among others.

Although these extensions target different scenarios and have heterogeneous semantics, they share an important set of common features, e.g. similar RDF stream models, window operators and continuous queries. There is still no standard set of these extensions, but there is an ongoing effort to agree on them in the community[3]. The RSP prototypes that have been presented so far focus almost exclusively in the query evaluation and the different optimizations that can be applied to their algebra operators. However, the prototypes do not consider a broader scenario where RDF stream systems can reactively produce and consume RDF events asynchronously, and deliver continuous results dynamically, depending on the demands of the stream consumer.

In this paper we introduce a model that describes RSP producers and consumers, and that is adaptable to the specific case of RSP query processing. This model is based on the *Actor Model*, where lightweight objects interact exclusively by interchanging immutable messages. This model allows composing networks of RSP engines in such a way that they are composable, yet independent, and we show how this can be implemented using existing frameworks in the family of the JVM (Java Virtual Machine) languages. In particular, we focus on specifying how RSP query results can be delivered in scenarios where the stream producer is faster than the consumer, and takes into account its demand to push only the volumes of triples that can be handled by the other end. This dynamic push delivery can be convenient on scenarios where receivers have lower storage and processing capabilities, such as constrained devices and sensors in the IoT. The remainder of the paper is structured as follows: we briefly describe RSP systems and some of their limitations in Sect. 2, then we present the actor-based model on Sect. 3. We provide details of the dynamic push delivery on Sect. 4, and the implementation and experimentation are described in Sect. 5. We present the related work on Sect. 6 before concluding in Sect. 7.

2   RSP Engines, Producers and Consumers

In general RSP query engines can be informally described as follows: given as input a set of RDF streams and graphs, and a set of continuous queries, the RSP engine will produce a stream of continuous answers matching the queries (see Fig. 1). This high-level model of an RSP engine is simple yet enough to describe

---

[3] W3C RDF Stream Processing Community Group http://www.w3.org/community/ rsp.

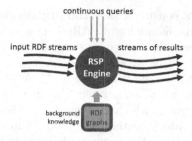

Fig. 1. Evaluation of continuous queries in RDF Stream Processing. The data stream flows through the engine, while continuous queries are registered and results that match them are streamed out.

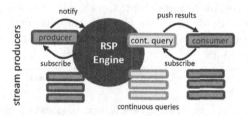

Fig. 2. Implementation of an RSP query engine based on tightly coupled publisher and subscribers.

most stream query processing scenarios. Nevertheless, this model, and the existing implementations of it, does not detail how stream producers communicate with RSP engines, and how stream consumers receive results from RSP engines. This ambiguity or lack of specification has resulted in different implementations that may result in a number of issues, especially regarding responsiveness, elasticity and resiliency.

2.1 RSP Query Engines

To illustrate these issues, let's consider first how streams are produced in these systems. On the producer side, RDF streams are entities to which the RSP engine subscribes, so that whenever a stream element is produced, the engine is notified (Fig. 2). The issues with this model arise from the fact that the RSP engine and the stream producer are tightly coupled. In some cases like C-SPARQL or SPARQL$_{stream}$, the coupling is at the process level, i.e. both the producer and the engine coexist in the same application process. A first issue regards scalability: it is not possible to dynamically route the stream items from the producer to a different engine or array of engines, since the subscription is hard-wired on the code. Moreover, if the stream producer is faster than the RSP engine, the subscription notifications can flood the latter, potentially overflowing its capacity. A second issue is related to resilience: failures on the stream producer can escalate and directly affect or even halt the RSP engine.

Looking at the stream consumer side, the situation is similar. The continuous queries, typically implemented as SPARQL extensions, are registered into the RSP engine, acting as subscription systems. Then, for each of the continuous queries, a consumer can be attached so that it can receive notifications of the continuous answers to the queries (see Fig. 2). Again, we face the problem of tightly coupled publisher and subscribers that have fixed routing configuration and shared process space, which may hinder the scalability, elasticity and resiliency of the system. Added to that, the delivery mode of the query results is fixed and cannot be tuned to the needs of the consumer.

It is possible to see these issues in concrete implementations: for instance in Listing 1 the C-SPARQL code produces an RDF stream. Here, the stream data structure is mixed with the execution of the stream producer (through a dedicated thread). Even more important, the tightly coupled publishing is done when the RDF quad is made available through the put method. The engine (in this case acting as a consumer) is forced to receive quad-by-quad whenever the RDF Stream has new data.

```
public class SensorsStreamer extends RdfStream implements Runnable {
  public void run() {
    while(true){
      RdfQuadruple q=new RdfQuadruple(subject,predicate,object,
                                      System.currentTimeMillis());
      this.put(q);
    }
  }
}
```

Listing 1. Example of generation of an RDF stream in C-SPARQL.

A similar scenario can be observed on query results recipient. The continuous listener code for the CQELS engine in Listing 2 represents a query registration (ContinuousSelect) to which one or more listeners can be attached. The subscription is tightly coupled, and results are pushed mapping by mapping, forcing the consumer to receive these updates and act accordingly.

```
String queryString ="SELECT ?person ?loc"
ContinuousSelect selQuery=context.registerSelect(queryString);
selQuery.register(new ContinuousListener() {
  public void update(Mapping mapping){
    String result="";
    for(Iterator<Var> vars=mapping.vars();vars.hasNext();){
      result+=""+context.engine().decode(mapping.get(vars.next()));
      System.out.println(result);
    }
  }
});
```

Listing 2. Example of generation of an RDF stream in CQELS.

2.2 Results Delivery for Constrained Consumers

In the previous section we discussed some of the general issues of current RSP engines regarding producing and consuming RDF streams. Now we focus on the particular case where a stream consumer is not necessarily able to cope with the rate of the stream producer, and furthermore, when the stream generation rate fluctuates. As an example, consider the case of an RDF stream of annotated geo-located triples that mobile phones communicate to stationary sensors that detect proximity (e.g. for a social networking application, or for public transportation congestion studies), In this scenario the number of RDF stream producers can greatly vary (from a handful to thousands, depending on how many people are nearby in a certain time of the day), and also the stream rate can fluctuate. In this and other examples the assumption that all consumers can handle any type of stream load does not always hold, and RSP engines need to consider this fact. Some approaches have used load shedding, eviction and discarding methods to alleviate the load, and could be applicable in these scenarios [1,9]. Complementary to that, it should be possible for stream producers to regulate the rate and the number of items they dispatch to a consumer, depending on the data needs and demand of the latter.

3   An Actor Architecture for RDF Stream Processing

A central issue in the previous systems is that several aspects are mixed into a single implementation. An RDF stream in these systems encapsulates not only the stream data structure, but also its execution environment (threading model) and the way that data is delivered (subscriptions). In distributed systems, one of the most successful models for decentralized asynchronous programming is the *Actor model* [2,10]. This paradigm introduces *actors*, lightweight objects that communicate through messages in an asynchronous manner, with no-shared mutable state between them. Each actor is responsible of managing its own state, which is not accessible by other actors. The only way for actors to interact is through asynchronous and immutable messages that they can send to each other either locally or remotely, as seen in Fig. 3.

We can characterize an actor A as a tuple: $A = (s, b, mb)$, where s is the actor state, b is the actor behavior and mb is its message box. The state s is accessible and modifiable only by the actor itself, and no other Actor can either read or write on it. The mailbox mb is a queue of messages m_i that are received from other actors. Each message $m_i = (a_i^s, a_i^r, d_i)$ is composed of a data item d_i, a reference to the sender actor a_i^s, and a reference to the receiver actor a_i^r. The behavior is a function $b(m_i, s)$ where m_i is a message received through

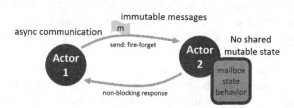

Fig. 3. Actor model: actors communicate through asynchronous messages that arrive to their mailboxes. There is no shared mutable state, as each actor handles its own state exclusively.

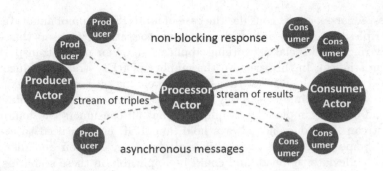

Fig. 4. RSP actors: RDF stream producers, processors and consumers. All actors send the stream elements as asynchronous messages. An RSP query engine is both a consumer (receives an input RDF stream) and a producer (produces a stream of continuous answers).

the mailbox. The behavior can change the actor state depending on the message acquired. Given a reference to an actor a, an actor can send a message m_i through the $send(m_i, a)$ operation. References to actors can be seen as addresses of an actor, which can be used for sending messages.

We propose a simple execution model for RDF stream processing that is composed of three generic types of actors: a stream producer, a processor and a consumer, as depicted in Fig. 4. A producer actor generates and transmits messages that encapsulate RDF streams to the consumer actors. The processor actor is a special case that implements both a producer (producer of results) and a consumer (consumes the input RDF streams), as well as some processing logic. Following the above definitions the data d_i of a message m_i emitted by a producer actor, or received by a consumer actor, is a set of timestamped triples. This model does not prevent these actors to receive and send also other types of messages.

In this model there is a clear separation of the data and the execution: the data stream is modeled as an infinite sequence of immutable event messages, each containing a set of RDF triples. Communication between producers and consumers is governed through asynchronous messaging that gets to the mailboxes of the actors. In that way, the subscribers are not tightly coupled with the producers of RDF streams, and in fact any consumer can feed from any stream generated by any producer. Moreover, this separation allows easily isolating failures in either end. Failures on consumers do not directly impact other consumers nor the producers, and vice-versa.

Event-driven asynchronous communication within RSP actors, as well as avoiding blocking operators, guarantees that the information flow is not stuck unnecessarily. Also, adaptive delivery of query results using dynamic push and pull, can prevent data bottlenecks and overflow, as we will see later. By handling stream delays, data out of order and reacting gracefully to failures, the system can maintain availability, even under stress or non-ideal conditions. Similarly, elasticity can boost the system overall responsiveness by efficiently distributing the load and adapting to the dynamic conditions of the system. The actor model results convenient for RDF stream processing, as it constitutes a basis for constructing what is commonly called a *reactive system*[4]. Reactive systems are characterized for being *event-driven, resilient, elastic*, and *responsive*.

4   Dynamic Push Delivery

In RSP engines there are typically two types of delivery modes for the stream of results associated to a continuous query: *pull* and *push*. In pull mode, the consumer actively requests the producer for more results, i.e. it has control of when the results are retrieved. While this mode has the advantage of guaranteeing that the consumer only receives the amount and rate of data that it needs, it may incur in delays that depend on the polling frequency. In the push mode, on the contrary, the producer pushes the data directly to the consumer, as soon as it is available. While this method can be more responsive and requires no active polling communication, it forces the consumer to deal with bursts of data, and potential message flooding. In some cases, when the consumer is *faster* than the producer, the push mode may be appropriate, but if the rate of messages exceeds the capacity of the consumer, then it may end up overloaded, causing system disruption, or requiring shedding or other techniques to deal with the problem (see Fig. 5a).

As an alternative, we propose using a dynamic push approach for delivering stream items to an RDF stream consumer, taking into consideration the capacity and availability of the latter (see Fig. 5b). The dynamic mechanism consists in allowing the consumer to explicitly indicate its demand to the producer. This can be simply done by issuing a message that indicates the capacity (e.g. volume of data) that it can handle. Then, knowing the demand of the consumer, the stream producer can push only the volume of data that is required, thus avoiding any overload on the consumer side. If the demand is lower than the supply, then this behavior results in a normal push scenario. Otherwise, the consumer can ask for more data, i.e. pull, when it is ready to do so. Notice that the consumer can at

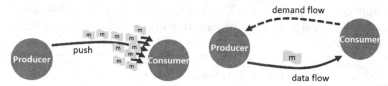

(a) Push overload if the producer pushes too fast.   (b) Dynamic push: demand on the side of the consumer.

Fig. 5. Delivery modes in RSP engines.

---

[4] The reactive manifesto http://www.reactivemanifesto.org/.

any point in time notify about its demand. If the consumer is overloaded with processing tasks for a period of time, it can notify a low demand until it is free again, and only then raise it and let the producer know about it.

5   Implementing RSP Dynamic Push

In order to validate the proposed model, and more specifically, to verify the feasibility of the dynamic push in a RSP engine, we have implemented this mechanism on top of an open-source RSP query processor. We have used the Akka library[5], which is available for both Java and Scala, to implement our RSP Actors. Akka provides a fully fledged implementation of the actor model, including routing, serialization, state machine support, remoting and failover, among other features. By using the Akka library, we were able to create producer and consumer actors that receive messages, i.e. streams of triples. For example, a Scala snippet of a consumer is detailed in Listing 3, where we declare a consumer that extends the Akka Actor class, and implements a `receive` method. The receive method is executed when the actor receives a message on its mailbox, i.e. in our case an RDF stream item.

```
class RDFConsumer extends Actor {
  def receive ={
    case d:Data =>
      // process the triples in the data message
  }
}
```

Listing 3. Scala code snippet of an RDF consumer actor.

To show that an RSP engine can be adapted to the actor model, we have used CQELS, which is open source and is written in Java, as it has demonstrated to be one of the most competitive prototype implementations, at least in terms of performance [12]. More concretely, we have added the dynamic push delivery of CQELS query results, so that a consumer actor can be fed with the results of a CQELS continuous query.

To show the feasibility of our approach and the implementation of the dynamic push, we used a synthetic stream generator based on the data and vocabularies of the SRBench [15] benchmark for RDF stream processing engines. As a sample query, consider the CQELS query in Listing 4 that constructs a stream of triples consisting of an observation event and its observed timestamp, for the last second.

```
PREFIX omOwl: http://knoesis.wright.edu/ssw/ont/sensor-observation.owl#.
CONSTRUCT {?observation <http://epfl.ch/stream/produces> ?time}
WHERE {
    STREAM <http://deri.org/streams/rfid> [RANGE 1000ms] {
      ?observation omOwl:timestamp ?time
    }
}
```

Listing 4. Example of generation of CQELS query over the SRBench dataset.

---

[5] Akka: http://akka.io/.

In the experiments, we focused on analyzing the processing throughput of the CQELS dynamic push, compared to the normal push operation. We tested using different processing latencies, i.e. considering that the processing on the consumer side can cause a delay of 10, 50, 100 and 500 milliseconds. This simulates a slow stream consumer, and we tested its behavior with different values for the fluctuating demand: e.g. from 5 to 10 thousand triples per execution. The results of these experiments are depicted in Fig. 6, where each plot corresponds to a different delay value, the Y axis is the throughput, and the X axis is the demand of the consumer.

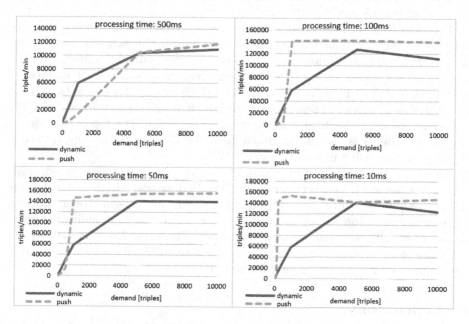

Fig. 6. Results of the experimentation: throughput of the results delivery after query processing for bot dynamic and normal push. The delay per processing execution is of 500, 100, 50, 10 milliseconds from left to right, top to bottom. The Y axis is the throughput, and the X axis is the demand.

As it can be seen, when the demand of the consumer is high, the behavior is similar to the push mode. However if the consumer specifies a high demand but has a slow processing time, the throughput is slowly degraded. When the processing time is fast (e.g. 10 ms), the push delivery throughput is almost constant, as expected, although it is important to notice that in this mode, if the supply is greater than the demand, the system simply drops and does not process the exceeding items. In that regard, the dynamic push can help alleviate this problem, although it has a minor penalty in terms of throughput.

6   Related Work and Discussion

RDF stream processors have emerged in the latest years as a response to the challenge of producing, querying and consuming streams of RDF events. These efforts resulted in a series of implementation and approaches in this area, proposing their own set of stream models and extensions to SPARQL [3,5,7,9,11]. These and other RSP engines have focused on the execution of SPARQL streaming queries and the possible optimization and techniques that can be applied in that context. However, their models and implementation do not include details about the stream producers and consumers, resulting in prototypes that overlook the issues described in Sect. 2.

For handling continuous queries over streams, several Data Stream Management Systems (DSMS) have been designed and built in the past years, exploiting the power of continuous query languages and providing pull and push-based data access. Other systems, cataloged as complex event processors (CEP), emphasize on pattern matching in query processing and defining complex events from basic ones through a series of operators [8]. Although none of the commercial CEP solutions provides semantically rich annotation capabilities on top of their query interfaces, systems as the ones dexfibed in [13,14] have proposed different types of semantic processing models on top of CEPs.

More recently, a new sort of stream processing platforms has emerged, spinning off the massively parallel distributed Map-Reduce based frameworks. Examples of this include Storm[6] or Spark Streaming[7], which represent stream processing as workflows of operators that can be deployed in the cloud, hiding the complexity of parallel and remote communication. The actor based model can be complementary to such platforms (e.g. Spark Streaming allows feeding streams from Akka Actors on its core implementation).

7   Conclusions

Event streams are one of the most prevalent and ubiquitous source of Big Data on the web, and it is a key challenge to design and build systems that cope with them in an effective and usable way. In this paper we have seen how RDF Stream Processing engines can be adapted to work in an architecture that responds to the principles of reactive systems. this model is based on the usage of lightweight actors that communicate via asynchronous event messages. We have shown that using this paradigm we can avoid the tight coupled design of current RSP engines, while opening the way for building more resilient, responsive and elastic systems. More specifically, we have shown a technique for delivering the continuous results of queries in an RSP engine through a dynamic push that takes into consideration the demand of the stream consumer. The resulting prototype implementation, on top of the well known CQELS engine, shows that is feasible to adapt an RSP to include this mode, while keeping a good throughput.

---

[6] http://storm.apache.org/.

[7] https://spark.apache.org/streaming/.

When processing streams of data, whether they are under the RDF umbrella or not, it is important to take architectural decisions that guarantee that the system aligns with the characteristics of a reactive system. Otherwise, regardless of how performant a RSP engine is, if it is not able to be responsive, resilient to failures and scalable, it will not be able to match the challenges of streaming applications such as the Internet of Things. we have seen that there are many pitfalls in systems design that prevent most of RSP engines to be *reactive*, in the sense that they do not always incorporate the traits of resilience, responsiveness, elasticity and message driven nature. We strongly believe that these principles have to be embraced at all levels of RDF stream processing to be successful.

As future work, we plan to extend the reactive actor model to all aspects of an RSP engine, including the stream generation, linking with stored datasets and dealing with entailment regimes. We also envision to use this architecture to show that different and heterogeneous RSP engines can be combined together, forming a network of producers and consumers that can communicate via messaging in a fully distributed scenario.

Acknowledgments. Partially supported by the SNSF-funded Osper and Nano-Tera OpenSense2 projects.

References

1. Abadi, D.J., Carney, D., Cetintemel, U., Cherniack, M., Convey, C., Lee, S., Stonebraker, M., Tatbul, N., Zdonik, S.: Aurora: a new model and architecture for data stream management. VLDB J. **12**(2), 120–139 (2003)
2. Agha, G.: Actors: A model of concurrent computation in distributed systems. Technical report, MIT (1985)
3. Anicic, D., Fodor, P., Rudolph, S., Stojanovic, N.: EP-SPARQL: a unified language for event processing and stream reasoning. In: WWW, pp. 635–644 (2011)
4. Barbieri, D.F., Braga, D., Ceri, S., Della Valle, E., Grossniklaus, M.: C-SPARQL: SPARQL for continuous querying. In: WWW, pp. 1061–1062 (2009)
5. Barbieri, D.F., Braga, D., Ceri, S., Della Valle, E., Grossniklaus, M.: Incremental reasoning on streams and rich background knowledge. In: Proceeding of 7th Extended Semantic Web Conference, pp. 1–15 (2010)
6. Calbimonte, J.-P., Corcho, O., Gray, A.J.G.: Enabling ontology-based access to streaming data sources. In: Patel-Schneider, P.F., Pan, Y., Hitzler, P., Mika, P., Zhang, L., Pan, J.Z., Horrocks, I., Glimm, B. (eds.) ISWC 2010, Part I. LNCS, vol. 6496, pp. 96–111. Springer, Heidelberg (2010)
7. Calbimonte, J.P., Jeung, H., Corcho, O., Aberer, K.: Enabling query technologies for the semantic sensor web. Int. J. Semant. Web Inf. Syst. (IJSWIS) **8**(1), 43–63 (2012)
8. Cugola, G., Margara, A.: Processing flows of information: from data stream to complex event processing. ACM Comput. Surv. **44**(3), 15:1–15:62 (2011)
9. Gao, S., Scharrenbach, T., Bernstein, A.: The CLOCK data-aware eviction approach: towards processing linked data streams with limited resources. In: Presutti, V., d'Amato, C., Gandon, F., d'Aquin, M., Staab, S., Tordai, A. (eds.) ESWC 2014. LNCS, vol. 8465, pp. 6–20. Springer, Heidelberg (2014)

10. Karmani, R.K., Shali, A., Agha, G.: Actor frameworks for the jvm platform: a comparative analysis. In: Proceedings of the 7th International Conference on Principles and Practice of Programming in Java. pp. 11–20. ACM (2009)
11. Le-Phuoc, D., Dao-Tran, M., Xavier Parreira, J., Hauswirth, M.: A native and adaptive approach for unified processing of linked streams and linked data. In: Aroyo, L., Welty, C., Alani, H., Taylor, J., Bernstein, A., Kagal, L., Noy, N., Blomqvist, E. (eds.) ISWC 2011, Part I. LNCS, vol. 7031, pp. 370–388. Springer, Heidelberg (2011)
12. Le-Phuoc, D., Nguyen-Mau, H.Q., Parreira, J.X., Hauswirth, M.: A middleware framework for scalable management of linked streams. Web Semant. Sci. Serv. Agents World Wide Web **16**, 42–51 (2012)
13. Paschke, A., Vincent, P., Alves, A., Moxey, C.: Tutorial on advanced design patterns in event processing. In: DEBS, pp. 324–334. ACM (2012)
14. Taylor, K., Leidinger, L.: Ontology-driven complex event processing in heterogeneous sensor networks. In: Antoniou, G., Grobelnik, M., Simperl, E., Parsia, B., Plexousakis, D., De Leenheer, P., Pan, J. (eds.) ESWC 2011, Part II. LNCS, vol. 6644, pp. 285–299. Springer, Heidelberg (2011)
15. Zhang, Y., Duc, P.M., Corcho, O., Calbimonte, J.-P.: SRBench: a streaming RDF/SPARQL benchmark. In: Cudré-Mauroux, P., et al. (eds.) ISWC 2012, Part I. LNCS, vol. 7649, pp. 641–657. Springer, Heidelberg (2012)

Author Index

Printed in the United States
by Baker & Taylor Publisher Services